The SAGE Handbook of
Early Childhood
Research

⊛SAGE | 50 YEARS

SAGE was founded in 1965 by Sara Miller McCune to support the dissemination of usable knowledge by publishing innovative and high-quality research and teaching content. Today, we publish more than 850 journals, including those of more than 300 learned societies, more than 800 new books per year, and a growing range of library products including archives, data, case studies, reports, and video. SAGE remains majority-owned by our founder, and after Sara's lifetime will become owned by a charitable trust that secures our continued independence.

Los Angeles | London | New Delhi | Singapore | Washington DC

The SAGE Handbook of
Early Childhood Research

Edited by

Ann Farrell, Sharon Lynn Kagan
and E. Kay M. Tisdall

$SAGE reference

Los Angeles | London | New Delhi
Singapore | Washington DC

◉SAGE

Los Angeles | London | New Delhi
Singapore | Washington DC

SAGE Publications Ltd
1 Oliver's Yard
55 City Road
London EC1Y 1SP

SAGE Publications Inc.
2455 Teller Road
Thousand Oaks, California 91320

SAGE Publications India Pvt Ltd
B 1/I 1 Mohan Cooperative Industrial Area
Mathura Road
New Delhi 110 044

SAGE Publications Asia-Pacific Pte Ltd
3 Church Street
#10-04 Samsung Hub
Singapore 049483

Editor: Mila Steele
Editorial assistant: Matthew Oldfield
Production editor: Shikha Jain
Copyeditor: Sharon Cawood
Proofreader: Jill Birch
Indexer: Avril Ehrlich
Marketing manager: Dilhara Attygalle
Cover design: Wendy Scott
Typeset by: Cenveo Publisher Services
Printed and bound by CPI Group (UK) Ltd,
Croydon, CR0 4YY [for Antony Rowe]

At SAGE we take sustainability seriously.
Most of our products are printed in the UK
using FSC papers and boards. When we
print overseas we ensure sustainable
papers are used as measured by the
Egmont grading system. We undertake an
annual audit to monitor our sustainability.

Library of Congress Control Number: 2015936048

British Library Cataloguing in Publication data

A catalogue record for this book is available from the British Library

ISBN 978-1-4462-7219-0

Contents

List of Figures

List of Tables

Notes on the Editors
and Contributors

THE EDITORS

Ann Farrell is Professor of Early Childhood and Head of the School of Early Childhood, Queensland University of Technology. Earning a PhD from the University of Queensland in 2006, she received an Honorary Doctorate from Gothenburg University (Sweden) in 2012. Her research expertise is in cross-jurisdictional childhood studies, research ethics, children's rights to participation and protection in the contexts of risk and early childhood education and care. She is an Australian Research Council (ARC) International Reader (IntReader) assessing ARC grants and collaborative bids between the ARC and the UK's Economic and Social Research Council; and is an External Assessor for Australia's National Health and Medical Research Council, the Social Sciences and Humanities Research Council of Canada and the National Research Foundation, Reviews and Evaluation Directorate of South Africa.

Sharon Lynn Kagan is the Virginia and Leonard Marx Professor of Early Childhood and Family Policy at Teachers College, Columbia University and Professor Adjunct at Yale University's Child Study Center. Author of over 250 articles, author/editor of 15 volumes and the recipient of scores of research grants, Kagan's work examines dimensions of early childhood policy. Using this scholarship to improve practice and policy, Kagan serves on numerous boards and consults with over 70 countries. A past president of the National Association for the Education of Young Children, she has received international and national honorary doctoral degrees, is a Fellow of the American Educational Research Association, a member of the National Academy of Education, a Fulbright recipient, and is the only woman in the USA to have received its three most prestigious awards: the Distinguished Service Award (Council of Chief State School Officers), the James Bryant Conant Award for Lifetime Service to Education, and the Harold W. McGraw, Jr. prize.

E. Kay M. Tisdall is Professor of Childhood Policy and co-Director of the Centre for Research on Families and Relationships (CRFR) (www.crfr.ac.uk) at the University of Edinburgh. She established the MSc in Childhood Studies at the University of Edinburgh (www.sps.ed.ac.uk/pgtcs), which is underlined by the UN Convention on the Rights of the Child, and specializes in research skills training in directly engaging with children and young people. She has undertaken a range of collaborative research, on such issues as children's involvement in family law, school complaints, and children with additional support needs. She has an extensive policy and academic interest in children and young people's participation, with collaborative projects funded by such organizations as the Leverhulme Trust and the UK's Economic and Social Research Council and ensuing publications in journals, chapters and books (e.g., *Children and Young People's Participation and its Transformative Potential: Learning from across Countries*, 2014).

THE CONTRIBUTORS

Mike Anderson is Dean of the School of Psychology and Exercise Science at Murdoch University and Research Director of the Project KIDS neurodevelopmental research program. His core area of research expertise is in individual differences and the development of intelligence, and his key theoretical contribution is the Minimal Cognitive Architecture theory of intelligence. Professor Anderson's current projects include an exploration of neurodevelopment in children with Type 1 Diabetes Mellitus, children born extremely preterm, and typically developing children. MRI, ERP and psychometric data from these studies are illuminating similarities and differences in the structures and processes of brain function in children with different developmental challenges.

Maria Caridad Araujo is a Lead Economist in the Social Protection and Health Division of the Inter-American Development Bank. Her work at the IDB has focused on issues of early childhood development and poverty alleviation. From 2003 to 2005, she taught on Georgetown University's masters-level program in Public Policy. Between 2003 and 2009, she worked at the World Bank in the areas of poverty and inequality, education and social protection, in East and Central Asia and Latin America. Maria Caridad's work has been published in peer-reviewed journals and she is the author and co-author of book chapters on social protection, poverty, and the political economy of policy-making processes. She is Ecuadorian and she holds a PhD in agricultural and natural resource economics from the University of California, Berkeley.

Emily Ashton is a Doctoral Student in the School of Child and Youth Care at the University of Victoria, Canada. She is a graduate of the Critical Studies in Education Master's program at the University of New Brunswick. Her current research interests include the intersection of critical and settler colonial theories in the context of early childhood education in Canada, in addition to postcolonial and reconceptualist reimaginings of early years' research in Sub-Saharan Africa.

Jeanne Brooks-Gunn PhD is the Virginia and Leonard Marx Professor of Child Development and Education at Teachers College and the College of Physicians and Surgeons at Columbia University and co-directs the National Center for Children and Families. She examines factors contributing to both positive and negative outcomes across childhood, adolescence, and adulthood, and has designed and evaluated intervention programs for children and parents (Early Head Start, Infant Health and Development Program, Head Start Quality Program). Other large-scale longitudinal studies include the Fragile Families and Child Well-being Study and the Project on Human Development in Chicago Neighborhoods. She is the author of 4 books and over 350 publications. She has been elected into the Institute of Medicine of the National Academies and has received life-time achievement awards from the Society for Research in Child Development, American Academy of Political and Social Science, the American Psychological Society, American Psychological Association, and Society for Research on Adolescence.

Malcolm Bush is an Affiliated Scholar at Chapin Hall at the University of Chicago and Senior Adviser to the International Center for Research and Policy on Childhood at the Pontifical Catholic University of Rio de Janeiro. His publications include research in the USA and Brazil on community economic development, low-income children and families, and workforce development. He is fluent in Brazilian Portuguese. He was a regular faculty member at the University of Chicago and for 15 years the president of Woodstock Institute in Chicago, a national economic development think tank. He has served on the Community Advisory Council of the US Federal Reserve Board and, at Woodstock, was awarded the MacArthur Foundation's international award for creative and effective organizations. His BA is in modern history from Oxford University, his MA in American History and Economics from the University of Pennsylvania, and he holds a PhD from Northwestern University in Social Psychology and Urban Affairs.

Margaret Carr is Director of the Early Years Research Centre at the University of Waikato. Her research interests have focused primarily on assessment practices and pedagogy in early childhood centers and the early years of school. Three books describe these interests. The first is a 2010 volume entitled *Learning in the Making* (Sense, Rotterdam), in which 14 children's learning journeys were traced from their last year in an early childhood center to their first few months at school, with three dispositions in mind: reciprocity, resilience and imagination. Two books (SAGE, 2001 and 2012) are about learning stories as narrative formative assessments. The second of these – *Learning Stories: Constructing Learner Identities in Early Education* – is written in collaboration with Wendy Lee (Director of Educational Learning Project). Her current research is on children's learning in museums, in collaboration with Jeanette Clarkin-Phillips and Bronwen Cowie (from early childhood center and a primary school) and Brenda Soutar (te kōhanga reo and te kura kaupapa Māori).

D. Jean Clandinin is Professor and Founding Director of the Centre for Research for Teacher Education and Development at the University of Alberta. She teaches in the areas of curriculum theory, teacher knowledge, teacher education and narrative inquiry. Her research interests are at the intersection of children's, families' and teachers' stories of school; narrative reflective practice in medicine; the experiences of youth who leave school early; and the educational experiences of Aboriginal youth and families.

Gordon Cleveland is Senior Lecturer in Economics in the Department of Management at University of Toronto Scarborough. He is part of the Qualité Éducative des Services de Garde et Petite Enfance research team centred at the Université du Québec à Montréal and has been Honorary Senior Fellow at the Graduate School of Education, University of Melbourne. His research focuses on the determinants of the affordability and quality of early childhood education services, including non-profit status, and on the effects of early childhood services on children's development and mothers' employment. He has a particular interest in the design of effective early childhood policies.

Bronwen Cohen is Honorary Professor in the School of Social and Political Science at the University of Edinburgh. She has over 35 years' experience in social and educational policy and research at NGO, government and university levels. Her current area of research is place-based learning in Scotland, Norway and the USA. Her recent publications include 'Education in Norway and Scotland: developing and re-forming the systems', in *Northern Neighbours: Scotland and Norway since 1800*, with Wenche Rønning (Edinburgh University Press, 2015); 'Place-based learning in early years services: approaches and examples from Norway and Scotland', in *International Perspectives in the Early Years*, with Wenche Rønning (SAGE, 2014); and 'Developing ECEC services in regionalised administrations: Scotland's post-devolution experience', in the *International Journal of Early Childhood* (2013).

Bronwen Cowie is Director of the Wilf Malcolm Institute of Educational Research at the University of Waikato. Her research has focused on formative assessment practices in primary and secondary classrooms, with a particular interest in student voice and cultural responsiveness. Other areas of interest include curriculum implementation and the role of information and communication technologies in teaching and learning science and making the science conducted by New Zealand scientists accessible to New Zealand teachers and students. She is currently working on a three year Teaching and Learning Research Initiative project focused on developing the mathematical thinking that student teachers need for the breadth of their professional role – teaching and learning across the school curriculum, data literacy and administration. Her other current research is on children's learning in museums, in collaboration with Margaret Carr and Jeanette Clarkin-Phillips (from early childhood centre and a primary school) and Brenda Soutar (te kōhanga reo and te kura kaupapa Māori).

Yyannú Cruz Aguayo is an Economist for the office of the Manager of the Social Sector of the Inter-American Development Bank, where she specializes in impact evaluation of social programs. Prior to joining the IADB, Yyannú worked at the research departments of the World Bank and the Central Bank in Mexico in the areas of labor markets, productivity and education, and taught undergraduate micro-economics at the Instituto Tecnológico Autónomo de México. Yyannú's work has been published in peer-reviewed journals and is the author and co-author of book chapters on the effectiveness of social programs in Latin America and the Caribbean. Yyannú's current research is mostly focused on teaching quality. She is Mexican and holds an MA and PhD from the University of Maryland, College Park.

Carmen Dalli is Professor of Early Childhood Education, Director of the Institute for Early Childhood Studies, and Associate Dean (Research) at the Faculty of Education, Victoria University of Wellington, New Zealand. Her research spans issues of policy and pedagogy and their impact on children's experiences in group-based early childhood settings. Most recently, her research has focused on early childhood services for infants and toddlers and teachers' views of professional practice. She regularly publishes commentaries on early childhood education policy in New Zealand, co-convenes a special interest group on ECEC professionalism within the European Early Childhood Education Research Association, and has co-edited two books on this topic: *Professionalism in Early Childhood Education and Care: International Perspectives* (Routledge, 2010) and *Early Childhood Grows Up: Towards a Critical Ecology of the Profession* (Springer, 2012).With E. Jayne White she is co-editor of a new book series (Springer) entitled *Policy and Pedagogy with Under-three Year Olds: Cross-disciplinary Insights and Innovations.*

Sibnath Deb is Professor in Department of Applied Psychology, Pondicherry University (A Central University), India and Adjunct Professor, School of Public Health and Social Work, Queensland University of Technology (QUT), Brisbane, Australia. He has 26 years of teaching and research experience, and is currently coordinator of the UGC SAP project. In 2009, he was visiting faculty at the School of Public Health, QUT, Brisbane, Australia. He has supervised ten PhDs and successfully coordinated more than 50 large-scale qualitative and quantitative studies in addition to publishing more than 100 research papers, writing eight books and editing four. Professor Deb is on the editorial board of the *Journal of Interpersonal Violence*. In 2004–08, he served as Council Member of the International Society for Prevention of Child Abuse and Neglect (ISPCAN). He has received three international and three national awards for his contributions to the fields of child safety and applied psychology. His current areas of research interest include child safety/protection, students' mental health, adolescent reproductive health, HIV/AIDS and applied social psychology.

Katrien De Graeve is a Postdoctoral Research Fellow at the Research Foundation Flanders, affiliated to the Department of Languages and Cultures of Ghent University, Belgium. In 2013–2014, she worked as a fellow of the Helsinki Collegium for Advanced Studies, Finland. She holds a PhD in Comparative Sciences of Culture from Ghent University and her doctoral thesis examined parenting practices and belonging in Belgian–Ethiopian adoption. Her research interests are situated at the intersection of critical care, kinship and family studies, and the anthropology of migration and postcoloniality, with transnational adoption and guardianships of refugee minors a specific empirical focus.

Hasina Banu Ebrahim is Professor of Early Childhood at the University of South Africa and a rated researcher with the National Research Foundation in South Africa. She is also the President of the South African Research Association for Early Childhood Education (SARAECE). She is currently developing the research theme of early childhood at the margins through a focus on practice, policy and teacher development, and is involved in developing early childhood researchers in national and African contexts.

Lesley Anne Gallacher is a Senior Lecturer in the Department of Social Work and Communities at Northumbria University. Her background is in human geography and she has published on the geographies of early childhood, methodological issues surrounding children's participation in research and youth cultures (in particular, English-speaking people's engagement with Japanese popular cultures).

Eugene E. Garcia is Professor Emeritus of Education at Arizona State University (ASU). He served as Vice President and Dean at ASU before assuming emeritus status. He continues to do research in areas of bilingual development and the education of bilingual children, particularly those living in families from immigrant backgrounds.

Anjali Gireesan has been carrying out her doctoral research in the Department of Applied Psychology, Pondicherry University, under the supervision of Sibnath Deb. She is currently teaching in college as an assistant professor in Psychology. Prior to joining the college, she worked on a research project on Academic Stress of School Students, funded by the University Grants Commission, New Delhi as a Project Fellow. She also has a PG Diploma in Industrial Psychology from Pondicherry University and cleared the National Eligibility Test (NET). She has published seven research papers.

Jennifer Glickman received her Masters of Education in Educational Research, Measurement, and Evaluation from Boston College. She is currently a senior research analyst at the Center for Effective Philanthropy, where she conducts research on foundation and nonprofit practices to enhance funder–grantee relationships. She recently co-authored a report with her colleagues entitled, 'Assessing to Achieve High Performance: What Nonprofits are Doing and How Foundations Can Help', which explores the ways in which nonprofit organizations assess and manage their performance.

Janice Huber is Associate Professor and Director of the Centre for Research for Teacher Education and Development at the University of Alberta. She teaches in the areas of early childhood education, narrative inquiry, and curriculum studies. Her research interests are in the educational experiences of Aboriginal children and families and in the experiences of teachers of Aboriginal heritage.

Analía Jaimovich is an Education Specialist in the Education Division of the Inter-American Development Bank. Prior to joining the IADB, Analía worked for the Human Development Network of the World Bank, Research Triangle International, the Academy for Educational Development (now FHI 360), and in the Ministries of Education of Argentina, Mexico, and Peru. A recipient of both the Fulbright and Gates grants for graduate study, Analía holds an MPhil in Politics and Education from the University of Cambridge, and an EdM in International Education Policy from Harvard University, where she is finishing her doctoral studies. Analía's research is mostly focused on the institutional architecture of education governance in Latin America.

Kristina Konstantoni is a Lecturer in Childhood Studies, Programme Director of the BA Childhood Practice and the co-Director of the Centre for Education for Racial Equality in Scotland at the University of Edinburgh. Her main research interests are in children's social identities and attitudes, diversity, social justice and children's rights and participation, and how the latter are taken forward in policy, research and practice.

Marta Korintus is Senior Adviser and Childcare Expert at the General Directorate of Social Affairs and Child Protection in Hungary which supports ECEC, family policy, child welfare and child protection. She has been involved in research and development work and international projects related to services for children for more than 30 years with a particular focus on children under the age of 3 years, including the OECD Thematic Review of Early Childhood Education and Care, and the EU research projects Care Work in Europe and YIPPEE. Her recent publications include 'Early childhood socialization: societal context and childrearing values in Hungary', in the *Journal of Early Childhood Research*, with April Brayfield (2011); 'Work–life balance in Hungary', in *Work–Life Balance Policy in Czech Republic, Hungary, Poland and Slovakia, 1989–2009: Twenty Years of Transformation*, with Luca Koltai (Dom Wydawniczy Harasimowicz Poznan, 2010).

Marlies Kustatscher is a Lecturer in Childhood Studies at the University of Edinburgh. Her interests include children's social identities and experiences of social inequalities, children's participation in research, policy and practice, and children's emotions and relationships, particularly in educational settings.

Alexis R. Lauricella is the Associate Director of the Center on Media and Human Development at Northwestern University and a Lecturer in the department of Communication Studies. Dr Lauricella earned her PhD in Developmental Psychology and her Master's degree in Public Policy from Georgetown University. Her research focuses on children's learning from media, and parents' and teachers' attitudes toward and use of media with young children. Dr Lauricella is also the founder of www.playlearnparent.com, a website that translates child-development research for parents.

Michael H. Levine is the Executive Director of the Joan Ganz Cooney Center at Sesame Workshop. The Center conducts research and convenes leaders to promote investments in high-quality media experiences for children. He previously oversaw the Carnegie Corporation of New York's groundbreaking work in early childhood development and was a senior advisor to the New York City Schools Chancellor, where he directed dropout prevention, afterschool, and early childhood initiatives. Dr Levine serves on New York City's Universal Pre-Kindergarten Scientific Advisory Council, and is a Pahara-Aspen Education Reform Fellow. Michael received his PhD in Social Policy from Brandeis University's Florence Heller School and his BS from Cornell University.

Jackie Marsh is Professor of Education at the University of Sheffield. Her research is focused on the digital literacy practices of young children in homes, schools and early years settings and communities. Her most recent publication is *Changing Play: Play, Media and Commercial Culture from the 1950s to the Present Day* (Open University Press, 2014, with Bishop). She is an editor of the *Journal of Early Childhood Literacy*.

Jinny Menon is a Doctoral Student enrolled in the Teacher Education Program in Elementary Education at the University of Alberta. She is interested in narrative inquiry as a relational methodology.

Linda Mitchell is Associate Director of the Early Years Research Centre at the University of Waikato. Her research interests are focused on the idea of early years services as democratic communities for citizenship and social justice. These ideas can be linked to policy and curriculum. Linda has led several evaluations of national ECE policies, including of New Zealand's strategic plan for ECE and her current evaluation of the government's ECE Participation Programme. A key aspect of these evaluations is interviews with families about their views and experiences of early childhood education. Her current research includes a community research project with Congolese refugee families, examining experiences of resettlement and of early childhood education, and a project analysing teaching and learning in culturally diverse early childhood settings. Recently, she worked with a research team for the data collection of the Continuity of Early Learning: Learning Progress and Outcomes in the Early Years project, investigating assessment documentation gathered in ECE services and primary schools, and how information is exchanged at transition points.

Marisa Morin BA is a Doctoral Student in Developmental Psychology at Teachers College, Columbia University. She is a graduate research fellow at the National Center for Children and Families (NCCF) at Teachers College, which focuses on policy research on children and families (www.policyforchildren.org). Her research interests focus on the effects of poverty on child and family well-being. She has previously conducted research examining the quality of parent–child interactions within the juvenile justice system. Currently, she is examining how contextual factors, such as religion, affect parenting practices and subsequent child development in low-income populations. In addition, she is involved with NCCF in a national evaluation of home visiting programs within the United States (Mother Infant Home Visiting Program Evaluation).

Peter Moss is an Emeritus Professor at the Thomas Coram Research Unit, UCL Institute of Education, University College London. He has a wide range of interests including education (early childhood and subsequently), the relationship between care, employment and gender, and social pedagogy. He is currently editing a book of the selected writings and speeches of Loris Malaguzzi, the great Italian educator from Reggio Emilia. His latest book, published in the Contesting Early Childhood series, is *Transformative Change and Real Utopias in Early Childhood Education: The Story of Democracy, Experimentation and Potentiality* (Routledge, 2014).

M. Shaun Murphy is an Associate Professor in the Department of Educational Foundations at the University of Saskatchewan. His research interests are based in relational narrative inquiry and focus on familial and school curriculum making; the interwoven lives of children, families, and teachers; and teacher education.

Claire O'Kane is a Child Rights Practitioner, Researcher and Advocate with two decades of international experience working in development and humanitarian contexts, particularly in Asia and Africa. She worked with Save the Children for many years, and has been an international child rights consultant since 2011. She was a lead researcher for a two-year research and evaluation process on children's participation in armed conflict, post-conflict and peace building with Save the Children Norway (2006–2007). Claire has published a number of articles, reports and programme guidance on child rights, child protection, children's citizenship, participation and peace building.

Auma Okwany is an Assistant Professor of Social Policy at the International Institute of Social Studies of Erasmus University Rotterdam in the Netherlands. Her research interests center on the relationship between policy, practice and theory in childhood and youth issues in development from a critical perspective. She is lead author of *The Role of Local Knowledge and Culture in Childcare in Africa: A sociological study of several ethnic groups in Kenya and Uganda* (Edwin Mellen Press, 2011). Her most recent research focuses on child sensitive social protection and a volume on social protection for which she is editor is forthcoming. She is currently co-editing a book on Girls' Secondary Education in Africa.

Alan Pence is UNESCO Chair for Early Childhood Education, Care and Development, and a and Professor, University of Victoria, Canada. He was the founding director of the First Nations Partnerships Program at the University, the Unit for Early Years Research and Development, and founder and current director of the Early Childhood Development Virtual University (ECDVU), a graduate-level web-based leadership and capacity-building program active in Sub-Saharan Africa since 2000. The author of over 130 articles and chapters, two of his thirteen books that relate closely to this article are *Africa's Future, Africa's Challenge: Early Childhood Care and Development in Sub-Saharan Africa* (edited with Garcia and Evans, 2008), and *Complexities, Capacities, Communities: Changing Development Narratives in Early Childhood Education, Care and Development* (with Benner, 2015).

Helen Penn is Emeritus Professor of Early Childhood in the Cass School of Education, University of East London (UEL), and is a co-Director of the International Centre for the Study of the Mixed Economy of Childcare at UEL. She has been carrying out research and development in low- and middle-income countries in Africa and Central Asia for the last 20 years, for a variety of international agencies including the EU, the Asian Development Bank, UNICEF, UNESCO and Save the Children UK.

Nirmala Rao is Serena H C Yang Professor in Early Childhood Development and Education, Professor, Faculty of Education and Dean, Graduate School, The University of Hong Kong. She is a developmental and chartered (educational) psychologist who is internationally recognized for her research on early childhood development and education in Asian cultural contexts. This research has focused on the development, evaluation and dissemination of evidence-based programmes directed at children in the early childhood stage of development, with the objective of finding out why they have the effects that they do. She has published widely in the areas of early childhood development and education, child development and educational policy, and educational psychology and has been a consultant/expert on early childhood development and education for UN agencies.

Corinne Reid is a Clinical Psychologist and Academic Chair of the postgraduate clinical training program at Murdoch University. Her focus is on translational clinical research that builds bridges between research and practice. Dr Reid's primary research interest is in working with vulnerable groups of children to better understand their developmental trajectories and to help practitioners design individualized interventions that have a good fit with the needs of each child and their family. She also works with several remote indigenous communities to learn about the needs of young children and families living in diverse cultural contexts.

Irene Rizzini is a Professor at the Pontifical Catholic University of Rio de Janeiro (PUC-Rio), Brazil and Director of the International Center for Research on Childhood (CIESPI) at PUC-Rio. She was President of the Childwatch International Research Network from 2002 to 2009. Rizzini held the Visiting Chair in Brazilian Studies at the Kellogg Institute for International Studies at the University of Notre Dame in 2006, and was appointed a John Simon Guggenheim Memorial Foundation fellow in 2008. She is the author of a number of books, including: *Globalization and children*; *The art of governing children: the history of social policies, legislation and child welfare in Brazil*; *Disinherited from society: street children in Latin America*; *The lost century: the historical roots of public policies on children in Brazil*; *Children and the law in Brazil: revisiting the history (1822–2000)*; *The human rights of children and adolescents: twenty years of the [Brazilian] statute [on the child and the adolescent]*.

Ingrid Pramling Samuelsson is a Professor at the University of Gothenburg, Sweden. Her main research field is young children's learning and curriculum questions of early years education. Her many research studies of children's learning and play in the preschool context have led to the development of a didactics approach, labelled developmental pedagogy. One of her most popular books is *The Playing-Learning Child* (originally in Swedish, but also translated into German), which is based on the idea that children are playing-learning individuals and is subsequently why preschool didactics need to integrate play and learning. Her latest research concerns children's possibilities of learning in relation to group size. She is the UNESCO Chair in Early Childhood Education and Sustainable Development and is the former World President of OMEP (Organisation Mondiale pour l'Èducation Présolaire).

Jack Sidnell is Full Professor of Anthropology at the University of Toronto with a cross-appointment to the Department of Linguistics. His research focuses on the structures of talk and interaction. In addition to research in the Caribbean and Vietnam, he has examined talk in court and among young children. He is the author of *Conversation Analysis: An Introduction* (2010), the editor of *Conversation Analysis: Comparative Perspectives* (2009) and co-editor of *Conversational Repair and Human Understanding* (2013), *The Handbook of Conversation Analysis* (2012) and *The Cambridge Handbook of Linguistic Anthropology* (2014).

Jin Sun is an Assistant Professor in the Department of Early Childhood Education, The Hong Kong Institute of Education. Her research interests include international comparisons of early child development and education, assessment of early learning and development, interventions for socially and economically disadvantaged children, early self-regulation development, and Chinese socialization. She also has experience in data mining and analyses of large datasets.

Cindy Swanson is a PhD student in the Centre for Research for Teacher Education and Development in the Faculty of Elementary Education at the University of Alberta. Prior to entering the doctoral program, she taught for 12 years and completed her MEd thesis,

'An Autobiographical Narrative Inquiry into the Lived Tensions Between Familial and School Curriculum-Making Worlds'. Her doctoral studies focus on making visible the importance of familial curriculum-making worlds in school curriculum-making worlds, not only as places of becoming and of shaping identities, but also as engaging and sustaining places for children, families, and teachers.

Ying Wang is currently a Post-doctoral Fellow at the Faculty of Education at The University of Hong Kong. She received her PhD in Psychology from the Chinese University of Hong Kong. Her research is primarily focused on intervention studies designed to facilitate children's literacy and cognitive skills. She has published articles in journals that focus on child development and education.

Ellen Wartella is the Sheikh Hamad bin Khalifa Al-thani Professor of Communication and a Professor of psychology, human development and social policy, and medical social sciences at Northwestern University. She is director of the Center on Media and Human Development and chair of the Department of Communication Studies. She is a leading scholar of the role of media in children's development and serves on a variety of national and international boards and committees on children's issues. She is co-principal investigator on two National Science Foundation projects: a three-year multi-site grant entitled 'Media Characters: the Unhidden Persuaders in Food Marketing to Children (2013–2016)' and a five-year multi-site grant entitled 'Collaborative Research: Using Educational DVDs to Enhance Young Children's STEM Education (2013–2018)'. Dr Wartella earned her PhD in Mass Communication from the University of Minnesota in 1977 and completed post-doctoral research in developmental psychology at the University of Kansas.

E. Jayne White is an Associate Professor at the University of Waikato, New Zealand, where she is Associate Director of the Centre for Global Studies. Jayne's work focuses on the complex processes and practices of meaning-making in contemporary 'open' societies. At the heart of her practice lies a strong emphasis on dialogic pedagogy and the ways in which teachers can best engage within complex learning relationships. Jayne's work focuses on the early years, with a particular emphasis on practices and pedagogies for teachers working with under threes in ECE. She has pioneered the use of polyphonic video in generating visual data that provokes deeper understandings of these encounters. She is associate editor of the *International Journal of Early Childhood* and the *Video Journal of Pedagogy*, regularly reviews for a variety of other journals including *Educational Philosophy and Theory*, has edited two books, and recently published a sole-authored book entitled *Introducing Dialogic Pedagogy: Provocations for the Early Years* (Routledge). With Carmen Dalli she is co-editor of a new book series entitled *Policy and Pedagogy with Under-three Year Olds: Cross-disciplinary Insights and Innovations* (Springer).

Elizabeth Wood is Professor of Education at the University of Sheffield and Director for Research in the School of Education. She specializes in early childhood and primary education, and has conducted research into teachers' professional knowledge and beliefs; progression and continuity; play and pedagogy; children's choices during free play; critical perspectives on early childhood policy and practice; gender and underachievement. Elizabeth's research on play, pedagogy and curriculum in early childhood has had international reach and impact. She has worked with many organizations and policy makers to promote informed ways of valuing and integrating children's free play within curriculum frameworks.

Jason C. Yip is an Assistant Professor of Digital Youth at the Information School at the University of Washington – Seattle. Dr Yip examines how new technologies support children's engagement in participatory cultures. He is the co-principal investigator on a four-year National Science Foundation project (2014–2018) exploring how the design of social media technologies for science can support participatory learning for children across domains. He has also worked with a number of organizations and companies, such as Nickelodeon, the National Parks Service, Google, and National Geographic to partner together with children to develop new technologies for children. Dr Yip earned his PhD in Curriculum and Instruction from the University of Maryland – College Park and completed his post-doctoral research at the Joan Ganz Cooney Center at Sesame Workshop.

Mary E. Young is a Pediatrician and Global Health and Child Development Specialist with broad experience in both developed and developing countries. For the past three decades at the World Bank, she has led global efforts to inform world leaders about early childhood development. Dr Young has advised clients through policy dialogues, sector analyses and project design and management. Her experience spans the globe – from China to Eastern Europe and Central Asia, to the Middle East and North Africa, and to Latin America and the Caribbean. Currently, she is Senior Fellow of the China Development Research Foundation, co-leader (with James Heckman) of the Early Childhood Intervention Network/HCEO Working Group at the University of Chicago, and Senior Advisor to Harvard University's Center on the Developing Child, and Adjunct Professor of Pediatrics at University of Hawaii Medical Center.

Stephen R. Zubrick holds a Professorial appointment in the Centre for Child Health Research at the University of Western Australia and is a Senior Principal Research Fellow at the Telethon Kids Institute. He is Chairman of the Consortium Advisory Group for the Australian Longitudinal Study of Australian Children and is a member of the Steering Committee for the Longitudinal Study of Indigenous Children. He holds several national and international competitive research grants and his research interests include the study of the social determinants of health and mental health in children, studies of the genetic and environmental determinants of language development, and large-scale psychosocial survey work in non-Indigenous and Indigenous populations.

Early Childhood Research: An Expanding Field

Ann Farrell, Sharon Lynn Kagan
and E. Kay M. Tisdall

INTRODUCTION: THE CONTEMPORARY STATE OF EARLY CHILDHOOD AND THE CALL FOR EARLY CHILDHOOD RESEARCH

Early childhood is an expanding research field that is concerned with young children, their families, and their communities. Drawn from a range of disciplines and conducted within a range of contexts, empirical evidence generated within this field demonstrates the importance of the early years for individual, community, and global outcomes. Strengthened international and national commitments to early childhood are inviting new high-stakes questions for researchers, practitioners, and policy makers. These questions are occasioning a heightened focus on research concerned with young children and heralding a call for new insights into its design, conduct, and impact. Against this backcloth, this volume provides thought-provoking, empirically-based insights into the range of extant early childhood research

that addresses the diverse contexts of children's lives and speaks to the transformative conditions under which children's rights are fostered and their developmental and life chances are optimized.

The issue has captured much attention. On the international stage, early childhood research has been an empirical driver of many notable efforts to bring young children and their life chances to the forefront of policy. Prominent international bodies such as the Organisation for Economic Cooperation and Development (OECD) (2001, 2006, 2012) and the United Nations Children's Fund (UNICEF) (2008, 2014) attest to the importance of early childhood research in shaping government and non-government priorities across a range of jurisdictions. A key catalyst for early childhood research influencing priorities is the 'starting strong' agenda. Exemplified in a series of OECD international comparative reports on Early Childhood Education and Care (ECEC) (2001, 2006, 2012). Starting Strong agenda draws upon early childhood research and its methodologies within human development, sociology, children's rights, and econometrics to demonstrate the affordances of investment in quality ECEC. Early childhood research has, therefore, become part of an internationally recognized discourse, pushing for the strongest possible start for children's life chances and life outcomes. Starting Strong is a significant global challenge given that the world's 2.2 billion children (UNICEF, 2014) represent the largest and most complex population of children in human history and a generation who face the unprecedented and seismic challenges of new technologies and geo-political shifts. The rhetoric of Starting Strong resonates with the United Nations Convention on the Rights of the Child (UNCRC, 1989), with its focus on children's rights to participation, provision, and protection in areas of their everyday lives. The UNCRC, in concert with traditional and emerging theoretical understandings of young children and their lives, has come to shape the expanding and complex field that is the focus of this volume.

EARLY CHILDHOOD AND EARLY CHILDHOOD RESEARCH DEFINED

Given this attention, it is important to underscore that early childhood and research in early childhood take place within a complex field, replete with undergirding theories, content, and methodology, all of which demand examination. Indeed, because this handbook addresses these issues and because the field is diverse, it is important to begin by presenting diverse definitions and constructions of early childhood, which in turn frame early childhood research. To do so, we provide an orientation to what is 'considered' as early childhood research in a range of contexts and what 'counts' as credible and robust research within those contexts.

There is no universal definition of early childhood and, indeed, no universal definition of early childhood research with regard

to the terms used to define it and to the ages of children it includes. With respect to the former, the field is peppered with many and varied terms, including early years, early childhood development, early care, early care and education, and early childhood education and care. While definitions abound and debates are lively, the terms 'early childhood' and 'early years' are among the two most popular internationally, and are often used interchangeably by researchers and policy personnel. Thus, the two terms 'early childhood' and 'early years' are largely used throughout this volume.

There is also controversy regarding the age span of children that should be included in early childhood, with most using the term to refer to children from birth to age 8. Some, however, suggest that the pre-natal period should be included, and others proffer that early childhood should include children up to 12 years of age. Despite the contested nature of the ages to be included in early childhood education, the vast majority of the international world adopts the nomenclature of early childhood or early years as embracing birth to age 8 years. As such, we adopt this age span as we consider early childhood services and research, whilst fully acknowledging debates over terms and age-based definitions.

Beyond the issues of terms and ages to be used when discussing young children, there is also controversy regarding the range of services to be examined. In many countries, the context is regarded somewhat narrowly, to include center-based provision primarily. In other settings, the context includes an array of services for young children, including center-based and home-based services, as well as those that include health, mental health, nutrition, and protection services. We adopt the more inclusive definition of early childhood services. Further, in examining early childhood research, we note that it is not confined to services, but embraces broader contexts, such as neighborhoods, communities, as well as political, social, and policy contexts.

EARLY CHILDHOOD RESEARCH: A COMPLEX CONCEPTUAL AND METHODOLOGICAL FIELD

The field of early childhood research is conceptually and methodologically complex, with different disciplinary and professional lineages, multiple methodological and analytic approaches and multiple stakeholders. Its conceptual underpinnings of respect for childhood and child competence, for example, have given rise to methodologies that open up possibilities for children's participation in, and decision-making regarding, research. The rhetoric around child competence and child participation, theorized within childhood studies (c.f. Qvortrup, 2000), for example, has been accompanied by legislative and policy concern for children's rights in research that affects their everyday lives and life chances.

So too, the contexts in which early childhood research occur and the governance of its contexts predispose the field to complexity. Health services as sites of research, for example, are often distinct from education and care services, bringing their own corporate governance cultures and structures that, in turn, contour the research that is sanctioned, facilitated, and disseminated. Institutional and disciplinary orientations are difficult to overcome, given the long histories and methods associated with each. Another layer of complexity is that research is bounded by human and fiscal resources, budget cycles, labor force patterns, and the push towards using research to advance speedy policy decisions. Such factors mean that research can be truncated due to financial or human factors outside the researcher's control. So too, there is the cycle of research dissemination that can oscillate between rapid knowledge transfer, on the one hand, and protracted or even stymied dissemination of findings, on the other. Moreover, mapping the field of early childhood research is beset by the frailty of the published literature to represent accurately the research that is occurring and by the temporal factors of time, space, and resources. The exponential change in policy and the press to translate research into policy and practice, with greater rapidity, thus, contribute to unprecedented complexity and urgency in the conduct and dissemination of research.

TRENDS IN EARLY CHILDHOOD RESEARCH

A Growing Range of Research Studies

Against the backcloth of these challenges and complexities, research in early childhood services has yielded a wealth of studies, both in quantity and diversity. Barnett's (2008) review of a range of significant preschool education studies, for example, reveals the depth and breadth of empirical work which has come to justify investment in the early years. Barnett's (2008) sample of studies includes: randomized control trials (e.g., *Abecedarian Program*, Campbell et al., 2012; *Head Start National Impact Study*, Puma et al., 2001); quasi-experimental studies (e.g., *Michigan School Readiness Program*, Xiang and Schweinhart, 2002); and longitudinal studies (e.g., *Effective Provision of Preschool Education*, Melhuish et al., 2008). So too, a meta-analysis of early education intervention studies produced by Camilli, Vargas, Ryan, and Barnett (2010) provides a snapshot of the impact of early intervention on children's cognitive and social development. Such analyses complement the growing corpus of cost-benefit studies (Cunha et al., 2005; Heckman, 2011) to show the merit of early intervention and, in turn, to justify systematic research in this area.

While these works are concerned (predominantly) with program-based intervention, other large-scale, longitudinal cohort studies are concerned with wider health and social matters for children and their families. Examples include: *Longitudinal Effects of Parenting on Children's Academic Achievement in African American Families* (Qi, 2006) in the USA; the *Avon Longitudinal Study of Parents and Children* (since 1991) (2012) in the UK; and the *Longitudinal Study of Australian Children* (since 2004) (2011), *Effective Early Childhood Education Experiences Study* (E4Kids) (since 2009) (Tayler and Thorpe, 2012) in Australia, and a range of birth cohort studies from South East Asia and the Eastern Mediterranean regions (McKinnon and Campbell, 2011). Thus, studies of intervention in early childhood services, as well as studies of young children's experience in a range of other contexts, reveal the complexity of the field that has come to be known as early childhood research.

A sobering point is that reviews of widely cited and influential studies show a preponderance of work from the Global North, that is, from those countries or regions that are wealthier in education and in social and economic resources than those of the Global South. Barnett's (2008) sample of 28 studies (by research strength), for example, features only three from outside the USA: the *Mauritius Study* (Raine et al., 2003), *Effective Provision of Preschool Education* (EPPE) (Melhuish et al., 2008), and *Effective Preschool Provision in Northern Ireland* (EPPNI) (Melhuish et al., 2006). Such reviews reveal differential research resources, research infrastructure, research personnel, and research networks across and within the Global North/Global South configuration. Reducing the disparity between those rich in resources and those with much less was the remit of the United Nations' *Millennium Development Goals* (2010). Although such declarations are not ostensibly focused on research, they form part of the macro-context for the volume's examination of early childhood research.

There is lively debate about what constitutes *bona fide* early childhood research. A case-in-point is the debate as to whether evaluation is research and/or a sub-set of research or whether research and evaluation are mutually exclusive (Beney, 2011; Donaldson, Christie and Mark, 2009; Mark, 2009; Patton, 2008, 2014; Renger, 2014; Scriven, 1991, 2003, 2013). We find research publications peppered with evaluation studies, research bodies with evaluation studies in their cadre of funded works, and the emergence of scholarly journals devoted to evaluation – a scenario likely spurred by an imperative for research-to-practice evidence, using impact studies for government and other stakeholders.

Patton (2014) distinguishes between research and evaluation, arguing that research is concerned with empirical evidence, theory testing, peer review, and generalizability of results, while evaluation is concerned with determining the effectiveness, quality, or impact of a specific program or model and drawing evaluative conclusions for stakeholders and end-users. Renger (2014), in turn, refers to the continued blurring of evaluation and research as hybridized terms and the frequent use of similar designs in both research and evaluation, such that confusion over their distinctiveness is inevitable (see also Levin-Rozalis, 2003; Renger et al., 2013). A related newcomer is the field of 'evaluation capacity building' (ECB), a design and implementation process that seeks to assist individuals, groups, and organizations to develop an evaluative stance (see Labin, 2014; Preskill and Boyle, 2008). While not explicitly addressed as an extant field within this volume, these ideas and practices form part of the context in which early childhood research practitioners, policy makers, and end users operate.

A Growing Range of Researchers

Not only has the field seen a growing range of research studies and approaches, it has seen the emergence of a growing range of researchers. Once the primary province of university-based research academics, early childhood research, in embracing *in situ* approaches and methodologies, has welcomed new research players such as those from non-traditional disciplines such as neuroscience or economics, along with parents and, indeed, children. A particular category of early childhood researcher to emerge is the early childhood practitioner-researcher, particularly in the UK, the USA, Australia, and New Zealand. Practitioner research is defined by Goodfellow (2005: 48) as 'systematic inquiry-based efforts directed toward creating and extending professional knowledge and associated understandings of professional practice.' In England, for example, early childhood practitioner research has proliferated in tandem with the universal rollout of the *Early Years Foundation Stage* (EYFS) for children up to 5 years of age. The Mosaic approach championed by Clark and colleagues (2005) in the UK and addressed in Chapter 5, for example, has been taken up by early years practitioner-researchers to make 'listening' visible through documentation and reflection (see Clark and Moss, 2001; Clark et al., 2005). So, too, there has been exponential growth in research resources for use by early years practitioners (Arnold, 2012; Mukherji and Albon, 2009).

Indeed, the growing prominence of early years practitioner-research is seen in the named category of research award sponsored by SAGE Publications and the *British Educational Research Association* (2012), and another similar award sponsored by Routledge and the *European Early Childhood Education Research Association* (2012). In Australia, early childhood practitioner research is featured in the Research in Practice series published by Australia's premier professional body *Early Childhood Australia* (Goodfellow, 2009; Goodfellow and Hedges, 2007). While located within the field of professional practice, conducted (typically) in early childhood services, the phenomenon of the specialist early childhood researcher is emblematic of the broader uptake of early childhood research and the shaping of the field of early childhood research. It is fair to say that the work of the early childhood practitioner-researcher has generated a significant corpus of (predominantly) qualitative data, yet the influence and impact of such activity are yet to be examined in any systematic way.

EARLY CHILDHOOD RESEARCH: POSSIBILITIES FOR TRANSFORMATION

The transformative potential of research is to enable change in the research setting and those within it. Possibilities of research for transformation can be seen through the everyday practices of life in: home and family contexts; out-of-home contexts such as services for young children and their families; and broader societal and global contexts that pose challenges and risks for young children. Possibilities for transformation lie in conceptual understandings of research *with* children rather than research *on* or *about* children (Kellet, 2005), where children are seen as holding rights as active participants and competent interpreters of their own worlds, as persons with the right to be seen and heard within their sites of experience on issues that affect them (Christensen and James, 1998; Mayall, 2003; Qvortrup, 2000; Tisdall, 2012). Such sociological understandings contrast with and contest traditional developmental understandings of children as pre-competent (Danby, 2002; Mackay, 1991), as under-developed 'human becomings' (Phillips and Alderson, 2002: 6), who, one day, may become competent adults.

Early childhood research, in turn, has the transformative potential to tackle 'wicked' problems (see Rittel and Webber, 1973), which beset children, families, and communities. Wicked problems include the adverse impacts of climate change and geo-political instability, child poverty, rapid urbanization, transnational displacement, and food shortages. UNICEF's (2014: 3) report on the *State of the World's Children*, for example, shows that, of the 18,000 children under 5 years old who die every day, a disproportionate number are from parts of cities or the countryside that are cut off from services because of poverty or geography, and the world's poorest children are 2.7 times less likely than the richest ones to have a skilled attendant at their birth. Despite the stark situation for children evidenced by UNICEF's current Multiple Indicator Cluster Surveys (MICS) (250 surveys conducted in more than 100 countries and areas since 1995), UNICEF (2014: 15) avows that 'Children drive change. Children are experts on their own lives. They can contribute valuable knowledge to validate and enrich the evidence base – if only they have a chance to be heard.' Evidence such as this points to the urgent need for research-for-transformation of the settings in which children operate.

Another 'wicked' problem that shapes research foci and settings of concern to many adults is child consumerism and children's engagement with globalized social media. Buckingham (2011) concedes:

> From the moment they are born, children today are already consumers. Contemporary childhoods are lived out in a world of commercial goods and services. Marketing to children is by no means new, but children now play an increasingly important role, both as consumers in their own right and as influences on parents ... Yet far from being welcome or celebrated, children's consumption has often been perceived as an urgent social problem. (p. 5)

The pervasiveness of social media, albeit for those resourced for access, forms part of the context in which research occurs. Some argue that the phenomenon of children operating as consumers of new technologies, online services, and social media, particularly in the Global North, is posing opportunities and challenges for children, families, and communities, and in turn, for early childhood research. A quest for antidotes to exponential social and technological change and children's participation in it has seen the emergence of new fields of inquiry, such as studies of human 'happiness'. One that goes beyond the conventional correlates such as poverty to explore new evidences of wellbeing. In summary, the social conditions under which children and adults operate and the social and technological resources at their disposal inform the context in which research occurs and, to some extent, inform the methodological approaches that are taken up in research.

This whirlwind review suggests several things about early childhood research. It sits at the convergence of multiple disciplinary domains, each with their respective research traditions and orientations. While aspiring to a shared focus, the domains have historically competed with each other for recognition and influence in the policy and research funding landscape. Further, the review recognizes that the field is strong in conceptual and methodological diversity, and relatively weak in giving coherent and convincing arguments of evidence in favor of young children and their life chances. The review shows that early childhood research, however complex, is critical particularly in light of the urgent need for evidence to drive the decisions that governments and others are making on behalf of children. Despite challenges, it is worthy of thoughtful investigation, interrogation, and reflection, such as is provided within this volume.

OVERVIEW OF THE HANDBOOK

This handbook provides an overview of the field of early childhood research, incorporating its conceptual underpinnings, research methodologies and future possibilities in the contexts in which young children, their families, and communities operate. It reveals the weight of evidence from human development, educational research, and economics to show that the lived experiences of children, now, impact their life chances in the future. It maps developing areas of research and research methods and notes the changing players and practices to enter the field. In turn, from a human rights perspective, the volume shows the importance of young children, in their own right, in the here and now, as worthy of ethical research and policy attention. The volume recognizes that contexts shape the contours of children's everyday lives, in home and out-of-home settings and shape the design, conduct, and dissemination of the research that ensues.

A thread running through the volume is the importance of the ethical conduct of research with children in the contexts of their everyday lives, a substantive point made, with acuity, in those chapters that deal with the Global South and post-colonial situations of war and conflict. Another thread is the need for critique of burgeoning interest in econometrics and cost-benefit studies and a reliance on dominant neo-liberal Western formulations in shaping policy and practice.

In compiling the volume, the editors faced the challenge of a preponderance of work from the Global North and a favoring (in published work and citations) of Western research traditions and approaches. The editors embarked on a quest to enlist work from the Global South and appreciated the connections made, and contributions *from* as well as *on* the Global South. The combination of work from the Global North and the Global South extended theory, methods, and policy and practice implications, thereby showing the potential of cross-country conversations. While challenging, the initiative to include work from both the Global North and the Global South opened up a rich seam of scholarship from a number of post-colonial regions, such that new research identities and groupings are beginning to emerge in regions traditionally eclipsed in works such as this.

The volume is organized into five parts, each drawing upon specific cases to illuminate their diverse foci and to optimize applicability to the relevant context of practice:

Part I. Situating early childhood research (context focus)
Part II. Theorizing early childhood research (theoretical focus)
Part III. Conducting early childhood research (methodology focus)
Part IV. Applying early childhood research (issues focus)

Part V. Considering the future of early childhood research (prospective focus)

Each chapter considers early childhood research within its respective area of focus, the theoretical and methodological approaches that are used therein, issues of relevance for the broader field of early childhood research and/or policy, and new developments or perspectives that the area brings to the early childhood agenda. In designing the Handbook, the editors encouraged the authors to consider diversity and equity related to issues germane to their chapter and to be mindful of the geo-political contexts in which the work is located. That said, a volume of this scale and scope does not assure equal coverage of such matters across its five parts.

Part I begins by setting early childhood research, as a complex and expanding field, within its historical, conceptual, and policy contexts and identifies the significant contributions of early childhood research to the context of children's lives, thereby demonstrating the impact of research on children and on the contexts in which they operate. Morin, Glickman and Brooks-Gunn provide a thorough examination of home and family contexts for research, while Dalli and White locate their systematic analysis within the context of group-based care for very young children. Cohen and Korintus' consideration of the child and the community in context is an illuminating examination of child and community contexts in different locales.

Part II explores the significant theoretical underpinnings of early childhood research. This section opens with Tisdall's examination of young children's participation that shows affordances of children's rights in everyday research contexts. Moss's theoretical perspectives on the positionality of the researcher, her language and pedagogy, within the research context. Moss's chapter is complemented by De Graeve's theoretical understandings of identity politics, intersectionality, and discourses of citizenship, using notions of motherhood and parenthood to show the ways in which particular discourses in particular communities normalize, pathologize, and devalue parenting. Gallacher provides a theorization of young children's spaces and children's rights in research. Young's analysis of the applications of the science of early human development into action in order to close the gap between what we know and what we do. The part moves to Anderson and Reid's consideration of theorizations from neuroscience and neuroplasticity, as highly influential in early childhood policy, and thus, affording critique Finally, the section concludes with a chapter on systems theory within the context of Latin America and the Caribbean, by Kagan, Araujo, Jaimovich, and Aguoyo.

Part III is devoted to conducting early childhood research, its focus being research design and the methodological and analytic aspects of undertaking research in the contexts of children's lives. The part opens with Farrell's chapter on ethics in research with young children. Its historical overview of research ethics in child research provides a conceptual platform for consideration of the design, conduct, and dissemination of early childhood research. Zubrick's chapter, in turn, contributes conceptual and methodological insights into the scope and scale of longitudinal research as a global technology, its affordances being demonstrated for data sharing, data mining, and policy formation. The part moves to a different methodological field in Konstantoni and Kustatscher's chapter on ethnographic research and its focus on child participation, participant observation, and reflexivity.

The section moves to a chapter by Clandinin, Huber, Menon, Murphy, and Swanson on narrative inquiry as a methodology in child research. Drawing on the work of Dewey, the authors discuss the importance of the ethical aspects of relationships involving children and adults in research contexts, be they in educational, family, or health care. Sidnell's chapter, in turn, highlights the conceptual and methodological contribution of conversation analysis in research with young children, in a range of everyday contexts. The chapter authored by Carr, Cowie, and Mitchell demonstrates the

research merit of documentation of young children's learning in early childhood education and care contexts, while Wood's chapter that follows demonstrates the complexity and context specificity of young children's play in intrepretivist research. The final chapter in the section, Cleveland's chapter on econometrics in early childhood research, argues for its fit-for-purpose in tackling major social issues.

Part IV considers the applications of early childhood research in the increasingly globalized, yet uneven and often inequitable, worlds of children. The section opens with Deb and Giraseen's chapter draws on evidence, largely from the Indian sub-continent, to exemplify the range of risks young children face and the importance of legislation and policy in tackling problems such as childhood illness, malnutrition, and crimes against children. O'Kane's analysis of applied research, involving young children in conflict situations within the Global South, argues for a greater prominence of child participation, ethics, children's rights to child-friendly spaces, and greater funding of collaborative humanitarian initiatives to ameliorate the adverse effects of war and its ravages on children.

Garcia's chapter on dual-language learners draws upon key examples from the Head Start program in the USA and collaborative work between the USA and Mexico, while Pence and Ashton's chapter charts the development of early childhood research in Sub-Saharan Africa since the 1970s, from a six-culture study of socialization to the growing voice of African researchers. The chapter by Yip, Levine, Lauricella and Wartella while based largely in the USA, considers the role and impact of electronic media on young children's development, with particular reference to the impact of media use on children's sleep. Their recommendations for further research into the link between media and early childhood learning stand to inform future research agendas. Rizzini and Bush draw upon early childhood research in Brazil to examine legislative, legal, and law enforcement initiatives to increase community safety and to enact the United Nations Declaration on the Rights of the Child. Rizzini and Bush use their work to illustrate how university researchers can form networks and alliances with community organizations to engage in public discussion and impact on policy making. The chapter authored by Okwany and Ebrahim critiques dominant narratives of early childhood development, using Africa as an example to consider epistemology and contextualization of research with local scholars, children, caregivers, and communities. Drawing on postcolonial theorists, they critique the application, efficacy, and relevance of Western scholarship and early childhood development studies about Africa. They assert that there is no singular childcare narrative and that the adage 'who writes and listens what about whom' requires challenging. The part finishes with a review and discussion of cognitive research in Global South by Rao, Sun and Wang.

Part V concludes the volume with an exploration of the expanding field of early childhood research and future possibilities within increasingly complex political and social landscapes.

This part opens with Penn's analysis of neo-liberal, post-colonial, social, economic, and political aspects of early childhood education and care interventions in economically disadvantaged countries. In so doing, it provides a theoretical platform for consideration of Western paradigms and methodologies that predominate early childhood research. Marsh examines the ever-changing digital technologies in children's worlds and futures, referring to empirical evidence around children using technologies in home and out-of-home contexts. Against the backcloth of the United Nations Millennium Development Goals, Pramling Samuelsson addresses the future of an environmental sustainability agenda in early childhood education by presenting some key case studies of sustainability-in-action projects.

The final chapter draws together key substantive issues addressed in the Handbook and sets the stage for future early childhood research, within changing contexts, methodologies, and agendas. The volume provides a platform from which to present powerful

next-step imperatives for early childhood research into the future.

REFERENCES

Arnold, C. (ed.) (2012) *Improving Your Reflective Practice through Stories of Practitioner Research.* London: Routledge.

Barnett, W. S. (2008) *Preschool Education and its Lasting Effects: Research and Policy Implications.* Boulder, CO and Tempe, AZ: Education and the Public Interest Center & Education Policy Research Unit. Available at: http://epicpolicy.org/publication/preschooleducation

Beney, T. (2011) *Distinguishing Evaluation from Research.* Available at: http://www.uniteforsight.org/evaluation-course/module10 (accessed 1 June 2015).

Buckingham, D. (2011) *The Material Child: Growing up in a Consumer Culture.* Cambridge: Polity Press.

Camilli, G., Vargas, S., Ryan, S. and Barnett, S. W. (2010) 'Meta-analysis of the effects of early education interventions on cognitive and social development', *Teachers College Record*, 112(3): 579–620.

Campbell, F. A., Pungello, E. P., Kainz, K., Burchinal, M., Pan, Y., Wasik, B. H., … Ramey, C. T. (2012) 'Adult outcomes as a function of an early childhood educational program: an abecedarian project follow-up', *Developmental Psychology*, 48(4): 1033–1043.

Christensen, P. and James, A. (eds) (1998) *Research with Children: Perspectives and Practices.* London: Falmer Press.

Clark, A., Kjørholt, A. and Moss, P. (2005) *Beyond Listening. Children's Perspectives on Early Childhood Services.* Bristol: Policy Press.

Clark, A. and Moss, P. (2001) *Listening to Young Children: The Mosaic Approach.* London: National Children's Bureau for the Joseph Rowntree Foundation.

Cunha, F., Heckman, J., Lochner, L. and Masterov, D. (2005) *Interpreting the Evidence of Life-cycle Skill Formation.* ISA Discussion Paper Series, No. 1575, Institute for the Study of Labour, Bonn, Germany.

Danby, S. (2002) 'The communicative competence of young children', *Australian Journal of Early Childhood*, 27(3): 25–30.

Donaldson, S. I., Christie, C. A. and Mark, M. M. (2009) *What Counts as Credible Evidence in Applied Research and Evaluation Practice?* Los Angeles: Sage Publications.

Goodfellow, J. (2005) 'Researching with/for whom? Stepping in and out of practitioner research', *Australian Journal of Early Childhood*, 30(4): 48–57.

Goodfellow, J. (2009) *The Early Years Learning Framework: Getting Started.* Deakin West, ACT: Early Childhood Australia. Available at: http://www.earlychildhoodaustralia.org.au/nqsplp/wp-content/uploads/2012/05/RIP0904_EYLFsample.pdf (accessed 1 June 2015).

Goodfellow, J. and Hedges, H. (2007) 'Practitioner research "centre stage": Contexts, contributions and challenges', in L. Keesing-Styles and H. Hedges (eds), *Theorising Early Childhood Practice: Emerging Dialogues.* Castle Hill, NSW: Pademelon Press.

Heckman, J. (2011) 'The economics of inequality: the value of early childhood education', *American Educator*, Spring: 31–47.

Kellett, M. (2005) *Children as Active Researchers: A New Research Paradigm for the 21st Century?* UK: ESRC. Available at: http://oro.open.ac.uk/7539/1/ (accessed 1 June 2015).

Labin, S. N. (2014) 'Developing common measures in evaluation capacity building: an iterative science and practice process', *American Journal of Evaluation*, 35: 107–15.

Levin-Rozalis, M. (2003) 'Evaluation and research: Differences and similarities', *Canadian Journal of Program Evaluation*, 18(2): 1–31.

Mackay, R. W. (1991) 'Conceptions of children and models of socialization', in F. C. Waksler (ed.), *Studying the Social Worlds of Children: Sociological Readings.* London: Falmer Press. pp. 23–37.

Mark, M. (2009) 'Credible evidence: Changing the terms of the debate', in S. I. Donaldson, C. Christie, and M. Mark (eds), *What Counts as Credible Evidence in Applied Research and Evaluation Practice?* Los Angeles, CA: Sage Publications. pp. 214–38. Available at: http://dx.doi.org/10.4135/9781412995634.d20 (accessed 1 June 2015).

Mayall, B. (2003) 'Sociologies of Childhood and Educational Thinking', professorial lecture presented at the Institute of Education, University of London, London.

McKinnon, R. and Campbell, H. (2011) 'Systematic review of birth cohort studies in South East Asia and the Eastern Mediterranean regions', *Journal of Global Health*, 1(1): 59–71. Available at: www.ncbi.nlm.nih.gov/pmc/articles/PMC3484744/ (accessed 16 February 2015).

Melhuish, E., Quinn, L., Hanna, K., Sylva, K., Siraj-Blatchford, I., Sammons, P. and Taggart, B. (2006) *The Effective Pre-school Provision in Northern Ireland Project, Summary Report.* Belfast: Stranmillis University Press. Available at: http://www.deni.gov.uk/researchreport41.pdf (accessed 1 June 2015).

Melhuish, E., Sammons, P., Siraj-Blatchford, I., Taggart, B. and Sylva, K. (2008) 'Towards the transformation of practice in early childhood education: the effective provision of pre-school education (EPPE) project', *Cambridge Journal of Education*, 38(1): 23–36.

Mukherji, P. and Albon, P. (2009) *Research Methods in Early Childhood: An Introductory Guide.* London: SAGE.

Organisation for Economic Cooperation and Development (OECD) (2001) *Starting Strong.* Paris: OECD.

Organisation for Economic Cooperation and Development (OECD) (2006) *Starting Strong II.* Paris: OECD.

Organisation for Economic Cooperation and Development (OECD) (2012) *Starting Strong III: A Quality Toolbox for ECEC.* Paris: OECD.

Patton, M. Q. (2008) *Utilization-focused Evaluation* (4th ed.). Thousand Oaks, CA: Sage Publications.

Patton, M. Q. (2014) *Qualitative Research & Evaluation Methods Integrating Theory and Practice* (4th ed.). Thousand Oaks, CA: Sage Publications. Available at: https://study.sagepub.com/patton4e (accessed 1 June 2015).

Phillips, B. and Alderson, P. (2003) 'Beyond anti-smacking: challenging violence and coercion in parent–child relations', *International Journal of Children's Rights*, 11(2):175–97.

Preskill, H. and Boyle, S. (2008) 'A multidisciplinary model of evaluation capacity building', *American Journal of Evaluation*, 29: 443–59.

Puma, M., Bell, S., Shapiro, G., Broene, P., Cook, R., Friedman, J. and Heid, C. (2001) *Building Futures: The Head Start Impact Study: Research Design Plan.* Available at:

http://www.acf.hhs.gov/sites/default/files/opre/impactstdy_resrch_plan.pdf (accessed 1 June 2015).

Qi, S. (2006) 'Longitudinal effects of parenting on children's academic achievement in African American families', *Journal of Negro Education*, 75(3): 415–29.

Qvortrup, J. (2000) 'Macroanalysis of childhood', in P. Christensen and A. James (eds), *Research with Children: Perspectives and Practices*. London: Falmer Press. pp. 77–97.

Raine, A., Mellingen, K., Liu J., Venables, P. and Mednick, S. A. (2003) 'Effects of environmental enrichment at ages 3–5 years on schizotypal personality and antisocial behavior at ages 17 and 23 years', *American Journal of Psychiatry*, 160: 1627–35.

Renger, R. (2014) 'Contributing factors to the continued blurring of evaluation and research: Strategies for moving forward', *The Canadian Journal of Program Evaluation*, 29(1): 104–17.

Renger, R., Bartel, G. and Foltysova, J. (2013) 'The reciprocal relationship between implementation theory and program theory in assisting decision-making'. *Canadian Journal of Program Evaluation*, 28(1): 27–41.

Rittel, H. and Webber, M. (1973) 'Dilemmas in a general theory of planning', *Policy Sciences*, 4: 155–69.

Scriven, M. (1991) *Evaluation Thesaurus* (4th ed.). Newbury Park, CA: Sage Publications.

Scriven, M. (2003) 'Reflecting on the past and future of evaluation', *The Evaluation Exchange*, 9(4). Available at: http://www.hfrp.org/evaluation/the-evaluation-exchange/issuearchive/reflecting-on-the-past-and-future-of-evaluation/michael-scriven-on-the-differences-between-evaluation-and-social-science-research (accessed 1 June 2015).

Scriven, M. (2013) 'The past, present, and future of evaluation', paper presented at The International Conference of the Australasian Evaluation Society, Brisbane, Australia.

Tayler, C. and Thorpe, K. (2012) 'Assessing the quality of Australian child care and kindergartens', *E4Kids: Effective Early Educational Experiences Research Bulletin*, 2: 1–6. Available at: http://web.education.unimelb.edu.au/E4Kids/news/pdfs/E4Kids_Research_Bulletin_Issue2.pdf (accessed 16 January 2015).

Tisdall, K. (2012) 'Children's services: working together', in M. Hill, G. Head, A. Lockyer, B. Reid and R. Taylor (eds), *Taking Forward Children's and Young People's Participation in Decision-Making*. London: Pearson Longman.

United Nations (1989) *Convention on the Rights of the Child (UNCRC)*. Available at: www.ohchr.org/en/professionalinterest/pages/crc.aspx (accessed 16 February 2015).

United Nations (2010) *United Nations Millennium Development Goals*. Available at: www.un.org/millenniumgoals/ (accessed 8 January 2015).

United Nations Children's Fund (UNICEF) (2008) *Innocenti Report Card. The Child Care Transition: A League Table of Early Childhood Education and Care in Economically Advanced Countries*. Florence: UNICEF Innocenti Research Centre.

United Nations Children's Fund (UNICEF) (2014) Children in an Urban World: State of the World's Children. Geneva: UNICEF.

Xiang, Z. and Schweinhart, L. J. (2002) Effects five years later: The Michigan School Readiness Program evaluation through age 10. Ypsilanti, MI: High/Scope Educational Research Foundation. Available at: http://www.highscope.org/file/Research/Effects%205%20Years%20Later.pdf (accessed 1 June 2015).

PART I

Situating Early Childhood Research

2

Parenting and the Home Environment

Marisa Morin, Jennifer Glickman
and Jeanne Brooks-Gunn

INTRODUCTION

Children develop within multiple contexts
that affect children and family over time
(Bronfenbrenner, 1986). In this chapter, we
examine two intersecting spheres of influence
on children's development – what parents do
with their children (often referred to by developmental psychologists as parenting) and
what the home environment is like for young
children. Clearly, parents are largely responsible for organizing the home environment
experienced by their children. However, parents are often constrained by what has been
called capital – economic capital (the amount
of monetary resources), human capital (the
amount of education), and social capital (the
number of relationships and ties to other individuals). Each of the forms of capital is often
studied by economists and sociologists. The
degree to which children benefit from capital
is determined by how well opportunities to
utilize capital are maximized (Becker and
Tomes, 1994). For example, Heckman (2006)

shows how families and childcare settings may
provide conditions for enhancing children's
learning. Child learning itself is a form of
human capital, as achieving in school is
linked to literacy and numeracy capabilities in
children, as well as to less easily quantified
capabilities such as perseverance and grit
(Borghans et al., 2008). These capabilities are
developed through experiences in the home
and educational settings. Feedback effects
are believed to operate such that children
who gain such abilities early on are better
able to take advantage of learning experiences
later on. In fact, early achievement scores at
kindergarten are associated with achievement
scores in high school, which are associated
with high school graduation, post-secondary
schooling, and, ultimately, higher lifetime
wages (Brooks-Gunn et al., 2014).

In this chapter, we review the extant literature on how parenting and the home environment reflect parents' economic and human
capital opportunities and constraints on children's development and on parents' behaviors

towards their children. We will discuss three aspects of family characteristics that influence parenting – family income, parental education, and family structure. Together, these three socioeconomic conditions give rise to large disparities in achievement and later educational and job success between children whose parents are single, low income, and/or not well educated compared to children whose parents are more advantaged. Of course, other family characteristics might influence parenting and the home environment, such as cultural beliefs, neighborhood characteristics, household composition and turbulence, discrimination, language spoken in the home, and immigration status. We focus on the three that have been studied most comprehensively here. In general, we refer to mothers rather than parents, because the bulk of the research to date has concentrated on mothers. However, there is ample evidence to suggest that fathers' parenting behaviors independently affect young children's behavior and cognition in the first five years of life as well (Martin et al., 2010; Parke, 2004; Tamis-LeMonda et al., 2004). We conclude with a discussion of interventions aimed at supporting parenting in the context of these three socioeconomic conditions.

It is important to note that this chapter focuses primarily on work that has been conducted within the USA, given that its research base is more comprehensive and has considered selection bias in more depth (e.g., examined whether links are likely to be causal). The USA is a particular context. Compared to other members of the Organization for Economic Cooperation and Development (OECD), the USA has very high rates of poverty in families with young children. In addition, while rates of unwed parenthood are high in many OECD countries, children in the USA experience more biological and father figure (e.g., maternal romantic partner) transitions moving in and out of their lives. Parental education levels, once higher in the USA, are now similar to many other OECD countries. Inequality in family income is very high in the USA. Therefore, the experience

of families in the USA is not uniformly or relatively better than that of families in other OECD countries. Research within the context of the USA is more relevant or generalizable to other OECD countries than to less affluent countries, especially those that are sometimes referred to as the Global South, where the vast majority of families are poor and adult educational levels are low. In the intervention section of this chapter, we present evidence of the effectiveness of two types of interventions – conditional cash transfers and home visiting – in such less affluent contexts.

FAMILY INCOME

In 2013, a family of two is considered to be living in poverty if the household income falls below $15,510 (Department of Health and Human Services (DHHS), 2013). A family of two is typically considered to be 'low-income' if the household income falls below 200% of this poverty line, or is less than $31,020 per year (DHHS, 2013). Almost one-third of all families who have an employed parent in the USA now fall into this 'low-income' category (DHHS, 2013). The percentage of children under the poverty threshold is approximately 22% (Federal Interagency Forum on Child and Family Statistics, 2014). In addition, another 20% of children live in families which have difficulty making ends meet (Edin and Lein, 1997). We often use poverty or poor children to refer to those children under the poverty threshold (22% of children), and low income to refer to those children who are poor or near poor (40% of children).

Two theoretical models are often used to explain how low income affects child development through parenting and the home environment. The first, known as the 'family stress model' (Conger et al., 1994; McLoyd, 1990), posits that economic hardship is a negative life event in families that disrupts marital bonds and increases parental psychological distress. In turn, such factors cause lower levels of supportive parenting (McLoyd, 1990). Lower-income parents tend to engage in harsher, less responsive interactions with their children (Bradley and Corwyn, 2002; Conger and Donnellan, 2007; Fuligni and Brooks-Gunn, 2013). These parents rely more on corporal punishment than higher-income families, and their diminished responsiveness can lead to less attention and social support to children's emotional needs. Less supportive parenting increases the likelihood that children will experience internalizing (anxiety, depression) and externalizing (aggression) problems (Evans and Kim, 2013). In short, this model asserts that the association between lower family income and greater child behavior problems is mediated by parental distress and consequent parenting behaviors (Conger et al., 1994).

The second model, often referred to as the 'investment model' or 'human capital model' (Becker, 1981; Duncan and Brooks-Gunn, 1997), argues that economic deprivation decreases families' access to goods and services that promote development, causing children to have lower cognitive skills and more behavioral problems. The investment model posits that low-income parents are less able to invest their time and money in services for their children, creating a less safe, stimulating and responsive home environment (Conger et al., 1994; Linver et al., 2002; McLoyd, 1990; Yeung et al., 2002). Past studies find that, as family income increases, the quality of a child's home environment increases. For example, each $10,000 increase in income is associated with a 0.08 standard deviation increase in cognitive stimulation in the home environment, indexed by how often someone reads to the child; helps him or her learn numbers, letters, colors, shapes, and sizes; and encourages the child to engage in extracurricular activities (Duncan et al., 1998; Votruba-Drzal, 2003). Changes in the lower end of income distribution seem to matter more than changes in the higher end of income distribution (Duncan et al., 1998).

While both the family stress model and the investment model have been shown to mediate the relationship between income and behavior outcomes (Conger et al., 1997; Elder, 1999; Guo and Harris, 2000), the investment model results in a stronger association with cognitive and academic achievement outcomes and the family stress model results in a stronger association with behavioral outcomes (Linver et al., 2002; Yeung et al., 2002). Other research shows that children in poverty, in particular, live in less cognitively stimulating environments than other children, which in part accounts for their lower cognitive outcomes. Specifically, children in poverty have fewer age-appropriate toys, fewer informal learning experiences, fewer educational materials, and more exposure to television (Duncan et al., 1994; Evans, 2004; Klebanov et al., 1998). Children living in economic hardship also have less verbal stimulation because fewer words are spoken to them and parents read to them less often (Hoff et al., 2002). On a broader scale, poor children are more likely to live in neighborhoods that have less social capital; more chaos, noise, crowding, toxins, and crime; and fewer places to engage in physical activity and access healthy foods (Evans, 2004).

Questions have arisen as to whether these links are casual. Dearing and Taylor (2007) argue that income affects the home environment, as opposed to both being a function of a third variable, such as competing investment demands, family preferences in parenting practices, or other financial or psychological constraints on parenting. Authors examined within-family changes in income over time (thereby using each family as its own control) and tested for corresponding changes in the home environment. Results indicated that an increase in income was indeed associated with an improvement in the home environment. This improvement was largest for families who started with the lowest income levels, but, in general, all families benefited (Dearing and Taylor, 2007). Sibling analyses have been used to make the same point (Duncan et al., 1998). Experiments also suggest that income has a casual impact (Morris et al., 2005).

MATERNAL EDUCATION

In the USA, 25.2% of mothers have no more than a high school degree, while 12.8% have less than a high school education (Child Trends Databank, 2014). Low levels of education are overrepresented for low-income families. Over 70% of low-income mothers have no more than a high school degree (Addy and Wight, 2012; Sabol and Chase-Lansdale, 2015).

Research has found that parenting is often the pathway through which parental education influences child cognitive outcomes (Brooks-Gunn and Markman, 2005; Chase-Lansdale and Brooks-Gunn, 2014; Mistry et al., 2008). In other words, maternal education primarily influences children through its impact on the quality of children's home environment (Votruba-Drzal, 2003), which has been shown to have an impact on cognitive outcomes (Klebanov et al., 1998). Mothers who are more highly educated tend to talk more to their children, ask more questions, and use a larger vocabulary (Hart and Risley, 1999; Hoff, 2003). Among low-income families, maternal education is especially influential through this type of language and literacy stimulation and supportiveness (Magnuson, 2007; Mistry et al., 2008). Davis-Kean (2005) also found that parents' education is related to children's academic achievement through their beliefs and behaviors as well as educational expectations.

The impact of maternal education on *how* a mother teaches her child is also mediated through the effects of positive and harsh parenting (Carr and Pike, 2012). Higher levels of maternal education are linked to a parenting environment characterized by affection and positive discipline, which in turn is associated with contingent shifting, or adaptations of teaching based on the success or failure of a child (Neitzel and Stright, 2004). Lower levels of maternal education, on the other hand, are associated with greater parent–child conflict and negative discipline. Mothers with less education more commonly employ 'fixed failure feedback' or teaching behaviors that remain constant despite changes in a child's ability or task performance (Carr and Pike, 2012). In other words, such mothers are less skilled at scaffolding their children's learning.

FAMILY STRUCTURE

In the USA, two-fifths of all children are born to mothers who are not married (Kennedy and Bumpass, 2008; Waldfogel et al., 2010). In fact, children are more likely to live in single-parent families in the USA than children in any other Westernized country (Cherlin, 2005). However, not all unmarried mothers live alone. Half of non-marital births are to cohabiting parents (Kennedy and Bumpass, 2008; McLanahan and Beck, 2010). Unfortunately, most cohabiting relationships do not last long after the child's birth (McLanahan and Beck, 2010). In 2002, over 50% of children born to cohabiting parents had experienced parental separation by age 9, compared to 20% of children born to married parents (Kennedy and Bumpass, 2008). In general, children in traditional families with married parents are associated with better developmental outcomes compared to children living in single-mother or cohabiting families (Waldfogel et al., 2010).

The main question is what mechanisms drive the effect of family structure on child outcomes. It is currently thought that family structure is linked to child wellbeing because it is associated with parental resources, parental mental health, parental relationship quality, parenting quality, instability, and father involvement (Waldfogel et al., 2010). Some of these factors are likely to influence whether a child's biological parents marry in the first place. First, non-marital families have fewer resources through which to support their children (Waldfogel et al., 2010). Parents who marry have more education and income than those who do not (McLanahan and Waldfogel, 2011). Second, various studies have found that married mothers have better mental health compared to single mothers, the same as for fathers (DeKlyen et al., 2006). Third, regardless of whether unmarried parents are cohabitating, married parents have higher-quality relationships, defined by self-reports of how encouraging and supportive partners are, than unmarried parents do (Carlson et al., 2011). And more positive couple relationships are linked to more sensitive parenting and better child outcomes (Cox et al., 1999).

To some extent, family structure reflects pre-existing characteristics of parents (income and education, mental health, relationship quality) that are known to affect children. However, family structure does seem to influence child development on its own. Married mothers generally score higher than single mothers in terms of parenting quality, and sometimes score higher than unmarried but cohabiting mothers. In one study, single mothers scored higher than both cohabiting and married mothers on negative affect, and cohabiting mothers scored lower than married mothers on cognitive stimulation (Gibson-Davis and Gassman-Pines, 2010). In another study, single and cohabiting mothers both scored lower than married mothers on supportive parenting behaviors (Aronson and Huston, 2004).

Approaching the question of how family structure influences child development with the family stress model in mind, one possible explanatory variable is the extent to which families are stable in their structures. Since transitions to and from marriage or cohabitation can place stress on the primary caregiver, such stress could spill over to affect parenting in a negative manner. In fact, non-marital families are more likely to experience instability in family structure than families in which the child is born to married parents (Osborne and McLanahan, 2007). Therefore, it is not surprising that increased family instability was found to be associated with parenting stress (Cooper et al., 2009). Research has shown that family stability may matter more than structure for cognitive and health outcomes (Waldfogel et al., 2010). In addition, unmarried families may experience further stressors if parents have additional births with different partners and if biological fathers are less involved in their children's lives. Multiple-partner fertility, in particular, is associated with poor quality parent relationships, low non-resident father involvement, and poor co-parenting quality (McLanahan and Beck, 2010). Lastly, unmarried fathers are typically less involved in their children's caregiving than married fathers (Carlson et al., 2008; Waldfogel et al., 2010).

Despite being, on average, less involved than married fathers are, a number of non-resident fathers maintain contact with their children and provide both formal and informal economic support for their children. Highest when children are young, approximately 63% of non-resident fathers report regular contact with their children (McLanahan and Beck, 2010). Yet, as children grow older, contact with non-resident fathers declines to approximately 55% when children are 3 years of age and declines to 51% when children are 5 years of age (as cited in McLanahan and Beck, 2010; see also Carlson et al., 2008).

CUMULATIVE RISK

Being low income, having no post-secondary education, and being a single parent are related and often highly correlated characteristics within families (Duncan et al., 1994). Under the cumulative risk model of development, children who experience a combination of these family characteristics are at an increased risk of adverse developmental outcomes (Sameroff et al., 1993). Children with all three have a higher likelihood of having low cognitive, linguistic, and achievement scores, of being unhealthy, and of exhibiting behavioral problems (Pressman et al., 2012; Sameroff and Fiese, 2000). Cumulative risk has been found to be similarly associated with negative outcomes for children in both pre-school and adolescence (Klebanov and Brooks-Gunn, 2006). In addition, early cumulative risk is predictive of later negative child outcomes (Sameroff et al., 1989; Seifer et al., 1992) and later negative adult outcomes (Pungello et al., 2010). The long reach of early cumulative risk is due, in part, to the fact that cumulative risk scores are highly correlated themselves between preschool and adolescence (Sameroff et al., 1993).

PARENTING AND THE HOME ENVIRONMENT AS MAJOR MEDIATORS OF LINKS BETWEEN FAMILY CHARACTERISTICS AND CHILD WELLBEING

There are a number of factors – maternal employment, maternal mental health, and the parent relationship – that are often seen as mediators between family characteristics and parenting. As pictured in Figure 2.1, the effects of family income, maternal education, and family structure on parenting practices are explained by the three factors' influence on maternal employment, maternal mental health, and the parent relationship. In addition, family income, maternal education, and family structure affect child wellbeing via their influence on these three mediating factors and their subsequent influence on parenting practices. Parenting practices have a proximate effect on child wellbeing. Moreover, there are transactional processes at work in which child characteristics and wellbeing influence parenting as

well. For example, children with high levels of behavioral problems are associated with high parent and child reports of corporal punishment (Schneider et al., 2014). Higher book reading practices are found in low-income families where children are more linguistically advanced, which suggest that more linguistically advanced children encourage increased parental engagement in joint book reading activities (Raikes et al., 2006). Lastly, reciprocal effects regarding co-parenting quality and paternal involvement have been shown, where co-parenting is a predictor of future non-resident father involvement and father involvement is a predictor of future co-parenting quality (Carlson et al., 2008). While these three mediating factors are not exclusively affected by the family characteristics discussed in the previous section, it is important to consider their effects on child wellbeing. In the next section, we will review the literature on maternal employment, maternal mental health, and parent relationship/co-parenting quality.

MATERNAL EMPLOYMENT

The employment rate for mothers with young children has increased dramatically

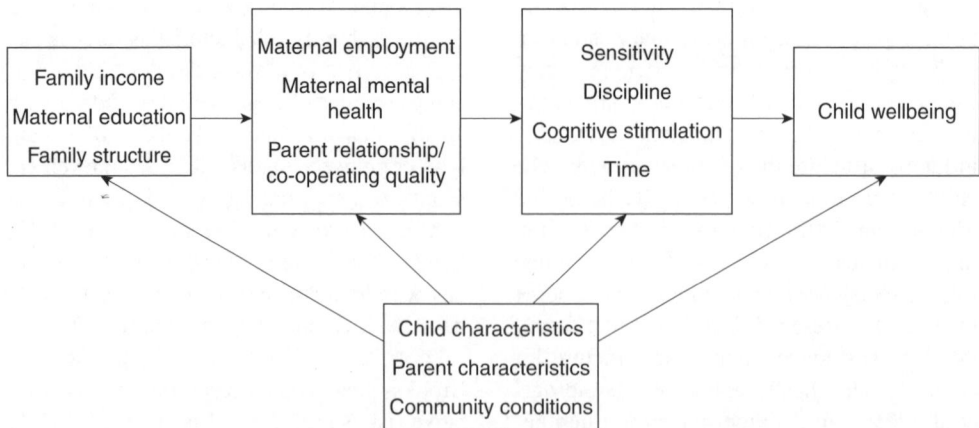

Figure 2.1   The effects of family income, maternal education, and family structure on parenting practices

over the past 25 years. In 2012, 65% of mothers with children under 6 years of age participated in the labor force (US Bureau of Labor Statistics, 2013). Of these working mothers, about 71% worked full time (US Bureau of Labor Statistics, 2013). The increases have been largest for mothers with infants (Brooks-Gunn, Han and Waldfogel, 2010). Working full time in a child's first year of life is associated with lower cognitive outcomes for children of white mothers, although these associations are mitigated by income brought into the family by employment and by high quality childcare (Brooks-Gunn, Han and Waldfogel, 2010). No associations between mothers' full-time employment in a child's first year of life and child cognitive outcomes are found for Hispanic and African American families (Chase-Lansdale, 1994; Coley and Lombardi, 2013), and positive associations are found for socioemotional outcomes for African American children (Coley and Lombardi, 2013). In general, maternal employment in the toddler or preschool years is not associated with child outcomes (although a few studies suggest a positive association). However, working non-standard hours is associated negatively with child outcomes throughout the preschool years (Han, 2008).

One of the reasons the research does not show that maternal employment is inherently bad for children is that employment, on average, does not negatively affect maternal investments in their children. Bianchi (2000) cites research that has shown that employed mothers and non-employed mothers devote the same amount of time to their children (Nock and Kingston, 1988). In addition, fathers today, especially married ones, are more likely to be involved with their children and to help working mothers meet the needs of their children. The problem arises when mothers are of low socioeconomic status. Such mothers have less choice in whether they pursue paid work, less choice regarding employment hours, and are less likely to be married and to benefit from the support of the biological father (Bianchi, 2000).

MATERNAL DEPRESSION

Some studies examine the effects of depressive symptomology and others examine the effects of clinical diagnoses of depression on child outcomes. Both bodies of literature suggest direct and indirect links between maternal depression and child outcomes. The direct pathway from maternal mental health to child development is explained by social learning theory, or the notion that children learn behaviors by observing others. Distressed mothers may role-model negative cognitions, poor emotional regulation, and ineffective problem solving that their children then emulate (Goodman, 2007).

The indirect pathway is mediated by parenting behaviors (Elder, 1999). Both depression and high stress in parents are strongly associated with irritability and hostility toward a child, and are somewhat correlated with familial disengagement (Lovejoy et al., 2000; Meadows et al., 2007). Depressed mothers engage in less sensitive behaviors and more punitive discipline. They respond less positively, frequently, and quickly to children's efforts of engagement, and they are more likely to control child behavior through coercion rather than negotiation or care (Downey and Coyne, 1990). Additionally, mothers who suffer from depression tend to have flatter speech (Lovejoy et al., 2000). Therefore, these negative parenting behaviors are one mechanism by which maternal depression is thought to contribute to childhood psychopathology (Goodman and Gotlib, 1999, 2002). Maternal depression has been found to be associated with young children's internalizing and externalizing behavior (Trapolini et al., 2007) and externalizing behavior in adolescents (Foster et al., 2008).

PARENT RELATIONSHIP AND CO-PARENTING QUALITY

In general, high quality co-parenting, or the relationship between two parent figures, is characterized by teamwork, mutual support, and consistent perceptions of the child (Bonds and Gondoli, 2007; Cox et al., 1999). Research has found that co-parenting is more predictive of parenting behaviors and child outcomes than is general marital quality, even after controlling for individual parent characteristics (Abidin and Brunner, 1995; Annemiek et al., 2008; Frosch et al., 2000). For example, how well parents work together is significantly associated with parenting style, whereas marital adjustment is not (Abidin and Brunner, 1995; Bearss and Eyberg, 1998; Carlson et al., 2008, 2011). Regardless of when romantic relationships dissolve, unmarried parents are capable of maintaining positive co-parenting relationships (McLanahan and Beck, 2010).

Improvements in maternal warmth over time are more closely determined by co-parenting support than by the quality of the actual marital relationship (Bonds and Gondoli, 2007). Co-parenting impacts parenting style, and the overall home environment, by influencing family affectivity, or the extent to which family members enjoy being together and are warm, affectionate, and comfortable with each other (Schoppe et al., 2001). A family with high negative affect is characterized by hostility, anger, or sarcasm (Schoppe et al., 2001). Such an affect can undermine children's emotional security (Davies and Cummings, 1998) or the extent to which a child feels confident in the certainty of his or her emotional wellbeing.

INTERVENTIONS FOCUSING ON PARENTS

Interventions can target each of the components shown in Figure 2.1. In other words, interventions can focus on the family characteristics influencing child wellbeing via increasing income, increasing maternal education, and decreasing unwed childbearing. In addition, interventions could alter maternal employment (the timing and stability of employment), reduce maternal depression, or enhance the relationship between mothers

and fathers. More direct programs focus on altering parenting behaviors specifically.

ENHANCING FAMILY INCOME AND EDUCATION

In the following section, we review programs seeking to increase family income, increase education, and support maternal employment. We name existing interventions, as well as present the literature available evaluating the effectiveness of such programs on enhancing family characteristics and influencing child wellbeing.

Income

There are a variety of federally administered programs in place to serve low-income families. Many of these programs fall into one of two categories: direct cash supplements and in-kind programs. Direct cash supplements can be conditional, in which families are required to do something in order to receive the benefits, or unconditional, in which families simply receive benefits if they qualify. In-kind programs offer services which otherwise cost money, such as nutrition, healthcare, subsidized childcare (Child Care and Development Block Grants), preschool programs (Head Start program and pre-kindergarten programs), and public housing (Housing Choice Voucher Program).

In terms of job assistance, many low-income working parents qualify for the Earned Income Tax Credit (EITC). The EITC is a refundable federal income tax credit given to low- to moderate-income workers to offset the burden of taxes and provide an incentive to work. Since qualifying for EITC requires employment, it is an example of a conditional program.

Temporary Assistance for Needy Families (TANF) is a mixture of conditional and in-kind programs. Originally, TANF was unconditional in that mothers who qualified were able to receive welfare if they were raising children. Since welfare reform in 1997, time limits were placed on receipt of TANF, so that it can now be seen as being partially conditional on time. TANF provides block grants to states to allow them to design and operate programs that will provide assistance to families, so that they can care for their children, reduce the dependency of needy parents by promoting work and marriage, reduce unplanned pregnancies among young adults, and/or encourage the maintenance of two-parent families. Because individual states administer TANF, the exact programs available to families vary.

Head Start is an early childhood care and education program designed to promote school readiness in children aged birth to 5 from low-income families and is an example of an in-kind program. The program supports children's growth in the areas of language and literacy, cognition, physical health, social and emotional development, and approaches to learning, while also emphasizing the role of the parent in family wellbeing and engagement.

Low-income families also have access to in-kind program services in the area of health and nutrition assistance. Examples of these programs include Medicaid; the Supplemental Nutrition Assistance Program (SNAP) and the Special Supplemental Nutrition Program for Women, Infants, and Children (WIC); and free or reduced-priced lunch and breakfast. Medicaid provides eligible children and parents who are not covered by a health plan with healthcare services. Both SNAP and WIC aim to provide individuals with the nutrition they need to survive. SNAP offers these services to all eligible low-income individuals and families, whereas WIC specifically targets pregnant, breastfeeding, non-breastfeeding postpartum mothers, and at-risk infants and children up to age 5. Additionally, WIC provides states with grants for health care referral and nutritional education for women. Free or reduced-price meals are provided at schools who participate in the National School Lunch Program to children from families with incomes at or below 185% of the poverty level. Children between 130% and 185% of the poverty level qualify for reduced-price lunch, meaning they will pay no more than 40 cents per meal, and children below 130% of the poverty level qualify for free lunch.

INCOME SUBSIDY EXPERIMENTS IN THE USA AND CANADA

Studies of several American antipoverty initiatives suggest that low-income children sometimes benefit when household income is supplemented. Two such programs were implemented in conjunction with American welfare reform in the mid-1990s, and aimed to force long-term recipients of public assistance off the welfare rolls and into the labor market. The Minnesota Family Investment Program (MFIP) and the Connecticut Jobs First program mandated employment among welfare recipients and, in exchange, granted earnings disregards to working parents. That is, the programs raised the threshold at which earnings triggered a reduction in welfare benefits, thereby allowing parents to keep some or all of their welfare benefits while working. The earnings disregards in both programs resulted in a net increase in income; thus, they can be considered income transfers. A comparison of the children of welfare recipients before and after the MFIP was implemented found that the MFIP had positive effects on children's academic performance and school engagement, but not on behavior (Knox et al., 2000). Contradictorily, a similar study of the Connecticut Jobs First program revealed positive effects on children's behavior but null or negative effects on academic performance (Bloom et al., 2002). An experimental study of a comparable program in Milwaukee called New Hope, which gave low-income parents income supplements in exchange for working, showed academic and behavioral benefits among children as many as five years after the program had ended (Huston et al., 2005). On the other hand, a

Canadian program (the Canadian Self-Sufficiency Program), which provided single parents with income supplements in exchange for leaving welfare and finding work, had positive effects on academic and health outcomes among school-age children in a three-year follow-up study, but no effects on outcomes among younger children, and negative effects on academic and behavioral outcomes among adolescents (Morris and Michalopoulos, 2003).

INTERNATIONAL INCOME SUBSIDY EXPERIMENTS

Recent studies of income transfer programs in the developing world also highlight the potential benefits of such initiatives for children. In a cash transfer program in rural Nicaragua, families received the equivalent of 15% of per capita expenditures made by families over that year (Maluccio and Flores, 2005). Nine months later, children in the treatment group scored higher than children in the control group on both cognitive and socioemotional outcomes. A similar cash transfer program in Ecuador assigned families within randomly selected communities to receive monthly cash payments of approximately 6–10% of household income (Fernald and Hidrobo, 2011). In rural but not urban areas, the children in the treatment group had better language scores than the comparison group and were more likely to have been bought a toy in the past six months (Fernald and Hidrobo, 2011). Many of these programs are conditional, in that parents are expected to take their children to health clinics and to school.

IMPLICATIONS OF PREVIOUS INCOME SUBSIDY EXPERIMENTS

The findings from the international experiments are consistent in that schooling and health are impacted. However, results are less

consistent in the USA and Canada. Many of the transfers involved mandated labor force participation. However, an interesting example of an unconditional cash transfer comes from a recent natural experiment in rural North Carolina. A casino opened on an Eastern Cherokee reservation approximately four years into an ongoing longitudinal study of 9-, 11-, and 13-year-old children that began in 1993 called the Great Smoky Mountains Study of Youth. A portion of the profits has been distributed to all adult American Indian tribal members (approximately $4,000 annually per adult) every six months since then. The income transfers are given only to adult tribal members, but there are no other stipulations attached to the receipt of the transfers, and no other programs or services accompany the transfer. Compared to a similar group of non-tribal children who did not receive the transfers, the tribal children showed greater gains in rates of high school graduation, overall educational attainment, and greater declines in involvement in minor delinquency (Copeland and Costello, 2010).

EDUCATION

It has been argued that low-income mothers might improve their child's life chances if mothers themselves obtain more schooling. Indeed, Magnuson (2007) found an association between mothers completing additional schooling and an improvement in child academic achievement, especially in reading and in the quality of the home environment. However, these results only applied to young mothers who initially had low levels of education. There was no association between increased maternal education and improved academic outcomes or home environments for children with older and more highly educated mothers (Magnuson, 2007).

However, it is not yet clear whether interventions designed to promote mothers' educational attainment actually result in higher degrees earned. College completion rates among unmarried parents are low, possibly due to either inadequate academic preparation or financial constraints. Financial burdens can often cause students to interrupt their studies or increase their work hours, both of which compromise the quality of their education and the outcomes for their children. Additionally, support from public programs available for education is not well coordinated or easily accessed. Loans are costly for families and only increase their financial burden. If families increase their work hours in order to pay back their loans, they may receive a reduction in public benefits without making enough money through the increased work to make up the difference (Goldrick-Rab and Sorensen, 2010).

A new approach to increasing mothers' human capital is pairing high quality early childhood education with programs to help mothers further their own education (known as two-generation programs; see Chase-Landsdale and Brooks-Gunn, 2014). The goal of a two-generation program is to increase the human capital of low-income parents and children in the same program. For example, a two-generation program could consist of an early childhood center for children, providing high-quality classrooms and family support services, as well as postsecondary education and workforce development services for parents.

EMPLOYMENT

Family leave policies are the only organized 'intervention' possibly reducing parenting stress and difficulties related to maternal employment. Currently, federal law only provides for unpaid leave. The Family and Medical Leave Act, most recently amended in 2008, requires employers to provide up to 12 weeks of job-protected, unpaid leave during any 12-month period to eligible employees who are incapacitated due to pregnancy, prenatal care, or child birth; who wish to care for their newborn child within one year of birth; who have adopted or taken

in a foster child; who must care for an immediate family member who has a serious health condition; or who has his or her own health condition that makes the employee unable to perform his or her job. To be eligible for leave, employees must have worked for a covered employer for at least 12 months, have completed 1,250 hours of service in the previous 12 months, and be working at a company that employs at least 50 employees within 75 miles. Three states have paid family leave.

While the research base is thin, family leave seems to be related to better maternal health. Having less than 12 weeks of maternal leave and less than eight weeks of paid maternal leave are both associated with increases in depressive symptoms and decreases in overall health status in mothers (Chatterji et al., 2011). Those mothers who most often take advantage of leave policies are typically married or more educated (Han et al., 2009), which is not surprising given that such mothers are more likely to be in jobs with family leave policies and are more likely to be able to take time off without pay given their income levels.

In other countries, findings depend on the outcome examined. Evaluations of family leave policies in Germany have failed to find any long-term outcomes for children. Extending unpaid parental leave from 18 to 36 months was not shown to increase selective high school attendance for German children (Dustmann and Schönberg, 2012). Yet, there is evidence from research examining parental leave policies for 16 European countries, the USA, and Japan between 1969 and 2000 that suggests paid parental leave, but not unpaid parental leave, decreases infant mortality within these countries (Tanaka, 2005). New laws might extend maternal leave to paid leave and/or promote longer periods of leave. Additionally, programs that provide postpartum health services that target mothers' mental and physical health and its impact on infants may be a useful support for mothers unsure of how to handle the work–family balance (Chatterji and Markowitz, 2012).

ENHANCING MATERNAL MENTAL HEALTH AND RELATIONSHIPS

In the following section, we review programs seeking to increase the wellbeing of mothers and their relationships with the biological fathers of their children. By supporting maternal mental health and parent relationship quality, such interventions are targeting mediating variables that affect a mother's ability to be sensitive, less punitive, and cognitively stimulating towards her child.

Maternal Depression

Interventions that focus on mothers who are mentally ill seek to help them become more sensitive and responsive to offspring, rather than directly treating their mental health problems. These efforts may be effective in helping children even when mothers continue to struggle with recurrent depression. One such intervention, Toddler–Parent Psychotherapy (Cicchetti et al., 2000), found that at age 3, children of depressed mothers who participated in the intervention had the same levels of cognitive functioning as children of non-depressed mothers (Cicchetti et al., 2000). By addressing features of the depressed mother–child interaction, Toddler–Parent Psychotherapy taught mothers how to interact positively with their children even with the continued persistence of contributors to depressive symptoms (Cicchetti et al., 2000). Other approaches are reviewed in Osborne et al. (2012).

Family Structure and Parent Relationship Quality

Despite the fact that public support of marriage is stronger in the USA than in most other developed countries and adults are more likely to marry, divorce rates are also higher in the USA than in other countries (Cherlin, 2005). The federal government supports public interventions to remediate conditions associated with single motherhood and family instability. The Deficit Reduction Act of 2005 provides $150 million of funding each year to healthy marriage promotion and fatherhood initiatives. At least $100 million of this funding must go towards specific marriage promotion activities, including marriage education, marriage skills training, public advertising campaigns, high school education on the value of marriage, and marriage mentoring programs. These programs, in general, have not been successful (Cowan et al., 2010).

However, the architects of these programs assume that the relationship between stable parents and child wellbeing is causal, when it appears to be due in large part to selection. That is, couples who get married tend to be more educated and have higher incomes than couples who do not. Both of these factors are associated with better child outcomes independent of marital status. In fact, using propensity score matching to rate parents' likelihood of marriage based on background characteristics, Ryan (2012) found that there was a positive association between parental marriage and cognitive outcomes for children at age 3 *only* for children with parents that were married at the child's birth. There were more positive associations between marriage and children's cognitive wellbeing when fathers possessed the human capital to influence cognitive development, such as education level (Ryan, 2012). Consequently, programs that enhance unwed fathers' capital and parenting skills may help make them more desirable for marriage and increase their capacity to enhance child development. Policymakers must balance marriage-based and marriage-neutral programs to provide assistance to needy families regardless of household structure, or children destined to live in single-parent and cohabiting families will not be helped (Cherlin, 2005).

Parenting Interventions

There are also interventions which target parenting itself. Such programs that focus on parenting are by definition two-generation programs. Beginning in 1965 with Head Start, two-generation programs aim to enhance young children's wellbeing through a focus on parenting and the home environment (Chase-Lansdale and Brooks-Gunn, 2014). Two-generation programs vary a great deal in structure and content. For example, two-generation programs can be delivered via center-based care, home visiting, or mothering groups. Home visiting may include case management, modeling of positive parenting behavior, provision of cognitively stimulating materials, social support, referrals to classes and services provided by outside agencies, mental health services, health information, or a combination of any of these. The same is true of center-based programs focusing on parents – all of the aforementioned services and supports might be offered to parents in addition to peer group support and modeling. Another aspect of some two-generation programs involves enhancing the human capital of parents (Chase-Lansdale and Brooks-Gunn, 2014). We have briefly considered these programs in an earlier section of this chapter.

Home-Visiting Programs

This type of intervention is used to enhance parenting and have an impact on the home environment of low-income households (Howard and Brooks-Gunn, 2009). While home-visiting programs differ substantially in design, size, and implementation (Nievar et al., 2010), most are based on Bronfenbrenner's (1986) Ecological Systems Theory, which underscores the importance of – and interactions among – the multiple contexts (e.g., family, school) that affect a child's development. For example, many home-visiting programs strive to improve parenting, which is theorized to improve parent–child interactions, and, consequently, the development of the child (Nievar et al., 2010). Some home-visiting programs target special parenting needs, such as providing parent training for families with young children who have already developed serious behavior problems.

For example, the Webster Stratton's Incredible Years parent-training program has been shown to be effective in reducing conduct problems in children both in the short term, at one month of age, and in the long term, at age 3 (Jones et al., 2008).

Home visiting, especially for poor young mothers, has been shown to increase the quality of a child's home environment by improving women's health-related behaviors, qualities of infant caregiving, and a mother's own life-course development (e.g., education and receipt of welfare) (Olds et al., 1998). Evidence is mixed as to whether these improvements in the home environment lead to enhanced cognitive development. Evidence is stronger for social and emotional development (Love et al., 2013). There is little evidence that home-visiting programs directly prevent child abuse and neglect (Howard and Brooks-Gunn, 2009). Nevertheless, programs like the Nurse–Family Partnership and Early Start have been shown to indirectly prevent maltreatment and childhood injuries by improving the parenting skills, attitudes, and behaviors associated with greater child wellbeing and decreased maltreatment (Howard and Brooks-Gunn, 2009). This improvement, in turn, enhances children's socioemotional outcomes (Sweet and Appelbaum, 2004).

International Home-Visiting Programs

Home-visiting programs exist in developing countries around the world as well. A home-visiting program in Jamaica provided nutritional supplementation and psychosocial stimulation to stunted children between the ages of 9 and 24 months (Engle et al., 2007). In weekly one-hour home visits, community health workers taught mothers how to improve interactions with their children within a play context. An initial evaluation of the intervention found significant benefits for children, helping them reach the developmental level of their non-stunted peers (Grantham-McGregor et al., 1991). Follow-up analyses when children were 17 to 18 years of age showed positive program effects on cognitive and educational outcomes (Walker et al., 2005). In addition, increased stimulation from the intervention has been shown to increase the average earnings by 42% for intervention participants at 20 years of age (Gertler et al., 2013). In Bolivia, home visits used along with a literacy program for indigenous women was found to be associated with higher test scores for intervention participants (Engle et al., 2007; Morenza et al., 2005). Lastly, Turkey and Bangladesh have used group session home visits with mothers. The Turkish program found positive short- and long-term effects on child development, whereas the Bangladeshi program found no intervention effects (Engle et al., 2007).

Parenting in the Context of Center-Based Care

There are also programs targeting parents within center-based care. For example, the Incredible Years Curriculum has been offered to families within Head Start. Utilizing the Incredible Years curriculum, parents meet as a group within a Head Start center to view and discuss videotaped vignettes depicting positive and negative parenting behaviors in response to child noncompliance. There are other programs within centers targeting parents' literacy behaviors with their children, such as Grover Whitehurst's dialogic reading program. In this program, mothers are trained not simply to read the text in books but rather to cultivate conversations with children by asking questions and making connections from the book and children's personal experiences (Brooks-Gunn and Markman, 2005).

CONCLUSION

The purpose of parenting interventions is to 'focus on creating opportunities for and meeting the needs of vulnerable children and

their parents together' (Lombardi et al., 2014: 4). Some but not all programs have been shown to influence parenting behaviors (St Pierre et al., 1995). Meta-analyses examining the effects of home-visiting programs on parent and child outcomes have found positive impacts but no program characteristics that consistently yield large effect sizes across participant subgroups (Kendrick et al., 2000; Nievar et al., 2010; Sweet and Appelbaum, 2004). Interestingly, most of these programs have not affected child well-being, with the exceptions of the Nurse–Family Partnership and Child Parent Center (Howard and Brooks-Gunn, 2009). Despite the mixed findings on effectiveness, parenting interventions continue to be valued by theorists and policymakers. With respective programs as guides for service providers, parenting interventions have the potential to be beneficial to both parents and children (Howard and Brooks-Gunn, 2009).

FURTHER READING

Becker, G. S. (2009). *Human Capital: A Theoretical and Empirical Analysis, with Special Reference to Education*. Chicago: University of Chicago Press.
Bornstein, M. (ed.) (2002). *Handbook of Parenting*, 2nd edn (Vols 1–3, pp. 3–44). Mahwah, NJ: Lawrence Erlbaum.
Bradley, R. H., & Corwyn, R. F. (2002). Socioeconomic status and child development. *Annual Review of Psychology*, 53, 371–99.

QUESTIONS FOR REFLECTION

1 What are the most effective ways to redress the differences in young children's home environments that cause more advantaged children to be more ready for school?
2 How might efforts focus on particular parenting practices or on the economic and social circumstances that give rise to these parenting practices?
3 What strategies might be used to enhance parent–child stimulation in low-income families?

ACKNOWLEDGEMENTS

We thank Anne Martin, Margo Gardner, and the Marx Family Foundation for their support.

REFERENCES

Abidin, R. R., & Brunner, J. F. (1995). Development of a parenting alliance inventory. *Journal of Clinical Child Psychology*, 24, 31–40.

Addy, S., & Wight, V. R. (2012). Basic facts about low-income children, 2010: Children under age 18 (NCCP Fact Sheet). New York: National Center for Children in Poverty.

Annemiek, K., van Tuijl, C., van Aken, M. A., & Dekovic, M. (2008). Parenting, coparenting, and effortful control in preschoolers. *Journal of Family Psychology*, 22(1), 30–40.

Aronson, S. R., & Huston, A. C. (2004). The mother–infant relationship in single, cohabiting, and married families: A case for marriage? *Journal of Family Psychology*, 18, 5–18.

Bearss, K. E., & Eyberg, S. (1998). A test of the parenting alliance theory. *Early Education & Development*, 9, 179–85.

Becker, G. S. (1981). *A Treatise on the Family*. Cambridge, MA: Harvard University Press.

Becker, G. S., & Tomes, N. (1994). Human capital and the rise and fall of families. In *Human Capital: A Theoretical and Empirical Analysis with Special Reference to Education*, 3rd edition (pp. 257–98). Chicago: University of Chicago Press.

Bianchi, S. M. (2000). Maternal employment and time with children: Dramatic change or surprising continuity? *Demographics*, 37(4), 401–14.

Bloom, D., Scrivener, S., Michalopoulos, C., Morris, P., Hendra, R., Adams-Ciardullo, D., & Walter, J. (2002). *Jobs First: Final Report on Connecticut's Welfare Reform Initiative*. New York: MDRC.

Bonds, D. D., & Gondoli, D. M. (2007). Examining the process by which marital adjustment affects maternal warmth: The role of coparenting support as a mediator. *Journal of Family Psychology*, 21(2), 288–96.

Borghans, L., Duckworth, A. L., Heckman, J. J., & Ter Weel, B. (2008). The economics and psychology of personality traits. *Journal of Human Resources*, 43(4), 972–1059.

Bornstein, M. (ed.) (2002). *Handbook of Parenting: Status and Social Conditions of Parenting* (Vols 1–4). Mahwah, NJ: Lawrence Erlbaum.

Bradley, R. H., & Corwyn, R. F. (2002). Socioeconomic status and child development. *Annual Review of Psychology*, 53, 371–99.

Bronfenbrenner, U. (1986). Ecology of the family as a context for human development: Research perspectives. *Developmental Psychology*, 22, 723–42.

Brooks-Gunn, J., & Markman, L. B. (2005). The contribution of parenting to ethnic and racial gaps in school readiness. *The Future of Children*, 15(1), 139–68.

Brooks-Gunn, J., Han, W. J., & Waldfogel, J. (2010). First-year maternal employment and child development in the first 7 years: III. What distinguishes women who work full-time, part-time, or not at all in the 1st year? *Monographs of the Society for Research in Child Development*, 75(2), 1–147.

Brooks-Gunn, J., Johnson, A., & Leventhal, T. (2010). Disorder, turbulence, and resources in children's homes and neighborhoods. In G. W. Evans, & T. D. Wachs (eds), *Chaos and its Influence on Children's Development: An Ecological Perspective* (pp. 155–70). Washington, DC: American Psychological Association Books.

Brooks-Gunn, J., Magnusson, K., & Waldfogel, J. (2014). Long-run economic effects of early childhood programs on adult earnings. Executive summary. Washington, DC: Partnership for America's Economic Success.

Caldwell, B., & Bradley, R. (1984). *Home Observation for Measurement of the Environment (HOME)*, revised edition. Little Rock, AK: University of Arkansas.

Carlson, M. J., McLanahan, S., & Brooks-Gunn, J. (2008). Coparenting and nonresident fathers' involvement with young children after a non-marital birth. *Demography*, 45, 461–88.

Carlson, M. J., Pilkauskas, N. V., McLanahan, S. S., & Brooks-Gunn, J. (2011). Couples as partners and parents over children's early years. *Journal of Marriage and Family*, 73, 317–34.

Carr, A., & Pike, A. (2012). Maternal scaffolding behavior: Links with parenting style and maternal education. *Developmental Psychology*, 48(2), 543–51.

Chase-Lansdale, L. (1994). Families and maternal employment during infancy: New linkages. In R. D. Parke and S. G. Kellam (eds), *Exploring Family Relationships with Other Social Contexts* (pp. 25–48). Hillsdale, NJ: Lawrence Erlbaum.

Chase-Landsdale, L., & Brooks-Gunn, J. (2014). Two-generation programs in the 21st century. *The Future of Children*, 24, 13–39.

Chatterji, P., & Markowitz, S. (2012). Family leave after childbirth and the mental health of new mothers. *Journal of Mental Health Policy and Economics*, 15, 61–76.

Chatterji, P., Markowitz, S., & Brooks-Gunn, J. (2011). *Early Maternal Employment and Family Wellbeing* (No. w17212). Cambridge, MA: National Bureau of Economic Research.

Cherlin, A. J. (2005). American marriage in the early twenty-first century. *Future of Children*, 15(2), 33–55.

Child Trends Databank (2014). *Parental Education: Indicators of Children and Youth*. Bethesda, MD: Child Trends Databank. Available at: www.childtrends.org/ ?indicators=parental-education

Cicchetti, D., Rogosch, F. A., & Toth, S. L. (2000). The efficacy of toddler–parent psychotherapy for fostering cognitive development in offspring of depressed mothers. *Journal of Abnormal Child Psychology*, 28(2), 135–48.

Coley, R. L., & Lombardi, C. M. (2013). Does maternal employment following childbirth support or inhibit low-income children's long-term development? *Child Development*, 84(1), 178–97.

Conger, R. D., & Donnellan, M. B. (2007). An interactionist perspective on the socioeconomic context of human development. *Annual Review of Psychology*, 58, 175–99.

Conger, R., Conger, K., & Elder, G. (1997). Family economic hardship and adolescent adjustment: Mediating and moderating processes. In G. Duncan & J. Brooks-Gunn (eds), *Consequences of Growing up Poor* (pp. 288–310). New York: Russell Sage Foundation.

Conger, R. D., Ge, X., Elder, G. H., Jr., Lorenz, F. O., & Simons, R. L. (1994). Economic stress, coercive family process, and developmental problems of adolescents. *Child Development*, 65(2), 541–61.

Cooper, C. E., McLanahan, S., Meadows, S., & Brooks-Gunn, J. (2009). Family structure transitions and maternal parenting stress. *Journal of Family and Marriage*, 71, 558–74.

Copeland, W., & Costello, E. J. (2010). Parents' incomes and children's outcomes: A quasi-experiment. *American Economic Journal: Applied Economics*, 2(1), 86.

Cowan, P. A., Cowan, C. P., & Knox, V. (2010). Marriage and fatherhood programs. *Future of Children*, 20, 87–112.

Cox, M., Brooks-Gunn, J., & Paley, B. (1999). Perspectives on conflict and cohesion in families. In M. Cox & J. Brooks-Gunn (eds), *Conflict and Cohesion: Causes and Consequences* (pp. 321–44). Mahwah, NJ: Lawrence Erlbaum.

Davidson, H. (1997). The legal aspects of corporal punishment in the home: When does physical discipline cross the line to become child abuse? *Children's Legal Rights Journal*, 17, 18–29.

Davies, P. T., & Cummings, E. M. (1998). Exploring children's emotional security as a mediator of the link between marital relations and child adjustment. *Child Development*, 69, 124–39.

Davis-Kean, P. E. (2005). The influence of parent education and family income on child achievement: The indirect role of parental expectations and the home environment. *Journal of Family Psychology*, 19(2), 294–304.

Dearing, E., & Taylor, B. A. (2007). Home improvements: Within-family associations between income and the quality of children's home environments. *Journal of Applied Developmental Psychology*, 28, 427–44.

DeKlyen, M., Brooks-Gunn, J., McLanahan, S., & Knab, J. (2006). The mental health of married, cohabitating, and non-coresident parents with infants. *Research and Practice*, 96(10), 1836–41.

Department of Health and Human Services. (2013). Annual update of the HHS poverty guidelines. *Federal Register*, 78(16), 5182–3.

Downey, G., & Coyne, J. C. (1990). Children of depressed parents: An integrative review. *Psychological Bulletin*, 108(1), 50–76.

Duncan, G. J., & Brooks-Gunn, J. (eds). (1997). *Consequences of Growing up Poor*. New York: Russell Sage Foundation.

Duncan, G. J., Brooks-Gunn, J., & Klebanov, P. (1994). Economic deprivation and early-childhood development. *Child Development*, 65(2), 296–318.

Duncan, G. J., Yeung, W. J., Brooks-Gunn, J., & Smith, J. R. (1998). How much does childhood poverty affect the life chances of children? *American Sociological Review*, 63, 406–23.

Dustmann, C., & Schönberg, U. (2012). Expansions in maternity leave coverage and children's long-term outcomes. *American Economic Journal: Applied Economics*, 4(3), 190–224.

Edin, K., & Lein, L. (1997). *Making Ends Meet: How Single Mothers Survive Welfare and Low-wage Work*. New York: Russell Sage Foundation.

Elder, G. H. (1999). *Children of the Great Depression: Social Change in Life Experience*. Boulder, CO: Westview Press.

Engle, P. L., Black, M. M., Behrman, J. R., Cabral de Mello, M., Gertler, P. J., Kapiriri, L., et al. (2007). Strategies to avoid the loss of developmental potential in more than 200 million children in the developing world. *The Lancet*, 369(9557), 229–42.

Evans, G. W. (2004). The environment of childhood poverty. *American Psychologist*, 59, 77–92.

Evans, G. W., & Kim, P. (2013). Childhood poverty, chronic stress, self-regulation, and coping. *Child Development Perspectives*, 7, 43–8.

Federal Interagency Forum on Child and Family Statistics. (2014). *At a Glance for 2014 America's Children: Key National Indicators of Well-being*. Washington, DC: US Government Printing Office.

Fernald, L. C., & Hidrobo, M. (2011). Effect of Ecuador's cash transfer program (Bono de Desarrollo Humano) on child development in infants and toddlers: A randomized effectiveness trial. *Social Science & Medicine*, 72(9), 1437–46.

Foster, C. J. E., Garber, J., & Durlak, J. A. (2008). Current and past maternal depression, maternal interaction behaviors, and children's externalizing and internalizing symptoms. *Journal of Abnormal Child Psychology*, 36(4), 527–37.

Frosch, C. A., Mangelsdorf, S. C., & McHale, J. L. (2000). Marital behavior and the security of preschooler–parent attachment relationships. *Journal of Family Psychology*, 14(1), 144–61.

Fuligni, A., & Brooks-Gunn, J. (2013). Mother–child interactions in Early Head Start: Age and ethnic differences in low-income dyads. *Parenting: Science and Practice*, 13, 1–26.

Fuligni, A., Brady-Smith, B., Tamis-LeMond, C., Bradley, R.H., Chazan-Cohen, R., Boyce, L., & Brooks-Gunn, J. (2013). Patterns of supportive mothering with 1-, 2-, and 3-year-olds by ethnicity in Early Head Start. *Parenting: Science and Practice*, 13, 44–57.

Fuligni, A., Han, W. J., & Brooks-Gunn, J. (2004). The infant-toddler HOME in the second and third years of life. *Parenting: Science and Practice*, 4(2–3), 139–59.

Gershoff, E. T. (2002). Corporal punishment by parents and associated child behaviors and experiences: A meta-analytic and theoretical review. *Psychological Bulletin*, 128, 539–79.

Gershoff, E. T. (2013). Spanking and child development: We know enough now to stop hitting our children. *Child development perspectives*, 7(3), 133–137.

Gershoff, E. T. and Bitensky, S. H. (2007). The case against corporal punishment of children: Converging evidence from social science research and international human rights law and implications for US public policy. *Psychology, Public Policy and Law*, 13(4), 231.

Gertler, P., Heckman, J., Pinto, R., Zanolini, A., Vermeersch, C., Walker, S., et al. (2013). *Labor Market Returns to Early Childhood Stimulation: A 20-year Follow up to an Experimental Intervention in Jamaica* (No. w19185). Cambridge, MA: National Bureau of Economic Research.

Gibson-Davis, C.M., & Gassman-Pines, A. (2010). Early childhood family structure and mother–child interactions: Variation by race and ethnicity. *Developmental Psychology*, 46, 151–64.

Goldrick-Rab, S., & Sorensen, K. (2010). Unmarried parents in college. *The Future of Children*, 20(2), 179–203.

Goodman, S. H. (2007). Depression in mothers. *Annual Review of Clinical Psychology*, 3, 107–35.

Goodman, S. H., & Gotlib, I. H. (1999). Risk for psychopathology in the children of depressed mothers: A developmental model for understanding mechanisms of transmission. *Psychological Review*, 106, 458–90.

Goodman, S. H., & Gotlib, I. H. (eds). (2002). *Children of Depressed Parents: Mechanisms of Risk and Implications for Treatment*. Washington, DC: APA.

Grantham-McGregor, S. M., Powell, C. A., Walker, S. P., & Himes, J. H. (1991). Nutritional supplementation, psychosocial stimulation, and mental development of stunted children: The Jamaican Study. *The Lancet*, 338, 1–5.

Guo, G., & Harris, K. M. (2000). The mechanisms mediating the effects of poverty on children's intellectual development. *Demography*, 37(4), 431–47.

Han, W. (2008). Shift work and child behavioral outcomes. *Work, Employment, and Society*, 22(1), 67–87.

Han, W., Ruhm, C., & Waldfogel, J. (2009). Parental leave policies and parents' employment and leave taking. *Journal of Policy Analysis and Management*, 28(1), 29–45.

Harkness, S., & Super, C. (1995). Culture and parenting. In M. Bornstein (ed.), *Handbook of Parenting, Vol. 2: Biology and Ecology of Parenting* (p. 211). Mahwah, NJ: Lawrence Erlbaum.

Hart, B., & Risley, T. (1999). *The Social World of Children Learning to Talk*. Baltimore, MD: Paul Brookes Publishing.

Heckman, J. J. (2006). Skill formation and the economics of investing in disadvantaged children. *Science*, 312(5782), 1900–1902.

Hoff, E. (2003). The specificity of environmental influence: Socioeconomic status affects early vocabulary development via maternal speech. *Child Development*, 74(5), 1368–78.

Hoff, E., Laursen, B., & Tardif, T. (2002). Socioeconomic status and parenting. In M. Bornstein (ed.), *Handbook of Parenting, Vol. 2: Biology and Ecology of Parenting*, 2nd edn (pp. 231–52). Mahwah, NJ: Lawrence Erlbaum.

Howard, K. S., & Brooks-Gunn, J. (2009). The role of home-visiting programs in preventing child abuse and neglect. *The Future of Children*, 19(2), 119–45.

Huston, A. C., Duncan, G. J., McLoyd, V. C., Crosby, D. A., Ripke, M. N., Weisner, T. S., & Eldred, C. A. (2005). Impacts on children of a policy to promote employment and reduce poverty for low-income parents: New hope after five years. *Developmental Psychology*, 41(6), 902.

Huttenlocher, J., Haight, W., Bryk, A., Seltzer, M., & Lyons, T. (1991). Early vocabulary growth: Relation to language input and gender. *Developmental Psychology*, 27(2), 236–48.

Ispa, J. M., Fine, M. A., Halgunseth, L. C., Harper, S., Robinson, J., Boyce, L., et al. (2004). Maternal intrusiveness, maternal warmth, and mother–toddler relationship outcomes: Variations across low-income ethnic and acculturation groups. *Child Development*, 75(6), 1613–31.

Jones, K., Daley, D., Hutchings, J., Bywater, T., & Eames, C. (2008). Efficacy of the incredible years programme as an early intervention for children with conduct problems and ADHD: Long-term follow-up. *Child: Care, Health, and Development*, 34(3), 380–90.

Kendrick, D., Elkan, R., Hewitt, M., Dewey, M., Blair, M., Robinson, J., et al. (2000). Does home visiting improve parenting and the quality of the home environment? A systematic review and meta-analysis. *Archives of Disease in Childhood*, 82, 443–51.

Kennedy, S., & Bumpass, L. (2008). Cohabitation and children's living arrangements: New estimates from the USA. *Demographic Research*, 19, 1663–92.

Klebanov, P., & Brooks-Gunn, J. (2006). Cumulative, human capital, and psychological risk in the context of early intervention. *Annals of the New York Academy of Sciences*, 1094(1), 63–82.

Klebanov, P. K., Brooks-Gunn, J., McCarton, C., & McCormick, M. C. (1998). The contribution of neighborhood and family income to developmental test scores over the first three years of life. *Child Development*, 69(5), 1420–36.

Knox, V. W., Miller, C., & Gennetian, L. A. (2000). *Reforming Welfare and Rewarding Work: A Summary of the Final Report on the Minnesota Family Investment Program* (Vol. 8). New York: Manpower Demonstration Research Corporation.

Linver, M. R., Brooks-Gunn, J., & Kohen, D. E. (2002). Family processes as pathways from income to young children's development. *Developmental Psychology*, 38(5), 719–34.

Lombardi, J., Mosle, A., Patel, N., Schumacher, R., & Stedron, J. (2014). *Gateways to Two Generations: The Potential for Early Childhood Programs and Partnerships to Support Children and Parents Together*. Washington, DC: Ascend at the Aspen Institute.

Love, J., Chazan-Cohen, R., Raikes, H., & Brooks-Gunn, J. (2013). What makes a difference? Early Head Start evaluation findings in a developmental context. *Monographs of the Society for Research in Child Development*, 78(1), 1–173.

Lovejoy, M. C., Graczyk, P. A., O'Hare, E., & Neuman, G. (2000). Maternal depression and parenting behavior: A meta-analytic review. *Clinical Psychology Review*, 20(5), 561–92.

MacKenzie, M.J., Nicklas, E., Waldfogel, J., & Brooks-Gunn, J. (2013). Spanking and child development across the first decade of life. *Pediatrics*, 132(5), e1118–25.

Magnuson, K. (2007). Maternal education and children's academic achievement during middle childhood. *Developmental Psychology*, 43(6), 1497.

Maluccio, J., & Flores, R. (2005). *Impact Evaluation of a Conditional Cash Transfer Program: The Nicaraguan Red de Protección Social*. Washington, DC: International Food Policy Research Institute.

Martin, A., Ryan, R. M., & Brooks-Gunn, J. (2010). When fathers' supportiveness matters most: Maternal and paternal parenting and children's school readiness. *Journal of Family Psychology*, 24, 145–55.

McLanahan, S., & Beck, A. N. (2010). Parental relationships in fragile families. *The Future of Children*, 20(2), 17–37.

McLanahan, S., & Waldfogel, J. (eds). (2011). Work and family. *The Future of Children*, 21, 1–214.

McLoyd, V. C. (1990). The impact of economic hardship on black families and children: Psychological distress, parenting, and socioemotional development. *Child Development*, 61(2), 311–46.

Meadows, S. O., McLanahan, S. S., & Brooks-Gunn, J. (2007). Parental depression and anxiety and early childhood behavior problems across family types. *Journal of Marriage and Family*, 69(5), 1162–77.

Mistry, R. S., Lowe, E. D., Renner, A. D., & Chien, N. (2008). Expanding the family economic stress model: Insights from a mixed-methods approach. *Journal of Marriage and Family*, 70(1), 196–209.

Morenza, L., Arrazola, O., Seleme, I., & Martinez, F. (2005) *Evaluacion Proyecto Kallpa Wawa* (pp. 1–130). Santa Cruz, Bolivia.

Morris, P., & Michalopoulos, C. (2003). Findings from the Self-Sufficiency Project: Effects on children and adolescents of a program that increased employment and income. *Journal of Applied Developmental Psychology*, 24(2), 201–39.

Morris, P., Gennetian, L., & Duncan, G. (2005). Effects of welfare and employment policies on young children: New findings on policy experiments conducted in the early 1990s. Social Policy Report, Society for Research in Child Development, XIX(2), 3–14.

Neitzel, C., & Stright, A. D. (2004). Parenting behaviours during child problem solving: The roles of child temperament, mother education and personality, and the problem-solving context. *International Journal of Behavioral Development*, 28, 166–79.

Nievar, M. A., Van Egeren, L. A., & Polland, S. (2010). A meta-analysis of home visiting programs: Moderators of improvements in maternal behavior. *Infant Mental Health Journal*, 31(5), 499–520.

Nock, S. L., & Kingston, P. W. (1988). Time with children: The impact of couples' work-time commitments. *Social Forces*, 67, 59–83.

Olds, D., Henderson, C., Jr., Kitzman, H., Eckenrode, J., Cole, R., & Tatelbaum, R. (1998). The promise of home visitation: Results of two randomized trials. *Journal of Community Psychology*, 26(1), 5–21.

Osborne, C., & McLanahan, S. (2007). Partnership instability and child well-being. *Journal of Marriage and Family*, 69(4), 1065–83.

Osborne, C., Berger, L., & Magnuson, K. (2012). Family structure transitions and changes in maternal depression and parenting. *Demography*, 49, 23–47.

Parke, R. D. (2004). Development in the family. *Annual Review of Psychology*, 55, 365–99.

Pressman, A. W., Klebanov, P. K., & Brooks-Gunn, J. (2012). New approaches to the notion of environmental risk. *A Developmental Environmental Measurement Handbook* (pp. 152–72).

Pungello, E. P., Kainz, K., Burchinal, M., Wasik, B. H., Sparling, J. J., Ramey, C. T., & Campbell, F. A. (2010). Early educational intervention, early cumulative risk, and the early home environment as predictors of young adult outcomes within a high-risk sample. *Child Development*, 81(1), 410–26.

Raikes, H., Pan, B. A., Luze, G., Tamis-LeMonda, C. S., Brooks-Gunn, J., Constantine, J., et al. (2006). Mother–child bookreading in low-income families: Correlates and outcomes during the first three years of life. *Child Development*, 77, 924–53.

Ryan, R. M. (2012). Marital birth and early child outcomes: The moderating influence of marriage propensity. *Child Development*, 83(5), 1085–101.

Ryan, R. M., Martin, A., & Brooks-Gunn, J. (2006). Is one good parent good enough? Patterns of father and mother parenting and their combined associations with concurrent child outcomes at 24 and 36 months. *Parenting: Science and Practice*, 6(2–3), 211–28.

Sabol, T. J., & Chase-Lansdale, P. L. (2015). The influence of low-income children's participation in Head Start on their parents' education and employment. *Journal of Policy Analysis and Management*, 34(1), 136–61.

Sameroff, A. J., & Fiese, B. H. (2000). Transactional regulation: The developmental ecology of early intervention. *Handbook of Early Childhood Intervention*, 2, 135–59.

Sameroff, A. J., Seifer, R., Baldwin, C., & Baldwin, A. (1989). Continuity of risk from early childhood to adolescence. In R. Barocas (Chair), *Development and Risk from Early Childhood to Adolescence: The Rochester Longitudinal Study.* Symposium presented at the Society for Research in Child Development meeting, Kansas City.

Sameroff, A. J., Seifer, R., Baldwin, A., & Baldwin, C. (1993). Stability of intelligence from preschool to adolescence: The influence of social and family risk factors. *Child Development*, 64(1), 80–97.

Schneider, W., MacKenzie, M., Waldfogel, J., & Brooks-Gunn, J. (2014). Parent and child reporting of corporal punishment: New evidence from the Fragile Families and Child Wellbeing Study. *Child Indicators Research*, August [online].

Schoppe, S. J., Mangelsdorf, S. C., & Frosch, C. A. (2001). Coparenting, family process, and family structure: Implications for preschoolers' externalizing behavior problems. *Journal of Family Psychology*, 15(3), 526–45.

Seifer, R., Sameroff, A. J., Baldwin, C. P., & Baldwin, A. (1992). Child and family factors that ameliorate risk between 4 and 13 years of age. *Journal of the American Academy of Child & Adolescent Psychiatry*, 31(5), 893–903.

Snow, C. (1991). The theoretical basis for relationships between language and literacy development. *Journal of Research in Childhood Education*, 6, 5.

Spiker, D., Ferguson, J., & Brooks-Gunn, J. (1993). Enhancing maternal interactive behavior and child social competence in low birth weight, premature infants. *Child Development*, 64, 754.

St Pierre, R. G., Layzer, J. I., & Barnes, H. V. (1995). Two-generation programs: Design, cost, and short-term effectiveness. *The Future of Children*, 5(3), 76–93.

Straus, M. A. (1994). Should the use of corporal punishment by parents be considered child abuse? Yes. In M. A. Mason & E. Gambrill (eds), *Debating Children's Lives: Current Controversies on Children and Adolescents* (pp. 197–203). Thousand Oaks, CA: SAGE.

Sweet, M. A., & Appelbaum, M. I. (2004). Is home visiting an effective strategy? A meta-analytic review of home visiting programs for families with young children. *Child Development*, 75(5), 1435–56.

Tamis-LeMonda, C. S., Shannon, J. D., Cabrera, N. J., & Lamb, M. E. (2004). Fathers and mothers at play with their 2- and 3-year-olds: Contributions to language and cognitive development. *Child Development*, 75, 1806–20.

Tanaka, S. (2005). Parental leave and child health across OECD countries. *The Economic Journal*, 115(501), F7–F28.

Trapolini, T., McMahon, C. A., & Ungerer, J. A. (2007). The effect of maternal depression and marital adjustment on young children's internalizing and externalizing behaviour problems. *Child: Care, Health and Development*, 33(6), 794–803.

US Bureau of Labor Statistics. (2013). Women in the labor force: A databook. *BLS Reports*, 1–104.

Votruba-Drzal, E. (2003). Income changes and cognitive stimulation in young children's home learning environments. *Journal of Marriage and Family*, 65, 341–55.

Waldfogel, J., Craigie, T., & Brooks-Gunn, J. (2010). Fragile families and child wellbeing. *The Future of Children*, 20, 87–112.

Walker, S. P., Chang, S. M., Powell, C. A., & Grantham-McGregor, S. M. (2005). Effects of early childhood psychosocial stimulation and nutritional supplementation on cognition and education in growth-stunted Jamaican children: Prospective cohort study. *The Lancet*, 366(9499), 1804–7.

Weizman, Z., & Snow, C. (2001). Lexical input as related to children's vocabulary acquisition: Effects of sophisticated exposure and support for meaning. *Developmental Psychology*, 37, 265.

Yeung, W. J., Linver, M. R., & Brooks-Gunn, J. (2002). How money matters for young children's development: Parental investment and family processes. *Child Development*, 73(6), 1861–79.

APPENDIX: COMPONENTS OF PARENTING

Discipline. Discipline refers to the ways in which parents respond to child behaviors that they deem appropriate or inappropriate. The appropriateness of a particular child behavior can depend on a child's age and gender and on parental beliefs and culture (Harkness & Super, 1995). Discipline is considered harsh or punitive when it involves spanking, slapping, or yelling (Davidson, 1997; Fuligni et al., 2004, 2013; Gershoff, 2002, 2013; Gershoff & Bitensky, 2007; MacKenzie et al., 2013; Straus, 1994). It differs from abuse in terms of severity (Bradley & Corwyn, 2002; Howard & Brooks-Gunn, 2009).

Language. Language as a parenting behavior refers to both the amount of language a child hears and the quality of that language, e.g., number of different words used, length of sentences, questions asked, elaborations of child's speech, and events discussed (Huttenlocher et al., 1991; Weizman & Snow, 2001). For example, when reading to a child, parents vary in how often they engage in optimal practices such as asking the child questions, expanding on elements of the story and/or going beyond the information given in the story, and seeing whether a child understands the meaning of particular words (Snow, 1991; Weizman & Snow, 2001).

Management and predictability. Management refers to the way parents schedule and complete scheduled events, as well as to the predictability and order of the household; the latter is often termed chaos (Brooks-Gunn & Markman, 2005; Brooks-Gunn, Johnson and Leventhal, 2010).

Materials. Overlapping with language and teaching are materials. Materials include the cognitively and linguistically stimulating items provided to children in a home. Many studies assess this aspect of parenting by observing children's home environment. Measures typically count the number and variety of books, educational toys, musical instruments, or drawing materials in the home (Bradley & Corwyn, 2002; Caldwell & Bradley, 1984).

Monitoring. Monitoring involves parental watchfulness and the extent to which a parent keeps track of a child. For young children, monitoring may include checking on a child who is playing in a room alone or keeping track of what a child is watching on television and ensuring that it is appropriate (Brooks-Gunn & Markman, 2005).

Sensitivity. Parenting behaviors have been categorized in various ways (Bornstein, 2002). One such system identifies nurturance, discipline, teaching, language, monitoring, management, and materials. As a key component (Brooks-Gunn & Markman, 2005), sensitivity involves the ways in which parents express love, affection, and care (Brooks-Gunn & Markman, 2005). Parents who display high nurturing behaviors are warm, responsive to a child's needs, and sensitive to changes in a child's behavior (Fuligni & Brooks-Gunn, 2013; Ispa et al., 2004; Ryan et al., 2006). Low nurturing behaviors, on the other hand, are characterized by detachment, intrusiveness, and negativity towards a child (Ispa et al., 2004; Ryan et al., 2006).

Supportive parenting. Overall, highly supportive parenting is defined by sensitivity and consistency in discipline and involvement, whereas low supportive parenting is defined by inconsistent, distant, restrictive, and punitive behaviors (McLoyd, 1990).

Teaching. Teaching involves the strategies that parents use to convey information and skills to a child. Strategies are often rated in terms of the quality of parent assistance. For example, parents that use scaffolding, or provide cues or prompts to help a child learn rather than take over or not help at all, are employing high quality teaching assistance (Spiker et al., 1993).

3

Group-Based Early Childhood Education and Care for Under-2-Year-Olds: Quality Debates, Pedagogy and Lived Experience

Carmen Dalli and E. Jayne White

INTRODUCTION

Across the Western world, the presence of under-2-year-olds in group-based ECEC settings first attracted research interest in the heyday of the feminist movement during the 1960s and 1970s. Defying societal views that the best place for infants was at home 'basking in the unwavering warmth, understanding and patience of their ever-adoring mothers' (Katz, 1985: 12), out-of-home services for young children raised both ideological debates as well as scientific interest in the effects of early 'daycare' (Belsky, 1986, 1988; Phillips et al., 1987). More recently, the controversies of the 1970s and 1980s have given way to consensus that high quality Early Childhood Education and Care (ECEC) benefits children and families as well as societies (OECD, 2012). As a consequence, governments increasingly see the provision of ECEC for the youngest children not only as a service that supports women in the paid workforce, but also as a means of intervention in cycles of poverty and family disadvantage, a mechanism for enhanced wellbeing for children (Britto et al., 2011), and a means of improving the overall economic health of their country (Heckman, 2011). There is recognition that the benefits of participation in ECEC are conditional on 'quality' provision for ECEC services (Camilli et al., 2010; OECD, 2013). Determining and ensuring high quality ECEC according to universal and/or local standards is, however, a complex proposition that remains a widespread policy challenge as well as an active area of research across diverse contexts (e.g., Landry et al., 2014).

In this chapter, we focus specifically on research that has direct relevance to the goal of ensuring high quality group-based ECEC for under-2-year-olds. The OECD uses the term ECEC to refer to all forms of early childhood education (ECE) and early childhood care (ECC) services 'under an integrated system which provides integrated pedagogical settings covering age zero or one to compulsory schooling age' (OECD, 2013, p. 1).

However, not all countries provide this integrated provision for under-2-year-olds; many jurisdictions separate out services for under-2-year-olds from those for older pre-schoolers in a range of provisions variously referred to as day-care or childcare centers, nurseries, crèches, playschools, and parent-run playgroups, as well as home-based family day-care run by licensed family day-care providers or networks of providers. Thus, research about ECEC for under-2-year-olds uses terminology that reflects this diversity. In this chapter, the term ECEC is used to refer to all types of group-based early childhood services for under-2-year-olds in both integrated as well as non-integrated settings.

Starting with a historical overview of the ways quality has been constructed and, latterly, contested in empirical research and scholarly debates, this chapter identifies key themes in contemporary research with implications for the provision of high quality group-based early childhood practice with under-2-year-olds. Pedagogical approaches consistent with these themes are then discussed. We also highlight promising and potential lines of future enquiry in a field that is increasingly inter-disciplinary and multi-theoretical. We argue that this new inter-disciplinarity, introducing alternative theoretical and philosophical perspectives, makes visible the complex lived experiences of infants and toddlers within the diverse spaces of their ECEC settings (Harrison and Sumsion, 2014).

THE QUESTION OF QUALITY: A HISTORICAL OVERVIEW

The notion of 'quality ECEC' has now accumulated a 40-year history of scholarship. By the 1990s scholars began to identify 'three waves' or generations of research associated with changing discourses about quality ECEC (Melhuish, 2001; Pence and Pacini-Ketchabaw, 2006). Crossing over into the new millennium additional lines of discourse became discernible that encompassed a more critical stance towards the notion of quality in ECEC: we call these post- 'waves' discourses.

Three Waves of Research: The 1970s to the 1990s

'First wave' research can be dated back to the emergence of under-2-year-olds in formal educational settings in the early 1970s and was linked to the question of whether out-of-home ECEC, or day-care, was bad for children, especially under-1-year-olds. Mostly carried out in North American contexts, first wave research often involved comparing children in day-care settings against home-reared ones using Bowlby's attachment theory framework and Ainsworth's strange situation (Ainsworth and Bowlby, 1991). Also influenced by the Freudian notion that the roots of our emotional life lie in infancy and early childhood, and by echoes of the *maternal deprivation hypothesis* of the late 1940s (e.g., Spitz and Wolf, 1946), the expectation was that if use of day-care was detrimental, children's attachment status to their mother would be less secure than that of home-reared children. Conflicting results across different studies were hotly debated on methodological and ideological grounds with the 'Belsky controversy'[1] of the mid-1980s illustrating the politically charged nature of this question (Belsky, 1986; Phillips et al., 1987). The eventual consensus from this line of inquiry that what matters for development is the quality of care experienced by children, regardless of setting (e.g., Phillips, 1987), opened the way to the next wave of research.

In 'second wave' ECEC research during the 1980s, the aim shifted to identifying specific elements of the ECEC setting – such as caregiver:child ratios, and the physical environment – that would be amenable to policy intervention to secure high quality (e.g., McCartney et al., 1982). Licensing regulations for ECEC services in various jurisdictions still reflect findings from these studies.

Particularly influential were the results of the United States National Day Care Study (Ruopp et al., 1979). Identifying the variables of group size, caregiver:child ratio, and caregiver qualifications as the three policy variables that make up the 'iron triangle' of quality, the study showed that less positive interactions and less advanced development were associated with larger groups in both center-based and family day-care services. Assessment tools to measure overall or global levels of quality in centers were also developed including the Early Childhood Environment Rating Scale (ECERS) (Harms and Clifford, 1980) and, later, its equivalent for infant and toddler settings, the Infant/Toddler Environment Rating Scale (ITERS) (Harms et al., 1998). These, as well as revised versions of both, remain in use in research requiring a global measure of quality (e.g., Scopelliti and Musatti, 2013). The more recently developed Classroom Assessment Scoring System (CLASS) (Pianta et al., 2008) similarly cites research from this period.

A more ecological conceptualization of quality emerged in 'third wave' research during the late 1980s and early 1990s. Marking the beginnings of a more nuanced approach to discussions about the meaning of 'quality', a key argument in this period was that quality outcomes for children's development – measured via a range of cognitive, linguistic, and socio-emotional tests – did not depend solely on the structural characteristics of the childcare environment but also on the links between these and 'process' variables, such as the nature of adult–child interactions. In a still-cited study, Howes et al. (1992; see also de Schipper et al., 2004; Munton et al., 2002) reported a predictable pathway from regulable, or structural, elements of quality to process quality, and thence to relationships with teachers and with peers. In their words, 'good things go together' (1992, p. 458).

Early results in the mid-1990s from the prospective longitudinal *Study of Early Child Care* initiated in 1991 by the US National Institute of Child Health and Human Development (NICHD) (Peth-Pierce, 1998)

served to support this conclusion. Set up partly in response to the re-opening of the debate about the impact of infant day-care sparked off by the previously mentioned 'Belsky controversy', this collaborative multi-site study aimed to 'move beyond the global questions about whether child care is good or bad for children' (Peth-Pierce, 1998, p. 2) and investigate relationships between a wide range of variables within the childcare and family environment and outcomes for children.

Meanwhile, as the search for evidence-based formulae of quality continued, studies in diverse cultural contexts (e.g., Tobin et al., 1989) drew attention to different views on quality within different communities, thus positioning the notion of quality not only as a multi-faceted phenomenon, but also as value-laden, relative and multi-perspectival. Outside of the world of research, indigenous communities such as Māori and Pacific Nations people in New Zealand had already expressed these views around policy tables and at sector conferences (e.g., Ete, 1993; Irwin, 1987). Researchers working in Third or Majority World countries (e.g., Woodhead, 1996) soon proposed that a distinction needed to be made between the quality issues faced in affluent Western societies and those faced in developing economies. Building on these views, caution about the use of quality measures such as the ECERS (Harms and Clifford, 1980) was raised, with critics noting that they were based on values that were culturally derived and thus not universally useful (e.g., Rosenthal, 1999). An expansion of scholarship emphasizing the need to re-conceptualize the disciplinary base of early childhood beyond its traditional child development focus (Singer, 1993; Stott and Bowman, 1996) strengthened this view. Cumulatively, these arguments created a strong case for looking beyond traditional psychological domains to other human science disciplines such as sociology, philosophy, anthropology and health sciences to inform quality practice in ECEC. They also opened the philosophical question of 'who says what is quality?', thus positioning the construct of quality increasingly as a post-structuralist concern – contestable, perspectival, located within discourses through which it might be critiqued and, consequently, de-stabilized (Dahlberg et al., 2007).

By the beginning of the new millennium there were thus two dominant lines of scholarly discussions distinguishable in the international literature on ECEC for under-2-year-olds. The first was concerned with untangling the impact of various day-care/childcare variables on child outcomes and the second focused on post-structural critique concerning the relevance of quality as a defining construct and expanding on notions of care, education and what it means to be an infant or toddler in contemporary society.

Post 'Waves' Discourses

Taking stock of quality debates in ECEC at the turn of the century, Melhuish (2001, p. 1) predicted that discussions about quality measures would continue but increasingly move away from measurements that relied primarily on observations of settings or a specific child, towards research aimed at gauging whether a particular institution attended by a child 'made demonstrable beneficial effects on child development' (2001, p. 4). Certainly, effectiveness studies, including programs aimed at under-2-year-olds living in adverse conditions, have focused increasingly on demonstrable differences, including the evaluation of Sure Start in the UK (e.g., Belsky et al., 2006) and Early Head Start in the USA (e.g., Love et al., 2005). The adoption of Quality Rating and Improvement Systems (QRISs) by many US jurisdictions as a market-based approach for improving early education, and to inform policy makers on investment decisions, are natural extensions of this type of effectiveness research. Nonetheless, debates continue on whether QRISs, often used in high stakes contexts such as informing parents and funding bodies about program outcomes, truly measure impacts on learning. For example, Sabol et al.'s analysis of how QRIS scores relate to child outcomes suggests that there is a need to re-emphasize process elements of quality as potentially the 'aspects of quality that matter most' (2013, p. 846).

Meanwhile, in post-third wave non-measurement oriented ECEC scholarship, critiques of the notion of quality continued. Across international contexts, scholars increasingly 'troubled' the concept of 'quality' as a one-word-fits-all construct (Moss and Dahlberg, 2008), challenging its potentially colonizing effects (Cannella and Viruru, 2004) and seeking to stimulate 'conversations so that the measures and enactments of quality can be as complex as the practice' (Graue, 2005, p. 522; see also Manning-Morton, 2006). For example, Nsamenang (2010) critiqued 'international childhood instruments and programmatic visions' used by 'elite ECD planners' (p. 22) as out of touch with the reality of children's lives in Africa. Similarly, writing within the context of Bangladesh, Islam (2010) emphasized the need to understand issues of quality in their cultural and historical context and argued for the use of 'little narratives' (petits récits), or more modest and localized narratives from diverse voices, including children's, as a way of achieving this.

Arising from these arguments, the past few years have witnessed both an increasing acceptance that indicators of quality have a role to play in policy and accountability discourses,[2] as well as a mounting acceptance of the need to revise, reconceptualize, diversify, and challenge existing indicators of quality in response to local contexts and populations. This engagement with how quality is conceptualized, enacted, and evaluated in ECEC is particularly important for pedagogical work with infants and toddlers. As research on what 'quality' learning and teaching entails for such young children gains momentum, what is deemed as good quality pedagogy is discursively shaped by these broader debates.

KEY THEMES IN CONTEMPORARY RESEARCH AND IMPLICATIONS FOR QUALITY GROUP-BASED ECEC FOR INFANTS AND TODDLERS

Over the past few decades, a flurry of research outside of the exclusive domain of ECEC provision has given rise to new understandings about infants and toddlers. Technological advances such as in magnetic resonance imaging (MRI) (Inder, 2002), robotics (Meltzoff et al., 2009), and the 'event-related potential' (ERP) technique (e.g., de Regnier, 2005),[3] as well as innovative research practices such as saliva tests to measure the stress hormone, cortisol, in very young children (e.g., Gunnar and Cheatham, 2003; Sims et al., 2005), have catapulted neurobiological and psychobiological research out of its traditional laboratory context of experiments with rodents and primates into the human experience, paving the way for investigations of the brain functioning of living young children. Greater understandings about neural patterns of 'synaptic "blooming" or "pruning"' (Fox and Rutter, 2010, p. 24) and about the effects of the perinatal environment on DNA structure (e.g., Meaney, 2010) have brought about a fundamental shift from seeing child development as 'a simple nature-versus-nurture situation' towards a 'nature *and* nurture or nature *with* nurture' proposition (Herrod, 2007, p. 199). A growing focus on translational studies has also emerged, emphasizing the advantages of pooling important insights across disciplines such as neuroscience, developmental psychology, and education to highlight the connectedness between the social, physical, linguistic, cognitive, and emotional experiences of infants (Shapiro and Applegate, 2002), and thus 'drive a new generation of early childhood policies and practices' (Shonkoff, 2010, p. 358). In this reconceptualization, attention has turned to the process aspects of ECEC enacted in relationships and pedagogy. The following sections highlight key themes that give rise to such emphases.

Sensitive Responsiveness, Emotional Regulation and Stress

Of significant import for the education and care of very young children has been the growing evidence from neuroscientific research that the brain is not a discreet organ but inextricably connected to environmental conditions, physical and relational (Fox et al., 2010; Meltzoff et al., 2009; Shonkoff, 2010). It is now accepted that emotion and cognition are 'an intricately bound developmental process' (Bell and Wolfe, 2004, p. 366) with shared neural mechanisms, thus leading to use of the term 'the social brain' (e.g., Fox and Rutter, 2010).

Additionally, clear links have been established between very young children's stress levels and the quality of their early care, whether at home or out of home, with excessive and prolonged exposure to 'toxic stress'[4] identified as a risk factor for the healthy development of infant brain circuits, hormonal systems, emotional wellbeing, and cognitive functioning (Davis and Sandman, 2010; Gunnar and Cheatham, 2003; Watamura et al., 2003).[5] Numerous studies of the stress hormone cortisol and behavior in children within the first five years of life have led to a focus on sensitive responsive caregiving as creating a 'buffer' against the damaging effects of stress, because 'when cared for responsively and sensitively, children anticipate that adults will protect them and thus that they can cope with threat' (Gunnar and Donzella, 2002, p. 215).

A connected theme is that sensitive responsive caregiving and emotional regulation are also linked to the executive functions of the brain, that group of skills related to the ability to remember and connect information (working memory), filter thoughts and impulses (inhibitory control), and adjust to changing demands (cognitive flexibility). These skills are seen as essential for both learning and social interaction and have been described as the 'biological foundation for school readiness' (Center on the Developing Child at Harvard University, 2011, p. 4). In the same way that infants are understood to learn to regulate their emotions through interactions with adults who are emotionally attuned to them in low stress environments, so they are understood to thrive when, as toddlers, they experience interactions with adults who provide them with opportunities to practise increasing autonomy in self-directed activities within safe and non-chaotic environments.

The First Years of Life: A Critical Period or a Window of Opportunity?

As knowledge about infant development in the very early years has accumulated, infancy and toddlerhood have been increasingly described as a critical and under-recognized period for learning and development. The National Scientific Council on the Developing Child (2007) has characterized the very early years of life as 'a succession of "sensitive periods", each associated with the formation of specific circuits that are associated with specific abilities' (p. 5). Fox and Rutter (2010) described the time as offering 'windows of opportunity' (p. 23) and significant potential for learning and development and, by implication, for teaching. Others (e.g., Keuroghlian and Knudsen, 2007, in their study of animals) have argued that the plasticity of the brain suggests a capacity to adapt over a lifetime. At the same time, Gunnar and Cheatham (2003) warned that the extent of plasticity in the human brain is a phenomenon that is yet to be fully understood. Irrespective of whether early damage is permanent or not, however, the conclusion that 'the longer a child is neglected, the higher the degree of developmental delay' (2003, p. 208) remains a salutary point to bear in mind for applied fields such as ECEC.

While these insights have seldom come from research conducted in ECEC contexts, they have impacted the ECEC field, dramatically creating a strongly compelling argument that is now often deployed when advocating for the improvement of quality ECEC provision at the policy table (Dalli et al., 2011; Mathers et al., 2014). Yet, these arguments are not wholly unproblematic and have contributed to the idea that ECEC can be the silver bullet to solve major societal problems (Farquhar and White, 2014). Some have argued that neurobiological arguments have assumed a disproportionate amount of authority in the field relative to other types of research and caution against simplistic extrapolation of 'causal relations between ECEC and future benefits instead of theorizing the correlations that are found' (Vandenbroeck et al., 2012, p. 542). Vandenbroeck and colleagues call for paradigmatic openness and researcher reflexivity as well as acknowledgment that all research is a value-laden political act that generates different ways of knowing.

The Competent Infant as an Intersubjective Partner

At the same time as these neurological debates were occurring, in child developmental research there was mounting evidence of infants' communicative competences and the complex meanings that under-1-year-olds can convey through the use of gestures, vocalizations, and other bodily movements (Crais et al., 2009). Detailed observations of newborns and their mothers, and documentation of the way that babies engage in careful experimentation with communication from birth (e.g., Reddy, 2008), have had significant impact for the field of ECEC. In particular, Trevarthen and Malloch's seminal (2002) examination of the reciprocal nature of such communication, which they likened to musical composition, has established important precedents for research in the field and contributed to a revised view of very young infants as intersubjective partners who are just as capable of moderating the behavior of adults as of having their own behavior modified (see also White, Peter and Redder, 2015). This positions infants as subjects, rather than merely objects, in relationship with others (Murray, 2014).

The concept of intersubjectivity is rooted in a number of scholarly disciplines including philosophy (e.g., Edmund Husserl;

Ludwig Wittgenstein) and sociology (G. H. Mead; Alfred Schutz) as well as psychology (e.g., Daniel Stern). Intersubjectivity is generally defined as a state of agreement between people about the meaning of an object, a sense of mutual understanding (Gillespie and Cornish, 2010), interpersonal communion (Stern, 1985), or person-to-person connectivity (Trevarthen, 1998), including in joint attention episodes (Tomasello, 1988). Examples of such episodes are dyadic proto-conversations between infants and adults in which they mutually attend to one another's cues, turn take, and mimic each other's emotional state, facial expressions, and cognitive interests. In sociology, intersubjectivity is considered central to social wellbeing and, as Gillespie and Cornish (2010, p. 20) pointed out, in psychology it 'lies just below the surface of widely used concepts such as decentration (Piaget and Inhelder, 1969), theory of mind (Doherty, 2008) and perspective taking (Martin et al., 2008)'.

Intersubjectivity and Joint Attention as the Basis of Pedagogy With Under-2-Year-Olds

Research in ECEC group settings for under-2-year-olds increasingly draws on all these perspectives in identifying intersubjective interactions between adults and children as central to high quality practice (Degotardi and Pearson, 2014; Goouch and Powell, 2013; White et al., 2015). Johansson (2004, p. 11) wrote of intersubjectivity as 'a pedagogical encounter in the child's life-world … approaching and trying to understand the child's whole being'. This statement positions pedagogy as a learning encounter that teachers initiate but which is deeply influenced by the infants themselves. As White (2013) argued, the teacher is not only a mirror but a compass for emotional response. Correspondingly, the 'curriculum' is enacted in the space of children's embodied, everyday experiences in close interrelation with others. It is based on subtle, nuanced engagement with teachers and peers. Additionally,

Johansson's statement merges intersubjectivity with the phenomenological notion of a person's 'lifeworld' being constituted by experience in the world. This makes learning the outcome of the experience of mutual engagement or 'joint attention' (e.g., Tomasello, 1988) and is influenced by physical proximity (White and Redder, 2015). The related concepts of attunement, caregiver sensitivity (de Wolff and Van IJzendoorn, 1997; Gerber et al., 2007), and presence and intimacy (Goodfellow, 2008) also feature strongly in contemporary pedagogical research converging on the cognate notions of *a pedagogy of listening* (Rinaldi, 2006), a *pedagogy of care* (Dalli and Kibble, 2010), and *relational pedagogy* (e.g., Papatheodorou, 2009).

PEDAGOGICAL APPROACHES WITH UNDER-2-YEAR-OLDS

Pedagogy has been described as both a science and an art (e.g., Watkins and Mortimore, 1999), a combination of skills, knowledge, dispositions, and associated strategies that reside in the domain of teacher practice, and can be strategically employed to promote learning. Farquhar and White (2014) have argued that pedagogy may, in fact, represent a form of manipulation in the hands of those who exert power over others and that this is an especially important consideration in the lives of infants and toddlers. Applied to work with under-2-year-olds, pedagogy can therefore be especially challenging to define since the unique characteristics of infants and toddlers require a re-visioning of taken-for-granted notions about the division between teaching and learning, and care as well as its conceptualization beyond 'nature-versus-nurture causalities' (Peers and Abenyega, 2014, p. 1509).

The Specialized Nature of Infant and Toddler Pedagogy

As Piaget (Piaget and Inhelder, 1969) has classically argued, infants learn about the world through their senses and bodily movements. Additionally, neuro-scientific research is clear that physical experiences such as being held, stroked and rocked, or engagement in rough and tumble play contribute to very young children's overall wellbeing, including a healthy immune system (e.g., Schore, 2001). Under-2-year-olds also communicate differently to older children and this makes them difficult to interpret. For these reasons, many have argued that pedagogy with under-2-year-olds is different from that with older pre-schoolers: it incorporates higher levels of physical care (Fleer and Linke, 1999; Manning-Morton, 2006) and requires heightened levels of intimacy and emotional nurturing (Dalli and Kibble, 2010; Elfer, 1996; Leavitt, 1994).

Contemporary pedagogical research and scholarship builds on these ideas, positioning learning in the very first years as an embodied process that requires an emotional, physical, and intellectual emphasis.

The Role of the Adult

Adult responsiveness to very young children's physicality as careful attunement to their agentic body is now viewed as central to high quality practice (Johansson and Løkken, 2014). This recognizes that, as argued by Hungarian pediatrician Emmi Pikler, the inspiration behind the RIE (Resources for Infant Educarers, 2006) approach, when the very young child has the freedom to move, the child not only learns 'to turn on the belly, to roll, creep, sit, stand and walk … but also how to learn. He learns to do something on his own, to be interested, to try out, to experiment. He learns to overcome difficulties' (Pikler, cited in Resources for Infant Educarers, 2006, p. xxiv). Young children's bodily agency is also displayed in their use of gestures, and in the nuanced changes of volume and pitch of their vocalizations as they gain increased sophistication in engaging others in communication (e.g., Trevarthen and Malloch, 2002). As Løkken (2006) put it, for the very young child, the modus operandi *is* the body, a point

also highlighted in White's (2009) analysis of video data of a toddler's experiences in an early childhood center collated through the child's visual field. Constant movement and constant seeking out of social partners were key features of the child's learning experiences in the early childhood center, as were the teacher's interpretations of such actions.

Care and Love in Infant and Toddler Pedagogy

In the public eye, the physicality of infants and toddlers, and the physical care this demands, is held in part responsible for positioning those who work with this age group as engaged in physical 'care' versus 'education' (Cheeseman et al., 2015) and thus as lesser professionals with consequent lower pay and working conditions (e.g., Manning-Morton, 2006). Critical feminist writers have examined teachers' practice as 'emotional labour' (Leavitt, 1994) that is marginalized and under-valued. From the teachers' perspective, however, the emotional side of their practice is a key and valued aspect (e.g., Goodfellow, 2008; Manning-Morton, 2006). Some have proposed that work with infants and toddlers needs to be re-theorized and underpinned by an 'ethic' of care (Dalli, 2006; Page, 2011). From this perspective, caring is not merely a physical activity but a relation, an interpersonal encounter in which the key principle is 'the unending obligation to meet the other as the one-caring' (Noddings, 1984, p. 24); in other words, with engrossment, full attention, and giving primacy to the goals and needs of the one cared for. Peers and Agbenyega (2014) call for a 'lovingly disarmed attention' (p. 1508) in a conceptualization of care that exceeds the parameters of maternal instinct to generate a more ambiguous stance of reflexivity. Together, these revised understandings of care shift high quality pedagogy with infants and toddlers (as well as with older pre-schoolers and young children) away from a focus on physical care towards a dialogic emphasis that places the teacher at the center of the curriculum. They pinpoint adult–child engagement in intimate acts of intersubjective interactions as the fulcrum of learning and summon the word 'love' to the pedagogical arena.

A Pedagogy of Listening and Relational Pedagogy

The term *pedagogy of listening* (Rinaldi, 2006) is often associated with the Reggio Emilia approach to early childhood education. It highlights the idea that the *pedagogista* – or teacher – should be keenly observant of children, listening out for the multi-modal semiotic ways in which they communicate, giving rise to the term: 'the hundred languages of children'. Similarly, *relational pedagogy* (Papatheodorou, 2009) requires adults to learn to know the child and their particular communicative idiosyncrasies including within their wider socio-cultural context (Araujo, 2012). It builds on the long-established finding that children's language is enhanced when adults are contingently responsive to children's communicative bids and therefore privilege their voice(s) (Johansson and White, 2011). It also rests on research which shows that responsive adults attend as much to gestures and bodily movements as to vocalizations in order to make communicative interpretations. The focus on movement and gesture in infant and toddler experience is a growing area of research (e.g., Crais et al., 2009; Southgate et al., 2007; White, 2009), linking up to an emerging line of enquiry exploring the potential of the notion of *dialogic pedagogy* for work with this age group (White, 2016). New visual technologies are now making it possible to interpret much more of the infant experience than was previously accessible (Johansson and White, 2011). These technologies bring with them increased opportunities to capture and interpret the complex language cues of infants and toddlers as a primary source of intersubjectivity on the part of teachers who wish to understand learners.

Relationships as Curriculum: Implications for Practice

Striving for intersubjective relationships between teachers and under-2-year-olds is clearly central to what is now understood to be infant pedagogy in ECEC. Several investigations of how adult–child relationships play out in real ECEC settings have emphasized that 'relationships are the curriculum' (e.g., Degotardi and Pearson, 2014; Gevers Deynoot-Schaub and Riksen-Walraven, 2008; Honig, 2002; Lee, 2006; Manning-Morton, 2006). For example, translating attachment research into implications for infant and toddler practice, Honig argued that 'building secure attachments can be considered a prime goal in early childhood education' (p. xi) since secure attachments are related to long-term emotional wellbeing, social competence, and emotional regulation.

Reflecting on her qualitative study of the relationship development process of infant–caregiver dyads in a university-affiliated childcare setting, Lee (2006, p. 148) proposed that ECEC professional preparation programs should promote the study of relationships and emotions and urged the development of 'practicum courses that make theory and practice come together'. Others have urged that specialized training programs are needed to support teachers in pedagogy which emphasizes intersubjectivity (Gevers Deynoot-Schaub and Riksen-Walraven, 2008; Manlove et al., 2008) and thus facilitates the successful 'reading' of infant and toddler cues and joint attentional initiations.

'Research-proven strategies' (Gallagher and Mayer, 2008, p. 80) that help develop and sustain high-quality relationships with children from birth have also been collated. Such strategies include interactions which are: gentle, responsive and individualized and involve sensitive and timely adjustments to children's verbal and non-verbal cues. Adults' interactions with under-2-year-olds should also be attentive to the child's temperament, cultural background, interests, and current 'zone of proximal development'. Adult positive affect, communicated via body language, tone of voice, and the way they handle infants' bodies, has also been highlighted as a component of high quality teacher–child interactions (Hammond, 2009) together with: comforting and supporting children's emotions; daily routines that create a sense of safety and security; and minimizing changes of staff (Gloeckler, 2006; Stephen et al., 2003). With toddlers, teachers also need to respect their need for 'autonomy with connectedness' which Thomason and La Paro (2009, p. 285) identified as more likely when there is: a positive climate; teacher sensitivity; regard for the child's perspective; behavior guidance; and language modeling. Clearly, these process dimensions of pedagogy now inform the quality agenda for ECEC.

Pedagogical Relationships and Structural Arrangements

Yet it is also clear that the traditional structural dimensions of quality, identified in the late 1970s as constituting the 'iron triangle' of quality (Ruopp et al., 1979), remain a persistent feature of the research landscape about infant-toddler pedagogy. Contemporary research continues to document that high adult:child ratios and small group size (Frank et al., 2006; Lee, 2006; Thomason and La Paro, 2009) provide optimum conditions for the development of attuned relationships since they allow both teacher and child the time needed to get to 'know' each other better (Gallagher and Mayer, 2008; Gevers Deynoot-Schaub and Riksen-Walraven, 2008; Lee, 2006).

Research has also led to specific guidelines on these regulable elements of quality suggesting an ideal adult:child ratio of 1:3 (Expert Advisory Panel on Quality ECE and Child Care, 2009; Munton et al., 2002). However, researchers also warn that, by themselves, ratios are only pre-conditions for quality since they interact with other factors such as levels of staff satisfaction, which interact with factors like appropriate levels of remuneration (Milgrom and Mietz, 2004).

High staff turnover (Gallagher and Mayer, 2008) and workforce status and working conditions (Sims et al., 2005) have also been persistently identified as having a significant impact on teachers' ability to demonstrate the practices necessary for effective infant and toddler pedagogy – otherwise referred to as process variables of quality.

Structural practices like the use of a primary caregiver/key worker system (e.g., Dalli and Kibble, 2010) are now widely considered as essential to support the development of attuned caregiving and a sense of security and attachment in centre-based education and care. Additionally, continuity of care, individualized or personalized care, cultural continuity, and inclusion of children with special needs have also been recommended and are among the program practices recommended by the *Program for Infant Toddler Care* (PITC) (Lally, 2009).

Together, these factors help define the possibilities and limitations of experiences for children and staff. They also highlight the multi-faceted challenge for teachers to be attuned to infants' and toddlers' realities and desires in order to support their sense of agency, enquiry, and identity. They further reflect the fact that infant and toddler pedagogy, with its emphasis on intersubjective, attuned relationships, takes place in a range of ECEC contexts: the context affects teachers' actions, and teachers affect the context in which they work.

FUTURE LINES OF ENQUIRY

Research related to group-based ECEC for under-2-year-olds has to date employed a remarkably diverse range of theoretical and methodological frameworks and sought to respond to multiple agendas that reflect, to a large extent, the complexity of ECEC provision for this age group. As participation in group-based ECEC services continues to grow in many OECD countries, presenting new issues and approaches to the topic, the diversity of research is likely to continue.

Policy Research on the Effects of ECEC for Under-2-Year-Olds

From a global policy perspective, it is clear that policy agencies continue to seek research that will inform policy and link it to practice; to improve quantity and quality; and to disseminate research internationally (OECD, 2012). Additionally, despite 'waves' or phases of research that suggest a sequential or evolutionary development of knowledge about ECEC for under-2-year-olds, there remains a call for more evidence on the effects of ECEC. In particular, governments are interested in 'robust' studies that deliver cost-benefit analyses of their investment in very young children as human capital (e.g., Barnett and Nores, 2012). As a primary rationale for research, this focus is problematic in the way that it positions very young children as beings of the future rather than as citizens of today. By contrast, the rich array of contemporary research across diverse disciplines points to the need for policy research to look beyond economic imperatives and reflect wider societal realities, including the new normality of very young children's childhoods, in all their complexities, lived in ECEC settings.

From Global to Local: Infants' and Toddlers' Lived Experiences in ECEC

A momentum of research is building which draws emphasis away from the identification of universal or even local 'variables' or notions of 'quality' towards the unique 'lived' experiences of infants and toddlers in ECEC.

Philosophically there is also an increasing interest in understanding what constitutes 'reality' for very young children and how reality is framed within the contemporary context of new right ideologies and rationalist discourses (Farquhar and White, 2014). In this domain, the traditional emphasis on measurable 'quality' is superseded by one that focuses on the way infancy is 'seen', 'experienced' and accordingly represented by and for

others (Cheeseman et al., 2015; Harrison and Sumsion, 2014; Johansson and White, 2011). A critique of research approaches that seek to determine what infants or toddlers might be thinking or doing is offered by Elwick et al. (2014) who summon the phenomenology of Merleau-Ponty to suggest, as Stern (1985) likewise did, that research which seeks to understand infant experience can, at best, only construct meaning based on researcher interpretations of infant languages. Hence, what can be 'known' from this standpoint is hermeneutic and, in consideration of Levinas, deeply ethical in relation to the 'other'. In keeping with this tenet, Sommer, Pramling Samuelsson and Hundeide (2010) call for a distinction between research on children's perspectives (which emphasizes forms of expression) and child perspectives (emphasizing adult understanding of the child). Without a reflexive consideration of this distinction, they argue, the young child may be objectified within the research. Such a stance has been deeply considered by contemporary researchers in their work with the very young (Johansson and White, 2011), leading to a more reflexive, ethical stance and a much more tentative position on the experiences of under-2-year-olds as 'know-able' phenomena.

There is also a shift away from the sociological view of infants and toddlers in a 'group' as a consensus-building notion (reinforced through democratic theories) to seeing the individual within the group, and the experience for this child in this *locale*. In contrast to the generic 'child' that is privileged in studies that seek to create correlations as truth, such a view creates significant provocations for the field in the sense that what was once 'certain' is now contested and deeply uncertain.

An emphasis on lived experience is also heralded through the theoretical positions of post-structural philosophy (e.g., Johansson and Løkken, 2014; Rutanen, 2014; Sumsion et al., 2014). In these cases, a deeply ethical agenda is articulated as one that underpins all research work in the field. Taguchi (2010) interprets this message for early childhood practice as one that 'doesn't treat pedagogical work as being exclusively about trying to get children, students and teachers to reach pre-set goals of pre-set learning contents as in contemporary developmentally appropriate practices, constructivist learning theory and learning studies' (Taguchi, 2010, p. 177). Rather, emphasis is placed on the potential of discovery to generate new ways of thinking about the early childhood experience rather than merely reporting on what 'already is'. An example of recent research in this domain is the philosophical work of Peers and Agbenyega (2014) who argue against the self-evident character of 'care' in ECEC to posit the view that 'the psychological profile of "care" as a maternal instinct is insufficient' (p. 1508). Their proposition, that care is both ambiguous and beyond causality, offers a welcome challenge to the field.

Research on Teaching by Teachers

Against this background, research focused on under-2-year-olds in group-based settings is rapidly expanding its areas of focus and theoretical and inter-disciplinary orientation (Rayna, 2010), including through the work of a growing number of teacher-researchers (Duncan and Conner, 2013). Teachers are increasingly not only participants *in* but also initiators *of* research alongside infants and toddlers, involved in participatory or praxeologic research that not only interrogates their practice in critical ways, but also seeks to reveal the unique characteristics of group care and education from ideological and cultural standpoints. These researchers are enriching the field with insights into their own lived experience of pedagogy with this age group and signaling the need to consider knowledge about best practice as a 'work in progress' (Berthelsen, 2010, p. 84). They are also contributing to revised interpretations of the ECEC setting as 'a culture characterized by its own values, conventions, manners and social relations which are developed, kept alive, and transmitted to new members of the small community by both pedagogues and children'

(Broström and Hansen, 2010, p. 99). Such emphases reveal the complexity of teachers' experiences and, in doing so, offer significant challenge to traditional discourses about universal dimensions of quality, 'reveal[ing] a sophisticated, complex world that may be [otherwise] unseen, overlooked or unacknowledged' (Press and Mitchell, 2014, p. 235).

Relationships in ECEC

Another promising line of inquiry is research which, in various ways, foregrounds relationships in early childhood research, reinstalling the adult into the research process as a co-participant. Some of these theoretical approaches emphasize democratic transformation based on the work of Freire, Deleuze and Guatarri, and others (e.g., Vandenbroeck et al., 2012); whilst others aim to interpret language as an ideological event of dialogue *between* infants, toddlers, peers, and adults in the ECEC setting (White et al., 2015). In these approaches, the perspectives and interpretations of all who participate in the event are brought into view, rather than simply the thoughts of the lone researcher. Notions of the event itself are also expanded upon – as silent or spoken dialogue with the past, present, and future. The body is also deeply implicated, especially the gaze as a central means of intersubjectivity (White et al., 2015).

CONCLUSION

This chapter has traced the history of research on group-based ECEC for under-2-year-olds from its origins in the controversial debates about the effects of early day-care during the 1970s through 'waves' of research which in the 1980s focused on identifying the structural elements of the ECEC environment that made a difference to quality, and in the 1990s identified that quality depended as much on 'process' variables as on structural ones. Moving into the new millennium, the focus on regulable elements of quality and how they interacted with other factors remained on the research agenda, but was supplemented by a new line of philosophical, post-structural and reconceptualist questioning of the notion of quality that positioned the concept as contestable, relative, and potentially harmful in its colonizing effects. Meanwhile, research outside the field of ECEC brought new understandings about infants and toddlers: neurobiological research highlighted the very early years as a period of intense brain activity that laid down the foundation for later learning and development, and child development research increasingly revealed the careful experimentation with communication that infants engage in from birth as they make sense of their interactional environment. These insights shone a spotlight on the importance of nurturing relationships in which infants experience sensitive responsive caregiving in conditions that are free from toxic stress. As such, they both created a useful tool in the hands of policy advocates for the improvement of ECEC provision for these youngest children, and constructed a discourse about ECEC for under-2-year-olds that some have warned might overshadow the importance of other types of research that are equally critical to ensure equitable responses to all children in diverse populations. In pedagogical research, the same insights have provided a platform for an upsurge of interest in relational pedagogies that emphasize adult–child attunement within structural arrangements that enable a 'culture of quality', thereby re-asserting a focus on aspects of process to the quality agenda. Taken together, both process and structural dimensions of quality, combined with interdisciplinary research concerning the developing (social) brain, the body, and language in its broadest sense, have posited a research and policy agenda that orients ECEC for under-2-year-olds towards a relationship encounter. The growing emphasis on how those relationships play out in real-life situations is accompanied by a more philosophical gaze into the origins of that experience. As a consequence, there is now a much greater critical orientation in research in this field, an orientation that constructs ECEC for infants and toddlers as deeply nuanced, complex, and uncertain.

Looking to the future, researchers are increasingly shifting their attention away from debates about universal or even local notions of 'quality' and towards investigating the unique 'lived' experience of the infant and toddler in ECEC. Such research seeks to suspend certainty in any universal sense while emphasizing experience as central to understanding. Elwick et al. (2014) suggest that too much certainty in the domain of ECEC is not only immoral but also profoundly limiting. Using methodologies that respect the developing infant or toddler as a person in their own right – albeit one who is infinitely shaped by past, present, and future people, places, and things – this new line of research is also a means of interrogating the realities of lived experiences in ECEC communities. Here, research emphasizes the hidden or 'underground' nature of infant experience rather than merely the privileged aspects of curriculum (e.g., White, 2013, 2016). Moreover, deliberate attempts are made to put seemingly disparate ideas into dialogue with one another in order to generate 'new conversations, insights and understandings' (Harrison and Sumsion, 2014, p. 12).

Given the diversity of provision, the challenges of high quality pedagogy with this unique age group, and the inter-disciplinary nature of inquiry, it is likely that this revised research agenda has the potential to promote new ways of thinking about ECEC for under-2-year-olds and what this means, not only as a future-oriented human capital outcome but also as a portal for understanding this unique period of life in a contemporary world.

FURTHER READING

Dalli, C., White, J., Rockel, J., Duhn, I., with Buchanan, E., Davidson, S., et al. (2011). Quality early childhood education for under-two-year-olds: what should it look like?

A literature review. Ministry of Education. Available at: www.educationcounts.govt.nz/publications/ECE/Quality_ECE_for_under-two-year-olds/965_QualityECE_Web-22032011.pdf

Harrison, L. & Sumsion, J. (2014). *Lived Spaces of Infant-Toddler Education and Care: Exploring Diverse Perspectives on Theory, Research, Practice and Policy*. Dordrecht: Springer.

Johansson, E. & White, E. J. (2011). *Educational Research with Our Youngest: Voices of Infants and Toddlers*. Dordrechdt: Springer.

QUESTIONS FOR REFLECTION

1 How should early childhood educators and policy makers 'read' the complex landscape of research on under-2-year-olds in ECEC?

2 What methodological and theoretical positions can best respond to the new normality of infants and toddlers in ECEC?

3 To what extent can or should diverse research paradigms speak to one another: from the laboratory into the ECEC setting; from correlations to speculations; from inferences to subjectivities; across disciplines?

4 How might we reconcile the complexity of certainty and uncertainty to understand more about the ECEC experience for under-2-year-olds?

5 What is privileged and/or silenced theoretically, methodologically, thematically within the contemporary research agenda?

NOTES

1 In 1986, Jay Belsky published a paper in which he claimed that a circumstantial case could be made that early infant non-maternal care (in any context) may be associated with an avoidant attachment to the mother, diminished compliance and cooperation, increased aggressiveness and greater social maladjustment in later years. Rebuttals by Phillips et al. (1987: 20) claimed that Belsky's argument was based on a selective and misinterpreted reading of available data, and called for more carefully controlled studies of infant day-care because the 'evidence on infant day care was not all in'.

2 This is evident in documents such as the *NAEYC Early Childhood Program Standards and Accreditation: All Criteria* (2014) available at: www.naeyc.org/files/academy/file/AllCriteriaDocument.pdf;

the *California Early Childhood Educator Competencies* (2011) California Department of Education and First 5, California Department of Education; and the Australian Guide to the National Quality Standard (Australian Children's Education and Care Authority, 2013), among others.

3 The 'event-related potential' (ERP) technique is used to record brain activity from the scalp in order to evaluate cognitive responses such as attention, memory, and language.

4 Toxic stress occurs in situations where children have no control over stressful events and no access to support from an adult who can soothe them.

5 Children in these studies ranged in age from 3 months to 29 months.

REFERENCES

Ainsworth, M. D. S. & Bowlby, J. (1991). An ethological approach to personality development. *The American Psychologist*, 46(4), 333–41.

Araujo, S. B. (2012). Researching change: A praxeological case study on toddlers' educational contexts. *European Early Childhood Education Research Journal*, 20(4), 505–17.

Barnett, W. S. & Nores, M. (2012). *The Investment and Productivity Argument for ECCE: An International Volume – Early Childhood Care and Education: Building the Wealth of Nations*. New Brunswick, NJ: National Institute for Early Education Research.

Bell, M. A. & Wolfe, C. D. (2004). Emotion and cognition: An intricately bound developmental process. *Child Development*, 75(2), 366–70.

Belsky, J. (1986). Infant day care: A cause for concern? *Zero to Three*, VI(5), 1–9.

Belsky, J. (1988). The effects of infant day care reconsidered. *Early Childhood Research Quarterly*, 3, 235–272.

Belsky, J., Melhuish, E., Barnes, J., Leyland, A. H., Romaniuk, H. & National Evaluation of Sure Start Research Team. (2006). Effects of Sure Start local programmes on children and families: Early findings from a quasi-experimental, cross-sectional study. *British Medical Journal*, 332, 1476–82.

Berthelsen, D. (2010). Introduction. *International Journal of Early Childhood*, 42: 81–6.

Britto, P. R., Yoshikawa, H. & Boller, K. (2011). *Quality of Early Childhood Development*

Programs in Global Contexts: Rationale for Investment, Conceptual Framework and Implications for Equity. Social Policy Report, 25(2). Society for Research in Child Development.

Broström, S. & Hansen, O. (2010). Care and education in the Danish creche. International Journal of Early Childhood, 42(2), 87–100.

Camilli, G., Vargas, S., Ryan, S. & Barnett, W. S. (2010). Meta-analysis of the effects of early education interventions on cognitive and social development. Teachers College Record, 112(3), 579–620.

Cannella, G. S. & Viruru, R. (2004). Childhood and Postcolonialisation: Power, Education, and Contemporary Practice. New York: RoutledgeFalmer.

Center on the Developing Child at Harvard University (2011). Building the Brain's 'Air Traffic Control' System: How Early Experiences Shape the Development of Executive Function. Working Paper No. 11. Available at: www.developingchild.harvard.edu

Cheeseman, S., Press, F. & Sumsion, J. (2015). An encounter with 'sayings' of curriculum: Levinas and the formalisation of infants' learning. Educational Philosophy and Theory, 47(8), 822–832.

Crais, E., Watson, L. & Baranek, G. (2009). Use of gesture development in profiling children's prelinguistic communication skills. American Journal of Speech-Language Pathology, 18(1), 95–108.

Dahlberg, G., Moss, P. & Pence, A. (2007). Beyond Quality in Early Childhood Education and Care: Languages of Evaluation. London. Routledge.

Dalli, C. (2006). Re-visioning love and care in early childhood: Constructing the future of our profession. The First Years New Zealand Journal of Infant and Toddler Education, 8(1), 5–11.

Dalli, C. & Kibble, N. (2010). Peaceful caregiving as curriculum: Insights on primary caregiving from action research. In A. Meade (ed.), Dispersing Waves: Innovation in Early Childhood Education (pp. 27–34). Wellington: NZCER.

Dalli, C., White, J., Rockel, J., Duhn, I., with Buchanan, E., Davidson, S., et al. (2011). Quality early childhood education for under-two-year-olds: what should it look like? A literature review. Ministry of Education. Available at:

www.educationcounts.govt.nz/publications/ECE/Quality_ECE_for_under-two-year-olds/965_QualityECE_Web-22032011.pdf

Davis, E. & Sandman, C. (2010). The timing of prenatal exposure to maternal cortisol and psychosocial stress is associated with human infant cognitive development. Child Development, 81(1), 131–48.

Degotardi, S. & Pearson, E. (2014). The Relationship Worlds of Infants and Toddlers: Multiple Perspectives from Early Years Theory and Practice. Maidenhead: Open University Press.

de Regnier, R. (2005). Neurophysiologic evaluation of early cognitive development in high-risk infants and toddlers. Mental Retardation and Developmental Disabilities Research Review, 11, 317–24.

de Schipper, J. C., Tavecchio, L. W. C., Van Ijzendoorn, M. H. & Van Zeijl, J. (2004). Goodness-of-fit in center day care: Relations of temperament, stability, and quality of care with the child's adjustment. Early Childhood Research Quarterly, 19(2), 257–72.

de Wolff, M. S. & van IJzendoorn, M. H. (1997). Sensitivity and attachment: A meta-analysis on parental antecedents of infant attachment. Child Development, 68, 571–91.

Doherty, M. (2008). Theory of Mind: How Children Understand Others' Thoughts and Feelings. Hove: Psychology Press.

Duncan, J. & Conner, L. (eds) (2013) Research Partnerships in Early Childhood Education: Teachers and Researchers in Collaboration. New York: Palgrave Macmillan.

Elfer, P. (1996) Building intimacy in relationships with young children in nurseries. Early Years, 16(2), 30–4.

Elwick, S., Bradley, B. & Sumsion, J. (2014). Creating space for infants to influence ECEC practice: The encounter, ecart, reversability and ethical reflection. Educational Philosophy and Theory, 46(8), 873–85.

Ete, F. (1993). Pacific Island early childhood centres (language nests): The role of the church in promoting early childhood education in Aotearoa. Paper presented at the NZCER seminar: What is government's role in early childhood education? Wellington, February.

Expert Advisory Panel on Quality Early Childhood Education and Child Care. (2009). Towards a national quality framework for early childhood education and care: Report of the expert advisory panel on quality early childhood education and care. Canberra, Australia: DEEWR.

Farquhar, S. & White, E. J. (2014). Philosophy and pedagogy of early childhood education. *Educational Philosophy and Theory*, 46(8), 821–32, 885.

Fleer, M. & Linke, P. (1999). Babies: Responding appropriately to infants. *Australian Early Childhood Research in Practice Series*, 6(2), 1–18.

Fox, N. A. & Rutter, M. (2010). Introduction to the special edition on the effects of early experience on development. *Child Development*, 81(1), 23–7.

Fox, S. E., Leavitt, P. & Nelson, C. A. (2010). How the timing and quality of early experiences influence the development of brain architecture. *Child Development*, 81(1), 28–40.

Frank, I., Stolarski, E. & Scher, A. (2006). Caregivers' mediation and toddlers' emotional responses in the child care context. *Early Child Development and Care*, 176(3–4), 239–51.

Gallagher, K. C. & Mayer, K. (2008). Enhancing development and learning through teacher–child relationships. *Young Children*, 63(6), 80–7.

Gerber, E. B., Whitebrook, M. & Weinstein, R. S. (2007). At the heart of child care: Predictors of teacher sensitivity in center-based child care. *Early Childhood Research Quarterly*, 22(3), 327–46.

Gevers Deynoot-Schaub, J. & Riksen-Walraven, J. M. (2008). Infants in group care: Their interactions with professional caregivers and parents across the second year of life. *Infant Behavior & Development*, 31(2), 181–9.

Gillespie, A. & Cornish, F. (2010). Intersubjectivity: Towards a dialogical analysis. *Journal for the Theory of Social Behaviour*, 40(1), 20–46.

Gloeckler, L. (2006). Teacher/caregiver practices influencing the early development of emotion regulation in toddlers. Unpublished PhD thesis, University of North Carolina at Greensboro, USA.

Goodfellow, J. (2008). Presence as a dimension of early childhood professional practice. *Australian Journal of Early Childhood*, 33(1), 17–22.

Goouch, K. & Powell, S. (2013). *The Baby Room: Principles, Policy and Practice*. Maidenhead: McGraw Hill/Open University Press.

Graue, E. (2005). Section III commentary: Qualifying quality. *Early Childhood Education & Development*, 16(4), 521–2.

Gunnar, M. R. & Cheatham, C. L. (2003). Brain and behaviour interface: Stress and the developing brain. *Infant Mental Health Journal*, 24(3), 195–211.

Gunnar, M. R. & Donzella, B. (2002). Social regulation of the cortisol levels in early human development. *Psychoneuroendocrinology*, 27, 199–220.

Hammond, R. A. (2009). *Respecting Babies: A New Look at Magda Gerber's RIE Approach*. Washington, DC: Zero to Three.

Harms, T. & Clifford, R. (eds). (1980). *Early Childhood Environmental Rating Scale*. New York: Teachers College Press.

Harms, T., Cryer, D. & Clifford, R. (1998). *Infant/Toddler Environment Rating Scale*. New York: Teachers College Press.

Harrison, L. & Sumsion, J. (2014). *Lived Spaces of Infant-Toddler Education and Care: Exploring Diverse Perspectives on Theory, Research, Practice and Policy*. Dordrecht: Springer.

Heckman, J. (2011). The economics of inequality: The value of early childhood education. *American Educator*, 35 (Spring), 31–47.

Herrod, H. G. (2007). Do first years really last a lifetime? *Clinical Pediatrics*, 46(3), 199–205.

Honig, A. S. (2002). *Secure Relationships: Nurturing Infant/Toddler Attachment in Early Care Settings*. Washington, DC: National Association for the Education of Young Children.

Howes, C., Phillips, D. & Whitebook, M. (1992). Thresholds of quality: Implications for the social development of children in center-based child care. *Child Development*, 63, 449–60.

Inder, T. (2002). Magnetic resonance techniques: Opening a window into our understandings of brain development in the newborn infant. *Childrenz Issues*, 6(2), 30–8.

Irwin, K. (1987). The Pakeha response to Kohanga Reo. *Childcare Quarterly*, 7(3), 28–30.

Islam, Z. (2010). From 'marginality' to 'mainstream': A narrative of early childhood professionalism in Bangladesh. *Contemporary Issues in Early Childhood*, 11(1), 29–38.

Johansson, E. (2004). Learning encounters in preschool: Interaction between atmosphere, view of children and of learning. *International Journal of Early Childhood*, 36(2), 9–26.

Johansson, E. & Løkken, G. (2014). Sensory pedagogy: Understanding and encountering children through the senses. *Educational Philosophy and Theory*, 46(8), 886–97.

Johansson, E. & White, E. J. (eds). (2011). *Educational Research with Our Youngest* (pp. 15–38). Dordrecht: Springer.

Katz, L. G. (1985) The nature of professions: Where is early childhood education? Address presented at Early Childhood Organization Conference at Bristol Polytechnic, Bristol, England, 20 September.

Keuroghlian, A. S. & Knudsen, E. I. (2007). Adaptive auditory plasticity in developing and adult animals. *Progress in Neurobiology*, 82, 109–21.

Lally, J. R. (2009). The science and psychology of infant-toddler care. *Zero to Three*, November, 34–40.

Landry, S. H., Zucker, T. A., Taylor, H. B., Swank, P. R., Williams, J. M., Assel, M., et al. (2014). Enhancing early child care quality and learning for toddlers at risk: The responsive early childhood program. *Developmental Psychology*, 50(2), 526–41.

Leavitt, R. L. (1994). Emotionally responsive, empowering childcare. In *Power and Emotion in Infant-Toddler Day Care* (pp. 69–90). New York: State University of New York Press.

Lee, S. Y. (2006). A journey to a close, secure, and synchronous relationship: Infant–caregiver relationship development in a childcare context. *Journal of Early Childhood Research*, 4(2), 133–51.

Løkken, G. (2006). The toddler as a social construct in early childhood education pedagogy. Paper presented at the Little Scientist, OMEP Conference, Tromso, Norway.

Love, J. M., Kisker, E., Ross, C. & Raikes, H. (2005). The effectiveness of Early Head Start for 3-year-old children and their parents: Lessons for policy and programs. *Developmental Psychology*, 41(6), 885.

Manlove, E. E., Vazquez, A. & Vernon-Feagans, L. (2008). The quality of caregiving in child care: Relations to teacher complexity of thinking and perceived supportiveness of the work environment. *Infant and Child Development*, 17(3), 203–22.

Manning-Morton, J. (2006). The personal is professional: Professionalism and the birth to threes practitioner. *Contemporary Issues in Early Childhood*, 7(1), 42–52.

Martin, J., Sokol, B. & Elfers, T. (2008). Taking and coordinating perspectives: From prereflective interactivity, through reflective intersubjectivity, to metareflective sociality. *Human Development*, 51(5–6), 294–317.

Mathers, S., Eisenstadt, N., Sylva, K., Soukakou, E. & Ereky-Sevens, K. (2014). Sound foundations: A review of the research evidence on quality of early childhood education and care for children under three – Implications for policy and practice. Oxford: University of Oxford and The Sutton Trust.

McCartney, M., Scarr, S., Phillips, D., Grajek. S. & Schwarz, J. C. (1982). Environmental differences among day care centres and their effects on children's development. In E. F. Zigler & E. W. Gordon (eds), *Day Care: Scientific and Social Policy Issues*. Boston: Auburn House.

Meaney, M. (2010). Epigenetics and the biological definition of gene x environment interactions. *Child Development*, 81(1), 41–79.

Melhuish, E. (2001). The quest for quality in early day care and preschool experience continues. *International Journal of Behavioural Development*, 25(1), 1–6.

Meltzoff, A. N., Kuhl, P. K., Movellan, J. & Sejnowski, T. (2009). Foundations for a new science of learning. *Science*, 325, 284–8.

Milgrom, J. & Mietz, A. (2004). Quality of infant experience in day care. *Australian Research in Early Childhood Education*, 11, 39–50.

Moss, P. & Dahlberg, G. (2008). Beyond quality in early childhood education and care: languages of evaluation. *New Zealand journal of teachers' work*, 5(1), 3–12.

Munton, T., Mooney, A., Moss, P., Petrie, P., Clark, A. & Woolner, J. (2002). Research on ratios, group size and staff qualifications and training in early years and childcare settings. Research Report No. 320. London: Thomas Coram Research Unit, Institute of Education, University of London.

Murray, L. (2014). *The Psychology of Babies: How Relationships Support Development from Birth to Two*. London: Constable & Robinson.

National Scientific Council on the Developing Child (2007). The science of early childhood development: Closing the gap between what we do and what we know. Harvard University. Available at: www.developing-child.harvard.edu

Noddings, N. (1984). *Caring*. Berkeley, CA: University of California Press.

Nsamenang, A. B. (2010). Issues in and challenges to professionalism in Africa's cultural settings. *Contemporary Issues in Early Childhood*, 11 (1), 20–8.

OECD (2012). *Starting Strong III: A Quality Toolbox for Early Childhood Education and Care*. Paris: OECD.

OECD (2013). Education Indicators. *In Focus*. 2013/02. February.

Page, J. (2011). Do mothers want professional carers to love their babies? *Journal of Early Childhood Research*, 9(3), 310–23.

Papatheodorou, T. (2009). Exploring relational pedagogy. In T. Papatheodorou & J. Moyles (eds), *Learning Together in the Early Years* (pp. 3–18). Oxon: Routledge.

Peers, C. & Agbenyega, J. (2014). Le Theatre de la Cruaute or When caring 'is'. *Educational Philosophy and Theory*, 46(14), 1496–510.

Pence, A. & Pacini-Ketchabaw, V. (2006). The investigating 'quality' project: Challenges and possibilities for Canada. *Interaction, CCCF*, Fall, 11–13.

Peth-Pierce, R. (1998). *The NICHD Study of Early Child Care*. Rockville, MD: National Institute of Child Health and Human Development, Public Information and Communications Branch.

Phillips, D. A. (ed.). (1987). Quality in child care: What does research tell us? *Research Monographs of the National Association for the Education of Young Children*, 1, 21–42.

Phillips, D., McCartney, K., Scarr, S. & Howes, C. (1987). Selective review of infant day care research: A cause for concern. *Zero to Three*, Feb., 18–21.

Piaget, J. & Inhelder, B. (1969). *The Psychology of the Child* (H. Weaver, trans.). New York: Basic Books.

Pianta, R. C., La Paro, K. M. & Hamre, B. K. (2008). *Classroom Assessment Scoring System Manual: Pre-K*. Baltimore, MD: Paul H. Brookes.

Press, F. & Mitchell, L. (2014). Lived spaces of infant-toddler education and care: Implications for policy. In L. Harrison & J. Sumsion (eds), *Lived Spaces of Infant-Toddler Education and Care: Exploring Diverse Perspectives on Theory, Research, Practice and Policy* (pp. 225–40). Dordrecht: Springer.

Rayna, S. (2010). Research and ECEC for children under three in France: A brief review. *International Journal of Early Childhood*, 42(2), 117–30.

Reddy, V. (2008). *How Infants Know Minds*. Cambridge, MA & London: Harvard University Press.

Resources for Infant Educarers (RIE). (2006). *Unfolding of Infants' Natural Gross Motor Development*. Los Angeles, CA: RIE.

Rinaldi, C. (2006). *In Dialogue with Reggio Emilia: Listening, Researching and Learning*. London: Routledge.

Rosenthal, M. (1999). Out of the home child care research: A cultural perspective. *International Journal of Behavioural Development*, 23, 477–518.

Ruopp, R., Travers, J., Glantz, F. & Coelen, C. (1979). *Children at the Center*. Cambridge, MA: Abt Associates.

Rutanen, N. (2014). Lived spaces in a toddler group: application of Lefebvre's spatial triad. In L. Harrison & J. Sumsion (eds). *Lived Spaces of Infant-Toddler Education and Care: Exploring Diverse Perspectives on Theory, Research, Practice and Policy* (pp. 17–18). Dordrecht: Springer.

Sabol, T. J., Soliday Hong, S. L., Pianta, R. C. & Burchinal, M. R. (2013). Can rating pre-K programs predict children's learning? *Science*, 341, 845–6.

Schore, A. N. (2001) How parent–infant interactions enhance or inhibit the growth of the developing brain. *Infant Mental Health Journal*, 22(1–2), 7–66.

Scopelliti, M. & Musatti, T. (2013). Parents' view of child care quality: Values, evaluations, and satisfaction. *Journal of Child and Family Studies*, 22(8), 1025–38.

Shapiro, J. & Applegate, J. S. (2002). Child care as a relational context for early development: Research in neurobiology and emerging roles for social work. *Child & Adolescent Social Work Journal*, 19(2), 97–114.

Shonkoff, J. P. (2010). Building a new biodevelopmental framework to guide the future of early childhood policy. *Child Development*, 81(1), 357–67.

Sims, M., Guilfoyle, A. & Parry, T. (2005). What children's cortisol levels tell us about quality in childcare centres. *Australian Journal of Early Childhood*, 30(2), 29–39.

Singer, E. (1993). Shared care for children. *Theory and Psychology*, 3(4), 429–49.

Sommer, D., Pramling-Samuelsson, I. & Hundeide, K. (2010). *Child Perspectives and*

Children's Perspectives in Theory and Practice. London: Springer.

Southgate, V., van Maanen, C. & Csibra, G. (2007). Infant pointing: Communication to cooperate or communication to learn? *Child Development*, 78(3), 735–40.

Spitz, R. & Wolf, K. (1946). Anaclytic depression. *Psychoanalytic Study of the Child*, 2, 313–42.

Stephen, C., Dunlop, A.-W. & Trevarthen, C. (2003). Meeting the needs of children from birth to three: Research evidence and implications for out-of-home provision. *Insight 6*. Edinburgh: Scottish Executive Education Department

Stern, D. (1985). *The Interpersonal World of the Infant*. New York: Basic Books.

Stott, F. & Bowman, B. (1996). Child development knowledge: A slippery base for practice. *Early Childhood Research Quarterly*, 11, 169–83.

Sumsion, J., Stratigos, T. & Bradley, B. (2014). Babies in space. In L. Harrison & J. Sumsion (eds). *Lived Spaces of Infant-Toddler Education and Care: Exploring Diverse Perspectives on Theory, Research, Practice and Policy* (pp. 43–58). Dordrecht: Springer.

Taguchi, H. L. (2010). *Going Beyond the Theory/Practice Divide in Early Childhood Education*. London & New York: Routledge.

Thomason, A. C. & La Paro, K. M. (2009). Measuring the quality of teacher–child interactions in toddler child care. *Early Education and Development*, 20(2), 285–304.

Tobin, J., Vu, D. & Davidson, D. (1989). *Preschool in Three Cultures*. New Haven, CT: Yale University Press.

Tomasello, M. (1988). The role of joint attentional processes in early language development. *Language Sciences*, 10(1), 69–88.

Trevarthen, C. (1998). The concept and foundations of infant intersubjectivity. In S. Bråten (ed.), *Intersubjective Communication and Emotion in Early Ontogeny* (pp. 15–46). Cambridge: Cambridge University Press.

Trevarthen, C. and Malloch, S. (2002). Musicality and music before three: Human vitality and invention shared with pride. *Zero to Three*, 23(1), 10–18.

Vandenbroeck, M., Roets, G. & Roose, R. (2012). Why the evidence-based paradigm in early childhood education and care is anything but evident. *European Early Childhood Education Research Journal*, 20(4), 537–52.

Watamura, S., Donzella, B., Alwin, J. & Gunnar, M. R. (2003). Morning-to-afternoon increases in cortisol concentrations for infants and toddlers at child care age differences and behavioural correlates. *Child Development*, 74(4), 1006–20.

Watkins, C. & Mortimore, P. (1999). Pedagogy: What do we know? In P. Mortimore (ed.), *Understanding Pedagogy and its Impact on Learning*. London: Paul Chapman.

White, E. J. (2009). A Bakhtinian homecoming: Operationalizing dialogism in the context of an early childhood education and care centre in Wellington, New Zealand. *Journal of Early Childhood Research*, 7(3), 299–323.

White, E. J. (2013). Cry, baby, cry: A dialogic response to emotion. *Mind, Culture, and Activity*, 20(1), 62–78.

White, E. J. (2016). *Introducing Dialogic Pedagogy: Provocations for the Early Years*. Routledge: London.

White, E. J. & Redder, B. (2015). Proximity with under two-year-olds in early childhood education: A silent pedagogical encounter. *Early Education and Care*, DOI: 10.1080/03004430.2015.1028386.

White, E. J., Peter, M. & Redder, B. (2015). Infant and teacher dialogue in education and care: A pedagogical imperative. *Early Childhood Research Quarterly*, 30, 160–73.

Woodhead, M. (1996). *In Search of the Rainbow: Pathways to Quality in Large-scale Programme for Young Disadvantaged Children*. The Hague: Bernard Van Leer Foundation.

4

Young Children in their Local Communities

Bronwen Cohen and Marta Korintus

INTRODUCTION

What meaning does 'community' have for young children and what difference can it make to their lives? Frequently mentioned in early childhood policies and research, it reflects our awareness of a wider world of physical, social, emotional, economic, aesthetic and cultural factors and relationships that shape our lives. Globalization and identity politics have led to a broader definition, encompassing other variables implicated in social networks, including 'non-place' networks and social media. However, local communities, in their diversity and varying contributions to the lives of young children, remain key areas for research. Research questions include the ways in which local communities support the agency of their youngest citizens, the different physical, climatic, aesthetic, social, political and cultural environments they provide and the role they play as meeting grounds between the different generations and diverse cultural groups.

As is well documented and described elsewhere in this book, for much of the last century children were most visible to research in terms of their development or 'becoming' within psychology, psychiatry and education. Child development was the most influential child research paradigm within the Global North and mostly focused on the 'universal' child and what children have in common, with less interest, until more recently, in diverse contexts and cultures (Woodhead, 2009: 47).

Those disciplines most concerned with social structure paid scant attention to children as members of their communities. As Qvortrup (2009: 21–2) put it: 'Despite eminent sociologists' impeccable record for appreciating the significance of social structure, they all, when it comes to children, fail to think in terms of *structure*, let alone of children as a *social group* or a *collective* – apart perhaps from the fact they are *all* heading towards adulthood'. Children shared their 'muted' status with women (Hardman, 1973: 85). As Montgomery (2008: 35–7) has noted, such silences were particularly true of British anthropology at the time, which was narrower in its focus than American anthropology. It was also echoed in other disciplines (Hill and Tisdall, 1997; Oakley, 1994).

Children's gradual loss of 'muted status' has been extensively described (Amit and Rapport, 2002; Hastrup and Fog Olwig, 1996; James, 2013; James and Prout, 1997; Qvortrup et al., 2009) and is discussed elsewhere in this book. We consider here some of the approaches that have been taken, and what has been learned, about the significance of 'community' in relation to the lives of young children. We look first at the changing understandings and different approaches that researchers have taken to the concept of community. We then examine its significance in early childhood, starting with the US cross-cultural and cross-disciplinary studies of child socialization initiated in the 1950s, and 'ecological' and 'contextualist' studies within this tradition (Bronfenbrenner, 1979; LeVine and LeVine, 1966; Rogoff, 2003: 10; Tudge, 2008; Whiting, 1963). Subsequently, we consider what has been learned about the relationship between preschools and community from cross-cultural studies and through research undertaken on specific models for delivering Early Childhood Education and Care (ECEC) (Dahlberg et al., 1999; Delgado, 2009; New, 1998, 1999; Tobin et al., 1989, 2009). We look at more recent educational pedagogies that emphasize collaboration with communities and consider how these relate to the pedagogies of diversity and democratic practice (Cohen and Rønning, 2015; Gruenewald and Smith, 2008; Moss, 2007; Vandenbroeck et al., 2009). Finally, we discuss what still needs to be learned and the gaps we see in current research.

UNDERSTANDINGS OF COMMUNITY

The German sociologist and philosopher, Ferdinand Tönnies (1887), first applied the terms *gemeinschaft* and *gesellschaft* to contrast the different types of relationships among individuals and between individuals and society. Since then, the concept and definitions of community have given rise to innumerable studies and much debate within and across different disciplines.[1]

Understandings and conceptualizations of community have changed considerably over the last century. For a variety of reasons, depending on their theoretical persuasions, sociologists focusing on modern industrial societies have found the concept of community unsatisfactory. For some, it conflicted with what they saw as the primary variable of class; for others, it did not acknowledge the overwhelming primacy of the state (e.g., Bell and Newby, 1971; Cohen, 1985; Frankenberg, 1969). In Eastern Europe during the socialist years, the nature of local communities changed and opportunities for local self-organization were minimal (Csathó, 2008). In Western Europe and the Anglophone countries in particular, community was treated by some as almost pre-industrial, and certainly as 'simple', by contrast with the 'complexity' of modern society (e.g., Hillery, 1955; Wirth, 1938). Over the years, numerous dichotomous representations of 'community' and 'modern' society appeared in the literature, the burden of which was to represent relationships in the former as being based on personal knowledge and in the latter on function – a specific 'role' (Wirth, 1938, 1964).

However, over the last century, community studies were to contribute extensively to the social sciences. Social anthropology developed through the study of small, bounded societies and place-based (and subsequently community) concepts of culture. It brought extensive insights into human behaviour from ethnographic studies. Community studies formed the basis for the development of the practice-based discipline of community development and have informed social and public policies and political debate.

The concept and definitions of community have long been contested and, over recent decades, the relationship between community and place has been increasingly questioned.

Social anthropology, with its focus on discrete societies and groups, became problematized by identity politics and globalization, leading one social anthropologist, Nigel Rapport, to comment: 'I do not find community "good to think with"', explaining his preference for the term 'cosmopolitanism' which deals with the 'ontological truths of the human condition' (Rapport, cited in Amit and Rapport, 2012: 211). Less radically, anthropology in general has broadened its concept of community from being essentially place-based to encompass other variables such as religion, occupation and shared interests of many and diverse kinds, including social networking sites (Hastrup and Fog Olwig, 1996).

Other disciplines have similarly felt the need to distinguish between place and community, acknowledging the blurring of physical boundaries and the development of new economic and social networks in an increasingly globalized world, and the emergence of the 'non-place' and the 'post-place' community (Bradshaw, 2013; Crow and Allen, 1994).

However, in all these disciplines, the wider and looser definitions that are now used have modified rather than removed the significance of community and its links with place. As Amit (2002) argues in her edited volume for the European Association of Social Anthropologists, community may be an over-used word and 'hackneyed concept', but it continues to resonate in our daily lives and engage the attention of sociologists and anthropologists: 'However much they may have bemoaned its sloppy manifestations', she notes, 'they have never entirely ceased their efforts to address it' (2002: 1).

Brennan, Frumento, Bridger and Alter (2013), in a volume that brings together new theoretical and empirical research in community development (including Ted Bradshaw's posthumously published chapter on non-place and post-place community), point to the need to update and modify rather than abandon our understanding of the significance of community as it relates to place. They highlight Bradshaw's observation based on survey evidence suggesting that, whilst people attribute increasing importance to social relations outside of their local communities, 'they still also remain attached to these local communities'[2] (Brennan et al., 2013: 3).

CONTEXTUALIZING EARLY CHILDHOOD IN COMMUNITY

Working within the tradition of American anthropology with its strong links with psychology, anthropologists John Whiting and his wife Beatrice Whiting initiated in 1954 what became known as the Six Cultures study (Whiting, 1963). A cross-cultural study of childrearing and development, it involved naturalistic observations of children's behaviour within ethnographic studies of communities within six countries (Japan, Kenya, Mexico, India, the Philippines and the USA) and inspired a generation of researchers to undertake cross-cultural ethnographic research on childrearing and development (LeVine, 2010; New, 2010; Rogoff, 1990, 2003). LeVine (2010: 518) (who took part in the Six Cultures study) and New (2010: 527) also describe the growing influence at this time in the USA of the Russian psychologist and educator, Lev Vygotsky. Although already known of, it was the English translations of Vygotsky's *Thought and Language* (1962/1986) and *Mind in Society* (1978) that brought greater awareness of his sociocultural theory and his emphasis on shared collaborative learning and cultural-historical contexts.

One of those inspired by the Whitings (1963) and Vygotsky (1978) was the American cognitive psychologist, Barbara Rogoff, whose work stems from a socio-cultural–historical approach. She draws on Vygotsky's view that, rather than trying to 'reveal the eternal child', the goal is to discover 'the historical child' (Rogoff, 2003: 10). A psychologist in cognitive development who has undertaken research for over 40 years in a Guatemalan Mayan city, Rogoff locates her work within an interdisciplinary approach 'involving psychology, anthropology, history, sociolinguistics, education, sociology and other fields' (2003: 10) and in direct descent from the Whitings (1975) and Bronfenbrenner (1979).

Apprenticeship in Thinking (Rogoff, 1990) is grounded in Vygotsky's theory of the cultural–historical formation of the mind. From this position, she develops the concept of 'guided participation', encompassing guidance and participation in culturally valued activities. The concept is explained through a detailed account of how children as 'apprentices in thinking' learn from a very young age from 'observing and participating with their peers and more skilled members of society' (Rogoff, 1990: 7). She described in an interview in 2011 why this became the focus of her research in Guatemala, after becoming curious about how Mayan children learned complex skills such as weaving intricate fabrics and being told that they were not taught these skills – they simply learned them: 'So I asked more questions and watched, and over the intervening three decades, I learned that the children learn through observing keenly and contributing to ongoing endeavours, with the support of their families' (Glăveaunu, 2011: 409).

Lave and Wenger's (1991) short but influential monograph, *Situated Learning*, published a year later, drew on somewhat similar observations of the actual process of apprenticeship of young people in varied settings. They reconceptualized learning as a process in which, rather than an individual learner 'internalizing' knowledge, learning is an evolving and continuously renewed set of relations within 'communities of practice' (1991: 47, 50). Further developed by Wenger (1998, 2000), the concept of 'communities of practice' can now be found in a wide range of areas from management to healthcare, as well as increasingly appearing in early childhood literature (Ampartzaki et al., 2013; Kuh, 2012; Waller et al., 2011).

Its application in this way has prompted questions within management studies over its use of the term 'community' and ambiguities over their definition (Handley et al., 2006; Roberts, 2006). The Finnish cultural-activity theorist, Yrjö Engeström, has pointed to its detachment from sociocultural contexts – describing it as an 'ahistorical way to conceptualize work communities' which fails to situate communities of practice 'in the history of real societies and patterns of organizing work' (Engeström, 2007: 1, 3). One looks in vain, he notes, 'for discussions on the conditions of implementing communities of practice in highly rationalized hierarchical mass production organizations, or in settings driven by financialization, outsourcing and fragmentation of work, or in various networks, partnerships and strategic alliances' (2007: 3).

These are not criticisms that could be made about Barbara Rogoff, who, following on from her earlier work, argues in *The Cultural Nature of Human Development* (2003) that people develop as participants in cultural communities and that their development can only be understood in this context. She was strongly critical of the extent to which the study of human development had been based on research and theory often assumed to apply universally, although based in middle-class communities in Europe and North America. She juxtaposed the segregation of children in specialized 'age-graded' institutions that has developed in industrialized societies from those in which children are integrated in the everyday activities of their communities. These provide them, she says, with 'opportunities to observe and pitch in to allow children to learn through keen attention to ongoing activities, rather than relying on lessons out of the context of using the knowledge and skills' (Rogoff, 2003: 9). From her own research and other ethnographic studies, Rogoff concludes that in some communities 'children are included in almost all community and family events, day and night, from infancy' (2003: 133).

Rogoff (2003: 292–7) describes how science, religion, proper behaviour, community tradition and history are taught and learned through narratives in many communities, with Maori children's learning emphasizing songs and genealogies central to family and community life and reinforced through community events.

'Intent participation' in these communities can enable children in almost the full range of community activities 'to observe and listen in on the ongoing processes of life and death, work and play that are important in their communities' (2003: 317). In this way, in such communities, children 'play actively central roles, along with their elders and other companions, in learning and extending the ways of their communities' (2003: 284–5). Rogoff and her colleagues have established an international research consortium focused on the Learning through Intent Community Participation approach (Glăveanu, 2011).[3]

Rogoff sees her ideas as having built on the psycho-cultural model of the Whitings (Whiting and Whiting, 1975) and on Bronfenbrenner's ecological system (Bronfenbrenner, 1979). However, her emphasis on participation leads Rogoff to criticize both the Whitings and Bronfenbrenner for the causal chains suggested in their use of diagrams, which does not allow for 'the mutual relationship of culture and human development' (Rogoff, 2003: 42–9). Her own emphasis on the impact of culture on human development has in turn been criticized for 'raising the fear' 'that the previous developmental determinism in child psychology has, to a certain degree, been substituted here with an equally powerful form of cultural determinism' (James, 2013: 130). James, albeit gently, takes issue with Rogoff's statement that people develop as participants in cultural communities and that 'their development can be understood only in light of the cultural practices and circumstances of their communities – which also change' (Rogoff, 2003: 3, cited in James, 2013: 131). James sees this as unnecessary in demonstrating the impact of culture on human development because 'it could be that it is through the *mutual interactions* between infant and carer that the attachment patterns specific to a society or culture are reproduced – or indeed changed over time' (James, 2013: 131). But it is also the case that Rogoff (2003: 283), like James, sees cultural learning as a two-way process in which children themselves play central roles along with their

elders in learning and, we would add, *extending* the ways of their communities.

Jonathan Tudge (2008) identifies himself, like Rogoff, as a contextualist and follows her in drawing on Vygotsky and Bronfenbrenner in constructing the cultural–ecological theory that underpins his research. He differentiates himself as a contextualist from Rogoff and colleagues by his dialectical approach in which individuals and their social worlds are seen as separate entities but treated as dynamically related (Tudge, 2008: 260). His dialectical approach contrasts with the holistic view of Rogoff and colleagues that, he says (2008: 260), denies any meaningful boundary between individual and context. Tudge says that his dialectical approach makes sense to him 'because it can consider at one and the same time the joint realities of the social world, and the individuals who make up that world by treating them in dynamic interaction' (2008: 263). He describes this approach as the 'essence' of cultural–ecological theory. Tudge's cross-cultural research project, *The Cultural Ecology of Young Children* (CEYC), includes 'within-societal' variations relating to social class and, in respect of the USA, ethnicity. This has enabled him to examine 'broader social structural forces that influence the relations of particular communities with other communities as well as larger groups, within the society (or culture) at large. Every society has a shared history, no matter the extent of within-society heterogeneity' (Tudge, 2008: 261–2).

CEYC is based on observations of 3-year-olds in the USA, Russia, Estonia, Finland, Korea, Kenya and Brazil with the children followed through their first years of school. The research focuses on 'typical' everyday activities with each child in the study observed for 20 hours in one week spread over different times of the day and different days of the week, and 'putting no restrictions on where they go or on the people who interact with them' (Tudge, 2008: 90).

Tudge raises a number of the methodological challenges himself. For example, he notes that although the observations are time-consuming, it is still not clear whether 20 hours is sufficient to get an adequate sense of the typically occurring daily activities and interactions (2008: 102–8). However, it may also be that the emphasis on 'everyday activities' is inadequate in revealing some cultural processes within communities. James (2009) has commented that although the book's data do underscore the importance of context for children's development, they reveal 'far less about children's active contribution to cultural change', and she feels that greater attention could perhaps have been paid to the descriptive material intended to flesh out the data. We would similarly say that the data contribute little information on children's involvement in collective community events or in recording ways in which young children are introduced to cultural traditions or the implicated roles of particular partners or activities in this. It is therefore less helpful in discovering the 'historical' child and how communities involve children in their cultural traditions through activities which are not, by definition, 'everyday' but can in some instances take on a greater significance in children's lives for being less frequent but more memorable. For example, seasonal celebrations and life events such as birth and death can highlight not only indigenous traditions but also heterogeneity, cultural mixing and 'cosmopolitanism'.

ECEC SERVICES AND COMMUNITIES

Tudge's study, although limited by the numbers attending preschool services, provides some comparison of children's experiences within and outside of childcare, including variation in forms of play and use of school-relevant material (2008: 189–98). There is little data on the role of extended family and community in care giving that can be found in Kenya in the Six Cultures study, a difference that Tudge partly attributes to the development of preschool education there since the first study (2008: 53).

Tudge's analysis touches on the different functions served by preschool services, with class and ethnic variation, in the cities studied in his project. He agrees with Tobin, Wu and Davidson (1989) that 'different societies may have different goals for child care' (Tudge, 2008: 188) but Tudge's main focus is on the activities that take place.

Preschool in Three Cultures, an earlier study begun by Joseph Tobin and colleagues (Tobin et al., 1989) was primarily focused on understanding the cultural goals of early childhood education within a nation. Drawing on the research team's wide range of expertise in human development, cultural anthropology, psychology and early childhood education, it addressed this through a comparative study of the role of preschools in three very different cultures, at a time when they were being seen as a 'solution to the problem of how to care for, socialize and educate children between infancy and the start of formal schooling' (Tobin et al., 1989: 2). The countries in which the research took place were Japan, China and the USA, and the method they used is known as 'video-cued multivocal ethnography' which, described simply, involves the recording of visual ethnographies of preschool everyday life and using this as the basis for discussion with administrators, teachers and parents about their own services and those from other cultures (Tobin et al., 1989: 4–9; 2009). The method was further modified for subsequent research undertaken by Tobin with two other researchers in 2002. This modification added an explicitly historical and diachronic dimension, intended to ensure that the systems described exist in time but are not assumed as being on the same time line and ahead or behind each other but within their own historical and cultural context. The method, now known as video-cued multivocal diachronic ethnography (VMDE), is discussed in a number of Tobin's later publications (Tobin and Davidson, 1991; Tobin and Hsueh, 2007; Tobin et al., 2009).

Both the 1989 and 2009 studies conclude that preschools, although a relatively new 'invention', are more a force of cultural continuity than cultural change (Tobin et al., 1989:

221; 2009). The most extensive changes taking place in preschools were in China where they still found evidence of continuity, including examples of culturally implicit practices such as socio-dramatic play activity (Tobin et al., 2009: Loc. 947). One of the strengths of VDME as a methodology lies in its combination of ethnography, interviews, survey and reflexive discussion and the opportunity this provides not only to study three cultures' preschools but also 'three cultures as seen through their preschools' (Tobin et al., 1989: 2). However, our insights into the latter are more limited than they might have been if discussion had, as Hess (1990: 307) has pointed out, been less focused on the preschool sector itself, and enabled further exploration of some points. This includes, for example, the observation that in the Chinese preschool, play was prioritized less within the school, possibly because in 1984/5 China remained a 'society of street life, public meetings, public squares and open markets, a society where children not enrolled in organized play groups or preschools still have many opportunities to enjoy spontaneous and varied interactions with peers' (Tobin et al., 1989: 202).

Coinciding with the publication in 2009 of *Preschool in Three Cultures Revisited*, a moderated discussion in the *Comparative Education Review* considered the material from the new book and the methodology used in both books in a generally positive way, although Steiner-Khamsi drew attention to the 'conceptual black hole' which exists in educational research around the relationship of school to society (Steiner-Khamsi, 2009: 273). Most recently, Watras (2014: 80) is more critical of the weaknesses around this point, commenting that in order to show the relation of the preschool to society, Tobin 'had to stretch the words of the teachers and make conjectures' and construct meanings with informants. Watras concluded that one of the lessons that may be drawn is that 'assumptions that arise outside available evidence should become hypotheses for new studies' (2014: 84).

Both the Tudge and Tobin studies help to illuminate the cultural goals of early childhood education but highlight the need for us to know more about the relationship between local communities, services and society. The studies we examine next focus on specific 'exemplar' community services which offer insights into what this relationship can involve.

CHILDHOOD AND ECEC AS A COMMUNITY PROJECT

The story of how Reggio Emilia, a small city in the Emilia Romagna region of Northern Italy, supported the development of its nursery co-operatives in the 1960s and 1970s is well known and referred to elsewhere in this volume. Informed by the ideas and work in Northern Italy of Loris Malaguzzi (1920–1994), these co-ops grew into a substantial and inspirational network of centres. In 1993, in one of his last interviews before his death, Malaguzzi described to the Swedish film director, Carlo Barsotti, the community solidarity that led the building of the first nursery school after the end of the 1939–45 war:

> It was an intuition of the women, a fierce determination on the part of the women, together with the solidarity shown by a small village of farmers, farm hands and workers. It was they who built the nursery school at Villa Cella between 1945 and 1947... and this is where the story begins. (Barsotti, 2004: 11)

Malaguzzi describes how families and community, for whom education was a new concept, were brought in to the learning process:

> If I remember correctly, we immediately held a series of exhibitions in the city. This was something completely new and original for the townspeople who began to see how children might be able to work and relate to each other, how they were able to converse, to reason and to create. (Barsotti, 2004: 12)

Local action in establishing these services as co-operatives, as well as political leadership at *comune* level in supporting this, characterized a number of Northern Italian *comuni* from the 1960s. Reggio Emilia has attracted many admirers. The American educator and cultural psychologist, Rebecca New, who first came to know it and other North and Central Italian exemplar systems of early childhood services during her doctoral studies on comparative child development in the early 1980s, believes much can be learned from such services but offers frequent warnings to over-zealous advocates wanting to import the model. Pointing to the substantial role played by the socio-cultural context of the Italian services manifest in the cultural value given to interdependent relationships and the political and financial support from radical local authorities, she notes that 'there is more to be gained by understanding Reggio Emilia interpretations of early childhood education both ideological and practical, than will be accomplished by direct emulation of their practices' (New, 1998: 265).

New's year-long ethnographic study of Italian infant care and social development was followed by her subsequent research on Italian conceptions of community, participation and social responsibility. She undertook these in collaboration with Reggio Emilia and four other north-central Italian cities, which she described as exemplars of cultural values, regional support and local interpretation (New, 1999). Using a mixture of methodologies, including ethnographic observation, questionnaires and structured interviews, enabled her to examine the services in context. Her findings pointed to the significance attributed to social relationships – reflecting the cultural value given to interdependent relationships – to be found at regional and national levels as well. She found a congruence between developmental goals for children and the communal or civic expectations of adults and pointed to the way in which children participated in local economic activities. For example, in Pistoia, a tradition of apprenticeship characterizes the curriculum, with an emphasis on needlework in one and carpentry in another:

> These diverse emphases were *not* selected because of children's initiatives; rather they represent areas of expertise and passionate pursuit among some of the adults in the school and

neighborhood settings. The explicit goal, in this case, is to create opportunities for children to work with and learn from the adults as a means of connecting them to each other and to the larger community. (New, 1999: n.p.)

What still appears distinctive in these Italian *comuni* (and San Miniato is another example; see Fortunati, 2006) is the extent to which community as well as families have become integral to the process. Nimmo (1998: 305–6) noted in 1998 the way that US and Australian teachers recognized the need to co-operate with families but sought to protect young children from a wider world of contacts. By contrast, he saw that in Reggio Emilia a more connected identity for children raised the possibility that young children could be active participants in the wider arena of neighbourhood and city contacts, whether through field trips into the life of the surrounding streets and countryside or curiosity about 'the workings of pipes under city roads or the annual grape harvest' (Nimmo, 1998: 306).

This way of working may also be seen as reinforcing community support for the services. As New (1998: 278) points out, theories of learning and development are products of social and political forces, as well as of experience and experimentation. In many parts of northern and central Italy, the principles of co-operation and economic co-operatives have long traditions. As we saw earlier, Reggio Emilia's first nursery school, Villa Cella, was created by farmers for whom agricultural co-operatives were part of their way of life. In her examination of collective models of nurseries as part of a wider examination of quality from an international perspective, Penn (2011) pointed to the significance of co-operative traditions in models for services in Italy and Spain. By contrast, she comments on the lack of this tradition in the programme of community nurseries funded in London in the 1970s and 1980s, initially through the Greater London Council (GLC) and subsequently on an England-wide programme 'outside the mainstream – neither fish nor fowl' (Penn, 2011: 38). She identified the key to the success of the Spanish and Italian nurseries as the input of the local authority:

> The co-operatives did not have to deal with routine day-to-day administration; they did not have to raise money; and they were pedagogically inspired by highly trained and articulate people. They had autonomy, but they also had practical support and imaginative guidance of a high order. (Penn, 2011: 141)

Although many of the GLC community nurseries closed, the Sheffield Children's Centre is still in existence. The history, ethos and work with families and community of this inner-city exemplar co-operative in South Yorkshire are described in a book authored by some of the co-operative's members and Marco Antonio Delgado, a then doctoral research student (Broadhead et al., 2008). In his forward to the book, Peter Moss (2008: xii) draws a comparison with a network of early childhood centres in a Northern Italian city referred to by the city's director as a 'local cultural project of childhood'. Moss points out that in both cases 'there has been a recognition of public responsibility to local children as valued citizens of their community, and a commitment, sustained over time, to giving culturally appropriate meaning to that responsibility'. Delgado's ethnographic research on the Sheffield centre contributed (in an anonymized form) to his more extensive study that compared examples of government and community-led initiatives in England and in Mexico where he is now based (Delgado, 2014). *Community Involvement in Services for Young Children* (Delgado, 2009) examines the nature of community involvement in four initiatives.

In Mexico, he contrasts an independent, community-based preschool scheme started in 1981 in the Mexico City shantytown of Ciudad Nezahualcóyotl with a six-year World Bank compensatory programme for socially excluded parents. In England the Sheffield Children's Centre, referred to as the 'Castle Children's Centre', is contrasted with a small team supporting established services and providing home visits and parenting courses and subsequently supported through the Sure Start local programme (Delgado, 2009).

Ciudad Nezahualcóyotl developed through rural migration and Nezahuapilli, the preschool co-operative, came from a partnership between educational researchers and local mothers at a time when preschool education had not been made compulsory in Mexico. Inspired by Paulo Freire's concept of creating public space for dialogic learning, it was established on the basis that the work with children could only have meaning alongside work with parents and the community, and through ongoing democratic dialogue at all levels, and, crucially, with those who kept them marginalized (2009: 41–4). Although Nezahuapilli worked with the whole community, the World Bank programme for socially excluded parents (PRODEI) worked exclusively with parents and did not in general help or encourage the communities they worked with to address the underlying issues behind their poverty and exclusion (Delgado, 2009: 52–6).

The English examples explore in a similar way the varying impact of Sheffield Children's Centre as a long-established co-operative children's centre and the outreach services of a local authority. Sheffield Children's Centre, in common with Nezahuapilli, is a community co-operative with its decisions taken collectively through dialogue and has, Delgado finds, become a social arena 'where community identity is forged' (Delgado, 2009: 117). The centre's role in this was strengthened in the wake of the devastatingly damaging UK miners' strike of 1984–5, reinforcing its wider role in the community through offering a variety of training courses, driving lessons and, for example, helping male ex-miners to retrain as childcare workers (Delgado, 2009: 122–3). In meeting the needs of the community, the centre provided full-time childcare services, in contrast with the local authority's part-time service, which were also seen as more culturally appropriate and sensitive to the needs of a diverse and disadvantaged inner-city area and important in recognizing the totality of children's lives. As one worker explains: 'We try to think that we can do something for the whole of the child's life. That's what we are looking at and the whole of their families' lives, like in *the whole of the community's life'* (Delgado, 2009: 132; emphasis own).

Delgado presents both Nezahuapilli and the Sheffield Children's Centre as social movements, in contrast to the local government and World Bank examples. But the difference is not between public and non-public providers per se. Delgado draws parallels between Nezahuapilli and the Sheffield Children's Centre and the public services of Reggio Emilia. The difference lies rather in the broader political approach involved, in a willingness to challenge not only current practice and discourse but also social and economic systems. As Dahlberg describes in her account of the partnership forged between Reggio Emilia and the district of Hammarby in Stockholm, Reggio Emilia had not only transgressed dominant discourses in early childhood pedagogy but also in 'organization and community' (Dahlberg et al., 1999: 131).

Delgado points to the definitional ambivalence that surrounds community involvement and the institutional obstacles that can confront governments – and the World Bank – in their aspirations to support community development. Similar issues concerning the approach of governments and the World Bank are raised by the Armenian sociologist Armenuhi Tadevosyan (2008) who describes some of the confusion now surrounding the recent focus on community development in the post-socialist countries of Eastern Europe. He argues that, apart from a general sense that community participation is 'something positive', there is no shared understanding between donors such as the World Bank and the Open Society Institute and the governments of what it entails:

> Few international projects promoting community participation pursue objectives commonly associated with participation in donor countries. Community participation does not necessarily mean more decision-making authority granted to the community, or more active involvement of the community in the school. (Tadevosyan, 2008: 81–2)[4]

Such accounts remind us that time and place do matter and highlight the importance of 'community projects of childhood' in fostering our understanding of this. From the 'intuition of the women' following a war that lead to the Reggio Emilia nurseries, to the Sheffield Children's Centre that drew strength from its role in the UK miners' strike in the early 1980s, they reflect, in different ways, the significance of their time, place and history, although, as Moss (2007: 11) comments, the required conditions, structures and processes are all important subjects for research.

PLACE, COMMUNITY AND YOUNG CHILDREN'S LEARNING

We noted earlier that the 'non-place' and the 'post-place' community, and 'communities of practice' all speak to definitions of community often detached from, or not dependent on, 'place'. In diverse societies and an increasingly globalized world, place, culture and identity can have multiple meanings for young children. But place itself, physically, socially, historically, aesthetically and emotionally and as a site and resource for learning, still forms part of this. Place-based learning (or place-based education as it is also known) is a pedagogy linked to active and collaborative learning and in a number of respects exemplifies the 'intent participation' described by Rogoff. Defined as 'an approach to learning that makes use of local economic activities and the unique history, culture and tradition and other community reference points to engage more effectively with children and young people in the context of their lives' (Cohen and Rønning, 2014: 112), it has drawn inspiration from the American educator John Dewey (1916/1997), as well as from Lev Vygotsky.

It developed in association with wider societal goals such as stemming rural depopulation and, arguably, the most systematic approach to place-based learning can be found in Norway where rural policy has been accorded high priority and local authorities have greater freedom in the delivery of services (Cohen and Rønning, 2014: 113).

Although it developed as a pedagogy for schools, its principles have been incorporated within Norway's extensive system of kindergartens (which now provide full-time places for all children between the ages of 1 and 6) and indeed is probably most evident now in this first stage of the Norwegian education system (Cohen and Rønning, 2015: 264).

Smith and Sobel (2010: iv) point out that, although it is often seen as a pedagogy for rural schools, in the USA 'some of the most exciting examples of place- and community-based education are flourishing in inner-city schools'. Gruenewald and Smith (2008: xiii) seek to make the case for place-based education as 'the educational counterpart of a broader movement towards reclaiming the significance of the local in the global age'. They refer to this broader social movement as the 'new localism' that emphasizes the importance of reconnecting the 'process of education, enculturation and human development to the well-being of community life' (Gruenewald and Smith, 2008: xvi).

In some countries, place-based learning has been associated with the use of outdoor environments, drawing inspiration from nature. This is a longstanding feature of ECEC provision in the Nordic countries and is increasingly popular in the UK where research is exploring the association of outdoor experiences with health and gender issues and child-initiated learning (Cameron, 2014; Maynard et al., 2013). However, other strands of place-based learning that are evident in Norway, including the nurturing and passing on of history and economic and cultural traditions, are less visible in the research literature. In Scotland, the links that are now developing between the new community-owned trusts and woodlands and schools are seen as a fruitful area for educational and socio-economic research (Cohen and Rønning, 2014: 121).

As ECEC services develop, their interface with the local environments, communities and wider society in which they are situated becomes increasingly critical. As Moss asks (2007: 9–12), are they to be defined as a public good or a private commodity? In the vision

he shares of the declaration of the Catalan educational reform movement, Rosa Sensat (2005), they are spaces 'where children and adults can dialogue, listen, and discuss in order to share meanings'.

In some countries, ECEC can be a popular site for launching policy documents or making announcements. Nimmo describes a qualitatively different relationship between Reggio Emilia and its community when it is undertaking its projects:

> When a project is in process, teachers spread news of the children's work in the local newspaper. When it is time for celebration of a completed project, it is likely that the Mayor or other community members will be invited. (Nimmo, 1998: 306)

Such engagement is not just a matter of 'bringing politics into the nursery' (Moss, 2007: 1) but also of enabling young children to contribute politically to their communities. And arguably one of the most important aspects of this is in the challenge provided to 'identity politics' through the meeting places that can be provided for the multiple or micro-communities associated with our increasingly globalized world. Vandenbroeck, Roets and Snoeck (2009) identify this dimension in their small-scale study of the experiences of immigrant mothers attending Flemish day-care centres and taking part in projects on 'respect for diversity'. Their account of the dialogues that opened up and the 'consequent productive cross-fertilization of values and subcultures' (Vandenbroeck et al., 2009: 212) highlight the role that ECEC can play as a democratic forum for micro-communities in diverse societies.

FINAL THOUGHTS

Interdisciplinary perspectives have been important in contributing to our understanding of young children and community and remain so. The trend in collaborative research has now been helped, as James has remarked (2013: 4), by the development of childhood studies since the 1990s as an interdisciplinary field of inquiry.

But if we are to understand better the socio-economic, cultural and political contexts in which young children live their lives, we need to challenge ourselves in the scope of our enquiries and the methodologies we use.

'Community' as a context within which young children live their lives is too often on the margins of research on ECEC and schools. The voices of young children still do not feature as they might in research on community and its institutions: children should be perceived as powerful rather than weak, as contributors to change rather than as the victims they may on occasion be. So it seems to us that we do need to know more about young children in their communities: not just in their everyday lives but also by capturing the calendrical and special events and activities in their lives through which young children may find meaning in their lives and develop their understanding of themselves. It is not for nothing that 'rituals' and less frequent community events have attracted the attention of anthropologists.

We also need to recognize, as Amit and Rapport (2012: 209) put it, that 'communities are plural in social space and personal lives and in time', and more needs to be known about the ways in which spaces, services and institutions can serve as meeting places in interpreting, negotiating and generating new concepts of community within our increasingly diverse societies. Such research suggests the continuing importance of ethnography measured in years rather than months – we have been struck by the contribution made by those whose research commitment has extended over decades.

Crow and Mah emphasize (2011–2012) that multiple perspectives are important in community research and we wonder whether, for example, social network analysis[5] might also have some value in examining the developing social networks of young children within and across their localities and multiple communities.

Finally, as time and place do matter, more attention needs to be paid to ways in which they can be examined. Comparative research remains an essential tool for this. The rich variety of approaches to ECEC and community within the European Union invite a much more open and exploratory research programme at an EU level than is currently the case, which might include closer examination of the impact of such far-reaching political events as the dissolution of the Soviet Union and the development of post-socialist regimes in East-Central Europe.[6] This could helpfully contribute to our understanding of the 'historical' child and the significance of place and community in their lives as well as a much better understanding of diversity in Europe.

SUMMARY

This chapter has considered some research perspectives on the significance of 'local community' in the lives of young children. Understandings and conceptualizations of community have changed considerably over the past century and it remains a contested concept. Whilst it is now seen as encompassing other variables such as religion and class and shared interests, place remains an important element within the concept of community, particularly in the lives of young children and in recognition of their contribution to their communities.

Children were for a long time largely invisible within community studies but have become more visible through cross-cultural ethnographic research on child rearing and development from the 1950s, informed by the growing influence of Vygotsky's socio-cultural theory, and directing attention to collaborative learning and cultural-historical contexts.

Our understanding of the relationship between ECEC and communities has been helped by studies of exemplar systems and may be further assisted by examining more closely the educational pedagogy of place-based learning, which is developing new kinds of relationship between ECEC, schools and communities.

Interdisciplinary perspectives remain key to improving our understanding of young children and community but more thought needs to be given to the scope and methodologies employed. Examining the 'everyday' activities of children over a relatively short period does not necessarily capture the calendrical and special events in the lives of young children that may contribute to their sense of identity and can obscure the heterogeneity of communities. More extensive ethnographic research and exploration of other methodologies such as social network analysis might prove beneficial.

FURTHER READING

Cohen, B. and Rønning, W. (2014) 'Place-based Learning in Early Years Services: Approaches and Examples from Norway and Scotland', in L. Miller and C. Cameron (eds), *International Perspectives in the Early Years*. London: SAGE. pp. 112–26.

Daniels, H., Cole, M. and Wertsch, J.V. (2007) *The Cambridge Companion to Vygotsky*. Cambridge: Cambridge University Press.

Nimmo, J. (1998) 'The Child in Community: Constraints from the Early Childhood Lore', in C. Edwards, L. Gandini and G. Forman (eds), *The Hundred Languages of Children: The Reggio Emilia Approach – Advanced Reflections*. Norwood, NJ: Ablex. pp. 295–312.

QUESTIONS FOR REFLECTION

1 How and why did Lev Vygotsky's socio-cultural theory impact on our understanding of community?
2 Why and in what ways does research on the meaning of community for young children require an interdisciplinary approach?
3 How can young children's contribution to communities be most effectively explored?

NOTES

1 Crow and Mah (2011–2012: 5) point to the following disciplines as having 'useful contributions to make to researching community both separately and together'. These include (in alphabetical order) architecture and planning, communications and information science, criminology,

development studies, disability studies, ecology, education, ethnic and racial studies, geography, history, housing studies, law, literature, media studies, philosophy, political science, psychology, social anthropology, social policy, social work and community development, sociology, theology and youth studies, amongst others.

2 Bradshaw (2013: 18–20) examines data collected over the period 1972–1998 from the University of Chicago General Social Survey showing that people are socializing over a broader geographical area, that social evenings within the neighbourhood are declining and that people have a weaker sense of place through their neighbourhood, while they feel stronger towards their city and state. However, the substantial majority of people want to stay where they are.

3 The Intent Community Participation website (www.intentcommunityparticipation.net) makes more explicit the advocacy of Rogoff and colleagues of an approach in which children are treated as 'regular participants in the community', with the paradigm shift required in thinking of learning as 'transformation of participation rather than as the accretion of knowledge and skills'.

4 In the former socialist countries, the concept of community was understood differently with only minimal opportunities for local self-organization. Csathó (2008) describes how after the political changes in Hungary in 1989/1990 former 'cultural workers' started to focus on community development work in the Western sense.

5 Social Network Analysis (SNA) is the mapping, measuring and analysis of social relationships, often represented in a social network diagram showing individuals or nodes as points and their relationships or ties through kinship, friendship and other groupings as lines (see, for example, Rodkin and Hanish, 2007).

6 Kamarás (2001) describes the emergence in post-socialist regimes in East-Central Europe of what is described as the badly understood concept of 'community participation' and the increasing, if still low involvement, of religious institutions in delivering services which require greater scrutiny than they are currently receiving.

REFERENCES

Amit, V. (2002) 'Reconceptualizing community', in V. Amit (ed.) *Realizing Community: Concepts, Social Relationships and Sentiments*. London: Routledge. pp. 1–21.

Amit, V. and Rapport, N. (2002) *The Trouble with Community: Anthropological Reflections* on Movement, Identity and Collectivity. London: Pluto Press.

Amit, V. and Rapport, N. (2012) Community, Cosmopolitanism and the Problem of Human Commonality. London: Pluto Press.

Ampartzaki, M., Kypriotaki, M. and Voreaudou, C. (2013) 'Communities of Practice and Participatory Action Research', Educational Action Research 21(1): 4–27.

Barsotti, C. (2004) Interview with Loris Malaguzzi in the film L'uomo di Reggio. Reproduced in 'Celebrating 40 years of Reggio Emilia', Children in Europe 6: 10–16.

Bell, C. and Newby, H. (1971) Community Studies. London: Allen & Unwin.

Bradshaw, T. (2013) 'The Post-Place Community: Contributions to the Debate about the Definition of Community', in M.A. Brennan, J.C. Bridger and T. Alter (eds), Theory, Practice and Community Development. New York: Routledge. pp. 11–25.

Brennan, M.A., Frumento, P.Z.C., Bridger, J.C. and Alter, T.R. (2013) 'Introduction: Theory, Practice, and Community Development', in M.A. Brennan, J.C. Bridger and T. Alter (eds), Theory, Practice and Community Development. New York: Routledge. pp. 1–11.

Broadhead, P., Meleady, C. and Delgado, M.A. (2008) Children, Families and Communities: Creating and Sustaining Integrated Services. Maidenhead: Open University Press.

Bronfenbrenner, U. (1979) The Ecology of Human Development. Cambridge, MA: Harvard University Press.

Cameron, C. (2014) 'Perceptions of Using the Outdoors in Early Childhood Education and Care Centres in England, Hungary and Denmark', in L. Miller and C. Cameron (eds), International Perspectives in the Early Years. London: SAGE. pp. 127–42.

Cohen, A.P. (1985) The Symbolic Construction of Community. Chichester: Ellis Horwood.

Cohen, B. and Rønning, W. (2014) 'Place-based Learning in Early Years Services: Approaches and Examples from Norway and Scotland', in L. Miller and C. Cameron (eds), International Perspectives in the Early Years. London: SAGE. pp. 112–26.

Cohen, B. and Rønning, W. (2015) 'Education in Norway and Scotland: Developing and Re-forming the Systems', in Northern Neighbours: Scotland and Norway since 1800. Edinburgh: Edinburgh University Press. pp. 250–268.

Crow, G. and Allen, G. (1994) Community Life: An Introduction to Local Social Relationships. London: Routledge.

Crow, G. and Mah, A. (2011–2012) Connected Communities: Conceptualisations and Meanings of 'Community Discussion Paper Unity' – The Theory and Operationalization of a Contested Concept. Discussion paper, annotated bibliography and final report. Arts and Humanities Research Council. Available at: www.community-methods.soton.ac.uk/

Csathó, T. (2008) 'A közösségfejlesztés és a helyi hatalomkapcsolata' (The relationship between community work and local power), PAROLA füzetek 2: 14. Közösségfejlesztők Egyesülete, Budapest. Available at: www.kka.hu/_Kozossegi_Adattar/PAROLAAR.NSF/cimsz/492ACF1AEA2E1F44C12574B9003A8C4D?OpenDocument

Dahlberg, G., Moss, P. and Pence, A. (1999) Beyond Quality in Early Childhood Education and Care: Post Modern Perspectives. London: RoutledgeFalmer.

Delgado, M.A. (2009) Community Involvement in Services for Young Children: Accepting, Resisting and Proposing Alternatives to Mainstream Views. Saarbrucken: VDM.

Delgado, M.A. (2014) Personal communication, 4 March.

Dewey, J. (1916/1997) Democracy and Education. New York: Simon & Schuster.

Engeström, Y. (2007) 'From Communities of Practice to Mycorrhizae', in J. Hughes, N. Jewson and L. Unwin (eds), Communities of Practice: Critical Perspectives. London: Routledge.

Fortunati, A. (2006) The Education of Young Children as a Community Project: The Experience of San Miniato. San Miniato: Edizione Junior.

Frankenberg, R. (1969) Communities in Britain. London: Penguin.

Glăveanu, V. (2011) 'On culture and human development: Interview with Barbara Rogoff', Europe's Journal of Psychology 7(3): 408–18.

Gruenewald, D.A. and Smith, G.A. (2008) Place-Based Education in the Global Age: Local Diversity. New York and Abingdon: Lawrence Erlbaum.

Handley, K., Sturdy, A., Fincham, R. and Clark, T. (2006) 'Within and Beyond Communities of Practice: Making Sense of Learning through Participation, Identity and Practice', Journal of Management Studies 43(3): 641–53.

Hardman, C. (1973) 'Can there Be an Anthropology of Childhood?', *Journal of the Anthropological Society of Oxford* 4: 85–9.

Hastrup, K. and Fog Olwig, K. (eds) (1996) *Siting Culture: The Shifting Anthropological Object*. London: Routledge.

Hess, R. (1990) 'Book review: Preschool in Three Cultures', *American Journal of Education* 98(3): 305–7.

Hill, M. and Tisdall, K. (1997) *Children and Society*. London: Longman.

Hillery, G.A. (1955) 'Definitions of Community: Areas of Agreement', *Rural Sociology* 20: 111–23.

James, A. (2009) 'Book Review of Tudge: The Everyday Lives of Young Children', *American Journal of Sociology* 115(2): 623–4.

James, A. (2013) *Socialising Children*. Basingstoke: Palgrave Macmillan.

James, A. and Prout, A. (eds) (1997) *Constructing and Reconstructing Childhood: Contemporary Issues in the Sociological Study of Childhood*, 2nd edn. London: Falmer Press.

Kamarás, I. (2001) 'Civil Society and Religion in Post-Communist Hungary', *Journal of Interdisciplinary Studies* 13(1/2): 117–34.

Kuh, L.P. (2012) 'Promoting Communities of Practice and Parallel Process in Early Childhood Settings', *Journal of Early Childhood Teacher Education* 33(1): 19–37.

Lave, J. and Wenger, E. (1991) *Situated Learning*. Cambridge: Cambridge University Press.

LeVine, R. (2010) 'The Six Cultures Study: Prologue to a History of a Landmark Project', *Journal of Cross-Cultural Psychology* 41: 513–21.

LeVine, R. and LeVine, B.B. (1966) *Nyansongo: A Gusii Community in Kenya*. New York: Wiley.

Maynard, T., Waters, J. and Clement, J. (2013) 'Child-initiated Learning, the Outdoor Environment and the "Underachieving" Child', *Early Years: Journal of International Research and Development* 33(3): 212–25.

Montgomery, H. (2008) *An Introduction to Childhood: Anthropological Perspectives on Children's Lives*. Oxford: Wiley-Blackwell.

Moss, P. (2007) 'Bringing Politics into the Nursery: Early Childhood Education as Democratic Practice', *European Early Childhood Education Research Journal* 15(1): 5–20.

Moss, P. (2008) 'Foreword', in P. Broadhead, C. Meleady and M.A. Delgado, *Children, Families and Communities: Creating and Sustaining Integrated Services*. Maidenhead: Open University Press.

New, R.S. (1998) 'Theory and Praxis in Reggio Emilia: They Know What They are Doing and Why', in C. Edwards, L. Gandini and G. Forman (eds), *The Hundred Languages of Children: The Reggio Emilia Approach – Advanced Reflections*. Norwood, NJ: Ablex.

New, R.S. (1999) 'What Should Children Learn? Making Choices and Taking Chances', *Early Childhood Research and Practice* 1(2): n.p.

New, R.S. (2010) 'Cross-Cultural Research on Children's Development: Deep Roots and New Branches', *Journal of Cross-Cultural Psychology* 41: 522–33.

Nimmo, J. (1998) 'The Child in Community: Constraints from the Early Childhood Lore', in C. Edwards, L. Gandini and G. Forman (eds), *The Hundred Languages of Children: The Reggio Emilia Approach – Advanced Reflections*. Norwood, NJ: Ablex. pp. 295–312.

Oakley, A. (1994) 'Women and Children First and Last: Parallels and Differences between Children's and Women's Studies', in B. Mayell (ed.), *Children's Childhoods: Observed and Experienced*. London: Falmer Press. pp.13–32.

Penn, H. (2011) *Quality in Early Childhood Services: An International Perspective*. Maidenhead: Open University Press.

Qvortrup, J. (2009) 'Childhood as a Structural Form', in J. Qvortrup, W.A. Corsaro and M.-S. Honig (eds), *The Palgrave Handbook of Childhood Studies*. Basingstoke: Palgrave Macmillan. pp. 21–34.

Qvortrup, J., Corsaro, W.A. and Honig, M.-S. (2009) 'Why Social Studies of Childhood? An Introduction to the Handbook', in *The Palgrave Handbook of Childhood Studies*. Basingstoke: Palgrave Macmillan. pp. 1–19.

Roberts, J. (2006) 'Limits to Communities of Practice', *Journal of Management Studies* 43(3): 623–38.

Rodkin, P.C. and Hanish, L.D. (2007) *Social network analysis and children's peer relationships*. Issue 118 of *New Directions for Child and Adolescent Development*, pp. 1–8. University of Michigan.

Rogoff, B. (1990) *Apprenticeship in Thinking: Cognitive Development in Social Context*. Oxford: Oxford University Press.

Rogoff, B. (2003) *The Cultural Nature of Human Development*. New York: Oxford University Press (e-book).

Rosa Sensat (2005) *For a New Public Education System*. Barcelona: Rosa Sensat.

Smith, G. and Sobel, D. (2010) *Place- and Community-based Education in Schools.* New York and London: Routledge.

Steiner-Khamsi, G. (2009) 'Statement in Bjork, C. (ed.) Preschool in Three Cultures Revisited: Moderated Discussion', *Comparative Education Review* 53(2): 272–3.

Tadevosyan, A. (2008) 'The Parallel Worlds of NGOs, Multilateral Aid and Development Banks: The Case of Community Schools in Armenia', in I. Silova and G. Steiner-Khamsi (eds), *How NGOs React: Globalization and Education Reform in the Caucasus, Central Asia and Mongolia.* Bloomfield, CT: Kumarian Press. pp. 81–2.

Tobin, J. and Davidson, D. (1991) 'Multivocal Ethnographies of Schools: Empowering vs. Textualizing Children and Teachers', *International Journal of Qualitative Educational Research* 3: 271–83.

Tobin, J. and Hsueh, Y. (2007) 'The Poetics and Pleasures of Video Ethnography of Education', in R. Goldman, R. Pea, B. Barron and S.J. Derry (eds), *Video Research in the Learning Sciences.* Mahwah, NJ: Lawrence Erlbaum. pp. 77–92.

Tobin, J.J., Hsueh, Y. and Karasawa, M. (2009) *Preschool in Three Cultures Revisited: China, Japan and the United States.* London: University of Chicago Press.

Tobin, J.J., Wu, D.Y. and Davidson, D.H. (1989) *Preschool in Three Cultures: Japan, China and the United States.* Newhaven, CT and London: Yale University Press.

Tönnies, F. (1887) *Gemeinschaft und Gesellschaft.* Leipzig: Fues's Verlag.

Tudge, J. (2008) *The Everyday Lives of Young Children: Culture, Class and Child Rearing in Diverse Societies.* Cambridge: Cambridge University Press.

Vandenbroeck, M., Roests, G. and Snoeck, A. (2009) 'Immigrant Mothers Crossing Borders: Nomadic Identities and Multiple Belongings in Early Childhood Education', *European Early Childhood Education Research Journal* 17(2): 203–16.

Vygotsky, L. (1962/1986) *Thought and Language.* Cambridge, MA: MIT Press.

Vygotsky, L. (1978) *Mind in Society: The Development of Higher Psychological Processes.* Cambridge, MA: Harvard University Press.

Waller, T., Whitmarsh, J. and Clarke, K. (2011) *Making Sense of Theory and Practice in Early Childhood: The Power of Ideas.* Maidenhead: Open University Press.

Watras, J. (2014) 'Ethnographic Research and Globalization: A Discussion of Joseph Tobin's Model of Video-Cued Multivocal Ethnography', *Journal of Ethnographic and Qualitative Research* 8: 76–84.

Wenger, E. (1998) *Communities of Practice: Learning, Meaning and Identity.* Cambridge: Cambridge University Press.

Wenger, E. (2000) 'Communities of Practice and Social Learning Systems', *Organization* 7(2): 225–46.

Whiting, B.B. (ed.) (1963) *Six Cultures: Studies of Child Rearing.* New York: John Wiley.

Whiting, B.B. and Whiting, J. (1975) *Children of Six Cultures: A Psycho-Cultural Analysis.* Cambridge, MA: Harvard University Press.

Wirth, L. (1938) 'Urbanism as a Way of Life', *Australian Journal of Sociology* 44: 3–89.

Wirth, L. (1964) *On Cities and Social Life.* Chicago: University of Chicago Press.

Woodhead, M. (2009) 'Child Development and the Development of Childhood', in J. Qvortrup, W.A. Corsaro and M.-S. Honig (eds), *The Palgrave Handbook of Childhood Studies.* Basingstoke: Palgrave Macmillan. pp. 46–62.

PART II

Theorizing Early Childhood Research

5

Participation, Rights and 'Participatory' Methods

E. Kay M. Tisdall

INTRODUCTION

A wave of interest in children's participation has swept across countries around the world, from Brazil to South Africa to the UK. This wave has been greatly assisted by the assertion of children's rights through the United Nations Convention on the Rights of the Child (UNCRC), ratified by all States Parties except the United States of America. The UNCRC covers the more 'traditional' rights of provision and protection. More radically, the UNCRC contains a range of rights frequently referred to as 'participation' rights.

The UNCRC applies to all children under the age of 18 (unless a child attains majority earlier), including young children. The United Nations (UN) Committee on the Rights of the Child (2005) detailed the Convention's application to young children, in its General Comment No. 7, *Implementing Child Rights in Early Childhood.* The document underlines families' and professionals' responsibilities to create opportunities for young children to exercise their rights progressively, adapting to and promoting children's 'interests, levels of understanding and preferred ways of communicating' (2005: 7).

These legal obligations have come together with other influences, such as sociological and anthropological interest in children as 'social actors' (James et al., 1998; Prout, 2005; Tisdall and Punch, 2012), to create debate, policies, training and research on young children's participation. Frequently, this interest is set up in opposition to 'traditional' childhood research, theorizations and practice. Such traditional research is criticized for its deficit approaches in child development, unhelpful age- and stage-based assumptions, and falsely presenting a universal, 'normal' childhood (e.g., see James et al., 1998; Moss and Petrie, 2002). Despite this critique of child development, the policy, practices, research and literatures addressing children's participation are frequently divided by age. Research or policy consultations, for example, may casually note that children under a certain age were not included. This may well be with-out explanation or, if an explanation is given, there is some comment that young children were unable to interact with the methodol-ogy or too difficult to reach if not at school (e.g., Bell, 2007). Policy and practice can also be fixated by ages, with a great deal of chil-dren's legislation in Global North countries guided by age thresholds and presumptions. The general 'childhood' literature on partici-pation frequently does not address the particu-larities of involving young children (e.g., Hart, 1992; Lansdown, 2003). A rich literature has developed within the early years, in regards to participation, but with its own theoretical debates, research patterns and findings. Both literatures lose by too little cross-fertilization and this chapter seeks to address this.

The chapter begins by considering the cur-rent definitions of participation within the children's rights literature – and critically evaluates their theoretical underpinnings. It brings in alternatives, such as the preference for 'listening' in the early years literature, and critiques, such as the long-standing challenges noted in the development studies literature. The chapter continues by considering 'par-ticipatory' methods in research, outlining what could constitute such methods and considering them critically. The chapter ends by consider-ing implications for policy and practice, and a summative conclusion.

WHAT IS MEANT BY PARTICIPATION?

Definitions of participation are many and varied. Dictionary definitions of participation are very broad: for example, 'the action of taking part in something' (Oxford Dictionary, 2014). A seminal author on children's par-ticipation, Hart defines participation as 'the process of sharing decisions which affect one's life and the life of the community in which one lives' (1992: 5). This definition emphasizes children's everyday lives and that children are part of their communities. But it concentrates on processes, and not

outcomes, and does not address impact. Writing in the context of the UNCRC, Lansdown incorporates outcomes and impact into her definition: 'Participation can be defined as children taking part in and influ-encing processes, decisions and activities that affect them, in order to achieve greater respect for their rights' (2003: 273).

For those writing on children's participa-tion in recent decades, participation is closely associated with rights. The UNCRC is a touchstone, recognized as a key catalyst for policy, practice and research. The UNCRC contains a range of articles grouped together as participation rights, which include free-dom of expression (Article 13), freedom of thought, conscience and religion (Article 14), freedom of association and peaceful assem-bly (Article 15) and access to information (Article 17). Considered a key overarching principle of the UNCRC, Article 12 states:

1 States Parties shall assure to the child who is capable of forming his or her own views the right to express those views freely in all matters affecting the child, the views of the child being given due weight in accordance with the age and maturity of the child.
2 For this purpose, the child shall in particular be provided the opportunity to be heard in any judi-cial and administrative proceedings affecting the child, either directly, or through a representative or an appropriate body, in a manner consistent with the procedural rules of national law.

Article 12 does not use the term participa-tion. The UN Committee on the Rights of the Child recognizes this, in its General Comment No.12, and puts forward a particular descrip-tion of participation:

> This term has evolved and is now widely used to describe ongoing processes, which include infor-mation-sharing and dialogue between children and adults based on mutual respect, and in which children can learn how their views and those of adults are taken into account and shape the out-come of such processes. (2009: 3)

The General Comment distinguishes between the right of an individual child to be heard and the right to be heard as applied to a group of children (2009: 5). Both types of right are required by Article 12. The General Comment emphasizes particular aspects of Article 12's wording and accompanying implications. Some of these are particularly important for including young children:

- Children should be supported to participate. They may need information to clarify their views and assistance to express them.
- Children's participation should not be undermined by unhelpful and inaccurate ideas of their capacity. A child should be presumed to have the capacity to form a view and it is not up to the child to prove this capacity.
- The right to express a view has no age threshold and children need not have comprehensive knowledge to be considered capable.
- Children should receive feedback on how their views have been taken into consideration.

The UN Committee on the Rights of the Child (2005) specifically emphasizes the right of young children to participate, in General Comment No. 7, *Implementing Child Rights in Early Childhood*. This General Comment stresses that children's participation rights should be implemented 'from the earliest stage in ways appropriate to the children's capacities, best interests, and rights to protection from harmful experiences' (2005: 7). The rights should be 'anchored' in children's daily lives, in a range of contexts from formal to informal (2005: 7). Both General Comments give considerable attention to the processes and systems required to support children's participation rights.

The participation rights have been held up as the most radical and controversial contribution of the UNCRC (Reid, 1994; Smith, 2013), compared to the more readily-accepted rights for protection and provision (Freeman, 1983). Article 12 and associated rights have been challenging and are often cited within policy, practice and the literature for recognizing children as citizens, encouraging more equitable power relationships between children and adults, and allowing children to influence decisions that affect them (e.g., see Jans, 2004; Cairns, 2006; Cockburn, 2012). However,

Article 12 is not as radical as such writings suggest. Children's political right to vote is not recognized in Article 12, even though this is a central citizenship right in a liberal democracy (Marshall, 1950). Article 12 may facilitate children to be involved in a wide range of decisions ('all matters that affect them') but it does not discuss self-determination – although this is a common mistake in the literature (Reynaert el al., 2012). A decision-maker must give 'due weight' to the child's views but this is qualified by a judgement about the 'age and maturity' of the child. Ultimately, the decision can be against or incongruent with the child's views. Article 3 of the UNCRC requires that a child's best interests be a primary consideration in all actions concerning children; the potential tensions between Articles 3 and 12 are well-rehearsed in the literature (e.g., see Marshall, 1997). A child's views can easily be silenced or sidelined, with adults privileging what they see as a child's 'best interests'. Thus, Article 12 is a very qualified political right.

Early on, typologies were extremely influential in promoting children's participation. The most widely known of is Hart's (1992) ladder of participation, which has eight rungs. The bottom three (manipulation, tokenism and decoration) are categorized as non-participation. The remaining top five represent varying levels of children's influence, from being 'assigned and informed' up to 'child-initiated, shared decisions with adults' (1992: 8). Reddy and Ratner (2002) criticize the linear nature of this ladder, as it gives the impression that the top rung of child-initiated and shared decisions is the ideal one. Hart himself cautions that the ladder should not be used as a 'simple measuring stick of quality' (1992: 11). Other models have been created in response, from Treseder's non-hierarchical circle (1997) to Shier's pathways to participation model, based on five levels of obligation (2001). These typologies have been highly successful in catalyzing change. When used in training and similar settings, they facilitate those involved to question where children's participation is presently and to show opportunities for different positions on the ladder. But the typologies are weak at recognizing the social, economic and cultural contexts of participation activities and changes over time and locations. They tend to set up a dichotomy between children and adults and thus ignore the diversity of individuals and relationships (see Tisdall et al., 2014 for further discussion).

Participation, in the children's rights literature, is frequently given normative value: those who promote it see participation as a human rights issue, something that should be done. Even with such values, fundamental questions need to be asked about 'participation': who is participating, in what and for whose benefit (Cornwall, 2008). These questions apply to this chapter, as critical questions when participation is advocated or practised.

CRITIQUES OF PARTICIPATION

In the early years literature, the use of 'participation' is more contested, with preferences for alternatives such as listening (e.g., see Clark and Moss, 2001; Bath, 2013) or involving children (e.g., see Miller, 2009). Moss and colleagues (2005) give a provocative reason for their preference for listening over participation. They first quote Rinaldi, who emphasizes listening as an approach rather than particular tasks, as part of the Reggio Emilia pedagogy:

> Listening is not only a technique and a didactic methodology, but a way of thinking and seeing ourselves in relation with others and the world. Listening is an element that connects and that is part of human biology and is in the concept of life itself … [It] is a right or better it is part of the essence of being human. (cited in Moss et al., 2005: 6)

Participation, write Moss and colleagues, is associated with 'influencing change and decision making' (2005: 8). A rights-based approach to participation can unduly rely on individual autonomy and self-realization and undermine relationships and community belonging (Moss et al., 2005: 11).

Such arguments touch upon a wider debate about the weaknesses of rights theory, replete in the philosophical literature. In the Global North, philosophy about rights (re)emerged in the Enlightenment period, as part of carving out the relationship between the individual citizen and the state (e.g., Locke, 1982; see Jones, 1994 for an accessible overview of rights theory). The concerns were about the legitimacy of state intervention that curtails individuals' autonomy and freedoms. The resulting theorizations led to rights being political 'trumps' (Dworkin, 1997: xi), God-given, inalienable and universal. Arneil summarizes the problems of such liberal theory, for children:

> Most importantly, while the concept of 'rights' has been extraordinarily elastic, it cannot escape its origins … a rights-based argument is ultimately concerned with a change in status for the individual, a state commitment to the principles of both non-interference and enforcement … and a society constituted by associational relationships of mutual self-interest. (2002: 86)

Much attention has been given to critiquing such liberal theory, from communitarian and related philosophers who question the autonomous individual and instead recognize people as social beings (e.g., Sandel, 1982), to those who argue that rights are but social constructions and neither God-Given nor universal basics (e.g., MacIntyre, 1990), to those arguing for revised theorizations based on interdependency or vulnerability (e.g., Kymlicka, 1990; Arneil, 2002; Fineman, 2010/11). Yet, the rights framework retains its 'moral coinage' (Freeman, 1997: 188) in a range of settings, promoted by international organizations like the UN and supported in numerous states by 'the rule of law' and legal structures within the state. Pascal and Bertram (2009), for example, write of how the early years field needs to engage with power: a rights framework provides one way to do so.

The universality of rights has been a particularly contentious issue in relation to the UNCRC. The Convention itself is criticized for failing to incorporate a range of issues particularly pertinent to the Global South, such as child marriage (Olsen, 1992). It is accused of promoting a Global North view of childhood, with damaging consequences for children in the Global South who are excluded. For example, Ennew (1995) comments on the Convention's reinforcement of the family, which ignores street children's own friendships and social networks on the street. Valentin and Meinert (2009) are sharply critical of the individualized and egalitarian notions of rights, which clash sharply with generational hierarchies and social structures that help cope with different economic, environmental, societal and regional pressures in parts of the Global South. They accuse children's rights of infantilizing the Global South and being a new form of colonization:

> Embedded in a discourse of children's participation and empowerment, organizations advocating children's rights nonetheless contribute to a civilizing project which is in essence close to that of the old Christian missions, namely correcting social and bodily behaviour of both children and guardians in order to produce proper civic persons. (2009: 27)

While there are counter-arguments (e.g., see Burman, 1996; Alderson, 2012), these writers provide salient criticisms about the universality of children's rights, and their application in practice and in principle to the diversity of children cross-culturally.

Dahlberg and Moss (2005) introduce a further critique: that rights-based approaches are technical and decontextualized, rather than ethical and political. Listening can be part of participation – but it also goes beyond, in terms of a way or 'ethic of relating to others' that is more than 'just about' decision-making (Moss et al., 2005: 8–9). Again, an alignment can be made between these debates and alternatives, and other literature on participation. While the literature on children's participation continues to promote it normatively while agonizing over the problems of tokenism and lack of impact (see Barnardo's Scotland et al., 2011–2012; Tisdall, 2012a), development studies has a long-standing interest in participation – and a long-standing critique (see Teamey and Hinton, 2014 for a more extensive overview). 'Participation' became a popular term during the social movements of the 1960s, with Freire (1970, 1973, 1976) being a leading proponent with his promotion of participative practices of transformation. 'Participation' and particularly participatory approaches became part of the development industry, a response to past practices in international development where interventions failed to pay sufficient attention to community contexts and local knowledge. Chambers (1983) and colleagues are well-known for developing 'bottom-up' participation approaches, particularly with those who risked being excluded from more formal consultations and research. Methods were developed that sought to be cost- and time-effective, using less structured data collection procedures such as timelines and group mapping rather than highly structured surveys (e.g., Chambers, 1981). The visual data enabled information and findings to be communicated easily to decision-makers.

While empowerment and transformation have long-standing associations with participation, the development literature is replete with failures to empower and transform in practice. Participation can be co-opted to enable those with power to maintain the status quo, a 'safety valve' to channel dissent (Freire, 1970; Illich, 1970). Poor quality data collection, using participatory research methods, can be extractive rather than transformative (see Cooke and Kothari, 2001; Gaventa, 2004). Leal (2010) argues that participation *techniques* have been emphasized rather than the *meaning* of participation, so that power and political problems are translated into technical problems that the existing order can easily accommodate. Too many activities concentrate on engaging people and too few activities ensure accountability to participants and impact on decisions (Hart, 2008). Such critiques from the development field are instructive for those promoting and seeking to practise participation in the early childhood field.

PARTICIPATORY RESEARCH?

If children's participation rights are promoted, then the need to engage children directly in research logically follows. In the past, research might have involved only parents, on children's issues, using them as a proxy for children's experiences and views. This trend has been strongly challenged by the childhood studies literature (see Tisdall and Punch, 2012), so that children should be seen as research participants within their own right. Rather than questioning whether children are competent and can communicate, the children's rights perspective challenges researchers to be competent enough to be able to communicate effectively and ethically with children (see Tisdall et al., 2009).

To fulfil these aspirations of communicating with children, multiple methods are frequently advocated (e.g., Pascal and Bertram, 2009; Harcourt et al., 2011; Green, 2012; Bath, 2013). The Mosaic Approach (Clark and Moss, 2001; Clark, 2005) is often specifically mentioned (e.g., see Harcourt et al., 2011; Dockett et al., 2012; Baird, 2013). The Mosaic Approach was originally developed and used in England, through a project with 3- and 4-year-olds in an early childhood institution. Clark describes it as 'a strength-based framework for viewing young children as competent, active, meaning makers and explorers of their environment' (2005: 29). She summarizes six elements of the approach, as seen in Table 5.1:

The approach draws upon the participation research methods, popular in development work, discussed above. The methods do not require literacy or numeracy and are not unduly hampered by the researcher or research participants having different languages. The approach also draws on Reggio Emilia ideas of the competent child and the pedagogy of listening and of relationships. Documentation is a key practice, within these ideas, to ensure listening and being listened to. Documentation provides 'traces/documents that testify to and make visible the ways of learning of the individuals and the group' and allows the group and the child 'to

Table 5.1   The six elements of the Mosaic Approach

1. Multi-method:	recognises the different 'voices' or languages of children
2. Participatory:	treats children as experts and agents in their own lives
3. Reflexive:	includes children, practitioners and parents in reflecting on meanings, and addresses the question of interpretation
4. Adaptable:	can be applied in a variety of early childhood institutions
5. Focused on children's lived experiences:	can be used for a variety of purposes including looking at lives lived rather than knowledge gained or care received
6. Embedded into practice:	a framework for listening that has the potential to be used both as an evaluative tool and to become embedded into early years practice.

Source: Clark (2005: 30–1)

observe themselves from an external point of view' (Rinaldi, 2005: 23).

Clark (2005) summarizes the seven methods used in the approach:

1   Qualitative observation
2   A short structured interview with children, either one to one or in a group
3   Children taking photographs of 'important things' and making books
4   Children directing and recording tours of the site
5   Children making two-dimensional maps of the site, using their photographs and drawings
6   Informal interviews with parents and practitioners
7   A slideshow of familiar and different places, with children sitting on a 'magic carpet' to do so. (paraphrased from Clark, 2005: 33, Table 3.1)

By 2005, the Mosaic Approach had three stages: (1) gathering children's and adults' perspectives; (2) discussing the material; and (3) deciding on areas of continuity and change. Analysis is thus undertaken in (2) and (3), and done together with researchers, children, parents and practitioners.

The Mosaic Approach was not especially novel in its methods but had considerable impact by bringing them together as an approach and demonstrating their practicability to meet research agendas. A host of other methods are described in the literature. For example, children are frequently asked to draw on a particular topic or question, and discuss the drawings. Persona dolls have been modified from their original intention to promote ethnic diversity, for use in research as ongoing personalities (with individual stories, ages, gender and personalities; for example, see Konstantoni, 2011 and Te One, 2011). Similarly, puppets have been used (see Dobbs et al., 2006). 'All about me' books (see Fajerman et al., 2004) emphasize the child's or children's selection of what to include, in a form of documentation. Within the above methods or separately, arts-based methods have proven popular with children and practitioners. An example would be the 'reality boxes' used by Winter (2010), which she piloted with looked-after children aged 4–7. Children were invited to construct an image of themselves reflecting how they come across externally – on the outside of the box. On the inside, children were encouraged to construct their 'private person'. This list of methods is not exhaustive: numerous toolkits have been put together describing methods for work with younger children (e.g., Lancaster and Broadbent, 2003; Miller, 2009; Dynamix, 2010; Hertfordshire Council, 2010).

At least three claims are made for such participatory methods, within the childhood studies literature: epistemological; ethical; and inclusive. First, 'participatory' methods are claimed to create better knowledge: they will, 'access and valorize previously neglected knowledge and provide more nuanced understandings of complex, social phenomena' (Kesby, 2000: 423). With better knowledge, the research will have better data, better decision-making and better results. Second, 'participatory' methods are seen as more ethical and respectful of children's rights than are more traditional social science research methods. Thomas and O'Kane, for example, link better knowledge with ethics:

Effective methodology and ethics go hand in hand ... the reliability and validity, and the ethical acceptability, of research with children can be augmented by using an approach which gives children

control over the research process and methods which are in tune with children's ways of seeing and relating to their world. (1998: 336–7)

Third, 'participatory' methods are more inclusive. This is particularly evident in the discussions of the Mosaic Approach, in working with young children. Following the pedagogy of Reggio Emilia, they write of the '100 languages of children': children communicate in all kinds of different ways and using a range of such 'participatory' methods can tap into these ways of communication. If one method does not work for a child, another method might.

These claims are largely reliant on anecdotal – if thought-provoking – reflections from (adult) researchers in the literature. Given the interest in participation, ironically there is little systematic evidence from children and young people themselves nor much comparative analysis of different methods. This particularly applies to research with young children.

Some exceptions can be found. For example, Williams (2010) compares different methods when undertaking consultation with 3- and 4-year-olds, about their free entitlement to early years education in England. The children were involved through their current early years settings and the practitioners there; the practitioners were invited to comment on the methods. Most practitioners rated the virtual tour with children, using a camera, as working the best and being popular with the children. Observations of children were rated quite well but were difficult to carry out in practice. Puppets received mixed views, with some children seeming to enjoy the role play and finding it easier to talk 'through' the puppet, while others were uncomfortable, unnerved or not interested in the puppet.

Drawing and photography have received the most critical attention. For both, the recommendation is to use these methods in tandem with discussion. Einarsdóttir and colleagues (2009) base an academic article around this, in relation to drawing. They react against the 'expert' psychological analysis of children's drawings, as describing developmental sequences or emotional adjustment. In contrast, they argue that drawings' analysis should focus on meaning-making rather than representation. This recognizes the importance of context and the need to consider children's narratives as they make and later discuss the drawing. The research team uses drawings in one-to-one interactions between researchers and children, in pre-school and school, as well as in group activities. Einarsdóttir and colleagues (2009) report the willingness of children to complete their drawings and the significant time they dedicate to doing so. They also note some challenges. The teacher and classroom context influence both the drawings and the surrounding conversations: children can see whatever is produced in the classroom as work, which can be graded as 'good' or 'poor'. Children at quite a young age can become judgemental about what counts as a 'good' drawing. The researchers find some children do not want to draw, with preschool children more likely to leave the paper blank or spend little time on their drawing than school children. Some children are uncomfortable with both drawing and talking, preferring to do only one at once. The research team concludes that 'we are uncomfortable about promoting drawing as a comfortable and positive experience for all children' (2009: 228).

The enthusiasm and competency of children using digital technology, in taking camera photographs, is frequently mentioned (e.g., Stephen et al., 2008; Bitou and Waller, 2011). Photographs may recognize elements that would otherwise remain in the background, 'making visible the invisible' (Schratz and Walker, 1995, paraphrased in Dockett and Perry, 2005a: 7). The 'active role' of children in this method is seen as positive (Dockett and Perry, 2005b). Further, with digital cameras, instant review of the photographs is possible, allowing for 'accidental shots' to be deleted (Dockett and Perry, 2005a, although see Böök and Mykkänen, 2014). Some practical concerns are noted, such as: early years settings do not always have the technology and resources to look at and print out digital photographs; adequate

supervision of children in certain areas and children wanting to go into 'out of bounds' areas; the subsequent use of photographs that contain people who have not given their consent to be photographed. As Dockett and Perry (2005a) write, photographs taken by children are not necessarily the 'most important' for children but rather the 'most important that could be photographed'. Further, children may not distinguish between, or adhere to, the researcher's purpose of using photographs: for example, children may take photographs to see how the camera works, for artistic expression or as 'holiday snaps', none of which necessarily answer the researcher's initial question (Cook and Hess, 2007). Again, the literature emphasizes the importance of discussing the photographs, to understand the context and the meanings attributed to them.

Dockett and Perry (2005a) provide one of the few comparative reflections between data produced by different methods. When children took photographs and commented upon them, friends were not an overwhelming focus. Conversational data with these same children did suggest friends were a very important part of school. They explain these differences largely due to constraints in photographing – for example, children being stopped from going 'out of bounds' or permission not being given to include particular people.

If there is little robust and comparative evidence about whether participatory methods fulfil the claims made for them, there are further suggestions in the literature that encourage reflection. Methods used are often familiar to the children, from other contexts. This may make the activities comfortable for the children but the children may interact with the activities as they are used to – rather than as the research might intend. This has been remarked upon in school settings, where a 'smiley face' may be selected on a questionnaire because of its association with teacher approval rather than a child's preference, or a drawing could be considered 'good' judged by external standards (Dockett and Perry, 2010). Clark and colleagues (2003) are concerned about children's privacy. The participatory methods that often seek to build trust and relationships, to go where children are and are comfortable, can invade their privacy and ask them to reveal aspects of their lives that they had protected from others (see also Sumsion et al., 2011). Green (2012) writes of a young boy revealing his secret hiding place in a chest, while taking her on a tour of his home; observed by his father, who was alarmed at the potential danger, the boy was prohibited from using the chest again.

Research *on* children's participation in various contexts, and particularly in relation to early childhood education and care (ECEC) settings, raises issues as well. For example, Sweden was held up for its participatory curriculum, in two OECD documents (2001 and 2006) advocating for ECEC investments. Yet Lindgren (2012) looks critically at the expression of participation in practice, and particularly at the use of documentation. She considers how documentation can be something done to children, with teachers very much in control and only extending the 'adult gaze' on, and surveillance of, children. It demonstrates the potential for increasing self-regulation of children, rather than emancipation (Prout, 2000). Frequently, research (see Theobald et al., 2011; Dockett et al., 2012) finds that adults focus on their perceptions of children's competency, as the necessary criterion of their involvement. If children are seen as incompetent, or less competent, then their involvement and contributions are less valued or not included. This fails to consider why competency is valued as the most relevant (and sometimes sole) criterion and how sound the valuation of competency is (on what basis is it being made?). Alternatives to competency are possible, such as valuing children's lived experiences, as stakeholders in their own lives and communities (Investing in Children, 2008). As Lundy and McEvoy (2012) and indeed the UNCRC recommend, a rights-based approach suggests children are supported with information and more, in order to recognize their participation rights.

Much research is now claiming to involve children as participants, in disciplines ranging from social anthropology, to human geography, to socio-legal studies. For those committed to children's participation, there has been a question about other roles in the research process: from research inception to research dissemination (see Kirby, 1999; Brownlie et al., 2006; Dockett et al., 2012). There has been an enthusiasm for involving children in research, as researchers. Numerous examples now exist of great success in this approach, where children were able to follow their own research agendas, develop their own skills and experiences, and produce research with impact (e.g., Child-to-Child Trust; Investing in Children[1]). Claims are made that involving children in this way will ensure necessary questions are asked, which might not have been asked by adult research teams, and that children will be better able to connect with their peers (and thus gather better information). Such claims may well be met in much of peer research and arguably more space and funding should be given to supporting children to follow their own research agendas – just as this has been developed in the disability rights movement (Tisdall, 2012b) and on feminist agendas. Involving children as researchers, however, does not always meet such claims. Structures and other power relationships can intervene, hence: it is often adult organizations and researchers who gain and control the finances rather than children; it is usually adult facilitators who are employed, while employment laws may preclude children from being equally recognized for their time; conventions of anonymity and confidentiality may lead to adults gaining career advancement and their names on publications, rather than the child researchers. Children are not necessarily involved in all stages of the research, from inception to analysis to dissemination, despite the rhetoric. And the idea that children may better relate to other children can treat children as a homogeneous group, and not recognize the diversity likely within any group whether by background characteristic or personality. Baker and Hinton (1999), for example, found that the 'skilling up' of young people in their research, in Nepal, differentiated their young researchers, making other young people less likely to share their views. This is not to be unduly negative about the potential for child-led research but rather to consider how it can move forward with due consideration and learning.

The development studies' critique of participation is testing. Cooke and Kothari write of the 'tyranny of participation'; their critiques can be summarized into three:

- The tyranny of decision-making and control: Do participative facilitators override existing legitimate decision-making processes?
- The tyranny of the group: Do group dynamics lead to participative decisions that reinforce the interests of the already powerful?
- The tyranny of method: Have participative methods driven out others which have advantages that participation cannot provide? (based on Cooke and Kothari, 2001: 8–9)

These critiques are provocative to apply to participatory research with children. Participation can be used to sideline and control concerns from the 'bottom up', rather than fulfil its claims as an ethical and emancipatory process. While the legitimacy of many decision-making processes may be questioned from a children's rights perspective, participation may divert attention from identifying and challenging this. There is a distinct tendency towards qualitative research in the literature on participatory methods with young children. Yet research with older children (Hill, 2006) found children valuing 'traditional' self-report questionnaires, for allowing more children to participate and more private or quiet individuals to share their views. Participatory methods may include some children but exclude others. Thus, referring back to the claims of participatory methods, they *may* provide better knowledge, be more ethical and more inclusive and they may be more likely to do so than other methods – but such potential is not guaranteed by merely utilizing such methods.

IMPLICATIONS FOR POLICY AND PRACTICE

The avowal of children's rights, in general, in their participation rights and their involvement in research, in particular, tends to be normative and value-based. Recommendations for research methods often start with putting forward certain principles, to help ensure that an ethos of participation is maintained (see MacNaughton et al., 2004; Think Tank, 2008). There is a passion in the early childhood participation literature, where authors and other researchers are deeply committed to recognizing, respecting and promoting children's participation rights. This passion connects with the ethical and political basis recommended by Dahlberg and Moss above (2005), avoiding a technical approach. But the recent critical considerations of documentation show that virtually any approach – whether it is called listening or participation or involving children – can fall into a 'tick-box exercise', a technical and technocratic approach, that fails to fulfil the emancipatory hopes of the proponents. In fact, it can be even more oppressive in its seeming promise of different power relationships, when in fact reifying or further deepening them.

The normative valuing of participation can also gloss over its difficulties. These can be difficulties in practice, where barriers created by gate-keepers or other decision-makers mean children's involvement never happens, is problematic or lacks impact. It can ignore the fact that not all participation is inevitably positive – it can be challenging, discriminatory and destructive. Freire, even within his emancipatory pedagogy, recognized the potential painfulness of transformation.

As the UNCRC and children's rights become more established, it is increasingly possible to consider them critically while still recognizing and promoting their possible contribution. The UNCRC is a political document, representing a minimum consensus emerging from the UN politics of the 1980s. It is part of a human rights regime, which has been accused of supporting and promoting neo-liberalism and new forms of colonialism – and thus oppression of the Global South (see Cornwall and Eade, 2010; Leal, 2010). The UNCRC was created with little (but some) participation of children (Van Bueren, 2011) and is not highly radical in its political emancipation of children. But as an internationally agreed standard of minimum rights for children, it has been a powerful 'trump card' in local, national and international settings. If rights are used as a basis for promoting participation, then the strengths and weaknesses of the rights framework can be recognized.

With this critical and reflective eye, there is now a wealth of inspiring examples: of sensitive research undertaken with young children, rather than on them; of the small but growing initiatives of child-led research; of practice that has sought to realize children's participation rights individually and collectively. Most of this research and practice, however, is instigated and led by committed individuals, rather than being systemic (e.g., see Tisdall, 2014). Now that the innovation of such research and practice is past in many contexts, there are questions about whether it is suitably mainstreamed to be realized on a regular basis for children.

SUMMARY

The UNCRC has come together with academic ideas about children as social actors and valuable research participants, to recognize and promote children's participation. The UNCRC articulates a range of participation rights for children, from the right to have their views given due weight in all matters that affect them, to the right to information and freedom of expression. Such rights challenge traditional ideas of childhood, which focus on dependency, vulnerability and incompetency, to place far more value on children's potential and actual contributions. In terms of research, the challenge becomes not *whether* children should be involved in

research but *how* they can effectively and ethically be involved.

The UNCRC applies to all children under the age of 18 (unless a child attains majority earlier). Thus, young children have all the rights of the UNCRC, and the UN Committee on the Rights of the Child has sought to emphasize this. The literature on children's rights generally, and participation in particular, have not always recognized and developed younger children's inclusion, but either implicitly or explicitly have concentrated on older children and young people. A largely separate literature has developed around younger children, often stemming from the increased involvement of young children in early years institutions, promoting young children's participation rights and research. This chapter has sought to bring key ideas of rights and methods together, from these literatures. Further, it has brought in the well-developed critique of participation in development studies, which has often been highly challenging of participatory activities and methods.

Participatory methods with children have been promoted by at least three claims: (1) compared to 'traditional' research methods, they will create better knowledge; (2) consequently, they will be more ethical than traditional methods; and (3) they are more inclusive in their flexibility and openness to varied methods of communication. This chapter suggests that these claims may well be met but not necessarily so. To meet the claims, duty-bearers – whether they be practitioners, policy-makers, parents, researchers or other children – need to be duly reflective and critical. Participation can be coercive, controlling and exclusive as well as inclusive. To fulfil their rights-based potential, participation rights need to be seen contextually and systematically, alongside celebrating fun and stimulating processes, and questioned about whether they are meeting their supposed claims.

As discussed in the chapter, rights theorizations can be criticized for a philosophical heritage privileging autonomy and individuals over relationships, communities and interdependencies. However, rights are strong claims for minorities who are oppressed. They provide minimum thresholds. They assist in challenging constructions of childhood that ignore children's potential and actual contributions to their own development, their families and their communities; they give a respect for children, that other theoretical frameworks do not (see Freeman, 2007). Recognizing that young children have rights can provide a pertinent antidote to seeing them solely as social investments and human capital or as property of their parents. Participation rights have influenced new ways of working and research with children, which still have much further to go.

FURTHER READING

Alderson, P. (2008) *Young Children's Rights*. London: Jessica Kingsley Publishers.

Harcourt, D., Perry, B. and Waller, T. (eds) (2011) *Researching Young Children's Perspectives*. Abingdon: Routledge.

Tisdall, E.K.M., Gadda, A.M. and Butler, U.M. (eds) (2014) *Children and Young People's Participation and Its Transformative Potential: Learning from across Countries*. Basingstoke: Palgrave.

QUESTIONS FOR REFLECTION

1   What are the benefits, challenges and problems with a rights-based approach for research with children? How do these apply in different contexts and cultures?
2   What concepts are used in your contexts to describe 'participation'? What are the advantages and disadvantages of these concepts, for policy, practice and research?
3   What are the advantages and disadvantages of the 'participatory' methods used with children? How could systematic information be gathered to evaluate how well they meet their claims to create better knowledge, to be more ethical and more inclusive?

NOTE

1   See Child-to-Child Trust at www.child-to-child. org/; and Investing in Children at www.iic-uk.org/.

ACKNOWLEDGEMENTS

The ideas in this chapter were developed through a range of collaborative projects, funded by the Big Lottery Fund, the British Academy, the Economic and Social Research Council (R451265206, RES-189-25-0174, RES-451-26-0685), the European Research Council, the Leverhulme Trust, the Royal Society of Edinburgh and Scotland's Commissioner for Children and Young People.

REFERENCES

Alderson, P. (2012) 'Young Children's Human Rights: A Sociological Analysis', *International Journal of Children's Rights*, 20: 177–98.

Arneil, B. (2002) 'Becoming versus Being: A Critical Analysis of the Child in Liberal Theory', in D. Archard and C.M. Macleod (eds), *The Moral and Political Status of Children*. Oxford: Oxford University Press. pp. 70–96.

Baird, K. (2013) 'Exploring a Methodology with Young Children: Reflections on Using the Mosaic and Ecocultural Approaches', *Australian Journal of Early Childhood*, 38(1): 35–40.

Baker, R. and Hinton, R. (1999) 'Do Focus Groups Facilitate Meaningful Participation in Social Research?', in J. Kitzinger and R. Barbour (eds), *Developing Focus Group Research*. London: SAGE. pp. 79–96.

Barnardo's Scotland, Children in Scotland, and the Centre for Research on Families and Relationships (2011–2012) *Children and Young People's Participation in Policy-Making* (http://www.crfr.ac.uk/assets/CRFR-CIS Participation-briefing.pdf).

Bath, C. (2013) 'Conceptualising Listening to Young Children as an Ethic of Care in Early Childhood Education and Care', *Children & Society*, 27(5): 361–71.

Bell, A. (2007) 'Designing and Testing Questionnaires for Children', *Journal of Research in Nursing*, 12(5): 461–9.

Bitou, A. and Waller, T. (2011) 'Researching the Rights of Children under Three Years Old to Participate in the Curriculum in Early Years Education and Care', in D. Harcourt, B. Perry and T. Waller (eds), *Researching Young Children's Perspectives*. London: Routledge. pp. 52–67.

Böök, M.L. and Mykkänen, J. (2014) 'Photo-narrative Processes with Children and Young People', *International Journal of Child, Youth and Family Studies,* 5(4.1): 611–28.

Brownlie, J., Anderson, S. and Ormston, R. (2006) *Children as Researchers*. Edinburgh: Scottish Executive. (www.scotland.gov.uk/Resource/Doc/925/0080040.pdf)

Burman, E. (1996) 'Local, Global or Globalized? Child Development and International Children's Rights Legislation', *Childhood*, 3(1): 45–66.

Cairns, L. (2006) 'Participation with a Purpose', in E.K.M. Tisdall, J.M. Davis, M. Hill and A. Prout (eds), *Children, Young People and Social Inclusion*. Bristol: Policy Press. pp. 217–34.

Chambers, R. (1981) 'Rapid Rural Appraisal: Rationale and Repertoire', *Public Administration and Development*, 1(2): 95–106.

Chambers, R. (1983) *Rural Development: Putting the Last First*. Harlow: Longman.

Clark, A. (2005) 'Ways of Seeing: Using the Mosaic Approach to Listen to Young Children's Perspectives', in A. Clark, A.T. Kjørholt and P. Moss (eds), *Beyond Listening: Children's Perspectives on Early Childhood Services*. Bristol: Policy Press. pp. 29–50.

Clark, A. and Moss, P. (2001) *Listening to Young Children: The Mosaic Approach*. London: National Children's Bureau and Joseph Rowntree Foundation.

Clark, A., McQuail, S. and Moss, P. (2003) Exploring the Field of Listening to and Consulting with Young Children. Research Report no. 445. London: DfES. (www.ness.bbk.ac.uk/support/GuidanceReports/documents/172.pdf)

Cockburn, T. (2012) *Rethinking Children's Citizenship*. Basingstoke: Palgrave.

Cook, T. and Hess, E. (2007) 'What Cameras See and From Whose Perspective: Fun Methodologies for Engaging Children in Enlightening Adults', *Childhood*, 14(1): 29–45.

Cooke, B. and Kothari, U. (2001) *Participation: The New Tyranny?* London: Zed Books.

Cornwall, A. (2008) 'Unpacking Participation: Models, Meanings and Practices', *Community Development Journal*, 43(3): 269–83.

Cornwall, A. and Eade, D. (eds) (2010) *Deconstructing Development Discourse: Buzzwords and Fuzzwords*. London: Oxfam.

Dahlberg, G. and Moss, P. (2005) *Ethics and Politics in Early Childhood Education*. London: Routledge.

Dobbs, T., Smith, A.B. and Taylor, N. (2006) '"No, We Don't Get a Say, Children Suffer the Consequences": Children Talk about Family Discipline', *International Journal of Children's Rights*, 14(2):137–56.

Dockett, S. and Perry, B. (2005a) '"You Need to Know How to Play Safe": Children's Experiences of Starting School', *Contemporary Issues in Early Childhood*, 6(1): 4–18.

Dockett, S. and Perry, B. (2005b) 'Researching with Children: Insights from the Starting School Research Project', *Early Child Development and Care*, 175(6): 507–21.

Dockett, S. and Perry, B. (2010) 'Researching with Young Children: Seeking Assent', *Child Indicators Research*, 4(3): 231–47.

Dockett, S., Kearney, E. and Perry, B. (2012) 'Recognising Young Children's Understandings and Experiences of Community', *International Journal of Early Childhood*, 44: 287–305.

Dworkin, R. (1977) *Taking Rights Seriously*. Boston, MA: Harvard University Press.

Dynamix (2010) 'Spice it Up': The Companion Toolkit for Under 11s (http://wales.gov.uk/docs/dcells/publications/100705spiceen.pdf).

Einarsdóttir, J., Dockett, S. and Perry, B. (2009) 'Making Meaning: Children's Perspectives Expressed through Drawings', *Early Child Development and Care*, 179(2): 217–32.

Ennew, J. (1995) 'Outside Childhood: Street Children's Rights', in B. Franklin (ed.), *The Handbook of Children's Rights*. London: Routledge. pp. 201–14.

Fajerman, L., Treseder, P. and Connor, J. (2004) *Children are Service Users Too: A Guide to Consulting Children and Young People*. London: Save the Children.

Fineman, M.A. (2010/11) 'The Vulnerable Subject and the Responsive State', *Emory Law Journal*, 60: 251–75.

Freeman, M.D.A. (1983) *The Rights and Wrongs of Children*. London: Francis Pinter.

Freeman, M.D.A. (1997) *The Moral Status of Children: Essays on the Rights of the Children*. London: Martinus Nijhoff.

Freeman, M.D.A. (2007) 'Why it Remains Important to Take Children's Rights Seriously', *International Journal of Children's Rights*, 15(1): 5–23.

Freire, P. (1970) *Pedagogy of the Oppressed*. New York: Continuum Books.

Freire, P. (1973) *Education for Critical Consciousness*. New York: Continuum Books.

Freire, P. (1976) *Education, the Practice of Freedom*. London: Writers & Readers Group.

Gaventa, J. (2004) *Representation, Community Leadership and Participation: Citizen Involvement in Neighbourhood Renewal and Local Governance* (www.dfid.gov.uk/r4d/PDF/Outputs/CentreOnCitizenship/JGNRU.pdf).

Green, C. (2012) 'Listening to Children: Exploring Intuitive Strategies and Interactive Methods in a Study of Children's Special Places', *International Journal of Early Childhood*, 44: 269–85.

Harcourt, D., Perry, B. and Waller, T. (eds) (2011) *Researching Young Children's Perspectives*. London: Routledge.

Hart, J. (2008) 'Children's Participation and International Development', *International Journal of Children's Rights*, 16: 407–18.

Hart, R. (1992) *Children's Participation: The Theory and Practice of Involving Young Citizens in Community Development and Environmental Care*. London: Earthscan.

Hertfordshire Council (2010) Early Years Participation Toolkit (www.hertsdirect.org/services/edlearn/schdevproj/bsf2011/bsfarchive/bsf/partool/).

Hill, M. (2006) 'Children's Voices on Ways of Having a Voice: Children's and Young People's Perspectives on Methods used in Research and Consultation', *Childhood*, 13(1): 69–89.

Illich, I. (1970) *De-Schooling Society*. New York: Harper & Row.

Investing in Children (2008) 'Case Study – Investing in Children: Supporting Young People as Researchers', in E.K.M. Tisdall, J.M. Davis and M. Gallagher (eds), *Research with Children and Young People: Research Design, Methods and Analysis*. London: SAGE. pp. 168–75.

James, A., Jenks, C. and Prout, A. (1998) *Theorizing Childhood*. Cambridge: Polity Press.

Jans, M. (2004) 'Children as Citizens: Towards a Contemporary Notion of Child Participation', *Childhood*, 11(1): 27–44.

Jones, P. (1994) *Rights*. Basingstoke: Palgrave.

Kesby, M. (2000) 'Participatory Diagramming: Deploying Qualitative Methods through an Action Research Epistemology', *Area*, 32(4): 423–35.

Kirby, P. (1999) *Involving Young Researchers*. York: Joseph Rowntree Foundation.

Konstantoni, K. (2011) Young Children's Perceptions and Constructions of Social Identities and Social Implications: Promoting Social Justice in Early Childhood. PhD dissertation, University of Edinburgh, Edinburgh (www.era.lib.ed.ac.uk/handle/1842/5572).

Kymlicka, W. (1990) *Contemporary Political Philosophy: An Introduction*. Oxford: Oxford University Press.

Lancaster, Y.P. and Broadbent, V. (2003) *Listening to Young Children*. Maidenhead: Open University Press.

Lansdown, G. (2003) 'The Participation of Children', in H. Montgomery, R. Burr and M. Woodhead (eds), *Changing Childhoods: Local and Global*. Milton Keynes: Open University Press. pp. 273–82.

Leal, P.A. (2010) 'Participation: The Ascendancy of a Buzzword in the Neo-liberal Era', in A. Cornwall and D. Eade (eds), *Deconstructing Development Discourse: Buzzwords and Fuzzwords*. London: Oxfam. pp. 89–100.

Lindgren, A. (2012) 'Ethical Issues in Pedagogical Documentation', *International Journal of Early Childhood*, 44: 327–40.

Locke, J. (1982) *Second Treatise of Government* (R. Cox, ed.). Arlington Heights, VA: Harlan Davidson.

Lundy, L. and McEvoy, L. (2012) 'Childhood, the United Nations Convention on the Rights of the Child and Research: What Constitutes a Rights-based Approach?', in M. Freeman (ed.), *Law and Childhood*. Oxford: Oxford University Press. pp. 75–91.

MacIntyre, A. (1990) *After Virtue: A Study in Moral Theory*. London: Duckworth.

MacNaughton, G., Smith, K. and Lawrence, H. (2004) *Hearing Young Children's Voices – ACT Children's Strategy: Consulting with Children Birth to Eight Years of Age* (www.children.act.gov.au/documents/PDF/under5report.pdf).

Marshall, K. (1997) *Children's Rights in the Balance: The Participation Protection Debate*. London: The Stationery Office.

Marshall, T.H. (1950) 'Citizenship and Social Class', in *Sociology at the Crossroads and Other Essays*. Cambridge: Cambridge University Press. pp. 1–85.

Miller, J. (2009) *Never Too Young: How Children Can Take Responsibility and Make Decisions*, 2nd edn. London: Save the Children.

Moss, P. and Petrie, P. (2002) *From Children's Services to Children's Spaces: Public Policy, Children and Childhood*. London: Routledge/Falmer Press.

Moss, P., Clark, A. and Kjørholt, A.T. (2005) 'Introduction', in A. Clark, A.T. Kjørholt and

P. Moss (eds), *Beyond Listening: Children's Perspectives on Early Childhood Services*. Bristol: Policy Press. pp. 1–16.

OECD (2001) *Starting Strong: Early Childhood Care and Education*. Paris: OECD. (www.oecd.org/newsroom/earlychildhoodeducationandcare.htm)

OECD (2006) *Starting Strong II: Early Childhood Care and Education*. Paris: OECD. (www.oecd.org/newsroom/37425999.pdf)

Olsen, F. (1992) 'Social Legislation – Sex Bias in International Law: The UN Convention on the Rights of the Child', *Indian Journal of Social Work*, 53(3): 491–516.

Oxford Dictionary (2014) Participation. (www.oxforddictionaries.com/definition/english/participation)

Pascal, C. and Bertram, T. (2009) 'Listening to Young Citizens: The Struggle to Make Real a Participatory Paradigm in Research with Young Children', *European Early Childhood Education Research Journal*, 17(2): 249–62.

Prout, A. (2000) 'Children's Participation: Control and Self-realisation in British Late Modernity', *Children & Society*, 14(4): 304–15.

Prout, A. (2005) *The Future of Childhood*. London: Routledge/Falmer.

Reddy, N. and Ratner, K. (2002) *A Journey in Children's Participation: By The Concerned for Working Children* (www.pronats.de/assets/Uploads/reddy-ratna-a-journey-in-childrens-participation.pdf).

Reid, R. (1994) 'Children's Rights: Radical Remedies for Critical Needs', in S. Asquith and M. Hill (eds), *Justice for Children*. London: Martinus Nijhoff. pp. 19–25.

Reynaert, D., Bouverne-De Bie, M. and Vandevelde, S. (2012) 'Between "Believers" and "Opponents": Critical Discussions in Children's Rights', *International Journal of Children's Rights*, 20: 155–68.

Rinaldi, C. (2005) 'Documentation and Assessment: What is the Relationship?', in A. Clark, A.T. Kjørholt and P. Moss (eds), *Beyond Listening: Children's Perspectives on Early Childhood Services*. Bristol: Policy Press. pp. 17–28.

Sandel, M. (1982) *Liberalism and the Limits of Justice*. Cambridge: Cambridge University Press.

Shier, H. (2001) 'Pathways to Participation: Openings, Opportunities and Obligations', *Children & Society*, 15(2): 107–17.

Smith, A.B. (2013) 'Links to Theory and Advocacy', *Australian Journal of Early Childhood* (www.earlychildhoodaustralia.org.au/australian_journal_of_early_childhood/ajec_index_abstracts/childrens_rights_and_early_childhood_education.html).

Stephen, C., McPake, J., Plowman, L. and Berch-Heyman, S. (2008) 'Learning from the Children: Exploring Preschool Children's Encounters with ICT at Home', *Journal of Early Childhood Research*, 6(2): 99–117.

Sumsion, J., Harrison, L., Press, F., McLeod, S., Goodfellow, J. and Bradley, B. (2011) 'Researching Infants' Experiences of Early Childhood Education and Care', in D. Harcourt, B. Perry and T. Waller (eds), *Researching Young Children's Perspectives*. London: Routledge. pp. 113–27.

Te One, S. (2011) 'Supporting Children's Participation Rights: Curriculum and Research Approaches', in D. Harcourt, B. Perry and T. Waller (eds), *Researching Young Children's Perspectives*. London: Routledge. pp. 85–99.

Teamey, K. and Hinton, R. (2014) 'Reflections on Participation and its Link with Transformative Processes', in E.K.M. Tisdall, A.M. Gadda and U.M. Butler (eds), *Children and Young People's Participation and its Transformative Potential*. Basingstoke: Palgrave. pp. 22–43.

Theobald, M., Danby, S. and Ailwood, J. (2011) 'Child Participation in the Early Years: Challenges for Education', *Australian Journal of Early Childhood*, 36(3): 19–27.

Think Tank co-hosted by Australian Research Alliance for Children and Youth and the NSW Commission for Children and Young People (2008) *Involving Children and Young People in Research* (www.childhealthresearch.org.au/media/54379/involvingchildrenandyoungpeopleinresearch_1_.pdf).

Thomas, N. and O'Kane, C. (1998) 'The Ethics of Participatory Research with Children', *Children & Society*, 12: 336–48.

Tisdall, E.K.M. (2012a) 'Taking Forward Children and Young People's Participation', in M. Hill, G. Head, A. Lockyer, B. Reid and R. Taylor (eds), *Children's Services: Working Together*. Harlow: Pearson. pp. 151–62.

Tisdall, E.K.M. (2012b) 'The Challenge and Challenging of Childhood Studies? Lessons from Disability Studies and Research with Disabled Children', *Children & Society*, 26(3): 181–91.

Tisdall, E.K.M. (2014) 'Children Should be Seen and Heard? Children and Young People's Participation in the UK', in E.K.M. Tisdall, A.M. Gadda and U.M. Butler (eds), *Children and Young People's Participation and its Transformative Potential*. Basingstoke: Palgrave. pp. 168–88.

Tisdall, E.K.M. and Punch, S. (2012) 'Not so "New"? Looking Critically at Childhood Studies', *Children's Geographies*, 10(3): 249–64.

Tisdall, E.K.M., Davis, J.D. and Gallagher, M. (eds) (2009) *Researching with Children and Young People*. London: SAGE.

Tisdall, E.K.M., Gadda, A.M. and Butler, U.M. (2014) 'Introduction: Children and Young People's Participation in Collective Decision-Making', in E.K.M. Tisdall, A.M. Gadda and U.M. Butler (eds), *Children and Young People's Participation and its Transformative Potential*. Basingstoke: Palgrave. pp. 1–21.

Treseder, P. (1997) *Empowering Children and Young People Training Manual: Promoting Involvement in Decision-making*. London: Save the Children.

UN Committee on the Rights of the Child (2005) *Implementing Child Rights in Early Childhood*, General Comment No. 7 (www.childrensrights.ie/files/CRC-GC7_EarlyChildhood05.pdf).

UN Committee on the Rights of the Child (2009) *The Right of the Child to be Heard*, General Comment No. 12 (www2.ohchr.org/english/bodies/crc/docs/AdvanceVersions/CRC-C-GC-12.doc).

United Nations (1989) Convention on the Rights of the Child (www.ohchr.org/en/professionalinterest/pages/crc.aspx).

Valentin, K. and Meinert, L. (2009) 'The Adult North and the Young South', *Anthropology Today*, 25(3): 23–8.

Van Bueren, G. (2011) 'Multigenerational Citizenship: The Importance of Recognizing Children as National and International Citizens', *The ANNALS of the American Academy of Political and Social Science*, 633(1): 30–51.

Williams, L. (2010) 'Am I Staying for Lunch Today?': A Consultation with 3 and 4 Year Olds to Find out about their Experience of the Free Entitlement (www.c4eo.org.uk/cypviews/files/Am_I_staying_for_lunch_today_consultation%20project.pdf).

Winter, K. (2010) *Building Relationships and Communicating with Young Children: A Practical Guide for Social Workers*. London: Routledge.

6

Where am I? Position and Perspective in Researching Early Childhood Education

Peter Moss

INTRODUCTION

Positionality and perspective, concepts that question, indeed contest, the positivistic idea(l) inscribed in much research in the social sciences, including education: a belief in the possibility of objective researchers gaining true or valid knowledge of a real world through the application of scientific method in a search for natural laws or generalizable conclusions that can be applied to achieve universal goals. But positionality and perspective deny this possibility, challenging the notion that researchers can extract themselves from the world they live in and the positions they occupy in that world, inciting incredulity at the idea that researchers can achieve a 'God's eye view' or aspire to 'the view from nowhere'. Instead, both researchers and researched are inescapably situated in particular positions, and knowledge, therefore, is unavoidably perspectival and contextualized. That, at least, is the contention of this chapter.

What I aim to do in this chapter is to elaborate on this contention, and support it with examples of positionality and perspective and their effects on research. Some readers will choose to dismiss the arguments and retain a belief in the power of research to tell it as it is – and such a choice is the reader's prerogative, and justified if she or he is acquainted with the arguments and the alternatives. But for those readers who find the arguments for positionality and perspective more appealing, even perhaps liberating, the question may well arise, where does this leave research? I will argue that it leaves research in good shape, as an important attitude of mind and activity, an important way of relating to the world – in short, an essential element in processes of meaning-making, theory-building, policy-making and practice development.

What acknowledgement of positionality and perspective does call for, and I will develop these points towards the end of the chapter, is for researchers to be more aware of their relationship to what is researched, how they create the subject that they study and how they construct the knowledge of that subject; and also to think more about their role in the making of policy and the development of practice. That raises issues about the place of science in democratic societies and what claims scientists can make for their trade – in particular, what questions citizens should ask of scientists and what sort of answers scientists should offer.

Why does this matter? Is it relevant? You, the reader, must decide, but for my part positionality and perspective matter very much and are highly relevant. Without recognizing, valuing and working with them, we stand, from my perspective, in danger of reducing education from being, first and foremost, a political and ethical practice, in which all citizens can and should participate, in which there are real and conflicting alternatives upon which we must deliberate and dialogue, to being a predominantly technical practice, in which all citizens wait upon scientists to tell them, from their 'God's eye view', what works and what the evidence insists must be done.

POSITIONALITY: THE SUBJECT OF RESEARCH POSITIONED IN CONTEXT

To argue the importance of positionality and perspective is hardly a new insight. The idea that any researcher inevitably occupies a position or, indeed, positions, and that these positions shape how the researcher defines research questions, understands research subjects, relates to the researched, as well as how she or he sees and then interprets what is seen, has been around for some time, especially in disciplines like anthropology and geography, and in particular in the work of feminist academics (England, 2005; Hopkins, 2007). 'Position' may be defined in terms of aspects of our personal identity: gender, race, class, disability and sexuality, for example. Extensions of this may include nationality, language (or rather mother tongue) and culture. But position may also extend to include what might be termed philosophical affiliation: which disciplinary, theoretical and paradigmatic positions we choose to adopt, not to mention what political

frames we use to make sense of the world. I will return to look more closely at the positionality of the researcher in the next section.

But the researched, the subject of the researcher's gaze, is positioned too, within a complex network of people, structures and relationships; think, for example, of Bronfenbrenner's much-cited ecological systems theory, in which the child is situated within interconnected and interacting layers, the micro-, meso-, exo- and macro-systems, all bearing on the child's development (Bronfenbrenner, 1979). The researched is thus positioned in a complex context, or what might be termed more specifically a 'social context' – because in fields such as education, the phenomena under study are social, human beings and their institutions, and not natural; needing contextualization and interpretation, not finding and revealing. This context-specific positioning has a direct bearing not only on the subject of research, but also on how the researcher sees and understands the researched, influencing the meaning-making process central to research.

If for no other reason than the significance of context, social scientists cannot emulate natural scientists. The latter may aspire to proposing universal laws and theories that govern natural phenomena, and to doing so in a relatively objective way; the former, because their subjects are situated in and interacting with specific social contexts, cannot. For, if there are many positions and a multiplicity of perspectives, and if what we research is also positioned in very particular contexts, our knowledge is always situated and local, partial and provisional, conditional and contingent.

If discussions about positionality and perspective are relatively common in certain disciplines and fields, this has not been the case in early childhood education, or at least not in that part of it that has attracted the largest research resources and gained the greatest attention from policy-makers. This dominant tendency has been informed by two disciplines, developmental psychology and economics, and by an accompanying positivistic model of research, which has taken natural science as an ideal and assumed the making of objective and generalizable truth claims to be not only possible, but also the main purpose of this activity: in short, adopting an *epistemic* model of social science, a concept to which I shall return.

This positivistic model of social science finds little or no place for positionality, perspective or context, but presents research findings as if they were the objective, 'God's view' revelation of universal knowledge. As such, these findings get taken up and reproduced in innumerable research reviews and policy documents, where they are presented as evidence of universal truths. Let me give an example, which focuses, in particular, on the positioning of the researched and on researchers' failure to take account of it.

Many of the assertions of the long-term and widespread benefits of early childhood education are based on findings from three longitudinal studies of local interventions undertaken in the USA: Perry High/Scope (begun in 1962), Abecedarian (1972) and Chicago Child–Parent Centres (1983). It is worth, therefore, paying some attention to what have been referred to as 'iconic studies' (NESSE, 2009: 29), and which have been, in Helen Penn's words, 'endlessly recycled in the literature' (2011: 39).

All three were situated in small areas of a very large country, with samples – 111, 123 and 1,539 children respectively – drawn mainly from one group – poor 'Afro-American' families. All three were commenced decades ago, since when much has altered, for example understanding of issues such as race and motherhood, together with actual economic and demographic transformations that have led to huge changes in employment and family life and massive growth, as will be seen, in income and wealth inequality. At the same time, the three studies differed from each other in a variety of ways, for example in scope, in curriculum, in the length of time the intervention was offered, and in the effects measured and the instruments used to measure the effects. The results were also somewhat contradictory; for example, one study found 'no

impact on crime ratings [in later life], which is the main source of cost savings in the other two studies' (Penn et al., 2006a: 3).

Given these circumstances, it is not surprising that a systematic review of the evidence on the 'long-term economic impact of centre-based early childhood interventions', conducted at the EPPI (Evidence for Policy and Practice Information and Coordinating) Centre of the Institute of Education, University of London, arrived at distinctly agnostic conclusions. The EPPI reviewers found that these three research studies were the only ones to meet their criteria for inclusion in the review, i.e., that studies should 'deal with the long-term economic outcomes of centre-based early childhood interventions'. Overall, they concluded that the studies 'provide evidence for the beneficial effects of centre based early years interventions for very poor black children living in deprived inner city areas of the USA in the late 1960's [sic] and early 1970's [sic]' (Penn et al., 2006b: 1).

But the conclusion is highly qualified: the evidence provided by the three studies needs contextualizing and interpreting with great care. The assessments of benefits are highly context-specific, depending on local school models and high US levels of imprisonment and victim compensation. So while there appeared to be 'some positive financial returns', the authors of the review point out that 'the magnitude of the return is very sensitive to the assumptions made in the cost estimates' (Penn et al., 2006a: 24). Above all, the reviewers caution against generalizing from research conducted in such very specific spatial and temporal contexts:

> These findings cannot be assumed to be generalizable elsewhere. The findings from these studies should not be used as justification for investment in similar enterprises in different populations and locations and time periods … [T]he results of the three studies are not easily transferable to modern contexts in countries such as England. The results indicated should therefore all be read with the caveat of 'for the specific population in these studies'. (Penn et al., 2006b: 1)

In a later literature review, Penn again concludes that '[t]o make long-range predictions on the back of them is problematic' (NESSE, 2009: 29).

Yet despite this warning, not only have the results of these three studies been frequently generalized to other affluent countries, but the World Bank has 'extrapolated [the information] from the United States context without caveats, and applied [it] to Africa and other regions' (Penn, 2011: 55). Instead of being treated as quantitative case studies providing local knowledge and requiring careful interpretation that should take account of spatial and temporal context, they are treated as bearers of universal and timeless truths, applicable any time, any place.

There is one further failure to take account of context that merits attention. These three studies, but also many other research studies and interventions in the USA, are often cited as evidence of the 'high returns' to be gained from 'investing' in 'early interventions', with claims of anything up to $17 in benefits for every $1 spent (Wave Trust, 2013: 38). Yet in interpreting these research studies and evaluations, attention is rarely paid to the larger picture, the wider context of young childhood in the USA – to Bronfenbrenner's macro-system, the wider politico-economic environment.

For if we look at the larger picture, the USA seems to have remarkably little to show for all this early childhood research and intervention work going back over four decades; the country has a persistently poor record when it comes to the health and welfare of its young citizens, especially when looked at in a comparative context – and this despite being one of the richest countries on earth, measured by per capita GDP. Let me give some examples of this poor record.

Poverty rates amongst American children were marginally higher in 2012, at nearly 22 per cent, than when Head Start (the large-scale US government early intervention programme) began in 1965 (Denavas-Walt et al., 2013, Table B-2). Out of 34 'economically advanced' countries in the late 2000s, the USA had the second highest level of child poverty (UNICEF, 2012, Table 1b); while among 34 OECD member states, child poverty levels in

2008 were only higher in Turkey, Romania, Mexico and Israel (OECD Family Database, Chart CO2.2.A). The USA has far and away the worst score out of 21 affluent countries for an index constructed from indicators of nine social and health problems (Wilkinson and Pickett, 2009: 19–20). Social mobility is low, with a stronger link in the USA between parental education and children's economic and educational outcomes than in any of the other countries included in the Pew Trusts' Economic Mobility Project (Stiglitz, 2013). A comparison with 16 other affluent countries on a range of health indices concludes that not only are American lives shorter, but they 'also have a long standing pattern of poorer health that is strikingly consistent and pervasive over the life course' – including faring worst on infant mortality and low birth weight (Institute of Medicine of the National Academies, 2013: 1–2). To round off this litany of failure, the USA comes 26 out of 29 countries in UNICEF's review of child well-being in rich countries, managing to beat only Lithuania, Latvia and Romania (UNICEF, 2013), and comes at the bottom of that same organization's league table for inequality in child well-being (UNICEF, 2010).

Not only have researchers and policy-makers failed to position researched subjects within their particular, local temporal and spatial context. They have failed to look at the larger context, the societal context, and indeed the wider international context, and have failed therefore to ask pertinent and critical questions about the effectiveness of early intervention. Why has it failed to better the position of American children over the last 40 years? If it is because of inadequate implementation, what are the cultural and political reasons for this? What conditions in American society, one of the materially richest in the world, contribute to the country's poor record on children's well-being? Why, at a time of rising inequality and the dominance of a neoliberal political economy, is so much research and policy attention being paid to the technical practice of early childhood intervention? Clearly, there are no easy answers to such questions. But unless research studies position their subjects, their findings and their conclusions in a wider context, unless they are aware of such questions, they risk being complicit in reducing early childhood education to a merely technical practice at the service of the powers that be and of the status quo.

POSITIONALITY: THE RESEARCHER AND HER PERSPECTIVES

These examples and critiques focus on one aspect of positionality: the failure of researchers and readers of research to take sufficient account of the position of the subjects being researched within the wider economic, social and political context. This arises, in part, from the disciplinary, theoretical and political positionality of the researchers themselves, which has shaped the way they have approached, studied and made meaning of what they have chosen to research. In other words, what the researchers did and how policy-makers and other readers have often responded, not least by ignoring the complexities of and questions raised by context, is in large part because of the positions they occupy and which influence the perspectives they adopt.

As I have already indicated, these positions are multiple, so I will focus on just three to try to better exemplify my point (though as a male researcher in the predominantly female world of early childhood education, I might and should perhaps have chosen the positioning of gender and its consequences). First, nationality: how you see and understand social phenomena, in your own or other countries, will be influenced by where you have been brought up and live. I will illustrate the point with a piece of research that does in fact start from a recognition of positioning, by asking the question of how early childhood workers in different countries understand early childhood work: in other words, the research starts from the premise that national positioning might be significant

in the meaning attached to pedagogical relationships and practice. The emphasis, therefore, is on the positioning of observers who are early childhood professionals, but the principle, that national position (with its complex interweaving of history, culture and language) produces a particular perspective, can easily be extended to researchers.

Here, a Danish researcher describes the method she has used and its provenance:

> The data gathering uses a research method where focus groups of pedagogues [professional practitioners of social pedagogy, who work *inter alia* in Danish early childhood services] and others involved with pedagogical work are shown half-hour films of everyday life and practice in centres for pre-school children in Denmark, England and Hungary; these films were made for an earlier European project in which I participated, *Care Work in Europe, Current Understandings and Future Directions* (Cameron and Moss, 2009). Each film focuses in particular on two members of staff, pedagogues in the case of the Danish centre. The method was inspired by Tobin et al. (1989) then developed further in the European project where we called it SOPHOS: Second Order Phenomenological Observation Scheme (Hansen and Jensen, 2004). The films pose an open interview question: What do you think when you see this? And through the responses of the focus groups to this question, what the pedagogues and others talk about and discuss, what we might call the provocation of the film, it is possible to investigate and create a picture of their ideals and their understandings of central values in pedagogical practice. (Jensen, 2011: 142)

While, earlier, the films had been shown to groups in England and Hungary, in this piece of research the focus was on just one country, Denmark, and the responses of Danes to the three films – how, from their position and its accompanying perspective, they understood what was going on in the three countries' preschools. During the course of the work, the films were shown to a number of small groups, mostly pedagogues from early childhood centres, but also educators of these workers as well as other academics. The discussion of the three films in each group was recorded and transcribed, and these transcriptions provided the primary empirical data.

The researcher is at pains to emphasize that the research is not a comparative study of practice in three countries but rather:

> A study into *Danish understandings* of good peda-gogical work using films of practice from other countries (and also Denmark) to provoke discussion and reflection; the films could, of course, be used in the same way to study understandings of good work in any country. So it is important to bear in mind that the Danish pedagogues' understandings do not necessarily tell us something about English and Hungarian practice. Rather, *they say something about how these practices are interpreted through Danish eyes*. Through the practice of other coun-tries and Danish practice viewed on film, as well as their professional knowledge and experiences, the pedagogues formulate and articulate how they view good practice. (2011: 143, emphasis added)

What the Danish workers see in the films, their perspective, is that the nursery in each country has its own peculiar logic, what the researcher characterizes as 'childhood', 'pre-school' and 'home/family' logic. And in making the statements they do about the Danish, English and Hungarian films, the Danish viewers reflect, directly and indirectly, their national position: the constructions, rationalities and practices that are valued in their society, their understanding from their perspective of what constitutes good work:

> They saw the Danish institutional logic as a 'child-hood logic', where an underpinning idea is that children are experts in their own lives. The aim assumed by this rationality is children's acquisition of experiences and experiences gained by children on their own terms. The staff role includes the pedagogue viewing the child as a playing and participating child. The interaction between chil-dren and adults takes place by way of respectful relations with dialogic communications ('apprecia-tive relations'). The pace, rhythm and atmosphere in day-to-day life are characterized by absorption in certain activities, unpredictability and humor. (2011: 146)

In contrast, the Danish pedagogues saw a 'pre-school logic' in the film of the *English* nursery, with a school rationality in control of practice. The aims and objectives are seen to be formal teaching and learning. The role of the staff is that of a pre-school teacher who views the children as learning children. The interaction between children and adults involves alternating activities, with adults dictating to children as the dominant form of communication. The pace, rhythm and atmosphere are characterized by a high number of shifts over the day, from one activ-ity to another, and activities involving the entire group of children.

> In the film of the *Hungarian* nursery, the pedagogue informants found an institutional logic character-ized by the good family life/home and where an image of the good family or home shapes the prac-tice. The aim is upbringing. The role of the staff is the careful 'mother' and educator who sees before her, in part at least, a fragile child. The interaction between the children and adults takes place by way of the adults taking the initiative and through differ-ent activities, and the dominant type of communica-tion is instruction. The pace, rhythm and atmosphere are characterized by regularity, order and calmness. The observers viewed the institution as a highly female universe. (2011: 146, emphasis in original)

The positioning illustrated here is, of course, more complex than simply nationality. The viewers of the films did so more than just as Danes; they also viewed them from a particular disciplinary position, that of social pedagogy, the predominant discipline in Denmark not only for working with pre-school children but also in a wide range of other services for older children, young people and adults. Nor, of course, should we assume that all Danes or even all Danish social pedagogues occupy an identical position; there are many other cross-cutting influences that might define the posi-tion in which any one person is situated. But the results from this research do suggest that nationality and discipline can have a powerful effect on how we see and understand the world.

One reason for this effect is my second example of positionality: language, for it is through language that we construct mean-ing, our understanding and knowledge of the world. So, to take another example from the Danish study, the Danish observers made sense of what they saw through the medium of the Danish language and the concepts the lan-guage provides. Thus, the Danish researcher notes that one reason for the differences that the Danish viewers see between the three nursery settings is *kropslighed*. This Danish word expresses a very important concept in Danish pedagogy, which (the Danish researcher notes) is difficult to translate into English; writing in English, she eventually chooses the word 'embodiment' as 'perhaps the nearest English translation for this important Danish pedagogical term, which is about the use and expression of the body'.

The pedagogues find that both children and adults show few expressions of *kropslighed* in the English and Hungarian films. One informant, an academic in the field of pedagogy, put it this way:

> you can say that the children have their body in a different way in the Danish film, and the pedagogues as well. The children's bodies are much more present. The body is allowed to be there ... Nursing of the body is a focal point in [the Hungarian film] and one way or the other the body has been reduced to a head in the English film. (2011: 150)

There are three points I want to make here. First, to re-iterate that we see, interpret and understand the world through language – it is an integral part of our positioning and the perspectives we adopt. Second, that the increasing dominance of English as a research language (not only in conducting cross-national research, but in reporting results in the English-language journals that all researchers today must publish in for career advancement) serves to reduce multiplicity and enhance homogeneity, making important concepts and ways of understanding increasingly invisible as everyone uses English terms and concepts and, therefore, adopts Anglo-American ways of understanding. Thus, to give another example, 'social pedagogy' and 'pedagogue' have often been incorrectly translated into English as 'education' and 'teacher', so making the Other into the Same and nullifying a long-established tradition and profession with an extensive presence in Continental Europe (for an English-language introduction to social pedagogy, see Cameron and Moss, 2011). Third, this trend towards the hegemony of the English language attracts

little critical attention, not least from its main beneficiaries, native English speakers, who too often take it for granted that everything translates readily and perfectly into English. Moreover, in these hegemonic conditions, native English speakers can avoid questioning the meanings inscribed in taken-for-granted terms widely used in their own language, such as 'day care' and 'childcare'.

It is rare to find anyone in the world of early childhood or other social research raising questions about the issue of language, the dominance of English and the implications of the linguistic position adopted for research purposes. So these comments from the multilingual Austrian scholar Walter Lorenz, commenting on the experience of participating in a cross-national European project, are not only trenchant but unusual:

> The actual difficulties, the resources required in acquiring a foreign language in the course of studies have been totally miscalculated at all levels. This has led to a pragmatism of settling for more commonly spoken languages and of course among them for the English language predominantly with all the associated exclusionary consequences ... There is always the need to get results, to be pragmatic, to overcome language differences as barriers, and not enough time and space to explore the subtleties of discovering meaning through non-comprehension, through the pain not only of working through interpreters but of clarifying terminology so that it can be used reliably by interpreters and shared among all participants. This seems to hold up the works, those representing lesser spoken languages come to regard this as their personal problem, their personal deficit, and the whole language project is tilted and distorted. And yet, *it would be precisely the non-understanding which could give us the most valuable clues to differences in meaning*, to the need for further clarification of familiar terms and concepts, to the transformation of taken-for-granted perspectives into creative, shared knowledge. (Lorenz, 1999: 20–1, emphasis added)

In other words, recognition of linguistic positionality might be turned into a strength in research, rather than being considered a problem to be ignored or controlled, by recognizing the significance of 'non-understanding' and its potential for challenging the taken-for-granted and provoking new and different questions.

My third and final example of positionality concerns paradigm, by which I mean the over-arching mindset that we adopt to help us make sense of the world and our position in it. What I would term the influential research in early childhood education, influential in the sense that it is much cited as justification for policy and practice, has been undertaken by researchers situated in a particular paradigmatic position, a position that is also occupied by most policy-makers: what has been termed the paradigm of regulatory modernity (Dahlberg and Moss, 2005) with its basic tenets or foundations. What are these? The stable and coherent self, the transparency of language, the rationality of humans, the ability of reason to overcome conflicts between truth, power and knowledge, and that freedom involves obeying rational laws (Flax, 1990); and the value given to certainty and mastery, linearity and *predetermined* outcomes, objectivity and universality. Ontology and epistemology are central to paradigm. Regulatory modernity believes in universals and essences that can be revealed and represented, to give us true knowledge of how the world really is:

[A prominent feature of the paradigm of modernity] is its claim to the transcendent status of irreducible universal knowledge. The basis for this claim lies in the idea that value-free, archetypal knowledge is possible and accessible by way of rational or dialectical scientific methods and standards of proof. One aspect of the superiority claimed by scientific knowledge is its purported insulation from the vagaries of human diversity and contingency by the exercise of reason. It is precisely because of this ostensible autonomy that modern knowledge lays claim to Universal Truth. (Otto, 1999: 17)

Regulatory modernity is just one paradigmatic position that can be chosen. Others exist, including one that has attracted increasing, though still minority, interest in early childhood education[1]: post-foundationalism, a paradigm that encompasses a variety of theoretical perspectives including post-modernisms, post-structualisms and post-colonialisms. This paradigm challenges the basic tenets, or foundations, of the paradigm of regulatory modernity. Post-foundationalism values complexity and context, uncertainty and provisionality, subjectivity and interpretation. Ontologically, it adopts a social constructionist approach, in which the world and our knowledge of it are socially constructed, a process in which all of us, as human beings, are active participants in relationship with others: 'the world is always *our* world, understood or constructed by ourselves, not in isolation but as part of a community of human agents, and through our active interaction and participation with other people in that community' (Dahlberg et al., 2013: 24, original emphasis). A process not only undertaken with others, but in context, so that knowledge of the world is understood to be not only 'socially constituted, [but] historically embedded and valuationally based' (Lather, 1991: 52).

Epistemologically, too, the paradigmatic position is very different:

Post-structuralists, building on critical philosophies of science, reject the possibility of absolute truths and universally ordered systems of knowledge. Instead, knowledge is understood as produced by an 'economy of discourses of truth' and meaning emerges from the interaction of competing knowledges. Some knowledges justify and support dominating meanings and practices while other knowledges, usually marginal, challenge hegemonic discourses ... This perspective doesn't make scientific knowledge 'untrue'. Rather, *it demands that we understand Truth in a different way, as the contingent product of particular, situated ways of comprehending the world and not as something that is absolute and immutable which pre-exists social relations and awaits discovery* ... [T]he central issues become those of understanding the conditions in which certain discourses or world-views are privileged and how the distinctions they produce between true and false can be contested. (Otto, 1999: 17, emphasis added)

From this paradigmatic perspective, there is not and cannot be some position outside the world from which objective, stable and universal knowledge can be revealed and dispassionate and irrefutable judgements made. It recognizes, too, the inextricable relationship between knowledge and power, in which power functions through knowledge and what is deemed knowledge is a function of power, and the inevitability of position and context. There can, for example, be no neutral, stable and generic measure of 'quality', nor can evidence 'tell' us anything. Instead, post-foundationalism views knowledge as unavoidably partial, perspectival and provisional. It offers a world of multiple local practices, perspectives and knowledges, so that different people will interpret – make meaning of – evidence in different ways and will arrive at different views about what constitutes, for example, good education in a process that is inescapably political. For the paradigm lends itself readily to the primacy of political practice, with its view of a world in which we constantly face conflicting alternatives.

There are, at least, two major problems with paradigm in early childhood education (or any other field, if it comes to that). First, there is virtually no dialogue between researchers occupying different paradigmatic positions; they make almost no reference to each others' work, even to contest it, and there are no spaces where their different positions and perspectives are acknowledged and discussed. Second, while the concept of positionality and perspective is readily admitted and welcomed by post-foundationalists, indeed relativism is at the heart of the paradigm, it is anathema to modernists, for whom the idea(l) of objective and decontextualized knowledge is at the heart of their paradigm. Positionality, and the post-foundational paradigm in which it thrives, is therefore a challenge to objectivity and modernity, a challenge that (at least in early childhood education) seems to simply be ignored.

WHAT IS TO BE DONE?

The lack of dialogue between modernists and post-foundationalists in early childhood education – what I have termed elsewhere 'the paradigmatic divide' (Moss, 2007), and its consequences, and the near total invisibility of the latter paradigm in the field of policy-making and practice seems to me to be a matter of utmost importance and deep concern. But

that inquest must be left to another occasion. I want to end by addressing a further problem of great importance. How might the issue of positionality and perspective be addressed in research in early childhood education?

A starting point is to recognize the issue, not sweep it under the carpet, and to assess carefully its consequences. This should start at an early stage of the higher education of future educators, administrators, policy-makers and researchers, introducing them to the importance of positionality and perspective, and challenging them to reflect, as a continuous process, on their own positions and perspectives. Patti Lather, for example, writes of her 'paradigm talk' with students, including 'paradigm mapping' in which she 'argues against a linear sense of development toward "one best way" and "consensus" approaches' and enacts, instead, a 'paradigm mapping that deliberately holds together necessary incompatibilities in the hope that such a chart can help us diagram the variety that characterizes contemporary approaches to educational research' (Lather, 2006: 36).

This process of cultivating self-awareness should continue into the conduct of research. Indeed, it is not unknown in other fields of study; for instance, such critical reflection 'upon the positionalities of the researcher and the researched is now regarded as accepted practice amongst many feminist and critical geographers' (Hopkins, 2007: 387). So researchers might be encouraged to think about and discuss their positioning and its implications for their research, acknowledging in the process the perspective through which they constitute and view their research subject – what are, to borrow the title of John Berger's famous book on viewing art, their 'ways of seeing' (Berger, 2008). To start, say, an article or report by discussing from what paradigmatic position the reported research has been undertaken would be an important development, as would discussion of the context of the researched subject. Journals and funders themselves could encourage this process by discussing their expectations in guidelines to researchers.

Similarly, and especially in cross-national research or where an author for whom English is not her mother tongue is writing in that language, it might be important to devote time to the question of language. This would mean addressing directly the linguistic issues that have arisen in the course of the research and writing, Lorenz's instances of 'non-comprehension' for example, and seeing them as a way of deepening understanding about the diversity and complexity of pedagogical concepts and practices. Multi-national research teams, such as are increasingly to be found working in Europe on comparative studies, have a great potential for making positioning and its implications visible – but only if the importance of this task is recognized and accorded the time and space it requires. But even where a study is within one country only and undertaken solely by researchers from that country, the issue of the positioning of the subject and the perspectives of the researcher(s) needs careful attention.

Positionality and perspective highlight the inescapable subjectivity of the social research endeavour. Of course, there is subjectivity and subjectivity, and the aim should always be for 'rigorous' subjectivity, seeking to avoid 'the danger of rampant subjectivity where one finds only what one is predisposed to look for, an outcome that parallels the "pointless precision" of objectivism' (Lather, 1991: 52). But having said that, there seems no way of escaping subjectivity, of avoiding saying that this is the perspective from my position, that what I can offer is situated knowledge, valuable and carefully considered, but ultimately local and partial and provisional. One question then is how to use that knowledge. What can the positioned researcher contribute to public understanding and the development of policy and practice, a contribution that offers neither overblown truth claims nor undue diffidence? Here, I think, the Danish economic geographer, Bent Flyvbjerg (2006), offers some interesting pointers.

Flyvbjerg rejects what he terms an 'epistemic model' of social science, which seeks to emulate the natural science model of doing science, with the aim of delivering universal theories and laws that govern social action. Epistemic researchers claim a privileged position, as the discoverers and bearers of true knowledge, which should form the basis for public intervention: they are technocrats 'who – through their insight into social theories and laws – may provide society with solutions to social ills' (p.39). Instead, Flyvbjerg favours a 'phronetic model' of social science, 'which takes as its point of departure that despite centuries of trying the natural science model still does not work in social science. No predictive models have been arrived at as yet' (p. 39). Recognizing positionality, perspective and context, and that all social science is based on interpretation, the phronetic social scientist does not claim to know the truth, which society then can implement, but rather offers herself as one contributor to a process of public deliberation following the rules of constitutional democracy:

> The work [of the researcher] is dialogical in the sense that it incorporates, and, if successful, is incorporated into a polyphony of voices. No one voice, including that of the researcher, may claim final authority. The goal is to produce input to dialogue and praxis in social affairs, rather than to generate ultimate, unequivocally verified 'knowledge' ... Thus, phronetic social science explicitly sees itself as not having a privileged position from which the final truth can be told and further discussion arrested ... [As Nietzsche (1969) says] '(t)here is *only* a perspective seeing, only a perspective "knowing", and the *more* affects we allow to speak about one thing, the *more* eyes, different eyes, we can use to observe one thing, the more complete will our "concept" of this thing, our "objectivity" be'. Hence 'objectivity' in phronetic social science is not 'contemplation without interest' but employment of 'a *variety* of perspectives and affective interpretations in the service of knowledge'. (Flyvbjerg, 2006: 41, original emphasis)

The researcher *may* carry more weight than many in this process of democratic deliberation, but on the basis of earned authority, persuading others of her wisdom, based on training and time spent researching a subject. But ultimately, citizens themselves have to take responsibility for reflecting on, discussing and evaluating the research that is on offer to them, weighing up the likely consequences of position and perspective, not uncritically accepting what is offered by researchers as if it were the tablets brought down from the mountain top. We, as citizens, cannot turn to researchers and beg them to reveal 'what the research tells us', for it can tell us nothing by itself, being rather the raw material for processes of meaning-making. Rather, citizens should invite researchers to talk about their perspectives and share their experience and understanding, as participants in democratic processes of dialogue. In short, we need a reflexive citizenry engaged with reflexive researchers.

This 'phronetic model' of research and its role in policy and practice have much in common with what has been, until now, a small-scale form of research into early childhood education: pedagogical documentation, originally developed in the early childhood centres of the Italian city of Reggio Emilia, but subsequently taken up and worked with in many other places. Pedagogical documentation makes learning, and other processes, visible through being documented in various ways (e.g., note-taking, video and audio recordings, the display of children's work), but then goes further by enabling the documentation to be shared and opened up to multiple perspectives, dialogue and interpretations, from both adults and children – citizens coming together to discuss, contest, reflect on and construct meanings from the documented pedagogical work placed before them. For Loris Malaguzzi, one of its pioneers, pedagogical documentation 'meant the possibility to discuss and to dialogue "everything with everyone"', but based on 'being able to discuss real, concrete things – not just theories or words, about which it is possible to reach easy and naïve agreement' (Hoyuelos, 2004: 7). It was about, too, the 'ideological and ethical concept of a transparent school and transparent education' (Hoyuelos, 2004: 7).

Pedagogical documentation can serve many purposes, including professional development, evaluation and research, in particular an ongoing research of children's learning conducted (in Reggio Emilia at least) by educators themselves. This is research conducted as part of a democratic deliberative process, in which different positions and perspectives are assumed, so setting high store on reflection, dialogue and confrontation between differing interpretations. Scaled up, pedagogical documentation could be applied to policy-making, practice development and large-scale evaluations of systems. In these cases, various research studies (including the three much recycled and iconic US studies) could be seen as constituting some of the documentation introduced into the process of democratic deliberation and which would involve a wide range of citizens (including politicians and administrators) questioning, reflecting, dialoguing, contesting and making meaning, a process in which a degree of consensus might emerge, informed by but not mandated by the research input, by research as food for thought in a democratic politics of early childhood education. (For more on pedagogical documentation, see Dahlberg et al., 2013: Chapter 7; also Dahlberg and Moss, 2005; Rinaldi, 2006; Vecchi, 2010.)

CONCLUSION

We can think of policy and practice evolution as particular instances of learning, in which theories are constructed, listened to and shared, tested and challenged, re-worked and reformulated before being subjected again to the same process. Research – whether by academic researchers, educators or others – has an important part to play in such a learning process, termed a 'pedagogy of listening' in Reggio Emilia (Dahlberg and Moss, 2005; Rinaldi, 2006) and described, in a different context, by Ray Pawson in his book on evidence-based policy and practice (2006). Pawson is critical of much of the 'evidence-based' discourse and its suppositions, including:

> the ludicrous idea that evaluators and reviewers are able to tell policy-makers and practitioners exactly what works in the world of policy interventions ... and the [continuing] assumption about a

one-to-one relationship between each past intervention, each evaluation and each future intervention. This is a foolhardy supposition. Social interventions are complex, active systems thrust into [other] complex, active systems and are never implemented the same way twice. (2006: 170)

Nevertheless, he does not abandon working with research, and other evidence, in what he terms a process of 'realist synthesis', in which evidence from studies of interventions in a common field is worked with not to produce clear, consistent and universal answers, but to help build theory: realist synthesis, he writes, operates through processes of 'policy abstraction and theory-building rather than data extraction and number crunching'. From his realist perspective, intervention programmes represent theories about how to change behaviour, and the results, carefully evaluated, enable theory to be continuously refined. Evidence in realist synthesis is always contextualized and perspectival; 'evidential truths are partial, provisional and conditional' (2006: 175). Such truths cannot tell us what to do nor guarantee effective interventions. But they are still worthwhile, with the possibility of 'achieving some small betterment' (2006: 167) and able to 'alert the policy community to caveats and considerations that should inform decisions' (2006: 100).

This, then, is research evidence not as a definitive answer, not as a substitute for thought, but rather as a provocation to thought, a form of documentation that contributes to reflection, dialogue and deliberation. In short, it is thinking in context and thinking the complex (Morin, 1999). What Pawson captures in his 'realist perspective' is an attitude to research that is modest and measured, sceptical but not dismissive, ready to use findings but not to treat them as objective, decontextualized and replicable truth. Position and perspective are inescapable, but not a cause for despair.

In this chapter, I have attempted to set out why my perspective on research, viewed from my particular position, has much in common with Pawson's. Perhaps, in conclusion, I should add that this perspective on research, indeed on early childhood education, has totally altered over the last 20 years with a shift in position, as I have undertaken cross-national

work with multi-lingual colleagues, as I have been exposed to new theoretical ideas, and as I have become aware of different paradigmatic positions and chosen to move from a modernist position to a more post-foundational one. I still read positivistic research, but do so more critically and no longer exclusively. The consequences of this altered perspective, this shift in position have been exhilarating and renewing.

FURTHER READING

Dahlberg, G., Moss, P. and Pence, A. (2013) *Beyond Quality in Early Childhood Education and Care: Languages of Evaluation*, 3rd edn. London: Routledge.

Flyvbjerg, B. (2006) 'Social science that matters', *Foresight Europe* (October 2005–March 2006): 38–42. (http://flyvbjerg.plan.aau.dk/Publications2006/ForesightNo2PRINT.pdf)

Jensen, J. (2011) 'Understandings of Danish pedagogical practice', in C. Cameron and P. Moss (eds), *Social Pedagogy and Working with Children and Young People*. London: Jessica Kingsley.

QUESTIONS FOR REFLECTION

1   In what paradigmatic position are you situated? How have you come to be in that position? What other paradigms are you aware of?
2   Choose some aspect of your own identity (e.g., gender, race, class, disability or sexuality). How might this influence your perspective on early childhood education?
3   Take a publication – an article, a book, a policy document – that you have recently read. Does it acknowledge the issue of positionality and perspective? If so, how does it do so and with what consequences? If not, how might it have done so and what might have been the consequences?

NOTE

1   Examples of early childhood researchers and practitioners working from a post-foundational paradigmatic position can be found in the *Contesting Early Childhood* book series (co-edited by

Gunilla Dahlberg and Peter Moss), more details at http://www.routledge.com/books/series/SE0623/; a wide range of journal articles for example *in Contemporary Issues in Early Childhood*; and papers given at the annual Reconceptualizing Early Childhood Education conference.

REFERENCES

Berger, J. (2008) *Ways of Seeing*. London: Penguin Books.

Bronfenbrenner, U. (1979) *The Ecology of Human Development*. Cambridge, MA: Harvard University Press.

Cameron, C. and Moss, P. (eds) (2011) *Social Pedagogy and Working with Children and Young People*. London: Jessica Kingsley.

Dahlberg, G. and Moss, P. (2005) *Ethics and Politics in Early Childhood Education*. London: Routledge.

Dahlberg, G., Moss, P. and Pence, A. (2013) *Beyond Quality in Early Childhood Education and Care: Languages of Evaluation*, 3rd edn. London: Routledge.

Denavas-Walt, C., Proctor, B.D. and Smith, J.C. (2013) *Income, Poverty, and Health Insurance Coverage in the US 2012*. Washington, DC: United States Census Bureau. (www.census.gov/prod/2013pubs/p60-245.pdf)

England, K.V.L. (2005) 'Getting personal: Reflexivity, positionality and feminist research', *The Professional Geographer,* 46 (1), 80–89.

Flax, J. (1990) *Thinking Fragments: Psychoanalysis, Feminism and Postmodernism in the Contemporary West*. Berkeley and Los Angeles, CA: University of California Press.

Flyvbjerg, B. (2006) 'Social science that matters', *Foresight Europe* (October 2005–March 2006), 38–42.

Hopkins, P. (2007) 'Positionalities and knowledge: negotiating ethics in practice', *ACME: An International E-Journal for Critical Geographers*, 6 (3), 386–94.

Hoyuelos, A. (2004) 'A pedagogy of transgression', *Children in Europe*, 6, 6–7.

Institute of Medicine of the National Academies (2013) *US Health in International Perspective: Shorter Lives, Poorer Health – Report Brief*. (www.iom.edu/~/media/Files/Report%20Files/2013/US-Health-International-Perspective/USHealth_Intl_PerspectiveRB.pdf)

Jensen, J. (2011) 'Understandings of Danish pedagogical practice', in C. Cameron and P. Moss (eds) *Social Pedagogy and Working with Children and Young People*. London: Jessica Kingsley.

Lather, P. (1991) *Getting Smart: Feminist Research and Pedagogy with/in the Postmodern*. London: Routledge.

Lather, P. (2006) 'Paradigm proliferation as a good thing to think with: teaching research in education as a wild profusion', *International Journal of Qualitative Studies in Education*, 19 (1), 35–57.

Lorenz, W. (1999) 'The ECSPRESS approach: guiding the social professions between national and global perspectives', in *European Dimensions in Training and Practice of Social Professions*. Boskovice: Verlag ALBERT.

Moss, P. (2007) 'Meetings across the paradigmatic divide', *Educational Philosophy and Theory*, 39 (3), 229–40.

NESSE (2009) *Early Childhood Education and Care: Key Lessons from Research for Policy Makers*. (www.nesse.fr/nesse/activities/reports/ecec-report-pdf)

Otto, D. (1999) 'Everything is dangerous: some poststructural tools for *human rights* law', *Australian Journal of Human Rights*, 5 (1), 17–47.

Pawson, R. (2006) *Evidence-based Policy: A Realist Perspective*. London: SAGE.

Penn, H. (2011) *Quality in Early Childhood Services: An International Perspective*. Maidenhead: Open University Press.

Penn, H., Burton, V., Lloyd, E., Mugford, M., Potter, S. and Sayeed, Z. (2006a) *Early Years: What is known about the long-term economic impact of centre-based early childhood interventions? Technical report*. London: EPPI-Centre, Institute of Education, University of London. (http://eppi.ioe.ac.uk/cms/LinkClick.aspx?fileticket=I5do4A7UCSo%3D&tabid=676&mid=1572)

Penn, H., Burton, V., Lloyd, E., Mugford, M., Potter, S. and Sayeed, Z. (2006b) *Early Years: What is known about the long-term economic impact of centre-based early childhood interventions? Summary*. London: EPPI-Centre, Institute of Education, University of London. (http://eppi.ioe.ac.uk/cms/LinkClick.aspx?fileticket=LrZZFRxoUr4%3d&tabid=676&mid=1572)

Rinaldi, C. (2006) *In Dialogue with Reggio Emilia: Listening, Researching and Learning*. London: Routledge.

Stiglitz, J.E. (2013) *The Price of Inequality*. London: Penguin Books.

Tobin, J., Wu, D.Y. and Davidson, D.H. (1989) *Preschool in Three Cultures*. New Haven, CT: Yale University Press.

UNICEF (2010) *The Children Left Behind: A League Table of Inequality in Child Well-Being in the World's Rich Countries*. Innocenti Report Card 9. Florence: UNICEF Office of Research – Innocenti. (www.unicef-irc.org/publications/pdf/rc9_eng.pdf)

UNICEF (2012) *Measuring Child Poverty: New League Tables of Child Poverty in the World's Rich Countries*. Innocenti Report Card 11. Florence: UNICEF Office of Research – Innocenti. (www.unicef-irc.org/publications/pdf/rc10_eng.pdf)

UNICEF (2013) *Child Well-being in Rich Countries: A Comparative Overview*. Innocenti Report Card 11. Florence: UNICEF Office of Research – Innocenti. (www.unicef.org.uk/Images/Campaigns/FINAL_RC11-ENG-LORES-fnl2.pdf)

Vecchi, V. (2010) *Art and Creativity in Reggio Emilia: Exploring the Role and Potentiality of Ateliers in Early Childhood Education*. London: Routledge.

Wave Trust (2013) *Conception to Age 2: The Age of Opportunity*. London: Wave Trust. (www.wavetrust.org/key-publications/reports/conception-to-age-2)

Wilkinson, R. and Pickett, K. (2009) *The Spirit Level: Why More Equal Societies Almost Always Do Better*. London: Allen Lane.

7

Theorizing Identities in Early Childhood

Katrien De Graeve

INTRODUCTION

Age has been identified as one of the many identity categories that shape our lives and influence the extent to which we are able to exercise agency. In the 1990s, Prout and James (1997: 8) stated that the new paradigm in childhood studies should consider age, and young age in particular, as a variable of social analysis, inseparable from other variables such as class, gender, or ethnicity. Children are increasingly the focus of research and policy. However, 'the child' is still often considered as a unified, universal category, and the intersection with other markers of difference and inequality is not always clearly articulated. The field of early childhood and education is no exception. Despite its focus on a specific age range (usually the period from birth to 8 years is considered as early childhood), the diversity of experiences and identities often tends to be subsumed under universal categorizations.

In this chapter, I aim to present some building blocks for a theoretical framework for the study of young children that takes into account the plurality of childhood experiences, and the parental and other cultures of early childhood education and care that surround the rearing of children. I review a growing body of empirical and theoretical research on cultures and identities that contributes to a better understanding of early childhood identities as processes that are enacted in conjunction with intersecting vectors of oppression and privilege, bio-political governing technologies, moral economies of care, and the politics of belonging and citizenship. By tracing some of the scholarly debates that took place at the intersection of childhood studies and theoretical work on identities and subjectivity, I hope to provide some useful concepts and frameworks for the study of young children's lives. I aim to do so in a way that critically engages with structural inequalities based on gender, disability, sexuality, ethnicity, and other social differences, and that contributes to a more complex and diversified view of childhood, away from universalist assumptions.

Moreover, to avoid reifying essentialist notions of identity, in this chapter on the identities that unfold around young children, I prefer to shift the focus from identity as such to 'identity work' (Faircloth, 2013; Kershaw, 2010; Longman et al., 2013). The concept of identity is a contested term, with a variety of meanings and usages, though, more than a decade after Brubaker and Cooper's (2000) call to discard the term as an analytical category, it is still widely used in analyses by social scientists in a broad range of disciplines. Brubaker and Cooper (2000: 8) rightly criticized the (over)use of the term with a tendency to conflate identity as a category of practice and a category of analysis and pointed to its 'multivalent, even contradictory theoretical burden'. Their plea 'to unbundle the thick tangle of meanings that have accumulated around the term' (2000: 14) is certainly to be taken seriously. In many cases, a range of other less 'congested' terms are better suited to capture the varied work condensed in the single concept of 'identity'. Yuval-Davis's (2010: 266–7) definition of identity seems very useful here, as she focuses on identities as narratives of people about themselves and others, verbal or constructed as specific practices. Moreover, a view on identity as a matter of narration (Prins, 2006: 281) fits within constructionist understandings that emphasize its fluidity and multiplicity. A narrative approach enables us to view identity, to use Malkki's phrase (1992: 37), as 'a creolized aggregate composed through bricolage'. This metaphor, which refers to the improvisational amassing and assembling work of the tinkerer, catches the complexity and messiness of identity work.

The chapter is organized in four sections. In the first section, I explore theories of subjectivity that can be used for the study of young children's identities and agency. In the second section, I present intersectionality and super-diversity as possible frameworks for the study of the diversity of early childhood identities. The third section focuses on the parental identities that are co-constituted with the figurations and identities of young children.

The last section discusses recent research that focuses on the political implications of identity work in and around young children. I present research that explores the ways in which childrearing might affect social inclusion and citizenship.

SUBJECTIVITY AND THE YOUNG CHILD

Bourdieu's (1990: 55) concept of 'habitus', Ortner's (1989: 198) concept of a 'loosely structured actor', and other critical theorizations of empowerment and agency capture the idea of actors whose identities and actions are restricted by structural positions, though not fully determined by them (e.g., Bilge, 2010; Chambers, 2008; Isin and Wood, 1999; McNay, 2000; Seymour, 2006). These poststructuralist and interactionist views see power as a creative rather than a solely repressive and constraining force on the individual, while not denying the fact that the construction of identities does not occur in a social vacuum. This first section investigates how theories of subjectivity and agency are being applied and further developed in the light of young children's lives, allowing a focus on the plurality of childhoods, while not diverting attention from childhood as a structural position that sets children apart from adults. With Butler's (2003) notion of 'performativity', the concept of 'agency of nature' applied by Castañeda (2002), Lee's (1998) notion of 'immature sociology', and the concept of 'relational autonomy' that has been developed in care ethics, I present some possible building blocks for the further development of a theory of young children's subjectivity and identities. Moreover, studying the agency of infants and young children makes us reconsider the very concept of agency, away from neoliberal understandings of the rational, self-reliant autonomous subject and lets us re-evaluate notions of dependency and becoming for children's lives and human existence more generally.

The 'new paradigm for the sociology of childhood' (Prout and James, 1997: 8) included as one of its key features the acknowledgment that childhood is a social construction, clearly distinguished from biological immaturity. The biological immaturity–childhood binary has provoked critiques similar to feminist reconsiderations of the sex–gender divide that move away from the idea that the body has an 'ontological status apart from the various acts which constitute its reality' (Butler, 2006: 185). These critiques (e.g., Dickenson, 2011) have begun to question constructionist accounts of childhood that claim biological immaturity is 'a universal and natural feature of human groups' (James and Prout, 1997: 3) and that the 'natural' child is a pre-discursive entity, prior to culture, a neutral surface upon which the social can act. For Butler, there is no subject prior to its constructions (Dickenson, 2011: 15), but 'a continual and incessant *materialization* of possibilities … conditioned and circumscribed by historical convention' (Butler, 2003: 417, original emphasis).

Through Butler's notion of 'performativity', the immature body can be understood as what Foucault (1978: 154) called 'a fictitious unity', which is as much a matter of culture as is childhood. In other words, we can view 'the "natural" child likewise as "a fiction of coherence and unity" imposed upon "an otherwise random or unrelated set of biological functions, sensations and pleasures"' (Dickenson, 2011: 50, citing Butler, 1996). This understanding of the immature body as fictive, of course, does not imply that no material differences between children and adults exist, yet it challenges social constructionist discourses that cast the binary distinction between adults and children in a pre-discursive domain, situating biological immaturity as 'a bodily given' and, therefore, beyond question. The notion of 'performativity' can help researchers in childhood studies 'to see the child as an effect of the various discourses, institutions and practices that name, regulate and constrain it' (Dickenson, 2011: 63). Butler's (2003: 415) notion of performativity evokes an understanding of the social agent; not as a unified

'I' that does its body, 'a choosing and constituting agent prior to language', but as 'an *object* rather than the subject of constitutive acts'. Or, as Dickenson (2011: 64) formulates it, 'the "doer", in this case the child-subject, is constructed and secured in its position as "child" only by repeatedly citing or "assuming" the cultural norms of childhood'.

However, this emphasis on the 'forcible reiteration of norms' does not mean that infants and young children must be considered as 'completely subject to structures imagined by adults, incapable of asserting any subjectivity' (Gottlieb, 2000: 127). Gottlieb (2000: 127) denounces what she calls the 'missing agency of infants' and pleads for an anthropology of infancy 'premised on a notion that infants themselves be social actors'. She argues that research methods must become attuned to 'somatic modes of communication'. Castañeda (2002: 166) conceptualizes the infant as a 'thoroughly social category and form of embodiment'. She borrows Haraway's (1988: 599) notion of 'the world's active agency', similar to the notion of the 'agency of nature', which is used in the field of science studies, to go beyond both constructionist understandings that ignore any agency outside the social, and bio-essentialist or positivist understandings that reduce nature to a passive object that can be known. Castañeda argues:

> [E]ven an infant is not simply the raw natural material of the future adult subject it will become but rather an entity that is the effect of the agency of nature and the discursive matrix through which it is formed and reformed. The infant 'is' a subject and has subjectivity that is particular to this interaction, such that everything from culturally specific birthing practices to particular modes of embodiment, including racialization, gendering, sexualization, and so on, are constitutive of this entity *as* an infant. What might be called the absence of language here, or rather the presence of particular modes of embodied communication that do not include language per se, does not constitute this entity as pre-subjective in this formulation, and as such it cannot be occupied by adult fantasies or desires. Instead, this entity's existence, and its embodiment are the ground of its subjectivity, where 'subjectivity' signifies embodied experience. (2002: 171)

Using Haraway's (1988) understanding of 'situated knowledges', Castañeda (2002: 170) pleads for a 'different mode of knowing, necessarily partial and situated'. She argues that we cannot fully know the infant as its 'existence is the effect of an agency that is excessive of adult knowledge' and thus implies the impossibility of a total claim on the real (2002: 168).

Another call for rethinking agency has been made by Lee (1998). He criticizes the understandings of agency and subjectivity underlying the sociological accounts of childhood that seek to theorize children and their relationships and cultures 'in their own right' (Prout and James, 1997: 8), considering them as 'already complete enough to be mobilised as causal and/or interpretative agents in sociological account-making' (Lee, 1998: 463). He questions the way these accounts seem to imply that 'the young cannot figure in their own right in sociological theory unless they are understood as somehow "mature" in their possession of agency' (1998: 460). As such, he says, the sociology of childhood remains wedded to neoliberal understandings of agential subjects and choice, in which language and self-representation seem to operate as conditions. He denounces this rhetoric of self-representation, as it keeps privileging the finished and the mature, and pleads for an 'immature sociology'. He argues:

> Rather than have children inhabit the static world of mature sociology, conforming them as a point on which sociologists can stand, immaturity moves sociology into an unfinished world in which the grounds for according privilege to adults, the mature and the finished have been removed. It composes an 'ethics of motion' rather than of position. (Lee, 1998: 474–5)

In other words, instead of having to turn children into adults to be able to conceptualize them as agents, Lee suggests we need to rethink agency. He questions the preference for independence, completion, and 'finishedness' and argues for 'a sensitivity to the dependencies that underlie even the most mature performances of independence' (Lee, 1998: 460).

Lee's view of agency strikes a chord with insights of the feminist ethics of care, which criticize the '"masculinist" ideal of self defined through separation' (Thorne, 1987: 104–5) and, through women's and children's experiences of relatedness, argue for a theorization that begins 'with selves defined through relationships with others, retaining full awareness of social hierarchies' (Thorne, 1987: 104–5). The idea of 'relational autonomy' incorporates 'a notion of autonomy not as opposed to relations with others, but dependent on them' (Hirschmann, 2008: 152). It sees a person (be it a child or an adult) not as 'separate and inherently distinct from all others, but connected through networks of relationships, and through physical, material, psychological, and emotional interdependence' (Hirschmann, 2008: 152). The 'concrete' other (in contrast to the generalized other) 'requires us to view each and every rational being as an individual with a concrete history, identity, and affective-emotional constitution' (Benhabib, 1986: 411) and operates on the principle of the 'relational' self being part of networks of 'care and dependence'.

A PLURALITY OF CHILDHOODS

In the previous section, I presented concepts that enable us to rethink subjectivity and agency, beyond the presumption of the existence of a natural, essential 'child' and of the autonomous, liberal subject, towards conceptualizations of subjectivity and agency as immature and relational. In this section, I explore possible frameworks for the study of the diversity of early childhood experiences that leave space for the agency of children (and their carers), which, however, acknowledge the regulative discourses in which this agency is located. More particularly, I discuss the concepts of intersectionality and superdiversity, and how they have been applied to the study of childhood identities.

Intersectionality originated in the critical writings of Black and so-called 'Third World' feminists in the 1970s, who criticized how White middle-class feminism ignored the differences and different power positions that women face. It was Crenshaw (1991) who coined the term to capture the 'merging and mingling of multiple markers of difference' (Ludvig, 2006: 246) and the way these markers do not act independently of one another, but, on the contrary, inter-relate, make up 'intersections' of multiple forms of discrimination and privilege. The primary focus on the intersection of race and gender shifted in the decades that followed to incorporate a variety of other markers of difference (including age), turning intersectionality into 'a generalized theory of identity' (rather than 'a theory of marginalized subjectivity') (Nash, 2008: 10).

Recently, Vertovec (2007) coined the term 'super-diversity' to grasp the complexity and plurality of identities in the context of globally heightened mobility. This concept, which is similar to the concept of intersectionality, was launched within immigration studies as a reaction against monolithic conceptions of multiculturalism. Vertovec sought to develop a model for understanding the conjunctions and interactions of social variables and inequalities within radically diversifying migration flows, a more adequate model than 'the false transparency and neatness' of multiculturalism (Arnaut, 2012: 4). The term not only seeks to underscore the extensiveness of contemporary mobility and transnationality, both in scale and complexity, but also points to the multidimensional character of diversity (Vertovec, 2007: 1026) and the need, when analysing diversity, to take into account the 'complex simultaneity' (Arnaut, 2012: 5) of the practices and processes of identification.

Although both concepts have been developed in other fields, they are easily transferable to, and have been picked up by, childhood studies. Both approaches resonate with the call within the sociological study of childhood for (1) acknowledging childhood as a variable of social analysis, and (2) analysing childhood as a plural concept, which 'can never be entirely divorced from other variables such as class, gender, or ethnicity' (Prout and James, 1997: 8). Within feminist scholarship, there have been calls for more 'complex analyses that address

multiple structures of domination, particularly those often relegated to the periphery, like age and ability' (Nash, 2010: 1). As such, pleas for 'more intersectionality' (beyond the categories of gender, race, and class) have advanced the visibility of the concerns of children, and the recognition that 'children's social relationships and cultures are worthy of study in their own right' (James and Prout, 1997: 4). On the other hand, accounts of super-diversity and intersectionality have proved to be useful in grasping the diversities of childhood and children's experiences. The concerns voiced by Black women of being marginalized both by feminism and anti-racism resonate with the concerns of, for instance, girls, who tend to be marginalized 'within the category of children as female, and within the category of women as minors' (Taefi, 2009: 345). The concepts of intersectionality and super-diversity enable understandings of the multifaceted and simultaneous intersections of the multiple dimensions of difference that shape young children's worlds.

Nevertheless, the emphasis on multiplicity has also been subject to critiques, one of them the argument that it risks weakening 'the political power of the singular category of childhood' and reducing its 'ability to draw attention to the way in which children everywhere are marginalized and made invisible in social and economic policy' (James, 2010: 488). Some childhood scholars (2010: 487) have warned against placing too much emphasis on plurality, as it risks diverting attention away from childhood as a social category and diminishing the political power of the project of children's rights. This point strikes a chord with more general critiques of the recent trends in research and policy of the depoliticization and 'whitening' of intersectionality by treating it as a universal rule rather than a theory of oppression. The calls for childhood-only approaches are similar to the plea for the strategic use of race-only approaches in critical race studies (Bilge, 2013) on the ground that too much emphasis on plurality undermines the critical and emancipatory potential of intersectionality and super-diversity.

'In an age saturated with a neoliberal culture of diversity' (Bilge, 2013: 407), an image of identities at the intersection of an infinite number of axes runs the risk of toning down the problem of structural discriminations, reinforcing a view of social life as the interaction of individual social entrepreneurs, and depicting identities as optional consumerist choices, merely a question of lifestyle. Moreover, the 'happy' stories that appear in super-diversity studies 'about plurality and non-ranked cultural difference' (Ferguson, 2006: 179), staging immigrants as the cosmopolitan hybrids par excellence, tend to be guilty of 'social romanticism', circumventing profound global inequalities and creating 'an illusion of equality in a highly asymmetrical world' (Makoni, 2012: 193).

James (2010: 494–5) argues for some kind of balance between considering the commonalities and the diversities of childhood and allowing 'our enquiries to range across the entire fabric of childhood studies, from whatever our perspective, without asserting that any one element of the fabric is more important than any other'. Similarly, Yuval-Davis (1999: 95) presents transversal politics as a tool for social movements to move beyond both universalistic politics, which strives for an equalization of rights and identity politics, which emphasizes peculiarities of certain groups. She points to the importance of differences, yet argues that 'notions of difference should encompass rather than replace notions of equality'. While the acknowledgment that identities are 'constituted by the intersection of multiple vectors of power' (Nash, 2008: 10) enables a dynamic and complex understanding of processes of identification, it seems clear that intersectionality and super-diversity, if they seek to theorize identities in a truly complex fashion without losing grip of inequality, need to include 'structure-sensitive notions' (Spotti and Arnaut, 2014: 6) and a sensitivity to the power mechanisms that produce social inequalities. For the study of early childhood in particular, this means that we need to acknowledge both the way in which young age works as an enabling/restraining structural element in the lives of infants and young children and the way in which young age interacts with other social categories, affecting children's individual experiences and agency.

PARENTING YOUNG CHILDREN AS IDENTITY WORK

The notion of 'figuration', coined by Castañeda (2002: 3–4), seems to be very useful for grasping 'the means through which the child is brought into being *as* a figure, as well as the bodies and worlds that this figure generates through a plurality of forms'. Semiotic and material practices, knowledges, and power construe historically, geographically, and culturally specific child figures. In the process, other identities are 'co-constituted with that of the child' (Baird, 2008: 298). With 'the profound transformation in economic and sentimental value of children … between the 1870s and 1930s' (Zelizer, 1985: 3), the rearing of children has become increasingly the domain of policing, moralization, and intense identity work. Several authors (Faircloth et al., 2013; Forsberg, 2009; Furedi, 2008; Hays, 1996) have described how over the last half-century in particular childrearing has dramatically changed and, in middle-class milieus in the Global North, 'an intensified, spatially circumscribed idea of childhood intersects with an ideology of intensive mothering' (Caputo, 2007; Thorne, 2007: 151). Childrearing has become an important frame through which women (and to a lesser extent also men) 'communicate and sustain their identity' (Faircloth, 2009: 15). In this section, I discuss research on parenting cultures that engages with the rearing of young children as identity work. This research focuses upon the ways childrearing and relatedness are enacted 'in conjunction with constructions of the self' (Faircloth, 2009: 15), and how this is done differently from different intersectional positions and contexts.

Feminist historical research has shown how the transition to capitalism increasingly confined women to reproductive labor, labor that, at the same time, became totally devalued (Federici, 2004: 74). Patriarchal 'women-and-children' discourses began to equate women's interests with those of children and relegated both women and children to the private sphere. The hierarchical distinction between public and private realms served to sustain a patriarchal public order, and to justify gender inequality (Fraser, 1990; Lister, 2007; Werbner and Yuval-Davis, 1999). The public became constructed as 'the distinctively human realm in which man transcends his animal nature, while the private realm of the household is seen as the natural region in which women merely reproduce the species' (Held, 1990: 334–5).

Gradually, women (and children) came to be defined as non-workers and their work at home as non-work (Federici, 2004: 92). The process of 'domestication of middle-class women in the nineteenth century' (Zelizer, 1985: 9) and the growing importance of the family as a distinct realm more generally, went hand in hand with a dramatic shift in children's value. Children were increasingly seen as 'economically "worthless" but emotionally "priceless"' (Zelizer, 1985: 3). As Furedi (2008: 40) argues, 'babies and infants are seen today as both intensely vulnerable and highly impressionable – above all to parental influences'. Children, young children, in particular, are seen as incompetent and totally dependent on the care of adults. They are predominantly valued for their potentiality (Burman and Stacey, 2010; Cockburn, 2005), and the maximum development of that potentiality is considered mainly the mothers' responsibility. This view goes hand in hand with 'the construction of the special site of "home" as the appropriate place for children, their exclusion from paid work and segregation into educational establishments, and the construction of particular dedicated public places such as playgrounds' (Ribbens McCarthy et al., 2000: 788). Owing to gendered divisions of labor, cultural expectations and norms (Park, 2006: 207), and a breakdown in adult solidarity (Faircloth, 2013: 215), mothers are disproportionally held responsible for parenting (Lewis and Lamb, 2003; Ruddick, 1997: 216), especially when their children are very young (Ruddick, 1997: 206).

The expansion of childrearing in societies in the Global North to an intensive and highly interventionist enterprise in which every dimension of children's lives is dramatized goes hand in hand with an enhanced influence of expert knowledge, which has become increasingly influential in policy and discourse about children and families (and in early childhood programs in particular). Foucault (2003: 239) uses the term 'bio-power' to refer to the ways the state interferes by means of 'subtle coercion' (Foucault, 1977: 137), making use of a range of technologies, knowledges, and discourses to analyze, control, and regulate human bodies and populations (Murphy, 2003: 434–5) and turn parents into self-regulating subjects. Psychologized and medicalized expert discourses, and associated normalizing judgments, construct a framework that is generally considered morally neutral and beyond power and politics. While messages and guidelines on how parents should care for their children often have powerful moral dimensions, they are often presented as health issues (Faircloth, 2013; Lee, 2007; Ramaekers and Suissa, 2012). In dominant discourses on childrearing, this framework is thought to touch the heart of how things just are (or at least as science at this precise moment knows how things are) and seems to exist beyond human subjectivity, power, or ideology. Within this framework, certain child behavior, certain parenting practices, certain ways of family building, certain ways of raising children are identified as (psychologically) healthy, as normal, and therefore as legitimate. At the same time, other practices are dismissed as psychologically unhealthy or even dangerous for a child (Murphy, 2003: 437). 'Technologies of subjectification' encourage people to locate themselves within particular psychological discourses and to subject themselves to dominant norms (Castañeda and Campbell, 2006; Rose, 1999).

Psychological concepts, such as 'development' and 'infant determinism', have dominated the discourse (and much of the study) of children. Looking at children through the psychological lens of development has contributed to a view of the child as going through 'maturational stages' that need particular forms of care and attention (Ribbens McCarthy and Edwards, 2011). This conceptualization of childhood as a 'natural' succession of predictable and universal phases inevitably creates categories of 'abnormal' children. Children tend to be scrutinized in every possible way and when their development or behavior deviates from what is considered normal, they are deemed 'in need of correction, usually through medical or "scientific intervention"' (Heydon and Iannacci, 2008: 1). The cause of deviation is largely sought in early childhood, or more specifically, in the way the child has been treated by her carers. 'Infant determinism' (Kagan, 1998: 3) defines early childhood (and even experiences in the womb) as the most crucial period in life in which, proponents of this theory claim, the foundations of a (sound) human personality are built (Cunningham, 2005; Ramaekers and Suissa, 2012; Zelizer, 1985). As a consequence, it is the carers' responsibility to accomplish a positive outcome.

While infant determinism has been dismissed as a myth (Kagan, 1998), it remains unwaveringly persistent as an explanatory frame when children exhibit 'deviant' behavior or psychological distress. It has also heavily influenced current conceptions of 'good' parenthood, and constructions of middle-class parental/maternal identities in the Global North. Further, although normality is generated from 'Western', 'first world', and middle-class contexts, developmental discourses and infant determinism have come to regulate and stigmatize children who live in other contexts, as well as the caring and parental practices of their parents (Burman and Stacey, 2010). Pathologizing discourses are structured by power relations (it is the people of the least powerful groups that are considered abnormal by the more powerful) (Heydon and Iannacci,

2008: 3) and are part of the 'long-established practices of regulation of the poor and the masses' (Walkerdine, 2000: 21). Critical studies have uncovered it as a mode of colonization (Heydon and Iannacci, 2008: 4) or 'intimate colonialism' (Summers, 1991), aimed at controlling the personal lives of colonial subjects (Lock and Nguyen, 2010).

What is more, mothering, as Faircloth (2013: 3) notes, is increasingly understood as 'a vehicle for personal fulfilment for women'. The 'scientific account of parenting' (Ramaekers and Suissa, 2012: 3) made mothering/parenting increasingly part of women's identity narratives (and to a lesser extent men's, as hegemonic masculinity tends to depict men as workers first, parents second (Wall and Arnold, 2007)). These identity narratives are fashioned by the women's choice for a particular child-raising method and their negotiations of normative ('Western', middle class) parenting scripts and of the available discourses on children and childrearing.

A growing body of research focuses on parenting identities and maternal subjectivity in Euro-American, middle-class contexts (Faircloth, 2014; Forsberg, 2009; Ramaekers and Suissa, 2012), describing and analyzing a range of parenting styles that can be subsumed under the rubric of 'intensive motherhood' (Hays, 1996; O'Brien Hallstein, 2006). This work shows how seemingly mundane tasks such as feeding and nursing small children have become closely tied to maternal identity work, operating 'as a highly moralized signifier dividing women into different camps along purported axes of child-centred or mother-centred forms of care' (Faircloth, 2013: 4).

These studies uncover 'intensive motherhood' as the hegemonic parenting model in Euro-American contexts. However, this hegemonic position does not imply that it is the only model or that it is followed in practice by all parents (Hays, 1996: 21). In sociology and anthropology, there is an increasing interest in the childrearing ideas and practices of other groups, such as the poor, the working classes, and immigrant groups (Berry, 2013; Erel, 2011; Vandenbroeck et al., 2009).

This body of research discusses the ways dominant childrearing ideologies are negotiated by parents in a diverse range of contexts and from different intersectional positions. These studies show that parenting is 'a globalising set of ideas and practices that cannot be separated from considerations of global power inequities' (Faircloth et al., 2013: 4). Some of these studies demonstrate how the decontextualized and purported neutral and technical discourses of expert-led, skills-based parenting can be used 'to whitewash the dangerous power dynamics inherent in current constructions of "good" parenting' (Berry, 2013: 87) and to devalue the parenting skills of low-income or immigrant parents (Berry, 2013). Other studies lay bare the ways in which parenting can be a site of resistance, confrontation, and citizenship work. The next section focuses on this political potential by presenting academic debates on the agential capacity of childrearing and its potential to affect inclusivity and recognition.

THE POLITICAL POTENTIAL OF CHILDREARING

Classic conceptualizations of citizenship situated women and their activities of bearing and rearing children (i.e., producing citizens) and 'subsidizing the welfare state through unpaid reproductive and care work in the home' outside the political arena and apart from citizenship (Erel, 2011: 696). 'Malestream' citizenship theory systematically lauded participation in the public sphere, such as paid work and political participation, at the expense of labor within the private sphere, such as childrearing and domestic labor. The strong dualism between the public and the private, which has traditionally grounded a male-oriented citizenship, has been deconstructed by feminist critics (Fraser, 1990; Lister, 1997; Porter, 2001). They revealed the strong intertwining of private decisions and practices with public institutions and state policies (Oleksy, 2009:

4) and called attention to the ways in which the work traditionally done by women is equally constitutive of citizenship as the tasks traditionally performed by men.

Discussions on the status of parenting work in the pursuit and performance of citizenship have often been polarized between advocates of the recognition of difference and advocates of the right to equality (Pateman, 1992). Maternalist views, on the one hand, tended to exalt motherhood as a political status as such, 'a major vehicle of women's incorporation into the political order' (Pateman, 1992: 19) (and thus as a source of citizenship for women). On the other hand, so-called equality feminism criticized the maternalists' emphasis on women's difference and their tendency to reduce female identity to motherhood. Moreover, they pleaded for defending political values, such as 'freedom, equality and community power' for both men and women (Dietz, 1985: 34).

Pateman (1992: 25), in trying to move beyond the difference–equality dichotomy, argues that 'for citizenship to be of equal worth, the substance of equality must differ according to the diverse circumstances and capacities of citizens, men and women'. Also, Lister (2007: 52) argues for conceptualizing citizenship towards more pluralization, 'without sacrificing citizenship's universalist emancipatory promise as expressed in the ideals of inclusion, participation and equal moral worth'. Moreover, rethinking citizenship requires understanding it not only as a status (legal membership of a nation-state), but also as a practice, which involves the social, political, cultural, and symbolic practices of making citizens (Isin and Nielsen, 2008: 17). Studying citizenship as a practice enables us to see the dialogical and relational aspects of citizenship and its inflection by a range of social and cultural factors such as identity, social status, cultural presuppositions, and belonging (Lister, 2007; Werbner and Yuval-Davis, 1999: 4). Lister (2007: 55) argues for a multi-tiered analysis that includes not only the nation-state, but also 'the intimate and domestic, the local, the urban, the regional and the global'.

While a growing number of studies treat parenting practices as constitutive of citizenship, the question of *how* they constitute citizenship is the subject of ongoing discussion (Erel, 2011; Kershaw, 2010; Lister, 2007; Longman et al., 2013). More particularly, feminist scholars differ in their view of whether care should count as political citizenship or merely as 'a resource for citizenship and an expression of social citizenship responsibility' (Lister, 2007: 56). Lister (2007: 56) defends the position that parenting work 'should be acknowledged as an expression of social citizenship responsibilities and should be accorded equal value with paid work obligations'. While Lister situates the value of parenting work in its *civic* contribution, Kershaw (2010) argues that in some cases parenting may constitute a form of *political* citizenship as well. He provides the example of ethnic minority mothers whose care work must compensate for messages within the public sphere that tend to brand their children as less valuable (Kershaw, 2010: 396). To enforce his argument, he refers to the work of Hill Collins (1994), who describes how the mothering work of women of color 'reflects the tensions inherent in trying to foster a meaningful racial identity in children within a society that denigrates people of color' (Collins, 1994: 57). Kershaw (2010) points out that what he calls 'caregiving for identity' (or what Collins (1994: 57) refers to as 'motherwork for identity') is a political act of resistance and citizenship that stretches beyond the homes in which the work is performed and contributes to a broader political project of community development (Kershaw, 2010: 396).

Erel (2011) draws attention to the ambiguous position of migrant mothers in the discussion of the paradoxical inclusion/exclusion of mothers as citizens. How to conceptualize the mothering work of women who are 'positioned near the boundary of citizenship' within multi-ethnic societies of present-day nation-states? Recognizing their work as citizenship work, and seeing them 'not simply as outsiders to citizenship, but as constitutive of the gendered and ethnicized boundaries of citizenship', Erel (2011: 696) argues, 'raises the question of how plural ethnic identities can relate to citizenship identities'. She describes how migrant mothers construct complex identities and belongings for themselves and their children and that their 'culture work' should not simply be seen as a failure to adapt to the 'universalized identity assumed to be neutral in the country of residence' (2011: 698). She points to strategies of cultural resistance to racism, but also to ways of constructing themselves as competent mothers in their narratives of good citizenship (for other examples of resisting dominant parenting ideologies, see Jaysane-Darr, 2013; Jiménez Sedano, 2013).

In constituting the kind of parenting work that is able to count as an act of political citizenship, Kershaw (2010: 403) tends to impose as a condition that parents act from a 'politicized attitude of mind through which they contemplate the wider impact of their activities'. Others (Longman et al., 2013) broaden this scope by pointing to the inherently political character of all parenting work, even when this work is performed unconsciously and from (partly) privileged positions. The work parents carry out consists both of 'practices' that tend to confirm the status quo of power positions and are often performed unconsciously, and of conscious 'acts of citizenship' that are able to cause social transformation (see Isin and Nielsen, 2008: 18). Longman et al. (2013) believe that mothers/parents and unconscious practice as well as their conscious acts, which may disrupt habitus (Isin and Nielsen, 2008: 18), can be analyzed as political citizenship work, in that they count as political interventions that affect power relations, both by reinforcing existing power structures and by challenging them. They show how the mothers in their study engage in creative practices of care work and empowering of their children, which both reproduce and contest hegemonic norms of belonging. They argue that 'the mothers want for themselves and their children to be recognized as formal and "good" citizens, [while] at the same time they are forging new and often hybrid subjectivities that disrupt those normative categories of identity and who counts as the normal or ideal citizen' (Longman et al., 2013: 391).

Although in a slightly different vein, drawing conclusions from their analysis of contemporary dominant parenting discourses in the Global North, Ramaekers and Suissa (2012) plead for a re-politicization of the family as well. They believe that what they call the 'scientisation of the parentchild relationship' (Ramaekers and Suissa, 2010), characterized by a language saturated with psychological terminology and a fixation on expertise and professionalization, 'strips childrearing of its potential for offering political experiences' and 'downplays the possibility of action' (Ramaekers and Suissa, 2012: 146). Therefore, they advocate opening up the arena of childrearing in a way which allows the ethical, existential, and political dimensions of childrearing to come to the fore (2012: 147).

CONCLUSION

In this chapter, I have presented some of the ongoing scholarly debates that have important implications for the study of young children, the cultures of care in which they are embedded, and the identities that are performed within these cultures. The theoretical perspectives presented here can contribute to the development of a critical framework for rethinking the field of early childhood and education, and for critically evaluating the advice and curriculum production it yields.

Insights from studies that critically engage with gender, disability, sexuality, ethnicity, and other social differences clearly contribute to a more complex and diversified view of childhoods, away from the universalist assumptions that often underlie studies in the field of early childhood care and education. It seems crucial that the study of early childhood takes into account not only the specificity of the situation of being a young child and the figurations of early childhood that circulate and shape young children's lives, but also looks at the way other markers of difference intersect to oppress and/or privilege both children and adults who relate to them.

Moreover, a focus on the identity work that is undertaken by both children and their caregivers enhances the understanding of children as active agents who have actual experiences. This is in contrast to earlier views of children, and young children in particular, in terms of their potentiality and as merely passive subjects of social processes and structures. However, a view of identities as performative and contextual enactments and of agency as relational and immature may also contribute to more recent re-evaluations of notions of dependency and becoming for children's lives and human existence more generally.

Finally, it seems important for the study of early childhood to be aware of the power relations that structure children's experiences and identity work (and the identity work that occurs around them), with the capacity for both reproducing and contesting hegemonic norms of belonging. But it is equally important to be reflexive about the power relations that structure research and how science is used in processes of objectification and de-politicization in early childhood and family policies. Conceptualizing parenting as inherently political further elucidates the interdependence of the public and private sphere and expounds parenting as 'a dual process of self-making and being-made within webs of power linked to the nation-state and civil society' (Ong, 1996). Acknowledging the political nature of the rearing of (young) children can offer novel avenues for the field of early childhood, as it can improve our understanding of how young children's lives are closely intertwined with different kinds of identity work that try to carve out spaces for belonging and recognition in a context of differential power and inequality.

FURTHER READING

Castañeda, C. (2002) *Figurations: Child, Bodies, Worlds*. Durham, NC: Duke University Press.
Faircloth, C., Hoffman, D. and Layne L. (2013) *Parenting in Global Perspective: Negotiating*

Ideologies of Kinship, Self and Politics. London; New York: Routledge.

Ramaekers, S. and Suissa, J. (2012) *The Claims of Parenting: Reasons, Responsibility and Society*. Dordrecht: Springer.

QUESTIONS FOR REFLECTION

1   In what concrete ways can an intersectional approach be integrated in the study of early childhood?
2   How can research and policy move away from the objectified medical-scientific accounts of early childhood and care? Is there a need for a radically different vocabulary?
3   How can we be sensitive, when studying young children, to the researcher's own positionality and the power inequalities that arise in the research process?

REFERENCES

Arnaut, K. (2012) 'Super-diversity: Elements of an Emerging Perspective', *Diversities*, 14(2): 1–16.

Baird, B. (2008) 'Child Politics, Feminist Analyses', *Australian Feminist Studies*, 23(57): 291–305.

Benhabib, S. (1986) *The Generalized and the Concrete Other: The Kohlberg-Gilligan Controversy and Feminist Theory in Feminism as Critique*. Oxford: Blackwell.

Berry, N. S. (2013) 'Problem Parents? Undocumented Migrants in America's New South and the Power Dynamics of Parenting Advice', in C. Faircloth, D. M. Hoffman and L. L. Layne (eds) *Parenting in Global Perspective: Negotiating Ideologies of Kinship, Self and Politics*. London; New York: Routledge. pp. 86–100.

Bilge, S. (2010) 'Beyond Subordination vs. Resistance: An Intersectional Approach to the Agency of Veiled Muslim Women', *Journal of Intercultural Studies*, 31(1): 9–28.

Bilge, S. (2013) 'Intersectionality Undone', *Du Bois Review: Social Science Research on Race*, 10(2): 405–24.

Bourdieu, P. (1990) *The Logic of Practice*. Cambridge: Polity Press.

Brubaker, R. and Cooper, F. (2000) 'Beyond "Identity"', *Theory and Society*, 29:1–47.

Burman, E. and Stacey, J. (2010) 'The Child and Childhood in Feminist Theory', *Feminist Theory*, 11(3): 227–40.

Butler, J. (2003) 'Performative Acts and Gender Constitution: An Essay in Phenomenology and Feminist Theory', in C. R. McCann and S.-K. Kim (eds) *Feminist Theory Reader: Local and Global Perspectives*. New York: Routledge. pp. 415–27.

Butler, J. (2006) *Gender Trouble: Feminism and the Subversion of Identity*. London: Routledge.

Caputo, V. (2007) 'She's from a "Good Family": Performing Childhood and Motherhood in a Canadian Private School Setting', *Childhood*, 14(2): 173–92.

Castañeda, C. (2002) *Figurations: Child, Bodies, Worlds*. Durham, NC: Duke University Press.

Castañeda, L. and Campbell, S. B. (2006) *News and Sexuality: Media Portraits of Diversity*. Thousand Oaks, CA: SAGE.

Chambers, C. (2008) *Sex, Culture, and Justice: The Limits of Choice*. University Park, PA: Pennsylvania State University Press.

Cockburn, T. (2005) 'Children and the Feminist Ethic of Care', *Childhood*, 12(1): 71–89.

Collins, P. H. (1994) 'Shifting the Center: Race, Class, and Feminist Theorizing about Motherhood', in E. N. Glenn, G. Chang and L. R. Forcey (eds) *Mothering: Ideology, Experience, and Agency*. New York: Routledge. pp. 45–65.

Crenshaw, K. (1991) 'Mapping the margins: Intersectionality, identity politics, and violence against women of color', *Stanford Law Review*, 43(6): 1241–99.

Cunningham, H. (2005) *Children and Childhood in Western Society since 1500*. Harlow; New York: Pearson Longman.

Dickenson, D. (2011) 'Performing Childhood: Media, Childhood and Identity'. PhD dissertation, Faculty of Human Sciences, Dept. of Education, Macquarie University, Sydney.

Dietz, M. G. (1985) 'Citizenship with a Feminist Face: The Problem with Maternal Thinking', *Political Theory*, 13(1): 19–37.

Erel, U. (2011) 'Reframing Migrant Mothers as Citizens', *Citizenship Studies*, 15: 695–709.

Faircloth, C. (2009) 'Mothering as Identity-Work: Long-term Breastfeeding and Intensive Motherhood', *Anthropology News*, 50(2): 15–17.

Faircloth, C. (2013) *Militant Lactivism? Attachment Parenting and Intensive Motherhood in the UK and France*. New York: Berghahn Books.

Faircloth, C. (2014) 'Intensive Parenting and the Expansion of Parenting', in E. Lee, J. Bristow, C. Faircloth and J. Macvarish (eds) *Parenting Culture Studies*. Basingstoke: Palgrave Macmillan. pp. 25–50.

Faircloth, C., Hoffman, D. M. and Layne, L. L. (2013) 'Introduction', in C. Faircloth, D. M. Hoffman and L. L. Layne (eds) *Parenting in Global Perspective: Negotiating Ideologies of Kinship, Self and Politics*. London; New York: Routledge. pp. 1–17.

Federici, S. (2004) *Caliban and the Witch: Women, the Body and Primitive Accumulation*. New York: Autonomedia.

Ferguson, J. (2006) 'Decomposing Modernity: History and Hierarchy after Development', in A. Loomba (ed.) *Postcolonial Studies and Beyond*. Durham, NC: Duke University Press. pp. 166–81.

Forsberg, L. (2009) 'Involved Parenthood: Everyday Lives of Swedish Middle-class Families', in C. Faircloth, D. M. Hoffman and L. L. Layne (2013) *Parenting in Global Perspective: Negotiating Ideologies of Kinship, Self and Politics*. London; New York: Routledge.

Foucault, M. (1977) *Discipline and Punish: The Birth of the Prison*. New York: Pantheon Books.

Foucault, M. (1978) *The History of Sexuality*. New York: Pantheon Books.

Foucault, M. (2003) *Society Must Be Defended: Lectures at the Collège De France, 1975–76*. New York: Picador.

Fraser, N. (1990) 'Rethinking the Public Sphere: A Contribution to the Critique of Actually Existing Democracy', *Social Text*, 25/26: 56–80.

Furedi, F. (2008) *Paranoid Parenting: Why Ignoring the Experts May Be Best for Your Child*. London: Continuum.

Gottlieb, A. (2000) 'Where Have All the Babies Gone? Toward an Anthropology of Infants (and their Caretakers)', *Anthropological Quarterly*, 73(3): 121–32.

Haraway, D. (1988) 'Situated Knowledges: The Science Question in Feminism and the Privilege of Partial Perspective', *Feminist Studies*, 14(3): 575–99.

Hays, S. (1996) *The Cultural Contradictions of Motherhood*. New Haven, CT: Yale University Press.

Held, V. (1990) 'Feminist Transformations of Moral Theory', *Philosophy and Phenomenological Research*, 50: 321–44.

Heydon, R. and Iannacci, L. (2008) *Early Childhood Curricula and the De-Pathologizing of Childhood*. Toronto; Buffalo: University of Toronto Press.

Hirschmann, N. J. (2008) 'Feminist Political Philosophy', in L. M. Alcoff and E. F. Kittay (eds) *The Blackwell Guide to Feminist Philosophy*. Oxford: Wiley-Blackwell. pp. 145–64.

Isin, E. F. and Nielsen, G. M. (2008) *Acts of Citizenship*. London: Zed Books.

Isin, E. F. and Wood, P. K. (1999) *Citizenship and Identity*. London: SAGE.

James, A. L. (2010) 'Competition or Integration? The Next Step in Childhood Studies?', *Childhood*, 17(4): 485–99.

James, A. and Prout, A. (1997) 'Introduction', in A. James and A. Prout (eds) *Constructing and Reconstructing Childhood: Contemporary Issues in the Sociological Study of Childhood*. London: Falmer Press. pp. 1–6.

Jaysane-Darr, A. (2013) 'Nurturing Sudanese, Producing Americans: Refugee Parents and Personhood', in C. Faircloth, D. M. Hoffman and L. L. Layne (eds) *Parenting in Global Perspective: Negotiating Ideologies of Kinship, Self and Politics*. Abingdon; New York: Routledge. pp. 101–16.

Jiménez Sedano, L. (2013) '"Spanish People don't Know how to Rear their Children!" Dominican Women's Resistance to Intensive Mothering in Madrid', in C. Faircloth, D. M. Hoffman and L. L. Layne (eds) *Parenting in Global Perspective: Negotiating Ideologies of Kinship, Self and Politics*. Abingdon; New York: Routledge. pp. 169–83.

Kagan, J. (1998) *Three Seductive Ideas*. Cambridge, MA: Harvard University Press.

Kershaw, P. (2010) 'Caregiving for Identity is Political: Implications for Citizenship Theory', *Citizenship Studies*, 14(4): 395–410.

Lee, E. (2007) 'Health, Morality, and Infant Feeding: British Mothers' Experiences of Formula Milk Use in the Early Weeks', *Sociology of Health & Illness*, 29(7): 1075–90.

Lee, N. (1998) 'Towards an Immature Sociology', *The Sociological Review*, 46(3): 458–81.

Lewis, C. and Lamb, M. E. (2003) 'Fathers' Influences on Children's Development: The Evidence from Two-Parent Families',

European Journal of Psychology of Education, XVIII: 211–28.

Lister, R. (1997) 'Citizenship: Towards a Feminist Synthesis', *Feminist Review*, 57: 28–48.

Lister, R. (2007) 'Inclusive Citizenship: Realizing the Potential', *Citizenship Studies*, 11: 49–62.

Lock, M. and Nguyen, V.-K. (2010) *An Anthropology of Biomedicine*. Malden, MA: Wiley-Blackwell.

Longman, C., De Graeve, K. and Brouckaert, T. (2013) 'Mothering as a Citizenship Practice: An Intersectional Analysis of "Carework" and "Culturework" in Non-Normative Mother–Child Identities', *Citizenship Studies*, 17: 385–99.

Ludvig, A. (2006) 'Differences between Women? Intersecting Voices in a Female Narrative', *European Journal of Women's Studies*, 13: 245–58.

Makoni, S. B. (2012) 'A Critique of Language, Languaging and Supervernacular', *Muitas Vozes*, 1: 189–99.

Malkki, L. H. (1992) 'National Geographic: The Rooting of Peoples and the Territorialization of National Identity among Scholars and Refugees', *Cultural Anthropology*, 7: 24–44.

McNay, L. (2000) *Gender and Agency: Reconfiguring the Subject in Feminist and Social Theory*. Cambridge: Polity Press.

Murphy, E. (2003) 'Expertise and Forms of Knowledge in the Government of Families', *The Sociological Review*, 51: 433–62.

Nash, J. (2008) 'Re-thinking Intersectionality', *Feminist Review*, 89: 1–15.

Nash, J. (2010) 'On Difficulty: Intersectionality and Feminist Labor', *S&F Online*, 8: 1–7.

O'Brien Hallstein, L. (2006) 'Conceiving Intensive Mothering', *Journal of the Association for Research on Mothering*, 8: 96–108.

Oleksy, E. H. (2009) 'Citizenship Revisited', in E. H. Oleksy (ed.) *Intimate Citizenships: Gender, Sexualities, Politics*. New York: Routledge. pp. 1–13.

Ong, A. (1996) 'Cultural Citizenship as Subject-Making: Immigrants Negotiate Racial and Cultural Boundaries in the United States', *Current Anthropology*, 37: 737–62.

Ortner, S. B. (1989) *High Religion: A Cultural and Political History of Sherpa Buddhism*. Princeton, NJ: Princeton University Press.

Park, S. M. (2006) 'Adoptive Maternal Bodies: A Queer Paradigm for Rethinking Mothering?', *Hypatia*, 21: 201–27.

Pateman, C. (1992) 'Equality, Difference, Subordination: The Politics of Motherhood and Women's Citizenship', in G. Bock and S. James (eds) *Beyond Equality and Difference: Citizenship, Feminist Politics, and Female Subjectivity*. London; New York: Routledge. pp. 14–27.

Porter, E. (2001) 'Interdependence, Parenting and Responsible Citizenship', *Journal of Gender Studies*, 10: 5–15.

Prins, B. (2006) 'Narrative Accounts of Origins a Blind Spot in the Intersectional Approach?', *European Journal of Women's Studies*, 13: 277–90.

Prout, A. and James, A. (1997) 'A New Paradigm for the Sociology of Childhood? Provenance, Promise and Problems', in A. James and A. Prout (eds) *Constructing and Reconstructing Childhood: Contemporary Issues in the Sociological Study of Childhood*, 2nd edn. London; New York: Routledge. pp. 7–33.

Ramaekers, S. and Suissa, J. (2010) 'The Scientization of the Parent–Child Relationship', in L. Hopkins, M. Macleod and W. C. Turgeon (eds) *Negotiating Childhood*. Oxford: Inter-Disciplinary Press.

Ramaekers, S. and Suissa, J. (2012) *The Claims of Parenting: Reasons, Responsibility and Society*. Dordrecht: Springer.

Ribbens McCarthy, J. and Edwards, R. (2011) *Key Concepts in Family Studies*. London: SAGE.

Ribbens McCarthy, J., Edwards, R. and Gillies, V. (2000) 'Moral Tales of the Child and the Adult: Narratives of Contemporary Family Lives under Changing Circumstances', *Sociology*, 34: 785–803.

Rose, N. (1999) *Governing the Soul: The Shaping of the Private Self*. London: Free Association Books.

Ruddick, S. (1997) 'The Idea of Fatherhood', in L. H. Nelson (ed.) *Feminism and Families*. New York: Routledge. pp. 205–20.

Seymour, S. (2006) 'Resistance', *Anthropological Theory*, 6: 303–21.

Spotti, M. and Arnaut, K. (2014) 'Super-Diversity Discourse', *Working Papers in Urban Language and Literacies*, paper 122.

Summers, C. (1991) 'Intimate Colonialism: The Imperial Production of Reproduction in Uganda, 1907–1925', *Signs*, 16: 787–807.

Taefi, N. (2009) 'The Synthesis of Age and Gender: Intersectionality, International Human Rights Law and the Marginalisation of the Girl-Child', *The International Journal of Children's Rights*, 17: 345–76.

Thorne, B. (1987) 'Re-Visioning Women and Social Change: Where Are the Children?', *Gender and Society*, 1: 85–109.

Thorne, B. (2007) 'Editorial: Crafting the Interdisciplinary Field of Childhood Studies', *Childhood,* 14: 147–52.

Vandenbroeck, M., Roets, G. and Snoeck, A. (2009) 'Immigrant Mothers Crossing Borders: Nomadic Identities and Multiple Belongings in Early Childhood Education', *European Early Childhood Education Research Journal*, 17: 203–16.

Vertovec, S. (2007) 'Super-Diversity and its Implications', *Ethnic & Racial Studies*, 30: 1024–54.

Walkerdine, V. (2000) 'Violent Boys and Precocious Girls: Regulating Childhood at the End of the Millennium', *Contemporary Issues in Early Childhood*, 1: 3–22.

Wall, G. and Arnold, S. (2007) 'How Involved is Involved Fathering? An Exploration of the Contemporary Culture of Fatherhood', *Gender & Society*, 21: 508–27.

Werbner, P. and Yuval-Davis, N. (1999) 'Introduction: Women and the New Discourse of Citizenship', in P. Werbner and N. Yuval-Davis (eds) *Women, Citizenship and Difference*. London: Zed Books.

Yuval-Davis, N. (1999) 'What is "Transversal Politics"?', *Soundings*, 12: 94–8.

Yuval-Davis, N. (2010) 'Theorizing Identity: Beyond the "Us" and "Them" Dichotomy', *Patterns of Prejudice*, 44: 261–80.

Zelizer, V. A. (1985) *Pricing the Priceless Child: The Changing Social Value of Children*. New York: Basic Books.

8

Theorizing Young Children's Spaces

Lesley Anne Gallacher

INTRODUCTION

In this chapter, I consider how we might theorize and engage with the spaces in which young children live their lives. I begin (in the next section) by considering the particular spatial arrangements that we, as a society, make for young children. I consider the various purposes that the spaces we (as a society and as individual adults) provide *for young children* are supposed to serve and how these relate to adult agendas for early childhood. However, young children are not passively molded by these spaces; they are able to participate in and contribute to the ongoing social life of the spaces they inhabit. With this in mind, section three counterposes the idea of *spaces for young children* with a notion of *young children's spaces*, which emphasizes the active role young children play in the world around them. In doing so, this section starts to rethink everyday understandings of space as an inert container for social life and instead emphasizes that spaces are relational, heterogeneous and

always under construction through new practices, interactions and processes.

Nonetheless, I am wary of side-lining the material aspects of spaces (and of young children themselves) in favor of the social, political, cultural and ethical relations that compose them. Therefore, section four reconsiders the materiality of young children's spaces. I draw upon examples from young children's motor skills development to explore how the material and the biological are inextricably intertwined with the social and cultural, such that it is impossible to separate out young children from the environments in which they live. As such, I argue that young children do not simply come to inhabit spaces but that those spaces also come to inhabit young children in myriad ways. In the final section, I consider the implications of thinking about young children's inhabitation of space for how we understand embodiment, agency and subjectivity and what this might mean for future study in early childhood.

Research on young children's spaces tends to come from within early childhood education and, as a result, much emphasis has been placed on the environments in which young children learn. This literature considers issues such as the quality of learning environments (e.g., Walsh and Gardner, 2005) and children's experiences within them (e.g., Greenfield, 2004; Clark, 2007). Children's geographers have also considered the spaces of early childhood education (e.g., Gallacher, 2005; Gallagher, 2013; Jupp, 2013). More recently, attention has spread to children's experiences in other educational environments, such as to Hackett's work on museum spaces (2014). However, spaces associated with early childhood are not simply educational; researchers have also considered the purposes and children's experiences of playgrounds (e.g., Ward, 1990; Gagen, 2000) and the spaces of home for young children (e.g., Luzia, 2011; Cieraad, 2013). The examples given in this chapter reflect this wider literature on early childhood spaces insofar as they predominantly focus on the minority world. Focusing on young children's inhabitation of space highlights the material and cultural specificity of young children and early childhood in other places and, therefore, suggests that there is a need for more empirical research on the peculiarities of early childhood in majority world contexts.

SPACES FOR YOUNG CHILDREN

Chris Jenks (2005) has likened children to weeds. Plants designated as 'weeds' are not necessarily problematic in themselves; the problem is that they are 'growing in the wrong place' (2005: 74). Similarly, children become particularly noticeable – and are viewed as more or less problematic – depending upon where they are. Children are very often placed in specially designated settings, such as (pre-)schools, their own bedrooms or play parks. As Jenks explains:

> Childhood, then, is that status of personhood which is by definition often in the wrong place, like the parental bedroom, Daddy's chair, the public house or even crossing a busy road. All people in any society are subject to geographical and spatial prohibitions, whether delineated by discretion, private possession or political embargo, but the child's experience of such parameters is particularly paradoxical, often unprincipled and certainly erratic. In terms of social space children are sited, insulated and distanced, and their very gradual emergence into wider, adult space is by accident, by degrees, as an award or as part of a gradualist rite de passage. (2005: 74)

Children may not be uniquely noticeable in relation to their location (other social groups have similarly weed-like characteristics), but spatial prohibitions and limitations do seem to be particularly fundamental to children's experiences. This is perhaps even more the case for young children, who have not yet completed as much of this 'rite of passage' process as older children.

David Sibley explains that socio-spatial orders are maintained through a range of practices and 'curious rituals' (1995: 72). The environments in which we live privilege and support certain social groups while, at the same time, marginalizing others. On the whole, space tends to be understood as 'adult territory' (Jenks, 2005: 74). This is particularly the case in relation to so-called 'public spaces'. While older children and young people's activities in public space are very often viewed with suspicion – they are all too often perceived to be 'up to no good' simply because they are young people (Weller, 2003) – young children are more likely to be perceived as vulnerable in relation to a wide range of dangers in public space. Fears about 'stranger dangers' and busy road conditions, among other things, mean that young children are very often prevented from accessing public spaces alone and are encouraged and expected to spend time in their homes or in specially provided spaces in which they can be kept safe and supervised by adults. It is not so much that young children are a reviled presence in public spaces, although that can sometimes be the case (see, for example, Giroux, 2001). Instead, common parental practices work to create the idea that public space is 'naturally' or 'normally' an adult space and that young children's presence there needs to be carefully managed (Valentine, 1996; Lupton, 2014).

When we think of 'young children's spaces', then, we are likely to think of those spaces that adults produce and provide in order to nurture and protect young children Such *spaces for young children* include the nursery school, young children's bedrooms at home, playgrounds in public parks, and commercial spaces like soft play centers. These spaces might appear to be absolutely benign spaces in which young children can play. However, George Sternlieb insists that they constitute a kind of 'quarantine' in which children must conform to a whole set of adult-imposed roles for behavior and which govern what constitutes 'proper play'. He gives the examples of the sandbox or sandpit within a playground in a public park:

> A sandbox is a place where adults park their children in order to converse, play or work with a minimum of interference. The adults having found a distraction for the children can get on with the serious things of life. There is some reward for the children in all this. The sandbox is given to them as their own turf. Occasionally, fresh sand or toys are put in this sandbox, along with an implicit admonition that these things are furnished to minimize the level of noise and nuisance. If the children do become noisy and distract their parents, fresh toys may be brought. If the occupants of the sandbox choose sides and start bashing each other over the head, the adults will come running, smack the juniors more or less indiscriminately, calm things down and then, perhaps in an act of semi-contrition, bring fresh sand and fresh toys, pat the occupants of the sandbox on the head, and disappear once again into their adult involvement and pursuits. (quoted in Ward, 1990: 176)

For Sternlieb, the sandbox appears to function to ensure that children do not interfere with the 'real' business of city life, which is undertaken by the adults around them. But these spaces are far more than simply 'fenced-off child ghettoes' (Ward, 1990); specialized spaces provided for young children represent a variety of adult visions of and agendas for early childhood (Laris, 2005; Kraftl, 2006).

Nikolas Rose (1999) argues that the expansion of nursery education provision in the UK in the early- to mid-twentieth century was caught up with a range of governmental aims. Here Rose is drawing upon Foucauldian notions of governmentality in which government is understood as a wide range of activities which comprise 'deliberate attempts to shape conduct in certain ways in relation to certain objectives' (1999: 4). Understood in this way, government is not simply a repressive force applied to individuals from the outside; instead government is most effective when (and because) it shapes individual subjectivities and encourages individuals (and groups) to govern themselves by internalizing the prevailing norms. For example, Rose argues that the playgroup movement that emerged in the post-war period in the UK had a range of governmental purposes and effects, not least that it co-opted the family, and mothers in particular, into what Rose refers to as 'the educational apparatus' (1999: 203). Alongside the guidance provided through the health visiting system and a whole range of parenting guidebooks, playgroups and other forms of early education encouraged parents to see their role in very particular ways. Good parents would strive to create homes and family environments that would support, and even enhance, their children's learning and development. Parents, then, assumed responsibility for their children's success or failure as a consequence of their ability to apply the right kinds of parenting skills and techniques, or to provide appropriately nurturing environments.

This is not simply an historical phenomenon. Contemporary neurobehavioral discourses, for example, encourage parents to view themselves as 'engineers and programmers charged with the task of making the correct inputs' (Wall, 2010: 254) so as to ensure their children's healthy development. A key aspect of this task is the need to provide an appropriately enriching and nurturing environment so as to ensure, and even maximize, children's brain development (Casteñeda, 2002; Nadesan, 2002). Similarly, those adults charged with designing and organizing spaces for young children outside the home are expected to produce spaces to ensure children's healthy development and learning. For example, Lynn Fendler (2001) uses the concept of 'developmentality' to describe how developmental discourse defines and governs the practice of early childhood education and shapes how practitioners understand their role in relation to providing spaces for young children. In this sense, spaces for young children are very often defined by adult agendas to do with children's 'healthy' or 'normal' development and their potential as productive future workers and citizens based on this (Moss and Petrie, 2002).

These are not the only kinds of adult agenda or vision for childhood that can characterize spaces for young children. The things people accumulate and display in their houses are never random or arbitrary; they tell stories about the people who live there and who have chosen to express themselves, at least in part, through the 'stuff' that makes up their home (Miller, 2010). In a study about how pregnant women prepare for motherhood, Mary Jane Kehily examined individual women's motives and aspirations as they created a nursery (a common term for an infant's bedroom) in preparation for the birth of their first child (Thompson et al., 2011). As a special space for the new baby within the family home, the nursery often became a kind of 'maternal project' which allowed prospective mothers to perform mothering (and particularly what they considered 'good mothering') through material culture. The nurseries these women created expressed a range of different ideas about what young children need and also the (anticipated) culture and values of their family. In this sense, the nursery can be understood as an expression of parents' hopes for the soon-to-be-born children.

Yet, Kehily explains that women's ideas about the material things and the nursery environment they'd so carefully and thoughtfully chosen during their pregnancy often changed a great deal during the baby's first year of life. This was, at least in part, because those nursery spaces were no longer an environment for an idealized future child but were inhabited by an infant who could affect the environment around them. We often think of very young children as passively worked upon or cared for by adults, but infant bodies are as thoroughly agential as other human bodies. Indeed, Deborah Lupton (2012) reminds us that infants 'grow their mothers' and other carers (see also Miller, 1997). The changed feelings of the mothers in Kehily's study (Thompson et al., 2011) may, to some degree at least, derive from their children's influence on them and the environment they inhabit. To an extent, the nurseries they created ceased to be simply spaces for young children and became *young children's spaces*. The next section will consider the implications of this theorization.

YOUNG CHILDREN'S SPACES

Kim Rasmussen (2003) makes a distinction between 'places for children' and 'children's places'. That is, she distinguished between those officially designated and adult-defined places for children discussed in the section above, and those places that young children might produce for themselves. Although there are various differences between concepts of space and place (and no necessary agreement over what is meant by either term; see Massey, 2005), these are less important for my purposes in this chapter than the ideas about children and power relations that are foregrounded in Rasmussen's distinction. As she explains:

> One could say that while 'places for children' display adults' ideas about children (toys, fences, etc.), 'children's places' make clear that children develop meaningful relationships to other places. This assessment takes place on the basis of what children tell, show and do themselves. (Rasmussen, 2003: 166)

A distinction between spaces for young children and young children's spaces would not produce a typology of spaces defined in terms of ownership by different demographic groups. Most spaces are occupied and used by a wide range of people of all ages, and their qualities and characteristics are usually produced through the interactions between people and the environment around them in the course of their activities.

This description invokes a quite different concept of space to that which we usually encounter in everyday language. Everyday understandings tend to conceptualize space as a container that is filled with things, people and actions: space is understood as the backdrop against which things happen. This idea of space as an inert surface over which we move and onto which we impose meaning is of limited analytic use because it tends to reduce the complexity of the world (Crang and Thrift, 2000). Instead, space can be thought of as intricately caught up in social relations. Doreen Massey (2005) outlines a set of principles that can help us to understand and engage with the dynamic relationships between space and human action. She argues that spaces are produced in and through the practices of social life. As a result, spaces cannot pre-exist or contain social activity because they are produced through interactions among people and things.

In addition to being *relational*, Massey insists that spaces are always heterogeneous. Many different relations and interactions can contribute to the constitution of a particular space. Spaces can be more or less hospitable to certain types of action or they might be imbued with identities or feeling, but these are never singular or stable; there are always alternatives. This means that space is never finished or complete. It is always under construction as it is (re)constituted through new interactions, new practices and new processes. To a certain degree, then, spaces might be thought of as the sum of the practices and processes that make them up, but this is only true insofar as we are willing to accept that the sum will never finally add up. Individual spaces can derive a kind of specificity from the endurance of the kinds of action from which they are constituted, but they always remain subject to other influences and connections.

This kind of approach to space foregrounds the relationships between people and places.

For example, several years ago I studied the power relations in the toddler room of a Scottish day nursery (Gallacher, 2005). It is, to some degree, possible to think about the nursery as a conflict between two separate worlds and agendas – that of the adult staff (expressed in the idea of the nursery as a space for young children) and that of the children (expressed in the idea of the nursery as a young children's space) – but this may not be the most useful way to understand the nursery. The toddler room had an 'official' structure and a very definite spatio-temporal routine. The staff set up the room in a variety of configurations and moved the children around throughout the day so as to facilitate a range of different activities which supported children's educational and personal care needs. This spatio-temporal routine was supported and enabled by a set of rules and practices which guided the smooth running of the nursery day.

Alongside this routine of 'official' activities, the toddler room also had what could be described as a peer culture 'underlife'. In his study of mental asylums, Erving Goffman (1961) argued that institutions invariably support a range of 'unofficial' practices through which inmates (or patients) are able to get around, break the rules or even bend the rules to their own purposes. The young children in the toddler room were able to adapt the use of equipment and spaces in various ways and to work around the official system and routine to produce their own peer-culture routines and activities. However, this was not simply a case of adults versus children (or spaces for young children versus young children's spaces). There were times when the children's own activities were not tolerated (for a whole range of different reasons), but, in general, the 'official' routine and the children's activities did not stand in opposition to each other. Instead, the adults and children worked together and negotiated the use of space throughout their everyday interactions. The children would improvise new games and adapt activities, and the staff would adapt to and take advantage of these activities. For example, one member of staff (whose name is italicized here) responded positively to the children's attempts to turn a table into a tunnel and even acted to ensure the game was not interrupted:

> *Nuala* was trying to read to some children in story-book corner but the children were more interested in crawling under a small red table. She decided to abandon the story and organize what the children were doing instead, encouraging the children to take turns and imposing a one-way system. Charlotte noticed the game and joined in. On his turn, Max decided to lie down under the table disrupting the games. *Nuala* warned him that she would move the table unless he moved so he started crawling again. Abbie and Liam began to push in front of each other, but *Nuala* stopped them explaining, 'It's not nice to push'. (Gallacher, 2005: 260)

As such, we can think of the nursery as a thoroughly negotiated space, which is contingent on the emergent practices of both the adults and the children.

Peter Moss and Pat Petrie's (2002) concept of *children's spaces* tries to capture the shared aspects of nurseries, and other provisions for children, as negotiated between adults and children. They argue that dominant discourses of childhood reduce public provisions for childhood to technical and instrumental sites for the production of pre-specified outcomes: good future workers and citizens. This model of provisions for childhood (which they refer to as the *children's services* model) encompasses many of the features of what I have called *spaces for young children* in the section above. Instead, Moss advocates a *children's spaces* model, which takes as its starting point the metaphor of the meeting place or public forum (Dahlberg and Moss, 2005). Understood as children's spaces, public provisions become places where people of all ages come together to explore and enact myriad possibilities. As Moss and Petrie put it, they are concerned with 'processes and relationships, not primarily for the production of prespecified outcomes' (Moss and Petrie, 2002: 106–7).

Perhaps the key part of this reconceptualization of public provisions for childhood,

at least for my purposes here, is the shift in the image of young children underlying the models. The children's services model draws upon and reaffirms dominant discourses of children as innocent, vulnerable and incompetent. It is also premised upon a future-oriented view of childhood, in which young children are positioned as futurities (or future-adults-in-the-making). In this way, childhood is understood as a key site for securing societal futures and children's services are tasked with ensuring the right kinds of outcomes are achieved. In contrast, Moss and Petrie explain that children's spaces should focus as much on children as they are now as for what they may become in the future. In doing so, children's spaces should start from and promote an alternative discourse of childhood in which 'children are understood as citizens, members of a social group, agents of their own lives (although not free agents, the constraints of society, the duties of citizenship all come in to play for children as for adults), as co-constructors of knowledge, identity and culture, constantly making meaning of their lives and of the world in which they live' (Moss and Petrie, 2002: 101). This research has been important in transforming how we think about young children and their position in society, nonetheless the next section considers the implications of privileging the social aspects of childhood over the material and biological aspects.

INHABITING YOUNG CHILDREN'S SPACES

Children's spaces are defined by the relationships between the people within them. They are, by necessity, thoroughly negotiated between all those who occupy them, both adults and children. The concept opens up our understandings of young children's spaces in various ways, not least by broadening the qualities we consider spaces to possess and accommodate. Moss and Petrie explain that children's spaces are never merely physical spaces; they are always thoroughly social, cultural and even political spaces. Yet, for all the flexibility and innovation of children's spaces, the metaphor remains one of a site where different things happen. The physical spaces themselves remain more or less inert containers for the plethora of relationships, ideas and practices produced by those who occupy them.

Returning to the physical and material aspects of space can provide us with a way of understanding the dynamic interactions between space and social life. To do so we need to rethink everyday accounts of materials as 'indifferent stuff' (Whatmore, 2006: 608) in the background of the social world. Ian Hodder (2012) explains that we so often associate materiality (or the physical world) with fixity and stability. As a result, our attempts to focus on the processes and relations that make up the world very often involve a shift in our attentions away from physical spaces towards the social, the cultural and/or the political. To a certain extent, this is what happens in Moss and Petrie (2002)'s concept of children's spaces. However, I do not want to argue that these other qualities of space are less important than the material, only that they are inseparable from the physical aspects of space.

This withdrawal from the material is often a result of fears about producing mere descriptions of the physicality of spaces, or what Divya Tolia-Kelly refers to as 'surface geographies'. Tolia-Kelly urges researchers to do more than detail 'the *surface* of matter' and, instead, to consider 'the productive power of materials' in the ongoing construction of space (2011: 154). She argues that doing so requires a change in perspective in research, from an approach which 'looks onto' the material world to one which focuses on 'being with' materials. This is similar to the distinction that Tim Ingold (2000) makes between what he calls the *building perspective* and the *dwelling perspective* (or *habitation* as he prefers in his more recent work – Ingold, 2007, 2011).

Like the notion of space as an inert container for human action, the building perspective imagines that people occupy a world that pre-exists them. This perspective encourages us to look onto and over the surface of the world and focus on what happens there. In contrast, the dwelling perspective views humans (and other organisms) as always already embedded within environments with which they must actively engage. Ingold's environments are never simply containers for human action; humans are never *beyond* their environments, but are always implicated in 'the world's transformation of itself' (Ingold, 2000: 6). That is, humans are shaped by the environments they inhabit as much as their environments are shaped by them.

These ideas of 'dwelling' or 'inhabitation' are a useful way of understanding young children's relationships to the spaces in which they live. Indeed, thinking about how young children dwell in or inhabit spaces allows us to return to and reconsider the concept of development in early childhood. However, this is not to return to the kind of universal and linear model of child development that has been the subject of much critique both within developmental psychology (e.g., Woodhead, 1999; Rogoff, 2003; Stern, 2006; Burman, 2008, 2012) and from the so-called 'new' sociology of childhood (e.g., James et al., 1998; Holloway and Valentine, 2000; James and James, 2004). These critiques focus on problematic constructions of children within much traditional developmental discourse; they reject understandings of children as passively shaped by the world (and the adults) around them and as 'futurities', nothing more than future-adults-in-the-making (Moss and Petrie, 2002).

Within developmental movement science, Adolph and Robinson (2013) have been equally critical of the dominant metaphors of development in early childhood. They explain that the pervasive metaphor of developmental milestones is inaccurate – they do not represent discrete or universal stages 'in a progression towards an ideal form' – as well as 'compelling and dangerous' insofar as the 'iconography' of developmental charts and tables 'has become reified as fact' (2013:

405). Indeed, by functioning as 'immutable mobiles' (Latour, 1987), such developmental milestone charts have almost come to supersede young children themselves; rather than abstracting from reality, '[t]hese images are far more concrete, far more real than the child' (Rose, 1999: 150). As a result, the 'normative templates' produced by developmental psychologists have come to be understood more 'as prescriptions of what is desired rather than relatively narrow descriptions of what may be acquired' (Karasik et al., 2010: 95).

Thelen and Smith (1996) describe this traditional, and largely teleological, view of development as taking a 'view from above' (or a view with 'low magnification'). Instead, they advocate that researchers should take a 'high magnification' approach to children's development (or a 'view from below'). Looking closely at individual children's development uncovers a large degree of variation, and firmly locates young children (and humans in general) within their wider environments by emphasizing the wide range of social and material factors that influence children's development. This 'view from below' is, in many ways, similar to Ingold's dwelling perspective insofar as both focus on the dynamic processes which constitute the 'human-being-in-its-environment' (2000: 391).

In the last 20 years, research taking this kind of 'high magnification' approach to movement as a dynamic perception-action system has demonstrated how young children are able to achieve goals by perceiving and adjusting to the physical (and social) properties of the world around them (Adolph et al., 2003). As such, the capacities and shape of young children's bodies (as well as their cognitive capacities and emotional development) are profoundly affected by the social and material characteristics of the spaces they inhabit. Indeed, human development is driven by experience (which always occurs within environments) rather than by the unfolding of innate abilities in time (Adolph et al., 2012). For example, how and when young children learn to climb stairs is influenced by a combination of parents' teaching strategies and infants' everyday access to and experience in navigating stairs (Berger et al., 2007). Even simple things like differences in dress or the use of nappies for toileting infants can affect young children's motor skills development. Cole and colleagues (2012) found that the use of nappies came at a 'functional cost' in terms of gait pattern and proficiency that was particularly pronounced in novice walkers.

In this way, young children cannot be separated out from the spaces they inhabit. Indeed, even bodily comportment cannot be viewed as a purely 'biological' attribute that stands apart from 'social', 'cultural' or 'material' practices. Ingold (2000) explains how all aspects of human life result from processes of dwelling in environments through the examples of walking and cycling. Often the tendency is to think of walking as a natural capacity that is immanent within young children, simply waiting to unfold in time. After all, all 'normal' children do learn to walk. In contrast, we understand cycling as a culturally acquired skill; children will not learn to cycle without opportunity, teaching and practice.

However, walking is not the inevitable part of human development that it appears to be. Thelen and Smith explain that all children learn to walk upright because of the confluence of a wide range of factors, including: 'anatomical and neural elements that have an ontogenetic history; strong motivation to move and to move more efficiently; a shared task environment such as support surfaces, gravity, and things to hold on to; and parenting that facilitates certain sensorimotor configurations' (1996: 72). Walking, therefore, is not simply something that happens to children at a particular point in their maturation; every child has to learn to walk within the everyday spaces they inhabit, and in conjunction with a range of social, cultural and material factors (Ingold, 2000).

For this reason, walking is not the homogeneous skill we imagine it to be. All sorts of differences can emerge depending on the particular configurations of the spaces people inhabit. Historical and anthropological research indicates that something as simple as the introduction of shoe wearing has a dramatic effect on both the shape and capacities of human feet (Ingold, 2011). Indeed, the material properties of different shoes can affect the ways in which people walk. Recent research on the use of so-called 'barefoot shoes' in South Africa indicates that footwear can have observable effects on children's foot morphology and gait pattern even over quite short time frames (Thompson et al., 2009).

Changes in how young children are handled and cared for can affect all aspects of their development (and, in doing so, all aspects of their lives). For example, highly successful campaigns intended to reduce the incidence of Sudden Infant Death Syndrome in Western societies have advised parents to place children on their back to sleep (rather than on their front or side). However, a side-effect of this change in care-giving practice has been to delay the emergence of motor skills like rolling and crawling in young children. To mitigate this effect, parents are now advised to introduce daily 'tummy time' for young children to allow them the opportunities and experience of lying on their front and, in so doing, to learn to roll and crawl more efficiently (Cole et al., 2012). Different childcare and handling practices do not only affect young children's physical development. Pushchair design, for example, can influence how young children develop language or develop emotionally (Zeedyk, 2008).

Cross-cultural research indicates that differences in childcare and handling practices can have pronounced effects on the shape and timing of developmental patterns in children living in majority world contexts (Karasik et al., 2010). Apparently 'accelerated' development in children living in many African countries in comparison with the developmental 'norms' for children living in the minority world, which has often been referred to as 'African Infant Precocity' (Adolph and Robinson, 2013), is the result of such differences. Similar patterns are associated with childrearing practices in Jamaica (Hopkins and Westra, 1990). Karen Adolph

and colleagues (2009) discuss several studies that have indicated that only certain areas of children's development, those skills which are supported and encouraged by cultural practices, can be considered 'accelerated' in these contexts. Similarly, this so-called 'precocity' does not manifest when childrearing practices are closer to those usually found in minority world contexts. The next section considers how the idea that young children inhabit spaces (and are also inhabited by them) affects our understanding of early childhood, and returns our focus to issues of difference and inequality.

YOUNG CHILDREN'S 'THING POWER'

Young children, then, are inextricably caught up in the spaces they inhabit. For Ingold, this observation has quite striking implications for how we understand what it is to be human at all. He argues that all human characteristics are the outcomes of processes of development that always occur within particular environments. In his words:

> [H]uman beings are not naturally pre-equipped for any kind of life; rather, such equipment that they have comes into existence as they live their lives, through a process of development. And this process is none other than that by which they acquire the skills appropriate to the particular kind of life they lead. What each of us begins with, then, is a developmental system. It follows that cultural differences – since they emerge within the process of development of the human organism in its environment – *are themselves biological.* (Ingold, 2000: 376, original emphasis)

Focusing on dwelling in or inhabitation of spaces in this way, means that it is impossible to separate out the material or biological aspects of young children's spaces, and to counterpose them to other aspects of life. The oppositional discourses that have tended to underpin so much research in early childhood (and so much of Western thought since the Enlightenment) are unhelpful and even counterproductive. Alan Prout explains that the paradigm that currently dominates much social or cultural research about childhood emerged as a 'reverse discourse' in response to earlier understandings of childhood as simply 'natural' or 'biological'. In contrast, this research has tended to emphasize the social or cultural aspects of childhood. Yet, while this may have been an important strategic move in the late twentieth century, Prout argues that 'the intellectual limits of [this] programme are increasingly apparent' (2005: 2). It has tended to produce a 'self-defeating loop' which attempts to separate out and ignore 'the very conditions of children's lives' (2005: 143–4).

Dualistic thinking, whether broken up as nature/culture, being/becoming, mind/body, brain/behavior or any other binary opposition, is not a useful way of understanding young children's development (Thelen and Smith, 1996) or any other aspect of their lives. It is, therefore, important to move away from and, indeed, challenge what has come to seem a 'common-sense opposition between the person and the thing, the animate and the inanimate, the subject and the object' (Miller, 2010: 5). Jane Bennett develops the concept of 'thing power' as a means of discussing how objects and materials can gain a sort of independence or aliveness, which enables them to affect the world around them, including humans and other organisms. As a result, it is much more difficult to distinguish between human being and what Bennett calls 'thinghood' (2010: 4).

Lee and Montzakau (2011) explain that life processes and social processes are always intertwined; there can be no meaningful boundary between the biological and the social. The implications of this are twofold. The first implication is that human bodies are always as social as they are biological. From infancy (and even before birth), humans are always already 'social bundles' rather than 'biobundles' which are then made social (Brownlie and Scheach Leith, 2011). The other implication is that 'we are always non-human', at least in part (Bennett, 2010: 4). What Bennett means here is that we are as much part of the material world (largely through the corporeality of our bodies) as the social world. Deborah Lupton (2012) explains that human embodiment is always interrelational. She is particularly interested in the processes and practices that constitute 'interembodiment' between infants and their caregivers. But this interrelationality encompasses a wide range of relations between humans and things, as well as among humans. It is for this reason that Prout describes children's bodies as 'hybrid entities […] inseparable from, produced in, represented by and performed through their connections with other objects' (2000: 2).

As such, spaces and environments inhabit young children as much as young children inhabit them. Rethinking young children's spaces in terms of habitation or dwelling (Ingold, 2000, 2007), therefore, requires a shift in how we think about young children's agency. One of the key themes of research within childhood studies over the two decades or so has been the need to take children 'seriously' as active agents in shaping their own lives and the world around them. As I discussed above (in the third section), there have been numerous studies which demonstrate young children's ability to act in and influence the spaces in which they live (see also Einarsdóttir, 2005; Clark, 2007; Konstantoni, 2012). Similarly, the motor skills research discussed above indicates that children are actively involved in their own development by assessing and using a wide range of different tools to perform a wide range of motor tasks in the environment around them (e.g., Adolph et al., 1993; Kretch et al., 2013; Berger et al., 2014).

Yet, while many studies have documented young children's ability to exercise agency, the concept of 'agency' itself is not always as well theorized as it could be (Prout, 2000). Prout draws upon Latour's sociology of translation (2005) to argue that agency is not something that children inherently possess, nor something that they can have more or less of than other humans. Instead, agency is an interrelational outcome; it emerges as an effect of connections made between 'a heterogenous array of materials, including bodies, representations and technologies' (Prout, 2000: 16). Also drawing upon Latour's work, Nick Lee (2001) argues that we should think of agency as a kind of dependency. That is, rather than viewing agency as an attribute that humans possess, independent of their surroundings, we can see agency as something that humans are only able to achieve because of their interdependence with a range of materials and other humans in the spaces they inhabit.

Ian Hodder (2012) suggests that we should think in terms of both *dependence* and *dependency* in understanding the social and material entanglements of everyday life. He argues that we need to consider not only how humans depend on things and other humans, but how things depend on humans and other things. By decentering agency in this way, we are able to open up young children's lives by asking questions about how (and why) they are more or less able to exercise agency in particular circumstances and in particular spaces. Agency, then, becomes the starting point for investigations rather than the ultimate answer (Prout, 2000), and refocuses our attention on the young-child-in-environment, rather than trying to separate out the two.

Lousie Holt (2013) insists on the importance of considering these 'material spatialities' of early childhood. She urges the researcher to produce 'lively ethnographies' of young children's everyday lives so as to consider not simply how agency is (or is not) achieved but also the broader consequences of this for children's subjection and subjectification. Such an approach would foreground the active role that children play in their own life worlds but without perpetuating 'the fiction of the sovereign agent' (Holt, 2013: 656). Focusing on young children as inhabitants of (and inhabited by) the world in this way allows us to develop open-ended and non-teleological accounts of young children's lives. As 'inhabitants', young children are embedded within the world; they '[participate] from within the very process of the world's coming into being, and […] in laying a trail of life [contribute] to its weave and texture' (Ingold, 2007: 81). Young children

are, therefore, always already embedded in the spaces in which they live their lives or, as Ingold puts it in *Being Alive*: 'Growing into the world, the world grows into them' (Ingold, 2011: 6).

CONCLUSION

Attending to young children's relationship to (and with) spaces allows us to think through their lives in a range of different ways. Indeed, the ways in which we think about young children's spaces is necessarily caught up with how we understand young children and early childhood. Different images of the young child are bound up in, and made possible through, different theorizations of young children's relationship to space. In this chapter, I have identified three broad ways in which we can theorize and engage with the spaces in which young children live their lives, and the implications of these approaches for how we understand early childhood and young children's role in the world.

Many of our ideas about young children and space are premised, at least in part, on images of young children as in need of particular kinds of provision (which can be produced and supplied by adults). A whole range of *spaces for young children* have emerged which are (more or less explicitly) designed both to protect them from the dangers of the (adult) world and to, at least try to, ensure the achievement of a range of desired outcomes (and to prevent undesirable outcomes) for individual children and society as a whole. As such, spaces like nursery schools, playgrounds and young children's bedrooms (or nurseries) demonstrate a variety of different ideas about early childhood and adult hopes and fears for what young children will become in the future. These ideas do not necessarily add up to a consistent account of early childhood, but reflect the ambivalence of societal attitudes to young children.

Such spaces for young children may have a wide range of governmental aims, but it is important to remember that young children are not passively molded by the spaces in which they live. As such, theories of *young children's spaces* emphasize the active role that young children play in responding to and shaping the spaces around them. These approaches begin from a more relational and processual approach to both young children and the spaces in which they live. In doing so, they present an image of young children as active participants in all sorts of relationships through which they can explore a whole range of different possibilities and negotiate their own outcomes.

However, the material aspects of spaces are no less relational or processual than political, ethical, social and cultural aspects that are usually emphasized in ideas of young children's spaces. Drawing upon Ingold's concept of *inhabitation* allows us to develop and consider a more vital account of the materiality of the spaces in which young children live. This approach tries to move beyond the dualistic accounts that have tended to dominate post-Enlightenment Western thought (and which shape many of our everyday ideas about the world). Rather than separating out the material and the biological from the social and the cultural, the concept of inhabitation situates young children within environments in which the social, material, cultural and biological are inextricably entangled together. In doing so, these accounts argue that young children do not simply inhabit spaces, but that those spaces also come to inhabit young children in myriad ways.

Thinking about the relationship between young children and space as one of (mutual) inhabitation alters the ways in which we think about both young children and space. In particular, it forces us to reconsider how we think about young children's embodiment, agency and subjectivity in terms of (inter)dependence. We might think of young children as possessing a kind of 'thing power' (Bennett, 2010) because all aspects of their lives (and indeed themselves) are simultaneously social and material; they are always caught up with the environments in which they live. Thinking in this way allows us to consider not only how young children are able to achieve agency in particular circumstances, but also the broader

repercussions of young children's subjectification in terms of how a whole range of inequalities are (re)produced and performed, and also how they might be transformed. These are important questions that research in early childhood should seek to address.

FURTHER READING

Clark A (2010) *Transforming Children's Spaces: Children's and Adults' Participation in Designing Learning Environments*. New York: Routledge.

Kraftl P and Adey P (2008) Architecture/affect/dwelling. *Annals of the Association of American Geographers* 98: 213–31.

Stevenson O and Prout A (2013) Space for play? Families' strategies for organizing domestic space in homes with young children. *Home Cultures* 10: 135–57.

QUESTIONS FOR REFLECTION

1   In what ways are particular provisions for young children bound up with ideas about early childhood, and how might changing provisions alter how we think of young children?
2   What kinds of spaces for young children are provided in other places (and at other times), and how do they reflect ideas about young children's role in different societies?
3   What are the consequences of exporting Western ideas of childrearing and early education to the majority world?
4   To what extent do young children need special spaces? Why?
5   Why might involving young children in the design and organization of the spaces in which they live be important for transforming inequalities in society?

REFERENCES

Adolph KE and Robinson SR (2013) The road to walking: what learning to walk tells us about development. In: Zelazo P (ed.) *Oxford Handbook of Developmental Psychology*. New York: Oxford University Press, 403–43.

Adolph K, Cole W, Komati M, et al. (2012) How do you learn to walk? Thousands of steps and dozens of falls per day. *Psychological Science* 23: 1387–94.

Adolph KE, Eppler MA and Gibson EJ (1993) Crawling versus walking: infants' perception of affordances for locomotion over sloping surfaces. *Child Development* 64: 1158–74.

Adolph KE, Karasik LB and Tamis-LeMonda CS (2009) Moving between cultures: cross-cultural research on motor development. In: Bornstein M (ed.) *Handbook of Cross-cultural Developmental Science, Vol. 1: Domains of Development across Cultures*. New York: Psychology Press, 61–88.

Adolph KE, Vereijken B and Shrout PE (2003) What changes in infant walking and why. *Child Development* 74: 475–97.

Bennett J (2010) *Vibrant Matter: A Political Ecology of Things*. Durham, NC: Duke University Press.

Berger S, Chan G and Adolph K (2014) What cruising infants learn about support for locomotion. *Infancy* 19: 117–37.

Berger SE, Theuring C and Adolph KE (2007) How and when infants learn to climb stairs. *Infant Behavior and Development* 30: 36–49.

Brownlie J and Scheach Leith V (2011) Social bundles: thinking through the infant body. *Childhood* 18: 196–210.

Burman E (2008) *Deconstructing Developmental Psychology*. London: Routledge.

Burman E (2012) Deconstructing neoliberal childhood: towards a feminist antipsychological childhood. *Childhood* 19: 423–38.

Casteñeda C (2002) *Figurations: Child, Bodies, Worlds*. Durham, NC: Duke University Press.

Cieraad I (2013) Children's home life in the past and present. *Home Cultures* 10: 213–26.

Clark A (2007) Views from inside the shed: young children's perspectives on the outdoor environment. *Education 3–13* 35: 349–63.

Cole W, Lingeman J and Adolph KE (2012) Go naked: diapers affect infant walking. *Developmental Science* 15: 783–90.

Crang M and Thrift N (2000) Introduction. In: Crang M and Thrift N (eds) *Thinking Space*. London: Routledge.

Dahlberg G and Moss P (2005) *Ethics and Politics in Early Childhood Education*. London: RoutledgeFalmer.

Einarsdóttir J (2005) We can decide what to play! Children's perception of quality in an Icelandic playschool. *Early Education and Development* 16: 469–88.

Fendler L (2001) Educating flexible souls. In: Hultqvist K and Dahlberg G (eds) *Governing the Child in the New Millennium*. London: RoutledgeFalmer.

Gagen EA (2000) An example to us all: child development and identity construction in early 20th-century playgrounds. *Environment and Planning A*: 599–616.

Gallacher L-A (2005) 'The terrible twos': gaining control in the nursery? *Children's Geographies* 3: 243–64.

Gallagher A (2013) At home in preschool care? Childcare policy and the negotiated spaces of educational care. *Children's Geographies* 11: 202–14.

Giroux H (2001) Mis/education and zero tolerance: disposible youth and the politics of domestic militarization. *Boundary* 2(28): 61–94.

Goffman E (1961) *Asylums*. New York: Anchor Books.

Greenfield C (2004) Transcript: 'Can run, play on bikes, jump the zoom slide, and play on the swings': exploring the value of outdoor play. *Australian Journal of Early Childhood* 29: 1–5.

Hackett A (2014) Zigging and zooming all over the place: young children's meaning making and movement in the museum. *Journal of Early Childhood Literacy* 14: 5–27.

Hodder I (2012) *Entangled: An Archaeology of the Relationships between Humans and Things*. New York: Wiley-Blackwell.

Holloway SL and Valentine G (2000) *Children's Geographies: Playing, Living, Learning*. London: Routledge.

Holt L (2013) Exploring the emergence of the subject in power: infant geographies. *Environment and Planning D: Society and Space* 31: 645–63.

Hopkins B and Westra T (1990) Motor development, maternal expectations and the role of handling. *Infant Behavior and Development* 13: 117–22.

Ingold T (2000) *The Perception of the Environment: Essays on Livelihood, Dwelling and Skill*. London: Routledge.

Ingold T (2007) *Lines: A Brief History*. London: Routledge.

Ingold T (2011) *Being Alive: Essays on Movement, Knowledge and Description*. London and New York: Routledge.

James A and James AL (2004) *Constructing Childhood: Theory, Law and Social Practice*. London: Palgrave Macmillan.

James A, Jenks C and Prout A (1998) *Theorising Childhood*. Cambridge: Polity Press.

Jenks C (2005) *Childhood*. London and New York: Routledge.

Jupp E (2013) Enacting parenting policy? The hybrid spaces of Sure Start Children's Centres. *Children's Geographies* 11: 173–87.

Karasik L, Adolph K, Tamis-LeMonda C, et al. (2010) WEIRD walking: cross-cultural differences in motor development. *Behaviour and Brain Sciences* 33: 95–6.

Konstantoni K (2012) Children's peer relationships and social identities: exploring cases of young children's agency and complex interdependencies from the Minority World. *Children's Geographies* 10: 337–46.

Kraftl P (2006) Building an idea: the material construction of an ideal childhood. *Transactions of the Institute of British Geographers* 31: 488–504.

Kretch K, Franchak J and Adolph KE (2013) Crawling and walking infants see the world differently. *Child Development* 85: 1503–18.

Laris M (2005) Designing for play. In: Dudek M (ed.) *Children's Spaces*. London: Architectural Press.

Latour B (1987) *Science in Action: How to Follow Scientists and Engineers through Society*. Milton Keynes: Open University Press.

Latour B (2005) *Reassembling the Social: An Introduction to Actor-Network-Theory*. Oxford: Oxford University Press.

Lee N (2001) *Childhood and Society: Growing up in an Age of Uncertainty*. Maidenhead: Open University Press.

Lee N and Montzakau J (2011) Navigating the biopolitics of childhood. *Childhood* 19: 7–19.

Lupton D (2012) Infant embodiment and inter-embodiment: a review of sociocultural perspectives. *Childhood* 20: 37–50.

Lupton D (2014) Precious, pure, uncivilised, vulnerable: infant embodiment in Australian popular media. *Children & Society* 28(5): 341–51.

Luzia K (2011) Growing home: reordering the deomestic geographies of 'throwntogetherness'. *Home Cultures* 8(3): 297–316.

Massey D (2005) *For Space*. London: SAGE.

Miller D (1997) How infants grow mothers in North London. *Theory, Culture, Society* 14: 67–88.

Miller D (2010) *Stuff*. Cambridge: Polity Press.

Moss P and Petrie P (2002) *From Children's Services to Children's Spaces: Public Policy, Children and Childhood*. London and New York: RoutledgeFalmer.

Nadesan M (2002) Engineering the entrepreneurial infant: brain science, infant development toys, and governmentality. *Cultural Studies* 16: 401–32.

Prout A (2000) Childhood bodies: construction, agency and hybridity. In: Prout A (ed.) *The Body, Childhood and Society*. London: Macmillan.

Prout A (2005) *The Future of Childhood*. London: RoutledgeFalmer.

Rasmussen K (2003) Places for children, children's places. *Childhood* 11: 155–73.

Rogoff B (2003) *The Cultural Nature of Human Development*. New York: Oxford University Press.

Rose N (1999) *Governing the Soul: The Shaping of the Private Self*. London: Free Association Books.

Sibley D (1995) *Geographies of Exclusion: Society and Difference in the West*. London: Routledge.

Stern D (2006) *The Interpersonal World of the Infant: A View from Psychoanalysis and Developmental Psychology*. New York: Basic Books.

Thelen E and Smith LB (1996) *A Dynamic Systems Approach to the Development of Cognition and Action*. Cambridge, MA: The MIT Press.

Thompson A, Zipfel B, McKibbin B, et al. (2009) 'Barefoot technology' in school shoes: gait pattern and functional improvement over an 8-week period. *Footwear Science* 1: 55–7.

Thompson R, Kehily MJ, Hadfield L, et al. (2011) *Making Modern Mothers*. Bristol: Policy Press.

Tolia-Kelly DP (2011) The geographies of cultural geography III: material geographies, vibrant matters and risking surface geographies. *Progress in Human Geography* 37: 153–60.

Valentine G (1996) Children should be seen and not heard: the production and transgression of adults' public space. *Urban Geography* 17: 205–20.

Wall G (2010) Mothers' experiences with intensive parenting and brain development discourse. *Women's Studies International Forum* 33: 253–63.

Walsh G and Gardner J (2005) Assessing the quality of early years learning environments. *Early Childhood Research and Practice* 7.

Ward C (1990) *The Child in the City*. London: Bedford Square Press.

Weller S (2003) 'Teach us something useful': contested spaces. *Space and Polity* 7: 153–71.

Whatmore S (2006) Materialist returns: practising cultural geography in and for a more-than-human world. *Cultural Geographies* 13: 600–9.

Woodhead M (1999) Reconstructing developmental psychology: some first steps. *Children & Society* 3: 3–19.

Zeedyk MS (2008) What's life in a baby buggy like? The impact of buggy orientation on parent–infant interaction and infant stress. London: National Literacy Trust. Available at: www.literacytrust.org.uk/assets/0000/2531/Buggy_research.pdf

9

Converting the Science of Early Human Development into Action: Closing the Gap between What We Know and What We Do

Mary E. Young

INTRODUCTION

Remarkable achievements have been made to reduce child mortality in developing countries over the past few decades. But one still has to ask, how are the children? Despite the achievements, many continue to suffer throughout the world. Authors of the 2007 and 2011 series in *The Lancet* (Engle et al., 2007, 2011; Walker et al., 2011) estimate that 200 million children under the age of 5 are at risk of poor developmental growth.

Most of the world's children who are vulnerable developmentally, malnourished, or in ill health are clustered geographically in sub-Saharan Africa and South Asia (Engle et al., 2007, 2011; Black et al., 2008; Liu et al., 2012). However, in all areas and across social classes, children's social environment affects their health, learning, and behavior, but not all classes or children are affected equally. Rather, the association between socioeconomic status (SES) and children's health (socioemotional, physical, and mental) is a graded one – which persists at each stage of their life course (Marmot Review Team, 2010).

Rapid advances have been made in the science and understanding of early human development through a convergence of disciplines (e.g., neuroscience, developmental psychology, molecular biology, and economics) focused on this topic. The science demonstrates conclusively that early childhood matters and that there is a critical need to support early human development from the earliest stages of life. In addition, an array of longitudinal studies indicate that many adult diseases have their origins in childhood (Danese et al., 2007; Boivin and Hertzman, 2012; Shonkoff, 2012; Shonkoff and Garner, 2012). Further, we now know that many, if not most, human morbidities are products of the interplay between genes and the environment (Rutter, 2006).

Thus, early experience *in utero* and during the early years of childhood affects learning and educational attainment throughout life and influences adults' physical and mental outcomes. Adverse early-life experiences in particular, such as abuse, neglect, or being cared for by individuals with mental illness, negatively affect children's developing brains and increase their risk of deficits in learning and physical and mental disorders later in life.

WHAT WE KNOW FROM RESEARCH

The evidence from neuroscience, developmental biology, and longitudinal social science research offers solid data on the impact and long reach of children's early years (i.e., early experience) on health, learning, and behavior. Early exposure to adverse experiences specifically translates into biological risk for disease later in life, such as depression or increased levels of inflammation (Danese et al., 2007, 2011), a known predictor of cardiovascular disease. Recent studies clearly show that experiences (good or bad) in the early years affect the brain's circuits and influence individuals' health and developmental trajectory over the life course. Research findings from genetics and epigenetics (the study of ways that environmental factors affect gene function in animal models and humans) are supported by longitudinal studies, which indicate that the mechanisms for setting trajectories are based on dynamic interactions between genes and the environment in early life.

Four concepts summarize what we now know about early human development:

1 Both the architecture of skills (e.g., coping abilities, cognitive and non-cognitive competencies, health) and the process of skill formation are strongly influenced by neural circuits that develop as a result of dynamic interactions between genes and early-life environments and experiences.
2 Development of neural pathways and the mastery of skills follow hierarchical rules in a sequence of events 'from the bottom up' such that later attainment is built upon foundations laid earlier.
3 Cognitive, social, emotional, and language competencies are interdependent. All are shaped by early experiences, and all contribute to the formation of lifelong capabilities.

4 Adaptation continues throughout life. Capabilities are formed in predictable sequences during sensitive periods when the development of specific neural circuits is most plastic and most receptive to environmental influences.

It is important to recognize that even though the most rapid and dramatic period of brain growth takes place during the early years of life, maturation of the brain continues throughout childhood and into adulthood (Rutter, 2011). Rutter (2011) notes that despite the sensitive periods or age-related differences that influence risk and risk protection, no single age period has a 'monopoly on risks' and there is no age beyond which it is generally too late to intervene.

We can intervene later, but what are the costs then? Clearly, it is far less costly to invest in the early years and 'get things right the first time' than try to remediate problems that arise later (Knudsen et al., 2006; Shonkoff et al., 2012).

Structure and Function of the Brain

Figure 9.1 depicts in detail the development of the brain's structure and function over time, from conception to death. The formation of synapses (connections) in the brain is experience-dependent, and synaptogenesis (the onset of synapse formation) begins prenatally. Development of the senses, language and speech, and higher cognitive functions occurs sequentially and is especially critical during peak sensitive periods, as noted in the figure.

Neural Pathways in the Brain

The brain's neural circuits and pathways are formed to carry out specific functions. The circuits and pathways connect and mature during the prenatal and early childhood periods and into middle childhood and adolescence. Simple circuits are built first and are then followed by more complex circuits.

Human Brain Development

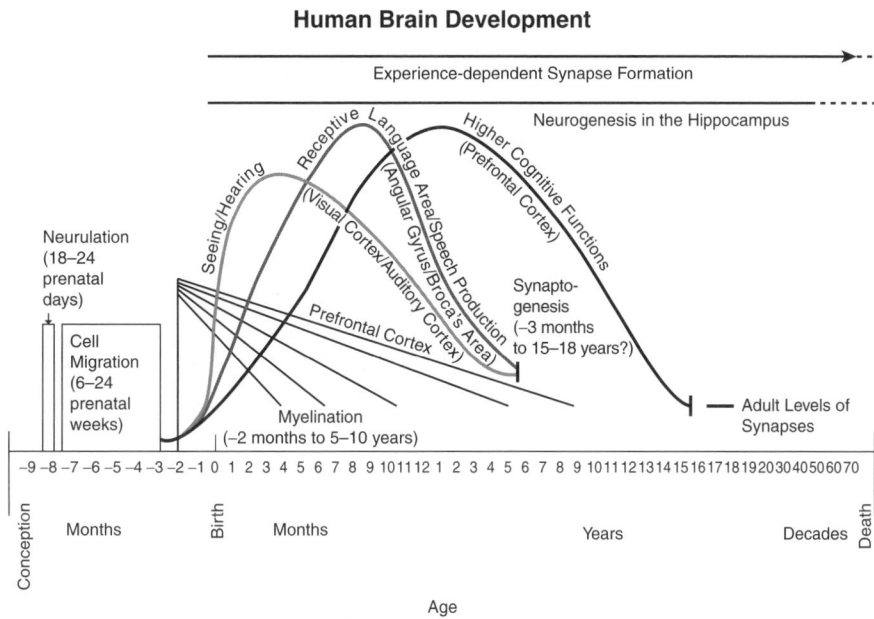

Figure 9.1   Development of the brain's structure and function

Source: Thompson and Nelson (2001); Figure provided by Nelson (2015)

For example, development of the sensing pathways for vision, hearing, touch, smell, and taste begins before birth and wanes by the age of 4 years. These sensory systems bring in information that children need for their subsequent development.

Development of the limbic system and the stress pathway also begins before birth and continues into the early years of childhood. The limbic system manages how we respond to challenges. The stress pathway – the neural network that operates between the limbic system and the adrenal glands and prefrontal cortex – determines how we respond and adapt to daily experiences and new challenges and situations.

The brain is the central organ of the stress response and adaptation. In summarizing the effect of stress on the brain, McEwen (2014) notes that the brain's circuits are remodeled by stress so as to change the balance between anxiety, mood control, memory, and decision making. The capacity to cope enables individuals to adapt to their environment,

and while the changes are adaptive in situations of danger (e.g., the fight-or-flight response), they may be maladaptive if they persist.

Among early-life experiences, the most potent stressors arise from the social environment. They can affect both the brain and the body, leading to wear and tear on tissues and organs and resulting in long-term, chronic mental and physical disease. McEwen notes that lower gradients of SES reflect a cumulative burden of coping with limited resources, toxic environments, and negative life events, as well as health-damaging behaviors, and the result is chronic, negative activation of physiological systems (McEwen, 2008a and b; Danese and McEwen, 2012; McEwen, 2014).

Gene–Environment Interactions

Early human development involves an intricate and dynamic interaction between nature and nurture – genes and the environment. Genes 'listen' to the environment, and the environment 'adapts' the genetic blueprint. In early life, nurturance, stimulation, and nutrition begin at gestation. In the fetus, the environment (i.e., a mother's health, well-being, level of stress, food and drug intake) interacts with genetic predispositions to sculpt the architecture of the brain and neural pathways, to influence learning, behavior, and physical and mental health for life.

The environment modifies the expression of genes (e.g., gene variants, phenotype) and can turn genes on and off through the epigenetic process, in which experiences leave a chemical signature, or epigenetic mark, that sits atop genes and can determine whether and how genes are switched on and off. Epigenetic mechanisms alter genetic expression without changing the DNA sequence, and although many of these changes are temporary, others seem to endure. Hence, our DNA blueprint carries a personalized signature.

Twin studies illustrate the effect of gene–environment interactions. Identical twins, which have the same DNA (i.e., genotype), can exhibit different gene expressions (i.e., phenotypes), as each twin will not have the same experience as the other in early life. Likewise, non-identical twins, who have different genes, but are exposed to the same environment, will also exhibit different gene expressions (McCain et al., 2011). In other words, the environment can affect individuals differently depending on their genetic endowment, and the same genetic endowment produces different outcomes depending on the environment (Hertzman and Boyce, 2010).

Effects of Poor Nurturing on Stress Pathways

Children begin life ready for relationships that 'drive' early brain development. An infant is primed to be interested in faces and to initiate non-verbal communication with others. When we respond to an infant's gaze, smile, or babbling, we set up a chain of back-and-forth exchanges that affect the wiring and sculpting of the child's limbic pathways.

Animal studies show how early experience shapes the architecture of the brain's neural circuits that are involved in the stress response and coping. Meaney and colleagues' seminal studies in rats (Meaney and Szyf, 2005) have helped to explain how mammals respond to environmental stimuli. They showed that rat pups that are poorly nurtured at birth and during infancy (i.e., the mothers do not adequately lick or groom them) have abnormal responses to stress in adulthood (e.g., an increased likelihood of addiction). The mothers' reduced licking and grooming (i.e., reduced touch) increase the cortisol levels in the rat pups' brains.

This research demonstrates how touch in early life influences the function of stress pathways in later life. The early rearing conditions of the rats permanently influence their brain circuits (i.e., the limbic system, hypothalamus-pituitary-adrenal (HPA) pathway, and autonomic nervous system) and their biological responses to stress throughout life. The effects are wide-ranging, as they influence the rats' temperament, behavior, learning, memory, metabolism, and reproduction.

Stimulation and Language Development

In humans, face-to-face interactions of newborns and infants with adults are critical for development of language. As shown in Figure 9.1, the development of neural pathways for language begins even before birth and sets the stage for the development of higher cognitive functions that continues into adolescence. Neural pathways related to language are dependent on the development of neural pathways for vision and sound and follow the development of neural pathways for stress responses and coping.

At approximately 7 months' gestation, the brain's sensory pathways for hearing are active and become sensitive to the rhythmic qualities of the particular language spoken at home. During the first 6–7 months after birth, babies gurgle and babble – they make the same babbling sounds regardless of a family's language. Scientists at the University of British Columbia, Canada, have noted that babies who are regularly exposed to two languages before birth can distinguish the difference between two languages after birth (McCain et al., 2011).

Early exposure to language at home predicts the size of children's vocabulary and their later verbal and literacy skills. In a study of US children, Hart and Risley (1995) showed that by the time children were 3 years old, parents in low-income circumstances had said fewer different words in their cumulative monthly vocabularies than had the parents of children in the most economically advantaged families during the same period.

Figure 9.2 shows the variability of children's early exposure to language in relation to family status and income. This evidence highlights the importance of good parent–child interactions and stimulation, especially for children in poorer socioeconomic settings, and the important role that families and communities have beyond just transmitting genes. The quality of children's early home environments *is* predictive of children's success.

Early Adversity Influences Later Cognitive and Non-Cognitive Development

Research from human and animal studies applying a wide array of tools in genetics, molecular biology, genomics, and brain imaging confirms that significant exposure to adversity, especially when sustained in early childhood and within a family environment of poverty and deprivation, can alter the structure and function of the brain's circuitry and related neurological pathways to negatively affect health (mental and physical), learning, and behavior for the life course.

Among pregnant women, low SES increases the likelihood of premature birth and fetal growth retardation, a fact that may be explained by high stress, higher rates of infection, and poor or inadequate nutrition. All of these factors increase cortisol levels in the mother and the fetus, and this increase can reduce fetal growth and trigger prematurity. The findings are consistent with those from studies in other primates (rhesus monkeys) which show that fetal exposure to increased levels of cortisol reduces the hippocampal volume of adults and that offspring of mothers who are stressed have lower birthweights, impaired neuromotor development, attention deficits, and emotional dysregulation across the lifespan.

Cumulative Vocabulary Experiences

Family status	Words heard per hour	Words heard in 3 years
Welfare	616	13 million
Working class	1,251	26 million
Professional	2,153	45 million

Cumulative Vocabulary at Age 3

Children from welfare families	500 words
Children from working-class families	700 words
Children from professional families	1,100 words

Figure 9.2   Meaningful differences: 30 million more words

Source: Based on Hart and Risley (1995)

In neuroscience, researchers are utilizing electroencephalograms and functional magnetic resonance imaging to identify the underlying affective and cognitive systems influenced by SES (Hackman et al., 2010). A better understanding of the mechanisms of this influence will make it possible to design more specific interventions to prevent and remediate the effects of low SES in childhood (Shonkoff et al., 2009; Hackman et al., 2010).

For example, we know that low SES postnatally is associated with greater depression in parents, compromised parent–child interactions (e.g., parents' use of harsh and inconsistent discipline, less sensitivity to their child's needs, reduced verbal communication), and insecure attachment of the child to the primary caregiver (Hackman et al., 2010). Hackman and colleagues cite studies which conclude that the quality of parenting not only correlates with a child's emotional and behavioral patterns, but also predicts the child's emotional and behavioral patterns later. Further, we know that the effect of SES on children's emotional and cognitive development occurs along a gradient according to parents' education or income. The development of children whose parents have the lowest quintiles of income, SES, or education is negatively affected the most, compared with children whose families have the highest income, SES, or education (Hackman et al., 2010).

Socioeconomic status affects some neurobiological systems more than others. Hart and Risley (1995) and other researchers have found that SES has the largest effect on language processing and moderate effects on executive function (i.e., working memory and cognitive control). Hackman, Farah, and Meaney (2010) point out that SES is positively correlated with the left part of the brain (left inferior frontal gyrus), which is activated during a language task, and that children with low SES exhibit decreased specialization of language function in the left hemisphere. Moreover, the researchers have evidence of SES-related differences in the neural processing of emotion (an executive function), as well as in cognitive and affective processes. They note that impairment in executive function is linked with less success in school performance.

Early Adversity Predicts Poor Health (mental, behavioral, physical) Outcomes

Numerous prospective, longitudinal studies conducted in developed countries illustrate that the severity of early-life experiences (e.g., socioeconomic deprivation, disruptive caregiving, harsh parenting) predicts difficulties in adult life. Among these studies are the 1958 British Cohort Study and the Avon Longitudinal Study of Parents and Children in the UK, the National Collaborative Perinatal Project and the Kauai Longitudinal Study in the USA, and the Quebec Longitudinal Study of Child Development in Canada. All have contributed to a better understanding of the gene-by-environment (GXE) interaction described by Hertzman and Boyce (2010).

New Zealand's Dunedin Multidisciplinary Health and Development Study, conducted by Caspi and colleagues, illustrates, in particular, how exposure to adversity in childhood predicts poor mental health (i.e., risk for depression) and substance use. In a birth cohort, the researchers (Caspi et al., 2003, 2010) showed that adverse conditions in early life (neglect or abuse) led to an increased risk of depression in adult life for individuals who had the short allele for the serotonin transporter gene. In the study, those with the short allele who were reared in good, caring environments were not at increased risk of depression, and those with the long allele who were brought up in adverse environments were also resilient.

Danese and colleagues (2007) have shown linkages between childhood stressors (e.g., maltreatment) and dysregulation of the immune system. Other long-term health effects of adversities that young children experience are also well documented and continue to be explored.

The Kaiser-Permanente's Adverse Early Childhood Experience (ACE) Study is a retrospective, longitudinal study in which 17,000 members of Kaiser-Permanente's health maintenance organization were surveyed about their history of adverse experiences before age 18. The study scored nine risk factors – recurrent physical abuse; recurrent emotional abuse; contact sexual abuse; alcohol and/or drug abuser in the household; incarcerated household member; chronically depressed, mentally ill, institutionalized, or suicidal household member; a mother treated violently; one or no parents; and emotional or physical neglect. The ACE survey showed that young children who were exposed to traumatic or abusive childhood events were predisposed as adults to a range of health problems, which included coronary artery disease, high blood pressure, type 2 diabetes, obesity, cancer, and mental and behavioral problems such as depression, alcoholism, smoking, and substance abuse (Felitti et al., 1998; Anda et al., 2006; Hertzman and Boyce, 2010).

The longitudinal studies do not show evidence of a unique relationship between an early risk factor and an outcome, but they do confirm a dose effect – that is, having a number of risk factors yields a cumulative risk. Moreover, the number of adverse early childhood experiences has a graded relationship to medical and public health problems, such as smoking, lung disease, alcohol abuse, HIV risk, suicide, depression, and teen sexual behavior. New Zealand's Dunedin Multidisciplinary Health and Development Study and the British Environment Risk (E-Risk) Longitudinal Twin Study showed a similar dose effect of the biological embedding of adverse risks in children (Danese, 2011; Nanni et al., 2012).

Violence and neglect have an especially severe impact on early brain development. A study of children caught in the Israel and Palestine conflict showed that children in the Gaza Strip had three times the rate of emotional and behavioral problems compared with middle-class children raised in Canada (Miller, 2000; McCain et al., 2007). Other extreme events such as epidemics (HIV/ AIDS) and orphanhood also have negative and lasting effects on the well-being of young children (Walque, 2011).

In addition, children who are reared in institutions may suffer profound deprivation, which has damaging effects on brain development (Nelson et al., 2009). These children tend to have lower IQs, stunted growth, and behavioral problems, and the longer their institutional deprivation is, the more pronounced their negative outcomes are. Rutter (2011) reports data which show that children who left an orphanage when they were younger than 6 months old had no detectable sequelae, but two-fifths of children adopted after that age had deficits. He concludes that profound institutional deprivation has lasting effects, which include a marked increase in deficits among children after the second half of the first year of their life. He notes that deprivation affected children's physical growth even among those who did not experience sub-nutrition and that the behavioral sequelae tended to be disinhibited attachment or quasi-autistic features, rather than the more usual features, such as emotional disturbance and disruptive behavior. Nevertheless, Rutter (2011) found a considerable heterogeneity in outcomes even among children who experienced the most prolonged deprivation.

The neurobiology of children in all these situations needs to be better understood, as the adversities they are experiencing have lasting effects on their mental, behavioral, and physical outcomes well into adulthood – and the costs to them and to society are huge.

What Money cannot Buy – Parenting

Longitudinal follow-up of interventions in early childhood have made it clear that parenting (i.e., adult–child interaction) in the early years is the essential stimulation for brain development, a finding that is supported by developmental biology research in animals. The interactions studied include back-and-forth communications with caregivers, vocalization, gestures, facial expressions, and body movements. The interactions may be warm expressions by mothers, physical contact and play, visual mutuality and/or vocal exchanges, and mothers' response to infants in timely and appropriate ways (Bornstein et al., 2008).

Parents' communication with their children and their sensitivity to the children's emotional needs mediate the effects of low SES on children's cognitive and socioemotional development (NICHD, 2006). Two domains of positive caregiving highlighted by Bornstein and Putnick (2012) are cognitive and socioemotional. Cognitive caregiving consists of strategies parents use to stimulate their children by providing opportunities for them to learn through practices such as reading, telling stories, naming, counting, and drawing. Socioemotional caregiving includes activities that engage children in interpersonal interactions such as playing and singing.

The features of caregiving that might contribute to altering the biological process (i.e., turning genes on or off) have the following properties: (a) they are present very early in life when the mother–infant dyad is closest; (b) they occur frequently, as in many times a day; and (c) they are iterative and repetitive, occurring more or less the same way each time. Importantly, this research shows that to effect a change in biological systems, caregiving behavior must happen through repeated small influences over time, rather than one large impact at a single point in time (Barr, 2011).

Intergenerational Transmission of Poor Parenting

Stress that is toxic in early childhood can create a vicious cycle that renders children more sensitive to stressful experiences later in life. As noted earlier, adverse experiences in childhood significantly increase the risk of mental health problems such as post-traumatic stress disorder, depression, substance abuse,

and other addictions. Neuroscience research shows that children who are maltreated have problems regulating their emotions.

The adversities experienced in early childhood may result in lowered stress tolerance and heightened stress reactivity in adulthood. When the children become adults, they too will have poor parenting skills. Mayes (2010, 2011) illustrates the impact of early adversity on parenting. Chronic stress impacts the brain's reward-and-stress regulator system. These systems are required to care for another – self-control, emotional regulation, distress tolerance, decision making, anticipation of consequences, and the capacity to maintain executive control function in a stressful situation.

For example, the presence of a new baby activates a parent's neural circuitry which is involved in balancing reward seeking and stress modulation. Parents who were securely attached emotionally while growing up will show greater activation of the brain's reward region when they interact with their own baby. In addition, they will respond to their infant's distress with future-focused action to meet the child's needs. In contrast, parents with addictions (i.e., with a brain disorder) experience less reward activation in response to a baby's positive emotions and are less sensitive and more stressed in response to the baby's cries. The baby's cues become stressful, rather than rewarding, because the parents are not able to anticipate the future reward of being successful when taking care of someone. Their stress increases a craving for them to do something habitual so as to decrease their stress, which, in turn, raises the potential for them to neglect or abuse the child. In this way, the early adversity that a child experiences becomes a repeating cycle (Leckman et al., 2004; Rutherford et al., 2011).

Poor parenting *is* transmitted intergenerationally. For this reason, interventions focused on at-risk children in early childhood must also include services for their parents. Parents need to understand their own responses in their parenting role, as well as the needs of their infants and young children (Mayes, 2011).

Not everyone is affected the same way, however. One predictor of resilience is having a secure, responsive adult relationship that can buffer stress. Also, some genes make children more susceptible to adverse early-life care. Boyce (2014) uses a metaphor of dandelions and orchids to describe how children differ in their sensitivity to social settings. These differences in neurobiological sensitivity are based on genetic *and* epigenetic variations. Indeed, researchers are finding that the same 'risky' genes appear to foster better-than-average development if a child grows up in a supportive environment.

CONVERTING KNOWLEDGE INTO ACTION: CLOSING THE GAP

So what is at stake? Societies that invest in mothers and children develop populations that enjoy better performance in education, health, and behavior than those that do not make this investment. The countries that do not invest in mothers and children pay the price in many ways – through higher expenditures for children's failure in school, special education, juvenile justice systems, and long-term social dependency. The costs are huge and include, as well, sub-optimal productivity and higher rates of lifelong, chronic diseases (e.g., hypertension, diabetes, mental illness).

For all countries, investing in mothers and children in the early years can be a powerful social equalizer and a prime tool for economic and social stability (Irwin et al., 2007). The facts are clear: investments in early human development have direct and positive effects on children's school performance, education attainment, and overall health for their entire lives. We cannot ignore the scientific findings gained over the past decade. This new, and accumulating, knowledge has profound implications for all nations as they establish and direct social, economic, and education policies and programs.

The fate of the world's young children must be at the forefront of discussions as national governments and the global development community look beyond the Millennium Development Goals set for 2015 and toward 2030. The three main tasks for the next decade and beyond are to:

- redirect social policies to focus on young children aged 0–8 years old
- transform medical and public health models to promote and optimize healthy development and incorporate the science of early child development (ECD)
- assess children's outcomes and link these to program and policy data.

1. Redirect Social Policies to Focus on Children Aged 0–8 Years Old

Social policies need to be redirected to the malleable, early years of life if we are to successfully reduce inequality and promote productivity by producing effective people (Heckman, 2013). This redirection of policy is beyond the purview of any single ministry. Rather, and ideally, governments will establish ministries of human development that would integrate into one system their health, education, family, and social protection services for children and families horizontally and longitudinally over the life span. Each ministry – health, education, family, and social protection – would have a role, and the objective would be to link evidence-based programs that support (and 'scaffold') children and families and enable them to withstand stressors that emerge during children's early years.

2. Transform Medical and Public Health Models to Promote and Optimize Healthy Development and Incorporate the Science of early Child Development

The paradigm for health care needs to shift from managing chronic diseases to preventing these diseases and optimizing health. The transformation will be dynamic, ongoing, and reiterative, and it will depend on an alignment of public and private sectors, the key ministries (health, education, family, social protection), and local and national stakeholders and communities. All parties must collaborate interactively in data collection; program design, planning, and implementation; monitoring and assessment of outcomes; and linkage of outcomes to program and policy data.

Currently, the medical care model is grounded in strategies to cure disease and to manage chronic diseases. The world's child survival agenda is grounded in public health measures – nutrition, clean water, sanitation, basic medical care, the Expanded Program on Immunization (EPI), early and exclusive breastfeeding, oral rehydration, micronutrients (e.g., vitamin A, folate), insecticide-treated bed nets, and the prevention of HIV infection. In recent years, strategies of child survival and human development have been strengthened by effective social interventions, such as cash transfers, parenting support, and center-based early child development services, which have helped to mitigate families' material deprivations and to enhance adult–child protective interactions.

The impact of these models of interventions, however, is limited in time and space. We can do so much more to improve the present and future of the world's children by adopting approaches that are broadly integrative and provide an enduring continuum of care for mothers and their children, beginning prenatally and continuing on into primary school and beyond. It is time to expand beyond traditional medical and public health care models to identify and incorporate innovations based on the science of early human development. The implications of this science is that we need to shift from the current paradigm of managing chronic diseases and providing remedial care, to focus on promoting and optimizing health from the beginning and throughout life and to invest in population health (Halfon, 2014).

In particular, we need to expand access to ECD programs (formal and non-formal) and to coordinate programs to ensure that mothers and their children receive a full continuum of care, from the prenatal period through pregnancy to the postnatal period and beyond. We need to:

- target both mothers and children and address their nutrition, health, and interactions in an integrated way
- assure the psychosocial well-being of mothers and children and educate and support parents in their roles
- deliver services to children (e.g., breastfeeding, nutrition, stimulation, essential health care, immunizations)
- develop caregivers' and teachers' capacities for ECD
- raise public awareness, through the media, of ECD knowledge and practices.

3. Assess Children's Outcomes and Link these to Program and Policy Data

Children's well-being depends on the opportunities and experiences they have during early childhood. To enhance children's chances in life and the quality of human capital formation, communities and countries need, first, a comprehensive database of children's outcomes. This database would go beyond small-scale research evaluations and provide the underpinning for converting knowledge into action. Currently, the health and education sectors do not have positive outcome measures of children's well-being or a population-level tool for measuring children's development.

Governments and policy makers are recognizing the importance of having a population-based measure of children's development from birth to age 8, and efforts are under way to develop consensus on population-level tools for measuring outcomes in early childhood. To develop a meaningful ECD data system (i.e., one that is applicable locally, nationally, and comparatively), we need to:

- collect, map, and analyze national and/or local data on ECD programs systematically and comparatively
- develop a population-level, multinational database of children's outcomes (with and without ECD interventions)

- link data on children's outcomes with program and policy data
- continue research to enhance the effectiveness and efficiency of ECD interventions.

AN AGENDA FOR THE FUTURE

The messages are clear:

- Start early, but don't stop there. Interventions in the very early years make a meaningful and lasting difference, and they are cost-effective. Plasticity in the brain continues, however, and thus interventions in early childhood must be aligned with later interventions to ensure a continuum of services and care for all children. Neither negates the need for the other.
- Focus on prevention and align efforts across all sectors and ministries that address the needs of young children. Shift society's emphasis on remedial services and the management of chronic health problems to the promotion and optimization of health and well-being.
- Explore innovative programs and policies that promote healthy human development and ameliorate early adverse experiences for at-risk pregnant mothers, young children, and families. Promote skills that encourage positive parent–child attachments and responsive caregiving. Empower and engage communities in the collection of data, planning of programs, and improvement of services to enhance their children's outcomes.

Research

This new framework – centered on early human development – is broad and all-encompassing. To uncover and fully understand the effects of experience-based brain development on health, behavior, and learning over the life course, researchers must come together and collaborate across disciplines. The work of neuroscientists, geneticists, biologists, social psychologists, and epidemiologists is essential to the field of early human development, and their insights must be coordinated with those of educators, other practitioners, and policy makers.

As the fields of developmental neurobiology, genetics, epigenetics, and population health converge on early human development and flourish, some questions of research interest and policy relevance include the following: How and by what mechanisms do genes and early social contexts co-determine trajectories of behavior and biological development? What mechanisms (mediators and effects of moderators) underpin associations among stress, development, and morbidity? When, at what ages, and in what subgroups do these associations hold? (Boyce and Hertzman, 2013).

New ideas and approaches in the science of early development are needed. We need to continue to learn from evaluations of ECD programs and interventions. Doing more of the same is no longer acceptable. Rather, we must systematically and comparatively identify what works and under what circumstances and then apply the lessons that have been learned to find ways to take effective interventions to scale.

Capacity Development

Along with research explorations, we need to develop the capacity for ECD among policy makers, as well as practitioners. The leveraging of public policies that foster effective ECD interventions depends on improving policy makers' understanding of and proficiency in early human development. Improving the quality of ECD practitioners and developing a cadre of quality practitioners and caregivers trained in early human development are essential for all countries. Sensitive, responsive caregiving is a key ingredient of quality for teachers and health workers, as well as parents.

CONCLUSION

Societies have a moral obligation to provide singular attentiveness to children (OECD, 2009). Given the knowledge we now have about how development of the brain in early life affects health, learning, and behavior until we die, countries and policy makers can no longer afford to do more of the same or nothing. Countries and policy makers must garner the political will and the skills to leverage and translate what we know into policies and practices that promote and protect children's early development – so that all children can reach their full potential as they develop, grow, and progress through life.

FURTHER READING

Britto, P. R., Engle, P. L. and Super, C. M. (eds) (2013). *Handbook of Early Childhood Development Research and its Impact on Global Policy*. New York: Oxford University Press.

Keating, D. P. (2011). *Nature and Nurture in Early Child Development*. New York: Cambridge University Press.

National Scientific Council on the Developing Child, Center on the Developing Child, Harvard University, Working Papers. Available at: www.developingchild.harvard.edu. See especially:

The Timing and Quality of Early Experiences Combine to Shape Brain Architecture. Working Paper No. 5 (2007).

Early Experiences Can Alter Gene Expression and Affect Long-Term Development. Working Paper No. 10 (2010).

Building the Brain's 'Air Traffic Control' System: How Early Experiences Shape the Development of Executive Function. Working Paper No. 11 (2011).

The Science of Neglect: The Persistent Absence of Responsive Care Disrupts the Developing Brain. Working Paper No. 12 (2012).

REFERENCES

Anda, R. F., V. J. Felitti, J. Walker, C. L. Whitfield, J. D. Bremner, B. D. Perry, et al. (2006). The Enduring Effects of Abuse and Related Adverse Experiences in Childhood: A Convergence of Evidence from Neurobiology and Epidemiology. *European Archives of Psychiatry and Clinical Neuroscience* 56(3): 174–86.

Barr, R. (2011). Mother and Child: Preparing for a Life. In D. P. Keating (ed.), *Nature and Nurture in Early Child Development*. New York: Cambridge University Press.

Black, R. E., L. H. Allen, Z. A. Bhutta, L. E. Caulfield, M. de Onis, M. Ezzati, et al. (2008). Maternal and Child Undernutrition Study Group – Maternal and Child Undernutrition: Global and Regional Exposures and Health Consequences. *The Lancet* 371(9608): 243–60.

Boivin, M. and C. Hertzman (eds) (2012). *Early Childhood Development: Adverse Experiences and Developmental Health*. The Royal Society of Canada – Canadian Academy of Health Sciences Expert Panel (with R. Barr, T. Boyce, A. Fleming, H. MacMillan, C. Odgers, M. Sokolowski, and N. Trocmé). Ottawa: Royal Society of Canada.

Bornstein, M. and D. Putnick (2012). Cognitive and Socioemotional Caregiving in Developing Countries. *Child Development: Society for Research in Child Development* 83 (Jan./Feb.) (1): 46–61.

Bornstein, M. H., C. S. Tamis-Lemonda, C. S. Hahn, and O. M. Haynes (2008). Maternal Responsiveness to Young Children at Three Ages: Longitudinal Analysis of a Multidimensional, Modular, and Specific Parenting Construct. *Developmental Psychology* 44 (May) (3): 867–74.

Boyce, W. T. (2014). From Science to Action: Clyde Hertzman's vision for a more just and generous world. Presentation at CIFAR Symposium: From Cell to Society, 6 February. Available at: www.cifar.ca/celltosociety vimeo.com/88309282

Boyce, W. T. and C. Hertzman (2013). Early Childhood Health and the Life Course: The State of the Science and Proposed Research Priorities. Background paper for the MCH Life Course Research Network. Presented at the Maternal and Child Health Life Course Research Agenda-Setting Meeting, Life Course Network, UCLA Center for Healthier Children, Families and Communities, Washington, DC, 20–22 February. Available at: www.mchb. hrsa.gov/research/project_info.asp?ID=164

Caspi, A., A. Hariri, A. Holmes, R. Uher, and T. E. Moffitt (2010). Genetic Sensitivity to the Environment: The Case of Serotonin Transporter Gene (5-HTT) and its Implications for Studying Complex Diseases and Traits. *American Journal of Psychiatry* 167: 509–27.

Caspi, A., K. Sugden, T. Moffitt, A. Taylor, I. Craig, H. Harrington, et al. (2003). Influence of Life Stress on Depression: Moderation by a Polymorphism in the 5-HTT Gene. *Science* 301: 386–9.

Danese, A. (2011). Biological Embedding of Adverse Childhood Experiences. Presentation at Early Brain & Biological Development: A Science in Society Symposium, Summary Report, Volume 3, 30 May to 3 June. Alberta Family Wellness Initiative, Banff, Alberta, Canada. www.albertafamilywellness.org

Danese, A. and B. S. McEwen (2012). Adverse Childhood Experiences, Allostasis, Allostatic Load, and Age-Related Disease. *Physiology and Behavior* 106(1): 29–39.

Danese, A., A. Caspi, B. Williams, A. Ambler, K. Sugden, J. Mika, et al. (2011). Biological Embedding of Stress through Inflammation Processes in Childhood. *Molecular Psychiatry* 16(3): 244–6.

Danese, A., C. Pariante, A. Caspi, A. Taylor, and R. Poulton (2007). Childhood Maltreatment Predicts Adult Inflammation in a Life-Course Study. *Proceedings of the National Academy of Sciences* 104: 1319–24.

Engle, P. L., M. M. Black, J. R. Behrman, M. Cabral de Mello, P. J. Gertler, L. Kapiriri, et al. (2007). Strategies to Avoid the Loss of Developmental Potential in More than 200 Million Children in the Developing World. *The Lancet* 369(9557): 229–42.

Engle, P. L., L. C. Fernald, H. Alderman, J. Behrman, C. O'Gara, A. Yousafzai, et al., and the Global Development Steering Group (2011). Strategies for Reducing Inequalities and Improving Developmental Outcomes for Young Children in Low-Income and Middle-Income Countries. *The Lancet* 378(9799): 1339–53.

Felitti, V. J., R. F. Anda, D. Nordenberg, D. F. Williamson, A. M. Spitz, V. Edwards, et al. (1998). The Relationship of Childhood Abuse and Household Dysfunction to Many of the Leading Causes of Death in Adults: The Adverse Childhood Experiences (ACE) Study. *American Journal of Preventive Medicine* 14 (May) (4): 245–58.

Hackman, D. A., M. J. Farah, and M. J. Meaney (2010). Socioeconomic Status and the Brain: Mechanistic Insights from Human and Animal Research. *Nature Reviews Neuroscience* 11: 651–9. Available at: www.nature.com/reviews/neuro

Halfon, N. (2014). Leveraging the Science of Health Development: Designing Systems that Help Children Thrive. Presentation at CIFAR Symposium: From Cell to Society, 6 February. Available at: www.cifar.ca/celltosociety vimeo.com88295979

Hart, T. and T. R. Risley (1995). *Meaningful Differences in the Everyday Experience of Young American Children*. Baltimore, MD: Paul H. Brookes.

Heckman, J. (2013). The Economics of Inequality and Human Development. Keynote presentation at the First National Congress meeting on Building a Legal Framework for Public Policies for Early Childhood, Brasilia, Brazil, 16 April.

Herztman, C. and T. Boyce (2010). How Experience Gets Under the Skin to Create Gradients in Developmental Health. *Annual Review of Public Health* 31: 329–47.

Irwin, L., A. Siddiqi, and C. Hertzman (2007). *Early Child Development: A Powerful Equalizer. Final Report for the World Health Organization's Commission on Social Determinants of Health*. Vancouver: University of British Columbia.

Knudsen, E., J. Heckman, J. Cameron, and J. Shonkoff (2006). Economic, Neurobiological, and Behavioral Perspectives on Building America's Future Workforce. *Proceedings of the National Academy of Sciences* 103(27): 10155–62.

Leckman, J. F., R. Feldman, J. E. Swain, V. Eicher, H. Thompson, and L. C. Mayes (2004). Primary Parental Preoccupation: Circuits, Genes and the Crucial Role of the Environment. *Journal of Neural Transmission* 111(7): 753–71.

Liu, L., H. L. Johnson, S. Cousens, J. Perin, S. Scott, J. E. Lawn, et al. (2012). Global, Regional, and National Causes of Child Mortality: An Updated Systematic Analysis for 2010 with Time Trends since 2000. *The Lancet* 379(9832): 2151–61.

Marmot Review Team (2010). *Fair Society, Healthy Lives*. London: UCL (University College London) Institute of Health Equity.

Available at: www.instituteofhealthequity.org/projects/fair-society-healthy-lives-the-marmot-review

Mayes, L. (2010). Stress & Parental Care: Intergenerational Transmission of Parenting Abilities. Presentation at Early Brain & Biological Development: A Science in Society Symposium, 31 May to 4 June. Alberta Family Wellness Initiative, Banff, Alberta, Canada. www.albertafamilywellness.org

Mayes, L. C. (2011). The Impact of Early Adversity on Parenting. Presentation at Early Brain & Biological Development: A Science in Society Symposium, 30 May to 3 June. Alberta Family Wellness Initiative, Banff, Alberta, Canada. www.albertafamilywellness.org

McCain, M., F. Mustard, and K. McCuaig (2011). *Early Years Study 3: Making Decisions, Taking Action*. Toronto: Margaret and Wallace McCain Family Foundation.

McCain, M., F. Mustard, and S. Shanker (2007). *Early Years 2: Putting Science into Action*. Ontario: Council for Early Child Development.

McEwen, B. S. (2008a). Central Effects of Stress Hormones in Health and Disease: Understanding the Protective and Damaging Effects of Stress and Stress Mediators. *European Journal of Pharmacology* 583(2–3): 174–85.

McEwen, B. S. (2008b). Understanding the Potency of Stressful Early Life Experiences on Brain and Body Function. *Metabolism Clinical and Experimental* 57(2): S11–15.

McEwen, B. S. (2014). The Brain on Stress: How the Social Environment 'Gets Under the Skin'. Presentation at CIFAR Symposium: From Cell to Society, 6 February. Available at: www.cifar.ca/celltosociety vimeo.com/88309282

Meaney, M. and Szyf, M. (2005). Maternal Care as a Model for Experience-Dependent Chromatin Plasticity. *Trends in Neuroscience* 28(9): 456–63.

Miller, T. (2000). Health of Children in War Zones: Gaza Child Health Survey. Hamilton, Ontario: McMaster University.

Nanni, V., R. Uher and A. Danese (2012). Childhood Maltreatment Predicts Unfavorable Course of Illness and Treatment Outcome in Depression: A Meta-Analysis. *American Journal of Psychiatry* 169(2): 141–51.

National Institute of Child Health and Human Development (NICHD) Early Child Care Research Network (2006). Child-Care Effect Sizes for the NICHD Study of Early Child Care and Youth Development. *American Psychologist* 61(2): 99–116.

National Scientific Council on the Developing Child, Center on the Developing Child, Harvard University, Working Papers Nos. 5, 10, 11, and 12. www.developingchild.harvard.edu.

Nelson, C. A., E. A. Furtado, N. A. Fox, and C. H. Zeanah (2009). The Deprived Human Brain. *American Science* 97: 222–9.

Organization for Economic Cooperation and Development (OECD) (2009). *Doing Better for Children: The Way Forward*. Paris: OECD.

Rutherford, H. J., S. K. Williams, S. Moy, L. C. Mayes, and J. M. Johns (2011). Disruption of Maternal Parenting Circuitry by Addictive Process: Rewiring of Reward and Stress Systems. *Frontiers in Psychiatry* 2: 37.

Rutter, M. (2006). *Genes and Behavior: Nature/Nurture Interplay Explained*. Oxford: Blackwell.

Rutter, M. (2011). Biological and Experiential Influences on Psychological Development. In D. P. Keating (ed.), *Nature and Nurture in Early Child Development*. New York: Cambridge University Press.

Shonkoff, J. (2012). Leveraging the Biology of Adversity to Address the Roots of Disparities in Health and Development. *Proceedings of the National Academy of Sciences* 109 (suppl. 2): 17302–7.

Shonkoff, J. and A. Garner (2012). The Lifelong Effects of Early Childhood Adversity and Toxic Stress. *Pediatrics* 129(1): e232–46.

Shonkoff, J., W. Boyce, and B. McEwen (2009). Neuroscience, Molecular Biology and the Childhood Roots of Health Disparities: Building a New Framework for Health Promotion and Disease Prevention. *JAMA* 301: 2252–9.

Shonkoff, J. P., L. Richter, J. van der Gaag, and Z. A. Bhutta (2012). The Biology of Adversity: Building an Integrated Science of Child Survival, Early Childhood Development, and Human Capital Formation. *Pediatrics* 129 (Feb.) (2): 1–13.

Thompson, R. A. and C. A. Nelson (2001). Developmental Science and the Media: Early Brain Development. *American Psychologist* 56(1): 5–15.

Walker, S. P., T. D. Wachs, S. Grantham-McGregor, M. Black, C. Nelson, S. Huffman, et al. (2011). Inequality in Early Childhood: Risk and

Protective Factors for Early Child Development. *The Lancet* 378(9799): 1325–38.

Walque, D. (2011). Conflicts, Epidemics and Orphanhood: The Impact of Extreme Events on the Health and Educational Achievement of Children. In H. Alderman (ed.), *No Small Matter: The Impact of Poverty, Shocks, and Human Capital Investment in Early Childhood Development*. Human Development Perspectives. Washington, DC: The World Bank.

10

Theoretical Insights from Neuroscience in Early Childhood Research

Mike Anderson and Corinne Reid

INTRODUCTION

In early childhood, practitioners see most clearly the interconnectedness of our sensory, motor, language, cognitive and social systems. Despite definitive categorical diagnostic traditions (i.e., DSM 5 and ICD-10) and brain research traditions focusing on localization of disorders in specific brain areas, complex presentations are the norm, with children often accumulating a number of different diagnoses by early school age (Kim, 2014; Landy and Bradley, 2013). Indeed, co-morbidity is the rule rather than the exception, as is the high clinical use of 'Not Otherwise Specified' (NOS) diagnostic classification, reflecting the challenge of fitting complex symptom presentation within existing categories (Fombonne, 2009; Regier et al., 2009). These practitioner and researcher observations have helped to drive a revolution in brain research toward understanding brain development in a trans-diagnostic and systemic neurodevelopmental way – it is a move away from seeking function-specific or disorder-specific localization which

has proven more potent for looking at causation in neurological, lesion-based conditions than complex psychological syndromes (Hyman, 2007, 2010; Insel et al., 2010; Kim, 2014; Regier et al., 2009).

We know, for example, that emotion dysregulation is a feature of many disorders of childhood (ADHD, anxiety, autism spectrum disorder and conduct disorder to name a few) and that there is a brain-basis to emotion regulation (Franklin et al., 2015; Geise et al., 2014). Blair and Raver (2105) for example, recently presented a trans-diagnostic view of school readiness by focussing on the central relevance of individual differences in brain-based self-regulation in setting the scene for school learning. Points of connection between conditions (rather than points of separation) are thus pointing to new understandings and to trans-diagnostic treatment possibilities, in this case using models of neuroplasticity to inform the training of neural cognitive control pathways. Working with parenting and teaching practice around the management of behavior can be enriched with understandings about neurodevelopmental pathways to self regulation. In addition, innovative cognitive 'brain training games' and neuro-feedback techniques offer the potential to more directly strengthen relevant aspects of brain function (Price et al., 2013, Rabipour and Raz, 2012). This new paradigm also requires bridging traditionally separate disciplines spanning different levels of explanation, from biology (brain) to cognition, to behavior (Anderson and Reid, 2009; Howard Jones and Fenton, 2012). Encouraging discourse between brain-based research and cognitive models of intellectual and emotional functioning is perhaps the most important aspect of this new paradigm and is re-invigorating both fields. This chapter will re-consider how we might best view developmental deficits and delays from a neurocognitive perspective in the light of emerging evidence about the nature of the developing brain. Perhaps the best place to start is to explore what is happening in the absence of a neurocognitive framework as brain technology outruns our development of conceptual models.

NEUROSCIENCE IN EARLY CHILDHOOD EDUCATION

Knowing a lot about brain development does not guarantee that we know a lot about what will work in training our brains though we do know that education is 'the best cognitive enhancer of all' (Center for the Developing Child, 2007: 1). In the absence of neurocognitive theory and translational research methodology that connects what we know from brain research with what we know from clinical practice, neuro-myths are flourishing and impacting international policy and daily practice in early childhood education, health and mental health.

Perhaps the most striking neuro-myth in international educational policy for early childhood is the inference that well-established evidence for unparalleled synaptic growth during the first three years of life (Davis, 2011) implicates the

need for access to formalized schooling at this age to ensure that optimal learning takes places and that this 'critical developmental window' is not missed (Howard Jones, 2014; Shonkoff 2011; Vandenbroeck, M., 2014). In fact there is no clear evidence to suggest that periods of synaptic growth are especially implicated in better learning (Alferink and Farmer-Dougan, 2010), nor that early formalized education is particularly beneficial for learning unless children are experiencing particularly impoverished environments at home (Loeb et al., 2005, Miller et al., 2011; National Scientific Council on the Developing Child, 2007; Schweinhart et al., 1993). This brain-centric misinterpretation of early childhood development is having increasingly broad implications for education policy and practice around the globe and is just one example of influential neuro-mythology.

The framing of a neurocognitive architecture for early childhood development will help to join the dots between brain research and cognitive research and must be a precursor to mapping this knowledge effectively onto early childhood practice to prevent similar leaps of faith and reverse logic (Anderson and Della Sala, 2012; Della Sala and Anderson, 2012; Goswami, 2006; Howard Jones, 2010; Reid and Anderson, 2012). Where to begin?

MIND THE GAP: WHAT DO WE KNOW? WHAT DO WE NEED TO KNOW? WHERE IS THE NEW GROUND?

Thanks to significant technological advances in the past decade, we know a fair bit about the developing brain (although of course there is much, much, more to know). We know even more about cognitive development from nearly 50 years of experimental work in Psychology. But we know very little about neurocognitive development. It is not so long ago that psychologists did not see much relevance of the brain for understanding cognition, education or mental health. Similarly, for some time we sensed that those interested in the brain and its development had tired of the core constructs of cognitive psychology and ultimately questioned its utility (Anderson, 2005; Churchland, 2007; Marshall, 2009). Most of what we claim to know is a rag bag that contains all that we do know about cognitive development along with the fair bit of knowledge about brain development. The contents are occasionally shuffled and then disgorged onto pages of journals and books whose focus is a new field with as yet little in the way of new ideas. Initially the collision of cognitive development and brain development was managed pretty much like an armistice of two former opponents who now tentatively agree that each has something to say. This left a 'no man's land' that was filled with treatment services that joined the dots for themselves.

Perhaps the most well known example of this is the Dore program which is described on its website as 'a unique and personalized program of physical exercises which aims to improve the efficiency of the cerebellum, for people with learning difficulties such as dyslexia, dyspraxia and ADHD'. Dore founders pointed to (i) sound evidence that the cerebellum is implicated in a number of language-related disorders including dyslexia and dyspraxia; and (ii) sound evidence that the cerebellum is centrally implicated in motor movement. The Dore program claimed to have designed a program that was able to ameliorate these language-related developmental disorders by stimulation of the cerebellum through physical activity. While the brain-based research implicating the cerebellum for a number of developmental disorders was sound, making the leap to designing an intervention based on physical activity on the basis of the known function of the cerebellum, was not warranted (Bishop, 2007). Not only would we need to find out how the cerebellum is involved in language processing, and in particular that part of language processing implicated in developmental disorders, but we would need to know how physical activity could change those features of the cerebellum and in such a way that it could restore a function that already has a

developmental trajectory. By the time this neuro-myth was exposed, many families had paid considerable sums of money at the more than 50 Dore centers around the world.

Events such as these impelled a more active rapprochement between scientific disciplines, yet while the barriers have broken down nothing truly new has emerged. We believe that indeed there really is value in a new field of neurocognitive development but that we need to stop and take stock to prevent further 'parallel play' between brain scientists and cognitive psychologists and to impede the further proliferation of neuro-myths in education, health and mental health care.

If we look at where the research impact of the new approach has been greatest it is in the field of developmental disorders and it is here that the shortcomings are most obvious. Laying side-by-side our knowledge of cognitive development on the one hand with our knowledge of brain development on the other highlights two major deficiencies in the newly emerging field of the neurocognitive basis of developmental disorders: (i) an outmoded atheoretical classificatory system and (ii) a neglect of our understanding of 'typical' development. For example, some of the most exciting work in developmental neurocognition is that of Philip Shaw and colleagues (at the Neurobehavioral Clinical Research Section, National Human Genome Research Institute, Bethesda) on the effect of different trajectories of brain development on neurocognitive outcomes (Shaw et al., 2006, 2011, 2012, 2013; Shaw, 2014). They have shown, for example, that children diagnosed with ADHD show characteristically different developmental trajectories for thickness of cortical grey matter. But this exciting research is handicapped by a hidden and longer term problem – the research group has inherited what we and others consider to be an outmoded classificatory system for developmental disorders (for detailed recent reviews of the limitations of the DSM diagnostic system, see Demazeux and Singy 2015; Nigg, 2015). In this kind of research we must act as if we 'know' what ADHD is and we act as if we know which children 'have' it and which don't and our analytical strategies (distinguishing developmental trajectories of cortical thickness between a group of children with ADHD and those who are developing 'typically') are predicated on this. But we would submit that the classification of children as having ADHD or whatever will ultimately be knowledge generated *from* the research program itself rather than being a foundation on which the research program progresses. Thus we will argue that the new focus on the relationship between trajectories of brain development and developmental outcomes compels us to change the way we think about atypical development, and particularly how we classify developmental disorders. More specifically, rather than thinking of these as discrete entities (or typologies) with specific single causes we will explore the idea that they reflect multiple and interacting atypical developmental pathways and consequently supposedly discrete disorders have much in common with alternative diagnostic categories – these differences are dimensional and multiple rather than categorical and singular. Certainly we have an overwhelming prima facie case for this proposition given the ubiquity of comorbidity in diagnoses of developmental disorders. This new approach requires a renewed interest in what constitutes typical developmental trajectories, what constitutes significant deviations from the typical and, ultimately, what categories of deviation attract which particular kinds of diagnostic label. Let's begin by looking at what we know about typical and atypical brain development and then what cognitive models tell us about typical development and developmental disorders as a prelude to considering an innovative neurocognitive research framework.

TYPICAL AND ATYPICAL BRAIN DEVELOPMENT IN EARLY CHILDHOOD

The number of neurons in the newborn brain is staggeringly large (~100 billion) and yet it is only about one quarter of the volume of the adult brain. It is also interesting that by 6 years of age total brain volume has reached about 95% of its adult value but by many accounts full structural development does not reach its peak until the early 20s (see Giedd and Rapoport, 2010 for a review). Our knowledge of brain development until relatively recently used to be founded on histological examination of post-mortem brains. But in the last 20 years or so there have been major technological advances in both structural (mainly MRI) and functional (mainly fMRI and EEG) brain imaging. Magnetic Resonance Imaging (MRI) uses an extremely powerful magnetic field to realign hydrogen atoms and by switching this field on and off the energy emitted by the atoms as they move between states is detected and is converted into images that correspond to the underlying brain tissue. The MRI scanner takes many 'slices' through the head in three dimensions and software can reassemble these images into 3-D models of the underlying brain structure. MRI allows us to see and measure white matter tracts and integrity as well as features of grey matter (such as surface areas, volumes and densities) as either global or localized features of brain anatomy. MRI has proved particularly popular because it is non-invasive, unlike other technologies such as Positron Emission Tomography (PET) that rely on detecting the movement of radioactive isotopes through the brain. However PET is more functional than MRI in that it detects changes in the brain as a consequence of concurrent cognitive (and other) activity. So it was the addition of an f in fMRI (functional magnetic resonance imaging) that led to a major research development. fMRI uses essentially the same recording hardware as MRI but it utilizes the fact that oxygenated blood has less of an influence on a magnetic field than de-oxygenated blood. The change in blood oxygen levels is reflected in the BOLD signal which although slow (taking a number of seconds to respond) gives excellent 'localization' (i.e., where in the brain activity is).

Electroencephalograms (EEG) have been around for many years and they work by recording tiny voltage changes via sensors on the scalp that are reflective of activity in the brain. In particular the development of techniques in measuring averaged waveforms in response to particular kinds of stimuli or responses (evoked potentials) has played an important role in our understanding of cognitive processes where, for example, different components (peaks and troughs occurring at different times after onset) have become indices of different process, e.g. N2 is considered to reflect early attentional processes whereas P3 reflects later 'thoughtful' stimulus evaluation. However, more recent research has seen a shift back to considering the phase and power of different frequencies recorded – such as alpha (8–12 Hz) and theta (4–8 Hz). The advantage of EEG over fMRI is that much of the functional activity in the brain that we are interested in takes place in milliseconds rather than seconds and EEG can record at the faster rate. However the advantages of speed are counterbalanced by the disadvantage of localizing the source of the activity. Nevertheless, modern systems with many more sensors (128 or 256) and accompanied by much more sophisticated signal processing are becoming much better at also localizing the source of the brain activity. The increasing efficiency of the hardware and the increasing sophistication in signal processing and analysis are generating unparalleled data on the development of both structure and function.

Many structural processes take place over the huge period of 'growth' in early childhood including myelination, dendritic branching of neurons and, in a curious twist, a great deal of neural pruning (Changeux, 2012). The two main structural components of the brain are grey matter and white matter, the former consisting mainly of neuronal bodies and dendrites and the latter myelinated axons that helps speed up connections around the brain, and they have quite different developmental trajectories. White matter increases roughly linearly until about 20 years of age whereas grey matter undergoes an inverted U-shaped function where the grey-matter volume of a 7-year-old exceeds that of a young adult. Aside from questions

about this general developmental pattern there are two other important considerations. The first is that individual development trajectories of brain development seem to be predictive of both psychiatric and cognitive developmental outcomes. As previously described, Shaw and colleagues have shown convincingly that in the case of children diagnosed with ADHD for example the trajectory of grey matter cortical thickness exhibits a delay of as much as two years. The second is that despite the generality of these global patterns of developmental change the brain can still be divided into regions and these regions themselves show different developmental profiles. So, for example, we have shown using EEG data that processing in primary auditory cortex shows every indication of being fully mature by 7 years old (Bishop et al., 2011) whereas a great deal of MRI, fMRI and EEG data indicates that frontal regions mature later (Brydges et al., 2013, 2014) and may still be developing in the late teens/early 20s (Gogtay et al., 2004; Giedd and Rapoport, 2010; Vidal et al., 2012).

What is clear is that both neural circuitry and structure impact on developmental outcomes at school, in daily life and in behavioral and mental health profiles.

COGNITIVE MODELS OF TYPICAL AND ATYPICAL DEVELOPMENT: THE MINIMAL COGNITIVE ARCHITECTURE

Rather than brain structure, cognitive psychology has traditionally been interested in the higher order 'mental processes' or information-processing mechanisms that affect behavior. These include processes such as attention, memory, perception, language and metacognition. Some models also consider systemic or overarching information-processing frameworks such as models of general processing capacity, also known as intelligence (or 'g') that theorize ways in which these sub-processes may result from, and/or operate as part of, a broader system of perceiving, thinking and problem solving that both enables and constrains our learning and daily functioning (Anderson, 1992, 2009, 2013). These general models are based around the measurement of intelligence with IQ tests. IQ tests are excellent predictors of life-outcomes such as occupation, welfare provision, crime and health – even of mortality (Deary, 2012). They remain the bedrock of educational assessment and policy making as well as diagnosis of developmental disorders and profiling of the impact of neurological insult. Increasingly they are also becoming central to understanding the neurodevelopmental footprint of psychological disorders, chronic illness and neonatal trauma. Notably, cognitive experimental paradigms have existed relatively independently of brain-based paradigms and have been most popularly adopted in educational fields rather than in the medical fields associated with brain-based research.

The cognitive model favored by our research team is that of the Minimal Cognitive Architecture (MCA) designed by the first author (Anderson, 1992, 2009, 2013; see Figure 10.1).

This model uniquely helps us to differentiate developmental disorders on the basis of different routes to manifest cognitive abilities. Rather than seeing each disorder as unconnected, the model shows elements of shared and differentiable features of cognitive development that may cross traditional disorder categorizations in ways that uniquely align with new thinking about brain structure and function. Specifically, the Minimal Cognitive Architecture proposes two routes to knowledge or cognitive functioning:

1   The first pathway involves thinking and problem solving. Functioning is constrained by the speed at which an individual can process information. All information, whether verbal or non verbal, will be impacted by the speed with which the system can operate. The speed of processing difficulties can thus create a global deficit from a specific cognitive limitation.

2   The second pathway is unconstrained by this fundamental feature of 'thinking speed'. Rather it is determined by automated systems, or 'modules' that carry complex but specific processing mechanisms

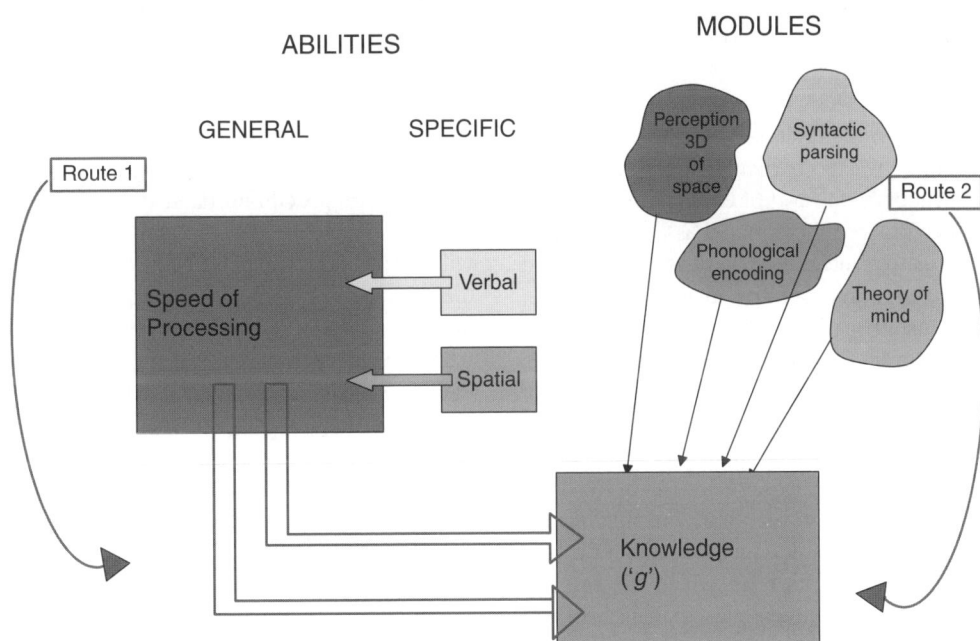

Figure 10.1   Anderson's minimal cognitive architecture

Source: Anderson (1992)

to facilitate evolutionarily advantageous functions. Modules may include face perception, 3D perception, language acquisition devices and socially relevant modules such as the theory of mind, implicated in autism. These may be delayed in coming 'on line' in some children whilst in others they may be absent, creating a permanent deficit. The nature of the modules means that delays or deficits may be innate or acquired and may manifest as learning-related difficulties, social and communication difficulties, motor difficulties and mental health difficulties. Executive dysfunctions, for example, are implicated in each of these domains. Emotional and behavioral dysregulation are key features of many disorders. Similarly, communication difficulties are common to many disorders.

BRAIN FUNCTION, COGNITION AND NEUROCOGNITIVE MODELS OF DEVELOPMENT AND INTERVENTION: THE MINIMAL NEUROCOGNITIVE ARCHITECTURE

The coming together of brain research and cognitive research has encouraged us to further develop the Minimal Cognitive Architecture (MCA). In the original instantiation of the MCA it was proposed that speed of processing may relate to neural efficiency but there was no particular focus on the biological or brain level of explanation. We will utilize this cognitive model as an example of how active integration between brain-based knowledge and cognitive models can result in new understandings and unique predictions that warrant the formalization of a new discipline called neurocognitive development.

The theory of the Minimal NeuroCognitive Architecture (MNCA) maintains its cognitive foundation and proposes a new set of hypotheses about the brain-basis of general intelligence (g) in children, built on a foundation of robust empirical regularities for which the original MCA has a novel theoretical explanation. The empirical regularities are:

1   There are substantial correlations between speed of information processing (SoP) and g;

2   There are substantial correlations between measures of executive functioning, or cognitive control (CC), and g;
3   There are substantial correlations between indices of alpha EEG and g;
4   There are substantial correlations between indices of theta EEG and g;
5   There is a robust relationship between properties of a specific brain-based fronto-parietal network (the Multiple Demand system) and g (Duncan, 2013; Giedd and Rapoport, 2010).

The MNCA proposes that there are two dimensions to g, one related to individual differences and speed of processing and the other related to developmental change in modular systems, primarily those related to cognitive control (Anderson, 1992, 2001). Linking these robust data via these theoretical positions leads us to an exciting conjecture about the brain-basis of g: one dimension of g is related to speed of information processing, is indexed psychophysiologically by EEG alpha and is related to white matter integrity; the other dimension of g is related to CC, is indexed psychophysiologically by EEG theta and is related to properties of the Multiple Demand system. This is one example of how developments in the understanding of brain function can significantly extend cognitive theory and how cognitive theory can provide impetus and a way of making sense of complex brain data. It is our view that understanding developmental disorders will not be dominated by what areas of the brain might be responsible for what disorder (as it was largely 20 years ago) but rather by what deviations from typical trajectories are likely to lead to developmental delays or deficits in learning and also in social-emotional functioning. This is but one example.

Thus, the reinstatement of a model of the nature of intelligence as central to assisting us in understanding early childhood development across educational, health, mental health and social relationship domains is an example of how brain science, cognitive science and early childhood practice can usefully inform one another. Nevertheless, at this point, there remains a separation between these three disciplines. A shared language in the form of a common model for understanding cognitive development is a beginning. The next step is the development of a shared research agenda and rigorous research methodologies that are contextually valid.

METHODOLOGIES OF RESEARCH AND INTERVENTION

One thing that is clear in current thinking about brain related research is the importance of building new conceptual, organizational and methodological frameworks to enable us to develop truly transdisciplinary research and practice. This need was one of the key points of recommendation in a report presented to the Australian parliament recently outlining a new national brain research agenda (AAS, 2013).

Research Domain Criteria

In response to the limitations of the ICD and DSM systems in illuminating mental health aetiology, there is currently a team developing new Research Domain Criteria (RDoC) that draw upon genomics and neuroscience as well as clinical observation (Cuthbert, 2014; Insel et al., 2010). The RDoC framework classifies mental illness as brain disorders of neural circuitry (rather than site-specific lesions associated with neurological conditions). While the RDoC focus is on re-defining and treating mental illness, we also consider it relevant in the broader context of developmental disorders. According to this view, aetiological and intervention research will be advanced by (Cuthbert, 2014; Sanislow et al., 2010; Shaw et al., 2010):

1 Conceptualization of disorders using multiple layers of explanation and interpretation with units of analysis including genetic, molecular, cellular, neural circuits, physiology, behavior and self-report.

2 Rather than categorical phenotypic systems (clusters of behavioral symptoms), an understanding of dimensional domains of neuro-functioning (rather than symptom phenotype) such as negative valence systems (that impact perception of threat, loss or non reward); positive valence systems (that impact responsiveness, habit or perception of reward); cognitive systems (such as attention, memory, executive control and language behavior); social processes (such as affiliation, attachment, and sense of self); and modulatory systems (such as sleeping or arousal). Defining normality and abnormality then is a distinction of quantity rather than quality.

3 Augmentation of traditional symptom-based assessments with imaging, genomic sequencing and tasks targeting underlying cognitive pathways.

Ultimately proponents expect that this process may result in a different classification system for mental health disorders (Cuthbert, 2014). Given the likely shared basis of mental health disorders and other developmental disorders illuminated by the Minimal NeuroCognitive Architecture it is likely that a new system would accommodate all developmental disorders. Indeed, the dimensional domains of neuro-functioning proposed by the RDoC criteria, parallel the modular and individual difference factors highlighted by the Minimal NeuroCognitive Architecture. For all developmental disorders then, gold standard research design is likely to prioritize:

1 Interdisciplinarity to consider these multiple levels of explanation from different vantage points.

2 Samples in research which are likely to span more than one diagnostic category but share a core neurodevelopmental feature such as executive dysfunction or impaired reward circuits. This may also include clients with pre-clinical symptoms who do not fit any DSM or ICD category.

3 Longitudinal design, incorporating multi-methods concurrently capturing multiple indices of development for each individual to look at neural trajectories and interactive pathways over the course of development; the impact of genes and environment; and the epigenetic shaping of behavior and behavior regulation (Leckman and Yazgan, 2010).

4 Consideration of developmental notions such as equifinality and equipotentiality when looking at the complex relationships between brain function and behavioral symptom (Franklin et al., 2015).
5 Working with real-world samples – given the different developmental trajectories associated with psychopathologies, working with analogue samples in laboratories will no longer be considered adequate to understand the mechanisms of psychopathology.
6 Understanding normal or typical development as a critical context for understanding atypical trajectories (Cuthbert, 2014; Sanislow et al., 2010; Shaw et al., 2010).

The theory of the Minimal NeuroCognitive Architecture has a goodness-of-fit with the RDoC system in which priority is given to trans-diagnostic cross-domain constructs such as speed of information processing as well as to modular constructs such as executive functioning and inhibition. Moreover, there is a theoretical framework provided for how these constructs relate to different levels of explanation from brain to behavior in multiple domains such as education and mental health and how they are expected to change over time. Thus, developmental theories such as this provide a framework from which to make and test predictions to inform understanding of causality and change trajectories and intervention in early childhood development and disorder (Casey et al., 2014; Franklin et al., 2015; Sonuga-Barke, 2014). How to go about operationalizing this new research framework is equally important, especially in the context of early childhood. Before we address this issue we will briefly consider a companion issue of the importance of connecting research with practice through research design.

Translational Research

The notion of plasticity is a central tenet of current research. Neurocognitive models of development will increasingly highlight possibilities for intervention in circumstances that would previously have seemed immutable (Morris et al., 2014). For example animal

models have demonstrated the potential for reversing neuronal and behavioral abnormalities associated with Rett syndrome as a result of the finding that the disorder involves the absence of a gene needed to sustain early brain development (Guy et al., 2007; Robinson et al., 2012; Happé and Frith, 2014). Brain-based causation affords as yet unknown potential for a generation of new technologies, pharmacology and environmental rehabilitation options.

Early childhood is likely to be the most impacted by neurocognitive intervention developments where policy provides an economic and moral imperative for early intervention. Research supports the idea that early childhood is a sensitive (though not necessarily critical) window for development with potential cascading effects throughout the lifespan, though also with incredible plasticity and resilience – both qualities demand neuroscience informed intervention to help guide the nature and timing of our practice (Happé and Frith, 2014; Wachs et al., 2014).

Translational research offers more promise than applied research in addressing the educational policy need with brain-based research findings. Currently, the translational literature, still in its infancy, is continuing to evolve in a somewhat haphazard way, expanding from conversations about two counterpoints ('bench' and 'bedside' research) into a taxonomy of sequenced stages as we seek to fill the gap between research conducted in the laboratory, or at the 'bench', to practice, or 'bedside' application. These have evolved into four stages with T1 referring to research that supports basic science moving to human science; T2, human testing into clinical practice; T3, translation into practice and clinical service; and T4, promoting the adoption of evidence-based recommendations by health practitioners and evaluating that real world application (Khoury et al., 2007). Delineating and distilling this taxonomy has been a significant advancement in plugging some of the gaps between research and inference to clinical application. Nevertheless, it is currently limited by the disjuncture between studies, which typically fall into one or other of these stages and are knitted together conceptually to make the link from basic research to application. Nowhere is this more evident than in the neuroscience of education. As discussed there is almost ubiquitous recourse to neuroscience in justifying any new form of practice.

While being aware of this existing taxonomy of research types and associated methodologies is important in not mistaking inference for evidence, it requires methodological innovation to bring this translation to fruition conceptually and pragmatically. An ideal scenario would involve one integrated methodology that will minimize the need for multiple, independent, studies to get from bench to bedside. This would move early childhood research from a taxonomic, linear, unidirectional model of innovation or a 'transitional' system to a truly translational model. While the former is characterized by independent studies that can be categorized along the continuum of bench to bedside methodologies aimed at filling 'gaps' in the research evidence base, the latter is characterized by a formulated process of integrated research with an explicitly translational agenda and a 'programme theory' (Molas-Gallart et al., 2014). The latter is infinitely more challenging as it brings conflicting transdisciplinary, epistemic cultures into contact (Knorr-Cetina, 1999; Sauermann and Stephan, 2013) and requires the development of new frameworks and shared theoretical platforms and language.

PROJECT KIDS NEURODEVELOPMENTAL RESEARCH PROGRAM: A NEUROCOGNITIVE MODEL, WITH NEUROCOGNITIVE METHODOLOGY TO ANSWER NEUROCOGNITIVE QUESTIONS AND INFORM NEUROCOGNITIVE INTERVENTIONS

The Project KIDS neurodevelopmental research program is one example of a bespoke research methodology designed to evaluate

hypotheses about neurocognitive development and to translate this into practice. It has been specifically designed to test the theory of the Minimal Neurocognitive Architecture. It has also been designed in a way that is responsive to the conceptual design issues outlined in the RDoC. Specifically Project KIDS prioritizes:

- Contextual validity: children attend a 'holiday activity day' for two days during which all standardized assessments are embedded within games and activities. This child-centric methodology is both ethically desirable (so that failure-sensitive clinical samples of children enjoy their experience) and critical to creating an environment in which motivation to complete tasks is maximized and best effort is given (Reid, 2013). The game-day format lends itself to modification according to the age and developmental stage of the children in attendance – assessment days with younger children have an underwater adventure theme, older children enjoy a brain explorer theme. Up to 12 children attend each day so that there is a socially supportive and 'real-world' environment in which to conduct the assessments. Each child in a clinical sample is invited to bring a same-age friend, which achieves the dual goals of creating a supportive environment and providing a matched control group. All sessions are 30 minutes in length in recognition of the attentional capacities of young children. After 30 minutes children change to a different type of assessment session (e.g., brain-based recording to word puzzles to computer game assessment of speed of information processing) to maintain novelty and motivation. Some sessions are held in a more classroom-like context while others involve informal play or structured dyadic tasks – each gives an important insight into how children respond to diverse real life contexts.
- Developmental responsiveness: the child-friendly methodology means that longitudinal studies are more possible with return rates of more than 90% of children over the course of three years. While cross-sectional designs are also used, longitudinal designs are preferred as they give a cleaner developmental dataset.
- Targeting different levels of explanation in the one study, so that comparison can be directly made rather than made between studies: throughout the course of the two assessment days psychometric measures of cognitive development are

completed as well as brain-based measures such as ERP and observation of behavior in structured and unstructured social and individual contexts. Taken together, this information provides much deeper analytic and comparative potential than multiple studies each targeting one or two variables within one or two levels of explanation.

- A profiling approach rather than many studies targeting a single neurodevelopmental issue with single indices in a hit-and-miss approach: the two days are designed to provide assessment of verbal and spatial abilities, academic achievement, executive functioning and social-emotional development for each child. This has uniquely allowed us to look beyond specific hypotheses to broader relationships, which has been instructive in seeing connections between educational, physical health and mental health domains.
- Multiple informants: we recognize the value of comparing parent-report with child performance on experimental tasks or with behavioral observation. We also have each child complete assessments with more than one tester during the course of the day so that there are multiple points of comparison about test taking behavior, motivation, attention and performance.
- Multiple types of measures: all core constructs are assessed with more than one measure. For example we use several psychometric measures of executive functioning as well as computer-based tasks such as the flanker task while conducting ERP assessments. We also conduct behavioral observations of executive skills such as turn taking, task switching and task organization. Triangulation of multiple measures allows us to look for points of confluence and disjuncture to differentiate global abilities from specific abilities.
- Transdisciplinary partnerships: more than merely multidisciplinary partnerships, the team seeks to work with one theoretical framework that offers meaningful points of contact for each discipline. Having the Minimal NeuroCognitive Architecture to guide our work facilitates the development of a shared point of contact for all disciplines.

In sum, Project KIDS provides a platform for elucidating the brain-cognition-behavior relationship in childhood. It is also designed to provide a direct and integrated pathway to the design and evaluation of intervention options including behavioral, cognitive and neurofeedback treatments. This integrated translational quality remains rare but offers significant potential for robust intervention design and evaluation. A child may enter the program as a research participant contributing to our scientific understanding of, say, preterm birth. Their neurodevelopmental profile will be added to group data analysis but will also be reviewed by our clinicians for suitability for neuro-rehabilitation pilot programs. The scientist-practitioner will then utilize the profile as a baseline for individualized intervention planning and progress monitoring. The tight interconnection between nomothetic and idiographic levels of data analysis affords a further opportunity for rich understanding of development in action.

CONCLUSION

Early childhood is an important developmental phase for investigation of the brain-based contribution to the typical and atypical, intersecting and independent trajectories of development impacting education, physical health, mental health and social relationships. A strong partnership is required between researchers and practitioners to avoid the proliferation of neuro-myths in early childhood practice. The proliferation of such fiction will only cease when there is clear and credible evidence of alternative translational possibilities. There is much to be excited about in this partnership between neuroscience and early childhood practice, but also much to be wary of.

Developing a shared language between researchers and practitioners is critical in building bridges between experimental findings and everyday applications (The Royal Society, 2011). In turn, a shared language will assist practitioners to inform researchers of paradoxes and priorities that need investigation. This language will come in the form of theories that can span biology and behavior and in doing so, bring together different professional domains. In this chapter we have presented the theory of the Minimal NeuroCognitive Architecture and outlined its potential for creating this bridge and advancing our understanding of both typical development and developmental disorders. Further, we have shown how this theory frames the research process and how innovative research methodologies designed with a neurocognitive frame of reference can further potentiate an evidence-base for this era of brain-informed practice.

The Project KIDS methodology is one example of developing a contextually valid, integrated translational research methodology that can bring together research and practice priorities to improve outcomes for children and their families. Methodologies such as this afford us unique opportunities to understand neurodevelopment as it unfolds in a real-world context. It provides an ethical approach to collecting complex data with vulnerable populations and at the same time makes the research process accessible and meaningful to practitioners and directly translatable into multidisciplinary practice. In this way, the emerging field of neurocognitive development has the potential to be the long-missing link between neuroscience and early childhood practice.

If the neurocognitive paradigm is successful, what we might expect to see 10 years from now is a new diagnostic framework for developmental disorders predicated on a multidimensional understanding of causation rather than merely reflecting symptom presentation; moreover, one with a dimensional rather than categorical frame of reference. We might also expect to have a more personalized approach to treatment based on individual neurocognitive profiling informed by neurocognitive theory that spans biology (brain) to environment (behavior). Integrated translational research methodologies will be the gold standard and will finally bring early childhood practitioners and scientists to the same table to close the gap between research and practice.

QUESTIONS FOR REFLECTION

1 What are the major differences between DSM 5 and the RDoC approach to classification of developmental disorders?

2 What are the advantages and disadvantages of EEG and MRI as imaging techniques?
3 The theory of the MNCA says there are two dimensions to general intelligence – what are they?

FURTHER READING

Della Sala, S., and Anderson, M. (eds). (2012) *Neuroscience in Education: The good, the bad, and the ugly*. Oxford University Press.

Krueger, R. F., and Eaton, N. R. (2015) 'Transdiagnostic factors of mental disorders', *World Psychiatry*, 14(1): 27–29.

Sanislow, C. A., Quinn, K. J., and Sypher, I. (2015) NIMH Research Domain Criteria (RDoC). *The Encyclopedia of Clinical Psychology*. Wiley online library

Vandenbroeck, M. (2014) The brainification of early childhood education and other challenges to academic rigour. *European Early Childhood Education Research Journal*, 22(1): 1–3.

REFERENCES

Alferink, L.A., and Farmer-Dougan, V. (2010) 'Brain-(not) based education: dangers of misunderstanding and misapplication of neuroscience research and brain based education', *Exceptionality*, 18(1): 42–52.

Anderson, M. (1992) *Intelligence and Development: A Cognitive Theory*. Oxford: Blackwell.

Anderson, M. (2001) 'Conceptions of intelligence', *Journal of Child Psychology and Psychiatry*, 42(3): 287–298.

Anderson, M. (2005) 'Marrying intelligence and cognition: A developmental view', in R.J. Sternberg and J.E. Pretz (eds), *Cognition and Intelligence: Identifying Mechanisms of the Mind*. Cambridge: Cambridge University Press, pp. 268–287.

Anderson, M. (2009) 'The concept and development of general intellectual ability', in Reed, J., and Warner-Rogers, J. (eds), *Child Neuropsychology: Concepts, Theory, and Practice*. Oxford: Wiley-Blackwell, pp. 112–135.

Anderson, M. (2013) 'Individual differences in intelligence', in K. Kirsner, C. Speelman, M. Maybery, A. O'Brien-Malone and M. Anderson (eds), *Implicit and Explicit Mental Processes*. London: Psychology Press, pp. 171–186.

Anderson, M., and Della Sala, S. (2012) 'Neuroscience in education: an (opinionated) introduction', in S. Della Sala and M. Anderson (eds), *Neuroscience in Education: The Good, The Bad and The Ugly*. Oxford: Oxford University Press, pp. 3–12.

Anderson, M., and Reid, C. (2009) 'Don't forget about levels of explanation', *Cortex*, 45(4): 560–561.

Australian Academy of Science (AAS) (2013) Inspiring smarter brain research in Australia: Recommendations from the 2013 Theo Murphy High Flyers Think Tank. https://www.science.org.au/sites/default/files/user-content/documents/thinktank-2013-recommendations.pdf (accessed 15 March 2015).

Bishop, D.V.M. (2007) 'Curing dyslexia and attention-deficit hyperactivity disorder by training motor co-ordination: miracle or myth?', *Journal of Paediatrics and Child Health*, 43: 653–655.

Bishop, D. V., Anderson, M., Reid, C., and Fox, A. M. (2011) 'Auditory development between 7 and 11 years: An event-related potential (ERP) study', *PloS one*, 6(5): e18993.

Blair, C., and Raver, C. C. (2015) 'School Readiness and Self-Regulation: A Developmental Psychobiological Approach', *Annual Review of Psychology*, 66: 711–731.

Brydges, C. R., Anderson, M., Reid, C. L., and Fox, A. M. (2013) 'Maturation of cognitive control: delineating response inhibition and interference suppression', *PloS one*, 8(7): e69826.

Brydges, C. R., Fox, A. M., Reid, C. L., and Anderson, M. (2014) 'The differentiation of executive functions in middle and late childhood: A longitudinal latent-variable analysis', *Intelligence*, 47: 34–43.

Casey, B.J., Oliveri, M.E., and Insel, T. (2014) 'A neurodevelopmental perspective on the Research Domain Criteria (RDoC) framework', *Biological Psychiatry*, 76(5): 350–353.

Center for the Developing Child at Harvard University. *A Science-based Framework for Early Childhood Policy: Using Evidence to Improve Outcomes in Learning, Behavior, and Health for Vulnerable Children*. Cambridge, MA: Center on the Developing Child at Harvard University; 2007. Available at: http://developingchild.harvard.edu/library/reports_and_working_papers/policy_framework/. Accessed July 2014.

Changeux, J. P. (2012) 'Synaptic Epigenesis and the Evolution of Higher Brain Functions', in *Epigenetics, Brain and Behavior* (pp. 11–22). Springer Berlin Heidelberg.

Churchland, P. (2007) *Neurophilosophy at Work*. Cambridge: Cambridge University Press.

Cuthbert, B. N. (2014) 'The RDoC framework: facilitating transition from ICD/DSM to dimensional approaches that integrate neuroscience and psychopathology', *World Psychiatry*, 13(1): 28–35.

Davis, A. (2011) (ed.) *Handbook of Pediatric Neuropsychology*. New York: Springer Press.

Deary, I. J. (2012) 'Human intelligence', *Annual Review of Psychology*, 63: 453–482.

Della Sala, S., and Anderson, M. (eds). (2012) *Neuroscience in Education: The Good, the Bad, and the Ugly*. Oxford: Oxford University Press.

Demazeux, S., and Singy, P. (eds) (2015) *The DSM-5 in Perspective: Philosophical Reflections on the Psychiatric Babel* (pp. 25–42). Netherlands: Springer.

Duncan, J. (2013) 'The structure of cognition: Attentional episodes in mind and brain', *Neuron*, 80(1): 35–50.

Fombonne, E. (2009) 'Epidemiology of pervasive developmental disorders', *Pediatric Research*, 65(6): 591–598.

Franklin, J. C., Jamieson, J. P., Glenn, C. R., and Nock, M. K. (2015) 'How Developmental Psychopathology Theory and Research Can Inform the Research Domain Criteria (RDoC) project', *Journal of Clinical Child and Adolescent Psychology*, 44: 280–290.

Geise, C., Barzman, D., and Strakowski, S. (2014) 'Pediatric Emotion Dysregulation: Biological and Developmental Evidence for a Dimensional Approach', *Psychiatric Quarterly*, 1–7.

Giedd, J. N., and Rapoport, J. L. (2010) 'Structural MRI of pediatric brain development: what have we learned and where are we going?', *Neuron*, 67(5): 728–734.

Gogtay, N., Giedd, J.N., Lusk, L., Hayashi, K.M., Greenstein, D., Vaituzis, A.C., Nugent, T.F., Herman, D.H., Clasen, L.S., Toga, A.W., Rapoport, J.L., and Thompson, P.M. (2004) *Dynamic Mapping of Human Cortical Development During Childhood Through Early Adulthood. Proceedings of the National*

Academy of Sciences (USA), 101, 8174–8179.

Goswami, U. (2006) 'Neuroscience and education: from research to practice?', *Nature Review of Neuroscience*, 7(5): 406–11.

Guy, J., Gan, J., Selfridge, J., Cobb, S., and Bird, A. (2007) 'Reversal of neurological defects in a mouse model of Rett syndrome', *Science*, 315(5815): 1143–1147.

Happé, F., and Frith, U. (2014) 'Annual Research Review: Towards a developmental neuroscience of atypical social cognition', *Journal of Child Psychology and Psychiatry*, 55(6): 553–577.

Howard Jones, P. (2010) *Introducing Neuroscience Research: Neuroscience, Education and the Brain*. New York: Routledge.

Howard Jones, P. A. (2014) 'Neuroscience and education: myths and messages', *Nature Reviews Neuroscience*, 15(12): 817–824.

Howard Jones, P. A., and Fenton, K. D. (2012) 'The need for interdisciplinary dialogue in developing ethical approaches to neuroeducational research', *Neuroethics*, 5(2):119–134.

Hyman, S (2007) 'Can neuroscience be integrated into the DSM-V?', *Nature Review of Neuroscience*, 8:725–732

Hyman, S. E. (2010) 'The diagnosis of mental disorders: the problem of reification', *Annual Review of Clinical Psychology*, 6: 155–179.

Insel, T., Cuthbert, B., Garvey, M., Heinssen, R., Pine, D. S., Quinn, K., ... and Wang, P. (2010) 'Research domain criteria (RDoC): toward a new classification framework for research on mental disorders', *American Journal of Psychiatry*, 167(7): 748–751.

Khoury, M. J., Gwinn, M., Yoon, P. W., Dowling, N., Moore, C. A., and Bradley, L. (2007) 'The continuum of translation research in genomic medicine: How can we accelerate the appropriate integration of human genome discoveries into health care and disease prevention?', *Genetics in Medicine*, 9(10): 665–674.

Kim, Y.S. (2014) 'Recent challenges to the psychiatric diagnostic nosology: a focus on the genetics and genomics of neurodevelopmental disorders', *International Journal of Epidemiology*, 43(2): 465–475.

Knorr-Cetina, K. (1999) *Epistemic Cultures. How the Sciences Make Knowledge*. Cambridge, MA: Harvard University Press.

Landy, S., and Bradley, S. (2013) *Children with Multiple Mental Health Challenges: An Integrated Approach to Intervention*. New York: Springer.

Leckman, J. F., and Yazgan, M. Y. (2010) 'Editorial: developmental transitions to psychopathology: from genomics and epigenomics to social policy', *Journal of Child Psychology and Psychiatry*, 51(4): 333–340.

Loeb, S., Bridges, M., Bassok, D., Fuller, B. and Rumberger, R. (2005) How much is too much? The influence of preschool centers on children's social and cognitive development. NBER Working Paper No. 11812, December, JEL No. I2, I3.

Marshall, P. J. (2009) 'Relating psychology and neuroscience: Taking up the challenges', *Perspectives on psychological science*, 4(2): 113–125.

Miller, S., Maguire, L.K., Macdonald, G. (2011) Home-based child development interventions for preschool children from socially disadvantaged families, Cochrane Database of Systematic Reviews, 12, Art. No. CD008131. DOI:10.1002/14651858.CD008131.pub2.

Molas-Gallart, J., D'Este, P., Llopis, Ó., and Rafols, I. (2014) *Towards an alternative framework for the evaluation of translational research initiatives* (No. 201403). Ingenio (CSIC-UPV).

Morris, S. E., Rumsey, J. M., and Cuthbert, B. N. (2014). 'Rethinking mental disorders: the role of learning and brain plasticity', *Restorative Neurology and Neuroscience*, 32(1): 5–23.

National Scientific Council on the Developing Child. (2007) *The Timing and Quality of Early Experiences Combine to Shape Brain Architecture*. Cambridge, MA: National Scientific Council on the Developing Child Working Paper No. 5. Available at: http://developingchild.harvard.edu/library/reports_and_working_papers/wp5/. Accessed July 2014.

Nigg, J. (2015) 'ADHD: New Approaches to Subtyping and Nosology', *The ADHD Report*, 23(2): 6–9.

Price, R. B., Paul, B., Schneider, W., and Siegle, G. J. (2013) 'Neural correlates of three neurocognitive intervention strategies: a preliminary step towards personalized treatment for psychological disorders', *Cognitive Therapy and Research*, 37(4): 657–672.

Rabipour, S., and Raz, A. (2012) 'Training the brain: Fact and fad in cognitive and behavioral remediation', *Brain and Cognition*, 79(2): 159–179.

Regier, D.A., Narrow, W.E., Kuhl, E.A., and Kupfer, D.J. (2009) 'The conceptual development of DSM-V', *The American Journal of Psychiatry,* 166: 1–7.

Reid, C. (2013) 'Developing a research framework to inform an evidence base for person-centered medicine: Keeping the person at the centre', *European Journal for Person Centered Healthcare*, 1(2): 336–342.

Reid, C., and Anderson, M.(2012) 'Left-brain, Right-brain, Braingames and Beanbags: Neuromyths in Education', in P. Adey and J. Dillon (eds), *Bad Education*. Berkshire, UK: Open University Press, pp. 179–198.

Robinson, L., Guy, J., McKay, L., Brockett, E., Spike, R. C., Selfridge, J., ... and Cobb, S. R. (2012) 'Morphological and functional reversal of phenotypes in a mouse model of Rett syndrome', *Brain*, aws096.

Sanislow, C. A., Pine, D. S., Quinn, K. J., Kozak, M. J., Garvey, M. A., Heinssen, R. K., ... and Cuthbert, B. N. (2010) 'Developing constructs for psychopathology research: research domain criteria', *Journal of Abnormal Psychology*, 119(4): 631.

Sauermann, H., and Stephan, P. (2013) 'Conflicting Logics? Multidimensional View of Industrial and Academic Science', *Organization Science*, 24(3): 889–909.

Schweinhart, L.J., Barnes, H., and Weikart, D. (1993) Significant Benefits: The High/Scope Perry Preschool Study Through Age 27. Ypsilanti, MI: High-Scope Educational Research Foundation, Monograph #10.

Shaw, P. (2014) 'The shape of things to come in attention deficit hyperactivity disorder. Am J Psychiatry', April 2010, *American Psychiatric Association Editorial*, 167: 363–365 http://ajp.psychiatryonline.org/cgi/content/full/ajp;167/4/363

Shaw, P., Lerch, J., Greenstein, D., Sharp, W., Clasen, L., Evans, A., ... and Rapoport, J. (2006) 'Longitudinal mapping of cortical thickness and clinical outcome in children and adolescents with attention-deficit/hyperactivity disorder', *Archives of General Psychiatry*, 63(5): 540–549.

Shaw, P., Gogtay, N., and Rapoport, J. (2010). 'Childhood psychiatric disorders as anomalies in neurodevelopmental trajectories', *Human Brain Mapping*, 31: 917–925.

Shaw, P., Gilliam, M., Liverpool, M., Weddle, C., Malek, M., Sharp, W., and Giedd, J. (2011) 'Cortical development in typically developing children with symptoms of hyperactivity and impulsivity: support for a dimensional view of attention deficit hyperactivity disorder', *American Journal of Psychiatry*, 168(2): 143–151.

Shaw, P., Malek, M., Watson, B., Sharp, W., Evans, A., and Greenstein, D. (2012) 'Development of cortical surface area and gyrification in attention-deficit/hyperactivity disorder', *Biological Psychiatry*, 72(3): 191–197.

Shaw, P., Malek, M., Watson, B., Greenstein, D., de Rossi, P., and Sharp, W. (2013) 'Trajectories of cerebral cortical development in childhood and adolescence and adult attention-deficit/hyperactivity disorder', *Biological Psychiatry*, 74(8): 599–606.

Shonkoff, J. P. (2011) 'Protecting brains, not simply stimulating minds', *Science*, 333(6045): 982–983.

Sonuga-Barke, E. J. (2014) 'Editorial: 'What's up,(R) DoC?' – can identifying core dimensions of early functioning help us understand, and then reduce, developmental risk for mental disorders?', *Journal of Child Psychology and Psychiatry*, 55(8): 849–851.

The Royal Society (2011) *Brain Waves Module 2: Neuroscience: Implications for Education and Lifelong Learning*. Policy document.

Vandenbroeck, M. (2014) 'The brainification of early childhood education and other challenges to academic rigour', *European Early Childhood Education Research Journal*, 22(1): 1–3.

Vidal, J., Mills, T., Pang, E. W., and Taylor, M. J. (2012) 'Response inhibition in adults and teenagers: spatiotemporal differences in the prefrontal cortex', *Brain and Cognition*, 79(1): 49–59.

Wachs, T. D., Georgieff, M., Cusick, S., and McEwen, B. S. (2014) 'Issues in the timing of integrated early interventions: contributions from nutrition, neuroscience, and psychological research', *Annals of the New York Academy of Sciences*, 1308(1): 89–106.

11

Understanding Systems Theory and Thinking: Early Childhood Education in Latin America and the Caribbean

Sharon Lynn Kagan, Maria Caridad Araujo,
Analía Jaimovich and Yyannú Cruz Aguayo

RATIONALE AND BACKGROUND: THE WHY

Systems Thinking and Early Childhood Education

Traditionally, early childhood research has focused primarily on elements of children's growth and development, pedagogical inputs and dynamics, the evaluation of specific programs or interventions, and the social contexts that influence young children and their development. Much of the present-day research has mobilized political and financial commitments, resulting in the considerably expanded attention now being accorded young children and early childhood education (ECE)[1] by governments around the world.

Augmenting these approaches to early childhood research, additional lines of inquiry – notably systems theory – exist and, we suggest, have importance for understanding the delivery of early childhood services. Broadly conceptualized, systems theory is a paradigmatic perspective that views all phenomena as a web of relationships among elements, a system (Laszlo, 1996; von Bertalanffy, 1968). It suggests that all systems, whether social, biological, or even electrical, share common properties and patterns of interactions that can be examined to better understand complex phenomena. In examining regularly interacting elements (laws, models, principles, activities, institutions, people), systems theory suggests that individual parts cannot be fully understood when they are separated from the whole. Quite popular, systems theory has been widely applied to a range of disciplines including cybernetics, kinetics, ecology, sociology, and psychology, and is manifest in a number of related theories including catastrophe theory, chaos theory, and decision-making theory. It has also influenced disciplines proximally related to human learning and development: education (Senge, 1990), learning theory (Piaget, 1972), family theory (Bowen, 1966), and developmental theory (Bronfenbrenner, 1979). So, broadly construed, systems theory is not new, nor is it new to work related to young children.

Closely aligned with systems theory, two explanatory theories are salient when discussing early childhood systems: new institutional theory and complex adaptive theory. Dating back to the work of Meyer and Rowan (1977) and DiMaggio and Powell (1983), new institutional theory stresses the fundamental role that institutions play in shaping the delivery of services. To do so, it explores the normative culture in and across institutions, as well as the influence that contextual environments have on institutional and organizational behavior (Scott, 2001; Scott and Davies, 2007). Institutional theory rejects the notion of organizations as fixed and static entities (e.g., rationalist theories); rather, it notes that institutions, like people, change in response to the temporal and cultural zeitgeist (e.g., adaptist theories). As such, institutional theory allows us to examine child and family outcomes from the stance that they may accrue not only as a result of what children, families, and early childhood teachers do, but as a partial result of a complex (and somewhat understudied) array of changing policies, non-familial institutions, and contexts.

Closely aligned with new institutional theory, complex adaptive theory suggests that, given the complexities of contemporary society, social changes are now normative and non-linear (Joachim and May, 2010). It posits that change cannot be understood by looking only at one institution, program, or policy, but must be examined systemically to discern how diverse elements relate to and impact one another. Stated simply, complex adaptive theory suggests that studying any one policy or institution in isolation from its systemic context renders that analysis incomplete. In this chapter, we use these theories, posit an adaptation of them, and seek to discern how systems theory can be appropriate for studying and understanding ECE. To do so, we provide an example of how systems work is unfolding in one region of the world, Latin America and the Caribbean (LAC).

To those accustomed to more traditional lines of inquiry when studying young children, the use of the above theories or any cohesive set of propositions about complex and interacting organizations may seem somewhat remote from the study of young children and the nature and quality of the services they receive. We suggest the opposite; systems theory is a complementary way of understanding early childhood practices that is nicely synchronized with, and can augment, current ecological and developmental theories. Paralleling and fitting firmly within the Bronfenbrennerian tradition of ecological thinking (Bronfenbrenner, 1979) and the learning theory of Piaget (Piaget, 1972), systems thinking acknowledges that children develop amidst a complex array of interconnected systems, each of which exerts differential impacts on their development and learning. Systems thinking also respects holistic developmental theory in that it seeks to understand how diverse disciplines and their related institutional entities – education, health and nutrition, mental health, and social protection – interact. Like ecological and developmental theory, systems theory presumes that the end results of effective early childhood policies are positive and can impact outcomes for children and families. Systems theory generally, and new institutional theory specifically, differ from conventional thinking in that they are concerned with multiple institutions and phenomena including the laws, policies, regulations, guidelines, and institutional structures that shape the nature of services offered to young children and their families. Complex adaptive theory provides a lens for examining the nature of changes associated with these intricate and interactive phenomena.

Our focus on systems, as well as new institutional and complex adaptive theories shifts not only the unit of analysis, but inspires the examination of outcomes that differ from more conventional child, family, classroom, or program outcomes. Using these theories, and as a means of operationalizing them, we suggest that there are three macro-level system outcomes that transcend and influence child and family outcomes (Kagan, 2015). Less well examined, we propose that (i) the quality of services and supports, (ii) their equitable distribution, and (iii) their sustainability over time profoundly impact early childhood services and are essential pre-requisites for successful child and family outcomes. As such, they become a focus for our analysis and, potentially, for other analyses of early childhood systems.

These three systemic outcomes – equity, quality, and sustainability – are all the result of an effective ECE system, as well as the foundations of one that can last over time. Quality refers to the set of attributes of ECE programs, of the providers, and of the staff employed in them that are necessary to provide families with support and protection to attain well-being and to allow children to reach their potential. Equity refers to an allocation of resources – over time, across territories, and between different sectors, populations, and age groups – that seeks to equalize opportunities and protect people from extreme deprivation in outcomes (World Bank, 2006). Sustainability is understood as the set of financial, political, and contextual variables that ensure the system can operate effectively over time and adapt to changing circumstances – without affecting families' or children's services. The underlying hypothesis of this work is that, only if the ECE system is built on the foundations of quality, equity, and sustainability will it be able to adapt to dynamic circumstances in the political, economic, and environmental systems that encase it, and thus perpetuate positive child and family well-being.

In this sense, systems theory expands the domains of analysis and insists that outcomes for *individual* children and families matter, as do the rights and outcomes for *all* children and families, over time. It also varies from more conventional ECE theory in that it presumes that institutions, replete with their own cultures, and the ways in which they interact, bear considerable weight in altering children's life trajectories. Moreover, in altering what is examined, systems theory begs for new research approaches and tools; as such, it warrants examination in this volume.

Systems Theory: Why Now?

Historically, a great deal of research has focused on discerning the programmatic effects of ECE on children's development. Promising and highly publicized, this line of inquiry has substantiated the need for, and the benefits of, investing in high-quality ECE. Less well noted and well publicized, however, are data that attest to the actual lack of quality and the lack of a system to produce quality outcomes. With regard to the former, some research affirms the pervasive lack of quality services for young children in the USA and globally (Berlinski and Schady, 2015; Mashburn et al., 2008; Peisner-Feinberg et al., 2001). With regard to the latter, scholars and practitioners have documented the lack of a system and the lack of the institutional architecture to deliver quality services (Britto et al., 2014; Bruner, 1996; Kagan and Cohen, 1996; Kagan and Kauerz, 2012; Neuman and Devercelli, 2013; Sugarman, 1981; Vargas-Baron, 2013). These scholars suggest that, without attending to the institutional architecture associated with ECE, comprehensive quality services are unlikely to become a reality. Indeed, programmatic expansions that simply build on a dysfunctional structure are unlikely to produce significant gains for quality, much less for the equitable distribution of services or for their sustainability.

Beyond the need to enhance the quality of ECE services, three additional contextual factors accelerate the urgency for systemic thinking in ECE. First, there is a strong precedent in the ECE field to use data to justify service expansion. Globally, policy makers rely on ECE research to inform their decisions. But if scholars continue to produce the same kinds of research on the same topics, there is likely to be little improvement in the way ECE is conceptualized and delivered. There is a need for new thinking about how quality is produced, how services can be more equitably distributed, and how societies can prevent the 'here-today, gone-tomorrow' approach to ECE policies. Second, as important as quality services are to children's development, they alone do not reveal a comprehensive picture of what is happening to the myriad investments being made on behalf of young children and their families. Rather, despite some work in this area, there is a need to examine the array of services and the mechanisms being established to span them to obtain a more robust picture of the nature of ECE services. Conventional boundaries need to be spanned so that ECE services can be opportunely delivered, coordinated with one another, and targeted to those most in need across multiple service delivery structures; examining a single ministry or a single level of government cannot provide such understandings. Third, presently the growth of ECE is burgeoning. The time to influence its trajectory is now. Precisely because so much activity is taking place in ECE, it is imperative to better understand it from a structural and systems perspective. Indeed, to capitalize on present-day momentum, forthcoming policies need to be based on much stronger conceptualizations of change, the change process, and the architecture that needs to be in place to promote quality services and, hence, to achieve more generalizable outcomes.

Systems Thinking: Why Latin America and the Caribbean?

Latin America and the Caribbean (LAC) provide fertile ground for such an examination of systems theory in that ECE progress in this region has been rapid and inventive. Services for young children have expanded significantly in nearly all countries in the region. Diverse approaches to such expansion are taking place, with many innovative strategies being tried. Studying systems theory in this context is also interesting because the 27 countries in Latin America and the Caribbean represent diverse ideas about, and approaches to, the nature and amount of government intervention in children's services deemed wise; such differences are also tied to diverse conceptions

about the role of the private sector, and governments' relationship to it. The countries also vary in the degree to which they centralize/decentralize their service provision and in the ministries accorded authority for children. Moreover, even though LAC has experienced a reduction in overall poverty rates in the past 10 years, economically it still remains the most unequal region in the world. Despite major efforts to reduce these disparities and to enhance growth, it has been very difficult to reverse this trend. But ECE policies do have the potential to help redress these situations and to even the playing field early on in life; therefore, they are particularly relevant for the LAC context. In short, a combination of diverse governmental values, institutions, and processes, coupled with increasing commitments to young children, makes LAC an ideal context in which to examine ECE systems theory and development.

ECE SYSTEMS THEORY AND SYSTEMS THINKING: THE WHAT

A Systems Framework

In attempting to understand theory-driven research as it applies to ECE systems, several conditions need to be met. First, the theory needs to be expressed through a conceptual framework that is broad enough to encase diverse programs and services for young children and their families, that pays attention to contextual and architectural variables, and that can be applied within and across diverse institutional settings. Second, the framework must incorporate the theoretical work upon which it is built and which it hopes to advance. Third, it must demonstrate the nature and trajectory of social change within a swirl of concurrent and rapidly changing political and economic events that characterize both the current ECE field and the social conditions of the involved countries. Fourth, the theory needs to be respectful of several guiding assumptions related to

ECE, specifically: (i) quality is a non-negotiable factor that influences the social and economic utility/benefit of ECE services; and (ii) quality is contingent on a number of important yet under-studied infrastructural elements.

With regard to the former assumption, considerable data, some of it cited in the preceding section, suggest that ECE programs are not delivering outcomes commensurate with their intentions. Studies unequivocally link program quality with outcomes, noting that positive outcomes for children accrue and are more likely to be sustained only when the ECE programs are of high quality. But indeed, the majority of youngsters languish in poor- to mediocre-quality programs. True in many countries, ECE services in the LAC are not exceptions.

With regard to the second assumption, the theory suggests that quality is not easy to produce, but that production variables are known and can be examined. Indeed, based on the work of Kagan and Cohen (1996), this chapter posits that there are seven quality production variables that are necessary to produce an effective ECE system. These seven production variables function synergistically and they are: (i) governance; (ii) finance; (iii) program quality, standards, and transitions; (iv) assessment, data, and accountability; (v) human capacity development; (vi) family and community engagement; and (vii) linkages with external influencers. When these seven elements are joined with the programs and services themselves and with boundary-spanning entities, a system is created. All eight elements are necessary for an effective ECE system to exist; without any single element, there can be no effective ECE system.

Systems Theory of Change

Predicated on ecological, developmental, and systems theory, and building from new institutional and complex adaptive theory, a theory of change is proffered to guide

thinking and research. The utility of framing research analyses with a theory of change has been well documented (Fulbright-Anderson et al., 1998; Kagan, 1998; Yin, 1992). It has been defined as a theory of how and why things change (Weiss, 1997) or as a 'systematic and cumulative study of the links between activities, outcomes, and the contexts of the initiative' (Connell and Kubisch, 1998, p. 16). As such, it is a potent tool, an initial framework, and a functional hypothesis that guides more nuanced understandings about how change occurs. Given the complexity associated with understanding ECE systems, we have adopted the theory of change summarized in Figure 11.1 (Kagan, 2015). Figure 11.1 suggests that socio-cultural [H] (values, beliefs, heritages, and religions) and temporal [G] (political, economic, and environmental) variables both frame and contour the context in which policies and programs exist. These are represented by rectangles that encase the systems theory being advanced. Working backwards, our theory of change suggests that improved child and family well-being [F] will only be achieved when systemic outcomes (defined as equitably distributed, high-quality, and sustainable [D]) are combined with family outcomes (defined as meaningfully involved and organizationally supported [E]).[2] In order for these conditions to exist, a well-conceptualized, well-designed, effective ECE system [C] must be in place. Scatter-shot, scatter-funded programs and services cannot deliver equitably distributed, quality services at scale; only a system can do that. To render such a system operational, programs and services (including boundary-spanning efforts) [A] must be supported by an infrastructure articulated around essential production variables [B], which, in turn, must be clear, linked, and deemed worthy of support.

Working forwards, the theory of change suggests that programs and services (including boundary-spanning efforts) and the production variables *together* constitute the system, which, in turn, has the potential to produce positive systemic and familial

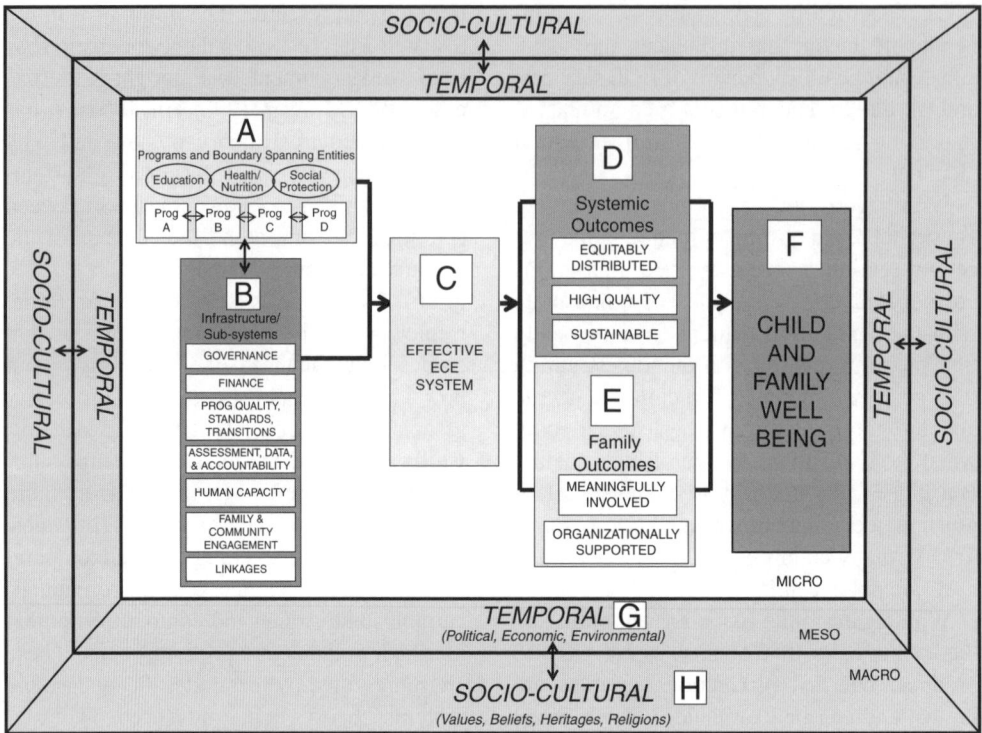

Figure 11.1   Conceptual map

Source: Kagan (2015)

outcomes that provide the best chance to improve the well-being of young children and their families. In other words, the framework described here suggests that: A + B are the requisite conditions that lead to C; when in place, C leads to D and E; and D + E are the precursors that enable the production of F.

Systems Thinking and ECE Research

Systems thinking suggests that all elements must be examined if one is to gather a sense of the potency of any country, region, or municipality to deliver quality, equitable, and sustainable services for young children. Using this framework, new research questions can be marshalled, giving us the opportunity to examine and design implementation more thoroughly and more deeply: Which production variables are understood and

operationalized? Was, and how was, each of the production variables manifest? To what degree did they interact with one another? To what degree are they supported? To what degree and how are they integrated into mainstream programs and services? Further, the framework provides the opportunity to posit different questions about outcomes: To what degree and how do the production variables foster service quality and integration? Which contextual variables, including political, economic, legal, and cultural factors, contour the production variables, the programs and services (including boundary-spanning efforts), and ultimately the ECE system? In short, the framework and the theory of change can work together to frame an inquiry that should render new insights on how ECE efforts are produced, and to gauge their likelihood of producing high quality, equitably distributed and sustainable services.

EXAMINING ECE SYSTEMS IN LATIN AMERICA AND THE CARIBBEAN: USING AND APPLYING SYSTEMS THINKING – THE HOW

The Research Questions

Interested in gaining deeper insight into *why* and *under what conditions* ECE is a powerful economic, social, and developmental change agent, we engaged in a prototype systems study in five countries in LAC. The study was designed to produce relevant findings regarding the region and to spur thinking about systems theory and its application to future research in ECE. We offer it as an example of a systems analysis, with the hope that its structure, method, and findings will be useful for future systemic analyses in ECE.

Given that ECE is coming to be defined as including programs and services for children from conception through age 8, we accepted this as our working definition of the ages of children whose services would be included in the study. Second, committed to a holistic perspective on ECE and given the unique design of system theory, our work looked at major efforts attendant to this age range in the education, health, social protection, social assistance, and justice sectors. It probed extant services and sought to understand the contextual, legal, fiscal, and implementation variables and conditions that converge to impact the accessibility, quality, and sustainability of ECE services.

Specifically, the study sought to address the following research questions:

- What are the major institutional and legal frameworks that shape the amount, nature, and delivery of early childhood development policies, programs, and services? What are the characteristics of each system's production variables?
- What linkages and coordination mechanisms exist among the above policies, programs, and services? Are there any boundary-spanning entities that give structure to that coordination and what are their most salient attributes?
- What are the main challenges that limit the country's ECE system capacity to produce systemic outcomes of equity, quality, and sustainability?

Data Collection and Analysis[3]

To address these questions from a systems perspective, we developed a three-phased methodology: (i) site selection, (ii) data design, and (iii) data collection and analysis. With regard to site selection, we considered that this systems analysis was designed to understand the driving phenomena that shape the *architecture* and *delivery* of ECE services. Five countries were selected: Brazil, Chile, Colombia, Guatemala, and Trinidad and Tobago, aiming to represent a continuum of economic and political conditions, as well as of institutional environments.

The data design phase included the amplification of the basic research questions presented above and the development of a set of protocol questions, including those concerned with legal and historical context; current programmatic and boundary-spanning efforts; infrastructure or architectural elements; and equity, quality, and sustainability. To enrich the protocol questions and to help prepare for the site visits, data collection began with lengthy desk reviews that documented: information about the countries' social, political, and economic contexts; legal efforts on behalf of children; current conditions of children and their families; services delivered; emerging efforts; and challenges. Using these data, formative case study reports were prepared; these enabled the team to tailor our questions and determine the appropriate informants for country site visits, each of one week's duration. Informants included current ministry heads and employees, prior ministry employees, representatives of political parties, elected officials, key NGO leaders, private philanthropy representatives, key ECE practitioners and researchers, as well as national and community advocates. Interviews were by and large concentrated in the capital city of the country (with some exceptions in Brazil, Colombia, and Trinidad and Tobago). Due to resource and time constraints, in all cases visits could not include extensive interviews with local authorities and program-executing offices at the subnational or local level.

This limited information about the challenges of implementation at all levels.

Using the formative case study material, and after careful discussion and analysis of the data gathered during the country site visits, case studies were amplified, fact checked, reviewed, and finalized. Five individual case studies, one for each country, were produced, and provided the main input for a comprehensive cross-case analysis (Araujo et al., in press).

As is suggested above, the methodology employed carefully respected the conceptual framework and the guiding theory of change. The overall advantage of a systems approach is that it provides a meaningful way to collect systemic data that vary over time and place. It also yields multiple perspectives on phenomena and events. As a result, not only is the data-gathering process complex, but the findings are layered, nuanced, and sometimes inconsistent. Data emanating from different sources need to be verified and examined for systematic variation by geographic locale, political party, governmental agency, and/or role within that agency. They also need to be integrated and reported in a way that reveals a story. Taken together, then, the process, the data, and the reporting render the results of any systematic analysis complex. To explore the merits of a systems approach for ECE research within and across countries, we present our results in the following sections: implementation findings, the relationship between systems theory and equity, the relationship between systems theory and quality, and, finally, the linkages between systems theory and sustainability.

IMPLEMENTING ECE SYSTEMS

In discussing the implementation of ECE in LAC from a systems perspective, three topics are presented. First, we focus on the broad context for systems work as being one that is changing rapidly, conceptually, and practically; second, we discuss some of the accomplishments that have accrued; and, third, we turn to a discussion of the challenges related to systems work.

Changing Conceptions of ECE and its Impact on Systems Thinking

The way in which a country regards its obligation to young children is embedded in its socio-cultural history, defining not only what services should be delivered, but also how and to whom they are delivered. In LAC, there have been three recent shifts in the way governments think about ECE which, in turn, make systems thinking particularly relevant in this era of important change.

First, there is an increasing recognition of the importance of ECE, accompanied by a diversification of the kinds of services delivered and an expansion of services in number and targeted ages. While the institutional mechanisms for the implementation of such expansion vary from country to country, there is a common conception that ECE services need to be expanded. From the point of view of systems analysis, an expansion of this sort brings about challenges to the key systemic outcomes of interest. It challenges sustainability, as countries ought to find the financial resources needed to permanently maintain the expansion and include it in their national budgets. This implies an important political commitment to early childhood, strong enough to mobilize a sustained, fiscal commitment. Expanding services also challenges quality, as the rapid increase in coverage demands a large enough supply of qualified human resources – often unavailable in the short term. Lastly, expansion challenges equity, as policy makers need to make decisions about where to start (in which territories), what populations to target (minorities, age groups), and what specific programs or services to expand more rapidly.

A second shift in LAC governments' thinking about ECE is the presence of a growing consensus that ECE is a universal human right that should be guaranteed by the state.

This guarantee is accomplished either through direct public provision or through the financing and regulation of private provision. Some countries, like Brazil, prioritize direct public provision as the policy option to ensure this right. Other countries, like Trinidad and Tobago, have voiced a commitment to young children, but, to date, have provided comparatively limited public service provision, and have relied on private providers who are partially financed by government subsidies.

The third shift is conceptual in nature, a shift towards comprehensive and integrated ECE service provision rather than a series of discrete and differentiated early childhood services (e.g., health, education, welfare). Conceptually, integration implies a move away from services organized from the point of view of the provider, towards services organized around the comprehensive development and needs of each child and his/her family. Thus, ECE is being increasingly understood as a multi-disciplinary phenomenon. In some countries, service integration has been associated with the creation of policy mechanisms to promote cross-sectorial collaboration. These cross-sectorial collaboration mechanisms, referred to here as boundary-spanning entities (BSEs), would be difficult to identify and analyze if it were not for systems thinking. In the model presented in the earlier section, the BSEs together with programs and services and the production variables, are the key elements of ECE systems. It is important to mention that the conceptual shift described here is not yet fully implemented on the ground. This means that in the countries studied, the conceptual move towards comprehensive ECE service provision still remains, to some extent, at a rhetorical level rather than at a practical one.

While these changing conceptualizations are promoting discourse and some institutional changes, comprehensive ECE is still far from being fully realized in most countries. None of the studied countries is addressing all elements of the system in a way that is likely to produce effects associated with the posited theory of change. Moreover, a consistent and dedicated focus on quality, equity, and sustainability is still lacking in the region.

Systems Accomplishments

Among the most important systemic efforts commanding attention in the early years are those that seek to link programs and services. Known collectively as BSEs, these efforts are manifest in different countries, with the two most notable examples being Chile (Chile Crece Contigo) and Colombia (De Cero a Siempre). BSEs act as integrated governance mechanisms among the various sectors and institutions that are responsible for ECE programs and policies, aiming to organize services around the comprehensive development and needs of each child and his/her family, rather than around those of service providers. In order to achieve this aim, BSEs have developed both horizontal and vertical coordination mechanisms. Horizontal coordination aims to link service provision among sectors such as health, nutrition, sanitation, education, culture, sports, labor, and social protection. Vertical coordination mechanisms aim to promote coherence in service provision across national, subnational, and local levels of government. Both the structure and level of BSE development vary substantially across the countries in this study. In some cases, where such BSEs have not formally emerged, other efforts to link services across traditional ministerial lines are evident as in the case of Brazil's integrated data systems.

To date, BSEs have been successful in improving the visibility of ECE services, mobilizing political support for ECE agencies, and promoting coordination across ECE institutions. BSEs have also encountered implementation difficulties, however, due to a lack of human resources and intermittent funding. Moreover, conflict is intrinsic to the very existence of BSEs. BSEs attempt to realign deeply rooted practices and conceptions in line ministries. Coordination with other sectors requires specific knowledge and skills, as well as accountability structures that incorporate coordination among the criteria for which employees and managers in line ministries are held accountable. Instead, line ministry employees often see cross-sectorial coordination as an add-on to already heavy workloads. Successful coordination mechanisms require changing deep-rooted practices and conceptions, human and financial resources, new incentive structures that promote coordination, and improvements in human capacity. A comprehensive move to an integrated ECE system requires extensive time and effort. Despite the many challenges faced by BSEs, they represent an inventive institutional response to the systemic thinking in ECE policy and practice.

Systems Challenges

As noted above, the idea of comprehensive and innovative services is taking hold in LAC. Yet, despite the exciting work of the BSEs and other efforts noted herein, mainstream ECE policies in LAC generally still favor individual programmatic efforts over a systemic approach. This may be attributed to several factors. First, while comprehensive framework documents provide compelling rationales that underscore the importance of the early years, the need for investments in them and the need to think inventively across sectors and services often render them aspirational in nature. Sometimes they are proffered as guides in contrast to legally enforceable documents; other times they are not sufficiently specific to foster comprehensive planning; and often they are not accompanied by the resources, guidance, and accountability mechanisms to ensure their implementation. In part, this may be due to the diverse nature of framework documents in general. It may also be attributed to the fact that these framework documents are so comparatively new that accompanying tools,

resources, and guidelines that could foster implementation are yet to be developed. Still fragile, however, ECE needs to have frameworks bolstered by adjunctive policy tools and by resources, which, no matter how great the commitment, may be scarce in some LAC countries.

Second, in many LAC countries, attention to the institutional architecture, however well regarded, is less urgent than meeting the immediate service demands of the population. Couple such pressing and immediate needs with proven, effective approaches to service delivery, and it is quite natural that some policy efforts favor more programmatic options. For example, conditional cash transfers (CCTs) are a widely used policy tool in the region, and have been very effective in increasing the utilization of public health and education services (Fiszbein and Schady, 2009). As such, CCTs command considerable attention. In well-developed fields such as primary education, where there are schools built and an apparatus for preparing and placing teachers, CCT's can boost attendance. ECE, as yet, is not such a sector; rather, it is a sector where physical and human infrastructure supports are either limited or simply lacking. So, CCTs alone, however viable in related fields, cannot be parachuted into ECE without according attention to infrastructural and human capacity constraints. Indeed, no single funding mechanism will be sufficient to support the integrated comprehensive approaches needed to meaningfully advance the emerging ECE services.

Third, a systemic approach to ECE is very complex to achieve. It requires clear and enjoined intentionality, a firm understanding of the needs of young children and their families, and a durable commitment to major social and institutional reforms. It commands leadership at the highest levels of government, and support from communities and non-governmental organizations. Durable resources coupled with an integrated vision are imperative. Thus, even under the most favorable circumstances, systems implementation is neither simple nor short-term.

SYSTEMS THEORY AND EQUITY

Systems theory is especially potent for examining equity issues because it acknowledges that the commitment to equity is not consistent across and even within countries; it acknowledges these contextual realities and notes their importance for framing critical policy decisions. Moreover, systems theory permits a cross-ministry, cross-program, and cross-policy perspective. Rather than examining the functioning of one institution, it can tackle the cross-institutional equity from three elements of service provision: (i) equitable access to services; (ii) equitable distribution of budgets; and (iii) equitable distribution and remuneration of personnel. Each is discussed below.

Equitable Access to Services

Throughout LAC, equitable access to ECE services, while improving, is compromised. In general, young children in LAC under the age of 5 have better access to health services than to home-based or center-based education services. The reasons for differential access to education services are numerous, with some countries justifying the strategic decision to target, most typically, poor populations, although not always relying on the best targeting systems to reach them. In some cases, targeted services to those most in need are regarded as a policy preamble to expanding services for all children. Inequity also exists because services are more limited in rural and remote areas, and, when they do exist, their quality is often compromised. This is in sharp contrast to examples of vibrant ECE services being offered to children in certain large, urban municipalities. Access inequities often exist by age, with more services being offered to pre-school-aged children than to infants and toddlers, although several notable community-based efforts valiantly seek to alleviate this discrepancy.

Limitations in accessibility may both reflect and contradict country policy. They reflect country policies in that adherence to decentralized decision-making is widespread in LAC. On the surface, localized decision-making seems respectful of community demands and needs, but this is not always equitable. This is particularly true when serious economic, contextual, and cultural disparities characterize different regions of the country, as is the case in many LAC countries. These differences are also evident in the capacity to implement policies and manage resources of the different levels of government and in the heterogeneity across them. Inequitable service distribution also contradicts country policy, particularly when it rhetorically adopts a rights-based stance. Inherent in a commitment to rights-based approaches is a pledge to universal service provision. Representing a worthy goal, universal ECE service provision in LAC is not widespread.

Despite the evident inequality in the provision of ECE services in LAC, there are some notable examples in which the region is making important strides to resolve its equity issues. One such example is the use of national targeting systems to allocate the limited supply of ECE services towards the poorest and most disadvantaged populations, as is manifest in Colombia and Chile. Systems theory has enabled an analysis of access that transcends any single program and conveys a broad picture of the degree to which young children have or do not have equitable access to services. This analysis in itself provides a powerful tool for the identification of areas in which efforts to reduce inequalities are most needed.

Equitable Distribution of Budgets

Despite the fact that there have been large increases in the overall amount of funds available to support ECE in LAC, there are serious inequities in the ways in which these funds are distributed. Such distribution often favors one ministry or one region over another. Regional and sub-regional variation may be due to the reliance on decentralized administrative units, such as municipal governments.

Often larger and wealthier local governments supplement federal funding with their own resources, thereby enhancing the percentages of children who are able to access services. Given that these localities are also likely to be the ones with the strongest technical and implementation capacities, they are capable of providing higher quality services, further exacerbating inequities between richer and poorer districts. For example, in Colombia, there is considerable reliance on municipalities' own commitments to ECE, which vary depending on the municipalities' available financial resources and on the preferences of elected authorities. In Brazil, where the provision of ECE services is the direct responsibility of the municipal governments, funding allocation is extremely unequal, particularly between the Northern and Southern municipalities. The federal government has implemented policies and programs that aim to compensate for the disparities across localities. For example, additional funding is provided to localities that are unable to guarantee a minimum level of expenditure per child per year. Strategies like this are being put in place as data from systems analyses convey the dimensions of budgetary inequities.

Equitable Distribution and Remuneration of Personnel

Since personnel costs are the largest part of ECE budgets, and because personnel quality has a great impact on the success of ECE, it is important to examine their equitable distribution and remuneration schemes. First, common to the countries studied, there are significant regional differences in the availability of qualified EC professionals to work in the health and education sectors, proportional to city size and levels of urbanization. In other words, smaller communities are not only likely to get fewer professionals, but they are also likely to get those who are less qualified. This reality can make it virtually impossible to hire staff who meet minimum qualifications in certain locations. As has been noted, differences

among municipalities can be exacerbated given the fact that, in better-endowed municipalities, governments may mobilize additional resources for EC education. To reverse this trend, salary incentives could and are being used by the health sector in countries like Brazil, to attract qualified staff to the most difficult-to-reach areas.

Second, complicating matters and disincentivizing personnel into the profession, EC educators have lower remunerations than, and different evaluations and career paths from, primary school teachers. This difference in salary has been found in Chile, Colombia, and Trinidad and Tobago. Lower salaries mean that, given a choice, teachers will opt for primary schools, leaving a smaller and often less qualified pool for ECE. This means that children in their earliest years may not have equal access to quality personnel. Moreover, quality personnel may be unevenly distributed throughout a single country, with urban children having greater access to more qualified teachers than children living in rural areas. Geography is not the only variable that can evoke inequity; differences in compensation paid by programs, irrespective of geographic locale, do so as well. For example, in Chile, the two largest programs providing childcare services, Integra and JUNJI, require similar qualifications and offer different compensations to their staff. Lower remuneration for workers in the public sector (compared to those in the private sector) is also common in some countries in the region. In Guatemala and in Trinidad and Tobago, professional careers in the public sector do not seem to attract the professional quality that is needed. A shortage of high-skilled workers in the public sector has been identified as a major challenge to the equitable distribution of quality personnel that is so essential to reduce academic disparities.

SYSTEMS THEORY AND QUALITY

Although debates about what constitutes quality and how it is best measured are prevalent, two generally agreed-upon elements guide the production and provision of quality services for young children: the existence of pedagogical frameworks and standards, and the existence of meaningful professional preparation and development. Guided by a systemic framework that examines quality across delivery systems, each is discussed below, as is an overall review of the trends in quality in the region.

Quantity Before Quality: LAC Trends

In examining multiple efforts in diverse LAC countries, much of the recent and rapid ECE growth has focused on generating programs and spaces for young children, with the result that quality efforts have been less prominent than those focused on quantity. Not unique to LAC, the quantity over quality orientation is sometimes presented as a staged strategy; that is, efforts are mounted with the anticipation that their quality will be improved over time. Taking advantage of current policy opportunities to launch programs seems to be an overriding imperative. Regardless of rationale, a more concerted focus on the production of quality ECE is necessary.

Quality is not totally absent. Indeed, models from other countries are in evidence, as are home-based approaches that show a deep respect for cultural variation. Moreover, there is a fairly clear understanding that quality outcomes are contingent upon quality personnel; this recognition exists despite the fact that the countries face serious personnel shortages. Moreover, concrete tools and instruments that are crucial to produce quality are also less apparent. For example, efforts to address the diverse languages of children, as well as efforts to address children with special needs, are not abundant. Effective program monitoring and child assessments for instructional improvement are policy tools that appear to be used inconsistently. Transition efforts, traditionally associated with quality, are also absent (except in Chile and Trinidad and Tobago).

Pedagogical Frameworks and Standards

Despite the fact that quality has not taken precedence over quantity in LAC, the importance of quality has been recognized and some key quality tools have been put in place. Standards, for example, are generally regarded to be among the most potent of policy tools that can be used to promote quality. Within each of the major sectors that comprise ECE (education, health, and social protection), at least three types of standards exist. The first type of standards, often called child outcome standards, specifies the precise and measurable *outcomes* children should derive as a result of receiving services. The second kind of standards, often referred to as program standards, relates to those that specify the nature of the *services* children should receive. The third kind of standards relates to the professional certifications that specify what teachers, doctors, nurses, and social workers need to know and be able to do to deliver services effectively.

Among the countries studied, nearly all had program standards for the major educational components of their ECE efforts. Program/service standards exist for most health and social protection programs as well. The mere existence of standards, however, is not a complete barometer of success; their quality must be examined. Often and across sectors, program standards focus on what could be easily counted. In education sector programs, this is manifest in an abundance of standards that address structural variables such as group size, child–adult ratios, and teacher pre-service training requirements. Requisite attention to process variables, for example teacher–child interactions, was less prevalent in all of the countries, despite the fact that they are most directly linked to child outcomes. Standards specifying what young children should know and be able to do were particularly lacking, partly due to fear that the results from standards-based assessments could be used to unfairly label or track young children. It is important to note, however, that although many countries do not have precise standards for children's outcomes, they have rather comprehensive approaches to curriculum, albeit weak mechanisms to monitor curriculum implementation. Structured transitions from home to center-based care programs and from programs to schools to ensure children's continuity of experience are still incipient as a key element of quality across most of LAC.

In the health sector, the existence of standards for health delivery is prevalent and visible. In general, however, program standards in the health sector focus on the number of services delivered coming from administrative data, rather than on parameters of service quality. As compared to education, health outcomes for children were more routinely specified in the countries studied, as they are often based on international norms that relate to pre- and post-natal care, growth, nutrition, and immunization.

Countries use their program standards in different ways. In some places, program standards are essentially used as licensing criteria to which providers must adhere before they are granted permission to operate. Other countries place less regulatory weight on program standards and recommend that they be used as guides for operation. Whatever the use, program standards are often very difficult to implement.

Because program standards are typically developed for a single program, it is common for countries to have several sets of standards for diverse efforts, even for those that deliver very similar services. The existence of multiple sets of program standards generates unintended inequities for children served by providers with varying levels of quality, even within public programs. This is especially clear where local and national government programs coexist. Moreover, because standards do not apply to both public and private sector providers in many countries, a 'double standard' that exacerbates inequity and inequality is created. Beyond implementation, standards are challenging to monitor. In the LAC countries studied, limited resources are allocated to program monitoring and to

quality compliance; monitoring staff are limited in number, and, in some cases, limited in competence. Monitoring mechanisms tend to be considered more as an accountability vehicle than as a quality improvement mechanism.

Meaningful Professional Preparation and Development

Despite general acknowledgement of the importance of teacher preparation and development to quality programs, human capacity in ECE is still weak in the region. For example, several large ECE programs in LAC are community-based provision models that rely on community mothers as service providers. Often the community mothers, armed with knowledge of the community context, have no pre-service training in ECE and no entry credentials. Moreover, community mothers often have very low levels of education themselves and exhibit large turnover. Even where there are professionals involved in ECE, the general understanding is that ECE is a field of specialization different from primary education. This is reflected by the fact that there are multiple efforts specifically designed to train ECE educators. Differentiation is commendable because it can allow for the acquisition of the appropriate skill set demanded in high-quality ECE classrooms. An unintended consequence of differentiation, present also in the countries studied, is that it can segregate ECE educators from the teaching profession, which provides justification for lower remuneration and/or a less attractive career path.

In the area of in-service training, efforts in LAC are still scattered and not always aligned to salary incentives or to evaluation schemes. One notable case is that of Brazil, which does not have an official pre-service credential for ECE educators. To resolve this omission, universities are retraining basic education teachers as ECE educators; such training is based on defined guidelines for teacher expectations. One encouraging finding was that the national budget allocates funds to local governments and mandates that they be used specifically for the purposes of carrying out in-service training initiatives. Some countries, like Guatemala, have also opted to retrain primary school teachers. While these efforts are important, they are not a permanent solution to compensate for the absence of pre-service training and credentialing for EC educators. Questions remain as to whether the retraining of primary school teachers has the capacity to produce enough qualified educators for the large and growing number of ECE classrooms and, more broadly, whether the system can produce enough staff for the rapidly growing array of EC services expanding their coverage.

SYSTEMS THEORY AND SUSTAINABILITY

Systems theory provides the opportunity to consider current policies and programmatic efforts in light of their durability and overall longevity. In discussing sustainability, we refer to the actual continuation of the direct services provided to children and to the supports needed to sustain those services. In LAC, several critical components of sustainability are discussed below: financing, durable data and accountability systems, and political and public support.

Financing and Sustainability

Central to any service system are the funds that are provided over time to support it. Often ECE efforts are proposed by one political leader, only to be dismounted when a successor takes office. Increasingly then, in addition to the quest for quality and equity, durable funding is essential to the longevity of ECE. This issue can be analyzed from two perspectives: first, the sufficiency of the funds for present-day service provision, and, second, the durability of the funding source over time. With regard to the former, the renewed

interest in ECE has resulted in an increase in public funding for such services. This increase, however, is not consistent across countries, and generally is insufficient to cover the growing needs of service provision. Compared to budgets allocated to primary education, for example, ECE budgets are still extremely low, particularly taking into account that good quality ECE services may be more expensive per child than primary education. Moreover, the move towards comprehensive service provision may require larger fiscal commitments. So although budgets allocated to ECE have expanded, they are still insufficient.

In the quest to fund programs quickly, the sector often relies on unsustainable sources of funding. In some countries, funding relies on the use of surpluses or royalties related to natural resource exports, which fluctuate over time. Further, funding is often contingent on matches required from the private sector; these may be prevalent while an idea or program is new, but are not likely to be sustained over time. Some countries have recognized the precariousness of these strategies and sought more durable funding mechanisms. But even in these countries, ECE is still a second-tier area. In the case of Brazil, expenditure floors for education are set in the Constitution. These general expenditures are not specifically earmarked for ECE, although they do comprise ECE expenditures. In short, this analysis suggests that sustainable funding is a critical but often overlooked systems issue.

Data/Accountability Systems and Sustainability

Data and accountability are essential to the sustainability of any system since they provide the information tools to monitor implementation and evaluate performance – two prerequisites for long-term planning. Indeed, it is difficult to consider systemic effectiveness or program sustainability without devoting considerable effort to data and accountability. Within LAC, there is an overall acknowledgement of the importance of data to inform policy decisions that may evoke greater program and service longevity. Despite this recognition, data and accountability systems vary widely across countries. Several key factors condition data generation and use: the conceptualization of the social utility of data, data timeliness, and the level of aggregation. Equally important is the issue of institutional capacity for data generation, management, and use.

Conceptually, data systems designed by individual ministries seem to be regarded as repositories for service delivery information, rather than as living vehicles for quality enhancement and policy development. As such, they tend to hold information on programmatic inputs (e.g., number of clinical cases, children in school, beneficiaries of a specific program), which translates into the use of such information for accountability purposes against output standards (e.g., number of children per classroom, amount spent on materials). Much less attention is devoted to collecting indicators of results, outcomes, or impacts (e.g., developmental indicators at the child level). This limits the use of available data for accountability that goes beyond inputs. Further complicating matters, data may not be current or available in a timely way to end users. In some of the studied countries, the data for children were aggregated for youngsters from birth to age 18, making it impossible to disaggregate information for any single age group.

Institutional capacity is associated with all of the challenges that arise in the effort to generate, manage, and use information systems. In some countries (and in less-developed regions within all countries), there are also technological gaps and connectivity problems that still impose constraints on the construction of modern data systems. With respect to technical and institutional capacity, there is a great variation not only between countries, but also across different sectors, institutions, and regions within each country. An additional layer of complexity emerges in the effort to construct integrated cross-sectorial data systems like the ones that would be necessary in order to track different outcomes associated with the well-being of young children and their families.

Despite these limitations, it is important to note that countries recognize the importance of transitioning to nominal data systems, where the unit of analysis is the individual, so that persons can be tracked throughout their life trajectory within a given sector, or ultimately merged across sectors. As the need for generating nominal data systems becomes more evident, some countries have initiated commendable efforts to produce such systems by using the rosters associated with conditional cash transfers as platforms on which to build these systems. The Colombian SISBEN, the national targeting system used to determine eligibility for social programs, is one example of an effort to produce a comprehensive data framework used across sectors.

The move to a more comprehensive approach in ECE and the creation of BSEs point to the need to build integrated data systems that articulate information about children, families, providers, human capacity, and programs from different sectors and levels of government. These data systems are necessary for planning, monitoring, and accountability purposes. They can facilitate transitions across services and allow for the implementation of quality assurance processes (e.g., incentives, licensing, or accreditation). Conceiving quality from a systemic perspective requires thinking beyond programmatic data collection efforts and towards more systemic ones. Systematic data collection efforts do not need to be integrated into one central database. Instead, they can still be housed in the sectors. What makes them systemic is that the different data sets are linked so that they can easily be merged, so that different parties have access to each other's information. This type of organization requires a strong central planning effort. In some of the countries studied, BSEs seem to have promoted the emergence of consolidated data systems, fostering data integration.

Political/Public Support and Sustainability

A third element related to service sustainability is the breadth of the base that supports it. In responsive democracies, diverse players have the ability to contour the policy agenda. To that end, program sustainability can be enhanced through public and private support. Systems analysis takes this into account when it examines the diverse phenomena that lead to sustainable efforts.

ECE in LAC has recognized this and has taken diverse positive steps to engage an array of governmental and non-governmental actors. Indeed, the increased focus on young children's issues in the policy agenda is the result of not only the discourse and actions of government agencies and officials, but the active participation of non-governmental actors. These external influencers include individuals from civil society, grassroots organizations, academics, the business sector, and international organizations, all of whom have strong voices in matters relating to the protection and development of young children. Often these external influencers' voices and opinions are expressed through their partnerships with governmental initiatives for young children. The National Early Childhood Network (*Rede Nacional Primeira Infância*) in Brazil is a good example of this type of partnership. The network is formed by a group of civil society organizations, government agencies, and the private sector. Together, they advocate for early childhood. In Trinidad and Tobago, the influence of non-governmental actors on escalating the importance of ECE is conspicuous; a remarkable example is the importance of academic input on practical issues such as the implementation of transition-specific curricula and teacher training for pre-primary teachers. These are but a few examples of the many efforts underway in LAC to create partnerships that advance ECE in the region.

ANALYSIS OF SYSTEMS THEORY FOR UNDERSTANDING THE STRUCTURAL ELEMENTS OF ECE

This analysis regarding the application of systems theory and systems thinking to LAC is helpful in a number of ways. First, it proffers a refreshing and innovative way to frame ECE research, with the goal of evoking new lines of inquiry, new methodologies, and new findings that may help guide constructive policy and practice. Second, it provides important lessons regarding the viability of applying such theory to practice in diverse countries with significantly different policy approaches. Third, it points out the limitations of systems theory and leads the authors to suggest modifications for reform.

New Lines of Inquiry and Methodology

Research in ECE has, to date, heavily favored programmatic and pedagogical analyses, with a large emphasis on evaluative studies (Does program X work for a, b, c children, and under which conditions?). By breaking the mold on these lines of inquiry, we move beyond the conventional issues to examine all elements of the institutional architecture of ECE systems in order to discern the roles they play individually and collectively in supporting good quality, equitable, and sustainable service provision. Rather than focusing on, for instance, the relationship between the characteristics of certain programs and individual child outcomes, systems research prioritizes how elements of the ECE architecture (governance mechanisms, funding schemes, human capital development, and quality assurance) interact with one another. Moreover, systems theory holds systemic outcomes to a different level of scrutiny. Supporting child and family outcomes as the desirable units of outcomes, systems theory posits that beyond them, interim systemic outcomes (e.g., quality, equity, and sustainability) must be present. In positing these as viable, children's right to ECE services is positioned front and center.

Systems research in ECE draws from a variety of existing methodologies and approaches. It can benefit from both quantitative and qualitative data collection and analysis methodologies that are common to other approaches. What is different about systems research in ECE, and what makes it so complex, is the need to constantly juggle various analytic levels and foci. This requires the researcher to simultaneously uncover and understand elements that play at the program and system levels across disciplines (education, health, social protection), and across levels of government (national, subnational, local). While the main focus is on understanding how such elements *interact* (the systemic focus), such understanding requires an exploration of the characteristics of each individual element. For example, an understanding of the sustainability of ECE services in a certain country will require an understanding of funding mechanisms across national, subnational, and local levels of government, an understanding of how funding decisions are made, and whether such decisions vary depending on the object of the funding (Is it pre-primary education? Is it health programs? Is it comprehensive services?), among many other elements.

This approach cannot be developed or implemented without suitable allocations of time, funds, and expertise. Time must be sufficient to ensure data collection across levels of government, and to gather perspectives from policy-makers, providers, parents, teachers, doctors, nurses, caregivers, and community members. Funding needs to be adequate to allow for intense follow-up and to confirm information. Such studies are best undertaken by those who conceptualize ECE broadly and understand its funding and governance mechanisms. Finally, those who undertake systems work must keep their eye on the past, present, and future simultaneously; they must understand that the elements that compose the ECE institutional architecture are impermanent, and that new organizations (e.g., boundary-spanning entities) may emerge with huge

fanfare, only to be curtailed or eliminated with a new political administration. Even within any given administration, ministries and ministry personnel are reshuffled with increasing regularity as are conventional powers and authorities. Understanding how institutional change takes place and how and why past changes in the institutional architecture have occurred is a critical part of understanding the current state of systems.

Applying Systems Theory in Diverse Contexts

Conducting systems research in just one context is difficult enough. Adopting a comparative perspective (as we have done in the case of the analysis of ECE systems in Latin America and the Caribbean) complicates matters even further. All elements of the research (from the formation of basic research questions, to the discernment of informants, to the scheduling and verification of interviews and interview data) must be designed so that each culture is taken into account. Culture and context may affect the extent to which informants are amenable to sharing crucial information, how researchers' intentions are viewed and trusted (or not), and the time and mechanisms that are needed to gain access to do fieldwork, among many other issues. In particular, the positionality of the researcher, an important consideration in all research, becomes crucial in comparative research. Researcher biases and interests must be revealed, both externally (to participants) and internally (to the researchers themselves). Taking into account how our own biases affect the ways in which we interpret information plays a crucial role in comparative research. Equally necessary is the ability to understand phenomena from the point of view of the participants, while simultaneously stepping back to see how similar phenomena are differently understood in different contexts.

Despite the additional difficulties that it brings to the analysis, a comparative perspective on systems research can yield important benefits. The comparative approach illuminates the extent of what is possible and challenges what is considered a given in a specific context. Different countries implement different solutions to similar problems. By analyzing such different solutions, the comparative approach helps uncover the relationships between culture, context, and institutional path dependency in a country's policy choices. At any point in the development of the ECE system, a country could have chosen a different path. The comparative analysis provides insights into the menu of possible alternative paths, while at the same time highlighting the contextual elements that lead a country to opt for a specific one.

Considerations Regarding Research on ECE Systems

As helpful as systems theory can be for documenting and understanding previously under-addressed elements of the ECE system, there are important limitations to be noted. First, conducting this type of systems research requires an interdisciplinary team that can provide attention to all the elements that compose the system. By definition, ECE systems involve several disciplines. Balancing attention so that all elements that impact young children, including their health, education, social protection, and well-being, and those of their parents, can be captured is a huge challenge in systems work. Often analyses may end up favoring some disciplines over others, and this needs to be acknowledged in the conclusions that are drawn from the analysis.

Second, decisions need to be made with regard to how deeply we need to understand each element of the system in order to be able to draw inferences about how the system works as a whole. The level of detail of the information collected may be affected by time and resource constraints, but this is also a crucial methodological decision: how much do we need to know about each element of the system in order to be able to infer the basic principles on which this system operates? Systems research may not provide enough information

to fully understand each element of the system. A reader may not find a fine-grain account of, for instance, the governance mechanisms for ECE in a given country. S/he will find, instead, enough elements to understand how governance interacts with financing schemes, accountability structures, and other elements of the system, and how such interactions affect the quality, equity, and sustainability of service provision.

Finally, systems research focuses on how systems work, and the likelihood that they will produce good quality, equitable, and sustainable ECE service provision. It cannot attest to the comparative effectiveness of specific governance mechanisms, finance schemes, quality assurance systems, or human capacity development programs.

Benefits of Research on ECE Systems

As noted throughout this chapter, ECE systems research is challenging to conduct, interpret, and apply. Given these issues, is systems work worth pursuing as an element of the ECE research repertoire? Not surprisingly, our answer is resoundingly yes. Still embryonic in ECE, systems thinking and systems research should be advanced as a meaningful way to understand how services can be manipulated, improved, and tailored to meet the needs of children and families. Systems research lets those concerned about young children see the whole picture. As ECE pedagogical theory and practice do not allow a focus on only one domain of development, systems thinking is required for policy. Indeed, seeing the system whole is an essential prelude to servicing the whole child. Moreover, systems thinking has helped to advance work on the outcomes of ECE; it is respectful of the importance of child outcomes, but sees quality, equity, and sustainability as requisite to such outcomes. Systems thinking expands the conceptual universe of ECE to a place where children, families, and the institutions that serve them are positioned front and center.

FURTHER READING

Araujo, M. C., Lopez-Boo, F. and Puyana, J. M. (2013). *Overview of early childhood development services in Latin American and the Caribbean*. Washington, DC: Inter-American Development Bank, Social Protection and Health Division.

Berlinski, S. and Norbert, S. (eds) (in press). *The early years*. Washington, DC: Inter-American Development Bank.

Harris-Van Keuren, C. and Rodriguez, D. (2013). *Early childhood learning guidelines in Latin America and the Caribbean*. Washington, DC: Inter-American Development Bank, Social Protection and Health Division.

Kagan, S. L. and Gomez, R. (eds) (2015). *Early childhood governance: Choices and consequences*. New York: Teachers College Press.

Levy, S. and Schady, N. (2013). Latin America's social policy challenge: Education, social insurance, redistribution. *Journal of Economic Perspectives*, 7(2), 193–218.

Naudeau, S., Kataoka, N., Valerio, A., Neuman, M. and Kennedy Elder, L. (2010) *Investing in young children*. Washington, DC: The World Bank.

OECD. (2012). *Starting strong III: A quality toolbox for early childhood education and care*. Paris: OECD.

Schady, N., Behrman, J., Araujo, M. C., Azuero, R., Bernal, R., Bravo, D., et al. (in press). Wealth gradients in early childhood development in five Latin American countries. *Journal of Human Resources*.

Vegas, E. and Santibanez, L. (2010). *The promise of ECD in Latin America and the Caribbean*. Washington, DC: The World Bank.

QUESTIONS FOR REFLECTION

1 To what extent are the discussed conceptual shifts and trends presented for LAC similar to or different from other regions of the world? Why might this be the case?

2 Are equity, quality, and sustainability the most important/effective systemic outcomes? Are there others that should be included?

3 How do equity, quality, and sustainability relate to one another conceptually? What were elements common to these three outcomes in the LAC analysis discussed in the chapter?

4 Are the challenges that pertain to systems thinking and theory applicable across contexts?

5 How do traditional theories upon which ECE research is based reflect systems thinking?

6 To what extent can systems thinking be applied to the pedagogy of the classroom?

7 What are different ways to operationalize the family outcomes of 'meaningfully involved' and 'organizationally supported'? What are the implications of these definitions for future ECE research?

NOTES

1 The systems approach used in this chapter proposes a broader view of policies and programs aimed at reaching children during the early years of their lives, beyond that of the discipline of education. As such, it is more aligned with the notion of early childhood development.

2 By meaningfully involved, we mean families that provide their children with high quality interactions and experiences, characterized by warmth, responsiveness, sensitivity, rich in language and learning opportunities. By organizationally supported, we mean families that have the means to satisfy their basic needs and to engage in productive activities.

3 The authors would like to acknowledge with great appreciation the work associated with this project carried out by Emily Fox, Martha Kluttig, Victoria Parra, and Juan Carlos Reyes.

REFERENCES

Araujo, M. C., Aguayo, Y. C., Jaimovich, A. and Kagan, S. L. (in press). The institutional architecture of early childhood development policies and programs in Latin America and the Caribbean. In S. Berlinski and N. Schady (eds), *The early years*, 1st edn. Washington, DC: Inter-American Development Bank.

Berlinski, S. and Schady, N. (eds) (2015). *The early years*. Washington, DC: Inter-American Development Bank.

Bowen, M. (1966). The use of family theory in clinical practice. *Comprehensive Psychiatry*, 7(5), 345–74.

Britto, P. R., Yoshikawa, H., Van Ravens, J., Ponguta, L. A., Reyes, M., Oh, S. S., Dimaya, R., Nieto, A. M. and Sede, R. (2014). Strengthening systems for integrated early childhood development services: A cross-national analysis of governance. *Annals of the New York Academy of Sciences*, 1308, 245–55.

Bronfenbrenner, U. (1979). The ecology of human development: Experiments by nature and design. Cambridge, MA: Harvard University Press. (Republished in 2006.)

Bruner, C. (1996). Where's the beef? Getting real about what comprehensive means. In R. Stone (ed.), *Core issues in comprehensive community-building initiatives* (pp. 85–6). Chicago, IL: Chapin Hall Center for Children.

Connell, J. B. and Kubisch, A. (1998). Applying a theory of change approach to the evaluation of comprehensive community initiations: Progress, prospects, and problems. In K. Fulbright-Anderson, A. Kubisch and J. B. Connell (eds), *New approaches to evaluating community initiatives* (pp. 15–44). Washington, DC: The Aspen Institute.

Constitution of Brazil, available at: www.planalto.gov.br/ccivil_03/constituicao/constituicaocompilado.htm (accessed February 2015).

DiMaggio, P. J. and Powell, W. W. (1983). The iron cage revisited: Institutional isomorphism and collective rationality in organizational fields. *American Sociological Review*, 48(2), 147–60.

Fiszbein, A. and Schady, N. (2009). *Conditional cash transfers: Reducing present and future poverty*. Washington, DC: The World Bank.

Fulbright-Anderson, K., Kubisch, A. and Connell, J.B. (eds) (1998). *New approaches to evaluating community initiatives*. Washington, DC: The Aspen Institute.

Joachim, A. and May, J. R. (2010). Beyond subsystems: Policy regimes and governance. *Policy Studies Journal*, 38(2), 303–27.

Kagan, S. L. (1998). Using a theory of change approach in a national evaluation of family support programs. In K. Fulbright-Anderson, A. Kubisch and J.B. Connell (eds), *New approaches to evaluating community initiatives* (pp. 113–22). Washington, DC: The Aspen Institute.

Kagan, S. L. (2015). Conceptualizing ECE governance: Not the elephant in the room. In S. L. Kagan and R. E. Gomez (eds), *Early childhood governance: Choices and consequences* (pp. 9–29). New York: Teachers College Press.

Kagan, S. L. and Cohen, N. (eds) (1996). *Reinventing early care and education: A vision for a quality system*. San Francisco, CA: Jossey-Bass.

Kagan, S. L. and Kauerz, K. (eds) (2012). *Early childhood systems: Transforming early learning*. New York: Teachers College Press.

Laszlo, E. (1996). *The systems view of the world: A holistic vision for our time*. New York: Hampton Press.

Mashburn, A. J., Pianta, R. C., Hamre, B. K., Downer, J. T., Barbarin, O. A., Bryant, D., et al. (2008). Measures of classroom quality in prekindergarten and children's development of academic, language, and social skills. *Child Development*, 79, 732–49.

Meyer, J. R. and Rowan, B. (1977). Institutionalized organizations: Formal structure as myth and ceremony. *American Journal of Sociology*, 83(2), 340–63.

Neuman, M. and Devercelli, A. E. (2013). *What matters most for early childhood development: A framework paper* (Working Paper No. 5). Available at: http://wbgfiles.worldbank.org/documents/hdn/ed/saber/supporting_doc/Background/ECD/Framework_SABER-ECD.pdf

Piaget, J. (1972). *The psychology of intelligence*. Totowa, NJ: Littlefield.

Peisner-Feinberg, E. S., Burchinal, M. R., Clifford, R. M., Culkin, M. L., Howes, C., Kagan, S. L. and Yazejian, N. (2001). The relation of preschool child-care quality to children's cognitive and social development trajectories through second grade. *Child Development*, 72, 1534–53.

Scott, W. R. (2001). *Institutions and organizations*, 2nd edn. Thousand Oaks, CA: SAGE.

Scott, W. R. and Davies, G. F. (2007). *Organizations and organizing: Rational, natural, and open system perspectives*. Upper Saddle River, NJ: Prentice Hall.

Senge, P. (1990). *The fifth discipline: The art and practice of the learning organization*. New York: Doubleday.

Sugarman, J. M. (1981). *Building early childhood systems: A resource handbook*. Washington, DC: Child Welfare League of America.

Vargas-Baron, E. (2013). Building and strengthening national systems for early childhood development. In P. Britto, P. Engle and

C. M. Super (eds), *Handbook of early child-hood development research and its impact on global policy* (pp. 443–66). New York: Oxford University Press.

Von Bertalanffy, L. (1968). *General system theory: Foundations, development, applications*. New York: George Braziller.

Weiss, C. H. (1997). How can theory-based evaluation make greater headway? *Evaluation Review*, 21(4), 501–24.

World Bank, The (2006). *World development report 2006: Equity and development*. Washington, DC: The World Bank.

Yin, R. K. (1992). The role of theory in doing case study research and evaluations. In H. Chen and P. Rossi (eds), *Using theory to improve program and policy evaluations*. New York: Greenwood Press.

PART III

Conducting Early Childhood Research

Ethics in Early Childhood Research

Ann Farrell

INTRODUCTION

Increasing international interest in young children's life experiences and life chances has paralleled an upsurge in conceptual and methodological interest in research involving young children and those around them. Early childhood has been the focus of heightened policy and empirical attention, such that peak bodies such as the Organization for Economic Cooperation and Development (OECD) (2001, 2006, 2012) and the United Nations Children's Fund (UNICEF) (2008, 2012) have produced international comparative reports on early childhood education and care and children's life chances, respectively. In turn, the United Nations Department of Economic and Social Affairs (UNDESA) (2011) has shown the ways in which geo-political shifts, rapid urbanization and child poverty reveal and, indeed, produce unequal life outcomes for the world's children. So too, recent empirical evidence from developmental and neuroscientific research and from cost-benefit analyses (Cunha et al., 2006; Camilli et al., 2010; Heckman, 2011) reveal unprecedented global interest in young children, their everyday lives and their life outcomes. Such evidence forms the policy and legislative backcloth to this chapter's consideration of ethical research with children.

The global focus on young children has been accompanied by growing awareness of the ethical conduct of child research, in light of global recognition (although not necessarily ratification) of the United Nations Convention on the Rights of the Child (UNCRC) (United Nations, 1989). The children's rights agenda has been attended by a global trend towards accountability, surveillance and regulation of research with young children, albeit under the guise of children's rights to participation and protection. Children's rights have come to underpin the frameworks and guidelines used by many professional bodies, research ethics committees and institutional review boards, as they work with those who conduct research with young children.

Within this context, the chapter sets out to map the international field of early childhood research ethics. First, the chapter will examine the historical antecedents that have contributed to global trends and local practices within the field of ethical research with young children. Second, it will examine the conceptual underpinnings and practical outworkings of ethical research with children, revealing the ways in which the field draws from a range of cognate disciplines such as developmental science, sociology, health sciences and human rights frameworks. It will consider the pivotal understandings of the competence of young children to participate in research *in situ* (and to agree to participate) as reliable, voluntary informants on matters that affect them. In so doing, the chapter will examine the key issues of informed consent and confidentiality in child research. Moreover, the chapter will provide a conceptual scaffold for exploring theoretical understandings and the practical implications of ethical research with children. Its purpose in doing so is to inform and challenge theorists, practitioners, policy workers and communities who contribute to, advocate for and govern ethical research with children and those around them.

GLOBAL TRENDS IN ETHICAL RESEARCH WITH CHILDREN

Global empirical interest in young children and their life chances, along with increased global attention to children's rights to participation and protection, have piqued global interest in the ethical conduct of research with children, in what can be seen now as an extant field of scholarship and practice (Farrell, 2013a, b). Theoretically, globalization can be seen as a phenomenon experienced and enacted in varied, yet uneven, ways by people across different times and places (Singh, 2004) or *locales* (Giddens, 2001). Globalization is manifest in global flows of people, practices, ideas and technologies,

which impact on local practices, including practices that relate to research with children.

How is ethics defined? Dictionary definitions of ethics are (characteristically) wide-ranging. The Oxford Dictionary (2014), for example, defines ethics as 'Moral principles that govern a person's behavior or the conduct of an activity (as in medical ethics)' and 'The branch of knowledge that deals with moral principles'. In theoretical terms, ethics can be seen as a justificatory discourse concerned with human values and judgments, invoking rules of behavior or conformity to a code or set of principles (Kimmel, 1988). Cribb (2004) argues that 'ethical behaviour springs from a desire to act properly in all circumstances, not just those which have been identified by rule-makers. Ethics exists as a characteristic of humankind precisely because law is inadequate to the task of creating morally good behaviour' (p. 55).

So too, the field of ethics has a long history: from the Hippocratic School of Ancient Greece (Smith, 1996) to the 18th century work of German philosopher Immanuel Kant (1781/2003; 1785/1995) in relation to ethics or moral laws as categorical imperatives, to the 19th century work, typified by Thomas Percival (1803/1997), on ethical imperatives for medical practice and clinical research ethics (Newsom, 1990; Smith, 1996; Emmanuel et al., 2008).

Since then, the most significant pivot-point for research ethics with humans was the Nuremberg Military Tribunal (NMT) (1949) and its ten basic principles for ethical research with humans. Central to the mandate of the NMT were obligations to contribute to the good of society, to avoid unnecessary physical or mental harm to participants, and to ensure the voluntary consent of humans to participate in and withdraw from the research without force, deceit or coercion (Weithorn and Scherer, 1994). The focus on beneficence, that is, the relative benefit versus the risk of involvement in research, became an enduring feature of the fledgling field of research ethics. Soon after the NMT, the World Medical

Association (WMA) published its *Principles for Those in Research and Experimentation* (1954) and adopted it, in 1964, as the *Declaration of Helsinki* (WMA, 1964/2000). So too, the British Medical Research Association published its *Responsibility in Investigations on Human Subjects* (1964), a code of ethical conduct for research supervisors, professional associations and scholarly journals (Coughlin and Beauchamp, 1996). These markers and drivers of change saw the geography of global research ethics (albeit in medical research) begin to take shape. In time, professional associations and learned bodies (particularly in medical research in countries such as Australia, New Zealand, Sweden, the UK, and the USA) became increasingly articulate, systematic and international in their governance and regulation of scientific merit, risk assessment, institutional ethical review and publication of research findings (Bankowski, 1993; McNeill, 1993; Babbie, 1998; Milburn, 2001; Miller, 2003; National Research Council, 2003; Tschudin, 2003).

By the end of the 20th century, scholarly bodies in the social sciences had developed their own guidelines for the ethical conduct of social research (Kimmel, 1988; Burgess, 1989; Homan, 1991; May, 1997; Babbie, 1998; Ezzy, 2002). This trend paralleled a similar trend in the health sciences (Alderson, 1992; Coughlin and Beauchamp, 1996; Hoagwood et al., 1996; Ross, 1998; Fisher et al., 2002; Miller, 2003; Berg and Latin, 2004). The articulation and governance of research ethics in the social sciences and health sciences, in turn, sharpened global interest in ethical research with children in the late 20th century (Grodin and Glantz, 1994; Hood et al., 1996; Mahon et al., 1996; Morrow and Richards, 1996; Graue et al., 1998; Greig and Taylor, 1999; Christensen and James, 2000; Farrell, 2005, 2013b).

In the Global North, a culture of research regulation and surveillance, epitomized in health research, saw professional bodies, ethics committees and institutional review boards intensify their focus on research ethics. Despite the push for regulation and surveillance, the Global North featured cases of uneven compliance. One example in parts of the USA was in relation to voluntary consent and participant selection (Redshaw et al., 2004). Studies of ethical compliance in the Global South, in turn, revealed a stark difference in ethical standards, practices and governance, in comparison to (even) the lowest performing cases in the Global North. Challenges for ethical practice and regulation in the Global South were shown in the work of Rivera and Ezcurra (2001) in Latin America, Coker and McKee (2001) in Eastern Europe, Kass et al. (2007) in Africa, and the World Health Organization (WHO) (2002) in India. Such were some of the pressing challenges faced by research ethics in the late 20th and early 21st centuries.

Now, in the second decade of the 21st century, there has been an upsurge of interest in research ethics and the contexts in which ethical research with children operates. Heightened global interest in child research (and in its everyday contexts such as early childhood education) can be seen to be framed by three agendas: (i) the Starting Strong agenda; (ii) the accountability agenda; and (iii) the children's rights agenda (Farrell, 2013a; Farrell and Danby, 2013). The Starting Strong agenda focuses on a strong start for children and their life chances (OECD, 2001, 2006, 2012; Moss, 2007; UNICEF, 2008); the accountability agenda focuses on assessing and reporting children's achievements against international benchmarks (IEA, 2007; OECD, 2011); and the accountability agenda elides with a third agenda, that of children's rights to participation and protection (Alderson and Morrow, 2011). While the three agendas may not ostensibly speak to ethical research with children, their permeation of the contexts in which child research is likely to occur is noted. Thus, it is against the backcloth of these agendas that we consider the field of research ethics, as *international* in its history and practice, while being *local* in its legislative, policy, jurisdictional and institutional requirements.

THE GROWING FIELD OF RESEARCH ETHICS

Since the late 20th century, the field of research ethics has shown steady growth in its profile and reach, with a growing number and range of publications (monographs, technical reports and journals) designed to provide guidance to researchers, institutional review boards/ethics committees and research gatekeepers concerned with ethics in research with humans.

Numerous journals came to be dedicated to medical bioethics and ethics (e.g., *Clinical Ethics, Ethics, American Journal of Bioethics*, the *Journal of Bioethical Inquiry*, the *Journal of Ethics*, the *Journal of Medical Ethics* and *Monash Bioethics Review*). Some social science journals, although not ostensibly dedicated to research ethics, devoted special issues to ethical research with children (e.g., *Children and Society, Global Studies of Childhood*). So too, the field attracted annotated bibliographies such as that of Halasa (2009), sponsored by the Australian Association for Research in Education, and that of Farrell (2013b) designed to resource research practitioners to deal with conceptual, methodological and analytic issues in the design, conduct and dissemination of research with children. Other work included literature reviews of ethical issues in child and youth research such as those of Powell and colleagues (Graham et al., 2013; Powell et al., 2011, 2012).

While awareness of ethical issues in child research appears to have increased, a meta-analysis of ten international early childhood journals, conducted by Mayne and Howitt (2014) (for the period 2009 to 2012), shows considerable under-reporting of ethical issues in research articles. The paucity of information on ethical practice such as informed voluntary consent, for example, points to the need for even greater awareness of ethical protocols and practice in the reporting of research and in the publishing of research, than appeared to be the case in the works reviewed by Mayne and Howitt (2014).

In summary, despite the shortcomings identified by Mayne and Howitt (2014), the expanding yet modest field of scholarship in child research and its ethical considerations has provided a platform for considering conceptual and methodological understandings of child research. This has been particularly so in Scandinavia and the UK, where authoritative work, for example, by Christensen and James (2008), Alderson and Morrow (2004, 2011) and James and James (2004) has come to inform policy frameworks and initiatives for researchers and research gatekeepers (Fraser et al., 2004; Greig et al., 2007).

CONCEPTUAL UNDERSTANDINGS OF ETHICAL RESEARCH WITH CHILDREN

Recent decades have seen the emergence of new conceptual understandings of children and their participation in research, within fields of inquiry known (variously) as childhood studies and the sociology of childhood (see Qvortrup, 1994, 2000; Tobin, 1995; Waksler, 1996; Corsaro, 1997; Danby and Baker, 1998; Hutchby and Moran-Ellis, 1998; James et al., 1998; Jenks, 1999; Alanen and Mayall, 2001; Danby, 2002; Mayall, 2002, 2003, 2008; Danby and Farrell, 2005). While not necessarily focused on research ethics, this body of scholarship on children as participants speaks powerfully to the topic of this chapter.

Characteristic of this new set of conceptual understandings is an interest in listening to what children say and how they say it (Morrow, 2010), largely in light of children's rights to participation (MacNaughton et al., 2007; Alderson and Morrow, 2011), a process that has been theorized as listening and/or consulting with children about their everyday lives (Tisdall et al., 2009). Labeled as child participation, child consultation or child participatory research, it is concerned with the research-oriented engagement of children with adults and/or other children that invites children to account for and/or contribute views on matters that are important to them. According to social researcher Kellett (2005), its remit is research *with* children, rather than research *on* children or *about* children.

Within this framework, childhood is not seen as universal. Rather, it is seen to be co-constructed within specific places, times and settings, with children viewed as already competent participants in their everyday worlds (Mackay, 1991). Within this frame, children can be afforded opportunities, through interactional practices *in situ*, to display their communicative competence (Danby, 2002).

This set of conceptual and methodological approaches stands in contrast to traditional developmental understandings of children, where children tended to be seen as (i) pre-competent (Mackay, 1991; Danby, 2002); (ii) 'underdeveloped … thus *not something* rather than *something*' (Waksler, 1991: 63); or (iii) 'human becomings' (Phillips and Alderson, 2002: 6), that is, as one day becoming adult humans.

The field of contemporary child research has, thus, developed its own contours distinct from those prescribed by prevailing notions of child development, whereby young children's developmental status rendered them incapable or incompetent to engage as *bone fide* participants in child research by dint of their developmental immaturity and untrustworthiness (Keith-Spiegel, 1983; Touliatos and Compton, 1983; Hughes and Helling, 1991; Koocher and Keith-Spiegel, 1994; Hoagwood et al., 1996; Leikin, 1996).

Conceptual understanding also came to bear on notions of children's power and agency through participation (Holland et al., 2010). Christensen and Prout's (2002: 477) notion of 'ethical symmetry' in social research is of a dialogic research relationship between child and researcher.

Work on power, agency and symmetry follows an earlier body of work championed by Speier (1973, 1976), which conceptualized children as having restricted conversational rights to those of adults; that is, asymmetrical rights, by virtue of their position within the adult-oriented interactional order (Busch, 2011). With respect to children's asymmetrical rights, Speier argued:

> The manner in which they can participate in conversations with adults is controlled by an asymmetrical distribution of speaker's rights, when adults claim rights of local control over conversations with children and children are obliged to allow them that control. (1976: 101)

Taking a post-modern stance, Moss (2001: 1) theorizes ethics as an 'encounter' within the everyday context of early childhood education. Dahlberg and Moss (2005), in turn, see such encounters as reflecting dominant discourses (such as managerialism and regulation) inherent within those everyday contexts and within the systems that support the contexts. Within their theoretical frame, ethics includes the decision-making, practice and reflection that professionals enact as they interact with children, colleagues, families and communities.

Barker and Smith (2002) discussed the notion of the gendered 'positionality' of the researcher and child participant. A decade later, research by Theobald and Kultti (2012) revealed the institutional contexts, categories and practices inherent in participation, even in those sites such as early childhood classrooms that purport to practice child participation (Theobald et al., 2011). Such insights resonate with the work of David, Edwards and Alldred on the school-based contexts and pedagogical approaches that are 'inscribed with differential power relations' (2001: 347).

During the period of growth experienced by social research, the health sciences also saw an upsurge in child research that recognized the capacity of children as participants, capable of contributing to the research record and its veracity. Health researchers began to examine how young research participants operate and are seen to operate (Balen et al., 2006; Carter, 2009), with timely critique of research in health contexts being *with*, *by* and/or *on* children (Clavering and McLaughlin, 2010). A contentious issue in health research, particularly research involving medical intervention, is that of the informed voluntary consent of children in relation to parental/adult permission (Balen et al., 2006; Duncan et al., 2009). Concern over child consent in research is not, however, confined to health research and will be discussed later in the chapter. As discussed later in the chapter, child consent involves children being afforded the opportunity to indicate their willingness to be involved in the research (i.e., consent) and, conversely, to indicate their unwillingness to be involved (i.e., dissent), whether prior to or during the research.

CHILD COMPETENCE IN ACTION

A growing body of research across continents and regions speaks to the competence of children in managing their everyday worlds and in accounting for their everyday lives. The corpus of work includes work by Einarsdóttir (2007) in Scandinavia, work in the UK by Clark (2005), Greene and Hogan (2005), Tisdall et al. (2009) and Hill et al. (2004), and Australian work by Graham and Fitzgerald (2010), Fasoli (2001, 2003) and Farrell and Danby (2015).

Clark's (2005) international review of literature and practice with respect to listening to and consulting with young children, along with Greene and Hogan's (2005) coverage of theoretical and methodological paradigms within developmental psychology, anthropology and sociology, shows the breadth and depth of work in support of child competence. Fargas-Malet, McSherry, Larkin and Robinson (2010), in the UK, discuss the use of life narrative techniques (such as artwork, diaries) in participatory child research, while Cameron (2005), in the Australian context, considers the creative use of projective techniques using artwork, puppets and dolls in research. There is also the question of research that asks young children to wear or carry particular data collection devices, such as the helmet cameras used by Sumsion, Statigos and Bradley (2014) to capture the social interactions of infants and toddlers in long day care. Research ethics asks whether this is a fair and reasonable imposition on young children and whether the inconvenience and possible discomfort associated with the practice is warranted in relation to the possible benefits of the research to the children and those around them.

The type of data, be it videotaped, audiotaped interviews/conversations, observations and/or artefacts, and the methodology for its generation and analysis need critical consideration. While the novelty and seeming user-friendliness of such techniques may be attractive to practitioner-researchers, authors such as Punch (2002) call for reflexivity and criticality, such that criteria are their usefulness and relevance to the research design over apparent utility.

In recent years, Australia, New Zealand and the UK have seen an upsurge in practitioner research in early childhood education and care contexts. Its prominence is evident in practitioner research being a specific category of research award sponsored by the British Educational Research Association (2012) in collaboration with SAGE, and the European Early Childhood Education Research Association (EECERA) in collaboration with Routledge (2012). Australia hosts a *Research in Practice* series published by the nation's peak professional body, Early Childhood Australia (2012). Goodfellow notes this trend, in Australia, as evidence of 'systematic inquiry-based efforts directed towards creating and extending professional knowledge and associated understandings of professional practice' (2005: 48). Overall, there is a growing trend for early childhood practitioner research to be looped into a cycle of reflective practice whereby the professional is challenged to enact professional ethical and legal obligations to guarantee children the opportunities for meaningful and sustained education and care that will optimize life experiences and life outcomes.

While the examples of child research provided thus far are predominantly of social research located within everyday contexts such as early childhood education and/or home settings, other child research such as longitudinal research and/or randomized control trials (e.g., Newnham et al., 2004) also speak to issues such as child and/or parent consent in research.

Child Consent in Research

Increasingly, early childhood research is faced with issues of informed voluntary consent, participation and power. The earlier work of Kimmel (1988), drawing on case studies of ethical practice in social science research, and that of Grodin and Glantz (1994), in relation to biomedical and behavioral research, showed sustained scholarly interest in children's participation and power in social research, particularly in the Global North.

In Australia, Danby and Farrell (2005) examined the process by which young children provide consent in research, focusing on the 'openings' of the research conversations, that is, on the beginning phase of the interview that may be concurrent to completion of the consent form/protocol. Their examples show the ways in which the process of consent reveals the interactional and relational conditions under which research with young children typically occurs.

More recently, a body of work in Africa is challenging accepted principles of ethical conduct by providing insights into the socioethical research spaces in which children experience extreme dislocation and disadvantage (Abebe, 2009; Angucia et al., 2010). Abebe (2009), for example, draws upon research with disadvantaged children in two contrasting fieldwork settings in Ethiopia to show the challenges of applying 'Western' research ethics to social, cultural and economic contexts within the Global South. Other work, in Global North contexts, speaks to issues of child and/or parent consent in research in challenging contexts such as foster care (Bogolub and Thomas, 2005), economic disadvantage (Gorin et al., 2008), children with learning and behavioral challenges (Cocks, 2006),

child abuse (Mudaly and Goddard, 2009) and natural disasters (Barron Ausbrooks et al., 2009). The wide ranging contexts in which research is being conducted invites questions such as: How do children who are fleeing danger, seeking refuge or moving as unaccompanied minors have opportunities to participate in research relevant to their lives? What are the benefits of their participation? What appreciable difference will participation make to their lives today and to their life chances in the future?

In summary, international attention has focused on children's competence to give consent, to participate and to withdraw or dissent from research (Carroll-Lind et al., 2006; Heath et al., 2009), be it in school (David et al., 2001; Gallagher et al., 2010), in early childhood education (Flewitt, 2005) or in home contexts (Malone, 2003). A related issue is that of anonymity and confidentiality in early childhood research.

Confidentiality and Anonymity in Child Research

Understandings of child competence and children's rights have been an impetus to considerations of confidentiality and anonymity as ethical, conceptual, methodological and analytic considerations in child research (Flewitt, 2005; Williamson et al., 2005).

Giordano, O'Reilly, Taylor and Dogra (2007) contested conventional wisdom and practice about confidentiality and explored the possibility of participants opting for nonconfidentiality, that is, not requiring that their identity and research record remain confidential, as a means of exercising autonomous choice, while adhering to the recognized codes of ethics and ethics agreements. In short, the field of research ethics is typified by awareness of the difficulties of engaging in research with young children. In one respect, this may be due, in part, to medically derived approaches to research and developmental understandings of children's immaturity, which may preclude or curtail them from meaningful participation in research. In another respect, it may be due to concern for children's vulnerability and the risk of children being exposed to adverse adult activity. Another concern is the privacy and anonymity of children and families.

A criterion for inclusion/exclusion of some ethics committees/review boards and/ or research gatekeepers relates to children's chronological age, that is, that their young age and, therefore, their developmental status render them unsuitable to give voluntary informed consent and to participate in research in meaningful ways. This notion, however, has been successfully challenged on the basis of the Gillick *competence ruling* (1985), albeit in relation to medical consent, which emphasized 'that it is not chronological age which determines competence but sufficient understanding and intelligence to comprehend what is being proposed, and for the individual to make a choice in his or her own best interests' (Kellett et al., 2004: 331).

CONCLUSION

In conclusion, the growing field of ethics in child research is affording new possibilities for children, researchers and the broader contexts in which they operate. A new affordance is the opportunity to develop Sumsion's (2003: 18) notions of humility, reciprocity and community through research. These affordances may be impaired both by concern for children's immaturity, on the one hand, and romantic optimism about children's capacities to participate, on the other. That early childhood research presents both challenges and opportunities invites systematic consideration at the level of design, implementation and dissemination.

FURTHER READING

Christensen, P. and Prout, A. (2002) 'Working with ethical symmetry in social research with children', *Childhood*, 9(4): 477–97.

Goodfellow, J. (2005) 'Researching with/for whom? Stepping in and out of practitioner research', *Australasian Journal of Early Childhood*, 30(4): 48–57.

Holland, S., Renold, E., Ross, N. and Hillman, A. (2010) 'Power, agency and participatory agendas: A critical exploration of young people's engagement in participative qualitative research', *Childhood*, 17: 360–75.

QUESTIONS FOR REFLECTION

1 What agendas are shaping and producing the ethical design, conduct and dissemination of research?
2 How might researchers and research contexts shape new agendas for ethical research with children?
3 What are the major challenges for ethical research with children in the contexts in which children and their families operate?

REFERENCES

Abebe, T. (2009) 'Multiple methods, complex dilemmas: Negotiating socio-ethical spaces in participatory research with disadvantaged children', *Children's Geographies*, 7(4): 451–65.

Alanen, L. and Mayall, B. (eds) (2001) *Conceptualizing Child–Adult Relations*. London: RoutledgeFalmer.

Alderson, P. (1992) 'Rights of children and young people', in A. Coote (ed.), *The Welfare of Citizens: Developing New Social Rights*. London: Rivers Oram Press. pp. 168–80.

Alderson, P. and Morrow, V. (2004) *Ethics, Social Research and Consulting with Children and Young People*, 2nd edn. Essex: Barnardos. (1st edn, 1995.)

Alderson, P. and Morrow, V. (2011) *The Ethics of Research with Children and Young People: A Practical Handbook*, 2nd edn. London: SAGE. (1st edn, 1995.)

Angucia, M., Zeelen, J. and de Jong, G. (2010) 'Researching the reintegration of formerly abducted children in northern Uganda through action research: Experiences and reflections', *Journal of Community and Applied Social Psychology*, 20(3): 217–31.

Babbie, E. (1998) *The Practice of Social Research.* Belmont, CA: Wadsworth.

Balen, R., Blyth, E., Calabretto, H., Fraser, C., Horrocks, C. and Manby, M. (2006) 'Involving children in health and social research: "Human becomings" or "active beings?"', *Childhood*, 13(1): 29–48.

Bankowski, Z. (ed.) (1993) *International Ethical Guidelines for Biomedical Research Involving Human Subjects.* Geneva, Switzerland: Council for International Organizations of Medication Sciences (CIOMS).

Barron Ausbrooks, C., Barrett, E. and Martinez-Cosio, M. (2009) 'Ethical issues in disaster research: Lessons from Hurricane Katrina', *Population Research and Policy Review*, 28(1): 93–106.

Berg, K. F. and Latin, R. W. (2004) *Essentials of Research Methods in Health, Physical Education, Exercise Science, and Recreation.* Philadelphia: Lippincott, Williams and Wilkins.

Bogolub, E. and Thomas, N. (2005) 'Parental consent and the ethics of research with foster children: Beginning a cross-cultural dialogue', *Qualitative Social Work*, 4(3): 271–92.

British Educational Research Association (BERA) (2012) *Revised Ethical Guidelines for Educational Research* (Online). Available at: www.bera.ac.uk/news/berasage-practitioners-award (accessed 14 April 2014).

British Medical Research Association (BMRA) (1964) *Responsibility in Investigations on Human Subjects.* London: BMRA.

Burgess, R. G. (ed.) (1989) *The Ethics of Educational Research.* New York: Falmer Press.

Busch, G. (2011) 'The social orders of family mealtime'. PhD dissertation, Queensland University of Technology, Brisbane, Australia.

Cameron, H. (2005) 'Asking the tough questions: A guide to ethical practices in interviewing young children', *Early Child Development and Care*, 175(6): 597–610.

Camilli, G., Vargas, S., Ryan, S. and Barnett, S. W. (2010) 'Meta-analysis of the effects of early education interventions on cognitive and social development', *Teachers College Record*, 112(3): 579–620.

Carter, B. (2009) 'Tick box for child? The ethical positioning of children as vulnerable, researchers as barbarians and reviewers as overly cautious', *International Journal of Nursing Studies*, 46(6): 858–64.

Christensen, P. and James, A. (eds) (2000) *Research with Children: Perspectives and Practices.* London: Falmer Press.

Christensen, P. and James, A. (2008) *Research with Children: Perspectives and Practices*, 2nd edn. New York: Routledge.

Christensen, P. and Prout, A. (2002) 'Working with ethical symmetry in social research with children', *Childhood*, 9(4): 477–97.

Clark, A. (2005) 'The Mosaic Approach and research with young children', in A. Clark and P. Moss, *Spaces to Play: More Listening to Young Children Using the Mosaic Approach.* London: National Children's Bureau.

Clavering, E. and McLaughlin, J. (2010) 'Children's participation in health research: From objects to agents?', *Child: Care, Health and Development*, 36(5): 603–11.

Cocks, A. (2006) 'The ethical maze: Finding an inclusive path towards gaining children's agreement to research participation', *Childhood*, 13: 247–266.

Coker, R. and McKee, M. (2001) 'Ethical approval for health research in central and eastern Europe: An international survey', *Clinical Medicine*, 1: 197–9.

Corsaro, W. A. (1997) *The Sociology of Childhood.* Thousand Oaks, CA: Pine Forge Press.

Coughlin, S. and Beauchamp, T. (eds) (1996) *Ethics and Epidemiology.* New York: Oxford University Press.

Cribb, R. (2004) 'Ethical regulation and humanities research in Australia: Problems and consequences', *Monash Bioethics Review*, 23(3): 39–57.

Cunha, F., Heckman, J. J., Lochner, L. J. and Masterov, D. V. (2006) 'Interpreting the evidence on life cycle skill formation', in E. Hanushek and F. Welch (eds), *Handbook of the Economics of Education.* Amsterdam: Elsevier. pp. 697–812.

Dahlberg, G. and Moss, P. (2005) *Ethics and Politics in Early Childhood Education: Contesting Early Childhood.* Hove: Psychology Press/Taylor & Francis.

Danby, S. (2002) 'The communicative competence of young children', *Australian Journal of Early Childhood*, 27(3): 25–30.

Danby, S. and Baker, C. (1998) '"What's the problem?": Restoring social order in the pre-school classroom', in I. Hutchby and J. Moran-Ellis (eds), *Children and Social*

Competence: Arenas of Action. London: Falmer Press. pp. 157–86.

Danby, S. and Farrell, A. (2005) 'Opening the research conversation', in A. Farrell (ed.), *Ethical Research with Children*. Milton Keynes: Open University Press. pp. 15–26.

David, M. Edwards, R. and Alldred, P. (2001) 'Children and school-based research: "Informed consent" or "educated consent"?', *British Educational Research Journal*, 27(3): 347–65.

Duncan, R., Drew, S., Hodgson, J. and Sawyer, S. (2009) '"Is my Mum going to hear this?" Methodological and ethical challenges in qualitative health research with young people', *Social Science and Medicine*, 69(11): 1691–9.

Early Childhood Australia (ECA) (2012) *Research in Practice*. Available at: www.early childhoodaustralia.org.au/research_in_practice_series/about_rips.html (accessed 14 June 2012).

Emmanuel, E., Grady, C., Crouch, R., Lie, R., Miller, F. and Wendler, D. (2008) *The Oxford Textbook of Clinical Research Ethics*. Oxford: Oxford University Press.

European Early Childhood Education Research Association (EECERA) (2012) *Practitioner Research Award*. Available at: www. eecera2012.ipp.pt/practitioners-research-award (accessed 14 June 2013).

Ezzy, D. (2002) *Qualitative Analysis: Practice and Innovation*. Crows Nest, NSW: Allen & Unwin.

Fargas-Malet, M., McSherry, D., Larkin, E. and Robinson, C. (2010) 'Research with children: Methodological issues and innovative techniques', *Journal of Early Childhood Research,* 8: 175–192.

Farrell, A. (2005) 'New times in ethical research with children', in A. Farrell (ed.), *Ethical Research with Children*. Milton Keynes: Open University Press/McGraw-Hill. pp. 166–75.

Farrell, A. (2013a) 'Early years research', in F. Veale (ed.), *Early Years*. Abingdon, Oxon: Hodder & Stoughton. pp. 361–77.

Farrell, A. (2013b) 'Ethics in research with children', in H. Montgomery (ed.), *Oxford Bibliographies in Childhood Studies*. New York: Oxford University Press.

Farrell, A. and Danby, S. (2015) 'How does homework "work" for young children? Children's accounts of homework in their everyday lives', *British Journal of Sociology of Education,* 36(2): 250–69.

Fasoli, L. (2001) 'Research with children: Ethical mind-fields', *Australian Journal of Early Childhood*, 26(4): 7–11.

Fasoli, L. (2003) 'Reflections on doing research with young children', *Australian Journal of Early Childhood*, 28(1): 7–11.

Fisher, C., Hoagwood, K. and Boyce, C. (2002) 'Research ethics for mental health science involving minority children', *American Psychologist*, 57(12): 1024–40.

Flewitt, R. (2005) 'Conducting research with young children: Some ethical considerations', *Early Child Development and Care*, 175(6): 553–65.

Fraser, S., Lewis, V., Ding, S., Kellett, M. and Robinson, C. (2004) *Doing Research with Children and Young People*. London: SAGE.

Gallagher, M., Haywood, S., Jones, M. and Milne, S. (2010) 'Negotiating informed consent with children in school-based research: A critical review', *Children and Society*, 24: 471–82.

Giddens, A. (2001) *Sociology*, 4th edn. Cambridge: Polity Press. (1st edn, 1982.)

Giordano, J., O'Reilly, M., Taylor, H. and Dogra, N. (2007) 'Confidentiality and autonomy: The challenge(s) of offering research participants a choice of disclosing their identity', *Qualitative Health Research*, 17(2): 264–75.

Goodfellow, J. (2005) 'Researching with/for whom? Stepping in and out of practitioner research', *Australasian Journal of Early Childhood*, 30(4): 48–57.

Gorin, S., Hooper, C., Dyson, C. and Cabral, C. (2008) 'Ethical challenges in conducting research with hard to reach families', *Child Abuse Review*, 17: 275–87.

Graham, A. and Fitzgerald, R. (2010) 'Children's participation in research: Some possibilities and constraints in the current Australian research environment', *Journal of Sociology*, 46: 133–47.

Graham, A., Powell, M. Taylor, N., Anderson, D. and Ftizgerald, R. (2013) *Ethical Research Involving Children*. Florence: UNICEF Office of Research – Innocenti.

Graue, M.E., Walsh, D. and Ceglowski, D. (1998) *Studying Children in Context: Theories, Methods and Ethics*. Thousand Oaks, CA: SAGE.

Greene, S. and Hogan, D. (eds) (2005) *Researching Children's Experience: Methods and Approaches*. London: Sage Publications.

Greig, A. and Taylor, J. (1999) *Doing Research with Children*. London: SAGE.

Greig, A., Taylor, J. and MacKay, T. (2007) *Doing Research with Children*, 2nd edn. Los Angeles, CA: SAGE. (1st edn, 1999.)

Grodin, M. and Glantz, L. (eds) (1994) *Children as Research Subjects: Science, Ethics and Law*. New York: Oxford University Press.

Halasa, K. (ed.) (2009) *Annotated Bibliography: Ethics in Educational Research*. Australian Association for Research in Education. Available at: www1.aare.edu.au/pages/static/aareethc.htm#summ

Heath, S., Brooks, R., Cleaver, E. and Ireland, E. (2009) *Researching Young People's Lives*. London: Sage Publications.

Heckman, J. (2011) 'The economics of inequality: The value of early childhood education', *American Educator*, Spring, 31–47.

Hill, M., Davis, J., Prout, A. and Tisdall, K. (2004) 'Moving the participation agenda forward', *Children and Society*, 18: 77–96.

Hoagwood, K., Jensen, P. and Fisher, C. (eds) (1996) *Ethical Issues in Mental Health Research with Children and Adolescents*. Malwah, NJ: Lawrence Erlbaum Associates.

Holland, S., Renold, E., Ross, N. and Hillman, A. (2010) 'Power, agency and participatory agendas: A critical exploration of young people's engagement in participative qualitative research', *Childhood*, 17: 360–75.

Homan, R. (1991) *The Ethics of Social Research*. London: Longman.

Hood, S., Kelly, P. and Mayall, B. (1996) 'Child as research subjects: A risky enterprise', *Children and Society*, 10(2): 117–28.

Hughes, T. and Helling, M. (1991) 'A case for obtaining informed consent from young children', *Early Childhood Research Quarterly*, 6: 225–32.

Hutchby, I. and Moran-Ellis, J. (1998) 'Situating children's social competence', in I. Hutchby and J. Moran-Ellis (eds), *Children and Social Competence: Arenas of Action*. London: Falmer Press. pp. 7–26.

International Association for the Evaluation of Educational Achievement (IEA) (2007) *Trends in International Mathematics and Science Study* (TIMSS). Boston, MA: Boston College.

James, A. and James, A. (2004) *Constructing Childhood: Theory, Policy and Social Practice*. Basingstoke: Palgrave Macmillan.

James, A., Jenks, C. and Prout, A. (1998) *Theorising Childhood*. Cambridge: Polity Press.

Jenks, C. (1999) *Childhood*. London: Routledge.

Kant, I. (1781/2003) *Critique of Pure Reason* (tr. N. Kemp-Smith). Basingstoke: Palgrave Macmillan.

Kant, I. (1785/1995) *Foundations of the Metaphysical of Morals and What is Enlightenment* (tr. L.W. Beck). Upper Saddle River, NJ: Prentice Hall.

Kass, N., Hyder, A., Ajuwon, A., Appiah-Poku, J., Barsdorf, N., Elsayed, D., et al. (2007) 'The structure and function of research ethics committees in Africa: A case study', *PLoS Med*, 4(1): 3.

Keith-Spiegel, P. (1983) 'Children and consent to participate in research', in G.B. Melton, G.P. Koocher and M.J. Saks (eds), *Children's Competence to Consent*. New York: Plenum. pp. 179–211.

Kellett, M. (2005) *Children as Active Researchers: A New Research Paradigm for the 21st Century?* NCTM Methods Review Papers, NCRM/003. London: Economic and Social Research Council/National Centre for Research Methods.

Kellett, M., Forrest, R., Dent, N. and Ward, S. (2004) '"Just teach us the skills please, we'll do the rest": Empowering ten-year-olds as active researchers', *Children & Society*, 18: 329–43.

Kimmel, A.J. (1988) *Ethics and Values in Applied Social Research*. Newbury Park, CA: SAGE.

Koocher, G.P. and Keith-Spiegel, P. (1994) 'Scientific issues in psychosocial and educational research with children', in M.A. Grodin and L.H. Glantz (eds), *Children as Research Subjects: Science, Ethics and Law*. New York: Oxford University Press. pp. 47–80.

Leikin, S. (1996) 'Ethical issues in epidemiologic research with children', in S.S. Coughlin and T. Beauchamp (eds), *Ethics and Epidemiology*. New York: Oxford University Press. pp. 199–218.

Mackay, R.W. (1991) 'Conceptions of children and models of socialization', in F.C. Waksler (ed.), *Studying the Social Worlds of Children: Sociological Readings*. London: Falmer Press. pp. 23–37.

MacNaughton, G., Hughes, P. and Smith, K. (2007) 'Young children's rights and public policy: Practices and possibilities for citizenship in the early years', *Children & Society*, 21: 458–69.

Mahon, A., Glendinning, C., Clarke, K. and Craig, G. (1996) 'Researching children: Methods and ethics', *Children and Society*, 10(2): 145–54.

Malone, S. (2003) 'Ethics at home: Informed consent in your own backyard', *International Journal of Qualitative Studies in Education*, 16: 797–815.

May, T. (1997) *Social Research: Issues, Methods and Process*. Buckingham: Open University Press.

Mayall, B. (2002) *Towards Sociology for Childhood: Thinking from Children's Lives*. Buckingham: Open University Press.

Mayall, B. (2003) 'Sociologies of Childhood and Educational Thinking', professorial lecture presented at the Institute of Education, University of London, London.

Mayall, B. (2008) 'Conversations with children: Working with generational issues', in P. Christensen and A. James (eds), *Research with Children: Perspectives and Practices*, 2nd edn. London: Routledge. pp. 109–22. (1st edn, 2000.)

Mayne, F. and Howitt, C. (2014) 'Reporting of ethics in early childhood journals: A meta-analysis of 10 journals from 2009 to 2012', *Australasian Journal of Early Childhood*, 39(2): 71–9.

McNeill, P.M. (1993) *The Ethics and Politics of Human Experimentation*. Cambridge: Cambridge University Press.

Milburn, M. (2001) *Informed Choice of Medical Services: Is the Law Just?* Aldershot: Ashgate.

Miller, R.B. (2003) *Children, Ethics and Modern Medicine*. Bloomington, IN: Indiana University Press.

Morrow, V. (2010) 'Child poverty, social exclusion and children's rights: A view from the sociology of childhood', in W. Vandenhole, J. Vranken and K. De Boyser (eds), *Poverty and Children's Rights*. Belgium: Intersentia Publishing.

Morrow, V. and Richards, M. (1996) 'The ethics of social research with children: An overview', *Children and Society*, 10: 90–105.

Moss, P. (2001) 'Making space for ethics', *Australian Journal of Early Childhood*, 26: 1–6.

Moss, P. (2007) 'Starting Strong: An exercise in international learning', *International Journal of Child Care and Education Policy*, 1(1): 11–21.

Mudaly, N. and Goddard, C. (2009) 'The ethics of involving children who have been abused in child abuse research', *International Journal of Children's Rights*, 17(2): 261–81.

National Research Council (2003) *Protecting Participants and Facilitating Social and Behavioral Sciences Research*. Washington, DC: The National Academies.

Newnham, J.P., Coherty, D.A., Kendall, G.E., Zubrick, S.R. and Stanley, F.J. (2004) 'Effects of repeated prenatal ultrasound examinations on childhood outcome up to 8 years of age: Follow-up of a randomised controlled trial', *Lancet*, 364(9450): 2038–44.

Newsom, B. (1990) 'Medical ethics: Thomas Percival', *JSCV Medical Association*, 86(3): 175.

Organisation for Economic Cooperation and Development (OECD) (2001) *Starting Strong*. Paris: OECD.

Organisation for Economic Cooperation and Development (OECD) (2006) *Starting Strong II*. Paris: OECD.

Organisation for Economic Cooperation and Development (OECD) (2011) *Program for International School Assessment* (PISA). Paris: OECD.

Organisation for Economic Cooperation and Development (OECD) (2012) *Starting Strong III: A Quality Toolbox for ECEC*. Paris: OECD.

Percival, T. (1803/1997) *Medical Ethics*. New York: Classics of Surgery Library.

Phillips, B. and Alderson, P. (2002) *Beyond 'Anti-Smacking': Challenging Violence and Coercion in Parent–Child Relations*. London: The Children's Society.

Powell, M., Fitzgerald, R., Taylor, N. and Graham, A. (2012) *International Literature Review: Ethical Issues in Undertaking Research with Children and Young People*. Dunedin, New Zealand: University of Otago, Centre for Research on Children and Families (http://epubs.scu.edu.au/cgi/viewcontent.cgi?article=1041&context=ccyp_pubs).

Powell, M., Graham, A., Taylor, N., Newell, S. and Fitzgerald, R. (2011) *Building Capacity for Ethical Research with Children and Young People: An International Research Project to Examine the Ethical Issues and Challenges in Undertaking Research with and for Children in Different Majority and Minority World Contexts*. Dunedin, New Zealand: University of Otago, Centre for Research on Children and Families (http://epubs.scu.edu.au/cgi/viewcontent.cgi?article=1033&context=ccyp_pubs).

Punch, S. (2002) 'Research with children: The same or different from research with adults?', *Childhood*, 9(3): 321–41.

Qvortrup, J. (1994) 'Childhood and modern society: A paradoxical relationship?', in J. Branner and M. Brien (eds), *Childhood and Parenthood: Proceedings of ISA Committee for Family Research Conference on Children and Families*. London: University of London, Institute of Education. pp. 189–98.

Qvortrup, J. (2000) 'Macroanalysis of childhood', in P. Christensen and A. James (eds), *Research with Children: Perspectives and Practices*. London: Falmer Press. pp. 77–97.

Redshaw, M., Harris, A. and Baum, J. (2004) 'Research ethics committee audit: Differences between communities', *Journal of Medical Ethics*, 22: 78–82.

Rivera, R. and Ezcurra, E. (2001) 'Composition and operation of selected research ethics review committees in Latin America', *IRB: Ethics and Human Research*, 23(5): 9–12.

Ross, L.F. (1998) *Children, Families and Health Care Decision Making*. Oxford: Clarendon Press.

Singh, P. (2004) 'Globalisation and education review essay', *Educational Theory*, 54(1): 103–15.

Smith, D. C. (1996) 'The Hippocratic Oath and modern medicine', *Journal of History and Medicine: Allied Sciences*, 51(4): 484–500.

Speier, M. (1973) *How to Observe Face-to-Face Communication: A Sociological Introduction*. Pacific Palisades, CA: Goodyear.

Speier, M. (1976) 'The child as conversationalist: Some cultural contact features of conversational interactions between adults and children', in M. Hammersley and P. Woods (eds), *The Process of Schooling: A Sociological Reader*. London: Routledge and Kegan Paul with the Open University Press. pp. 98–103.

Sumsion, J. (2003) 'Researching with children: Lessons in humility, reciprocity, and community', *Australian Journal of Early Childhood*, 28(1): 18–23.

Sumsion, J., Statigos, T. and Bradley, B. (2014) Babies in space. In L. Harrison and J. Sumsion (eds), *Lived Spaces of Infant-Toddler Education and Care: Diverse Perspectives on Theory, Methodology and Practice*. Dordrecht: Springer. pp. 43–58.

Theobald, M. and Kultti, A. (2012) 'Investigating child participation in the everyday talk of teacher and children in a preparatory year', *Contemporary Issues in Early Childhood*, 13(3): 210–25.

Theobald, M., Danby, S. and Ailwood, J. (2011) 'Child participation in the early years: Challenges for education', *Australasian Journal of Early Childhood*, 36(3): 19–26.

Tisdall, K., Davis, J. and Gallagher, M. (2009) *Researching with Children and Young People: Research Design, Methods and Analysis*. Los Angeles, CA: SAGE.

Tobin, J. (1995) 'Post-structural research in early childhood education', in J. Hatch (ed.), *Qualitative Research in Early Childhood Settings*. Westport, CT: Praeger. pp. 223–43.

Touliatos, J. and Compton, N.H. (1983) *Approaches to Child Study*. Minneapolis, MN: Burgess.

Tschudin, V. (2003) *Ethics in Nursing: The Caring Relationship*. London: Elsevier Science.

United Nations (1989) *Convention on the Rights of the Child*. Geneva: United Nations. Available at: www.ohchr.org/en/professional interest/pages/crc.aspx

United Nations Children's Fund (UNICEF) (2008) *The Child Care Transition: A League Table of Early Childhood Education and Care in Economically Advanced Countries*. Innocenti Report Card. Florence: UNICEF Innocenti Research Centre.

United Nations Children's Fund (UNICEF) (2012) *Children in an Urban World: State of the World's Children*. Geneva: UNICEF.

United Nations Department of Economic and Social Affairs (UNDESA) (2011) *Estimates of Urban Population*. New York: UNDESA.

Waksler, F. (1991) 'Studying children: Phenomenological insights', in F. Waksler (ed.), *Studying the Social Worlds of Children: Sociological Readings*. London: Falmer Press. pp. 60–9.

Waksler, F. (1996) *The Little Trials of Childhood and Children's Strategies for Dealing with Them*. London: Falmer Press.

Weithorn, L.A. and Scherer, D.G. (1994) 'Children's involvement in research participation decisions: Psychological considerations', in M.A. Grodin and L. Glanz (eds), *Children as Research Subjects: Science, Ethics and Law*. New York: Oxford University Press. pp. 133–79.

Williamson, E., Goodenough, T., Kent, J. and Ashcroft, R. (2005) 'Conducting research with children: The limits of confidentiality and child protection protocols', *Children and Society*, 19(5): 397–409.

World Health Organisation (WHO) South East Asian Regional Office (2002) *Ethics in Health Research*. New Delhi: World Health Organisation.

World Medical Association (WMA) (1954) *Principles for those in Research in Experience*. Fernay-Voltaire: WMA.

World Medical Association (WMA) (1964/2000) *Declaration of Helsinki*. Fernay-Voltaire: WMA.

World Medical Association (WMA) (2000) *Declaration of Helsinki: Ethical Principles for Medical Research Involving Human Subjects*. Fernay-Voltaire: WMA.

13

Longitudinal Research: Applications for the Design, Conduct and Dissemination of Early Childhood Research

Stephen R. Zubrick

INTRODUCTION

The scope of disciplinary activity brought to bear on child development is vast (Bynner et al., 2009: 3). The range of scholarly interest includes: psychology, biology, sociology, economics, demography, history, medicine, education, politics, philosophy and anthropology, to name but a few. All of these disciplines have one or more sub-specializations (e.g., medicine: paediatrics) representing an entire body of specialized knowledge about children and their development. This development is about growth and change in the early epochs of the life course – its prompts, facilitators and constraints. Of the methods to study developmental change, longitudinal methods are some of the most powerful. These methods employ repeated measures on the same subjects over time. Depending on the nature of the study and its aims, the time course for observing and measuring this change may vary from brief to extended periods that span years and lifetimes.

The *conduct* of longitudinal research in early childhood is the focus of this chapter. This focus moves the content away from a potentially vast methodological presentation of strategies, designs and statistical techniques to a narrower set of over-arching considerations that are often not immediately apparent in the creation and operation of studies with longitudinal designs (Binder, 1998; Eskenazi et al., 2005). These considerations include specifying the nature of developmental outcomes of interest to the study, anticipating and implementing measures of change, distinguishing sources of variation and making inferences about them, analytic approaches and capacities, and aspects less often written about such as study governance over time. They impact on the decisions made, not only about the creation and conduct of a proposed longitudinal study, but on a researcher's participation in, and use of, data from an existing or current longitudinal study.

LONGITUDINAL DESIGNS IN CHILD RESEARCH

Menard describes four basic designs for longitudinal research: total population designs, repeated cross-sectional designs, revolving panel designs and longitudinal panel designs (Menard, 2008). Each offers the researcher interested in children and their development a different mix of strengths and weaknesses from which to observe change. What unites them is their focus on the collection of data on the same sample elements on multiple occasions over time (Lynn, 2009). Note here the avoidance of the phrase same *individuals* on multiple occasions over time, this avoidance signalling that longitudinal studies, even of children, may not have as their principal unit of analysis the individual child.

Some of the study designs above are employed as foundation methods within specific disciplinary areas and have resulted in extensive statistical and methodological development or analytic conventions that may not necessarily have crossed disciplinary boundaries. Design specialization can occur within disciplinary specializations and results in highly refined and expert theoretical, analytical, statistical and interpretative frameworks not necessarily used in other disciplinary areas. For example, demographers frequently employ total population designs as a foundation method of their discipline for examining longitudinal changes in the composition and structure of populations within nations and/or between nations. Their studies provide not only vital descriptions about populations and subsamples of children but extend well beyond descriptive studies to encompass causal investigations of secular and historical population dynamics concerning children and childhood. This is not to imply that the discipline of demography uses only one longitudinal design, but rather to highlight that design specialization occurs within disciplinary boundaries and that this specialization can include highly refined and

expert theoretical, analytical, statistical and interpretative frameworks not necessarily present or used in other disciplinary areas. Researchers working in a particular disciplinary area on child development, using a particular longitudinal design, may need to – indeed should – collaboratively reach beyond their own discipline for specialized skills and comparative insights to enrich and interpret their own findings.

This chapter focuses on one particular design, the longitudinal panel design. This is the design that is most familiar to researchers across a wide range of disciplines. A longitudinal panel design typically recruits its subjects at a specific point in time, and then, at intervals, collects additional information on or from them. There is no entry of new subjects into the sample after the initial point of data collection. As Menard notes, 'the combination of measurement during more than one period and for more than one period represents, for some scholars, the only true longitudinal design, the only design that allows the measurement and analysis of intra-individual changes' (2008: 6). As will be demonstrated though, no one particular longitudinal design offers a totality of view across childhood, child development and its onward influence through the life course. However, contemporary research using longitudinal panel designs provides an expansive base from which to review challenges and opportunities in the conduct of longitudinal research in early childhood.

LONGITUDINAL STUDIES AS 'TECHNOLOGY'

There is no comprehensive summary of current longitudinal studies that focuses on children and childhood. There have been some overviews of collections of existing longitudinal studies that seek to address either specific developmental domains, such as health or ageing (Brown et al., 2006; Huguet et al., 2012), or some comprehensive summaries of longitudinal studies of children in specific global regions (Nicholson and Rempal, 2004; Sanson, 2002). The volatility in new study development and the sustainability of individual ongoing studies guarantee that any current summary of the global or regional effort will be at least partly outdated on publication.

Fortunately, there are many longitudinal studies that have been individually documented by their chief investigators or study team members (e.g., Boyd et al., 2013; Branum et al., 2003; Elliott and Shepherd, 2006; Fergusson, 1998; Fergusson and Horwood, 2013; Fraser et al., 2012; Hansen et al., 2010; Hirshfeld et al., 2011; Joshi, 2008; Power and Elliott, 2006; Silva and Stanton, 1996). For studies that have operated over extensive periods of time, proper documentation of the study, its evolution and current status require that this information be updated periodically.

Now, internet searches are also instrumental in connecting researchers seeking information about specific longitudinal studies. Numerous websites provide links to a range of longitudinal studies with their own study sites with descriptions of and access to protocols and questionnaires, research outputs, and the study teams and leaders.

The extent of the global effort and interest in longitudinal studies of children, the scope of their coverage, the breadth of their interdisciplinary collaboration, the diversity of their methodology, the analytic demands required in using their data and the extensive time spans now covered by many of them give support to the claim that longitudinal studies are a type of scientific technology. Longitudinal studies have emerged over the last 75 years, and more intensively so over the past 30 years at points of readiness in settings where researchers have been able to advocate for and procure research funding to (at least) initiate longitudinal work. Such funding has allowed some longitudinal studies to mature to the point where their value becomes evident and the ongoing work is able to attract more sustainable funding (Pearson, 2012). As the value of longitudinal research has become evident to governments, many nations have established scientific agendas and funding mechanisms that have called for longitudinal studies of children. Often, these calls require studies on a large collaborative scale, with designs entailing greater sample sizes, multiple informants from which to collect information, multiple sites of collection, and an implementation of an array of psychosocial, cognitive, physical, biological and administrative data linkage collection methodologies. They may involve the need for and use of a complex array of instruments and measures administered directly or indirectly to participating subjects. A prodigious logistic and technical effort is needed to bring this together and to manage the resultant data and information.

With this said, there are some challenges in what such studies can accomplish. One of these challenges is longitudinal studies of rare populations. While large population-based studies with representative sampling remain a key methodology, unless they are vast these studies have restricted power to observe important and rarer populations and their outcomes. With greater globalization of markets and labour arrangements, the threats of climate change, food security and regional destabilization, governments have an increasing focus on migrant and refugee populations, samples of the homeless, and families living in highly mobile settings that include the military as well as itinerate workers who are typically absent in longitudinal studies.

Finally, longitudinal studies are also typically expensive. They require core funding that supports the staff and an infrastructure that sustain the longitudinal study through and, particularly, between collection periods. This core funding needs to sit outside of the short-term or five-year research grant awards that investigator-led research teams usually bring to a study to investigate specific lines of enquiry.

CAUSAL PROCESSES AND LONGITUDINAL STUDIES

Longitudinal data collected on the same individuals observed over time can provide essential information about the nature of developmental change within individuals. These data enable the recording of the timing of events and experiences and the types of attitudes, feelings and behaviours that might accompany these. With well selected, calibrated and repeated measures, longitudinal data allow the measurement of individual growth – physical, intellectual, cognitive, social and economic. Longitudinal data also permit the direct estimation of risks associated with a variety of exposures and events and outcomes. Changes in status with respect to age can be observed. Both direct and indirect causal pathways can be illuminated through the use of longitudinal data (Rutter, 1988; Rutter et al., 2001). These are substantial advantages of longitudinal designs and one of the reasons they are turned to for testing a range of hypotheses.

However, notwithstanding the improved ability to observe and measure individual change and/or growth, longitudinal designs do not address many of the underlying dilemmas that researchers still face in arriving at valid conclusions about cause. Twenty years ago, Rutter (1994) noted several problems that remained out of the reach of longitudinal designs. Among these were the exclusion of third variable effects, the tracing of circular causal processes and of chain effects over time and the availability of appropriate statistical analyses to address problems of interest. At a broader level, the design and content of a longitudinal study may either enable or prohibit the ability to differentiate risk indicators from risk mechanisms. Risk indicators are estimates of statistical associations between variables – for example, the known association between maternal depression, on the one hand, and psychopathology in offspring, on the other. However, a statistically significant elevation in risk (i.e., the risk indicator) does not explain the causal process (i.e., the mechanism) that produces this association. The ability of a longitudinal design to move beyond documenting risk indicators and, instead, illuminate the causal pathways of this association depends upon the nature of the variables generated from the content and observations of the longitudinal data. This in turn rests on planning and decisions about the study design and its rationale and specific measures.

As will be seen in the following sections, prospects for addressing some of these challenges have improved over time with the availability of a greater range of analytic and statistical approaches. Additionally, some of these inferential challenges with regard to cause and effect, while not perfectly addressed, are better understood and, because of this, threats to the validity of these conclusions can be canvassed through better counterfactual analyses. Harmonization of measurement between longitudinal collections and with cross-sectional population studies has also strengthened the ability of researchers to compare within and across countries, settings and contexts. In some circumstances, data may be pooled to improve statistical power and to allow more appropriate selection of control and contrast populations and groups. In other cases, variables and effects that typically occur together can be isolated or pulled apart by comparing across contexts. In some instances, this can help distinguish between a risk association and a risk mechanism.

CHILDREN, CHILDHOOD AND THE LIFE COURSE

Consider for a moment the nature of the life course of a hypothetical child born in 1945 (Figure 13.1). This infant brings nine months of in-utero experience into the world along with its genetic and onward biological endowments. These will reciprocally interact and change in response to environmental

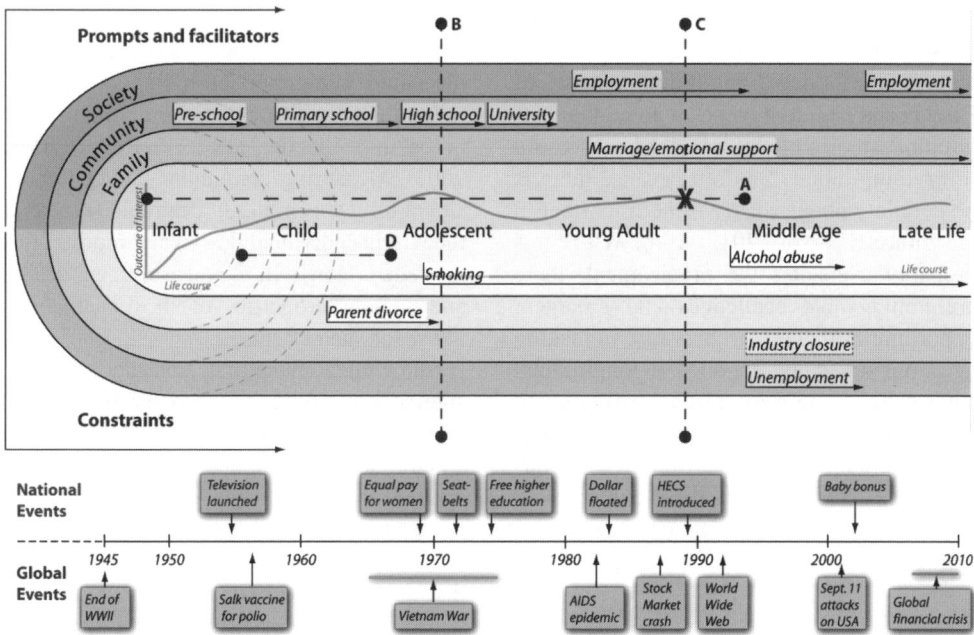

Figure 13.1   A hypothetical life course

Source: Zubrick et al. (2009)

contexts. These life-course environmental contexts include: the family, the community and wider society. There are elements of these contexts that can variously prompt and facilitate onward development, and there are those that may constrain this. Additionally, the wider contexts of both national and global environments are illustrated. As this child's hypothetical life course continues, it is possible to chart a variety of outcomes – this is represented by the line in the centre of the diagram.

Consider also that Figure 13.1 illustrates the course of a single life: longitudinal designs may cover thousands of lives. Various views of these lives are possible. In the full scope of time, they may be studied across many years (line A). There may be periodic cross-sectional studies of other samples and populations that intersect with the subjects in the longitudinal design (line B). Other cross-sectional designs may actually intersect to capture specific individual subjects (denoted by X) in the longitudinal

study as might occur through the linkage of administrative or census information about them to the longitudinal study (line C). Furthermore, the view may be restricted to a shorter developmental epoch (line D) either because this is a current point in the data collection or because the developmental questions of interest are restricted to this range.

Figure 13.1 also demonstrates that a longitudinal study is both *of* history and *in* history. So it is understandable that a focus on life-course outcomes from infancy and childhood onwards into adulthood may confront researchers with a fundamental question: What constitutes an 'outcome' of interest when so much of life and development are still ahead (Zubrick et al., 2009)? What guides the questions that a longitudinal study of children seeks to answer? How relevant will these questions be going into the future? What new opportunities will arise and how will history interact with the onward design of the study?

These types of questions may have been considerations of a former director of genetics for the Avon Longitudinal Study of Parents and Children when he noted that longitudinal studies of children need to measure 'everything' about children because there is no certainty about what will be important in the future (Pearson, 2012: 156). While this probably overstates the predicament, there are innumerable challenges and emergent opportunities that researchers face in making decisions about the conduct of longitudinal studies. Six of these are selected for comment here: challenges in longitudinal measurement; administrative data linkage; capturing area effects; enabling gene–environment hypotheses; mechanisms of social gradients; and the impact of study governance.

CHALLENGES IN LONGITUDINAL MEASUREMENT

One of the principal strengths of a longitudinal study is its capacity to observe and measure within-individual change. Measuring this change in the design of the study poses a perennial challenge to researchers. Often, the immediate need to design the study content and mode of collection at a specific developmental point in time can obscure the long-term view of how particular measures, and their scaling and mode of collection, may change over time and the impact that these changes have on being able to meaningfully observe and measure change. Measurement designs can also become overly dominated by categorical outcomes, reflecting the propensity of researchers to select brief item sets or indicator items over longer more continuous scales in order to save time and create space for other content. But the very notion of an outcome as a fixed state or a category to predict may be problematic in situations where the strength of the research design is in illuminating a chain of processes, a transitional stage, patterns of growth or the maintenance of stability. Moreover, the outcomes

and exposures of interest may be inherently dimensional: that is, they may operate and be measured along one or more continuums, rather than occur at a particular point or level or be in a specific category (Rutter, 2003, 2007). Measuring continuous and/or dimensional effects is a highly desirable feature of the within-individual design and more of this is needed. How will the measurement design and scaling properties of the observations allow for such effects?

Some phenomena offer constancy in measurement metric and are naturally responsive to growth and development across time: weight, height, girth, head circumference are such examples. Other developmental phenomena have relatively definable onset periods and early and rapid change with measures that permit growth to be estimated: early vocabulary development is an example of this. Puberty is another. Still others, such as cognitive measures, academic achievement measures, time-based activity measures, income and wealth have been developed with metrics that allow comparability across large developmental epochs. Repeated measurement at developmentally sensitive stages using the same measures with appropriate frequency is critical. It is widely accepted that use of such measures needs to encompass at least three observations (Singer and Willett, 2003), but practically, four or more repeated measures over time are required in order to permit informative growth modelling. For other types of measures, particularly subjective states and judgements based on ordinal scales, there are even greater challenges in charting their change over time. Longitudinal measurement invariance is one of these challenges.

Measurement invariance (e.g., factorial invariance or measurement equivalence) over time refers to the degree that measures at one time point assess the same things, and with the same precision, as they do at other time points. This is vital for longitudinal analyses. It permits greater confidence in interpreting the observed changes over time as being due to actual developmental change, rather than as being changes in the interpretation of items by the respondents or changes in the measurement precision of the items and scales over time. Simply put, are observed changes over time in individuals and between individuals entangled with changes in the meaning of the measures? Answering this question can become quite challenging in longitudinal developmental studies because the very content of items may also need to change while the focus of what these items measure remains the same. For example, parental monitoring is a feature of parental behaviour that can be measured across a large developmental period – however, the item content for this construct will, of necessity, be different for a child that is 4 years old as compared with when they are 14 years old.

Considerable advances have been made in item and scale development and in analytic procedures for assessing measurement invariance generally, and in ordinal categorical data specifically. The methodologies for this are analytically demanding and have evolved using both covariance approaches (Little et al., 2007; Millsap and Yun-Tein, 2004; Schmitt and Kuljanin, 2008; Vandenberg and Lance, 2000) and item response theory (Embretson, 2006, 2012; Kim and Yoon, 2011). As Embretson has noted though, 'applications of model-based measurement are rapidly increasing in the testing industry, but applications to psychological research are lagging' (Embretson, 2006: 50).

Not all researchers who are developing and implementing longitudinal studies have the breadth and depth of training required to appreciate the importance of new advances in measurement theories and the statistical methods that accompany them. As a result, research teams and consortia responsible for selecting content design understandably come to this task, more often than not, armed with knowledge from the past. While selection principles can be specified to guide the content that is ultimately recommended and collected, it is still the case that selection rests on what researchers have used in the past, the familiar or 'favourite', and the ease of its

access. Newer procedures are being proposed and developed that offer important opportunities for the design of longitudinal item pools for calibrated measures (Embretson, 2003). These newer model-based measurement methods have a critical relevance to the initial design and selection of items and scales. They can also be applied to existing data to inform onward decisions about subsequent item and scale selection. The point here is that innovations and advances in measurement methods need to be leveraged into the early stages of content selection for longitudinal studies. Capitalizing on these advantages requires anticipation, planning, analytic application and sustained vigilance over long periods (in many cases, years) of study implementation. It also requires scientists with the training and analytic skills to ensure that more of these advantages are realized in longitudinal designs and data collections.

Researchers charged with selecting measures for longitudinal studies also face the prospect of new technologies that are enabling new possibilities for data collection. Technological advances in communications and information are exerting fundamental changes in how people spend their time, do their work, maintain contact, make choices and understand their social world. Bioinformatics is also changing the way in which biological and genetic information is managed – particularly as this relates to longitudinal studies. These advances offer powerful opportunities for new approaches to involving participants in longitudinal studies and in gathering information about them. They also provide powerful avenues for their participation in the design of the study – it is no longer a one-way road from the researcher to the participant! Time-use diaries, digitized accelerometers, global positioning devices and real-time measures of mood, diet and activity provide avenues for understanding child and human development as never before. With them will come the demand for better analytic strategies.

Finally, the act of selecting and designing measures to gather observations on and from study participants in a longitudinal study has the propensity to reduce them to individuals who are predominately shaped by their environments and reacting to them. In truth, the situation is vastly different. While individuals do react to environments and events, they also select and shape them – they are *actors* in the way life unfolds (Bronfenbrenner, 1995). What individuals actually 'do' can be an extremely challenging aspect to capture dynamically in measures used in a longitudinal study. Some studies have turned to direct measures of study participants, gathering biological and behavioural observations in clinical or laboratory settings (e.g., Pearson, 2012). Other studies have implemented time-use diaries and event calendars to allow some greater capture of dynamic change in time and space as well as the pinpointing of specific events between data collection periods (e.g Mullan, 2014). With emerging internet and web-based telecommunications, possibilities for the real-time capture of information are becoming a reality.

There are other aspects of development, though, that are equally important but more challenging for measurement: an individual's possible choices and actual decisions at key points of transition, such as leaving school, commencing training or additional study, seeking employment, partnering, re-partnering and commencing a family, are examples of these. The reciprocal nature of development that is seen in emerging studies of gene–environment correlations and interactions is not well matched in the measurement designs employed on study participants. Measuring or capturing observations about the reciprocal nature of study participants' influence on the environment and their influence on others remains a significant challenge in onward longitudinal methodologies.

ADMINISTRATIVE DATA LINKAGE TO LONGITUDINAL STUDIES

The risk of over-burdening participants (i.e., respondent burden) with requests for their time is ever-present in the course of a longitudinal study. So too are the financial burdens associated with face-to-face or other interviewing techniques and data collection methods. In addition to concerns about burden and cost, the quality of information given by respondents can be subject to simple forgetting and selective recall, resulting in bias and inaccuracy in the collected data. These are reasons often invoked in seeking support for possible linkage to records of individual study participants in the administrative data regularly collected by government departments for public purposes. These administrative data may exist in a variety of forms across divergent domains: health records, school attendance and achievement tests, contacts with police, courts and justice systems, mental health records and collections of routine population information. The supplementation of longitudinal data through these means can provide powerful insights into the lives and circumstances of study participants (Jutte et al., 2011). Where population data registers are the basis of the linkage, then estimates derived from the longitudinal study may be examined for bias and generalizations from findings modified or extended. Counterfactual or comparison groups may also be created through linkage methodologies where important measures are common to both the longitudinal study and the source of linked data.

Where it is undertaken, data linkage to the participant data in a longitudinal study may occur at an aggregate level and/or at an individual level. In the former, this may occur at the level of small-area geography, whereby the specific address location of the study participant is linked to aggregate information describing the demographic and physical characteristics of the small area (e.g., census district, suburb, postcode) in which the study participant lives (e.g., an area SES indicator). In contrast, data linkage at an individual level may supplement each study participant's data with specific personal information about the individuals themselves (e.g., birthweight).

Data linkage is not possible in all places and under all circumstances. The feasibility of undertaking data linkage to a longitudinal study will inevitably reflect the jurisdictional regulatory environment in which such a study is positioned. In a global environment characterized by rapidly evolving communication and surveillance technologies, there are increasing public concerns about personal information and access to it (Allen et al., 2013; Holman, 2009; Huang et al., 2007). Statutory data are collected for public purposes and typically without the consent of the individual. The justification for restricting an individual's control over this information is the public benefit that is derived from its use. Community acceptance of this, however, rests on minimizing risks to individuals and their privacy and using the information for public benefit. The onward transmission of these statutory data, even when anonymized, requires robust regulatory frameworks that don't just govern the access to and release of such information, but also obligate researchers to adhere to legal and regulatory requirements (Allen et al., 2013). These requirements can restrict where a researcher analyses these types of data, how long they are retained and the conditions under which these data are kept and viewed.

With all of this said, where data linkage to longitudinal studies is undertaken, surprisingly encouraging rates of consent and rates of successful linkage can be achieved (da Silva et al., 2012; Sala et al., 2012; Soloff et al., 2007; Tate et al., 2006). Real benefits to scientific knowledge can be demonstrated in the resultant value adding of linked data to an existing or planned longitudinal study (Brook et al., 2008; Jutte et al., 2011).

In considering potential data linkage, researchers need to be mindful of the added complexity that is entailed in enabling data linkage, and that data linkage is not a 'quick fix'. Several considerations need to be kept in mind.

First, the beginning point for considering data linkage should be in a sound scientific rationale. What exactly does undertaking this enterprise enable in terms of gains in knowledge and reductions in respondent burden? Second, data linkage arrangements entail sustained high-level governance and administrative support for their establishment and onward management. These arrangements are typically labour intensive and need to operate in parallel with study design and content specification. Third, requiring participant consent for data linkage can be a potentially vexing methodological issue that threatens the validity or reduces the generalizability of the findings (Holman, 2009). Local administrative regulation and/or privacy legislation may establish the requirement for consent. Consent for data linkage, when needed, can be obtained from participants at the time of entry into the study. Preparation of the consent procedures and collection of the consent to include data linkage will entail justification and detailed training of interviewers to comply with regulatory requirements. The time window, or scope, of the consent for both retrospective and prospective data linkage requires detailed justification, ethical review and onward management. Fourth, management of the linkage process and the resultant data flows can entail quite elaborate arrangements to protect participant identities and adhere to confidentiality requirements (e.g., Kelman et al., 2002). Fifth, statistical and analytic training may be needed to handle the additional complexities of linked data. Finally, there are costs associated with undertaking the sequence of planning, enabling and supporting data linkage to a longitudinal study.

CAPTURING AREA EFFECTS

The relationship between the area in which a person lives and the subsequent formation of their capabilities, circumstances and life prospects has a long and worthy tradition in sociology and health (Durkheim, 1964; Rose, 1992) as well as in child development (Bronfenbrenner, 1995). There are several sources of evidence that demonstrate how area effects influence child development.

For example, experimental empirical studies have shown neighbourhood deprivation to be associated with conduct disorder, teenage pregnancy and substance use (Leventhal and Brooks-Gunn, 2003). Studies such as these consistently return findings that link area socioeconomic status to the developmental capabilities of the adults and children living in them. Other studies have attempted to disentangle the specific effects of individual-level SES from the effects of SES at the area level (Aaronson, 1998). In another example, Fone et al. have shown that income deprivation and social cohesion at the area level are significantly and independently associated with the poor mental health status of adults living in these areas (Fone et al., 2007) and demonstrate that this effect operates at the community level, not the individual level. Similar area-level effects have been observed in the impact of higher neighbourhood collective efficacy on the reduction of antisocial behaviour of children who live in deprived neighbourhoods (Odgers et al., 2009, 2012a, b). Taken together, these studies demonstrate that there are structural (e.g., urban decay, broken windows, green space, condition of walks and streets) and process (e.g., collective efficacy) elements in the local environment that need to be differentiated and measured and that have onward impact on child development.

For those undertaking the conduct of longitudinal studies, there are substantial challenges in study design that require anticipation and methodological planning in order to disentangle individual-level effects on development from those effects specifically attributable to the area level. Both structural and process factors of areas need to be assessed within the measurement design of a longitudinal study, if interests are focused on causal mechanisms (Sampson, 2011). Moreover, while such design preparation may provide greater clarity in the location of effects, it may not necessarily lead to insights about how these effects actually produce change at the level of the individual child. This is because, as levels are added to a model, measurements and specification of their effects need to be applied within each level in order to test the links between area effects of interest and the proposed mechanisms that operate to produce changes in individual-level outcomes.

At the practical level of conducting longitudinal studies, there is scope for improvements in methods for examining area-level effects on child development. First, most small-area analyses have been confined to populating individual subject records with aggregate information from census enumeration districts. There is now the need for studies that implement better methods for setting area boundaries around communities or neighbourhoods which are more meaningful in terms of the lived lives of individuals being studied. For example, new technologies and web-based opportunities using Google Street View for this have been described to reliably capture the defined neighbourhood conditions of families participating in longitudinal studies (Odgers et al., 2012a).

Second, consideration also needs to be given to what actually constitutes a 'measured' community. Raudenbush and Sampson (1999) have underscored ecological assessment as conceptually distinct from individual-level assessment (Sampson, 2011; Sampson and Raudenbush, 2004). They adapt and extend existing analytic strategies in psychometrics by applying them to survey-based measures of ecological settings gathered from survey respondents as well as to systematic social observations of the area that are independent of the perceptions of the survey respondents (i.e., 'econometrics').

Third, much of the extant literature on area effects is relatively silent on the effects of the material and built environment specifically on child development. Street layout, connectivity, paths and their walkability, residential density, traffic exposure, green space access and its quality and quantity, residential layout and land use are rarely mentioned and largely absent in the analytic space defined by longitudinal studies despite empirical dem-onstrations of their effects on health (Giles-Corti, 2011: 10; Villanueva et al., 2013: 103; Kimbro, 2011: 66).

Finally, there are several conceptual and analytic challenges in planning longitudinal designs that have the capacity to disentan-gle area-level effects (Sampson et al., 2013; Sastry et al., 2003). Collection of informa-tion particularly from independent observers about the wider physical and social environ-ments in which survey respondents move is rare and the practice is at a relatively early stage of development; sample sizes per clus-ter may be too small to permit reasonable estimation; and little or no information may be gathered on the circumstances of families moving in and out of the area as the study proceeds. These shortcomings can produce data sets that have high endogeneity among the predictors and outcomes of interest. Enthusiasm for the collection of these types of data and the use of these methods needs to be tempered by the arising practical and statistical challenges and coupled with rigour in the formulation of scientific questions for which answers are sought (Zubrick, 2007).

That said, there are pleasing advances in both theory, statistical treatments and practi-cal data collection that are bringing the esti-mation of meaningful area effects into the ambit of contemporary longitudinal studies. The principal challenges for the researchers are in articulating the key causal mechanisms to be captured, anticipating and designing measures for their collection, and keeping up with advances in technology that allow more of this into applied reach.

ENABLING GENE–ENVIRONMENT HYPOTHESES

Creators and stewards of longitudinal studies now face the opportunities and challenges of considering fundamental questions about the interplay of genes and environments and how these shape the lives of children from peri-conception onward to adulthood. To say that there has been a profound revolution in the understanding of the importance of this interplay would be an understatement. The emergent findings demonstrate that the once-presumed separation of the effects of genes from the effects of the environment on a variety of health and behavioural outcomes is not so distinct. Moreover, in the recent two decades, the broad initial interest in heritabil-ity has given way to a more focused pursuit of gene–environment correlations, gene–environment interactions and the processes of co-action that exist between genes and the environment (Rutter, 2007, 2009; Rutter et al., 2006). These have provided a more specific focus and critical challenge for researchers of developmental studies to better elucidate the causal processes under-pinning gene–environment interdependence.

Whether a longitudinal study should be genetically informed is a serious and sub-stantive methodological step and one that requires: careful scientific consideration and leadership; clarity and definition of purpose and potential gain in knowledge; access to technical expertise in genetics; sampling and biostatistics; and ultimately, methodological skills and supporting infra-structures for the collection and storage of specimens and their onward use. Ethics committees can be understandably sensitive to ambit applications of approval to collect participant DNA for future unspecified pur-poses. The issue of obtaining broad or open consent from parents for the future use of their children's specimens remains at best unresolved (Samuël et al., 2008). The man-agement of specimens and their future access and analysis impose significant and sub-stantial costs, along with demands for tech-nical support and ongoing expertise. That said, some ongoing longitudinal studies have added the collection of bio-specimens for the purpose of analysing specific gene–environment correlations and/or gene–environment inter-actions (Silva and Stanton, 1996). Other longitudinal studies have been designed at the outset with these purposes in mind

(Branum et al., 2003; Pembrey and ALSPAC Study Team, 2004).

Longitudinal studies may be genetically informative in a variety of ways apart from the collection of participant DNA. Twin studies which variously follow monozygotic and dizygotic twins have permitted insights into the contribution of genetics to a given condition or behavioural trait and allow the estimation of heritability, as well as estimation of the effects of shared and non-shared environments (Boomsma et al., 2002). The inclusion of other siblings in addition to the twin pair can permit deeper insights into gene–environment interactions. Family-level designs with intergenerational sampling also provide avenues for testing genetic hypotheses.

At a practical level, a full consideration of whether a longitudinal study should have a design that is genetically informed is beyond the scope of this review. What is clear in the conduct of longitudinal studies is that in addition to the decision to collect DNA or to enable other designs that permit inferences about genetic mechanisms, the design and selection of measures (e.g., phenotypes) – behavioural, physical and environmental – is equally critical to the quality of the science and resultant findings. As the findings have emerged documenting gene–environment co-actions, the dynamic nature of this field poses significant challenges to designers of longitudinal studies. Longitudinal measurement designs will require a better capture of the dynamic nature of study participants' behaviours, physical and emotional status (i.e., phenotypes) and the environments in which individuals live, work and move through and in which they (and others) act and respond.

MECHANISMS UNDERPINNING SOCIAL GRADIENTS

Social inequality, along with marked social gradient effects in developmental outcomes, is a significant global problem, with severe income disparity being the top risk facing many nations over the next ten years (World Economic Forum, 2012). The strong and almost universal relationship between social inequality and developmental outcomes has been clearly established across many populations (Keating and Hertzman, 1999; Marmot and Smith, 1991; Wilkinson, 1999). Poverty, homelessness, lack of education, ill-health, low levels of labour market participation and crime all feature as negative consequences of this disparity. A vexing feature of this disadvantage is the propensity for it to cluster in families and to be transmitted intergenerationally. This intergenerational disadvantage gives rise to significant transfers of public funds to support individuals and families experiencing these circumstances. While some of this assistance salvages these individuals and families from experiencing long-term failure in their sustainability, a significant proportion either fail to recover independent sustainability or, indeed, remain intergenerationally dependent on the public purse. This disadvantage is characterized by the impaired acquisition, poor accumulation, incomplete transfer or loss of human capital and human capability across the life course. It has proven persistently resistant to means of intervention by policies that differentially or universally alter choice and opportunity for individuals or, through direct intervention, alter the skills and knowledge of those individuals and families so affected. This persistence gives rise to considerable public policy interest in understanding these mechanisms and how longitudinal studies can contribute to our understanding of this.

For researchers conducting longitudinal studies of childhood, there are substantial opportunities and challenges in selecting study designs and measures that permit insights into the mechanisms of disadvantage. Recent international research has substantially elaborated on human capital theory in the past 20 years with vigorous expansion of the theoretical base and greater reference in recent times to human development across the lifespan (Carniero and Heckman, 2003; Keating and Hertzman, 1999). Theoretically, a focus on human capital building is, principally, a focus on achieving outcomes that will boost participation and productivity. This is because an increase in population stocks of human capital largely represents an increase in the agency of human beings as this is related to production possibilities (Richardson, 2005). In practical terms, this increase represents, at a more fundamental level, an increase in a person's actual skills, knowledge and effort. So, implementing study designs that define and measure the acquisition, accumulation, transfer and loss of skill, knowledge and effort as children grow through the life course are essential in addressing underlying mechanisms of disadvantage.

In addition to defining and measuring human capital, measures of the choices and constraints that influence an individual's use of human capital are also required. Human capability is a concept that describes the capacity of individuals to improve their health, wealth, knowledge and the opportunities available to facilitate these improvements, as well as manage the risks that pose barriers to these opportunities. The concept of human capability is linked to deep questions about the nature of individuals, their societies and their functions and purposes (e.g., Nussbaum, 2003). Human capability expansion is enabled by the nature of the distribution of equality, productivity, sustainability and empowerment within and between individuals and populations (Fukuda-Parr and Kumar, 2003). Thus, dimensions of existing human capability, such as health, education and vocational skills, can influence the uptake of policies and programs designed to improve life circumstances. Understanding these dimensions is critical for the development of policy and program content that matches the capability profile of populations in order to address its expansion.

Because productivity is one of the enablers of human capability, there is an explicit theoretical and practical association between human capability and the more narrowly (and commonly) measured concept of human capital. Economic growth occurs, in significant part, through human capital building. However, in achieving this growth, attention must be paid to its quality and distribution in populations, and to its link with human lives in the form of sustainability and the empowerment of meaningful choices (ul Haq, 2003). Given that such restrictions to human capital formation are increasingly recognized to have their origins in early disadvantage, the rationale for public policy to reduce early disadvantage is shifting from an equity focus to a focus on economic efficiency (Heckman, 2006).

Current international longitudinal data point to the potential longer-term benefits of investment early in the life course in the form of improved academic outcomes, crime reduction and higher workforce skill (World Bank, 2006). Governments around the world are now looking to develop effective strategies to build human capital through policies and programs that foster the development of children's cognitive and, particularly, social skills and abilities (Engle et al., 2007).

For the researcher seeking to address public policy, there are a number of questions about social inequality and social gradients that invite consideration through the conduct of longitudinal studies of children. First, what are the associations between human capital formation, the expansion of human capability and childhood determinants? Second, what are the measures and methods that can be used to chart population progress in terms of human capital formation and human capability expansion, and how are these operationalized in longitudinal studies? Third, is it possible to chart this progress and meaningfully interpret findings over time for public policy consumption? And finally, what are the mechanisms that link changes in human capital and human capability to developmental outcomes, and particularly to persistent intergenerational disadvantage?

As children develop, their skills, knowledge and effort undergo marked expansion and elaboration. This typically occurs in a family where these features are also changing in the adults and other family members.

Associations between measured capacities of children and their carers are often estimated in longitudinal studies. However, the requirement in emerging longitudinal studies is a more fundamental attention to mechanisms to determine how such developmental resources and capabilities in children and families are actually acquired, accumulated, transformed and lost.

THE IMPACT OF STUDY GOVERNANCE

As previously noted, longitudinal studies are exceptional in their requirement for 'core' funding that supports both the staff and the infrastructure that sustain the study through, and particularly between, collection periods. While they come in all shapes and sizes, as longitudinal studies increase in size with respect to participants, and broaden their scientific scope, the costs, and the value that they intend to contribute, can come under considerable scrutiny (e.g., National Research Council and Institute of Medicine, 2008). Their long time frames and extended horizons for the generation of knowledge and benefits can give rise to substantial governance demands. These demands can include decisions about ethical review; rules for deciding content, how respondents are recruited and consent is procured; data ownership, privacy and confidentiality; and reporting of, and expectations about, the translation of findings. Researchers need to be aware of and prepared for these.

Governance refers broadly to 'the system of administration and supervision through which research is managed, participants and staff are protected, and accountability is assured' (Shaw et al., 2005: 497). Establishing and maintaining governance can produce a considerable burden on the many parties involved – funders, researchers, regulators and participants. From time to time, study governance has been a source of concern for the potential waste it is perceived to produce relative to the risks that are managed

through it, with several recommendations on approaches for balancing these burdens to produce greater efficiencies (Chalmers et al., 2014; Ioannidis et al., 2014; Salman et al., 2014). The ethical regulation of studies with children has been covered previously (see the chapter by Farrell, this volume). There are, however, some features of the governance of ethical regulation for longitudinal studies commencing in childhood that merit comment here (Samuël et al., 2008).

Primary among these considerations is the time horizon for the scope of ethical coverage as the study children mature into late childhood, early adulthood and reach the jurisdictional age of consent and/or adulthood. Several legal instruments may be involved in shaping the consent procedures for a longitudinal study. These can entail the requirements of specific ethics committees which themselves are constituted by a variety of regulators. Researchers may be required to meet the ethical standards of granting authorities, religious institutions, health, medical and other registration bodies, schools and educational authorities, consumer and carer groups, as well as the privacy and freedom of information legislation. There may be added requirements arising through administrative data linkage processes. In all likelihood, several ethics committees and other regulators may simultaneously need to be involved in establishing the ethical governance of a longitudinal study.

Typically, parents or legal guardians are the individuals from whom consent is obtained for a study child's initial participation in a longitudinal study. However, when study children begin to transition into late childhood and early adulthood, there will be a need to seek their consent, often jointly with that of the guardian for a period, and then individually where children age to a defined point where they are deemed able to give their independent consent. This process requires careful planning and adherence to ethical and other regulatory requirements. It can add a burden to the interview process and introduce opportunities for study withdrawal through a need for the onward consent of the study child to participate.

Study governance is, of course, about far more than meeting the regulatory requirements for the ethical conduct of a longitudinal study. Particularly as longitudinal studies have grown in size and in cost, researchers are called upon to balance the desire and need for a study to be scientifically led with the need for a study to be policy-led – the latter often arising from the expectations of government funding agency(ies) and the onward involvement of community and other organizational 'stakeholders'. There can also be commercial interests that arise with, or as a result of, the ensuing research and its findings. Managing these forces can take a researcher's skills away from the scientific and knowledge-generation basis of a longitudinal study that comprise their expertise and interest and instead may propel them into the domain of managing the process, the people and their expectations – a role they may be ill-equipped to perform. It is unlikely though that there will be a return to the past where early longitudinal studies were solely established and led by a researcher or a small research team who was then faced not only with the foundation stages of the science and study and with meeting the existing ethical and regulatory frameworks of the time, but also was subsequently faced with meeting the onward and continuous challenge of procuring funding to sustain the study.

Many existing longitudinal studies now manage their onward sustainability and accountability through relatively elaborate governance mechanisms (Branum et al., 2003; Golding et al., 2002, 2004). Undoubtedly these governance arrangements, with their competing demands, open up the possibility of compromises to the scientific quality and novelty of some studies – in their content, design and methods. It is not clear just how this can be adequately addressed, although distinguishing between advisory capacities and executive decision-making capacities in this process is a critical step.

What are some of the practical considerations in governance that researchers should address in the establishment of a large longitudinal study of children? While the details of any specific longitudinal study will be guided by its scientific purpose or focus along with the expectations of the funders and jurisdictions, there are some broad issues to keep in mind.

First, the content of the information gathered in a longitudinal study interacts with the method(s) used to collect it. Just as children grow, change and develop so too do the methods used in collecting study information. While this seems completely self-evident, it needs to be stated and sometimes repeatedly. The initial planning stages of a longitudinal study may see several possible methodologies assessed and costed before the primary collection strategies are selected. Sometimes, the need for a particular content dictates the collection strategy. For studies with a relatively narrow focus and purpose, this stage may come together quickly with a specified methodology that optimizes content collection. For a larger, more broad-based omnibus study of child development, the interplay of content and methods can be quite protracted and lead to multiple collection scenarios. Piloting and dress rehearsal can be vital in supplying information about suitability and costs before final commitment to a method is determined.

Second, how will the actual content be chosen? Who will be involved and by what process will the selection and design of the content be achieved? How will expectations about this be established? In studies with relatively elaborate advisory and executive governance structures, the voices of scientists, funders, policy makers and other stakeholders need to be heard. How is this to be accomplished? By whom, or by what process, will the final decisions be made about what is collected? Where there is competing content or limited time for collection, how will priorities be established? Researchers can have high expectations and requirements where these affect the science of the study – its purpose and the quality of its methods and contents. Policy makers and funders may have an interest in more immediate outcomes and may sometimes be responding to more immediate pressures that shape their expectations about contents and their relevance to translation. There can be real conflicts between researchers and policy makers about novelty in methods or in taking risks on contents that may be seen to be more speculative or methods that pose both perceived and real risks to participants.

Third, the establishment phases and early data collection can result in a considerable delay in the production of descriptions and findings. Funds are spent without the immediate evidence of forward progress. The early phases of publication will, of necessity, have a higher proportion of descriptive and correlative findings relative to the future potential to produce findings that are more robust in terms of cause and effect. All of this requires careful management of communication – to researchers, funders and, critically, participants. This communication needs to be managed at the outset of the study and anticipated as an integral part of the study method and governance.

Fourth, how will the ongoing financial framework for sustainability be managed? Is this part of the concern or remit of the governance of the study? How will opportunities for leveraging of new funds into the study be managed: should this be encouraged, and if so, how?

Fifth, who 'owns' the data? Will there be a public release of confidentialized data? How will collaborators be approached?

Sixth, how will longitudinal fidelity be maintained? Some of this was discussed above with respect to measurement design. However, at a fundamental level a longitudinal study may operate over decades. Different method and content expertise and experts will undoubtedly be needed as the study participants and the study architects age and change. How will this process be managed with respect to what has come before? In addition, how is the corporate and scientific history of the study maintained through the lives of governments and funders? This is not a trivial issue. Politicians and government personnel change over time along with the policies that they produce. This can introduce discontinuity into how the study operates, in its perceived relevance and, more particularly, in pressures for differing contents and methods. These need to be balanced against the purposes of the study and the measurement framework over time.

Finally, a longitudinal study, as noted earlier, is a type of scientific technology. These studies are also sociological events of considerable historical interest. Quite apart from a careful documentation and publication of methods and content, by what process will the history of the study be recorded and made available? The experience of undertaking a longitudinal study is an experience of the creators, leaders, participants and agencies in shaping, reacting to and re-shaping the ongoing life of the study. Apart from scientific findings, where is this experience recorded? If the longitudinal study could tell its story, what would it have to say? For example, what was the contemporary scientific and policy context in which the study was initially established? Who specifically was involved at the initial stages and what were their roles and activities? Who left the study, when, and who joined? How much money was actually granted for the study in its various stages? From what sources did this funding come? What were the main challenges or threats in the ongoing work of the study and how were these met? What did those involved in collecting the data make of the experience? What were some of the unanticipated events in the conduct of the study? How did the work methodologically evolve? Not all of this history is absent in the extant literature, but nor is there a lot of it in relation to the history of many of the existing studies. The time to embark on documenting many of these aspects is not late in the life of the study or the researchers!

With regard to governance, Shaw et al. (2005: 501) noted: 'only time will tell if research governance procedures will achieve the goal of raising standards, protecting participants and assuring quality – and whether the inevitable constraints on research freedom will be worth the candle'. Whatever time will tell, the governance of a longitudinal study is exceptional for what it must accomplish. In addition to meeting regulatory requirements and protecting participants, governance must effectively create a sustained institutional arrangement that allows those involved (e.g., researchers, participants, policy makers and politicians) to experience substantive and situational social learning (Lin, 2004; Peterson, 1997) if the scientific findings are to gain wider policy and practical translation. The basis of this will require sensitive and generous participation and skilled leadership.

CONCLUSION

Longitudinal studies are one of the critical tools for understanding child and human development. They provide unique insights into the processes of change and growth.

Policies for 'liberating' longitudinal data and making them available for collaborative gain and teaching are now increasing the ranks of researchers who are capable and able to use such data to address important hypotheses. Data sharing arrangements, harmonization of data sets and the sheer diversity of interests and possibilities to which longitudinal data are put have further increased the reach of findings. Previously scant statistical and analytic approaches for longitudinal data are now more accessible, well described and within the reach of students and practitioners of longitudinal science (Singer and Willett, 2003). This is gratifying.

There is, of course, more to do. In reviewing the conduct of longitudinal studies, there is still the need for researchers to implement designs: that better measure and capture growth and change in physical, cognitive, emotional and social capabilities; that reveal more about the choices, decisions and actions taken (and not taken) by the child (and carers) as they grow to adulthood; and that capture the inputs and influences of these. Specific designs that study rare and hard-to-reach populations are needed. Methodologically, researchers using longitudinal data would also benefit from better documentation of longitudinal measurement fidelity and invariance characteristics, and when and how to use these properties in modelling data to investigate hypotheses.

At whatever point in the life course the study of child and human development commences, researchers will require not one, but a range of research designs and skills to test important hypotheses about developmental capabilities – their cause and effect, their growth and change, and their stability and instability. The driving forces in this interest encompass the need for basic knowledge but now also extend into balancing corporate and commercial interests, particularly from the health sector, with government interests that increasingly seek to derive translation from the research into policy outcomes across health, education and welfare. There is a notable interest from governments, not only in understanding the dynamic processes that lead to poor outcome in life prospects with resultant high dependencies on families, communities and social support benefits (Sampson et al., 2013), but also an increasing demand from governments to understand the processes that lead to typically good outcomes with reduced burdens and greater capabilities across the life course. These are high expectations for a study design that operates with a long time horizon for outcomes. Still, investments in new studies, along with the prodigious and growing output from established studies, suggest that many of these expectations are being met in the conduct of longitudinal studies of children.

FURTHER READING

Fergusson, D. M. and Horwood, L. J. (2013) The Christchurch Health and Development Study. In P. Joyce, G. Nicholls, K. Thomas and

T. Wilkinson (eds) *The Christchurch Experience: 40 Years of Research and Teaching.* Christchurch: University of Otago.

Rutter, M., Moffitt, T. E. and Caspi, A. (2006) Gene–environment interplay and psychopathology: Multiple varieties but real effects. *Journal of Child Psychology and Psychiatry*, 47, 226–61.

Sampson, R. J., Winship, C. and Knight, C. (2013) Translating causal claims. *Criminology and Public Policy*, 12, 587–616.

QUESTIONS FOR REFLECTION

1 Longitudinal studies are extolled for their value in providing insights into causal processes. How are individual differences and group differences revealed in longitudinal studies? Which longitudinal designs typically focus on these differences?

2 What are the distinguishing features and challenges of selecting measures for a longitudinal study?

3 Give an example of how administrative data linkage could be used to validate self-reported health status in longitudinal study participants.

ACKNOWLEDGEMENTS

The author is supported by grants from the National Health and Medical Research Council of Australia (#572742) and the Australian Research Council (CE140100027). Thanks particularly to Dr Judith Straton for providing helpful comments and guidance in preparation of this manuscript.

REFERENCES

Aaronson, D. (1998) Using sibling data to estimate the impact of neighborhoods on children's educational outcomes. *Journal of Human Resources*, 33(4), 915–46.

Allen, J., Holman, C. D. J., Meslin, E. M. and Stanley, F. (2013) Privacy protectionism and health information: Is there any redress for harms to health? *Journal of Law and Medicine*, 21, 473–85.

Binder, D. A. (1998) Longitudinal surveys: Why are these surveys different from all other surveys? *Survey Methodology*, 24(2), 101–8.

Boomsma, D., Busjahn, A. and Peltonen, L. (2002) Classical twin studies and beyond. *Nature Reviews Genetics*, 3(11), 872–82.

Boyd, A., Golding, J., Macleod, J., Lawlor, D. A., Fraser, A., Henderson, J., et al. (2013) Cohort Profile: The 'children of the 90s' – the index offspring of the Avon Longitudinal Study of Parents and Children. *International Journal of Epidemiology*, 42(1), 111–27.

Branum, A. M., Collman, G. W., Correa, A., Keim, S. A., Kessel, W., Kimmel, C. A., et al. (2003) The National Children's Study of environmental effects on child health and development. *Environmental Health Perspectives*, 11(3), 642–6.

Bronfenbrenner, U. (1995) Developmental ecology through space and time: A future perspective. In P. Moen, G. H. Elder and K. Luscher (eds), *Examining Lives in Context: Perspectives on the Ecology of Human Development* (pp. 599–647). Washington, DC: American Psychological Association.

Brook, E. L., Rosman, D. L. and Holman, C. D. J. (2008) Public good through data linkage: Measuring research outputs from the Western Australian Data Linkage System. *Australian and New Zealand Journal of Public Health*, 32(1), 19–23.

Brown, B., Zaslow, M. and Weitzman, M. (2006) Studying and tracking early child development from a health perspective: A review of available data sources. New York: The Commonwealth Fund.

Bynner, J., Erickson, R., Goldstein, H., Maughan, B. and Wadsworth, M. (2009) Longitudinal and Life Course Studies: a new journal. *Longitudinal and Life Course Studies: International Journal*, 1(1), 3–10.

Carniero, P. and Heckman, J. (2003) *Human Capital Policy* (Working Paper No. 9495). Cambridge, MA: National Bureau of Economic Research.

Chalmers, I., Bracken, M. B., Djulbegovic, B., Garattini, S., Grant, J., Gülmezoglu, A. M., et al. (2014) How to increase value and reduce waste when research priorities are set. *The Lancet*, 383(9912), 156–65.

da Silva, M. E. M., Coeli, C. M., Ventura, M., Palacios, M., Magnanini, M. M. F., Camargo, T. M. C. R. and Camargo, K. R. (2012) Informed consent for record linkage: A systematic review. *Journal of Medical Ethics*, 38(10), 639–42.

Durkheim, E. (1964) *The Rules of Sociological Method* (8th edn). New York: Free Press of Glencoe.

Elliott, J. and Shepherd, P. (2006) Cohort profile: 1970 British birth cohort (BCS70). *International Journal of Epidemiology*, 35(4), 836–43.

Embretson, S. E. (2003) *The Second Century of Ability Testing: Some Predictions and Speculations*. William H. Angoff Memorial Lecture Series. Princeton, NJ: Educational Testing Service.

Embretson, S. E. (2006) The continued search for nonarbitrary metrics in psychology. *American Psychologist*, 61(1), 50–5.

Embretson, S. E. (2012) Impact of measurement scale in modeling development processes and ecological factors. In T. D. Little, J. A. Bovaird and N. A. Card (eds), *Modeling Contextual Effects in Longitudinal Studies* (pp. 63–87). Hoboken, NJ: Taylor & Francis.

Engle, P. L., Black, M. M., Behrman, J. R., Cabral de Mello, M., Gertler, P. J., Kapiriri, L., et al. (2007) The International Child Development Steering Group: Strategies to avoid the loss of developmental potential in more than 200 million children in the developing world. *The Lancet*, 369, 229–42.

Eskenazi, B., Gladstone, E. A., Berkowitz, G. S., Drew, C. H., Faustman, E. M., Holland, N. T., et al. (2005) Methodologic and logistic issues in conducting longitudinal birth cohort studies: Lessons learned from the centers for children's environmental health and disease prevention research. *Environmental Health Perspectives*, 113(10), 1419–29.

Fergusson, D. M. (1998) The Christchurch health and development study: An overview and some key findings. *Social Policy Journal of New Zealand*, 10, 154–76.

Fergusson, D. M. and Horwood, L. J. (2013) The Christchurch Health and Development Study. In P. Joyce, G. Nicholls, K. Thomas and T. Wilkinson (eds), *The Christchurch Experience: 40 Years of Research and Teaching* (pp. 79–87). Christchurch: University of Otago.

Fone, D., Dunstan, F., Lloyd, K., Williams, G., Watkins, J. and Palmer, S. (2007) Does social cohesion modify the association between area income deprivation and mental health? A multilevel analysis. *International Journal of Epidemiology*, 36(2), 338–45.

Fraser, A., Macdonald-Wallis, C., Tilling, K., Boyd, A., Golding, J., Davey Smith, G., et al. (2012) Cohort Profile: The Avon Longitudinal Study of Parents and Children – ALSPAC mothers cohort. *International Journal of Epidemiology*, 42(1), 97–110.

Fukuda-Parr, S. and Kumar, A. K. S. (eds) (2003) *Readings in Human Development: Concepts, Measures and Policies for a Developmental Paradigm*. New Delhi: Oxford University Press.

Giles-Corti, B., Wood, G., Pikora, T., Learnihan, V., Bulsara, M., Van Niel, K., Timperio, A., McCormack, G. and Villanueva, K. (2011) School site and the potential to walk to school: The impact of street connectivity and traffic exposure in school neighborhoods. *Health & Place*, 17(2), 545–50.

Golding, J., Pembrey, M., Jones, R. and ALSPAC Study Team. (2002) ALSPAC – The Avon Longitudinal Study of Parents and Children I. Study methodology. *Paediatric and Perinatal Epidemiology*, 15(1), 74–87.

Golding, J. and ALSPAC Study Team. (2004) The Avon Longitudinal Study of Parents and Children (ALSPAC) – study design and collaborative opportunities. *European Journal of Endocrinology*, 151(Suppl), U119–U123.

Hansen, K., Joshi, H. and Dex, S. (eds) (2010) *Children of the 21st Century (Vol. 2): The First Five Years*. Bristol: Policy Press.

Heckman, J. J. (2006) *Investing in Disadvantaged Young Children is an Economically Efficient Policy*. New York: Committee for Economic Development/The Pew Charitable Trusts/PNC Financial Services Group Forum.

Hirshfeld, S., Songco, D., Kramer, B. S. and Guttmacher, A. E. (2011) National Children's Study: Status in 2010. *Mt Sanai Journal of Medicine*, 78(1), 119–25.

Holman, C. D. J. (2009) The impracticable nature of consent for research use of linked administrative health records. *Australian and New Zealand Journal of Public Health*, 25(5), 421–2.

Huang, N., Shih, S.-F., Chang, H.-Y. and Chou, Y.-J. (2007) Record linkage research and informed consent: who consents? *BMC Health Services Research*, 7(18). doi: 10.1186/1472-6963-7-18.

Huguet, N., Cunningham, S. D. and Newsom, J. T. (2012) Existing longitudinal data sets for the study of health and social aspects of aging. In J. T. Newsom, R. N. Jones and S. M. Hofer (eds), *Longitudinal Data Analysis: A Practical Guide for Researchers in Aging, Health and Social Sciences*. New York: Taylor & Francis Group.

Ioannidis, J. P. A., Greenland, S., Hlatky, M. A., Khoury, M. J., Macleod, M. R., Moher, D., et al. (2014) Increasing value and reducing waste in research design, conduct, and analysis. *The Lancet*, 383(9912), 166–75.

Joshi, H. (2008) The Millennium Cohort Study and mature national birth cohorts in Britain. In S. Menard (ed.), *Handbook of Longitudinal Research* (pp. 67–84). Burlington, MA: Elsevier Science.

Jutte, D. P., Roos, L. L. and Brownell, M. D. (2011) Administrative record linkage as a tool for public health research. *Annual Review of Public Health*, 32(1), 91–108.

Keating, D. P. and Hertzman, C. (eds) (1999) *Developmental Health and the Wealth of Nations: Social, Biological and Educational Dynamics*. New York: Guilford Press.

Kelman, C. W., Bass, A. J. and Holman, C. D. J. (2002) Research use of linked health data: A best practice protocol. *Australian and New Zealand Journal of Public Health*, 26(3), 251–5.

Kim, E. S. and Yoon, M. (2011) Testing measurement invariance: A comparison of multiple-group categorical CFA and IRT. *Structural Equation Modeling: A Multidisciplinary Journal*, 18(2), 212–28.

Kimbro, R. T., Brooks-Gunn, J. and McLanahan, S. (2011) Young children in urban areas: Links among neighborhood characteristics, weight status, outdoor play, and television watching. *Social Science & Medicine*, 72(5), 668–76.

Leventhal, T. and Brooks-Gunn, J. (2003) Children and youth in neighborhood contexts. *Current Directions in Psychological Science*, 12(1), 27–31.

Lin, V. (2004) From public health research to health promotion policy: On the 10 major contradictions. *Social and Preventive Medicine*, 49, 185–97.

Little, T. D., Preacher, K. J., Selig, J. P. and Card, N. A. (2007) New developments in latent variable panel analyses of longitudinal data. *International Journal of Behavioral Development*, 31(4), 357–65.

Lynn, P. (ed.) (2009) *Methodology of Longitudinal Surveys*. Chichester: Wiley.

Marmot, M. G. and Smith, G. D. (1991) Health inequalities among British civil servants: The Whitehall II study. *Lancet*, 337(8754), 1387–93.

Menard, S. (ed.) (2008) *Handbook of Longitudinal Research*. Burlington, MA: Elsevier Science.

Millsap, R. E. and Yun-Tein, J. (2004) Assessing factorial invariance in ordered-categorical measures. *Multivariate Behavioral Research*, 39(3), 479–515.

Mullan, K. (2014) Longitudinal analysis of LSAC time diary data: Considerations for data user. LSAC Technical Paper No. 11. Canberra: Department of Social Services, Australian Government (www.growingupinaustralia.gov.au/pubs/technical/tp11.pdf).

National Research Council and Institute of Medicine (2008) *The National Children's Study Research Plan: A Review – Panel to Review the National Children's Study Research Plan*. Committee on National Statistics, Division of Behavioral and Social Sciences and Education; Board on Children, Youth, and Families and Board on Population Health and Public Health Practice, Institute of Medicine. Washington, DC: The National Academies Press.

Nicholson, J. M. and Rempal, L. A. (2004) Australian and New Zealand birth cohort studies: Breadth, quality and contributions. *Journal of Paediatrics and Child Health*, 40, 87–95.

Nussbaum, M. C. (2003) Capabilities as fundamental entitlements: Sen and social justice. *Feminist Economics*, 9(2–3), 33–59.

Odgers, C. L., Caspi, A., Bates, C. J., Sampson, R. J. and Moffitt, T. E. (2012a) Systematic social observation of children's neighborhoods using Google Street View: A reliable and cost-effective method. *Journal of Child Psychology and Psychiatry*, 53(10), 1009–17.

Odgers, C. L., Caspi, A., Russell, M. A., Sampson, R. J., Arseneault, L. and Moffitt, T. E. (2012b) Supportive parenting mediates neighborhood socioeconomic disparities in children's antisocial behavior from ages

5 to 12. *Development and Psychopathology*, 24, 705–721.

Odgers, C. L., Moffitt, T. E., Tach, L. M., Sampson, R. J., Taylor, A., Matthews, C. L. and Caspi, A. (2009) The protective effects of neighborhood collective efficacy on British children growing up in deprivation: A developmental analysis. *Developmental Psychology*, 45(4), 942–57.

Pearson, H. (2012) Coming of age. *Nature*, 484(7393), 155–8.

Pembrey, M. and ALSPAC Study Team (2004) The Avon Longitudinal Study of Parents and Children (ALSPAC): A resource for genetic epidemiology. *European Journal of Endocrinology*, 2004(151), U125–9.

Peterson, M. (1997) The limits of social learning: Translating analysis into action. *Journal of Health, Politics, Policy and Law*, 22, 1077–114.

Power, C. and Elliott, J. (2006) Cohort profile: 1958 British birth cohort (National Child Development Study). *International Journal of Epidemiology*, 35(1), 34–41.

Raudenbush, S. W. and Sampson, R. J. (1999) Ecometrics: Toward a science of assessing ecological settings, with application to the systematic social observation of neighborhoods. *Sociological Methodology*, 29, 1–41.

Richardson, S. (2005) Children and the labour market. In S. Richardson and M. Prior (eds), *No Time to Lose: The Well-being of Australia's Children*. Melbourne: Academy of the Social Sciences in Australia and Melbourne University Press.

Rose, G. A. (1992) *The Strategy of Preventive Medicine*. Oxford: Oxford University Press.

Rutter, M. (1988) Longitudinal data in the study of causal processes: Some uses and some pitfalls. In M. Rutter (ed.), *Studies of Psychosocial Risk: The Power of Longitudinal Data* (pp. 1–28). New York: Cambridge University Press.

Rutter, M. (1994) Beyond longitudinal data: Causes, consequences, changes and continuity. *Journal of Consulting and Clinical Psychology*, 62(5), 928–40.

Rutter, M. (2003) Categories, dimensions and the mental health of children and adolescents. In C. F. King, J. A. Ferris and I. I. Lederhendler (eds), *Roots of Mental Illness* (pp. 11–21). New York: The New York Academy of Sciences.

Rutter, M. (2007) Gene–environment interdependence. *Developmental Science*, 10(1), 12–18.

Rutter, M. (2009) Understanding and testing risk mechanisms for mental disorders. *Journal of Child Psychology and Psychiatry*, 50(1–2), 44–52.

Rutter, M., Moffitt, T. E. and Caspi, A. (2006) Gene–environment interplay and psychopathology: Multiple varieties but real effects. *Journal of Child Psychology and Psychiatry*, 47(3–4), 226–61.

Rutter, M., Pickles, A., Murray, R. and Eaves, L. (2001) Testing hypotheses on specific environmental causal effects on behavior. *Psychological Bulletin*, 127(3), 291–324.

Sala, E., Burton, J. and Knies, G. (2012) Correlates of obtaining informed consent to data linkage: Respondent, interview and interviewer characteristics. *Sociological Methods and Research*, 41(3), 414–39.

Salman, R. A.-S., Beller, E., Kagan, J., Hemminki, E., Phillips, R. S., Savulescu, J., et al. (2014) Increasing value and reducing waste in biomedical research regulation and management. *The Lancet*, 383(9912), 176–85.

Sampson, R. J. (2011) Neighborhood effects, causal mechanisms, and the social structure of the city. In D. Pierre (ed.), *Analytical Sociology and Social Mechanisms* (pp. 227–50). Cambridge and New York: Cambridge University Press.

Sampson, R. J. and Raudenbush, S. W. (2004) Seeing disorder: Neighborhood stigma and the social construction of 'broken windows'. *Social Psychology Quarterly*, 67(4), 319–42.

Sampson, R. J., Winship, C. and Knight, C. (2013) Translating causal claims. *Criminology and Public Policy*, 12(4), 587–616.

Samuël, J., Ries, N. M., Malkin, D. and Knoppers, B. M. (2008) Biobanks and longitudinal studies: Where are the children? *GenEdit*, 6(3), 1–8.

Sanson, A. (ed.) (2002) *Children's Health and Development: New Directions for Australia*. Melbourne: Australian Institute of Family Studies, Commonwealth of Australia.

Sastry, N., Ghosh-Dastidar, B., Adams, J. and Pebly, A. (2003) *The Design of a Multilevel Survey of Children, Families, and Communities: The Los Angeles Family and Neighborhood Survey*. Office of Population Research, Princeton University, Working Paper Series. Santa Monica: RAND.

Schmitt, N. and Kuljanin, G. (2008) Measurement invariance: Review of practice and implications. *Human Resource Management Review*, 18(4), 210–22.

Shaw, S., Boynton, P. M. and Greenhalgh, T. (2005) Research governance: Where did it come from, what does it mean? *Journal of the Royal Society of Medicine*, 98(11), 496–502.

Silva, P. A. and Stanton, W. R. (eds) (1996) *From Child to Adult: The Dunedin Multidisciplinary Health and Development Study*. Auckland: Oxford University Press.

Singer, J. D. and Willett, J. B. (2003) *Applied Longitudinal Data Analysis: Modeling Change and Event Occurrence*. New York: Oxford University Press.

Soloff, C., Sanson, A., Wake, M. and Harrison, L. (2007) Enhancing longitudinal studies by linkage to national databases: Growing up in Australia, the Longitudinal Study of Australian Children. *International Journal of Social Research Methodology*, 10(5), 349–63.

Tate, A. R., Calderwood, L., Dezateux, C., Joshi, H. and The Millennium Cohort Study Child Health Group (2006) Mother's consent to linkage of survey data with her child's birth records in a multi-ethnic national cohort study. *International Journal of Epidemiology*, 35(2), 294–8.

ul Haq, M. (2003) The human development paradigm. In S. Fukuda-Parr and A. K. S. Kumar (eds), *Readings in Human Development: Concepts, Measures and Policies for a Developmental Paradigm* (pp. 17–34). New Delhi: Oxford University Press.

Vandenberg, R. J. and Lance, C. E. (2000) A review and synthesis of the measurement invariance literature: Suggestions, practices, and recommendations for organizational research. *Organizational Research Methods*, 3(1), 4–70.

Villanueva, K., Giles-Corti, B., Bulsara, M., Timperio, A., McCormack, G., Beesley, B., Trapp, G. and Middleton, N. (2013) Where Do Children Travel to and What Local Opportunities Are Available? The Relationship Between Neighborhood Destinations and Children's Independent Mobility. *Environment and Behavior*, 45(6), 679–705.

Wilkinson, R. G. (1999) Putting the picture together: Prosperity, redistribution, health, and welfare. In M. Marmot and R. G. Wilkinson (eds), *Social Determinants of Health* (pp. 256–74). Oxford: Oxford University Press.

World Bank (2006) *Equity and Development: World Development Report 2006*. New York: World Bank and Oxford University Press.

World Economic Forum (2012) *Global Risks 2012: Insight Report* (7th edn). Geneva: WEF.

Zubrick, S. R. (2007) Commentary: Area social cohesion, deprivation and mental health – Does misery love company? *International Journal of Epidemiology*, 36(April), 345–7.

Zubrick, S. R., Taylor, C. L., Lawrence, D. M., Mitrou, F. G., Christensen, D. and Dalby, R. (2009) The development of human capability across the lifecourse: Perspectives from childhood. *Australian Epidemiologist*, 16(3), 6–10.

14

Conducting Ethnographic Research in Early Childhood Research: Questions of Participation

Kristina Konstantoni and Marlies Kustatscher

INTRODUCTION

Ethnography is becoming the 'new ortho-doxy in childhood research' (James, 2007: 246; Qvortrup, 2000). In this chapter we provide an overview of ethnography in early childhood research. We begin by providing some historical background to the develop-ment of ethnography and how the theoretical assumptions informing it sit with doing research with young children. We outline the underlying principles and provide examples of early childhood ethnographic studies, before embarking on a discussion of (1) eth-nographic methods and research in practice, (2) the ethnographer's roles and the impor-tance of reflexivity, and (3) questions of ethics, particularly informed consent. These three overlapping areas constitute some of the main fields of debate in both ethno-graphic research and in research with chil-dren more generally, and are therefore crucial to consider in relation to ethnography with young children. We locate our discussion within a childhood studies paradigm which

recognizes children's competencies and agency (James et al., 1998; Tisdall and Punch, 2012), as well as against the backdrop of a worldwide growing interest in children's par-ticipation rights as engrained in the United Nations Convention on the Rights of the Child (UNCRC) (Tisdall, 2012). While we do not provide an in-depth discussion of chil-dren's participation (see Tisdall's chapter in this volume), we use it as a critical lens through which we explore the above points about early childhood ethnography. Since both the childhood studies as well as the chil-dren's rights field have been central in devel-oping research with children in recent years, this chapter contributes to the theoretical discussion of early childhood ethnography by situating it in relation to these paradigms.

WHAT IS ETHNOGRAPHY?

The term 'ethnography' derives from the ancient Greek words 'ethnos' and 'grapho' and means *writing about a particular folk or people* (Silverman, 2011: 114). Ethnographic research often involves multiple methods (most commonly participant observation and interviews) and data sources (e.g., talk, behaviour, interactions, texts).

Historically, the beginnings of ethnography are rooted in the discipline of anthropology, particularly in the works of Malinowski (1922) and Mead (1928), involving prolonged periods of fieldwork with tribes or cultures, embedded in a colonial paradigm. This was challenged as anthropologists became more diverse over time, and as ethnography spread into other disciplines: most notably, it entered sociology through the 'Chicago School' from the 1920s onwards and was applied to the study of communities and urban life in the Global North. Fields of interest at the time included, for example, gangs, subcultures, drug use, stigma or cultural consumption, with notable writers including Mead (1934), Becker (1963) and Goffman (1961). Throughout the twentieth century, ethnography was increasingly adopted by additional disciplines such as cultural studies, education, psychology and human geography (Hammersley and Atkinson, 2007). These historical developments went hand in hand with the influence of different theoretical and philosophical perspectives, from initially positivist (the researcher as an objective and distant collector of information), to naturalist, symbolic interactionist, constructionist, feminist and poststructuralist ideas (Hammersley and Atkinson, 2007).

Due to its complex history, and the influence of a number of theoretical approaches, there is no clear-cut definition of ethnography. In practice:

> ethnography usually involves the researcher participating, overtly or covertly, in people's daily lives for an extended period of time, watching what happens, listening to what is said, and/or asking questions through informal and formal interviews, collecting documents and artefacts – in fact, gathering whatever data are available to throw light on the issues that are the emerging focus of inquiry. (Hammersley and Atkinson, 2007: 3)

Research studies that adopt an ethnographic approach are mainly interested in in-depth and exploratory study and, thus, tend to focus on one or a few 'fairly small-scale' cases (Hammersley and Atkinson, 2007: 3). Ethnographers are interested in an understanding of people's everyday lives and practices in naturalistic settings, people's views and understandings of their social world and people's 'habits, beliefs and language' (Mukherji and Albon, 2010: 70).

While qualitative research generally considers the role and impact of the researcher in designing and analyzing the research, ethnographic approaches, in particular, stress the constructivist and reflexive nature of the research process (Hammersley and Atkinson, 2007). Ethnography, in turn, involves a description of culture through the lens of the ethnographer who locates the description within a context of meaningful structures – a process famously described as 'thick description':

> Culture is not a power, something to which social events, behaviors, institutions, or processes can be causally attributed; it is a context, something within which they can be intelligibly – that is, thickly – described. (Geertz, 1973: 14)

The emphasis of ethnography and participant observation as a deeply humanistic, interpretive approach is applicable to all social research which shares the idea that as researchers we cannot detach ourselves from the worlds we study. From this point of view, ethnography has been described as more than a qualitative research methodology: it is 'a mode of being-in-the-world characteristic of researchers' (Atkinson and Hammersley, 1994: 249), with particular ontological and epistemological properties. We will now spin this thought further and explore the underlying principles and effects of using ethnography in early childhood research. We begin by outlining debates and examples in ethnographic research with young children, and the particular underlying ontological and epistemological assumptions of such approaches. We then discuss various stages and methods of doing ethnographic research in practice (negotiating access, participant observation, writing field notes and questions of analysis). Following this, we move on to the interrelated issues of power dynamics, the researcher's roles and the importance of a reflexive stance in ethnographic research. Finally, we discuss ethical questions, particularly the concept of informed consent and our relational understanding of it. We link these issues to debates about children's participation throughout this chapter, and provide some reflections on the implications for policy and practice.

ETHNOGRAPHY AND EARLY CHILDHOOD RESEARCH

The methods that we, as researchers, choose for investigating early childhood reflect our ontological (what *is* a child?) and epistemological (what and how can we *know* about children and childhoods?) positions (Gallagher, 2009a). As described above, ethnographic approaches are far from homogeneous when it comes to their underlying theoretical frameworks. Earlier ethnographic studies *on* childhood did not focus on children's own perspectives. Rather, they saw the study of childhood as a 'means to a greater end' (James, 2007: 247), that is, the study of socialization processes (in which children were perceived to assume a rather passive role) and general development of cultures and 'civilizations'. More recently, and influenced by the 'new social studies of childhood' paradigm (James and Prout, 1997), there has been much debate about how ethnographic approaches conceptualize children and childhoods, and what the implications of these conceptualizations are for conducting research with children. It has been argued that ethnographic research entails a view of children as fundamentally different from adults, of childhood as a 'culture' that can and should be studied in its own right (James et al., 1998; Punch, 2002). On the other hand, ethnography has also been credited for enabling a shift from viewing children as the

objects of study, to children becoming *subjects* in the research process, since, 'what ethnography permits is a view of children as competent interpreters of the social world' (James, 2007: 246).

From this point of view, ethnography recognizes children as active contributors to their own lives and to how childhood and society are constructed in different cultural and historical contexts. As such, ethnography has been crucial in advancing the field of childhood studies. The field's focus on children's views and participation (James and Prout, 1997) has developed in parallel to ethnography becoming the most popular and accepted methodology for exploring children's views about their own and other people's lives in in-depth, small-scale projects (Qvortrup, 2000). Ethnographic research has highlighted the multifaceted nature of childhood (James, 2007) and has been used in different cultural contexts across the Global North and South and across academic disciplines.

The focus of ethnographic research with children has included a number of different areas to date. For example, it has focused on education and schooling (Gordon et al., 2001; Levinson et al., 1996), gender, identities and relationships (James, 1993; Punch and Tisdall, 2012; Renold, 2005; Thorne, 1993), family and home lives (Aarsand, 2007), experiences of health and care (Emond, 2002; Johnson and Vindrola-Padros, 2014), street children (Beazley, 2003; Gough and Franch, 2005; Hecht, 1998; Van Blerk, 2005), poverty, work and globalization (Cole and Durham, 2007; Liebel, 2004; Punch, 2001; Punch and Sugden, 2013; Scheper-Hughes and Sargent, 1998) and crises and war (Boyden and de Berry, 2005; De Waal and Argenti, 2002).

Ethnographic research in *early* childhood is often conducted on young children's experiences of or within particular services (Siraj-Blatchford, 2010), such as studies on play (Dau, 1999; Evaldson and Corsaro, 1998; Scott, 2002; Strandell, 1997), on service outcomes or experiences of specific programs (Kantor and Whalley, 1998; Sylva et al., 1999), or on young children's identities and relationships within educational settings (Connolly, 1998, 2000, 2003; Davies, 2003; Konstantoni, 2011, 2012, 2013; Kustatscher, 2015; Van Ausdale and Feagin, 2001). The majority of early childhood ethnographies that have been identified for this chapter were conducted in the Global North, and the fact that young children may not be institutionalized in age-segregating settings to the same extent in the Global South may be an explanation for this scenario.

Ethnographic research with children requires that researchers recognize their adult-centered views and preconceptions about childhood in the specific context of their research and set out to be 'taught' by the children how they shape and control their own worlds (Emond, 2005). Our ontological assumptions in terms of how we conceptualize childhood in general, especially in relation to adulthood, have implications for designing and conducting research about *early* childhood in particular. The principles underlying ethnographic research described so far apply to research with children, young people and adults. What then are the characteristics of ethnographic research with *young* children?

Whether research with children is the same, or different, from research with adults, and how such differences may be conceptualized, has been the subject of much debate in the field (for a detailed discussion, see Punch, 2002). Most researchers agree that children's competencies differ from those of adults (James et al., 1998) and that this needs to be taken into account when using so-called 'child-friendly' techniques within an ethnographic approach (e.g., photography or drawings). Such differing competencies may, for example, include taking account of young children's shorter attention span or different use of language. However, Punch (2002) warns of assuming such differences in a simplistic manner, since they are more often rooted in adults' assumptions about childhood and children's capabilities, as well as structural circumstances, than in inherent differences between different stages of child- and adulthood.

Developmental perspectives have been particularly powerful in constructing children as different (with a tendency towards a view of the child as deficient and incomplete) and it is important to remember that such perspectives are also historically and culturally situated (Punch, 2002; Woodhead, 1998). Constructs such as 'maturity' may differ from context to context (consider, for example, the differences between constructions of childhood when doing research in a primary school in the Global North or with child workers of the same age in the Global South). Thus, taking account of children's language and competencies in a meaningful way means being reflexive and sensitive to our own assumptions as researchers, to the fact that children are a heterogeneous group and to dynamics of power and the structural marginalization of childhood. Ethnography has been instrumental in overcoming purely developmental or biological conceptualizations of childhood by drawing attention to the importance of children's cultural contexts and contributions to it (James, 2007). Its recognition of children's 'huge amounts of knowledge' about their own worlds and relationships has drawn attention to children's situated competencies rather than adopting a deficit point of view of childhood (Aubrey et al., 2005: 115).

We now move on to discuss the practicalities of doing ethnographic research with young children, and analyze these in relation to children's participation.

ETHNOGRAPHY IN PRACTICE: A SPACE FOR YOUNG CHILDREN'S PARTICIPATION?

This section outlines some of the key issues of doing ethnographic research with young children in practice, namely matters of research access, the choice of methods available and questions around analysis. We link these issues to a discussion about the scope of children's participation within early childhood ethnographic research.

Since most ethnographic research with young children (that has been identified in this chapter) is conducted in institutional settings, researchers generally need to negotiate 'access' with gatekeepers (Heath et al., 2007; Powell and Smith, 2009; Troman, 1996). Often, procedural ethics, particularly informed consent, are a crucial element of these early stages of the research process, as will be discussed in more detail below. Gatekeepers may include parents/caregivers, professionals (e.g., teachers) and institutions (e.g., education authorities). The fact that young children are often ranked at the bottom of the access and consent 'hierarchy' (they are generally asked about their participation in the research last, after all other procedures have been followed; see, for example, Kustatscher (2014)) also serves to illustrate their structural positions in terms of power (Mayall, 1996). Such access procedures may also impact on the development of a participatory research design, since gatekeepers and institutional review boards often like to see a finalized research outline in advance of allowing researchers' interactions with children.

Once 'in the field' (although we would argue that negotiating access can allow ethnographic insights even before beginning the 'actual' fieldwork), ethnographers use a range of different methods. Traditionally, ethnographic research involves a combination of observations, informal conversations and interviews (mainly naturalistic rather than highly structured) (Mukherji and Albon, 2010: 74). Participant observation is generally considered to be the principal method in ethnography (and is indeed part of how ethnographers often define themselves). It involves participating in the social world of the participants of the research and 'reflecting on the products of that participation' (Hammersley and Atkinson, 2007: 15). Depending on the ethnographer's relationships with participants (Davis, 2000), there are various degrees of the researcher's 'participation', while observing. While some researchers have aimed at assuming a rather positivist position

of 'not disturbing the field', more recent reflexive ethnographic approaches recognize that such a detachment of the researcher is impossible (Mukherji and Albon, 2010: 70). However, while researchers may enter the field with a particular conceptualization of their degree of participation in mind, in practice this involves some negotiation with the children. Due to its long-term and immersive character, if carried out sensitively, ethnography is particularly suited to empowering young children to determine the degree of their engagement with the researcher, rather than just imposing the researcher's presence on them (Mukherji and Albon, 2010).

Data resulting from participant observation are traditionally captured in the form of field notes, whether handwritten or using technology such as tablets (Kustatscher, 2012). In addition to a 'running description of events' (Lofland, 1971: 232), field notes often include the researcher's own reflections and interpretations to differing degrees, and many ethnographers find it useful to keep a separate research diary in order to record and reflect on practical, emotional and intellectual difficulties (Punch, 2012).

Ethnographic research with children, particularly young children, has increasingly expanded its methodological repertoire in recent years (James et al., 1998), making use of the plethora of methods developed in the childhood studies field. Such methods may include task-based activities like drawings, mapping, stories, photography or role play, which are designed to engage with children's various interests and abilities. Particularly with young children, it has been argued that a multitude of methods can facilitate opportunities for different ways of communicating children's knowledge, such as through the 'Mosaic Approach' (Clark, 2011; Clark and Moss, 2001), and, thus, encourage children's participation in research (Christensen, 2004; Grover, 2004; Powell and Smith, 2009). However, the use of 'creative methods' needs to be considered carefully, and researchers need to reflect critically on their assumptions of what constitute 'appropriate' methods in relation to the children's preferences, abilities and social contexts (Holland et al., 2010; Hunleth, 2011; Punch, 2002). Participatory methods have also been critically discussed due to their potential of obscuring adult agendas whilst claiming to 'empower' children (Gallacher and Gallagher, 2008; see also Tisdall's chapter in this volume).

In the case of ethnography, children are often not involved in the decision about whether research will be conducted as an ethnographic study as they are usually only approached by the researcher once this decision has already been made.[1] However, during the fieldwork, children are able to participate in terms of negotiating the relationship and engagement with the researcher, direct the focus of the developing research and advise on the use of further research methods, depending on the researcher's sensitivity and flexibility (Christensen, 2004). Some researchers argue that the highest level of participation in research is for research to be 'chosen, carried out and disseminated by children themselves' (Tisdall et al., 2009: 214) and, thus, to involve children themselves as researchers (Kellett, 2010). In ethnography, this has been practiced to different extents. Clark and Moss (2001), for example, argue that research by children about children may provide more useful insights into children's lives than adult researchers' perspectives (although see Blaisdell (2012) for a critical view on this argument). Other researchers have involved former child research participants as ethnographers in later research, for example in Cheney's (2011) study on survival strategies of African orphans and vulnerable children.

The literature on research with children, including literature on ethnographic research more specifically, tends to pay relatively little attention to the process of analysis (Gallagher, 2009a). This may be due to the fact that, in ethnography, analysis is not an isolated stage of the research process, but an ongoing process beginning during fieldwork (Punch, 2009) and, therefore, not easily described in terms of 'how to' step-by-step guidelines. Instead, researchers need to identify a way of

analysis that is meaningful to their specific project in relation to its topic and context, their personal involvement and preferences, and of course the involvement of their participants. Ethnographic researchers generally adopt interpretivist or constructionist epistemological positions, and approaches to analysis may include thematic analysis, discourse analysis, content analysis or narrative analysis. Depending on the conceptualization of children's participation in research, they can be included to differing degrees during the analysis stage. For example, if children have been involved through taking photographs, many childhood studies researchers would argue that it is vital that their own explanations and interpretations of the pictures taken are sought (Barker and Weller, 2003).

However, the process of analysis also extends to the writing of ethnography, and it is therefore important to acknowledge that at this stage children do not participate but, instead, the researcher is key in shaping this process. However, engaging with children in the writing of ethnography, particularly in the shaping of this process, could be further explored and practiced by working closely with children. The next section will now take a closer look at the role of the researcher, in fieldwork and analysis, and the importance of power and relationships between researchers and participants.

POWER, ROLES AND REFLEXIVITY: CO-CONSTRUCTING PARTICIPATION

Ethnography is a fundamentally relational process, during which issues around power dynamics need to be considered and addressed. This is particularly evident when it comes to research with children (MacNaughton and Smith, 2005; Robinson and Kellett, 2004). Authors have highlighted that children are often marginalized in society by adults (for example, adults control children in various spheres of their lives) (Mayall, 2008) and this may be reflected within a researcher/adult–child/participant relationship. For example, a child may do things because of the presence of the adult researcher despite the child's own differing feelings (Greene and Hogan, 2005). However, other authors emphasize more dynamic, complex, context-specific and fluid power relations between adults/researchers and children/participants (Connolly, 2008; Konstantoni, 2011). Christensen (2004: 175) reminds us that 'in the process of research, power moves between different actors and different social positions, it is produced and negotiated in the social interactions of child to adult, child to child and adult to adult in the local setting of the research'. Power is also 'played out around the subject positions created through wider discourses on race, gender and childhood' (Connolly, 2008: 175), and children can actively resist and challenge power relationships between themselves and adults/researchers (Connolly, 2008).

Power relations are closely interlinked with the different roles that childhood ethnographers can assume in the field. The importance of the role of the researcher in ethnography – as the person who usually generates and analyses the data as well as writes up the research – has been recognized in ethnographic literature and the researcher has even been described as the 'key fieldwork tool' (Van Maanen et al., 1989: 5). In the literature on research with children, research roles have been the subject of much debate. For example, Mandell (1991) claimed that through adopting a 'least adult role', which involved joining the children in all activities in the playground (e.g., on swings and in the sandpit), she refused an adult authoritarian position and managed to become completely involved in the children's everyday life. This approach has been criticized, however, for assuming that structural power relations between adults and children can be dissolved through the researcher's individual behaviour (Mayall, 2008: 110). Other authors have advocated the role of an 'unusual adult', who 'is seriously interested in understanding how the social world looks from children's perspective but without making a dubious attempt to

be a child' (Christensen, 2004: 174), or the role of a 'friend' (Fine and Sandstrom, 1988). The role of an 'incompetent adult' who learns from the children about their lives and contexts, can allow the recognition of children's expertise, and may be further emphasized if ethnographers are foreign or speak a different language (Corsaro and Molinari, 2000: 180; Gregory and Ruby, 2011). This is similar to Mukherji and Albon's more general attitude of 'not knowing' (2010: 76), which requires children to explain to the researcher what they are doing. Other authors have highlighted the fact that both children and adults have multiple identities and challenge the adult–child binary (Tisdall et al., 2009). Davis and colleagues (2008: 213, 215) refer to more complex and contrasting roles like those of the 'friend/mediator/entertainer' and 'authoritarian/non-authoritarian/helper'.

In our own research, we have experienced such multiple and sometimes conflicting roles, for example as 'researcher/helper/friend/"unusual" adult' (see examples in Konstantoni, 2011: 92). We found that the particular dynamics at play in the institutional contexts of our research shaped the roles that we were able (or unable) to assume. In educational contexts, for example, researchers can be drawn into the authoritarian roles of 'teaching' or 'supervising' adults. While we found it helpful to reflect on the roles that we were planning to adopt prior to beginning fieldwork, in practice our situational roles were co-constructed between ourselves, the children and other participants in the context. Our roles also changed and evolved over the course of the research, allowing insights into how we were perceived by the children and how this impacted on our data (Hammersley and Atkinson, 2007).

In order to account for the multiple ways in which our positions as researchers and related dynamics of power and relationships shape the findings drawn from ethnographic research, there has been a call for reflexive research approaches (e.g., Clifford and Marcus, 1986; Van Maanen, 1988). Reflexivity has been described as a process of 'self-analysis and political awareness' (Callaway, 1992: 33) and a 'critical gaze' towards oneself (Finlay, 2003: 3). Reflexive approaches imply a view of research data as co-constructed and, therefore, argue for the presentation of research findings not as 'truth' or 'fact', but as situated, subjective and context-specific. In practice, reflexivity entails a process of 'detachment, internal dialogue and constant (and intensive) scrutiny' of what we know as researchers and how we have come to know it (Hertz, 1997: vii–viii). This means that reflexivity permeates the whole research process (Davis, 2000; Hertz, 1997) and requires researchers to examine critically their impact on the research, their interpretations (Finlay, 2003) and any personal preconceptions (Davis et al., 2008). While the notion of validity (which is concerned with the integrity and generalizability of findings) has been challenged in qualitative studies (Bryman, 2004), some authors suggest that reflexivity provides a tool to enable the production of valid and legitimate qualitative research (Pillow, 2003).

However, reflexive approaches have not been without critique. Reflexive researchers have been accused of navel-gazing, self-indulgence and narcissism, positioned as privileged academics worrying over unimportant representational issues, and questioned on whether 'all this self-reflexivity [will actually] produce better research?' (Patai, 1994: 69). While there is an agreement among most qualitative researchers that 'we do not escape from the consequences of our positions by talking about them endlessly' (Patai, 1994: 70), there are debates on '*how* it is we go about talking about our positions, that is how we practice reflexivity, and how these practices impact, open up, or limit the possibilities for critical representations' (Pillow, 2003: 177, original emphasis).

In childhood ethnography, common techniques to enable a reflexive research stance include the use of a reflexive diary (in which a record is kept of thoughts, feelings, theoretical ideas, notes on how the researcher's presence might have impacted on the environment, notes of the difficulties/challenges that the researcher has faced), the use of various methods (which could assist in cross-checking data or gaining further information), observing and challenging observed patterns, asking for participants' interpretations and having days away from the field (Konstantoni, 2011). Distancing oneself from the field involves both a 'step back' from what is happening in the actual interactions of the fieldwork and paying particular attention to how researchers themselves become part of and contribute to the very context that they set out to study (Connolly, 2008: 174). Such practices can aid a reflexive analytical stance and can be expressed in the writing of ethnographic research by enabling less authoritative and more self-critical texts (Finlay, 2003) and by 'providing multiple voices which may be contrary, complimentary or from different contexts' (Konstantoni, 2011: 79).

Thus, while there are no clear guidelines and tick boxes on how to do ethnographic research in a reflexive way, it is a process which questions our own interpretations and knowledge production, 'pushes towards the unfamiliar' and challenges the representations we come to, while at the same time acknowledging the political need to represent and find meaning (Pillow, 2003: 192). These are particularly important issues in research with children, given the above-described debates on power relations and roles in the research process.

RESEARCH ETHICS AND PARTICIPATION: THE IMPORTANCE OF RELATIONSHIPS

Ethics is an important part of research and tends to be especially highlighted in research with children (Alderson and Morrow, 2011; Morrow and Richards, 1996; see also Farrell's chapter, this volume). Ethical considerations in ethnographic research involve issues around anonymity, confidentiality and informed consent (Farrell, 2005; Tisdall et al., 2009).

General procedures to ensure confidentiality include keeping data stored securely and anonymized, and removing all identifying materials in publications and presentations about the research (Coady, 2010). Ethnographic researchers generally use pseudonyms in order to conceal the identity of their participants, and some childhood researchers have made this process more transparent and participatory by asking children to choose their own pseudonyms (Gallagher, 2009b). However, although most consent forms promise confidentiality and anonymity to participants, it is important to make children aware in advance that there are exceptions in certain circumstances (such as in the case of concerns about the child's safety). In research with young children, audiovisual methods (e.g., photographs, video, audio) are often used and this raises particular challenges in relation to anonymity. Even if the consent of the children has been sought at the time of the research, they might not approve of their pictures still being used when they are older (Coady, 2010), and therefore it is important for researchers to consider and make transparent their intentions of how such materials will be made publicly available.

A key aspect of research ethics extensively discussed in ethnographic research, and in research with children in particular, is the notion of informed consent. Informed consent refers to 'the invisible activity of evaluating information and making a decision, and the visible act of signifying the decision' (Alderson and Morrow, 2011: 101). The *informed* aspect of consent refers to participants' full understanding of the research content and process. This aspect has been criticized as a construct which is impossible to realize due to the open-ended and unpredictable nature of qualitative research (researchers themselves may not know where the research process will lead, much less participants) (Alderson and Morrow, 2011; Gallagher, 2009c).

Particularly in relation to research with children, there are also tensions between the childhood studies and children's rights fields that promote children's active participation and competence, on the one hand, and the ethical frameworks and institutional review boards which view children as 'vulnerable' and in need of protection, on the other (Bell, 2008; Kustatscher, 2014; Powell and Smith, 2009; Skelton, 2008). There is also a tension between the rather abstract and contractual way in which consent procedures are constructed by institutional review boards and the reality of *doing* research in practice, which may be 'messy' and produce unpredictable ethical challenges (Guillemin and Gillam, 2004). Although it is impossible to anticipate such challenges, it is useful for early childhood ethnographers to prepare by considering the potential scenarios that may produce ethical dilemmas (e.g., How will the researcher react in case of concerns about a child's safety? Which child protection procedures are in place? How can the research be realized if some children (or some parents/carers or staff) withdraw their consent? How inclusive is the research design of children's diverse backgrounds and abilities?).

Providing *information* about the research project can present challenges, not just because of the open-ended nature of ethnographic research, but also because of the complexities of appropriately adapting information to the participants' competencies and age. This may include written, visual or verbal forms of communicating information. Particularly with young children, or children in environments where writing is not a common form of communication, alternative methods of conveying information (such as photographs or video vignettes) may be useful (Graham et al., 2013).

In her research in a nursery setting, for example, Konstantoni (2011: 106) used a children's leaflet in the form of a book which was created with the help of the educators. Happy and sad faces, a stop card and a question mark were also created in order to support consent procedures and were kept in a commonly agreed place in the story corner. Informed and written consent was secured by the children, who were asked to create their own approval mark or to use the stamp that was provided under the smiley or sad face. Consent, however, was an ongoing process with the children, as with the adults, by being reminded that participation in the research was voluntary and how they could stop or join whenever they wanted to (for further discussion on this, see Konstantoni, 2011). As a way for the children to express their ongoing consent, Kustatscher (2013, 2014) introduced movable magnetic photographs in a primary classroom setting. The magnets consisted of the children's photographs and could be moved back and forth between an opt-in and an opt-out surface in the classroom at any time. While they fulfilled their purpose to some extent, they also pointed towards shortcomings of the contractual consent model. For example, it became clear that participation in research may not be conceptualized only in terms of the two extremes of 'opting in' or 'opting out', but that there can be grey areas in between. Children may want to interact with the researcher, but not want notes written down about their interactions. Children may also want to take part in certain activities of the research, but not others.

It is therefore important to remember that researchers need to be flexible with regards to ethics 'in practice'. Warming (2005: 62) argues that 'the most ethical practice might turn out to be unethical' if researchers fail to listen to and adapt to their participants. Especially in research with young children or babies, researchers need to be sensitive at all times throughout the fieldwork in order to pick up on children's ways of giving or withdrawing consent. Young children may withdraw their consent, for example, by being quiet, running away, crying, refusing to engage with any of the research materials or the researcher, or being angry (Langston et al., 2004). If the children do not know the researcher well, it can also be useful to involve the insights of parents/carers or staff (Mukherji and Albon, 2010). The relational aspect of ethnographic fieldwork is key to issues around informed consent, and through

being sensitive and flexible in relation to children's wishes researchers can allow them to actively participate in research on their own terms.

IMPLICATIONS FOR POLICY AND PRACTICE

James (2007: 246), drawing on Qvortrup (2000), states that ethnography has become the 'new orthodoxy in childhood research' due to its possibility of allowing children a 'direct voice and participation in the production of sociological data' (Prout and James, 1997: 8). Indeed, ethnographic studies of childhood have proliferated over the past two decades and there is now a wealth of literature illuminating children's everyday lives in different contexts and demonstrating their agency in co-constructing their lives. However, some questions arise in relation to this trend with respect to implications for policy and practice.

Qvortrup (2000: 78) argues that the tendency towards ethnographic research in the childhood studies field has shifted the sociological gaze towards a 'micro-orientation', neglecting the field's occupation with macro aspects of childhood (there are of course notable exceptions of large-scale studies, such as the Young Lives study (2014), an international study on childhood poverty). This raises questions about the potential policy impact that this kind of research can have, given current 'evidence hierarchies' of national and global policy makers which often privilege quantitative over qualitative research (Denzin, 2009). At the same time, many current ethnographic researchers subscribe to children's rights and participation value frameworks (see Tisdall, this volume) and are explicit about their intentions of driving policy development through their work. It can also be argued that ethnography is particularly useful in drawing attention to the various ways in which structural circumstances impact on children's individual lives, and therefore allows for critical reflection on universal policy frameworks.

However, while one of ethnography's advantages is exactly this detailed illumination of children's lives, it is also important to reflect on *which* children are given a 'voice' through ethnographic research, and which are being left out. With regards to early childhood, there is still a lack of research (and methodological debate) on and with very young participants – babies and infants – due to the perceived difficulty of gaining their first-hand perspectives (Thorne, 2008; Warming, 2011). The literature identified for this chapter has also showed that many early childhood ethnographies take place in some form of institution (nurseries, schools, day care centers, hospitals, residential care). This institutionalization, characteristic of the lives of many young children, particularly in the Global North, reifies early childhood as a specific age group and social category with implications for the representation of young children in research. In research which focuses on institutional settings, the lives of those children who are not institutionalized (as well as the aspects of children's lives beyond their time spent in institutions) may escape the ethnographic perspective, for example very young children or groups of children who are marginalized or who for different reasons may not be part of institutions (e.g., travelers). Particularly in the Global South, early childhood may be institutionalized to a lesser extent, and it may be understood in more relational terms rather than as a clearly defined and bounded social group. Studies in the Global South which include young children, alongside their families and communities, in ethnographic research, were not identified as 'early childhood ethnographies' for this chapter. This raises questions about the representation of young children in ethnographic research, and social research more widely, and illustrates that research is not only framed by but also contributes to particular understandings of childhood. Thus, reflecting on which young children are included in ethnographic research, and which

are not, also puts questions about marginality and the production of knowledge more generally on the agenda (van Blerk and Kesby, 2009).

CONCLUSION

This chapter has outlined the historical development and underlying principles of ethnographic research approaches, and their particular place in shaping the field of childhood studies. In relation to early childhood, ethnography has been helpful in critically reflecting on conceptualizations of childhood and particularly children's place and participation in research. Childhood ethnography has come a long way, in both epistemological and methodological developments, since early ethnographic studies in the twentieth century. A reflexive stance, with regards to the researcher's roles and relationships with participants, has become an accepted key practice of childhood ethnography. Childhood ethnographers have developed and made use of a plethora of methods. However, this chapter has also emphasized critical perspectives when it comes to the use of 'creative' methods and particularly assumptions about what constitute 'appropriate' methods in research with young children. Similar questions are important in deciding upon what constitutes 'ethical' ethnographic research with young children, for example in considering how information can be conveyed in a meaningful way and how children can be enabled to express their ongoing consent.

While the use of ethnography has contributed significantly to the development of the childhood studies field, researchers need to be reflexive about which groups of children are 'participating' and how ethnography can be developed in order to continue to drive the field further. In this chapter, we have reiterated the importance of relationships among researchers, participants, gatekeepers and institutions, for the ethnographic research process as a whole and more specifically for questions of ethics, the direction of research and data generation. Researchers make sense of children's worlds through relationships, and questions of power are crucial to consider in this context. We have showed that children's participation in ethnographic research (and beyond) is facilitated through these relationships. Ethnographic researchers need to be sensitive and flexible in their interactions with participants, and ethnography's reflexive attention to relational aspects holds the potential to contribute to and advance discussions around children's participation more widely.

FURTHER READING

James, A. (2007) 'Ethnography in the study of children and childhood', in P. Atkinson, A. Coffey, S. Delamont, J. Lofland and L. Lofland (eds), *Handbook of Ethnography*. London: SAGE. pp. 246–58.

Kustatscher, M. (2014) Informed consent in school-based ethnography – using visual magnets to explore participation, power and research relationships. *International Journal of Child, Youth and Family Studies*, 5 (4.1): 686–701.

Mukherji, P., and Albon, D. (2010) *Research Methods in Early Childhood: An Introductory Guide*. London: SAGE.

QUESTIONS FOR REFLECTION

1   What 'data' do you aim to produce with your ethnographic research? Which methods do you intend to employ?

2   How do you conceptualize children's participation in your research? What are the benefits and challenges of children's participation in ethnographic research?

3   What will your official role in the research context be (e.g., researcher, authoritative adult, unusual adult, helper)? How will different roles impact on the content and direction of your research?

4   Before beginning your ethnographic research, what ethical dilemmas can you anticipate and how would you resolve them? For example,

how would you react in the case of concerns about a child's safety, or if you witness bullying? Do you know the procedures in place for appropriate responses to concerns about child protection?

5   What challenges in relation to seeking informed consent can you anticipate, both in relation to children, parents/carers and others involved in the research? Consider, for example, your potential responses to the following scenario: you are observing a critical interaction between a group of children, whose parental consent you have, except for one child. What ethical issues arise and how do you deal with them?

NOTE

1   One exception is Emond's (2005) ethnographic study with older children (12–18) in residential care, in which case the young people had suggested that the best way to know more about their experiences would be for the researcher to come and live with them.

REFERENCES

Aarsand, P. A. (2007) 'Computer and video games in family life: the digital divide as a resource in intergenerational interactions', *Childhood*, 14(2): 235–56.

Alderson, P., and Morrow, V. (2011) *The Ethics of Research with Children and Young People: A Practical Handbook*. London: SAGE.

Atkinson, P., and Hammersley, M. (1994) 'Ethnography and participant observation', in N. K. Denzin and Y. Lincoln (eds), *Handbook of Qualitative Research*. London: SAGE. pp. 248–61.

Aubrey, C., David, T., Godfrey, R., and Thompson, L. (2005) *Early Childhood Educational Research: Issues in Methodology and Ethics*. London: RoutledgeFalmer.

Barker, J., and Weller, S. (2003) '"Is it fun?" Developing children-centred research methods', *International Journal of Sociology and Social Policy*, 23(1/2): 33–58.

Beazley, H. (2003) 'Voices from the margins: street children's subcultures in Indonesia', *Children's Geographies*, 1(2): 181–200.

Becker, H. S. (1963) *Outsiders: Studies in the Sociology of Deviance*. New York: The Free Press.

Bell, N. (2008) 'Ethics in child research: rights, reason and responsibilities', *Children's Geographies*, 6(1): 7–20.

Blaisdell, C. (2012) 'Inclusive or exclusive participation: paradigmatic tensions in the Mosaic approach and implications for childhood research', *Childhoods Today*, 6(1): 1–18.

Boyden, J., and de Berry, J. (2005) *Children and Youth on the Front Line: Ethnography, Armed Conflict and Displacement*. Oxford: Berghahn Books.

Bryman, A. (2004) *Social Research Methods*, 2nd edn. Oxford: University Press.

Callaway, H. (1992) 'Ethnography and experience: gender implications in fieldwork and texts', in J. Okely and H. Callaway (eds), *Anthropology and Autobiography*. New York: Routledge. pp. 29–49.

Cheney, K. E. (2011) 'Children as ethnographers: reflections on the importance of participatory research in assessing orphans' needs', *Childhood*, 18(2): 166–79.

Christensen, P. H. (2004) 'Children's participation in ethnographic research: issues of power and representation', *Children and Society*, 18(2): 165–76.

Clark, A. (2011) 'Multimodal map making with young children: exploring ethnographic and participatory methods', *Qualitative Research*, 11(3): 311–30.

Clark, A., and Moss, P. (2001) *Listening to Young Children: The MOSAIC Approach*. London: National Children's Bureau.

Clifford, J., and Marcus, G. (eds) (1986) *Writing Culture: The Poetics and Politics of Ethnography*. Berkeley, CA: University of California Press.

Coady, M. (2010) 'Ethics in early childhood research', in G. MacNaughton, S. A. Rolfe and I. Siraj-Blatchford (eds), *Doing Early Childhood Research: International Perspectives on Theory and Practice*, 2nd edn. Maidenhead: Open University Press. pp. 73–84.

Cole, J., and Durham, D. L. (2007) *Generations and Globalization: Youth, Age, and Family in the New World Economy*. Bloomington, IN: Indiana University Press.

Connolly, P. (1998) *Racism, Gender Identities, and Young Children: Social Relations in a Multi-ethnic, Inner-city Primary School*. London: Routledge.

Connolly, P. (2000) 'Racism and young girls' peer-group relations: the experiences of South Asian girls', *Sociology*, 34(3): 499–519.

Connolly, P. (2003) 'The development of young children's ethnic identities: implications for early years practice', in C. Vincent (ed.), *Social Justice, Education and Identity*. London: RoutledgeFalmer. pp. 165–82.

Connolly, P. (2008) 'Race, gender and critical reflexivity in research with young children', in P. Christensen and A. James (eds), *Research with Children: Perspectives and Practices*, 2nd edn. Oxford: Routledge. pp. 173–88.

Corsaro, W. A., and Molinari, L. (2000) 'Entering and observing in children's worlds: a reflection on a longitudinal ethnography of early education in Italy', in P. Christensen and A. James (eds), *Research with Children: Perspectives and Practices*. London/New York: RoutledgeFalmer. pp. 179–200.

Dau, E. (1999) *Child's Play: Revisiting Play in Early Childhood Settings*. Sydney, NSW: MacLennan and Petty.

Davies, B. (2003) *Frogs and Snails and Feminist Tales: Preschool Children and Gender*. Cresskill, NJ: Hampton Press.

Davis, J. M. (2000) 'Disability studies as ethnographic research and text: research strategies and roles for promoting social change?', *Disability and Society*, 15(2): 191–206.

Davis, J., Watson, N., and Cunningham-Burley, S. (2008) 'Disabled children, ethnography and unspoken understandings: the collaborative construction of diverse identities', in P. Christensen and A. James (eds), *Research with Children: Perspectives and Practices*, 2nd edn. Oxford: Routledge. pp. 220–38.

Denzin, N.K. (2009) 'The elephant in the living room: or extending the conversation about the politics of evidence', *Qualitative Research*, 9(2): 139–60.

De Waal, A., and Argenti, N. (2002) *Young Africa: Realising the Rights of Children and Youth*. Trenton, NJ: Africa World Press.

Emond, R. (2002) *Learning from their Lessons: A Study of Young People in Residential Care and their Experiences of Education*. Dublin: The Children's Research Centre.

Emond, R. (2005) 'Ethnographic research methods with children and young people', in S. Greene and D. Hogan (eds), *Researching*

Children's Experience: Approaches and Methods. London: SAGE. pp. 123–40.

Evaldson, A., and Corsaro, W. A. (1998) 'Play and games in the peer cultures of preschool and preadolescent children: an interpretative approach', *Childhood*, 5(4): 377–402.

Farrell, A. (2005) *Ethical Research with Children*. Maidenhead: Open University Press.

Fine, G.A., and Sandstrom, K.L. (1988) *Knowing Children: Participant Observation with Minors*. London: SAGE.

Finlay, L. (2003) 'The reflexive journey: mapping multiple routes', in L. Finlay and B. Gough (eds), *Reflexivity: A Practical Guide for Researchers in Health and Social Sciences*. Oxford: Blackwell. pp. 3–20.

Gallacher, L.A., and Gallagher, M. (2008) 'Methodological immaturity in childhood research? Thinking through "participatory methods"', *Childhood*, 15(4): 499–516.

Gallagher, M. (2009a) 'Data collection and analysis', in E. K. M. Tisdall, J. Davis and M. Gallagher (eds), *Researching with Children and Young People: Research Design, Methods and Analysis*. London: SAGE. pp. 65–127.

Gallagher, M. (2009b) 'Researching the geography of power in a primary school', in E. K. M. Tisdall, J. Davis and M. Gallagher (eds), *Researching with Children and Young People: Research Design, Methods and Analysis*. London: SAGE. pp. 57–64.

Gallagher, M. (2009c) 'Ethics', in E. K. M. Tisdall, J. Davis and M. Gallagher (eds), *Researching with Children and Young People: Research Design, Methods and Analysis*. London: SAGE. pp. 11–64.

Geertz, C. (1973) *The Interpretation of Culture: Selected Essays*. London: Hutchison.

Goffman, E. (1961) *Asylums: Essays on the Social Situation of Mental Patients and Other Inmates*. New York: Doubleday.

Gordon, T., Holland, J., and Lahelma, E. (2001) 'Ethnographic research in educational settings', in P. Atkinson, A. Coffey, S. Delamont, J. Lofland and L. Lofland (eds), *Handbook of Ethnography*. London: SAGE. pp. 188–203.

Gough, K. V., and Franch, M. (2005) 'Spaces of the street: socio-spatial mobility and exclusion of youth in Recife', *Children's Geographies*, 3(2): 149–66.

Graham, A., Powell, M., Taylor, N., Anderson, D., and Fitzgerald, R. (2013) *Ethical Research Involving Children*. Florence: UNICEF Office of Research – Innocenti.

Greene, S., and Hogan, D. (eds) (2005) *Researching Children's Experience: Approaches and Methods*. London: SAGE.

Gregory, E., and Ruby, M. (2011) 'The "insider/outsider" dilemma of ethnography: working with young children and their families in cross-cultural contexts', *Journal of Early Childhood Research*, 9(2): 162–74.

Grover, S. (2004) '"Why won't they listen to us?" On giving power and voice to children participating in social research', *Childhood*, 11(1): 81–93.

Guillemin, M., and Gillam, L. (2004) 'Ethics, reflexivity, and "ethically important moments" in research', *Qualitative Inquiry*, 10(2): 261–80.

Hammersley, M., and Atkinson, P. (2007) *Ethnography: Principles in Practice*. London: Routledge.

Heath, S., Charles, V., Crow, G., and Wiles, R. (2007) 'Informed consent, gatekeepers and go-betweens: negotiating consent in child- and youth-orientated institutions', *British Educational Research Journal*, 33(3): 403–17.

Hecht, T. (1998) *At Home in the Street: Street Children of Northeast Brazil*. Cambridge: Cambridge University Press.

Hertz, R. (1997) 'Introduction: reflexivity and voice', in R. Hertz (ed.), *Reflexivity and Voice*. London: SAGE. pp. vii–xviii.

Holland, S., Renold, E., Ross, N. J., and Hillman, A. (2010) 'Power, agency and participatory agendas: a critical exploration of young people's engagement in participative qualitative research', *Childhood*, 17(3): 360–75.

Hunleth, J. (2011) 'Beyond on or with: questioning power dynamics and knowledge production in "child-oriented" research methodology', *Childhood*, 18(1): 81–93.

James, A. (1993) *Childhood Identities: Self and Social Relationships in the Experience of the Child*. Edinburgh: Edinburgh University Press.

James, A. (2007) 'Ethnography in the study of children and childhood', in P. Atkinson, A. Coffey, S. Delamont, J. Lofland and L. Lofland (eds), *Handbook of Ethnography*. London: SAGE. pp. 246–58.

James, A., and Prout, A. (1997) *Constructing and Reconstructing Childhood: Contemporary Issues in the Sociological Study of Childhood*. London: RoutledgeFalmer.

James, A., Jenks, C., and Prout, A. (1998) *Theorizing Childhood*. Cambridge: Polity Press.

Johnson, G. A., and Vindrola-Padros, C. (2014) '"It's for the best": child movement in search of health in Njabini, Kenya', *Children's Geographies*, 12(2): 219–31.

Kantor, R., and Whalley, K. (1998) 'New ideas and existing frameworks: learning from Reggio Emilia', in C. P. Edwards, L. Gandini and G. E. Forman (eds), *The Hundred Languages of Children: The Reggio Emilia Approach – Advanced Reflections*. Norwood, NJ: Ablex. pp. 313–33.

Kellett, M. (2010) 'Small shoes, big steps! Empowering children as active researchers', *American Journal of Community Psychology*, 46(1/2): 195–203.

Konstantoni, K. (2011) Young Children's Perceptions and Constructions of Social Identities and Social Implications: Promoting Social Justice in Early Childhood. PhD thesis, University of Edinburgh.

Konstantoni, K. (2012) 'Children's peer relationships and social identities: exploring cases of young children's agency and complex interdependencies from the Minority World', *Children's Geographies*, 10(3): 337–46.

Konstantoni, K. (2013) 'Children's rights-based approaches: the challenges of listening to taboo/discriminatory issues and moving beyond children's participation', *International Journal of Early Years Education*, 21(4): 362–74.

Kustatscher, M. (2012) 'New technology and data generation: using an iPad in school-based research with children', paper presented at the BERA Annual Conference, University of Manchester, 4–6 September.

Kustatscher, M. (2013) 'Using magnets to visualise informed consent in school-based fieldwork with children', Ethical Research Involving Children (ERIC) website. Available at: http://childethics.com/wp-content/uploads/2013/10/ERIC_Compendium_Case-Studies_Informed-Consent_Marlies-Kustatscher.pdf

Kustatscher, M. (2014) 'Informed consent in school-based ethnography – using visual magnets to explore participation, power and research relationships', *International Journal of Child, Youth and Family Studies*, 5 (4.1): 686–701.

Kustatscher, M. (2015) *Exploring Young Children's Social Identities: Performing Social Class, Gender and Ethnicity in Primary School*, Unpublished PhD Thesis: The University of Edinburgh.

Langston, A., Abbot, L., Lewis, V., and Kellett, M. (2004) 'Early childhood', in S. Fraser, V. Lewis, S. Ding, M. Kellett and C. Robinson (eds), *Doing Research With Children and Young People*. London: SAGE. pp. 147–60.

Levinson, B. A., Foley, D. E., and Holland, D. C. (1996) *The Cultural Production of the Educated Person: Critical Ethnographies of Schooling and Local Practice*. New York: State University of New York Press.

Liebel, M. (2004) *A Will of Their Own: Cross-Cultural Perspectives on Working Children*. London/ New York: Zed Books.

Lofland, J. (1971) 'Field notes', in C. Seale (ed.), *Social Research Methods: A Reader*. New York: Routledge. pp. 232–5.

MacNaughton, G., and Smith, K. (2005) 'Transforming research ethics: the choices and challenges of researching with children', in A. Farrell (ed.), *Ethical Research with Children*. Buckingham: Open University Press. pp. 112–23.

Malinowski, B. (1922) *Argonauts of the Western Pacific: An Account of Native Enterprise and Adventure in the Archipelagoes of Melanesian New Guinea*. London: Routledge and Kegan Paul.

Mandell, N. (1991) 'The least-adult role in studying children', in F. C. Waksler (ed.), *Studying the Social Worlds of Children: Sociological Readings*. London: Falmer Press. pp. 38–59.

Mayall, B. (1996) *Children, Health and the Social Order*. Buckingham: Open University Press.

Mayall, B. (2008) 'Conversations with children: working with generational issues', in P. Christensen and A. James (eds), *Research with Children: Perspectives and Practices*, 2nd edn. Oxford: Routledge. pp. 109–24.

Mead, G. H. (1934) *Mind, Self, and Society*. Chicago: University of Chicago Press.

Mead, M. (1928) *Coming of Age in Samoa: A Psychological Study of Primitive Youth for Western Civilisation*. New York: Perennial Classics.

Morrow, V., and Richards, M. (1996) 'The ethics of social research with children: an overview', *Children and Society*, 10(2): 90–105.

Mukherji, P., and Albon, D. (2010) *Research Methods in Early Childhood: An Introductory Guide*. London: SAGE.

Patai, D. (1994) 'When method becomes power', in A. Gitlin (ed.), *Power and Method: Political Activism and Educational Research (Critical Social Thought)*. New York: Routledge. pp. 61–73.

Pillow, W. S. (2003) 'Confession, catharsis, or cure? Rethinking the uses of reflexivity as methodological power', *International Journal of Qualitative Studies in Education*, 16(2): 175–96.

Powell, M. A., and Smith, A. B. (2009) 'Children's participation rights in research', *Childhood*, 16(1): 124–42.

Prout, A., and James, A. (1997) 'A new paradigm for the sociology of childhood? Provenance, promise and problems', in A. James and A. Prout (eds), *Constructing and Reconstructing Childhood: Contemporary Issues in the Sociological Study of Childhood*. London: RoutledgeFalmer. pp. 7–32.

Punch, S. (2001) 'Household division of labour: generation, gender, age, birth order and sibling composition', *Work, Employment and Society*, 15(4): 803–23.

Punch, S. (2002) 'Research with children: the same or different from research with adults?', *Childhood*, 9(3): 321–41.

Punch, S. (2009) 'Case study: researching childhoods in rural Bolivia', in E. K. M. Tisdall, J. Davis and M. Gallagher (eds), *Researching with Children and Young People: Research Design, Methods and Analysis*. London: SAGE. pp. 89–96.

Punch, S. (2012) 'Hidden struggles of fieldwork: exploring the role and use of field diaries', *Emotion, Space and Society*, 5(2): 86–93.

Punch, S., and Sugden, F. (2013) 'Work, education and out-migration among children and youth in Upland Asia: changing patterns of labour and ecological knowledge in an era of globalisation', *Local Environment*, 18(3): 255–70.

Punch, S., and Tisdall, E. K. M. (2012) 'Exploring children and young people's relationships across majority and minority worlds', *Children's Geographies*, 10(3): 241–8.

Qvortrup, J. (2000) 'Macroanalysis of childhood', in P. Christensen and A. James (eds), *Research with Children: Perspectives and Practices*. London: Falmer. pp. 77–98.

Renold, E. (2005) *Girls, Boys and Junior Sexualities: Exploring Children's Gender and Sexual Relations in the Primary School*. London: RoutledgeFalmer.

Robinson, C., and Kellett, M. (2004) 'Power', in S. Fraser, V. Lewis, S. Ding, M. Kellett and C. Robinson (eds), *Doing Research With Children and Young People*. London: SAGE. pp. 81–96.

Scheper-Hughes, N., and Sargent, C. F. (1998) *Small Wars: The Cultural Politics of Childhood*. London: University of California Press.

Scott, K. (2002) '"You want to be a girl and not my friend": African-American/Black girls' play activities with and without boys', *Childhood*, 9(4): 397–414.

Silverman, D. (2011) *Interpreting Qualitative Data: A Guide to the Principles of Qualitative Research*. London: SAGE.

Siraj-Blatchford, I. (2010) 'An ethnographic approach to researching young children's learning', in G. MacNaughton, S. A. Rolfe and I. Siraj-Blatchford (eds), *Doing Early Childhood Research: International Perspectives on Theory and Practice*, 2nd edn. London: Allen & Unwin. pp. 271–90.

Skelton, T. (2008) 'Research with children and young people: exploring the tensions between ethics, competence and participation', *Children's Geographies*, 6(1): 21–36.

Strandell, H. (1997) 'Doing reality with play: play as a children's resource in organizing everyday life in daycare centres', *Childhood*, 4(4): 445–64.

Sylva, K., Siraj-Blatchford, I., Melhuish, E., Sammons, P., Taggart, B., and Evans, E. (1999) *Characteristics of the Centres in the EPPE Sample: Observational Profiles*. Technical Paper 6. London: Institute of Education and DfEE.

Thorne, B. (1993) *Gender Play: Girls and Boys in School*. New Brunswick, NJ: Rutgers University Press.

Thorne, B. (2008) 'What's in an age name?', *Childhood*, 15(4): 435–9.

Tisdall, E. K. M. (2012) 'The challenge and challenging of childhood studies? Learning from disability studies and research with disabled children', *Children and Society*, 26(3): 181–91.

Tisdall, E. K. M., and Punch, S. (2012) 'Not so "new"? Looking critically at childhood studies', *Children's Geographies*, 10(3): 249–64.

Tisdall, E.K.M., Davis, J. M., and Gallagher, M. (2009) *Researching with Children and Young People: Research Design, Methods and Analysis*. London: SAGE.

Troman, G. (1996) 'No entry signs: educational change and some problems encountered in negotiating entry to educational settings', *British Educational Research Journal*, 22(1): 71–88.

Van Ausdale, D., and Feagin, J. R. (2001) *The First R: How Children Learn Race and Racism*. Lanham, MD; Oxford: Rowman & Littlefield.

Van Blerk, L. (2005) 'Negotiating spatial identities: mobile perspectives on street life in Uganda', *Children's Geographies*, 3(1): 5–21.

Van Blerk, L., and Kesby, M. (eds) (2009) *Doing Children's Geographies: Methodological Issues in Research with Young People*. New York: Routledge.

Van Maanen, J. (1988) *Tales of the Field: On Writing Ethnography*. Chicago: University of Chicago Press.

Van Maanen, J., Manning, P., and Miller, M. (1989) 'Editor's introduction', in J. Hunt (ed.), *Psychoanalytic Aspects of Fieldwork* (Vol. 18, Qualitative Research Methods). London: SAGE. pp. 5–6.

Warming, H. (2005) 'Participant observation: a way to learn about children's perspectives', in A. Clark, A. Kjorholt and P. Moss (eds), *Beyond Listening: Children's Perspectives on Early Childhood Services*. Bristol: Policy Press. pp. 51–70.

Warming, H. (2011) 'Getting under their skins? Accessing young children's perspectives through ethnographic fieldwork', *Childhood*, 18(1): 39–53.

Woodhead, M. (1998) *Children's Perspectives on their Working Lives: A Participatory Study in Bangladesh, Ethiopia, The Philippines, Guatemala, El Salvador and Nicaragua*. Stockholm: Rädda Barnen.

Young Lives (2014) *Young Lives: An International Study of Childhood Poverty*, 5th edn, April. Colchester: UK Data Archive (www.younglives.org.uk/).

15

Narrative Inquiry: Conducting Research in Early Childhood

D. Jean Clandinin, Janice Huber, Jinny Menon,
M. Shaun Murphy and Cindy Swanson

INTRODUCTION

Narrative inquiry, the study of experience as storied phenomena, is used to study the experiences of young children, families, other caregivers, healthcare workers including physicians and nurses, social workers, and early childhood teachers. In this chapter, we foreground the definition of narrative inquiry used in the *Handbook of Narrative Inquiry: Mapping a Methodology* (Clandinin, 2007). The definition, as follows, was originally developed in 2006:

> People shape their daily lives by stories of who they and others are and as they interpret their past in terms of these stories. Story, in the current idiom, is a portal through which a person enters the world and by which their experience of the world is made personally meaningful. Narrative inquiry, the study of experience as story, then, is first and foremost a way of thinking about experience. Narrative inquiry as a methodology entails a view of the phenomenon. To use narrative inquiry methodology is to adopt a particular view of experience as phenomenon under study. (Connelly and Clandinin, 2006: 477)

This definition of narrative inquiry shows narrative inquiry as a methodology rather than a set of methods for data collection and analysis and draws attention to the methodological purpose as one of studying experience as a narrative phenomenon. Clandinin and Rosiek (2007) explained how the narrative inquiry conception of experience builds on Dewey's (1938) philosophy of experience:

> Framed within this view of experience, the focus of narrative inquiry is not only on an individual's experience but also on the social, cultural, and institutional narratives within which individuals' experiences are constituted, shaped, expressed, and enacted. Narrative inquirers study the individual's experience in the world, an experience that is storied both in the living and telling and that can be studied by listening, observing, living alongside another, and writing, and interpreting texts. (pp. 42–3)

The view of experience underlying narrative inquiry flows from the above definition in that experience is understood as relational, continuous, and both personal and social. While stories are personal and unique to each person, larger cultural, social, familial, and institutional narratives shape a person's experiences. The term relational draws attention to ways in which people are always in the midst of telling and living out stories.

In this chapter, we first outline the ways we reviewed the literature in early childhood with attention to key terms, databases, and processes used to identify relevant literature. We then provide a general outline of the contours of the literature. Following this, we outline eight design considerations in a narrative inquiry using one study as an exemplar. Finally, we outline key findings from the narrative inquiries and identify gaps and silences in the literature that point the way to future research programs.

REVIEWING THE LITERATURE

Methodology Used in the Literature Review

Criteria

Foregrounding narrative inquiry as a methodology in early childhood (birth to 8 years of age), we searched multiple disciplines: education, social work, psychology, medicine, public health, sociology, political science, and developmental sciences. Several databases were accessed through the University of Alberta library system: Academic Search Complete; Australian Education Index; CBCA Complete; CBCA Education; Child Development and Adolescent Studies; Cumulative Index to Nursing and Allied Health Literature (CINAHL); Education Research Complete; Educational Administration Abstracts; Educational Research Abstracts; Education and Research Archive (ERA); ERIC; Family Studies Abstracts; Medline; PsycINFO; Physical Education Index; Proquest Education Journals; Proquest Dissertations and Theses; PubMed; Social Sciences Citation Index; Teacher Reference; University of Alberta Theses and Dissertations; and the NEOS Libraries' catalogue. Within each database, a

systematic search was performed using the following terms or combination of terms to locate research in early childhood, framed within narrative inquiry: narrative inquiry OR narrative research OR narrative AND early childhood AND OR childhood OR children OR childhood infants OR child infancy OR infants OR babies AND OR preschool OR day care OR daycare OR day centres OR day homes OR nursery OR caregivers OR child care OR play OR playgrounds OR schools OR hospitals OR doctors OR nursing OR healthcare OR institutions. Our searches were limited to research dissertations, theses, books, and studies, published in English and found in scholarly or academic journals. Research identified as relevant emerged within the time frame of 1994 to 2013. Compiled articles were collectively reviewed by the authors and assessed for inclusion.

Process

Research matching the aforementioned criteria was transferred to an online database. Mining the databases yielded 193 matches, comprised of 89 theses and dissertations and 104 academic and scholarly journal articles, which were placed in a collective folder. Using multiple terms, we exhausted the database searches and returned to our initial possibilities. Following this, we scanned the literature to ensure narrative inquiry was utilized in the study, which resulted in 76 potential matches from the original 193 matches. Over several team meetings, we surveyed the literature and continued to attend closely to the methodology and age range of participants. Next, we further narrowed the research matches down to 26 articles, 25 theses and dissertations, seven books, and one book chapter. A summary template was created for a thorough exploration of the remaining research articles, theses, and dissertations, which included the following categories: *abstract, discipline/research site, whose experiences, starting points* (living and telling), *methodology, field texts, research texts, key findings*, as well as attending to the practical and theoretical research implications of *so what?* Collectively, we compiled 59 annotated bibliographical entries for consideration.

Throughout this process, we remained mindful of how narrative inquiry was unfolding throughout the research. After we carefully read the remaining 59 studies identified as using narrative inquiry, we recognized there were various interpretations of narrative inquiry at work, many of which did not resonate with what Clandinin and Caine (2012) describe as qualitative touchstones for narrative inquiry. They described the touchstones 'as a quality or example that is used to test the excellence or genuineness of others' or 'as a hard black stone, such as jasper or basalt, that was used to test the quality of gold or silver by comparing the streak left on the stone by one of these metals with that of a standard alloy' (p. 169). Clandinin and Caine 'wondered if we metaphorically touched or scratched a narrative inquiry, what kinds of streaks or marks would be left' (p. 169). When some studies did not appear to meet the touchstones of quality narrative inquiries, they were not included in this chapter. Subsequent discussions led to our acceptance and further review of 12 journal articles, nine thesis/dissertation studies, one book chapter, and seven books.

General Contours of the Literature

Through our review, we noted that narrative inquiry in early childhood is an emerging field. For the most part, when narrative inquirers engage with young children as research participants, they often come into these relationships through institutional contexts such as pre-school programs (Barrett, 2009, 2011) and elementary schools, including pre-kindergarten and kindergarten classrooms (Caine, 2010; Griffin, 2009; Houle, 2010; Huber and Clandinin, 2002; Huber et al., 2003, 2011; Murray Orr, 2005; Murray Orr et al., 2007; Norton, 2006; Oveson, 2012; Pearce, 2005; Tsai, 2007; Yeom, 1996). We were, therefore, not surprised to see that the

majority of narrative inquiries were undertaken by education researchers in institutions with an education focus. Only six inquiries were situated within non-education-focused institutions: Ellis' (2007) inquiry undertaken in a healthcare context; Greidanus' (2005) inquiry undertaken in a hospice context; Kinnunen's and Einarsdottir's (2013) inquiry undertaken in a family home; and Wingrove's (1994) inquiry undertaken in homes, health care spaces, and, eventually, in relation to school. Matheson (2000), who engaged with three mothers of preschool children who provided childcare to their own and other people's children, situated her narrative inquiry within each mother's home context. Paley (2010)[1] begins alongside a young boy, Eli, at a beach but also moves to a pre-school setting. As we noted this dominance of educational contexts, we wondered if it is not yet common among narrative inquirers to see young children, and families, as composing complex lives until they interact with educational institutions. Numerous studies were intentionally designed to include participation alongside children, and sometimes their families, within both institutional and familial contexts (Barrett, 2009, 2011; Clandinin et al., 2006; Griffin, 2009; Huber et al., 2011; Norton, 2006; Pearce, 2005).

The majority of narrative inquiries reviewed were situated within a North American context. Exceptions were those situated in Australia (Barrett, 2009, 2011), Finland (Kinnunen and Einarsdottir, 2013), and Taiwan (Tsai, 2007).

DESIGNING NARRATIVE INQUIRIES

In what follows we use eight design considerations outlined by Clandinin (2013). We do so to illustrate narrative inquiries in early childhood and represent one early childhood study as an exemplar of narrative inquiry. Houle (2012) conducted a multiperspectival narrative inquiry into the experiences of two boys identified in Grade 1 (the first required year of schooling in North America) as struggling readers, their mothers, and their teachers. Engaging in the study over two years, Houle first worked with the boys, their mothers, and their Grade 1 teacher, and, in the following year, with the boys, their mothers, and their Grade 2 teacher.

Design Consideration 1: Four Key Terms Structure a Narrative Inquiry

As noted earlier, narrative inquiry is both a methodology for the study of the phenomenon of experience and a narrative view of experience. Four key terms structure narrative inquiry: living stories, telling stories, retelling stories, and reliving stories (Clandinin and Connelly, 1998). Narrative inquirers understand that people live out stories and tell stories of that living. Narrative inquirers come alongside participants and engage in narrative inquiry into participants' lived and told stories. Part of the process of narrative inquiry involves retelling stories, that is, inquiring into the stories lived and told. Of necessity, researchers also engage in narrative inquiry into their own lived and told stories as they come alongside participants. Retelling stories may eventually result in reliving stories in changed actions. Narrative inquirers work within a three-dimensional narrative inquiry space (derived from Dewey's (1938) view of experience) with dimensions of temporality, sociality (personal and social), and place (Clandinin and Connelly, 2000; Connelly and Clandinin, 2006).

Houle (2012) began her narrative inquiry with an autobiographical narrative inquiry into her experiences as a mother of a daughter who struggled to learn to read in Grade 1, as well as into her experiences as a primary grade teacher, attending closely to who she was as a teacher in relation to children who struggled with reading and her experiences with the children's mothers. She designed her narrative inquiry to allow her to enter, first, into a Grade 1 classroom alongside a teacher who agreed to participate in the study. Houle

participated as a classroom volunteer, coming alongside a number of children initially while she engaged in conversations with the teacher about possible child participants. Two boys were identified as possible participants. Through meeting the mothers, they agreed both to be participants and to allow their sons to participate. Houle continued as a participant observer in the classroom. After gaining the boys' assent to participate, she spent one-on-one time with them both during and after school hours.

Design Consideration 2: Inquiry Starting Points

There are two starting points for narrative inquiry. The first begins with telling stories, a process where participants tell stories of their experiences. The second begins with participants' living stories, a process in which a narrative inquirer comes alongside participants as they live their lives. In all narrative inquiries, researchers situate themselves in more or less relational ways with participants in order to come to understand participants' stories. Relationships are central to the work of narrative inquirers. Not only is the relational space between researchers and participants integral to understanding the composition of field texts and research texts, but relationships are also a central way of making sense of the temporal and contextual aspects of narrative inquiry.

Houle's (2012) narrative inquiry began with living stories, that is, she lived alongside the children and teachers in the Grades 1 and 2 classrooms. However, with the mothers, the focus was mostly on telling stories; that is, over two years, the mothers told stories of their experiences with their sons.

Design Consideration 3: Attending to Justifications Throughout the Inquiry

There are three kinds of justifications to which narrative inquirers attend as they respond to the questions of 'so what?' and 'who cares?' that all social science researchers must be able to address. Personal justifications allow researchers to justify a particular narrative inquiry in the context of their life experiences and personal inquiry puzzles. Practical justifications allow researchers to justify a particular narrative inquiry in practical terms; that is, to attend to the importance of considering the possibility of shifting, or changing, practices. Social and/or theoretical justifications allow researchers to justify the work in terms of new methodological, disciplinary, or interdisciplinary knowledge. Researchers address all three justifications at the outset of the inquiry, throughout the inquiry, and at the end of the inquiry.

Houle's (2012) personal justification is related to her experiences as her daughter learned to read as well as to her early teaching experiences. Her practical justification attends to the importance of shifting or changing practices in curriculum making for children who struggle to learn to read. Houle's theoretical and social justifications involve contributions to the literature on curriculum making as she shows how teachers and parents need to attend to children's life writing and their identity making within the subject matter of early reading. Furthermore, Houle contributes to narrative inquiry as a methodology as she underscores the importance of relationships in narrative inquiry. Houle also takes up the challenge of co-composing research texts with young children. Houle's work contributes to the social justice aspect of identity work through interrupting the dominant discourses of subject matter as the sole starting point for curriculum making.

Design Consideration 4: Research Puzzles rather than Research Questions

Each narrative inquiry is composed around a particular wonder and, rather than framing a research question with a precise definition or

expectation of an answer, narrative inquirers frame a research puzzle that carries with it a sense of a 're-search', a searching again, that suggests 'a sense of continual reformulation' (Clandinin and Connelly, 2000: 124). This shift from framing a research question to framing a research puzzle opens up the possibilities of change over time in the inquiry as researchers and participants live out the inquiry. This shift

> creates reverberations as it bumps against dominant research narratives. The shift from question to puzzle is one that allows narrative inquirers to make explicit that narrative inquiry is different from other methodologies. We begin in the midst, and end in the midst of experience. (Clandinin, 2013: 43)

Houle's (2012) wonders about reading were not wonders about specific reading strategies but about the experiences of children, parents, and teachers. While Houle posed multiple questions, they were questions posed in relation to her larger puzzle about 'experiencing perceived delays in schools within the context of learning to read' (2012: 12).

Design Consideration 5: Entering into the Midst

Narrative inquirers enter into research relationships with participants in the midst of their ongoing personal and professional lives; in the midst of researchers' lives enacted within particular institutional narratives such as funded projects and graduate student research; in the midst of institutional narratives such as university or other organizational narratives; and in the midst of social, political, linguistic, cultural, and familial narratives. Participants are also always in the midst of their lives. So too are the places or sites of inquiry where researchers live alongside and/or meet with participants.

Houle (2012) made clear that her understanding of an inquiry situated in the midst of lives being lived is important. She understands the lives of young children, parents, and teachers as lives being lived, lives in progress. She also understands the rhetoric of reading instruction as something always evolving when she traces the literature on the development of theories of reading. Houle considered her presence on the landscape of Ramsey Elementary as a presence in an ever-changing place shaped by multiple lives and policies. Houle positioned herself as a researcher in the midst of her life, negotiated over time with her daughter, with her life as a graduate student in a post-secondary institution, and as a teacher.

Design Consideration 6: From Field to Field Texts

The field in a narrative inquiry can be ongoing conversations with participants where participants tell stories of living alongside participants in a particular place or places. Being in the field involves settling into the temporal unfolding of lives in place or places. We negotiate with participants 'an ongoing relational inquiry space' (Clandinin and Caine, 2012: 171), a relational space we call the field.

There are many ways to gather, compose, and create field texts (data) as we live in the field with participants. Field texts can be field notes of activities and events, transcripts of conversations or interviews, artifacts such as memory box items, photographs, work samples, documents, plans, policies, annals and chronicles, and so on (Clandinin and Connelly, 2000).

Houle (2012) detailed the multiple ways in which she was a researcher in the field. Always in reference to her relational responsibilities as a narrative inquirer, Houle described entry to the school and her meeting with the principal; she wrote of her living alongside two boys, Tiny Tim and Matson, in Grade 1 with Mrs. Taylor, in Grade 2 with Mrs. Henry, and in the boys' familial places. She refers often to meetings with the boys' mothers. Her field texts include recorded conversations with participants, artifacts created and/or used by the children, teacher, and

herself, field notes written about experiences in the classroom and out of school places, and a research journal. She includes two sections in her dissertation specifically on field texts titled, *Kinds of field texts* and *Co-composing field texts with children.*

Design Consideration 7: From Field Texts to Interim and Final Research Texts

Field texts are embedded within research relationships. Working within the three-dimensional narrative inquiry space, researchers work to shape field texts first into interim research texts and then into final research texts (narrative ways of thinking of data analysis and interpretation). This move from field texts to research texts is marked by tensions and uncertainties. As narrative inquirers inquire into field texts, they continue to think narratively, that is, to inquire into the field texts with attentiveness to the three-dimensional narrative inquiry space.

When researchers move from interim research texts to final research texts, both researchers and participants become aware that texts will become visible to public audiences. This highlights again the relational ethics, reminding narrative inquirers that their first ethical responsibility is to participants. As they compose final research texts, they return to the personal, practical, and social/theoretical justifications of the inquiry, reminding themselves why they have undertaken the inquiry and attending closely to how they are responding to the 'so what?' and 'who cares?' questions. Final research texts include academic publications, including books and articles, dissertations, theses, and presentations for academic and non-academic audiences. All research texts need to reflect temporality, sociality, and place.

As Houle (2012) moved from field texts to interim and final research texts, she engaged in multiple levels of negotiation. First, she carefully read and reread the field texts for each child, mother, and teacher. Working temporally, she created several interim narrative accounts, that is, accounts for her work with each boy in Grade 1, in the summer months between Grades 1 and 2, and the time in Grade 2. Working with each child's experiences at the heart of each account, she wove in transcript segments, field notes, and artifacts to create one narrative account for each child. She also engaged in multiple further conversations with each mother, teacher, and child. While the final narrative accounts were shared with each mother and teacher, she also created narrative accounts, modeled on a children's book, to represent each child's story. All accounts were negotiated with participants and included in the final research texts. As Houle maintained close contact with participants throughout her inquiry, relational ethics were a primary consideration in negotiating the interim and final research texts.

Design Consideration 8: Relational Ethics at the Heart of Narrative Inquiry – Relational Responsibilities

Ethical matters need to be narrated over the entire narrative inquiry process: 'ethical matters shift and change as we move through an inquiry. They are never far from the heart of our inquiries no matter where we are in the inquiry process' (Clandinin and Connelly, 2000: 170). What we term relational ethics, that is, the ethics of living in relational ways with participants, need to be continually at the heart of our narrative inquiries (Clandinin and Huber, 2002).

Narrative inquirers comply with the legal and procedural aspects of ethics held by institutional research boards. Working within fidelity to relationships (Noddings, 1984), ethical considerations are responsibilities negotiated by participants and narrative inquirers at all phases of an inquiry (Clandinin and Connelly, 2000). Issues of anonymity and confidentiality take on added importance as the complexity of lives is made visible in research texts.

Attention to ethical relations permeated Houle's (2012) narrative inquiry in negotiating relationships with school administrators, teachers, mothers, and children. Alongside attention to issues of trust and mutual vulnerability, Houle created ways that allowed her to attend to each person's experience as she negotiated field, interim, and final research texts.

KEY FINDINGS IN THE LITERATURE

In this section, we outline eight emerging findings discerned from the narrative inquiries reviewed.

Being 'in the Midst': Epistemological and Ontological Commitments

Narrative inquiry in early childhood is a field of inquiry that is in the midst. Over time, the epistemological and ontological commitments to experience and the relational have become increasingly emphasized in narrative inquiries. For example, since the early to mid-1990s when Wingrove (1994) and Yeom (1996) engaged in their narrative inquiries, there has been 'intensified talk about our stories, their function in our lives, and their place in composing our collective affairs' (Clandinin and Rosiek, 2007: 36). This increased attention shaped the need for 'greater philosophical precision in our use of the terms *narrative* and *narrative inquiry*' (Clandinin and Rosiek, 2007: 36, emphasis in original), which has, in turn, shaped a stronger 'sense of the epistemological and ontological commitments of those who work within the field' (Clandinin, 2013: 11). Tsai (2007) made a shift in her work from analyzing the speech acts of young children in a Taiwanese kindergarten class, to considering their experiences. This shift to understanding the experience of children highlights the ontological commitments of narrative inquiry and the fundamental interest of narrative inquirers.

While Connelly and Clandinin (1990) first

> wrote of narrative inquiry as both phenomenon and method, we quickly began to understand that it was a research methodology. What was apparent was how interwoven narrative ways of thinking about phenomena are with narrative inquiry as research methodology. It was 'the interweaving of narrative views of phenomena and narrative inquiry that marks the emerging field and that draws attention to the need for careful uses and distinctions of terms'. (Clandinin and Rosiek, 2007: 36)

As shown in Houle's (2012) dissertation and in Barrett's work (2009, 2011), it is now commonplace for these methodological understandings to be visible centrally in research texts through, for example, clearly articulated attentiveness to 'thinking narratively within the three commonplaces of narrative inquiry – temporality, sociality, and place' (Clandinin, 2013: 38). As Clandinin wrote:

> Thinking narratively about the phenomenon is necessary throughout each inquiry – that is, from framing the research puzzle, to being in the field, to composing field texts, and to composing research texts. Thinking in this way highlights the shifting, changing, personal, and social nature of the phenomenon under study. Thinking narratively about a phenomenon challenges the dominant story of phenomenon as fixed and unchanging throughout an inquiry. (2013: 38)

Increasing Use of Visual Field Texts and Visual Representations in Research Texts

Many narrative inquirers attend to ways in which children might express their experiences. This attention to children's potential ways of expressing their experience shaped the inquiries, particularly the co-composing of field, interim, and research texts. We highlighted this aspect in Houle's (2012) inquiry as she worked with field texts and the format of a children's book to compose research texts that the child participants would understand. Barrett's (2011) research puzzles of

'infants' and young children's early musical engagement as singers, song-makers, and music-makers' (p. 403) and 'ways young children and their families engage with and use music in their daily lives' (Barrett, 2009: 115) highlighted potential ways in which children might express their experiences. In Caine's (2010) narrative inquiry alongside children in a Grade 2/3 classroom, she engaged the children in explorations 'of community in artful ways' (p. 481). As 'the children photographed and wrote in what was often an iterative process, where writing/talking and photographing intermingled' (p. 481), they gradually, with Caine, drew upon these field texts to create an interim research text in the form of an alphabet book which showed their understandings of community. Griffin (2009) used photographs as field texts as she inquired with three girls in Grades 2 and 3 into their perspectives of their in- and out-of-school music experiences. Norton (2006) also included a visual component in her narrative inquiry. Weighill (2004), as a teacher researcher, engaged children and parents in a narrative inquiry and used photographs as field texts. Yeom (1996) 'took pictures of the children as they were involved in their activities' (p. 49), which she then used to begin subsequent conversations with the three children with whom she explored the transition from kindergarten to Grade 1.

Greidanus (2005) invited children to make 'various art expressions' (p. 39) as they participated in a grief support group where she first met the three children with whom she engaged in a narrative inquiry into their experiences of bereavement. Greidanus drew upon a story shared in a picture book[2] to create narrative accounts for each child, which were representative of the experiences shared by each child's storytelling (through artistic expressions, orally, and in writing), and with which the children might potentially interact in the future. Both Huber et al. (2003) and Murray Orr (2005) also included picture books in their narrative inquiries. In the first study, the picture books became significant in the field notes as Huber, Whelan, and

Clandinin (2003) wrote of their participation alongside children and a teacher in a Grade 3/4 classroom, while Murray Orr situated picture books as central in both field texts and interim research texts. In the midst of composing narrative accounts of three mothers, Matheson (2000) wove books, pictures, and cloth as a way to more deeply understand and inquire into their experiences.

Co-composition with Children of Field, Interim, and Final Research Texts

In our earlier review of Houle's (2012) narrative inquiry, we highlighted ways she engaged in co-composing field texts, something that is also evident in other studies. Narrative inquirers invited children as co-researchers and together children and researchers co-composed field texts as they made and talked about their visual texts (Ahn and Filipenko, 2007), photographs they had collected and created (Caine, 2010), photographs and journals (Griffin, 2009), various art expressions (Greidanus, 2005), and drawings of particular aspects of a child's experiences (Huber et al., 2011; Yeom, 1996). In addition, some children engaged in processes of 'spontaneous drawing stories' (Kinnunen and Einarsdottir, 2013: 366), in which drawing and storytelling happened simultaneously. Other narrative inquirers engaged with children as co-researchers through open-ended, unstructured conversations (Clandinin et al., 2006; Griffin, 2009; Huber and Clandinin, 2002; Murray Orr, 2005; Murray Orr et al., 2007; Pearce, 2005; Yeom, 1996) or by drawing upon the photographs taken by children (Weighill, 2004). While in some inquiries children were involved in the co-composition of field texts (Ahn and Filipenko, 2007), numerous inquirers simultaneously engaged both children and members of their families (Ellis, 2007; Greidanus, 2005; Kinnunen and Einarsdottir, 2013) or children and teachers (Paley, 2010) in the co-composition of field texts. Some narrative inquiries engaged

family members as co-researchers (Matheson, 2000; Oveson, 2012; Wingrove, 1994). Still other narrative inquiries simultaneously involved children, families, and teachers in the co-composition of field texts (Barrett, 2009, 2011; Caine, 2010; Clandinin et al., 2006; Griffin, 2009; Huber and Clandinin, 2002; Huber et al., 2011; Murray Orr et al., 2007; Norton, 2006; Pearce, 2005; Weighill, 2004; Yeom, 1996).

We noted that many narrative inquirers also engaged with participants in the co-composition of interim research texts as well as final research texts. Many narrative inquirers saw the co-composition of field, interim, and research texts as connected with the long-term relational ethics and responsibilities of narrative inquiry.

Multiperspectival Narrative Inquiries

Narrative inquiries are also sometimes multiperspectival in their attention to multiple plotlines of experience. The sociality dimension of narrative inquiry (Clandinin and Connelly, 2000) draws attention to lives in interaction. Yeom's (1996) dissertation was an early example of considering multiple lives in relation as she inquired into the experiences of three young children transitioning from kindergarten to Grade 1. In Caine's (2010) work, she explored children's knowledge of community and, as part of a larger study (Clandinin et al., 2006), invited multiple children to explore understandings alongside the school principal, the teacher, and the children's families. Houle (2010, 2012) inquired into the identity making of struggling readers in Grades 1 and 2.

Huber and Clandinin (2002), alongside a child, his parent, and his teacher, found that 'moral responsibility must fall toward the relationship rather than on what often counts as "good" nonrelational research' (p. 797). A significant finding was that 'researchers [might] imagine future relational narrative inquiries with children as co-researchers [that] could take them toward numerous storylines' (p. 800) by understanding that 'children's narrative authority was an uncommon plot-line on classroom, school, and research landscapes' (p. 792). Huber, Whelan, and Clandinin (2003) inquired into the experiences of diverse 8- and 9-year-old children and their teacher in a Grade 3/4 classroom in an inner-city school. Murray Orr, Murphy, and Pearce (2007) wrote about the experiences of children, families, teachers, researchers, and a principal.

Identity Making of Young Children

Trying to understand children's identities is becoming a common thread in narrative inquiries into the experiences of young children. In their narrative inquiry into kindergarten children's narratives, imaginative play, and art, Ahn and Filipenko (2007) considered the ways in which children's personal narratives establish the children's identities as moral, social, cultural and engendered, that children negotiate their roles (self) with others, and that children's reconstruction and re-imagination is concerned with ways in which they use narratives to grapple with abstract scientific, philosophical, and moral questions.

Barrett (2009, 2011) inquired into the ways that music shaped the identity-making experiences of young children ages 18–48 months in home and childcare settings. Huber, Whelan, and Clandinin (2003) examined issues of identity making for Year 3/4 children. Paley's (1981, 1986, 1992, 1997, 2010) work explores children's identity making in kindergarten classrooms. Her work considers children's relationships and identities in classroom community. In Tsai's (2007) work in Taiwanese classrooms, she found it was not speech patterns that interested her but the identities of the children as evidenced in their talk.

Beginning to Engage with Young Children in Places Beyond Institutional Contexts

While many narrative inquiries focus on children's experiences within educational contexts, we located four inquiries that shifted research puzzles to familial inquiry spaces, beginning in children's homes and community contexts. Wingrove (1994), positioning herself as a mother and then teacher-researcher, engaged in a narrative inquiry alongside her son Joshua, her husband, and another family to illuminate the experiences of two families living alongside two young children with chronic asthma and allergies. Her findings illustrate the need to attend to both children's and familial knowledge as 'know[ing] our children best, and that we are the ones who must have a great deal of input and control in the matter of caring for our children' (Wingrove, 1994: 109) within institutional contexts. This study highlights the need to attend first to multiple familial contexts, where children and families' knowledge is honoured, validated, and viewed as equally important to other knowledge, in order to establish collaboration between institutions, such as schools and health care institutions.

Ellis (2007) focused on preverbal children's narrative experiences through engaging in a narrative inquiry alongside familial knowledge and experiences in the home. Her inquiry highlights the importance of attending to the familial aspects of parents' personal practical knowledge (Connelly and Clandinin, 1988). This inquiry makes visible the co-construction of preverbal and non-verbal children's experiences and wordless narrations. Similarly, beginning an inquiry within the home alongside the researcher mother, Kinnunen and Einarsdottir (2013) explored the nature of children's aesthetic experiences as they narrate their life changes over time. Attending to children's experiences as holistic and multimodal, this study recognizes children's abilities to narratively construct their lives and provides an 'understanding of why and how children tell in certain contexts, reflecting the surrounding cultures in which they live' (Kinnunen and Einarsdottir, 2013: 381). They point out the importance of attending to children's multimodal narration within the home as a tool for understanding processes of responding to multiple life changes.

Greidanus (2005) positioned her study within a community theological ministry hospice where children aged 5 and 6 shared their experiences of loss, grief, and mourning, alongside other children. Greidanus' work illustrates the need for bereaved children to express themselves within safe spaces and over time. This study recognizes and honors children's individual experiences while reflecting on how children experience loss, grief, and mourning in multiple ways, which may not follow the mourning experiences of adults.

All four studies drew attention to the recognition that institutional contexts are not the only places where we may learn about the experiences of children and families.

Beginning in the Living of Lives in Narrative Inquiries with Young Children

The ethical and relational aspects throughout the inquiry are of concern in all narrative inquiries. Matheson (2000), for instance, began with the telling of stories of three caregivers and mothers who weave relational threads of friendship and children in their experiences. In inviting Black and Latina/o first-grade children to be co-researchers, Norton (2006) encouraged them to interview family members about their spiritual beliefs and, in the process of sharing, finds that counter stories are constructed as a means of ameliorating deficiency thinking.

Other narrative inquirers began their inquiries living alongside participants. Greidanus (2005) found that her roles as both a researcher and bereavement counselor were shaped by the lived interactions of the 'young

co-researchers' in the support group she facilitated. While Wingrove's (1994) inquiry unfolded along autobiographical lines, we saw this as another way of beginning with living stories, that is, as a mother inquiring into her experiences of parenting a child with asthma. Ellis's (2007) narrative inquiry alongside her son suggested how 'a preverbal or non-speaking child may be able to share an experience, recount an event, and tell a story in collaboration with an intimate adult who provides the words for the narration' (p. 113). Yeom (1996), inquiring into the experiences of children transitioning from kindergarten to Grade 1, sought to live alongside three children and their teachers. We found it very interesting that Yeom came alongside the children's parents in school places *as well as* in familial places. Weighill's (2004) inquiry differed in that her positioning as a teacher-researcher in her Year 1 classroom provided her with, perhaps, more opportunities to wonder 'how each child could express his/her story within the institution of school' (p. 7).

A Relational Methodology between Young Children and their Families

Young children's experiences are often studied in narrative inquiries in relation to their familial experiences, that is, children's experiences are understood in relation to their families. Barrett (2009, 2011), in longitudinal work around children's experiences with song-making and music engagement, involved parents as field text (data) collectors as she asked them to record video and written diaries of children's experiences, as well as to participate in interviews and conversations as participants. As the parents engaged in field text composition, we saw this as highlighting the relationality between families and young children in narrative inquiries. Further, children's experiences of music-making were shaped by the familial contexts at the same time as their experiences shaped the familial contexts. Through narrative inquiry, Barrett (2009) showed the function of joint music making in relation to family experiences. Houle (2012) made visible how parents/families were integrally involved in the narrative inquiry as both storytellers of their sons' experiences and as tellers of their own experiences of parenting their sons as they encountered reading in schools.

GAPS OR SILENCES AND IMAGINING FORWARD

We noted earlier that it might not yet be commonplace for narrative inquirers to see young children, and families, as composing complex and interesting lives, until they interact with institutional contexts. We know that *education* is most often seen as connected with an institutional context (i.e., children and youth attend early learning and school contexts where they are educated or parents attend parent education classes offered by hospitals, local nursing clinics, schools, and so on where they are educated on various topics). The images of childhood, and of families, which flow from this view of education often situate children, and their families, as deficit and in need of fixing (Steeves, 2006). We see, for example, that in the midst of the current increasing plotline of school readiness, children are commonly seen as lacking when they do not enter pre-kindergarten contexts already demonstrating pre-determined numeracy, literacy, or social skills.

We also noted questions about the view of young children held in research. We wondered if there is a dominant narrative in which children are not considered trustworthy participants; that is, children may be thought incapable of storying the 'truth' of their experiences, of their lives.

A third wonder was in relation to images of childhood, which may dominate institutional and social narratives of childhood. We wondered if situating children in research as objects that are storied through second-hand accounts is shaped by a lingering narrative of childhood as a happy, carefree time in a person's life. We wondered if researchers were not directly engaging in inquiry with children because they did not want to disrupt the apparent worry-free, non-complex nature of a child's life. Might it be for this reason that some researchers choose only to hear stories *of* children, that is, stories told from the perspectives of the adults with whom children interact?

As we identified gaps and noted trends toward increasing numbers of narrative inquiries alongside young children and families, we wondered about the increased potential for counter stories which seek to interrupt plotlines in which children's experiences, children's lives outside of institutional contexts, are seen as non-education related. Our review has shown that this shift is already beginning as narrative inquirers seek to respect children's, and families', everyday lives and experiences (Barrett, 2009; Clandinin, 2013). This attending to children's experiences not only in institutional places is important given that children compose their lives in the midst of many places, relationships, and situations. In this movement both inclusive of, and beyond, institutional places, we sense a return to Dewey's (1938) understanding of experience as education. Understanding education as experience holds tremendous potential for shaping educative reverberations in the lives of children and families, and in the lives of people with whom young children and families interact in institutional places, such as teachers and childcare providers, doctors, nurses, social workers, and so on. Understanding education as experience also holds potential for reshaping the dominant plotlines, such as those noted above, which currently structure institutions. Narrative inquiries are possible ways forward for composing counter stories.

FURTHER READING

Barrett, M. S. (2009) Sounding lives in and through music: A narrative inquiry of the 'everyday' musical engagement of a young child. *Journal of Early Childhood Research*, 7(2): 115–34.

Clandinin, D. J. (2013) *Engaging in narrative inquiry.* Walnut Creek, CA: Left Coast Press.

Paley, V. (2010) *The boy on the beach: Building community through play.* Chicago, IL: University of Chicago Press.

QUESTIONS FOR REFLECTION

1   What views of children as individuals and childhood as a part of life underlie narrative inquiry?

2   How does attending to children's experiences in narrative inquiries shape new methodological understandings?

3   What are the ethical complexities and considerations of engaging in narrative inquiries with children and families?

4   What are the barriers to engaging in narrative inquiry with young children?

5   What kinds of experiences do we, as researchers, need in order to engage in narrative inquiry with children?

NOTES

1   Although Paley does not name herself as a narrative inquirer, given that much of her work occurred at the laboratory school originally created by John Dewey and that his, hers, and our commitment is to an ontology of experience, we include her work. In *You can't say you can't play*, Paley (1992) wrote, 'Story is never enough, nor is talk' (p. 110). We see Paley's work as both contributing to, and an example of, narrative inquiry shaped through a sustained commitment to experience.

2   In North America, picture books are commonly understood as texts that weave together a story told in images and words. These kinds of books are common in children's homes, childcare, and school places.

REFERENCES

Ahn, J., and Filipenko, M. (2007) Narrative, imaginary play, art, and self: Intersecting worlds. *Early Childhood Education Journal*, 34(4): 279–89.

Barrett, M. S. (2009) Sounding lives in and through music: A narrative inquiry of the 'everyday' musical engagement of a young child. *Journal of Early Childhood Research*, 7(2): 115–34.

Barrett, M. S. (2011) Musical narratives: A study of a young child's identity work in and through music-making. *Psychology of Music*, 39(4): 403–23.

Caine, V. (2010) Visualizing community: Understanding narrative inquiry as action research. *Educational Action Research*, 18(4): 481–96.

Clandinin, D. J. (ed.) (2007) *Handbook of narrative inquiry: Mapping a methodology.* Thousand Oaks, CA: SAGE.

Clandinin, D. J. (2013) *Engaging in narrative inquiry.* Walnut Creek, CA: Left Coast Press.

Clandinin, D. J., and Caine, V. (2012) Narrative inquiry. In A. A. Trainor and E. Graue (eds), *Reviewing qualitative research in the social sciences* (pp. 166–79). New York: Routledge.

Clandinin, D. J., and Connelly, F. M. (1998) Asking questions about telling stories. In C. Kridel (ed.), *Writing educational biography: Explorations in qualitative research* (pp. 243–53). New York: Garland.

Clandinin, D. J., and Connelly, F. M. (2000) *Narrative inquiry: Experience and story in qualitative research.* San Francisco, CA: Jossey-Bass.

Clandinin, D. J., and Huber, J. (2002) Narrative inquiry: Toward understanding life's artistry. *Curriculum Inquiry*, 32(2): 161–70.

Clandinin, D. J., and Rosiek, J. (2007) Mapping a landscape of narrative inquiry: Borderland spaces and tensions. In D. J. Clandinin (ed.), *Handbook of narrative inquiry: Mapping a methodology* (pp. 35–75). Thousand Oaks, CA: SAGE.

Clandinin, D. J., Huber, J., Huber, M., Murphy, M. S., Murray Orr, A., Pearce, M., and Steeves, P. (2006) *Composing diverse identities: Narrative inquiries into the interwoven lives of children and teachers.* London and New York: Routledge.

Connelly, F. M., and Clandinin, D. J. (1988) *Teachers as curriculum planners: Narratives of experience*. New York: Teachers College Press.

Connelly, F. M., and Clandinin, D. J. (1990) Stories of experience and narrative inquiry. *Educational Researcher*, 19(5): 2–14.

Connelly, F. M., and Clandinin, D. J. (2006) Narrative inquiry. In J. Green, G. Camilli and P. Elmore (eds), *Handbook of complementary methods in education research*, 3rd edn (pp. 477–87). Mahwah, NJ: Lawrence Erlbaum.

Dewey, J. (1938). *Experience and education*. New York: Collier Books.

Ellis, V. (2007) The narrative matrix and wordless narrations: A research note. *Augmentative and Alternative Communication*, 23(2): 113–25.

Greidanus, J. A. (2005) A narrative inquiry into the experiences of bereaved children. Doctoral dissertation, ProQuest Dissertations and Theses NR18086.

Griffin, S. M. (2009) Listening to children's music perspectives: In- and out-of-school thoughts. *Research Studies in Music Education*, 31(2): 161–77.

Houle, S. T. (2010) Not making the grade: A narrative inquiry into Timmy's experiences with the mandated curriculum. *In Education*, 16(2): 30–40.

Houle, S. T. (2012) A narrative inquiry into the lived curriculum of grade 1 children identified as struggling readers: Experiences of children, parents, and teachers. Doctoral dissertation, ProQuest Dissertations and Theses NR89855.

Huber, J., and Clandinin, D. J. (2002) Ethical dilemmas in relational narrative inquiry with children. *Qualitative Inquiry*, 8(6): 785–803.

Huber, J., Murphy, M. S., and Clandinin, D. J. (2011) *Places of curriculum making: Narrative inquiries into children's lives in motion*. Bingley, UK: Emerald Group.

Huber, J., Whelan, K. K., and Clandinin, D. J. (2003) Children's narrative identity-making: Becoming intentional about negotiating classroom spaces. *Journal of Curriculum Studies*, 35(3): 303–18.

Kinnunen, S., and Einarsdottir, J. (2013) Feeling, wondering, sharing and constructing life: Aesthetic experience and life changes in young children's drawing stories. *International Journal of Early Childhood*, 45(3): 359–85.

Matheson, M. L. (2000) A narrative inquiry into mothering and child caregiving. Unpublished Master's thesis, University of Alberta, Edmonton, Alberta, Canada.

Murray Orr, A. (2005) Stories to live by: Book conversations as spaces for attending to children's lives in school. Doctoral dissertation, ProQuest Dissertations and Theses NR08704.

Murray Orr, A. E. M., Murphy, M. S., and Pearce, M. (2007) Stories of school, stories in school: Understanding two aboriginal children's competing and conflicting stories of curriculum. *Canadian Journal of Native Education*, 30(2): 275–88, 322.

Noddings, N. (1984) *Caring: A feminine approach to ethics and moral education*. Berkeley, CA: University of California Press.

Norton, N. E. L. (2006) Talking spirituality with family members: Black and Latina/o children co-researcher methodologies. *The Urban Review*, 38(4): 313–34.

Oveson, J. (2012) A narrative inquiry into Thai families' lived experiences in Canadian early childhood settings. Master's thesis, ProQuest Dissertations and Theses MR90526.

Paley, V. G. (1981) *Wally's stories*. Cambridge, MA: Harvard University Press.

Paley, V. G. (1986) *Mollie is three: Growing up in school*. Chicago, IL: University of Chicago Press.

Paley, V. G. (1992) *You can't say you can't play*. Cambridge, MA: Harvard University Press.

Paley, V. G. (1997) *The girl with the brown crayon*. Cambridge, MA: Harvard University Press.

Paley, V. (2010) *The boy on the beach: Building community through play*. Chicago, IL: University of Chicago Press.

Pearce, M. P. (2005) Community as relationship: A narrative inquiry into the school experiences of two children. Doctoral dissertation, ProQuest Dissertations and Theses NR08714.

Steeves, P. (2006) Sliding doors: Opening our world. *Equity and Excellence in Education*, 39(2): 105–14.

Tsai, M. (2007) Understanding young children's personal narratives: What I have learned from young children's sharing time narratives in a Taiwanese kindergarten classroom. In D. J. Clandinin (ed.), *Handbook of narrative inquiry: Mapping a methodology* (pp. 461–88). Thousand Oaks, CA: SAGE.

Weighill, C. L. (2004) Narrative underpaintings: An inquiry into curriculum making in a grade one classroom. Master's thesis, ProQuest Dissertations and Theses MQ96431.

Wingrove, D. A. (1994) The lived world of a family with a child with asthma: Implications for education. Master's thesis, ProQuest Dissertations and Theses MM94974.

Yeom, J. (1996) From the voices of children: Transition stories from kindergarten to grade one. Doctoral dissertation, ProQuest Dissertations and Theses NN10656.

16

A Conversation Analytic Approach to Research on Early Childhood

Jack Sidnell

INTRODUCTION

In the late 1950s and early 1960s, two pioneers of the social and behavioral sciences – Erving Goffman and Harold Garfinkel – identified significant gaps in the study of human social life. Goffman, who had trained with sociologists and anthropologists in the methods of ethnography, wrote of the 'neglected situation' – that substratum of co-present interaction that runs underneath and provides the foundation for all social life (see Goffman 1964, 1967). Garfinkel, a student of Talcott Parsons who had been inspired by the writings of Alfred Schutz and other phenomenologists, noted that social order was the product of members' methodic procedures for producing and recognizing such order and thus that social life is fundamentally a matter of practical reasoning (see Garfinkel 1967). These insights provided the basis for an approach to social interaction known as conversation analysis (hereafter, CA). The founders of CA, Harvey Sacks and Emanuel

Schegloff, studied with Goffman at Berkeley in the mid- to late 1960s and Sacks went on to work with Garfinkel on a research project that examined calls to a suicide prevention hotline. Together with Gail Jefferson, Sacks and Schegloff developed the methods of conversation analysis in such a way as to allow for the systematic study of the practical reasoning and endogenous methods that members of society use in order to engage in interaction with one another. Although CA is concerned with interaction in general, language figures centrally in human social life and as a result CA is often primarily concerned with talk-in-interaction.

Rooted in the pioneering work of Sacks, Schegloff and Jefferson, contemporary work in conversation analysis seeks to understand the underlying organizations of human interaction through an investigation of the practices by which it is carried out. A very basic idea within CA is that conduct in interaction is orderly at a fine level of detail. Indeed, Sacks once proposed that interaction is orderly 'at all points' (see Sacks 1995: v1, 484). The orderliness of interaction is a result of participants' pervasive orientation to norms in both its production and interpretation (see Sacks 1984; Robinson 2007). So, for instance, if one person asks another a question, whatever is produced next by the recipient of the question will be understood in terms of how it might be a response (and preferably an answer) to that question. If no response is produced, if the recipient of the question does not look up from what he is doing, that too will be understood in light of the norm that specifies that the recipient of an addressed question is obliged to produce a response – perhaps he did not hear, perhaps he is thinking, perhaps he is very angry with me, and so on (see Heritage 1984).[1]

Participants can readily be seen to orient to these norms in interaction. One pervasive way in which they do so is by conducting themselves in a way that is observably compliant with the norm (i.e., a passenger on the bus maintains an appropriate distance between himself and the person in the next seat, the addressed recipient produces an answer to a question without delay, etc.). Another way they orient is by doing or saying something that acknowledges a departure from the norm. So, for instance, when asked a question, an addressed recipient may account for not answering by saying 'I don't know' or may account for not immediately responding by looking at the questioner while visibly chewing. On the other hand, the one asking the question may orient to such a departure as not receiving an answer by pursuing one with a follow-up question or, where no response at all has been produced, by attempting to elicit one by use of an address term (see, inter alia, Pomerantz 1984; Stivers and Rossano 2010).

Research within this tradition has focused on ways in which participants operate within these normative structures of talk in interaction (Sidnell 2010a; Raymond and Sidnell 2014). For instance, one set of studies has examined the organizational structures that allow for the orderly distribution of opportunities to participate in talk or what we describe as 'turn-taking' (Sacks et al. 1974; Ford et al. 1996; Lerner 2003; Stivers et al. 2009). Another set of studies has considered the organization of action into sequences (Schegloff 1968, 2007; Raymond 2003; Stivers 2012). And there is also a large body of work that considers the practices by which participants in interaction locate, identify and attempt to resolve problems of speaking, hearing or understanding (Schegloff et al. 1977; Kitzinger 2012; Hayashi et al. 2013).

While the vast majority of this work has focused primarily on adults, some has either purposefully or coincidentally examined interaction among children. There are several strands of research here (see Kidwell 2012 for an overview). First, there is research that examines the organization of interaction (e.g., turn-taking, action sequencing, repair) among children (see e.g., Wootton 1981a, 1981b, 1994, 1997, 2007, 2010; Tarplee 1996, 2010; Wells and Corrin 2004; Sidnell 2010b). Some of these studies, having located differences between children and adults, go on to ask how children's behavior changes over time as they come to approximate the patterns observed in interaction among adults (Filipi 2009). Second, there are studies that attempt to describe the special properties of children's interaction (Sacks 1972; Maynard 1985; Goodwin and Goodwin 1987; Goodwin 1990; Kidwell 2011) or interaction between adults and children (Drew 1981; Stivers and Majid 2007; Clemente 2009; Cahill 2010; Hutchby and O'Reilly 2010). For instance, the research by Kidwell, Zimmerman and Lerner that I discuss below has focused on interaction among and with very young children who have limited linguistic abilities and resources. How, they ask, do children make their way within the normative structures of interaction in a daycare setting? Another set of studies within this second group tends to focus on slightly older, linguistically more proficient children and attempts to describe the special concerns of interaction, especially various kinds of play interaction, among them (Whalen 1995; Butler and Weatherall 2006; Sidnell 2011).

This chapter reviews a range of work within CA on children aged nine months to about 8 or 9 years old. The emphasis though is on younger children and on studies that articulate with other accounts (such as those from psychology) of interaction among children of this age. Through a consideration of several key studies, I aim to show that the methods and analytical focus of CA provide a unique perspective on the social lives of young children. Specifically, through detailed attention to the talk and other conduct of children in interaction, it is possible to identify the particular social phenomena to which they are themselves oriented. We can thus hope to develop a study of children's worlds that is directly responsive to their own experience. Furthermore, by combining the methods of CA with a longitudinal and/or comparative approach, we can start to describe the ways in which children develop, over the course of their maturation, a deepening sensitivity to the normative structures constitutive of human societies.

THE PERSPECTIVE OF CA: SOCIAL ACCOUNTABILITY VS INDIVIDUAL ABILITY

Much of the research on young children and early childhood is primarily concerned with individual *ability*. Work on first-language acquisition focuses on the child's abilities of production and comprehension (see e.g., Tomasello et al. 2005). Work on theory of mind focuses on the child's increasingly sophisticated ability to attribute mental states to others, as well as the child's understanding of others' attributions, and so on (Astington 1994). Classic work in psychology on egocentrism is premised on the assumption that, through the course of development, a child becomes increasingly able to take the perspectives and experiences of others into account (in, for instance, designing speech that is fitted to them) (see e.g., Wertsch 1985). In contrast, work in CA is more

concerned with *accountability* than with *ability* per se. Here I mean to point to the fact that, from the perspective of CA at least, the process of becoming a social being involves not only developing ability but also an increasing awareness of, and accountability to, the normative structures by which interaction is organized. So, as Schegloff points out with respect to turn-taking:

> Children have to learn not to talk when another is talking … And when overlapping talk occurs anyway, they have to learn to listen while talking, or talk while listening, so that the simultaneous talk can be adjusted to that of the other. Then, they have to learn to recognize when another is talking – for example, that another can 'be talking' even though not at the moment producing sounds as, for example, when they are trying to remember a name in the course of an as yet unfinished sentence/utterance. Then … they have to learn that they can still be thought to be interrupting even though the speaker has finished a sentence – for example, when a story is in progress … In other words, children have to learn that talk-by-one-person is nonetheless an outcome, which it takes the whole assemblage to produce. Sometimes that involves others-than-the-speaker remaining quiet; at other times it involves them in talking as well, in brief increments, precisely placed in the continuing talk of the primary speaker, the absence of such talk (or cognate body behavior; see Goodwin, 1979, 1980, 1981) being able to induce considerable modification, even disruption, in the talk of 'the speaker.' The 'talk of the speaker' is then an interactional product, in one sense of the term. (1989: 140)

Of course, the contrast between ability and accountability is not absolute but rather a matter of emphasis. After all, an emerging accountability is clearly rooted in an increasing *ability* to identify and recognize the formal structures of interaction (e.g., the phased, ordered-event structures of activities like serving a meal, the structures from which a possible turn-at-talk is composed, and so on). Moreover, for the most part, persons are treated as the accountable agents of their own actions if and only if they are *able* to make choices, that is, *able* to do otherwise (see Enfield 2013).

An important point here is that notions of accountability attach to interactionally relevant, context-tied 'categories' rather than 'objectively identifiable' criteria obtained from outside the setting of inter-action. In much work in psychology and linguistics, the child's abilities are assessed in relation to absolute age. In interaction, however, normative accountability does not attach to absolute age but rather to a specifically relevant or currently activated category. So, for instance, a 'child', as opposed to an 'infant', may be expected to understand simple instructions from a par-ent or caregiver, or may be expected not to interrupt ongoing talk and, more generally, contribute to that talk in such a way as to show attentiveness to the contributions of others, and so on. An 'infant', in contrast, is typically not expected to behave in such ways and thus is not held accountable for perceived failures or shortcomings in this respect. Moreover, accountability attaches to multiple, overlapping categories drawn from different orders of relevance at any given moment in interaction. Thus, the child may be accountable as 'speaker,' 'story-teller', 'pre-schooler', 'student', 'boy', etc. simultaneously. For this reason, we cannot assume that all conduct in interaction is organized by reference to the participant's status as a child (or infant or adult, etc.). To paraphrase McElhinny (2003: 33), even though a child may be speaking, that does not mean that s/he is always speaking 'as a child'. So, while some aspects of a par-ticipant's conduct may be produced with an orientation to that participant's status as a child, other aspects may be produced with an orientation to that participant's status as a boy, as the second oldest in a family, as a member of a soccer team or whatever else.

Adopting a 'developmental' perspective, we can ask when a person actually becomes accountable to various interactional norms, this being equivalent to asking when they are treated, by others, as accountable to those norms. Forrester and Reason (2006), draw-ing on suggestions from Garfinkel and Sacks (1970), argue that this crucially involves an attribution, by others, of mastery of language,

that mastery of language is treated as criterial for membership. It is not clear, to me at least, however, what is meant by 'membership' in this context. As we will see below, the stud-ies of Kidwell, Zimmerman and Lerner show clearly that children are treated as account-able agents of their actions well before they acquire substantial linguistic competence (let alone mastery). As such, it may be that we need to think of this in much more local terms. Accountability attaches locally as cat-egories (or statuses) are made interactionally relevant. Consider, in this respect, a case such as the following in which three 4-year-olds are playing with blocks. Erika has created a tower-like structure and when Jude acciden-tally bumps the table she produces the turn in line 1:

1   Kids_JKT1.mov 10:55[2]

```
01 E:    Ju::de: yer makin' (me)
02       knock it dow:n.
03       (0.4)
04       be more careful next time.
05 J:    I: wi:ll:. I we:ll, I will,
06       I will.
07 T: -> He sounds like a (actin) hhh
08  ->   kinda like (ss) (0.2) ba::by,
09       (0.8)
10 J:    Ba::by?
11       (0.4)
12 T:    he he ha ha oh .hhhh
13 J:    sshhh.
14       (0.2)
15       You sound like a baby ((to adult researcher))
```

This begins with Erika complaining that, by shaking the table, Jude is making her knock down the structure she is building. She enjoins him to 'be more careful next time', to which he responds with 'I: wi:ll:. I we:ll, I will, I will'. Now although in saying this Jude acquiesces and accepts responsibility for 'not being careful', the manner in which he says it – with multiple repetition and a whining intonation – conveys also that he is treating the complaint as less than com-pletely serious. Tina picks up on the some-what peculiar way Jude says this in her talk at lines 5–6, remarking that Jude 'sounds like

– kinda like a baby'. While this possible insult is later collaboratively recast as a joke (see Sidnell 2010a: 13–14), the important point for present purposes is that it involves Tina likening Jude's behavior (specifically his talk) to that of a member of the category 'baby'. Clearly, if Jude *actually* were a baby there would be nothing remarkable here. Tina's talk only makes sense then to the extent that Jude is a member of an alternate age-based category (not 'baby' but 'child') to which his behavior (and specifically here his talk) is not fitted (see Schegloff 2002).

PARTICIPATION, OBSERVABILITY AND JOINT ATTENTION

If we take 'interaction' in its broadest possible sense, it is clear that infants participate in it within the first few days, indeed perhaps the first few hours, of life. Developmental psychologists such as Trevarthen (1977) have, for instance, shown that infants react differently depending on whether they are confronted by an object or by their mother. Moreover, there seems to be some sense in which they are capable of responding to another person through imitation from a very young age. Interaction during this early period is, however, strictly dyadic. As is now well documented, at about nine months, infants reach a developmental milestone when they start to engage in triadic, joint attentional behaviors (Tomasello 1999, 2008). This first manifests in the child checking the attention of an adult-caregiver when confronted with some obstacle and also in simple showing behaviors. At about 11 months, the child starts to follow a caregiver's attention as indicated by gaze or pointing. And at roughly 13 months, normally developing children will start to direct another's attention through pointing (see Tomasello 1999; Brown 2011). These forms of joint attentional behavior, along with a range of other motoric and verbal abilities (standing, walking, producing one-word utterances), provide a foundation for more complex forms of interactional engagement with others. For instance, Kidwell and Zimmerman (2006) show that children as young as 1 year monitor the attentional focus of their caregivers when they are engaged in acts that are possibly sanctionable (e.g., pushing a peer). In such situations, even at this age, children organize their conduct so as to evade a caregiver's attention to these events. Kidwell and Zimmerman propose that, in these and other contexts, children are pervasively orientated to the 'organization of observability', being 'the systematic ways in which objects in the environment, including people and their actions, come to be available to others for assessment. This includes opportunities to manage whether, and how, they may be viewed by others' (2006: 2). For instance, in one case (Kidwell and Zimmerman 2006; see also Kidwell 2011) Natalie (24 months) hits Jessica (around 14 to 18 months) several times on the head with a toy lizard. Jessica, apparently searching for the caregiver, looks out into the yard where the caregiver is talking to another child. Natalie follows Jessica's gaze while dropping the striking arm to her side and, finding that the caregiver is otherwise preoccupied and not looking in her direction, 'lunges into' Jessica 'for a very hard poke' (Kidwell and Zimmerman 2006). When Jessica now begins to cry loudly, Natalie orients to the possibility that this will draw the caregiver's attention (which it indeed does) and, while still looking in the caregiver's direction, walks away from the crying child.

Natalie then begins to hit a tree with the toy lizard several feet away from where Jessica is still standing. As Kidwell writes, in doing so,

she redeploys the object in a new, innocuous and thereby unincriminating line of activity and, moreover, at some distance from Jessica. In this way, Natalie treats Jessica's actions, her crying, as inevitably drawing the caregiver to the scene (which it does), and her proximity to the crying child, and a particular arrangement of objects (her hand, the toy lizard in it) in relation to the child, as implicating her in the activity that has instigated Jessica's crying. In concealing the object, putting distance between herself and the other child, and then redeploying the object in a new activity, Natalie prepares for a somewhat different contingency from that of the caregiver *actually* seeing her strike the other child: she prepares for the contingency that the caregiver – having not actually witnessed these events – will nonetheless draw a link between her and these various 'evidences' (the crying child, Natalie's proximity to her, and the object in her hand) to infer something about what has transpired previously, and she manages her actions to thwart this inference. (2011: 276)

In cases such as these, young children assess the attentional states of others and, in organizing their own conduct, take account of both *what* those others see and *how* they are likely to see it (i.e., what inferences they can be expected to draw from what they see). In related work on the same corpus of recordings, Lerner et al. (2011) consider the way in which very young children engage in an interactionally organized social world before they are able to speak, suggesting that various pre-verbal modes of conduct such as gesture, gaze, body posture and the deployment of objects along with non-linguistic vocalizations serve as 'resources for composing orderly and recognizable actions in interaction with others'. A key issue for these authors is the way the child positions his or her conduct in relation to the context of ongoing action. Positioning relative to an activity context provides the child with a key resource in the production of their own actions. In the case they examine, from a recording made at a daycare center, 'an adult caregiver is serving a meal to a young child, Charlene (15 mo), as two other children, Ryan (14 mo) and especially Laura (16 mo) attempt to join in'. The authors show that, in a bid to be included in the activity, Laura positions her actions to fit into the structure of the ongoing activity of meal service. For instance, as Charlene is being readied to eat by the caregiver, both Charlene and Laura watch her. 'Laura looks on as the Caregiver unfolds and drapes the bib over Charlene. Just as the Caregiver begins to fasten the bib – that is, just as the bibbing task is reaching its possible completion – Laura launches her

first overt appeal' (2011: 47), first raising her left hand in a point toward the railing while producing a squeal and then moving her gaze away from the railing and back to where the caregiver is placing the bib on Charlene. The authors write, 'as she gazes toward the site of the Caregiver's action, Laura splays her fingers into what has been termed a "non-effortful reach"' (Bruner et al. 1982), while at the same time voicing the possible protoword 'BAeh? baeh!' (Lerner et al. 2011: 47).

A careful examination of this episode shows that very young children parse the conduct of others so as to find in it what the authors describe as the 'formal structure of practical tasks'. In her appeals to get some food, the authors argue, Laura has displayed a 'procedural grasp of the emergent routine' (2011: 56), which she employs to 'design and implement actions fitted to its unfolding realization' (2011: 57). They suggest that:

> very young children only require the *in situ* practiced capacities required to recognize, in each particular case, the formal structures of the in-progress actions that recurrently fill their social-interactional world and the practical skills to participate in each context-specific realization of those structures of action as they are progressively realized and as each next element in its progressive realization projects a next constituent of that structure. (2011: 57)

While the authors do not deny the importance of cognitive capacities that might underwrite the interaction order, in their study they emphasize the often underappreciated importance of sequentially organized and locally realized practical activity.

In a final study worth considering here, Kidwell and Zimmerman (2007) describe some of the practices very young children use in initiating, establishing and sustaining bouts of what Michael Tomasello and others term 'joint attention' or 'shared intentionality' (see e.g., Tomasello and Carpenter 2007). Of particular interest is the action that Kidwell and Zimmerman describe as 'showing'. In a typical showing sequence, a young child will approach another (typically an adult) with an outstretched arm and an object in hand. The other then produces a response that identifies the object ('Watermelon'), expresses a social-relational feature of the object ('Your shoe') or appreciates it in some way ('Oh wow, a pretty hat'). The showing child then withdraws the object from view and/or moves out of the recipient's line of vision, either returning to the activity she was engaged in before the showing or initiating some new activity.

In these 'showings', children establish the triadic, joint attentional interaction configuration that Tomasello and others argue provides the foundation for our more sophisticated use of language in later years. Consider then the following examples from Kidwell and Zimmerman's study. In the first of these, the child, Juanita, runs across the room toward Sarah, the cameraperson (not visible), holding a shoe in each hand. As she approaches Sarah, she raises one of the shoes and holds it out toward her.

2   VYC- Kidwell and Zimmerman

```
01  J:   ((Runs across room toward S, holding a shoe
02       in each hand. Looking at S, raises shoe,
03       holds for 1.5 seconds. Lowers shoe))
04  S:   That's your shoe.
05       (1.6) ((J holds gaze toward S))
06       (0.1) ((J raises other shoe higher,
07       beginning to look at it))
08  S:   Those are your shoe:s.
09  J:   ((lowers shoe))
10       (([lowers gaze, nodding slightly))
12       (([smiles))
13       ((walks away))
```

The authors note that the practices Juanita uses to attract Sarah's attention and subsequently to focus it first on one shoe and then the other are recurrent and stable across many instances of showing. Notice that even in these perhaps most basic forms of triadic interaction – joint attentional engagements – showing is a complex act that involves selecting a particular recipient, attracting that recipient's attention and focusing the selected recipient's attention on the object to be shown – that is, foregrounding this object from the range of things that might be shown.

Moreover, there is a recurrent, stable organization of actions here in which Sarah recognizes Juanita's bodily orientation and gaze, as well as her presentation of the shoe as a first action which establishes the relevance of a response from her. Sarah's response is in turn treated by Juanita as evidence that the first action has been recognized for what it was intended to be.

Kidwell and Zimmerman go on to consider cases in which the child encounters 'inattentive others' and must pursue them in order to have the initiating show action recognized. For instance, in the following case the caregiver is initially sitting with Alex and another child. However, as she produces the talk in line 1 she gets up and begins to 'put things away'. While doing this, she is talking to the camera person – an activity which makes her temporarily unavailable as a recipient for the show-action that Alex produces in line 6.

3   VYC- Kidwell and Zimmerman

```
01  CG:  We never got one from Rachelle?
02       (1.2)
03  CP:  I: know:: I can't believe that huh::,
04       (3.7)
05  CG:  [We've got to [(have) (we found)
06  A: ->  [WAter: : Melo[n:: ((shifts gaze to CG))
07  CP:                  [An' an Rosa's mom.
08  CG:  [We found almost all of the middle
         group.
09  A: ->  [WATer: Melon:: ((raises, then lowers
10       watermelon)) (0.5)
11  CP:  Oh that's [grea:t,
12  CG:            [((CG shifts gaze to))
13  A: ->  °water° [MElon
14              [((A shifts gaze to CG))
15  CP:  okay.
16  CG:  [.hhh! Wa[termelon:::!
17          [((A lowers watermelon))
```

Here, when the first attempt to show the watermelon fails to secure an attending recipient (and as such a relevant response), Alex redoes the show first at line 9 and then again at line 13. As the authors note, Alex produces the first show here as he stands up without signaling to the recipient that a show (or any other action) directed at her is on the way. His urgency here perhaps suggests that this place has been selected as an appropriate one on the basis of the lull in conversation that precedes it (the 3.7 seconds of silence at line 4).

When Alex receives no response from the CG/Show recipient, he stays close to her, producing a show-identification again at line 9. This second attempt likewise fails to attract the attention of the caregiver and Alex brings the object to his mouth, apparently chewing it. However, even while he does this he is producing the word 'watermelon' a third time. Over the word 'water', the caregiver brings her gaze to Alex and he removes the object from his mouth, raising it up and holding it directly in the caregiver's line of vision as she says 'watermelon' at line 16. As she finishes the word/turn, Alex returns the object to what may be thought of as its home position and gazes at it, apparently satisfied that his show has been properly recognized and the object properly appreciated.

Taken together, the studies of Kidwell, Zimmerman and Lerner reviewed here show how conversation analysis can be applied to the interactional conduct of very young children to reveal the various methods they use to accomplish social action. Moreover, this strand of research provides a useful illustration of the way in which many phenomena of interest within the psychology of human development (e.g., attention, joint attention, the child's understanding of others' mental states) may be reconceptualized in terms of the practices through which their interactions with others are organized.

MAKING REQUESTS

A basic finding that emerges from the studies discussed in the previous section is that, from a very early age, children are able to identify formal structures of practical activities and design their own contributions in ways that are fitted to these structures. As the child gains linguistic competence and the linguistic repertoire becomes more elaborate, new forms of engagement become possible. Specifically, the child comes to have alternate forms or practices that may be used in ways fitted to particular interactional contingencies.

In a series of studies, Wootton has shown that, at about 2 years old, children begin to work with sequentially based, local understandings in designing their talk and other conduct. For instance, in a study of 4-year-olds, Wootton (1981b) showed that children respond differently to alternate formats for the rejection of their requests. In a related study, Wootton (1981a) showed that 4-year-olds use alternate request forms in different situations. Thus, *I want X* tends to be used to re-request after an initial rejection, that is, 'to request that which recipient is not prepared to grant' (Wootton 1981a: 513). In contrast, *Can I X* is used to re-request after the recipient has failed to respond or has responded with hesitation or deferment, that is, where eventual compliance with the request seems possible. Moreover, when used to re-request, *Can I X* is typically constructed in a modified form which takes into account and attempts to obviate the recipient's previously conveyed grounds for rejection or deferment. Wootton (1981a: 516) writes that these subsequent requests are 'not so much constructed to change recipient's mind as to find a version of the request which might be acceptable to recipient' (1981a: 516). These early studies showed then that, when designing action, children of this age take into account what has previously transpired in an interaction. Different request forms, for instance, appear to be fitted to different situations. Specifically, the *I want X* format is used to plead in the face of initial refusal, whereas *Can I X* is used where an eventual granting of the request seems possible if that request is appropriately modified. These generalizations also hold across other sequential positions (after a directive, sequence initial).

The position Wootton develops in this work contrasts with one in which the selection of some particular format (e.g., *I want X, Can I X*) is understood to be shaped by factors that have trans-situational application. Two variants of this approach can be identified, one based on a concept of 'scripts' and the other on a notion of 'sociolinguistic' variables. In the first case, it is suggested that young children are faced with the task of learning routines or scripts and that these are then played out in particular situations to achieve particular goals. In the second case, it is suggested that children assess a situation in which they find themselves in terms of socially significant coordinates – for example, the age and gender of speaker and recipient and the relative distance between them. On the basis of such an assessment of the situation, they then select an appropriate format (see e.g., Ervin-Tripp 1977). Wootton's approach differs in emphasizing not a trans-situational knowledge store (i.e., scripts) or objective, external characteristics (e.g., sex, age, gender) but instead local 'understandings' that are arrived at *within* the interaction itself.

In a study of one child aged 2–4 years, Wootton develops this sequentially-based account in an analysis of various request formats. He writes:

> Instead of seeing the young child's actions as shaped and constrained by an emerging, general knowledge store, I shall argue that the critical knowledge on which she is drawing is intimately linked with the particular sequence of action in which she is engaged. In the course of participating in sequences of action the child develops a capacity to take into account what I shall call *understandings* which have arisen either from events earlier in the same sequence of talk or from ones occurring in a sequence in the relatively recent past. (1997: 7)

Wootton argues that, in the third year of life, the child tends to use imperatives (e.g., 'Lift out now, dad') in those cases where some understanding as to the permissibility and/or feasibility of the proposed action has been reached earlier in the interaction. In contrast, the alternative linguistic devices used for making requests at this age such as 'I want X' or 'I like X' are used where no such understanding has been reached. The imperative construction, it could be suggested, indexes some presupposed, previously arrived at understanding whereas other request formats do not. A comparison of two examples illustrates this:

4 2;l/4524

Amy and her father sit at the table, mother standing close by off camera. A has just been playing with F, giving him bread that she knows he doesn't want. Then F says:

```
01 F:   Would you like any more to eat?
02 M:   D'you [want any more
03 A:        [No:
04 F:   No ((confirmatory in intonation))
05 M:   No?=
06 F:   =D'you want to get down now,
07 A:   Yes=
08 M:   Mm: right I think its probably medicine
09      time again now
```

((56 secs))

((M is now out of room and gum ointment put away; A, standing in her high-chair, then gives F another medicine box; F puts it to the other end of the table and says:))

```
10 F:   That's for mummy isn't it to do your eyes ((to A))
11 M:   Well I think I generally let her do more
12      things so then she assumes that in other
13      ways she can= ((to F, linking back to
14      earlier talk))
15 A:   =Lift out[dad, ((as she says this A begins to climb
16      up on to the tray of her high-chair))
17 F:           [Mm ((to M))
18 M:   Do more= ((to F, completes NTs prior turn))
19 F:   Okay ((to A; raises his arms to lift her out of
20      the chair))
```

In example 4, the child Amy is in her high chair when the father asks if she would like anymore to eat. The sequence runs its course with Amy indicating that she would not and the father subsequently offering to get her out of the chair (line 6). Amy immediately accepts the offer (line 7) but thereupon Mom interjects that it might be time for Amy to have her medicine. The medicine is administered in the 56 seconds not shown here and at line 15 Amy produces the imperative construction 'Lift out, dad'. Compare now example 5:

5   2;l/4479

Amy, in her chair at the table, has just been asking for some orange, and told that we do not have any. She then turns down an offer of some banana, and after eating two bits of apple on her tray begins to climb out of her seat. As she does this she says:

01   A: Like get out now ((*still in process of lifting*
02   *herself up*))
03   F: Get out now?=But you haven't finished your
04   apple
05   A: (But) like get out, ((*by end of this turn she is*
06   *in a crouched position with her feet on the*
07   *seat of her chair*))
08   F: Finish your apple first
09   A: Like get out no:w, ((*kneeling on seat by*
10   *the end of this turn, looking directly at F*))
11   Can't you finish those pieces of apple first
12   A: No:::::::::: ((*starts high pitch and gradually*
13   *descends in song-like intonations; as she*
14   *says this she remains stilled, looking steadily*
15   *slightly away from F*))

Here, in contrast to example 4, no previous understanding with respect to Amy's release from the high chair has been established in the prior talk. Rather than link back indexically to such an understanding, Amy's 'Like get out now' is a new proposal and one that the father, as can be seen from what follows, resists. Wootton's analysis thus shows that, when the child uses the imperative, she typically has a basis for supposing that 'what she is asking the parent to do is compatible with an earlier understanding' (Wootton 1997: 80).

Wootton shows that this analysis can be extended in various ways. So, for instance, it is possible to see what are commonly referred to as 'temper tantrums' and what Wootton terms 'distressing incidents', as arising in situations where a child sees a previously established understanding as having been violated. For instance, in one case the child requests some honey from her mother and this is granted on the condition that she first clean some

chalk from her hands. When the father then approaches with the honey, the child becomes immediately distressed saying, '=No: No: le:t mummy: ge:t i::t=' while sharply moving her head and flailing her arm in the direction of the honey. Thus, according to this analysis, certain forms of otherwise mysterious and seemingly unprovoked distraught behavior become intelligible when seen in the light of previously established, relevant understandings – here that the mother, rather than the father, should provide the child with the honey.

In these ways, the child treats such understandings as a relevant context for the actions in which she engages; indeed, one might say that in orienting to such understandings the child's capacity to respect aspects of the context in which she acts undergoes a major transformation when contrasted with her behavior at, say, 16 months. She is now in a position to take account of and adjust her behavior in the light of local, sequence-specific knowledge. The sequence in which she is involved is thus permitted to inform and shape what she does, and what she does can display a sensitivity to these local circumstances.

Wootton also extends the analysis forward in developmental time, asking why, in the later part of her third year, the child should develop such a variety of ways of making requests. What is the functional advantage of having multiple formats for the making of requests and why can the child not operate just as effectively employing a single format? Wootton explains:

> Clearly, a single format would not suffice because it would not permit the child to differentiate, along the lines I have identified, the types of interactional circumstance in which she finds herself. This question becomes even more pointed, however, during her third year of life because at this time important further developments within her request system take place. During this year although the child continues to use most of the request forms that I have been examining, such as imperatives, she also comes to use a number of further request forms, notably interrogatives such as 'Can I have x?'. (1997: 138)

Wootton shows that the child employs this new form in cases where no 'sequential warrant' in the form of a previously arrived at understanding has been established. Tracing Wootton's argument, it appears that early in the third year imperative constructions become specialized to make requests in those cases where what is being asked for has already been agreed to by the parent where, that is, some understanding has been reached in the prior talk. In other situations, the child uses a range of forms. About midway through the third year, however, the interrogative 'Can I have X?' format comes to be used specifically for the situation in which there is no previously established understanding with the parent. Wootton writes, 'At the core of my argument is the claim that the motivation for the adoption of these designs is an interactional one, that these designs serve to encode and further differentiate forms of understanding which are either present or imminent within the child's interactional system' (1997: 140).

It is important to see then that Wootton's focus here is not the linguistic forms *per se* (imperative, interrogative) but rather the distinctions that they make between different types of interactional environment and thus the orientations they reveal to different interactional contingencies. Tracking the emergence and use of different request forms then allows us to see how the child is attending to different aspects of the interactional context, which aspects of it are treated by the child as relevant, and so on.

RESPONDING TO QUESTIONS

Conversational interaction is, as already noted, pervasively organized at a fine level of detail by norms. As such, a question emerges as to when and how the child comes to appreciate this and display in their own conduct a reflexive accountability to such norms.

In recent work, Stivers, Sidnell and Bergen (2015) address this issue by examining spontaneously produced questions and their responses as a window into the interaction order. There is substantial evidence to suggest that questioning is part of an underlying foundational infrastructure which gives human social life its distinctive character (see Levinson 2006; Enfield and Sidnell 2014). First, children begin to ask questions in the first year of life (Chouinard 2007). Second, in adult interaction, questions are used to perform a wide variety of different actions including requesting information, proposing activities, requesting objects, asking for clarification and more (Schegloff 1984; Stivers and Rossano 2010). Third, all languages have some special lexical, morphological or syntactic means to mark that an utterance is a question (Dryer 2008, 2011). Fourth, the asking and answering of questions is organized via a very robust set of social norms that are essentially inescapable in adult interaction.

To examine how, whether and to what extent children 'orient' to these social norms, Stivers, Sidnell and Bergen (2015) investigate how children interact with same-age peers. They show that, in this environment, while children generally adhere to interactional norms that organize sequences initiated by a question-turn, these norms are instantiated with some differences. These differences, the authors contend, help us to understand what constitutes the 'child-like' aspect of children's interactions. Moreover, the authors show that the norms to which children orient least consistently are those that are particularly important for managing social relationships because they allow speakers to indicate affiliation and cooperation even in the context of otherwise face-threatening action.

Particular actions are inevitably understood by participants as either in accord with or departing from interactional norms. Moreover, the degree of fit with normative expectations is, itself, communicative. For instance, an immediately produced 'no' in response to a question such as 'do you like it?' will be understood quite differently from a response which is delayed and hedged, such as, 'Uhm. Well, it's not really to my taste, no', even though both are disconfirmations. As Heritage puts it, norms provide 'both for the intelligibility and accountability of "continuing and developing the scene as normal" and for the visibility of other, alternative courses of action' (Heritage 1984: 108).

Following on from work by Stivers et al. (2009, 2010), Stivers, Sidnell and Bergen (2015) focus on four norms that govern the way adult speakers respond to questions in interaction. Specifically, the production of a Yes–No or polar question makes relevant, (1) a response that is, (2) an answer, (3) confirmation of the supposition conveyed and, (4) delivered without significant delay. To see the cumulative effect of participants' orientation to these norms on the organization of question–answer sequences among adult speakers, consider some examples. First, consider some cases in which a question is followed by significant delay, suggesting that no response is forthcoming (see also Pomerantz 1984; Stivers and Robinson 2006; Stivers and Rossano 2010).

6   Drew and Atkinson(1979), Levinson (1983)

```
01 Alex:   Is there something bothering you or not?
02         (1.0)
03         Yes or no.
04         (1.5)
05         Eh?
06 Bob:    No.
```

Here, in example 6, when Alex's query 'Is there something bothering you or not?' receives no response, he follows up (after a substantial delay) with 'yes or no'. When this again receives no response, Alex pursues a response with 'eh?'. These follow-up pursuits, designed as increasingly minimal anaphoric prompts, suggest that Alex sees the problem here as simple recalcitrance with no associated problem of hearing or understanding. In contrast, in example 7, when Rose's query 'en that went wro:ng' receives no immediate response and, subsequently, a turn beginning with 'hh We:ll? Uh:m', she follows up by repairing 'that' with 'that surgery' in line 9, thereby suggesting that she understands a lack of comprehension to have prevented Bea from answering.

7   SBL:I:I:IO:R

```
01 Rose:   A:nd uh (0.3) h Isn't she quite a young
02         woman? only in her fifties?=
03 Bea:    =^Ye:s uh hah,
04         (.)
05 Rose:   Oh how sa:d, En that went wro:ng,
06         (0.6)
07 Bea:    hh We:ll? uh:m
08         (0.4)
09 Rose:   That surgery ah mean.
10         (0.4)
11 Bea:    I don't=
```

Finally, in example 8, when Adam asks 'D'they have a good cook there?' and Jay does not respond, Adam follows up with 'nothing special?', thereby reversing the valence of the question. Such a modification suggests that Adam has heard Jay's failure to promptly respond as a sign of impending disagreement. The follow-up question, by reversing the assessment, is apparently designed to allow Jay to respond with agreement.

8   Pomerantz (1984, P. 77)

```
01 Adam:   D'they have a good cook there?
02         (1.7)
03         Nothing special?
04 Jay:    No. Every- everybody takes their turns.
```

In each of these cases then, we see participants' orientation to the robust norm that questions require a response. In their subsequent behavior here, questioners not only orient to the relevance of response but, also, in the design of their talk, display an understanding of what accounts for the norm violation.

Second, we can observe what happens when the response to a question is something other than an answer (see also Stivers and Hayashi 2010). Routinely, in this situation, a recipient either accounts for not answering the question (the most common account being 'I don't know') or makes a suggestion as to how an answer might be found (e.g., suggesting that it be directed to another who might be able to answer the question).

Notice, then, that in examples 9 and 10, the recipient accounts for not answering by explaining that he or she 'does not know'. In example 9, moreover, the recipient goes on to propose that he could 'go by and see' and thus acquire the information that the question seeks, while in 10, Dick's laughter-infused 'okay' marks Deb's non-delayed, non-answer, unaccounted-for response as a norm violation. In example 11, the operator suggests that Guy would need to ask someone else, thereby implying that she does not know herself and, moreover, is not professionally obligated to know.

9 NB I:1:r

```
01 Guy:   Think he'd like tih go:?
02 Jon:   u-I: uh,h I don't -kno:w, uh:heh heh hu:h
03        huh.hhh Ah(h)'ll I(c) I c'd go by 'n' see:,
```

10 YYZ – Deb and Dick

```
01 Dick:  Are the:y leaving today,
02 Deb:   I=don't=know.
03 Dick:  O-(hhh)-kay(hh)
```

11 NB 1.3 (Revised transcript)

```
01 Guy:   Now from, Balboa I jest- I don' haftuh dial
02        one or anything aheada that do I?
03 Oper:  Oh I'm sorry you'd haftuh ask yer "O"
04        Operator.
```

In each case, we see recipients orienting to the norm that a Yes–No question makes relevant an answer response. This orientation is displayed specifically in an account for not answering or in a suggestion as to how the question might be answered by someone other than its recipient.

Third, we can observe what happens in adult conversation when a Yes–No question receives an answer response that disconfirms rather than confirms what it supposes (see also Ford et al. 2004). In the first example below, taken from a family dinner, Virginia has been telling her brother Wesley and his girlfriend Prudence about going out to a bar on the weekend. Where the fragment begins, Wesley asks Virginia whether her

two companions, Beth and Legette, danced together. After Virginia answers (line 2), Prudence follows up with a question to Virginia in line 5. And in line 12, Wesley turns to Prudence and asks her, 'Is that the Paul that we know?'

12 Virginia

```
01 Wesley:   Did Beth and Legette dance any?
02 Virginia: N:o Beth- danced wi(th) Paul
03           mosta'time.
04           (0.9)
05 Prudence: Oh Paul uz there too.
06           (.)
07 Virginia: °Mm hm.
08           (2.0)
09 Virginia: Paul, an' Tom Kutnow, an' uhm (0.5)
10           Jeff Watson:,an'<Marshall Brigg(s).
11           (2.4)
12 Wesley:   Izzat- (1.9) ((chewing)) Paul th't
13           we know?
14 Prudence: Mm hm.
```

Each of these questions conveys its speaker's supposition or belief about what is the case and thus also their expectation as to how the question will be answered. Notice then that the questions in lines 5, 'Oh Paul uz there too', and 12–13, 'Izzat- (1.9) Paul th't we know?', are *confirmed* by 'mm hm'. In contrast, the question in line 1 is *disconfirmed*. What we want to notice is that these confirmations are done as simple token responses ('mm hm'), whereas the disconfirmation turn in line 2 is more elaborate. Specifically, the disconfirming 'no' is accompanied by something of an explanation as to why Beth did not dance with Legette (i.e., because she was dancing with someone else).

This pattern can be observed in other examples from the same occasion. Thus, in example 13, Virginia is proposing that her allowance should be raised from five to ten dollars a week. When mom follows up with the Y–N question, 'Ten dollahs a week?' in line 4, this is confirmed immediately in line 5 with 'mm hm'. However, when mom then asks 'just to throw away?' in line 6, there is a delay before Virginia disconfirms with 'Not to throw away, to spe:nd', using, as in the previous example, a more elaborate format to disconfirm than she did to confirm.

13 Virginia

```
01 Virginia:   But- you know, you have to have
02             enough mo:ney¿ I think ten
03             dollars'ud be good.
04             (0.4)
05 Mom:        ˙hhh Ten dollahs a week?
06 Virginia:   Mm hm.
07 Mom:        Just to throw away?
08             (0.5)
09 Virginia:   Not to throw away, to spe:nd.
```

And, finally, in example 14, after Wesley tells his mom that he jogged earlier in the evening, he returns the question asking, in line 6, 'Didjyou?'. When Mom disconfirms this, she adds the account "cause I didn' have tah:me.'.

14 Virginia

```
01 Mom:        Don't tell me you jogged tuh ni:ght!
02 Wesley:     >Mmhm.<
03 ???:        e[h huh! huh
04 Mom:         [Didju rea:lly?
05 ???:        ˙hhh[h
06 Wesley:          [Did[jyou?
07 Prudence:            [(He) jogs
08             [a:ll the time. ]
09 Mom:        [No, I didn' jog th]is mornin'
10             'cause I didn' have tah:me.
```

Across these examples (and many others), we see adult conversationalists' pervasive orientation to a set of norms that organize sequences of question and answer. Specifically, production of a question (here a Y–N question) makes relevant (1) a response, (2) which is an answer, (3) which confirms the supposition conveyed. Participants orient to these norms in conversation by holding both themselves and others accountable to them. Thus, where participants do not behave in conformity with expectation, an account for the deviation becomes relevant. Taken together, these norms constitute an underlying interactional architecture within which sequences of question and answer are produced.

We are now in a position to ask how children compare in this respect. Specifically, do they orient to these norms in the same way as adults? In a study that draws on quantitative evidence of timings as well as qualitative evidence of case-by-case analysis, Stivers, Sidnell and Bergen (2015) show that children aged 4–8 show an emerging reflexive awareness of these norms in peer interaction, though they do not consistently hold one another accountable to them. In the peer data, children typically respond to questions. Moreover, when no response is produced, they sometimes pursue it, thereby suggesting that they are oriented to the relevance of response.

In example 15, Jeremy, Benajmin and Paul are playing with wooden blocks known as Kapla. In line 1, Jeremy is looking directly at Benjamin when he asks, 'Can we dus- tch connect ou:rs sha-( )'. Benjamin, however, does not look up from what he is doing at the table and after 0.6 seconds Jeremy follows up with a name in an effort to pursue a response. At this point, Paul, who is on the other side of the table and who has not taken part in the discussion of joining the structures to this point, says something that appears to be a possible response to what Jeremy has said. Jeremy however ignores this and follows up again this time with 'Plea:::se', said while looking in Benjamin's direction. Rather than respond to Jeremy, Benjamin momentarily discontinues his building, looks towards the adult and says 'Where's the kapla. I need it.'

15 SK_T10 2:40

```
01 Jeremy:     Can we dus- tch connect ou:rs sha-( )
02             (0.6)
03             Benjamin.
04             (0.3)
05 Paul:       yeah we don' need tuh clean up.
06             (0.2) 'cause we wanna connec'
07             dis. [( )
08 Jeremy:          [Plea:::se
09 Benjamin:   Where's the kapla. I need it. ((to adult))
```

Notice then that Jeremy shows a clear orientation to the relevance of response from

Benjamin here by pursing one first with the name at line 3 and subsequently with 'please' at line 8. These can be seen as attempts by Jeremy to hold Benjamin accountable to the norm that question recipients are obligated to respond. Notice further that this is unsuccessful and that Benjamin, by not responding and, indeed, by completely ignoring Jeremy, treats response as optional.

There are other cases in the corpus where no response is ever produced and neither questioner nor recipient treats this as problematic. This kind of thing is vanishingly rare in adult conversation but relatively common among children, particularly 4- and 5-year-olds. Example 16 illustrates this well. Here Jude leans forward, gazing across the table at Kian and thus selecting her to answer a question that is fully in her epistemic domain (Heritage and Raymond 2005). Kian glances at him but does not respond. Although Jude maintains his gaze toward her for approximately 3 seconds, after that he continues his own building project. Neither pursues the matter.

16 JKT1 10:05

```
01        ((Kian's building fall collapses))
02 Jude:  Than- that's what you wanted
03        it to do?
04        (12.0)
05 Jude:  (I:::'m tumble wood!)
```

In sustaining gaze toward Kian after the production of his question, Jude shows some orientation to the normative expectation for response from Kian as the question recipient. However, he neither pursues response nor sanctions her lack of response. For her part, Kian offers no account for not responding and, indeed, appears to more or less completely ignore Jude throughout.

To summarize, these data suggest that children have an *emerging* accountability to a norm that obligates a question's recipient to respond. On the one hand, in the vast majority of cases, question recipients do in fact respond. Moreover, questioners orient to a response as due by looking at a recipient,

waiting for a response to be produced before continuing their own talk and by pursuing a response when it is not immediately delivered. On the other hand, child recipients of questions fail to respond much more frequently than adults do. Furthermore, child questioners do not pursue responses as consistently as adults. Question recipients who do eventually produce responses also typically treat the delayed response as unproblematic and do not account for delay nor attempt to minimize delay by the use of turn-initial elements such as *uh*, *uhm* or *well*.

With respect to the second norm described above, although children discriminate between answer and non-answer responses in terms of the frequency with which they produce each and the relative delay in their production, they do not exhibit a reflexive awareness of these categorical differences in the way that they *produce* their answers and non-answer responses. Instead, they tend to produce them in much the same way – relatively directly and with little in the way of account. In fact, although there were a few cases in which a child accounted for not answering a wh-question with an explanation such as 'I don't know', there were no cases in which they did this in response to a Yes–No question. Rather, non-answer responses to Yes–No questions took a variety of forms such as laughter, manual action or the initiation of repair. This suggests that children, unlike adults, do not treat non-answering responses as particularly problematic and in need of explanation or account.

While the frequency distributions and the relative timing of confirmations and disconfirmations suggest that children may be oriented to the preference for confirmation, the ways they design their disconfirming turns do not show a reflexive awareness of the norm. Adults produce disconfirmations less frequently than confirmations (see Stivers et al. 2010) and typically position them following delay. Adults also tend to push the disconfirmation items (i.e., words such as 'no') further into the turn through the use of prefaces, mitigations and hedges; and they may also provide accounts for not confirming. All of these practices are communicative and show a reflexive awareness on the part of the speaker that there has been a departure from the norm for confirmation. Children do not typically incorporate these design features into their disconfirmations and deliver both confirmations and disconfirmations directly and in essentially the same manner.

Consider example 17 where Roger invites David to build a marble run with him through a question. David's confirmation comes in slight overlap with the prepositional phrase, something that is common among adults delivering confirmations.

17 8 year old children

01 Roger: Devon do you wanna build a marble
02   run [with me?
03 David: [Yea::h s:ure:.

However, the design of David's confirmation is indistinguishable from Bill's disconfirmation in example 18: Here, Bill rejects Jason's offer quickly, without account or modulation.

18 5 year old children

01 Bill: Do you want these?, roo:fs:,
02 Jason: No.
03   (0.5)
04 Jason: Now I'm ((looks at adult)) transforming
05   it to people.

Similarly, in example 19, Honor claims that she has some knowledge of what a farm looks like in lines 1–2. Max offers a guess as to how she knows this, asking whether it might be because Honor lived on a farm when she was a baby (line 4).

19 4 year old children

01 Honor: This is a big fa:rm. This is not how (.)
02   a farm looks like when I saw one.
03   (1.0)
04 Max: Because when you were a baby you
05   lived in a farm?,
06 Honor: Nao.
07   (3.8)

08 Max: At the Santa Claus parade you saw
09   a farm?

At line 6, Honor responds to Max's guess with a response that disconfirms what he has suggested. She does this without any sign of reluctance such as *Uh/Uhm*, mitigation or modulation. Rather, she simply and directly disconfirms. In this way, she does not treat the form of her answer as having any implications for her relationship with Max. Furthermore, Honor provides no account to help Max reconcile Honor's earlier claim to know something about farms with her disconfirmation of having lived on a farm, and Max is left to offer another guess (line 8–9).

Even when children *do* design their disconfirmations in a way that shows an orientation to the dispreferred nature of their action, it usually also carries elements that are inconsistent with this orientation. For instance, in example 20, Jason makes a request. Bill provides an account for denying the request. However, the rejection of the request is done immediately and without prepositioned modifiers that might delay its production. Thus, although the account shows some orientation to the dispreferred nature of the rejection, the abrupt delivery of the rejection component cross-cuts this and potentially undermines any ameliorating effect it might have.

20 5 year old children

01 Jason: Could I: ha:ve i:::t.
02 Bill: No. I'm ma:king a new one.
03 Jason: A:ww:::?
04 Bill: A tiny one.

Together, these examples show that 4–8-year-old children generally do not display a fully developed orientation to the norm that prioritizes confirmations over disconfirmations. Although they regularly produce more confirmations than disconfirmations and produce confirmations more quickly than disconfirmations, they do not produce their confirmations and disconfirmations in ways that show a reflexive awareness of a norm governing this behavior and do not consistently make communicative use of the underlying norm. Thus, disconfirmations are no more likely than confirmations to be produced directly and without mitigation or accounts. For this reason, children appear to have an emerging sense of accountability within this domain, rather than having a fully developed orientation to the norm. Perhaps most importantly, children do not seem to treat the design of their confirming and nonconfirming turns as having consequences for the micro-management of social relations. A child will routinely issue a direct and immediate disconfirmation without thereby implying (or creating), and without being taken as implying, social-relational trouble.

CONCLUSION

If it is to persist over time, a society must constantly recruit and integrate new members. The research discussed in this chapter proposes that this happens largely through participation in social interaction. From within the first few days of life, children are treated as possible co-participants in interaction by adult members of society. After a period of roughly nine months, children begin to engage in a suite of joint attentional behaviors which allow them to play a more agentive role – following and also directing the attention of others. By the beginning of the third year, these joint attentional skills combine with an increasingly sophisticated linguistic ability to allow for still more complex forms of engagement. At the same time, children show an emerging awareness of the social norms that not only regulate social life but, moreover, provide for the intelligibility of social conduct. As the repertoire of practices within a particular domain becomes elaborated on (such as the set of practices used in the making of requests), children begin to distinguish between different interactional environments and select particular utterance formats to deal with specific

interactional contingencies. Even while these abilities develop, however, in their interactions with same-age peers, child up to the age of 8 show less accountability to norms than do adults in equivalent situations. Where adults design their conduct in interaction to carefully manage inferences about their relations with others, children appear to pay significantly less attention to the implications of their behavior in this respect.

Research into early childhood from a conversation-analytic perspective is still in its infancy. While we have some sense of the ways in which children participate in various activities, we still do not have detailed accounts of the ways in which the basic structures of conversational interaction (turn-taking, repair, etc.) develop over time. Moreover, to date, almost all the conversation-analytic research on children has focused on English-speaking communities, and as such we have little sense of the degree to which development in this area differs across communities (compare the extensive comparative work that has been done in the area of language socialization; see e.g., Duranti et al. 2012). That said, conversation analysis provides a rigorous method for the investigation of interaction that can readily be applied to interaction among children. Moreover, because conversation analysis involves a direct study of social life (at one basic point of production, i.e., interaction among members) and does not rely on the post hoc testimony or accounts of participants, it may offer a particularly useful tool in the investigation of children and human development.

FURTHER READING

Kidwell, M. and Zimmerman, D. H. (2007) 'Joint attention as action', *Journal of Pragmatics*, 39(3): 592–611.
Schegloff, E. A. (1989) 'Reflections on language, development, and the interactional character of talk-in-interaction', in M. H. Bornstein and J. S. Bruner (eds), *Interaction*

in human development. New York: Lawrence Erlbaum Associates. pp. 139–153.

Wootton, A. J. (1997) *Interaction and the development of mind*. Cambridge: Cambridge University Press.

QUESTIONS FOR REFLECTION

1 In what ways do participants orient to the underlying normative organization of interaction? How might children differ from adults in this respect?

2 If children less consistently orient to the underlying norms of conversation (e.g., failing to answer questions without accounting for that failure) what consequences might this have for their social relations?

3 What role, if any, is played by explicit commentary (e.g., 'you need to say "please"') and correction in the development of conversational and interactional competence and accountability? What practices other than explicit commentary and correction might play a role here?

NOTES

1 In a recent paper memorializing Mel Pollner, Heritage and Clayman (2012) describe such interactional norms as 'questions demand responses/ answers from their addressed recipients' as *incorrigible*. Relating their discussion to Pollner's consideration of mundane reasoning which was itself an elaboration of themes from Evans-Pritchard's masterful ethnography of Zande Oracles, the authors note that conduct that does not conform to the norm – such as the non-response in the imagined situation – does not in any way threaten the power of the rule/norm. Rather, any violation provides a catalyst for numerous 'secondary accounting devices', reasoning about why the person is not abiding by the norm. Such reasoning not only generates inferences about what a person 'intends' or 'means' in the current situation – 'what they are doing' – but also, in perfect feedback loop, insulates the norm or rule from challenge. These secondary accounting devices are premised on an assumption of *incorrigibility* (see 'the poison oracle does not err') which, in their operation, they also reinforce. And, of course, the system works just as

well in the reverse direction – e.g., if a recipient is annoyed by another's question, he may choose to convey that feeling by refusing to respond. To summarize, departures from a 'norm' do not threaten the norm but rather are understood to be produced 'for cause' – participants in interaction engage in interpretive work or local reasoning – to understand what that cause is, what the reason for the departure might be.

2 Examples are presented using the transcription conventions originally developed by Gail Jefferson. For present purposes, the most important symbols are the period ('.') which indicates falling and final intonation, the question mark ('?') indicating rising intonation, and brackets ('[" and"]') marking the onset and resolution of overlapping talk between two speakers. Equal signs, which come in pairs – one at the end of a line and another at the start of the next line or one shortly thereafter – are used to indicate that the second line followed the first with no discernable silence between them, i.e. it was 'latched' to it. Numbers in parentheses (e.g. (0.5)) indicate silence, represented in tenths of a second. Colons are used to indicate prolongation or stretching of the sound preceding them. The more colons, the longer the stretching. Double parenthesis enclose descriptions, in italics, of non-verbal, bodily behavior. For an explanation of other symbols see Sacks, Schegloff and Jefferson 1974; Sidnell 2010a).

REFERENCES

Astington, J. (1994) *The child's discovery of the mind*. Cambridge, MA: Harvard University Press.

Atkinson, J. M. and Drew, P. (1979) *Order in court: The organisation of verbal interaction in judicial settings*. London: Macmillan.

Brown, P. (2011) 'The cultural organization of attention', in A. Duranti, E. Ochs and B. B. Schieffelin (eds), *The handbook of language socialization*. Malden, MA: Wiley-Blackwell. pp. 29–55.

Bruner, J. S., Roy, C. and Ratner, N. (1982) 'The beginnings of request', in K. E. Nelson (ed.), *Children's language* (Vol. 3). Hillsdale, NJ: Lawrence Erlbaum. pp. 91–138.

Butler, C. and Weatherall, A. (2006) '"No, we're not playing families": Membership categorization in children's play,' *Research on Language and Social Interaction*, 39(4): 441–470.

Cahill, P. (2010) 'Children's participation in their primary care consultations', in H. Gardner and M. A. Forrester (eds), *Analysing interactions in childhood: Insights from conversation analysis.* Chichester: Wiley. pp. 128–145.

Chouinard, M. M. (2007) 'Children's questions: A mechanism for cognitive development', *Monographs of the Society for Research in Child Development*, 72(1): 1–112.

Clemente, I. (2009) 'Progressivity and participation: Children's management of parental assistance in pediatric chronic pain encounters', *Sociology of Health & Illness*, 31(6): 83–98.

Drew, P. (1981) 'Adults' corrections of children's mistakes', in P. French and M. MacLure (eds), *Adult–child conversations*. London: Croom Helm. pp. 244–267.

Dryer, M. S. (2008) 'Polar questions', in M. S. Dryer and M. Haspelmath (eds), *The World Atlas of Language Structures Online*. Munich: Max Planck Digital Library.

Dryer, M. S. (2011) 'Position of interrogative phrases in content questions', in M. S. Dryer and M. Haspelmath (eds), *The World Atlas of Language Structures Online*. Munich: Max Planck Digital Library.

Duranti, A., Ochs, E. and Schieffelin, B. B. (eds) (2012) *Handbook of language socialization*. Malden, MA: Wiley-Blackwell.

Enfield, N. J. (2013) *Relationship thinking: Agency, enchrony and human sociality*. Oxford/New York: Oxford University Press.

Enfield, N. J. and Sidnell, J. (2014) 'Language presupposes an enchronic infrastructure for social interaction', in D. Dor, C. Knight and J. Lewis (eds), *The social origins of language*. Oxford: Oxford University Press. pp. 92–104.

Ervin-Tripp, S. M. (1977) 'Wait for me, rollerskate', in C. Mitchell-Kernan and S. Ervin-Tripp (eds), *Child discourse*. New York: Academic Press. pp. 165–188.

Filipi, A. (2009) *Toddler and parent interaction: The organisation of gaze, pointing and vocalisation*. Amsterdam: John Benjamins.

Ford, C. E., Fox, B. A. and Hellerman, J. (2004) 'Getting past *no*', in E. Couper-Kuhlen and C. E. Ford (eds), *Sound patterns in interaction: Cross-linguistic studies from conversation*. Amsterdam: John Benjamins. pp. 233–269.

Ford, C. E., Fox, B. A. and Thompson, S. A. (1996) 'Practices in the construction of turns: The TCU revisted', *Pragmatics*, 6(3): 427–454.

Forrester, M. A. and Reason, D. (2006) 'Competency and participation in acquiring a mastery of language: A reconsideration of the idea of membership', *Sociological Review*, 54(3): 446–466.

Garfinkel, H. (1967) *Studies in Ethnomethodology*. Englewood Cliffs, NJ: Prentice-Hall.

Garfinkel, H. and Sacks, H. (1970) 'On formal structures of practical actions', in J. C. McKinney and E. A. Tiryakian (eds) *Theoretical Sociology: Perspectives and Developments*. New York: Appleton-Century-Crofts. pp. 337–366.

Goffman, E. (1964) 'The neglected situation', *American Anthropologist*, 66(6, pt. 2): 133–136.

Goffman, E. (1967) *Interaction ritual: Essays in face to face behavior*. Garden City, NY: Doubleday.

Goodwin, C. (1979) 'The interactive construction of a sentence in natural conversation', in G. Psathas (ed.), *Everyday language: Studies in ethnomethodology*. New York: Irvington. pp. 97–121.

Goodwin, C. (1980) 'Restarts, pauses, and the achievement of a state of mutual gaze at turn-beginning', *Sociological Inquiry*, 50: 272–302.

Goodwin, C. (1981) *Conversational organization: Interaction between speakers and hearers*. New York: Academic Press.

Goodwin, M. H. (1990) *He-said-she-said: Talk as social organization among Black children*. Bloomington, IN: Indiana University Press.

Goodwin, M. H. and Goodwin, C. (1987) 'Children's arguing', in S. Philips, S. Steele and C. Tanz (eds), *Language, gender, and sex in comparative perspective*. Cambridge: Cambridge University Press. pp. 200–248.

Hayashi, M., Raymond, G. and Sidnell, J. (eds) (2013) *Conversational repair and human understanding*. Cambridge: Cambridge University Press.

Heritage, J. (1984) *Garfinkel and ethnomethodology*. Cambridge: Polity Press.

Heritage, J. and Clayman, S. (2012) 'Melvin Pollner: A view from the suburbs', *American Sociologist*, 43: 99–108.

Heritage, J. and Raymond, G. (2005) 'The terms of agreement: Indexing epistemic authority and subordination in assessment sequences', *Social Psychology Quarterly*, 68(1): 15–38.

Hutchby, I. and O'Reilly, M. (2010) 'Children's participation and the familial moral order in family therapy', *Discourse Studies*, 12(1): 49–64.

Kidwell, M. (2011) 'Epistemics and embodiment in the interactions of very young children', in T. Stivers, J. Steensig and L. Mondada (eds), *The morality of knowledge in conversation*. Cambridge: Cambridge University Press. pp. 29–57.

Kidwell, M. (2012) 'Interaction among Children', in J. Sidnell and T. Stivers (eds), The Handbook of Conversation Analysis. Oxford: Blackwell. pp. 511–532.

Kidwell, M. and Zimmerman, D. H. (2006) '"Observability" in the interactions of very young children', *Communication Monographs*, 73(1): 1–28.

Kidwell, M. and Zimmerman, D. H. (2007) 'Joint attention as action', *Journal of Pragmatics*, 39(3): 592–611.

Kitzinger, C. (2012) 'Repair', in J. Sidnell and T. Stivers (eds), *The handbook of conversation analysis*. Oxford: Blackwell/Wiley. pp. 229–256.

Lerner, G. H. (2003) 'Selecting next speaker: The context sensitive operation of a context-free organization', *Language in Society*, 32: 177–201.

Lerner, G. H., Zimmerman, D. H. and Kidwell, M. (2011) 'Formal structures of practical tasks: A resource for action in the social lives of very young children', in C. Goodwin, C. Le Baron and J. Streeck (eds), *Multimodality and human activity: Research on human behavior, action and communication*. Cambridge: Cambridge University Press. pp. 44–58.

Levinson, S. C. (1983) *Pragmatics*. Cambridge: Cambridge University Press.

Levinson, S. C. (2006) 'On the human "interaction engine"', in N. J. Enfield and S. C. Levinson (eds), *Roots of human sociality: Culture, cognition, and interaction*. Oxford: Berg. pp. 39–69.

Maynard, D. W. (1985) 'On the functions of social conflict among children', *American Sociological Review*, 50: 207–223.

McElhinny, B. (2003) 'Theorizing gender in sociolinguistics and linguistic anthropology', in J. Holmes and M. Meyerhoff (eds), *The handbook of language and gender*. Oxford: Blackwell. pp. 21–42.

Pomerantz, A. M. (1984) 'Agreeing and disagreeing with assessments: Some features of preferred/dispreferred turn shapes', in J. M. Atkinson and J. Heritage (eds), *Structures of social action: Studies in conversation analysis*. Cambridge: Cambridge University Press. pp. 57–101.

Raymond, G. (2003) 'Grammar and social organization: Yes/no interrogatives and the structure of responding', *American Sociological Review*, 68: 939–967.

Raymond, G. and Sidnell, J. (2014) 'Conversation analysis', in A. Jaworski and N. Coupland (eds), *The Discourse Reader*, 3rd edn. New York: Routledge. pp. 249–263.

Robinson, J. D. (2007) 'The role of numbers and statistics within conversation analysis', *Communication Methods and Measures*, 1: 65–75.

Sacks, H. (1972) 'On the analyzability of stories by children', in J. J. Gumperz and D. Hymes (eds), *Directions in sociolinguistics: The ethnography of communication*. New York: Holt, Rinehart and Winston. pp. 325–345.

Sacks, H. (1984) 'Notes on methodology', in J. M. Atkinson and J. Heritage (eds), *Structures of social action: Studies in conversation analysis*. Cambridge: Cambridge University Press. pp. 21–27.

Sacks, H. (1995) *Lectures on conversation*, Volumes I & II. Oxford: Basil Blackwell.

Sacks, H., Schegloff, E. A. and Jefferson, G. (1974) 'A simplest systematics for the organization of turn-taking for conversation', *Language*, 50(4): 696–735.

Schegloff, E. A. (1968) 'Sequencing in conversational openings', *American Anthropologist*, 70(6): 1075–1095.

Schegloff, E. A. (1984) 'On some questions and ambiguities in conversation', in J. M. Atkinson and J. Heritage (eds), *Structures of social action: Studies in conversation analysis*. Cambridge: Cambridge University Press. pp. 28–52.

Schegloff, E. A. (1989) 'Reflections on language, development, and the interactional character of talk-in-interaction', in M. H. Bornstein and J. S. Bruner (eds), *Interaction in human development*. New York: Lawrence Erlbaum. pp. 139–153.

Schegloff, E. A. (2002) 'Conversation analysis, then and now', Plenary Address for the Inaugural Session of the Section-in-Formation on Ethnomethodology and Conversation Analysis of the American Sociological Association, Chicago, IL.

Schegloff, E. A. (2007) *Sequence organization in interaction: A primer in conversation analysis*. Cambridge: Cambridge University Press.

Schegloff, E. A., Jefferson, G. and Sacks, H. (1977) 'The preference for self-correction in the organization of repair in conversation', *Language*, 53(2): 361–382.

Sidnell, J. (2010a) *Conversation analysis: An introduction*. Oxford: Wiley-Blackwell.

Sidnell, J. (2010b) 'Questioning repeats in the talk of four-year-old children', in H. Gardner and M. A. Forrester (eds), *Analyzing interactions in childhood: Insights from conversation analysis*. Oxford: Wiley-Blackwell. pp. 103–127.

Sidnell, J. (2011) 'The epistemics of make-believe', in T. Stivers, L. Mondada and J. Steensig (eds), *The morality of knowledge in conversation*. Cambridge: Cambridge University Press. pp. 131–156.

Stivers, T. (2012) 'Sequence organization', in J. Sidnell and T. Stivers (eds), *The handbook of conversation analysis*. Oxford: Wiley-Blackwell. pp. 191–209.

Stivers, T. and Hayashi, M. (2010) 'Transformative answers: One way to resist a question's constraints', *Language in Society*, 39(1): 1–25.

Stivers, T. and Majid, A. (2007) 'Questioning children: Interactional evidence of implicit bias in medical interviews', *Social Psychology Quarterly*, 70: 424–441.

Stivers, T. and Robinson, J. D. (2006) 'A preference for progressivity in interaction', *Language in Society*, 35(3): 367–392.

Stivers, T. and Rossano, F. (2010) 'Mobilizing response', *Research on Language and Social Interaction*, 43(1): 3–31.

Stivers, T., Enfield, N. J., Brown, P., Englert, C., Hayashi, M., Heinemann, T., et al. (2009) 'Universals and cultural variation in turn-taking in conversation', *Proceedings of the National Academy of Sciences of the USA*, 106(26): 10587–10592.

Stivers, T., Enfield, N. J. and Levinson, S. C. (eds) (2010) 'Question–response sequences in conversation: A comparison across 10 languages', *Journal of Pragmatics*, 42(10): 2615–2619.

Stivers, T., Sidnell, J. and Bergen, C. (2015) 'Children's responses to questions in peer interaction: A window into the ontogenesis of interactional competence', unpublished manuscript.

Tarplee, C. (1996) 'Working on young children's utterances: Prosodic aspects of repetition during picture labeling', in E. Couper-Kuhlen and M. Selting (eds), *Prosody in conversation: Interactional studies*. Cambridge: Cambridge University Press. pp. 436–461.

Tarplee, C. (2010) 'Next turn and intersubjectivity: A conversation analytic perspective on the role of "feedback" in children's language acquisition', in H. Gardner and M. A. Forrester (eds), *Analyzing interactions in childhood: Insights from conversation analysis*. Oxford: Wiley-Blackwell. pp. 3–22.

Tomasello, M. (1999) *The cultural origins of human cognition*. Cambridge, MA: Harvard University Press.

Tomasello, M. (2008) *Origins of human communication*. Cambridge, MA: MIT Press.

Tomasello, M. and Carpenter, M. (2007) 'Shared intentionality', *Developmental Science*, 10: 121–125.

Tomasello, M., Carpenter, M., Call, J., Behne, T. and Moll, H. (2005) 'Understanding and sharing intentions: The origins of cultural cognition', *Behavioral and Brain Sciences*, 28(5): 675–735.

Trevarthen, C. (1977) 'Descriptive analyses of infant communicative behaviour', in H. R. Schaffer (ed.), *Studies in mother–infant interaction*. London: Academic Press. pp. 227–270.

Wells, W. H. G. and Corrin, J. (2004) 'Prosodic resources, turn-taking and overlap in children's talk-in-interaction', in E. Couper-Kuhlen and C. E. Ford (eds), *Sound patterns in interaction: Cross-linguistic studies from conversation*. Amsterdam: John Benjamins. pp. 119–144.

Wertsch, J. V. (1985) *Vygotsky and the social formation of mind*. Cambridge, MA: Harvard University Press.

Whalen, M. R. (1995) 'Working toward play: Complexity in children's fantasy activities', *Language in Society*, 24: 315–348.

Wootton, A. J. (1981a) 'Two request forms for four year olds', *Journal of Pragmatics*, 5: 511–523.

Wootton, A. J. (1981b) 'The management of grantings and rejections by parents in request sequences', *Semiotica*, 37: 59–89.

Wootton, A. J. (1994) 'Object transfer, intersubjectivity and third position repair: Early developmental observations of one child', *Journal of Child Language*, 21(3): 543–564.

Wootton, A. J. (1997) *Interaction and the development of mind*. Cambridge: Cambridge University Press.

Wootton, A. J. (2007) 'A puzzle about please: Repair, increments, and related matters in the speech of a young child', *Research on Language and Social Interaction*, 40(2–3): 171–198.

Wootton, A. J. (2010) 'The sequential skills of a two year old: One child's use of the word "actually"', in H. Gardner and M. A. Forrester (eds), *Analyzing interactions in childhood: Insights from conversation analysis*. Oxford: Wiley-Blackwell. pp. 59–73.

17

Documentation in Early Childhood Research: Practice and Research Informing each Other

Margaret Carr, Bronwen Cowie and Linda Mitchell

INTRODUCTION

A Definition of Documentation

The discussion of documentation in the early years owes much to the writing on teaching and learning from Carlina Rinaldi and Reggio Emilia about the role of documentation and the theory of 'the hundred languages'. Referring back to a volume entitled *Making Learning Visible* (Project Zero and Reggio Children, 2001), produced as a collaboration between Project Zero (at Harvard University) and Reggio Children (at Reggio Emilia), Rinaldi writes about the shift in meaning of the concept of 'documentation'. She advocates for the role of documentation in ongoing mutual engagement, as a possibility for reflection:

> The concept of documentation as a collection of documents used for demonstrating the truth of a fact or confirming a thesis is historically correlated to the birth and evolution of scientific thought and a conceptualisation of knowledge as an objective and demonstrable entity. It is thus tied to a certain historical period and to profound reasons of a cultural, social and political nature that I will not examine here. Rather, I find it interesting to underscore how the concept of documentation, which has only recently moved into the scholastic environment, and more specifically into the pedagogical-didactic sphere, has undergone substantial modifications that partially alter its definition. In this context, documentation is interpreted and used for its value as a tool for recalling; that is, as a possibility for reflection. Rinaldi (2006: 62)

Mara Krechevsky and colleagues, writing from Harvard's Project Zero, define documentation as 'the practice of observing, recording, interpreting, and sharing through a variety of media the processes and products of learning in order to deepen learning' (Krechevsky et al., 2010: 65).

Similarly, in this chapter, documentation is defined as material communication tools appropriated or developed by teachers/practitioners or researchers for the purpose of recalling, reflecting on, re-thinking and re-shaping learning, teaching, knowledge and understanding. Curriculum documents only appear as background. The examples come from New Zealand early years contexts, which include a number of features that are especially relevant to this topic: (i) an early childhood curriculum, Te Whāriki, that includes an explicitly stated socio-cultural and ecological stance on teaching and learning, (ii) two curriculum documents (early childhood and school) in which there is a cross-sector alignment of early childhood curriculum strands with school key competences, (iii) teacher freedom, in both sectors, to create their own forms of documentation, (iv) an established repertoire of narrative assessments in the early childhood sector, (v) an early years sector that includes te reo Māori (Māori language) immersion early childhood centres (ngā kōhanga reo) and schools (kura kaupapa Māori), and (vi) a number of opportunities for funding and publishing collaborative practitioner-researcher projects. We follow New Zealand practice to refer to practitioners in both sectors as teachers.

Purpose

The definition of documentation assumes a context and a purpose. In 2014 a paper in *Educational Researcher* discussed new initiatives in the Institute of Education Sciences (the IES) within the US Department of Education that emphasise 'relevance to practice' as a criterion for rigorous research. New programmes at the IES include researcher-practitioner partnerships where the problems are 'relevant to education practice and policy' and stakeholders deem them to be important. The paper questions 'scientific' research strategies that have prescribed and relied on random assignment studies of programme effects, and argues that 'rigor in studies that aim to draw causal inferences about policies, programmes, and practices requires in-depth qualitative research' (Gutierrez and Penuel, 2014: 19). The authors add:

> Studying the 'social life of interventions' moves us away from imagining interventions as fixed passages

of strategies with readily measurable outcomes and toward more open-ended social or socially embedded experiments that involve ongoing mutual engagement. (Gutierrez and Penuel, 2014: 20)

They look for 'new' approaches and tools to inform research that is designed to be directly relevant to practice and policy, and that uses direct observations of practice to 'generate insights into what works, when, why and for whom'. And they ask: 'How can practice and research inform one another?' This chapter explores and exemplifies the opportunities that documentation, in various ways, can assist with this quest.

Plan

There are four parts to this chapter. In the first section, we describe *teachers as researchers* who add a research component to their everyday work of using and creating documentation during teaching and formative assessment practice. Research projects are described in which teachers take the lead to develop the research questions and the direction of the research. The purpose of the documentation is to assist in the construction of learner identities and learning journeys, and to include others in the local community in discussions about learning. The audience is primarily the children, the teachers, the families and interested parties in the local community.

In the second section, we explore the different ways in which documentation can also become data in *collaborative teacher-researcher projects*. These projects may also construct documents to assist in the development of new knowledge and theoretical frameworks that will travel beyond the early childhood centre or the school and their immediate communities. In this case, documentation assists in connecting two communities of practice: teachers and external researchers. The audience includes the research community, policy-makers and the wider national and international education community.

The third section describes some research where documentation that is generated by teachers crosses the boundary from an early childhood centre to a school – and, in the New Zealand case, crosses from one curriculum to another. It does some unique learning journey and identity work. Etienne Wenger (1998) describes the significance for 'what it means to be a person' of this boundary-crossing, and this section explains how documentation can play a central role in this shift from one community to another:

> (W)hen a child moves from a family to a classroom, when an immigrant moves from one culture to another, or when an employee moves from the ranks to a management position, learning involves more than appropriating new pieces of information. Learners must often deal with conflicting forms of individuality and competence as defined in different communities. (Wenger, 1998: 160)

The final section summarises the story of the chapter and reflects back on the previous discussions to consider some particular conditions that enhance the ability of documentation to do its educational work. We will suggest that in order to be effective at crossing boundaries of time and place, the documentation must invite and/or construct re-contextualising in some way.

TEACHERS AS RESEARCHERS: USING DOCUMENTATION TO ASSIST IN THE CONSTRUCTION OF LEARNING JOURNEYS AND LEARNER IDENTITIES

In a number of early childhood (0–8 years) educational research projects in New Zealand, the teachers' everyday documentation forms the backbone of the data. In 2002, as part of the New Zealand Government's 10-year strategic plan for early childhood education policy – *Pathways to the Future/ Ngā Huarahi Arataki* – an early childhood education Centre of Innovation (COI) programme began. To be considered as a COI, an early childhood service had to be doing something innovative, worthy of a research

project, and have staff who were willing and able to undertake research. The teachers then invited researchers from tertiary research communities to provide advice and support and to assist with dissemination. Fifteen projects were completed (Meade, 2005, 2006, 2007 and 2010).

During one of the projects (Ryder and Wright, 2005; the teacher as first author), the 'profile books' (portfolios of documented assessments) were shifted from the office into the centre and became an integral part of the programme. This happened after the teachers asked 'Who do the books actually belong to?' The teachers researched the ways the children built autobiographical narratives around this documentation.

Two kōhanga reo became Centres of Innovation. One of these was Te Kōhanga Reo o Puau Te Moananui a Kiwa. During this project, videotapes were made of teaching episodes, and these were revisited over and over again, as a valuable stimulation for debate and change. Practical changes were made to increase the opportunities for conversational reo (Māori language). Outcomes from this project included an increase in the documentation of their practice. As well as the videos, this included photographs, written records of the teachers (kaiako and kaiāwhina) reflection on the video, and portfolios of the children's learning. A theme for their project became documentation and dialogue (Kaimahi of Te Kōhanga Reo o Puau Te Moananui a Kiwa, with H. Poatu and K. Stokes, 2005).

In another kōhanga from this programme, Brenda Soutar with Te Whānau o Mana Tamariki (2010) described the research task for the Mana Tamariki Kōhanga Reo: to strengthen the reciprocal relationships between (i) children as high achievers who exemplify the hopes and aspirations of their people, (ii) whānau (families in the widest sense), (iii) te reo (Māori language) and (iv) paki ako. Paki ako are an adaptation of Learning Stories (Carr and Lee, 2012). Learning Stories are formative assessment documents in story format that include a description of a learning episode (for one or more children), photographs, an evaluative commentary on the learning and suggestions for the future. The commentary in paki ako includes an emphasis on Māori values, practices and aspirations for children. Te Kōhanga Reo o Mana Tamariki also became a case study in a book on Te Whāriki, illustrating ways in which the Te Whāriki curriculum principle of *whakamana* (translated in the curriculum document as 'empowerment') is supported in practice.

> This principle connects with notions of agency and identity. In some curriculum documents it is referred to as 'self regulation', a label that is more psychological and individual than whakamana/empowerment, in which the concept of agency is more likely to refer to a context. Children are positioned with, or construct, agency in particular contexts, and may begin to recognise or construct these opportunities in other places: to assume the lead or to take responsibility. (Lee et al., 2013: 78)

That chapter describes the implementation of Te Whāriki from a Māori perspective, illustrating this with paki ako documentation. One of the paki ako (Lee et al., 2013: 80–82) describes a conversation about an act of vandalism in which the teacher (kaiako) writes that the children were 'guided by their cultural practices and values': they shifted the direction of the talk to consider vandalism as disrespect to the community, the building and the ancestors. This written account is revisited for discussion and reflection with the children by the kaiako and the families; paki ako are often printed in poster format and displayed on the walls of the centre for the same purpose.

In the volume *Learning Stories: Constructing Learner Identities in Early Education* (Carr and Lee, 2012), examples of teachers' documentation, including 37 Learning Stories, are analysed and annotated for their role in recalling and reflecting on the learning. Here is Naomi (Carr and Lee, 2012: 5), a teacher, reflecting on revisiting documentation with three- and four-year-old children:

> I have instigated many of these revisiting conversations and sometimes I have not chosen my timing well and the conversation has reflected this; the

child doesn't seem too interested and so I am having to lead the discussion; this often leads to my asking too many questions and the child does not say much. Today my timing was different in that I could see Rose was looking for someone to share her portfolio with and I seized the moment, offering to be that person for her. What a difference between this conversation and the first one I initiated with Rose. For the most part she led the conversation and I followed; I think this shows in comparing the length of my first conversation with Rose [18 verbal turns] and this one [six weeks later: 74 verbal turns].

Narrative Assessment Documents from Early Childhood Practice, Collected Together with Related Research as Exemplars for Teachers

A professional development resource, 20 booklets on documented assessments from early childhood centres in New Zealand, was commissioned by the Ministry of Education and published in 2004, 2007 and 2009: *Kei Tua o te Pae. Assessment for Learning: Early childhood exemplars* (2004, 2007a, 2009). These booklets integrated research-related and theoretical discussions with narrative formative assessments from everyday practice in centres, together with references and reflective questions for professional development. *Kei Tua o te Pae* is a quote from a lullaby or oriori by Hirini Melbourne; it is translated as Beyond the Horizon and Book One explains the use of this metaphor:

> In an ever changing world, we know that young children's horizons will expand and change in ways that cannot be foreseen. Children will travel beyond the current horizon, and early childhood is part of that. (Ministry of Education, 2004, Book 1: 5)

This resource was distributed to all early childhood centres and primary schools in the country, and its publication was followed by a Ministry of Education professional development programme for all early childhood teachers that focused on documentation as a means of formative assessment – using the exemplars in *Kei Tua o te Pae* for reflexive discussion and debate. This publication and accompanying professional development was another policy initiative under the government's 2002 strategic plan for early childhood education, aimed to improve quality teaching and learning practices. The locality-based evaluation of the strategic plan (Mitchell et al., 2011) that tracked the same early childhood services over 2004, 2006 and 2009 found particularly marked improvements in assessment, planning and evaluation practices and teachers' conceptual understanding of Te Whāriki, gains that were linked to the continuing and high usage of Kei Tua o te Pae, Centre of Innovation publications, workshops and professional development. Parent surveys showed marked increases in the percentage of parents who were contributing to assessment documentation and to the planning for their own child over the term of the evaluation. Teachers' understanding of socio-cultural theory was enhanced; as described in the introduction to the national early childhood curriculum, this theoretical stance was outlined as follows:

> This curriculum emphasises the critical role of socially and culturally mediated learning and of reciprocal and responsive relationships with people, places, and things. Children learn through collaboration with adults and peers, through guided participation and observation of others, as well as through exploration and reflection. (Ministry of Education, 1996: 9)

These findings were supported by a 2006 cross-sectional evaluation of the same resource by Stuart and colleagues (2008). That study also noted shifts in the quality of assessment practices and the associated documentation towards socio-cultural approaches that build an assessment community inclusive of children, families and teachers.

Documentation Designed to Engage Families and Children in Assessment with an Emphasis on Social Competence, Communication and Literacy

Book 7 (Continuity) of *Kei Tua o te Pae* (Ministry of Education, 2004: 27–39) provides examples of documentation enabling family engagement in assessment. In one of the exemplars, ten learning stories over time in Fe'ao's portfolio document the progress in his learning in social competence, communication and literacy. A number of these learning stories include a parent comment, hand written, indicating that these documents have been revisited with Fe'ao at home and adding some comments of connection with the home (sometimes in answer to a question posed in the portfolio by a teacher). Examples include: 'Fe'ao talk a lot at home about his kite experience at kindy with Aminiasi. He does fly kite at home. He asked his Dad to make up a kite', and 'Fe'ao came home with his pizza made at kindy … he explained how he made it at school – good experience as now he wants to help Mum do baking and he helped'.

Commentary also adds that a note about Fe'ao finding it a challenge to express his needs was followed by a number of episodes in which he shared his ideas, helped others and was open to suggestions (Ministry of Education, 2004: 38). In one of the entries, the teacher had recognised that when Fe'ao dictated a story to go with his painting, he was also referring to another child's book about clouds. She assisted Fe'ao to construct his own book: he chose cloud pictures from the Internet, added his own paintings and dictated the accompanying story. A parent added a comment:

> When Fe'ao arrived home with his school folder, he wanted to show everyone what [was] inside the folder. He explain what he was doing on the photos. He will name each person appear on the photos. If he notice anyone looking up his folder, he will not leave that person look alone, he will come sit next to that person and explain all inside the folder. (Ministry of Education, 2004, Book 7: 28)

From Checklists to Narratives in Special Education, Enabling Two Models of Development and Assessment to Come Together

A research project tracked the process when Learning Stories were used by teams surrounding two New Zealand children with high and complex needs (Williamson et al., 2006). The Learning Stories highlighted strength- and interest-based learning in natural settings, and this contrasted with the specialists' assessments, which highlighted decontextualised developmental skills. Team members, including parents, teachers, support workers, health and education professionals, shared the narrative documentation in Learning Stories, as well as the specialist assessments, at individual planning (IP) meetings. Goals for the children were collaboratively developed, drawing upon the different perspectives team members brought to the interpretation of the Learning Stories:

> This project showed that early childhood teachers, special education specialists, support workers and parents could effectively use the same narrative assessment tool to assess and plan for children with high and complex needs. Learning stories brought together two different assessment models (skills- and strength-based) and harmonised them in such a way that they could be viewed as complementary rather than divisive. The stories included the richness of the multiple perspectives inherent in the team. The lens for assessment was broadened and the focus shifted to include the child's strengths, the holistic view of the child and the teaching and learning context, which aligns well with family understandings and early childhood philosophies, beliefs and practices. Early intervention professionals were adept at 'backgrounding' developmental information pertinent to their expertise. (Williamson et al., 2006: 28)

COLLABORATIVE TEACHER-RESEARCHER PROJECTS: COMMUNITIES OF PRACTICE AND BOUNDARY PROCESSES

The discussion by Gutierrez and Penuel (2014), earlier in this chapter, invited us to consider research discussions that are socially embedded and involve ongoing mutual engagement. In 1996, Jean Lave, too, had emphasised a reconsideration of learning as social:

> Common theories of learning begin and end with individuals (although these days they often nod at 'the social' or 'the environment' in between). Such theories are deeply concerned with individual differences, with notions of better and worse, more or less learning, and with comparison of these things across groups-of-individuals. Psychological theories of learning prescribe ideals and pathways to excellence and identify the kinds of individuals (by no means all) who should arrive ... A reconsideration of learning as a social, collective, rather than individual, psychological phenomenon offers the only way beyond the current state of affairs that I can envision at the present time ... The argument developed by Etienne Wenger and myself (Lave and Wenger, 1991) is that learning is an aspect of changing participation in changing 'communities of practice' everywhere. (Lave, 1996: 149)

A key feature of a community of practice is the dynamic relationship between reification (making the practice of the community public in some way, as in documentation) and participation (Wenger, 1998). Documents can also *connect* communities of practice and significantly transform them in the process. In practice, documents can become 'boundary objects'. The concept of a boundary object first appeared in a model that described the divergent viewpoints of participants in the development of the Museum of Vertebrate Zoology at the University of California (Star and Griesemer, 1989). This was a study of 'institutional ecology' in which the authors wrote about the heterogeneity of viewpoints of the participants and the way in which boundary objects – objects that highlighted and coordinated the different perspectives – assisted in collaboration around a common task. To do this recontextualisation and collaboration work, documentation needs to be 'both plastic enough to adapt to local needs and the constraints of the several parties employing them, yet robust enough to maintain a common identity across sites' (Star and Griesemer, 1989: 393). Later, in 2010, Leigh Star reflects further on this concept. She explains that the notion of a 'boundary' encompasses 'a shared space, where exactly that sense of here and there are confounded' (Star, 2010: 602–603). Documents and documentation can provide a space for practice and research to inform each other within and across teacher-researcher collaboration. They can provide a focus and a forum for dialogue, collaborative theorising, iterative design decisions and publication partnerships.

Collaborative Research Projects that Develop Documents, Artefacts and Boundary Objects

A New Zealand research fund that has been influential in promoting and supporting practice and research to inform one another has been the Teaching and Learning Research Initiative (TLRI), funded by the Ministry of Education and administered by the New Zealand Council for Education Research (NZCER). Their website provides examples (www.tlri.org.nz). The TLRI programme is designed with five principles in mind, two of which emphasise the connection between practice and research: (i) the research projects within the TLRI will address themes of strategic importance to New Zealand, (ii) the TLRI research projects will build on New Zealand-based research evidence, draw on related international research and be forward thinking, (iii) the TLRI research projects will be designed to enable substantive and robust findings, (iv) the research projects within the TLRI will be undertaken as a partnership between researchers and practitioners, and (v) the TLRI research projects will recognise the central role of teachers and students in learning, and the importance of the work being useful in practice.

In a TLRI early years research project on kindergarten children and their teachers visiting a museum, the authors described the role of documentation as 'boundary objects' as young children developed meaning-making practices in a museum, assisted by their teachers and families:

> In this project, data were collected by the university researchers as they recorded reflective discussions with the teachers. All of us made observations and recorded children's conversations, and we worked together to identify and develop resources that would assist the project aims. The teachers also documented learning episodes for the children's assessment portfolios. This documentation, an aspect of everyday pedagogy, is kept in portfolios and regularly taken home. As we will discuss later, we began to see this assessment practice as providing 'boundary objects' that enabled the teachers to comment on the connections between the kindergarten and the museum. (Carr et al., 2012: 55)

Research has emphasised the key role that family expectations play in children's expectations. The synthesis of over 800 meta-analyses relating to educational achievement by John Hattie (2009: 70) found that parental expectations are far more powerful than many of the structural factors of the home (e.g., single- or two-parent families, families with resident or non-resident fathers, divorced parents, adopted or non-adopted children, only children or non-only children). Documents as 'Home Learning Books' played a key role in a TLRI project on culturally responsive pedagogy in primary science (Parkinson et al., 2011). These were already in use by one of the teachers to exchange ideas between home and school. The children recorded questions and topics in their home learning books at school and notes of conversations with their family at home. Ideas and examples were shared with the class. On occasion, family members came in to class to talk further about their experiences and teachers adapted the class curriculum to explicitly take into account these experiences. Like the assessment portfolios in early childhood centres, these books were treasured sources of information for teachers and students and for their families. In the example of the Home Learning Books, the documentation pushed out the boundary of the classroom to include the families in mutually meaningful ways. As Wenger has commented:

> A learning community must push its boundaries and interact with other communities of practice. But in order to go beyond just imagination, these contacts must take place in the course of seeking alignment for some meaningful purpose. (1998: 274)

Opportunities to Publish Create Another Level of Documents that Widen the Audience Beyond the Classroom or Centre

Two New Zealand journals, *set: Research Information for Teachers* and *Early Childhood Folio*, designed for readership by teachers, students, tertiary education professors and lecturers, have provided opportunities for publication that enable research and practice to inform one another. These articles themselves are documents, or boundary objects, that make research accessible to teachers and enable discussions across the practice–research divide.

The first of these journals to be established was *set*, published by the New Zealand Council for Educational Research (NZCER). For example, in 2008, a TLRI research project on science and technology, the InSiTE project, published three papers in *set* (Cowie et al., 2008a, 2008b; Moreland et al., 2008), as well as having four booklets published by NZCER for the TLRI programme. This project centred on Years 1–8 teachers and their students in science and technology classrooms. It examined (i) interactions that support learning in science and technology, (ii) connected and coherent teaching and learning of science and technology, (iii) student understandings of the nature of science and technology and (iv) subject ideas, skills and pedagogies that teachers see as important for student learning in science and technology, and their impact on classroom interactions. In the summary for Booklet 2, the role of multiple modes, documents and artefacts is highlighted:

> This booklet illustrates the multimodal nature of interactions between teachers and students in primary science and technology ... We found that when teachers made use of tasks that provided students with opportunities to make and express meaning through combining several modes, such as engaging with images, drawing, talking, dramatisation, writing and making products, students became actively involved in building and making meaning. These multimodal interactions helped teachers and students work together to negotiate

> and create shared understandings ... Teachers were able to provide richer feedback when they used multiple modes in their interactions with students. It also helped to provide students with multiple ways to represent, engage with and make sense of their world. (Cowie et al., 2010: 3)

The authors emphasise the opportunity for documents to cross boundaries between students and across locations and time:

> Teachers used artefacts, such as worksheets and templates, real-life artefacts and wall displays, to provide settings and resources for interaction with students. In whole-class settings, easily visible and accessible artefacts directed, guided and supported interactions between students and across locations and time. Artefacts helped students work together in groups and across locations and time ... This booklet includes examples that tease out the multiple modes used by teachers and students during their interactions. There are prompt questions and suggestions for teachers to try out. (Cowie et al., 2010: 3–4)

The second New Zealand journal, *Early Childhood Folio: A collection of recent research*, published twice a year by the New Zealand Council for Educational Research (NZCER), has also provided further opportunities for publication partnerships. It is aimed at an audience of primarily teachers, head teachers and supervisors, but also of students, lecturers and parents. The NZCER website (www.nzcer.org.nz) describes the journal as 'thought provoking and forward looking', 'ideal for staff discussions', 'a source of practical ideas for centre programmes' and 'a research base for critical and reflective thinking'. These, ideals to write for a practitioner audience, are reflected in the many articles written by partnerships of teachers and researchers, as well as teachers writing from their centres and classrooms, or from postgraduate research studies, with data gathered from within their own early childhood settings. Many of these research-based articles use documented data to show shifts in teaching and learning, explicating the roles of teachers, families and children in enriching the curriculum. Often, teachers report the process of critical analysis and discussion of data that generated new understandings. We highlight two examples here from the 2013 issues, and a Special Issue in 2011.

Combining Different Modes of Documentation to Define and Sustain Democratic Pedagogy

Simon Archard (2013) carried out a small case study in his own early childhood centre, where he was the supervisor. Data came from his MEd thesis and he was supported in the research by his academic supervisor. The article explored three experiences involving children and teachers in relational teaching and learning with ICT. It added teacher reflection to examples of documented assessment to explore how ICT can be used to help define and sustain democratic pedagogy and practices in early childhood settings. Notably, the author gathered data from perspectives of families (in semi-structured interviews), Learning Stories based on observation and discussion with the child/ren, and his own critique of his practice. His article was read widely and Simon was invited to be a keynote speaker at a conference of kindergarten teachers – an indication of how much teachers like to learn from other teachers who are researching teaching and learning in early childhood settings.

Critiquing the Role of Documentation in Engaging with Families

Maria Cooper and Helen Hedges worked as researchers with Daniel Lovatt and Trish Murphy as teachers (2013) in a TLRI project asking 'How might ways of engaging with families set Pasifika children up for learning success?' The article built on the teachers' documented and analysed interests for a Pasifika child, including families' and teachers' perspectives, and it added theoretical understanding from the literature on funds of knowledge and thinking about identity. These researchers and teacher-researchers argued that deeper interpretations may help teachers

to avoid stereotyping children or providing a 'tourist curriculum'.

Teachers Publishing Working Papers During a Research Project

A special issue in the *Early Childhood Folio* published six articles from another TLRI project, entitled 'Key Learning Competencies across Place and Time'. This project crossed the sectors of early childhood and school, researching the alignment of the key competencies in the school curriculum with the curriculum strands in the early childhood curriculum. These articles, all authored by teachers (one of them with a university lecturer partner; two of them with professional development providers who were also on the research team), were developed from Working Papers during the research. In every case, a document or documents are constructed to enable research and practice to inform one another. In the first paper, a metaphor – *te tuangi* (the clam) – for teaching and learning and the key competencies is developed to explain the Māori concept of *ako* which means teaching *and* learning (Simpson and Williams, 2011). A second paper calls on a series of documents as 'centre stories' to argue for and illustrate the notion of an *intentional* teacher (Robinson and Bartlett, 2011). The third paper includes assessment documents in a school classroom to illustrate 'split-screen pedagogy and analysis', analysing the teaching and children's learning from two perspectives – learning areas and key competencies – in the same assessment document (Smith et al., 2011). The fourth paper sets out the documentation of six stories about 'relating to others' (a key competency in the school curriculum) as three layers of knowing (Wilson-Tukaki and Davis, 2011). A fifth paper critiques and re-writes analytical language in Learning Stories for infants and toddlers (Bashford and Bartlett, 2011). The final paper uses classroom documentation to describe the complexity of a learning journey for one child in an early years school classroom (O'Connor and Greenslade, 2011).

DOCUMENTATION THAT CROSSES THE BOUNDARY BETWEEN EARLY CHILDHOOD AND SCHOOL, FROM ONE CURRICULUM TO ANOTHER

One of the Centres of Innovation completed a book on its strategies for the children's transition to school, entitled *Crossing the Border: A Community Negotiates the Transition to School* (Hartley et al., 2012; three of the authors are the teachers). The 'border-crossing' theoretical frame in the text of the book centrally includes a range of documentation tools, illustrated by photographs: (i) children sharing a portfolio of learning stories with a teacher at kindergarten (p. 19), (ii) teacher portfolios (p. 21), (iii) a child sharing his portfolio with two other children, (iv) a Visit to School learning story (p. 24), (v) a specially constructed place for children's early childhood portfolios to be housed in the school classroom (p. 26), (vi) a 'transition to school' photo display board at the kindergarten, a board that includes photographs of the school teachers and of the school buddies (p. 30), (vii) information pamphlets and parent packs (pp. 41–42), (viii) children sharing their school visits in individualized 'school visit books' (p. 39), and (ix) a drawing by Ben alongside a letter from the school about when he will meet his buddy.

Children's Portfolios

One of the chapters in the *Crossing the Border* book describes the use of portfolios as tools for enhancing learning 'across the borders' between the early childhood centre and school; another was a re-analysis of the documentation in one child's assessment portfolio, with the school curriculum's five key competencies as the unit of analysis. The introduction to the chapter on portfolios includes the following commentary on 'border crossing':

> As a form of formative assessment, Learning Stories focus on the relationship between learner

and context, documenting the interactions of the learner and reflecting the sociocultural view of learning implicit in *Te Whāriki* ... This paradigm shift to assessment as a sociocultural activity supports the use of the portfolio not only as an individual record of learning in one setting, but as an assessment and documentation tool that can cross the borders between settings. (2012: 17)

In another project, a commentary by a teacher, Robyn, illustrates the opportunity for documentation that crosses a boundary from one place to another (in this case from an early childhood centre to the nearby school library) to have apparent implications for identity:

> Today I was quietly surrounded by three children. We were revisiting their folders together. Children were exclaiming over the photos of themselves and their friends and recalling what was happening. Sela was leaning on the sofa behind us revisiting her folder alone carefully turning the pages and talking to herself. I was very aware of her and I hadn't seen her show this level of interest in her folder before. She was looking at some photos of herself where she is sitting with one of the school librarians in the school library. Then I heard her say to herself 'I'm a library girl, I'm a library girl' in a sweet singy-songy chant. She said this in a proud way smiling and to herself. I was astonished as I had never heard Sela speaking in English apart from the odd word. (Carr and Lee, 2012: 10)

The Concept of Teacher Portfolios

Teacher portfolios have been developed in some early childhood centres. These originated from an idea about 'bio-boards' from Curtis and Carter (2003); they contain stories and photos of the teachers' professional and home life and are stored with the children's portfolios, readily accessible for children and families to read. In the *Crossing the Border* project, these portfolios began as a page about each teacher in the children's portfolios. The teacher portfolios became a popular source of conversation with families and children. The teachers comment:

> The children constantly access the teachers' portfolios, discussing where teachers live, their families, pets and interests outside of the kindergarten.

They discuss our photos, investigating the relationships portrayed, and build a picture of the teacher as a learner as well as a participant in the life of the children and families in the kindergarten community. (Hartley et al., 2012: 21)

They add (p. 21):

More recently, William, a toy guinea pig, joined one of the teachers [Carol] on a holiday in London and began sending emails and photos back from London with Carol. He now has his own portfolio and the children are able to take William for adventures on family holidays … All of this documentation contributes to the funds of knowledge about the children, families and teachers (Gonzalez, Moll and Amanti, 2005). These visual records are highly accessible, able to be read, revisited and shared.

Transition to School Portfolios

Inspired by the 2007 New Zealand (school) Curriculum, which includes *key competencies* as outcomes, a number of early childhood centres in New Zealand have prepared Transition to School portfolios. These include a selection of recent Learning Stories, chosen by the teachers in consultation with the children and sometimes the families. At least one chosen story makes connection with one of the five key competencies in the school curriculum: thinking, using language symbols and texts, managing self, relating to others, or participating and contributing. An alignment between these five key competencies and the five curriculum strands in the early childhood curriculum, Te Whāriki, is published as a diagram in the school curriculum document (Ministry of Education, 2007b: 42). This diagram also makes an eloquent connection with learning beyond schooling, and it is included in the front of the Transition to School portfolios. The first trial was at Taitoko Kindergarten when interviews with two new entrant teachers at the local school suggested a number of consequences for these documents (Carr et al., 2013). Consequences were described as: facilitating 'getting to know you' conversations as the new entrant teacher discovers what interests

the child and together they can reflect on the stories, a language and literacy artefact that can be read and revisited by the child, a tool for facilitating a sense of belonging in a new environment as the transition to school portfolios were included in the display of early reading books in the classroom, a clear indication for families of the learning pathway from early childhood to school because the alignment with key competencies was included and discussed in the portfolio, and a reification – published evidence – for families of the valued learning that their children were taking to school. The Transition to School portfolio, too, provided a bridge between two communities of practice with different curriculum documents that reify the expected learning, and different forms of participation: the community in and around the early childhood centre and the community in and around the school. It provided an opportunity for early childhood teachers and teachers of junior classes to get together to construct indicators of learning that apply to both the learning dispositions in the strands of Te Whāriki and the key competencies in the New Zealand (school) Curriculum.

CONCLUSION

In this concluding section, we return to Carlina Rinaldi's analysis of documentation and its role in the early years, introduced in the first section. She pointed out that in recent times, and exemplified in the Reggio Emilia schools, 'documentation is interpreted and used for its value as a tool for recalling; that is, as a possibility for reflection'. We have emphasised the opportunity for children, families, teachers and researchers to use documentation to recall and reflect for a range of purposes. To do this, we called on experience in New Zealand of researching in early years centres and schools. Three contexts have been discussed and illustrated. The first was teachers researching their own practice, assisted in this work by sharing and revisiting their documentation in various ways and sometimes with the assistance of external researchers. This context emphasised the purpose as the construction of learning over time, children's identities as learners and the local community as the audience. A second context was collaborative projects where the documentation did some of the work of connecting two communities of practice: researching scholars and researching teachers. This introduced the notion of documents as boundary objects, contributing to the development of conversations and mutual understandings about learning and research. A third context was research projects that crossed the boundary between early childhood and school.

Some opportunities for both researching scholars and researching teachers working in these spaces were made apparent. The first of these is research funding opportunities where proposals must include partnerships, and 'relevance to practice' is a criterion for rigorous research. This imperative was introduced in the description of purpose early in this chapter via the quote from Kris Gutierrez and William Penuel (2014: 20); it gives value to research projects that are 'open-ended social or socially embedded experiments that involve ongoing mutual engagement'. The second opportunity is a place for researching teachers to publish short papers that are accessible and interesting to other teachers. Frequently, these are co-authored by university researchers, and often they are followed by longer publications and books.

As a final conclusion, this chapter might encourage debate about what kind of documentation is best able to strengthen the purposes in each of these three contexts and to position educational research in open-ended social or socially embedded spaces. We suggest that documentation will need to invite and/or construct recontextualising: vertically (over time and as socially constructed learning journeys) and horizontally (across places and communities of practice, building bridges for understanding). Five reflective questions to further these conversations follow.

QUESTIONS FOR REFLECTION

From your teaching and/or research experience:

1 If, as Gutierrez and Penuel suggest, we assume that educational research is about moving away from 'imagining interventions as fixed passages of strategies with readily measurable outcomes and toward more open-ended social or socially embedded experiments that involve ongoing mutual engagement', how might documentation play a part?
2 What documentation assists teachers to research their own pedagogy in the contexts that are most familiar to you, and how does it do this?
3 In the contexts that you know best, what documentation might enable and encourage families and/or the wider community to become engaged in discussions about education?
4 What documentation in those contexts has research value, as Carlina Rinaldi asks, as a tool for recall and as a possibility for reflection by the wider research audience amongst the national and international education community and policy-makers?
5 Given an interesting document and willing conversation partners from different education sectors, what might a valuable collaborative reflection look like?

FURTHER READING

Carr, M., and Lee, W. (2012) *Learning Stories: Constructing Learner Identities in Early Education*. London: SAGE.
Gutierrez, K. D., and Penuel, W. R. (2014) 'Relevance to practice as a criterion for rigor', *Educational Researcher*, 43(1): 19–23.
Rinaldi, C. (2006) *In Dialogue with Reggio Emilia: Listening, Researching and Learning*. London: Routledge.

REFERENCES

Archard, S. (2013) 'Democracy in early childhood education: How information and communication technology contributes to democratic pedagogy and practices', *Early Childhood Folio*, 17(2): 27–32.

Bashford, N., and Bartlett, C. (2011) 'Reshaping the learning disposition domains: Rethinking the language for infants and toddlers', *Early Childhood Folio*, 15(2): 25–29.

Carr, M., and Lee, W. (2012) *Learning Stories: Constructing Learner Identities in Early Education*. London: SAGE.

Carr, M., Clarkin-Phillips, J., Beer, A., Thomas, R., and Waitai, M. (2012) 'Young children developing meaning-making practices in a museum: The role of boundary objects', *Museum Management and Curatorship*, 27(1): 53–66.

Carr, M., Clarkin-Phillips, J., Resink, C., Anderson, M., and Jack, T. (2013) 'Toku matauranga oranga: Making visible the learning journey from early childhood into school', *Early Childhood Folio*, 17(1): 36–40.

Cooper, M., Hedges, H., Lovatt, D., and Murphy, T. (2013) 'Responding authentically to Pasifika children's learning and identity development', *Early Childhood Folio*, 17(1): 6–11.

Cowie, B., Moreland, J., Otrel-Cass, K., and Jones, A. (2008a) 'Making connections in the teaching of science and technology', *set: Research Information for Teachers*, 3: 42–44.

Cowie, B., Moreland, J., Otrel-Cass, K., and Jones, A. (2008b) 'More than talk and writing: Exploring the multimodal nature of classroom interactions', *set: Research Information for Teachers*, 3: 45–48.

Cowie, B., Moreland, J., Otrel-Cass, K., and Jones, A. (2010) *Teaching Primary Science and Technology: Ideas from the InSite Project*. Overview and summaries of Booklets 1, 2, 3 and 4. Wellington: NZCER Press.

Curtis, D., and Carter, M. (2003) *Designs for Living and Learning: Transforming Early Childhood Environments*. St Paul, MN: Redleaf Press.

Gonzalez, N., Moll, L., and Amanti, C. (2005) 'Introduction: Theorizing practice', in N. Gonzalez, L. Moll, and C. Amanti (eds.), *Funds of knowledge. Theorizing practices in households, communities, and classrooms*. New York, NY: Routledge. pp. 1–28.

Gutierrez, K. D., and Penuel, W. R. (2014) 'Relevance to practice as a criterion for rigor', *Educational Researcher*, 43(1): 19–23.

Hartley, C., Rogers, P., Smith, J., Peters, S., and Carr, M. (2012) *Crossing the Border: A Community Negotiates the Transition from Early Childhood to Primary School*. Wellington: NZCER Press.

Hattie, J. (2009) *Visible Learning: A Synthesis of over 800 Meta-analyses Relating to Achievement*. London: Routledge.

Kaimahi of Te Kōhanga Reo o Puau Te Moananui a Kiwa, with Poatu H., and Stokes, K. (2005) 'Te Kōhanga Reo o Puau Te Moananui a Kiwa', in A. Meade (ed.), *Catching the Waves: Innovation in Early Childhood Education*. Wellington: NZCER Press. pp. 38–44.

Krechevsky, M., Rivard, M., and Burton, F. R. (2010) 'Accountability in three realms: Making learning visible inside and outside the classroom', *Theory into Practice*, 49(1): 64–71.

Lave, J. (1996) 'Teaching, as learning, in practice', *Mind Culture and Activity*, 3(3): 149–164.

Lave, J., and Wenger, E. (1991) *Situated Learning: Legitimate Peripheral Participation*. Cambridge: Cambridge University Press.

Lee, W., Carr, M., Soutar, B., and Mitchell, L. (2013) *Understanding the Te Whāriki Approach*. London: Routledge.

Meade, A. (ed.) (2005) *Catching the Waves: Innovation in Early Childhood Education*. Wellington: NZCER Press.

Meade, A. (ed.) (2006) *Riding the Waves: Innovation in Early Childhood Education*. Wellington: NZCER Press.

Meade, A. (ed.) (2007) *Cresting the Waves: Innovation in Early Childhood Education*. Wellington: NZCER Press.

Meade, A. (ed.) (2010) *Dispersing the Waves: Innovation in Early Childhood Education*. Wellington: NZCER Press.

Ministry of Education (1996) Te Whāriki. He whāriki mātauranga mo ngā mokopuna o aotearoa. Early childhood curriculum. Wellington: Learning Media. Retrieved from www.educate.ece.govt.nz/learning/curriculumAndLearning/TeWhariki.aspx

Ministry of Education (2004) Kei Tua o te Pae. Assessment for learning: Early childhood exemplars. Books 1–9. Wellington: Learning Media. Retrieved from www.educate.ece.govt.nz/learning/curriculumAndLearning/Assessmentforlearning/KeiTuaotePae.aspx

Ministry of Education (2007a) Kei Tua o te Pae. Assessment for learning: Early childhood exemplars. Books 10–15. Wellington: Learning Media. Retrieved from www.educate.ece.govt.nz/learning/curriculumAndLearning/Assessmentforlearning/KeiTuaotePae.aspx

Ministry of Education (2007b) *The New Zealand Curriculum*. Wellington: Learning Media.

Ministry of Education (2009) Kei Tua o te Pae. Assessment for learning: Early childhood exemplars. Books 16–20. Wellington: Learning Media. Retrieved from www.educate. ece.govt.nz/learning/curriculumAndLearning/Assessmentforlearning/KeiTuaotePae.aspx

Mitchell, L., Meagher Lundberg, P., Mara, D., Cubey, P., and Whitford, M. (2011) Locality-based evaluation of Pathways to the Future: Nga Huarahi Arataki. Integrated report 2004, 2006 and 2009. Wellington: Ministry of Education. Retrieved from www.education-counts.govt.nz/publications/ece/locality-based-evaluation-of-pathways-to-the-future-ng-huarahi-arataki

Moreland, J., Cowie, B., Jones, A., and Otrel-Cass, K. (2008) 'Developing teacher knowledge in primary technology', *set: Research Information for Teachers*, 3: 38–41.

O'Connor, N., and Greenslade, S. (2011) 'Co-constructed pathways of learning: A case study', *Early Childhood Folio*, 15(2): 30–34.

Parkinson, A., Doyle, J., Cowie, B., Otrel-Cass, K., and Glynn, T. (2011) 'Engaging whānau with children's science learning', *set: Research Information for Educational Research*, 1: 3–9.

Project Zero and Reggio Children (2001) *Making Learning Visible: Children as Individual and Group Learners*. Reggio Emilia: Reggio Children.

Rinaldi, C. (2006) *In Dialogue with Reggio Emilia: Listening, Researching and Learning*. London: Routledge.

Robinson, P., and Bartlett, C. (2011) '"Stone crazy": A space where intentional teachers and intentional learners meet', *Early Childhood Folio*, 15(2): 10–14.

Ryder, D., and Wright, J. (2005) 'Innovations in New Beginnings pre-school', in A. Meade (ed.), *Catching the Waves: Innovation in Early Childhood Education*. Wellington: NZCER Press. pp. 15–24.

Simpson, M., and Williams, T. (2011) 'Te tuangi (the clam): A metaphor for teaching, learning and the key competencies', *Early Childhood Folio*, 15(2): 4–9.

Smith, Y., Davis, K., and Molloy, S. (2011) 'Assessment of key competencies, literacy and numeracy: Can these be combined?', *Early Childhood Folio*, 15(2): 15–19.

Soutar, B., with Te Whānau o Mana Tamariki (2010) 'Growing raukura', in A. Meade (ed.), *Dispersing the Waves: Innovation in Early Childhood Education*. Wellington: NZCER Press. pp. 35–40.

Star, S. L. (2010) 'This is not a boundary object: Reflections on the origin of a concept', *Science, Technology and Human Values*, 35(5): 601–617.

Star, S. L. and Griesemer, J. R. (1989) 'Institutional ecology, "translations" and boundary objects: Amateurs and professionals in Berkeley's museum of vertebrate zoology, 1907–39', *Social Studies of Science*, 19(3): 387–420.

Stuart, D. W., Aitken, H., Gould, K., and Meade, A. (2008) *Impact Evaluation of the Kei Tua o te Pae 2006 Professional Development*. Wellington: Ministry of Education.

Wenger, E. (1998) *Communities of Practice: Learning, Meaning and Identity*. Cambridge: Cambridge University Press.

Williamson, D., Cullen, J., and Lepper, C. (2006) 'From checklists to narratives in special education', *Australian Journal of Early Childhood*, 31(3): 20–30.

Wilson-Tukaki, A., and Davis, K. (2011) 'Relating to others: Three layers of knowing', *Early Childhood Folio*, 15(2): 20–24.

18

Understanding Complexity in Play through Interpretivist Research

Elizabeth Wood

INTRODUCTION

The field of play scholarship is eclectic in terms of the disciplinary, theoretical and methodological orientations that are used to understand play in its many forms and manifestations, across cultures, communities and life stages (Sutton-Smith, 2001; Dell Clark, 2011; Brooker et al., 2014). Whilst the continued search for definitions reflects this eclecticism, there have been moves away from the traditional dichotomies of pure play/non-play, play/work, free/structured play (Pellegrini, 2009). Free play is typically defined as being motivated, chosen and led by the child or group of children, with little or no intervention from adults. However, Wood (2013a) presents a synthesis of definitions to show that play can be understood across a continuum of activities from pure play to non-play, and can include playful engagement between adults and children in home and educational settings, and playful approaches to learning.

Although play is the ultimate 'mash-up' in terms of its multiple meanings and purposes for children, the focus on children's knowledge making has been overshadowed by the developmental and educational benefits that arise from both child-initiated and adult-led activities. However, as new forms of play have developed over time, so too have new ways of understanding, researching and defining play, notably concepts about intertextuality, hybridity and multi-modality (Wohlwend, 2009) and blended forms of digital and traditional play (Marsh, 2010; McPake et al., 2012; Edwards, 2013). These developments have taken place alongside methodological shifts towards understanding not just what play does for children, but the ways in which children create their own play cultures, practices and meanings (Alcock, 2010; Edmiston, 2010; Broadhead and Burt, 2012; Papadopoulou, 2013). Children's voices, perspectives and interpretations have become central to contemporary interpretivist research, sometimes blending with methods such as tests, rating scales and interviews. Digital methods of recording and analyzing play have also added new tools and affordances for researchers and participants to document play, in an attempt to provide more culturally nuanced understanding of children's perspectives and choices.

At the same time, there are: ongoing debates regarding ontological and epistemological orientations to researching play; ethical considerations of gaining access and consent; the positionality that researchers bring to research sites, including personal histories, beliefs, cultures and experiences; and the ways in which policy contexts determine what counts as play, typically in educational settings. Because the field of play scholarship is too broad to encompass in one chapter, the focus here will be on interpretivist research, using predominantly qualitative methods, including digital modes of data collection. This is not to deny the utility of research studies that rely on quantitative measures of developmental characteristics, styles and behaviors. However, the dominant developmental ontology is that play has specific characteristics and stages, is immediately valuable to children and leads to the skills, knowledge and dispositions that are subsequently valuable in later life. Consequently, the powerful alliance between developmental, educational and policy discourses reifies planned and purposeful play in which 'what counts as play' often relies on adults' rather than children's perspectives (Wood, 2013a). In contrast, interpretive research aims to illuminate what children do in their play, specifically the situated nature of their cultural routines and practices, their meanings and intentions, and their varied modes of communication, as they act as knowledge makers and knowledge users. Although many of the studies reviewed here are small-scale, they have contributed different ways of understanding play from children's perspectives, and have built cumulative knowledge that illuminates these intricacies and structural complexities.

The first section examines the ontological, epistemological and methodological concerns in interpretivist research. This is followed by exemplification of key studies, ranging from single case, in-depth ethnographies to studies that span home and school contexts. The intention is to indicate current directions in play scholarship within an interpretivist paradigm, and to critically consider culturally responsive ways of understanding play. The second section examines ethical concerns, particularly those that have arisen as a result of digital methods for conducting research, and how these align with contemporary concerns for children's rights, voices, consent and participation. The conclusion considers possible future directions for interpretive methods in play scholarship in light of current trends in children's play lives.

INTERPRETIVISM AT PLAY

This section will address three key themes: (1) interpretivism in play scholarship across cultures and communities, (2) the challenges of positionality and perspective, and (3) ethical approaches to research. Each of these themes will be examined in light of methodological developments and debates, and will be exemplified in relation to the challenges that play scholars have addressed.

Interpretivism in Play Scholarship

It is not the intention here to revisit well-trodden arguments regarding the relative merits of interpretivism versus positivism. Interpretivism has secured a place in the study of children and young people across diverse disciplines such as anthropology, sociology, education, geography, architecture and playwork (Sutton-Smith, 2001). The need for interpretivist research, using qualitative methods, has developed alongside (and not just as an antidote to) scientific research with a positivist orientation.

Historically, the scientific ontology of developmental psychology has dominated play scholarship in order to establish developmental patterns in young children, the general mechanisms or social processes that cause development and change, and the specific psychological processes that connect play to learning. Although the canon was consolidated during the twentieth century by psychologists such as Susan Isaacs, Anna Freud, Melanie Klein, Jean Piaget, Lev Vygotsky and Jerome Bruner, they did not share the same theoretical orientations, coming as they did from developmental, cognitive, educational, cultural-historical, socio-biological and psycho-analytical perspectives. Although a shared aspiration was establishing scientific approaches to the study of children, the knowledge they generated has been taken up in different ways and in different sites; for example, in informing policy and practice in health, welfare and education. The ontological position of the scientific paradigm is to discover and provide explanations of particular events or phenomena, and to establish general laws that govern relationships between certain variables. The tools of enquiry typically involve large-scale sample sizes and data sets, randomized control trials (RCTs), experimental or quasi-experimental designs, rating/measurement scales, tests, closed questionnaires and non-participant observation schedules. The theoretical outcomes include the specification of developmental stages, categories and norms, and the social construction of the 'universal child'. Concepts such as validity, reliability and generalizability act as disciplinary benchmarks, and inform the practical application of tools, scales and measures in different countries and contexts.

The coupling of scientific approaches to studying children and the formation of social policy has created a powerful discourse that can be discerned in minority and majority world countries, with economics adding a strong voice in determining what policies and interventions are likely to raise standards and improve outcomes in relation to cost-effectiveness. In such contexts, the scientific paradigm remains the gold standard for evidence-informed policy, but is counterbalanced by ongoing debates about the emphasis on narrow constructions of 'effectiveness' and 'what works' (Lowenstein, 2011; Shonkoff and Bales, 2011). As Wood (2013b) has argued, play sits uneasily within these discourses because it eludes the certainties and regularities that are implied in policy frameworks.

So how has interpretivist research managed to get under this ontological radar and, in particular, to establish a strong presence in the field of play scholarship? The commitment to scientific research has included a degree of skepticism and recognition of the need for 'mixed methods'. For example, in her extensive research on young children, Isaacs (1933) was cautious about the use of rating scales, unless they are used to support professionals in their observations and to provide insights into the significance of small aspects of children's behavior that might otherwise go unnoticed (1933: 6). Isaacs also noted that 'the major error into which quantitative studies handling large masses of quantitative data fall is the over-simplification of the problem and the treatment of very different situations as being essentially the same' (1933: 6).

The development of data analysis via computer programs and multi-level modeling may further compound the potential for this major error, but remain appealing to government policy makers because certain variables can be manipulated, for example in establishing causal relationships, correlations and effect sizes. In contrast, the ontological position in an interpretivist paradigm proposes that different elements intersect and interact in multiple ways that produce outcomes, such as change over time, but with no universal directionality to the changes and no need to prove that X has caused Y for one group and could therefore be generalized to other groups.

Although generalization, or 'scaling-up' interventions or practices, is not an outcome of interpretivist research, mixed methods are used. The skills of observation, categorization, description and analysis sit within both positivist and interpretivist methodologies, but a key distinction is whether research aims to specify broad typologies and classifications or to characterize variations and complexity. For example, the legacy of Susan Isaacs can be seen in the work of Chazan (2012) who developed the Children's Play Therapy Instrument and the Children's Developmental Play Instrument to identify children's play styles, based on four categories: adaptive, conflicted/inhibited, impulsive, disorganized. These instruments serve different purposes. First, the tools enable the observer to integrate an understanding of the child's play activity that includes affective, cognitive, narrative, social level, developmental level, and the interaction between players (Chazan, 2012: 298). The second purpose is for the instruments to aid parents' and practitioners' understanding of children's play activities, to explore children's play styles and to develop their skills of observation and analysis. Their third purpose is as teaching tools, including learning the skills of observation, categorization, description and analysis. However, a key question regarding measures such as rating scales is whether they allow flexibility for cultural variations and interpretations. In the dominant discourse of normalization, play is a means of promoting 'typical' developmental or educational pathways. Therefore, the danger is that research does not look at play, but looks through play in order to explain specific benefits and characteristics that can justify its presence in children's lives.

In contrast, interpretivist ontology and epistemologies offer scope for understanding variations within and across contexts, and cultural-historical influences on children's play repertoires. This explains the eclectic nature of play scholarship, for example on types of play such as block play, sociodramatic play, virtual play, rough and tumble, risky play, and on specific themes such as gender, friendships, social skills, emergent literacy and numeracy, creativity, and communicative practices (Saracho, 2012; Brooker et al., 2014). The challenge for interpretivist research is to reveal the 'small narratives' of children's play and to appreciate their wider significance, not just for developmental or educational progress, but for understanding play for its own sake and in its own right, and for understanding how children invent and perform their own childhoods. Central to this challenge is the task of understanding positionality and perspective from different interpretivist orientations.

The Challenges of Positionality and Perspective

Interpretive studies rely mainly on qualitative methods to understand the perspectives of children in the context of their freely-chosen play activities. The intentions are to describe as accurately as possible their activities, actions, interactions and communicative practices, and then to construct analyses and interpretations of, and explanations for, their intentions and meanings. However, because play takes place in the moment, and events are located within the boundaries of play, even with the best methodological intentions, adults' interpretations may be different from, or even in conflict with, those of the players. Children's meanings are often imbued with their cultural knowledge, their interests and their desire to act more knowledgeably, more skillfully and with a sense of agency. Their interests and preoccupations range across sharks and monsters, domestic practices and routines, magical and superhero powers, to the big existential questions of life, death, justice, power and ethics. Research on play can reveal not just children's understanding of their own worlds, but their interpretation of the forms of power that are enacted by adults, and the forms of resistance that are possible (particularly in education settings) (Wood, 2014).

The methodological challenges of researching play across cultures and communities are considerable, not least because of the amount of time needed to address ethical considerations and for immersion in the field. However, small-scale studies open up spaces for contestation of some of the 'grand narratives' of play that have emerged from dominant psychological discourses. Studies that focus on these smaller narratives explore variations in play and amongst players, by taking account of cultural orientations and re-framing what counts as play from children's perspectives. Theoretically, many contemporary studies exemplify the turn towards critical, post-colonial and post-modern perspectives, including the ways in which play incorporates issues of power, agency and control as children assert their identities and construct shared cultural repertoires (Grieshaber and McArdle, 2010; Sellers, 2013). This theoretical turn contests play as the 'natural activity of childhood' and as a space of freedom and innocence, challenges, stereotypes and uncritical assumptions, and decolonizes research through the process of 'valuing, reclaiming, and foregrounding indigenous voices and epistemologies' (Swadener and Mutua, 2007: 186). However, the challenge here is to portray cultural constructions of play from within communities both as a means of understanding different perspectives and contesting dominant discourses, particularly where characteristics of typically Euro-American forms of play are constructed as desirable developmental pathways and as curriculum goals in early childhood settings. In contrast, children bring culturally situated and culturally valued knowledges to their freely chosen activities and create their own play cultures. Children do things in play that they have not been taught explicitly by adults, and thereby learn what knowledge, skills and dispositions are relevant to managing and sustaining play. Motivations to play are focused on becoming a more skilled player, extending their play repertoires and engaging in more complex forms of play. Therefore, the task for research is to understand those variations and how they are manifest in different contexts.

Ethnographic approaches are particularly suited to revealing these intricacies, particularly if the researcher (or team of researchers) has scope for deep immersion in the context for a sustained period of time. Many ethnographic studies exemplify contemporary shifts towards involving children as research participants in documenting and narrating their play lives, rather than relying on rating scales and measures that reflect adults' categorizations of play skills and characteristics. The work of Kelly-Byrne (1989) and Edmiston (2008) exemplifies this approach, each of them focusing on one child, using participatory ethnographic methods. Kelly-Byrne's detailed documentation of the play life of Helen (age 6–7 years during the study) involved participant observation at her request and under her direction, and included both solitary and peer group play. Kelly-Byrne was able to portray the qualities of Helen's play, which was often 'irrational, exuberant, combative, unbridled, and grotesque in its moments of intense passion' (1989: 216).

Using similar ethnographic methods, Edmiston (2008) documented the play life of his own son, Michael, including child–adult interactions, adopting the dual position of participant and narrator. The themes of identity, power and agency resonate with Helen's play life, with similar challenges to assumptions about 'mythic play', including the meaning of superhero narratives and role models, rough and tumble and war play. Edmiston (2008, 2010) argues that these activities create social aesthetic spaces in which children and adults construct moral dilemmas based on themes such as oppressive and constructive uses of power. These two ethnographies reveal complexity in terms of children's interests and preoccupations, including the ways in which their everyday knowledges (including popular culture) inform and intersect with their play lives. The authors' narratives are not of developmental progress or regularities, but of the complex intersections between positional and relational identities, and the ways in which language is used to create the internal logic of play, based on blending and transforming the everyday and the imaginary. Edmiston (2010: 200) connects the concept of identity with Bakhtin's idea of an authoring self that acts in the moment and makes connections with others over time. Edmiston argues that

> How adults or children identify with others and act in present social arrangements is interrelated with both how they have acted, been identified and identified themselves with others in the past, as well as how they hope to act and identify with people in the future. Dramatic playing can be significant in shaping identities because it relies on past experience and anticipation of future actions and relationships, thus establishing a liminal space in which possibilities – rather than certainties – for being and identifying can be explored. (2010: 200)

Such insights provoke a challenge to more idealized and sanitized views of children's play where the exhortation to 'play nicely' is often invoked as a means of adults controlling approved forms of play.

Observation is central to interpretive research (Broadhead, 2006), but there are varied approaches, each of which carries methodological implications. For example, Shin (2010) conducted a qualitative study of how infants share and experience friendships, focusing on two girls, age 13 and 14 months. The study also followed and examined the caregivers' behaviors in and responses to the social experiences of the two girls. The study was conducted in the infant room of a university-based childcare center, where the researcher was able to conduct non-participant observations through a one-way mirror in an observation booth adjacent to the infant room. Running records and videotaping were used to capture events and interactions over time, resulting in both quantitative and qualitative analysis of the observed episodes. In terms of positionality, the data are interpreted from the perspective of the researcher: 'the focus of the data analysis was heavily on qualitative exploration of the content of social interactions involving emergent and intuitive processes' (Shin, 2010: 296). These emergent and intuitive processes are evident in much interpretive research, where patterns, themes and categories emerge from the data, informed by the researcher's theoretical and methodological positions. But even when

these positions are explicated, the researcher's own positionality is often less clear, for example what knowledge and experience inform 'intuitive processes', including the possibility for bias or distortion within interpretive processes. However well-informed these intuitive processes may be, a question remains about the efficacy of non-participant observations from the position of a one-way mirror for understanding children's perspectives and intentions.

Using participant and non-participant observation, Papadopoulou (2013) focused on the ecology of role play in order to examine the evolutionary function of pretense. The study focused on 18 children between 4 and 5 years old in a Greek primary school, and the data analysis identified four themes: sheltered families; the battle between good and bad; disobedience and punishment; and the world of protectors and their protégés. The processes of cultural adaptation and cultural production were evident as children played with familiar themes in their lives, but from the perspective of play as a child-led cultural activity. Familiar themes included the everyday and the existential, including culturally-specific narratives derived from Greek mythology. Papadopoulou reveals how these themes are also narrative expressions of power, control and agency that enabled the children to explore risk and uncertainty, both physical and emotional.

Pretense is the essential characteristic that creates the 'what if' and 'as if' qualities that operate within the liminality of play, but is often difficult to discern from the position of the researcher. Therefore, observing, analyzing and interpreting the complex social processes that make up children's play require sustained periods of time and sensitive methodological skills, especially as much of what happens is not directly observable, but needs to be inferred from children's actions. Communicative competence in play is embodied in many different modes, through gestures, mime and facial expressions (Broadhead, 2004; Ebrahim, 2010), through rhythmic, musical and aesthetic modes (Alcock, 2008, 2010), through arts-based approaches (Hall, 2010) and through the use of artefacts, tools and symbols (Wood, 2014). These are active and enactive modes which have distinct purposes within the flow of play. Exploring the links between play and drawing in children aged 4–5 years old, Wood and Hall (2011) conceptualize drawings as places for intellectual play, through the processes of playing at, in and with their drawings:

> The content of children's imaginative play is often expressed through signs and symbols which serve particular functions, and convey meanings which are often created at a meta-level, in that children simultaneously create imaginative transformations, and communicate these in different modes. Therefore children are not just 'acquiring' cultural tools, but are using them as intellectual tools in inventive and transformative ways. In imaginative play activities, children act via mediated social interactions, and via relationships between the players, in ways that lead towards intersubjective attunement and shared perspectives that are essential to maintaining play. Thus the role of drawings may be enhanced, because these take on the meta-communicative status of symbolic tools and artefacts which mediate collaborative activities. (2011: 271)

For Wohlwend (2009), these multi-modal activities are all part of children's social and communicative practices, including how they construct relational agency. As a result, multi-modal approaches to collecting data have been used to portray complex meanings from multiple perspectives and to consider how children's cultural perspectives and interpretations can be understood. Although digital tools have facilitated this endeavor, they have also brought methodological and ethical challenges.

Positionality in interpretive research is important because the processes of analysis and interpretation often result in re-interpretations through stories, narratives, vignettes or visual profiles of children's play such as mash-ups of drawings, artefacts and photographs. Successive acts of interpretation are required to categorize, connect, represent and re-present the data, often over time as researchers create patterns from fragmented

events and narrate these as complex wholes. Accordingly, the two processes of analysis and interpretation need to be made clear in research reports, particularly where digital modes have been used. A key feature of play is that it takes place 'in the moment', as children transcend temporal and spatial boundaries through acts of imagination and invention. Post-hoc reflective dialogues are used to understand children's perspectives, often prompted by digital images which have been taken either by children or by the researcher/s. In a study of self-regulation and metacognition in young children's play, Robson (2010) used qualitative methods of videotaping episodes of children's play and audiotaping discussions of the children's post-hoc Reflective Dialogues. Robson's study involved 12 children aged from 3.10 to 4.10 years, and the Reflective Dialogues took place between the children and their key person about the videotaped play activities (2010: 230). A key issue in Robson's study is that the success of play activities (especially role play and pretense) relies on children's abilities to share their knowledge and thinking in order to plan, manage and sustain the play, and, over time, to develop the complexity and challenge that is documented in ethnographic research. However, thinking is not always 'visible' through verbal utterances or interactions, because of the embodied and multi-modal characteristics of children's communication. As Robson (2010: 237) argues, the opportunity for children to engage in reflective dialogues makes visible what is implicit or understood by the players. These processes contribute to respecting children's interpretations and to promoting analytical clarity.

Davidson (2010) argues that analytical clarity should also extend to the process of transcription which is often regarded as a technical chore. Davidson proposes that a conversational analysis (CA) approach (see Sidnell, Chapter 16, this volume) includes, for example, notation of different types of overlap in talk; length of silences, pauses and gaps; inflection and intonation; degrees of emphasis; and visual actions that accompany talk, and nonverbal actions (2010: 120–121). Davidson argues for more methodical and deliberate coding because 'the CA transcript does double duty in the analysis; it produces features of talk and interaction for analysis and it enables the explication and description of the analysis' (2010: 128). Furthermore, CA establishes the orientations of the research participants and the researcher/s. Although conversational analysis offers a detailed approach to notation, the emphasis remains on linking talk and interaction. Digital tools allow new possibilities for documenting young children's activities, including the multi-modal nature of their social and communicative acts.

White (2009) conducted a study of the potential of metaphoric acts for providing insights into the world of toddlers (aged 18 to 24 months), and of teachers' assessment practices, in a New Zealand kindergarten. White used digital cameras, including 'cam-hats' for the children and teachers, and a hand-held camera for the researcher, to provide three views of the same events. (A cam-hat is a headband with a miniature camera attached.) These digital tools enabled White to record the multi-modal language acts of the children and to infer their symbolic meanings, using a Bakhtinian theoretical framework. Digital methods of representing and analyzing the data allowed for detailed interpretation by the teachers and the researcher of the children's metaphoric acts, based on a split-screen, time-synchronized format that displayed these three perspectives (White, 2009).

In the ethnographic studies of Edmiston and Kelly-Byrne, the children and the researchers were similar in their social class and ethnicity. But what are the issues for scholars whose research takes place within and across different cultural groups, whose cultures and practices may not be immediately accessible or easily interpreted? Although play is considered to be a universal characteristic of human development, there are considerable variations in the form of play and in the variability amongst players (Sutton-Smith,

2001). Furthermore, dimensions of diversity intersect to influence this variability (such as age, gender, ethnicity, social class, special or additional needs, languages, sexualities, religious affiliations). Therefore, researching play across cultures and communities brings additional considerations, because of the need to situate research in local cultural meanings and practices.

There has been a significant shift towards rights-based perspectives in researching children and their families in indigenous, minority and marginalized communities (Ebrahim, 2010; Kangas et al., 2012), with the implication that research should start from the position that people hold different ways of understanding and being in the world and different systems of belief, which influence how they explain and interpret 'reality'. Those systems include beliefs about childhood, development, play, as well as varying expectations of schooling, notably in adult–child relationships, and behavioral expectations such as independence, autonomy and agency that are typically constructed from Euro-American perspectives (Sellers, 2013).

Levinson (2005, 2008) reports his ethnographic research into Gypsy, Roma and Traveller (GRT) communities, including the ways in which children traverse the borders between home and school contexts. Consistent with the findings of other interpretive research, play reveals the ways in which children construct and maintain their cultural identities. However, as children traverse those borders, issues of cultural distance and dissonance arise when their play is not consistent with the expectations and cultures of school, particularly where 'free choice' is interpreted to imply levels of freedom and choice that are not actually permitted. Levinson questions uncritical assumptions about child-centered approaches in school settings, particularly in relation to the skills and interests that the children in his studies developed at home, whether these are transferable across home and school, and even whether these are recognized as valued forms of learning.

In summary, much interpretive research indicates that children use play (including technological play) to bridge home, community and school practices (Marsh and Burke, 2013). The ways in which children negotiate play across and within these different contexts reveal further complexities that can be captured through a range of methods, where the focus is not on measuring play styles or characteristics but on understanding children's cultural repertoires. Such a focus also requires detailed attention to the ethical dilemmas and challenges of conducting interpretive research.

THE ETHICAL DILEMMAS OF RESEARCHING PLAY

Play as Private or Public Activity

Ethics are integral to the conceptualization and conduct of interpretivist research, and often incorporate the rhetorics of co-production, community engagement, children-as-participants and 'giving children a voice'. The extent to which these rhetorics are addressed remains a methodological challenge within play scholarship, particularly in the intersections between private and public spaces.

Ebrahim (2010) conducted research on the constructions of childhood by children in two early childhood centers in KwaZulu-Natal, South Africa, and documented the moral and ethical complexities that arose during the study. Ebrahim argues that research ethics should be situated, negotiated, responsive and relational, all of which raise significant challenges for research on children's play. Although much contemporary play scholarship aims to respect children as participants and co-producers of knowledge about their play lives, there remain tensions between children as participants in, or as subjects of, research. Play is often considered to be a private or secret space for the development of childhood cultures, where secret spaces

(physical and imaginative) are constructed or defined by children (Moore, 2010; Wood, 2014). But at the same time, this privacy is open to scrutiny and forms of adult control, particularly in pre-school and school settings. So what happens when children and their play are subjected to the adult gaze, whether through traditional observation or digital methods?

Digital tools have undoubtedly facilitated the study of play (Dell Clark, 2011), but the technological progress towards their miniaturization calls into question children's rights to refuse their assent/consent either prior to or during a study. In her study of toddler metaphoricity, White (2009) records that children occasionally removed the cam-hats, and many studies report that children become so used to a video recorder in the setting that they occasionally perform for the camera, or eventually ignore it. But making data collection tools comfortable, wearable and familiar can also be interpreted as a form of coercion which children might find difficult to resist. Clearly, there are benefits and risks in using digital tools in data collection and analysis. Although digital tools are invaluable for facilitating micro-analyses and documenting fine details, these need to be related back to the wider contexts of children's lives and experiences. Digital methods can capture everything that happens in the play events that are recorded, but the subsequent task of interpretation is influenced by the theoretical framing of the study, the interpretive stance and the units or focus for analysis. Thus, the ontological/epistemological gaze is always refracted through disciplinary lenses. Therefore, even with the best of intentions, the ethical endeavor to engage children as participants, to use child-friendly, multi-modal methods, and to include children's voices/perspectives will always be framed by adult-centered discourses and disciplinary practices.

Traditional observation techniques are not immune from these concerns: in an observational study of children's choices in a pre-school setting in England, Wood (2014) documents how children used visual cues to protect their play from the researcher's gaze, which included freezing play, turning away and becoming silent. This raises ethical questions about the extent to which observational and digital methods distort or influence the play or the post-hoc conversations about play. Children's narratives are not just about what they are doing in their play, but who and what they are being and possibly becoming, as documented by Kelly-Byrne (1989) and Edmiston (2008). Play is intrinsically bound up with the making and maintaining of identity, relationships, status and peer affiliation. Because play takes place 'in the moment', children's meanings may not be accurately captured after the event: being asked to recall events and meanings implies that play is open to rational review and explanation. However, children do not always readily engage in post-hoc reflections of their play, even where visual methods are used to prompt recall, and there may not always be direct links between what children were doing in their play and what they say they were doing in post-hoc conversations. Furthermore, from a critical perspective, the very act of interviewing children, however sensitively this is done, is a social construction, in which children may be positioned as having specific identities that reflect adults' perspectives and categorizations. These concerns reflect the need for situated ethics.

Situated Ethics

As previously stated, in children's play, meanings are not always visible but may become so over time as patterns and themes evolve, and through many different modes. Ebrahim (2010) examined the communicative cues in the children's activities, but was also sensitive to the fact that gestures, body positions, eye contact may also carry culturally specific cues that can only be interpreted with situated insights into collective and individual repertoires. Such practices can contribute to culturally responsive and responsible research, but at the same time

may incur possible restraints for the researcher. Ebrahim noted and responded to children's assent and dissent during the research process: 'There was much effort put into respecting children's choices even in the frustrating context of meeting deadlines and returning from sites without much significant data' (2010: 293).

This comment acts as a reminder of the institutional contexts and cultures that 'situate' research within the academy. Researchers are bound by the academic practices of publications, dissemination and impact activities. Therefore, whose voices and interpretations become privileged in the journey from children's meanings to researchers' interpretations and (re)presentations? The theoretical and methodological frame influences the details of the picture, as do the values, beliefs and prior knowledge that play scholars bring to researching and understanding play. All the methodological and theoretical tools discussed in this chapter constitute adults' ways of interpreting children's play, and indicate the ways in which researchers must situate themselves within the contexts of children's play as well as in the contexts of academic conventions. However, as Ebrahim (2010) has argued, negotiated and relational ethics can go some way towards addressing, if not dissolving, these imbalances of power.

Negotiated and Relational Ethics: Perspectives and Values

Challenges to established issues of consent and access arise from feminist, postmodern, postcolonial and critical perspectives, and include ethical considerations of information, authority, capacity, capability, voluntarity (Gallagher et al., 2010), agency, ownership and rights, as well as questions about voice and silence – who can speak in and for communities and individuals? (Ebrahim, 2010). Negotiating informed consent in play scholarship remains a challenging process because of the age of the children, assumptions about their understanding and maturity, and the tensions between play as a private/public activity. Young children generally trust adults and see them as a resource. Therefore, children may be open about discussing their play, even where it takes place in secret spaces (Moore, 2010) and includes existential interests in life and death (Hill, 2014) or everyday interests in relationships and family routines. Researchers may encounter personal revelations or areas of discomfort. For example, children exercise power, agency and control through their choices of friendship groups and use strategies for including and excluding their peers, including silence and withdrawal. How these phenomena are understood and reported in research carries ethical obligations where data are shared either with children or with teachers and family members. Many different stories or interpretations are possible (those of the child, the group of children or the adult) and can be related to different cultural, spatial and temporal contexts.

In summary, interpretive research requires considerable ethical reflexivity, which cannot be guaranteed through the single 'point in time' ethical review that precedes academic research, but emerges through continuous engagement within a framework of culturally informed values and beliefs about children, childhoods and play. For researchers, ethical reflexivity provokes questions about whose knowledges are foregrounded and how power relationships are acknowledged. These questions may also address whose truths are privileged in research and how the 'smaller narratives' of play contrast with, or even contest, some of the grand educational, developmental and policy narratives.

CONCLUSION

Interpretive research has revealed detailed insights into the complexity and variability of play and of the ways in which children as players develop patterns and themes over time. They act as knowledge users and knowledge makers as they create and invent their own narratives that draw upon the everyday and the existential, and their own playful interpretations of those experiences. Interpretivist play scholars value illumination and particularization, against policy demands for demonstrating the ways in which play can align with standards and effectiveness agendas that are colonizing practice in early childhood settings in many countries (Brooker et al., 2014). An important role for interpretive researchers is to connect these smaller, situated narratives to the larger, dominant narratives about play. Further challenges to play scholarship arise as new forms of play develop, such as the ways in which children blend traditional and digital forms of play, and how new forms of play arise from these contexts.

Methodologically, moves towards interdisciplinarity in play scholarship are facilitating these trends, alongside the endeavor to frame research in ways that are ethically respectful and responsive to local cultures and contexts. Deeper knowledge of play and diversity is needed about children, families and communities, and how this can inform the practice of professionals in educational, therapeutic and playwork contexts. This knowledge must come from within those communities, and through interpretive research that is multi-modal and multi-voiced. The illumination of complexity remains a practical and ethical endeavor for play scholars.

FURTHER READING

Ebrahim, H. B. (2010) Situated ethics: possibilities for young children as research participants in the South African context. *Early Child Development and Care*, 180 (3): 289–298.

This article provides some thoughtful provocations that encourage researchers to think critically about their own positions and assumptions. Ebrahim provides some practical strategies to ensure that research is ethically and culturally responsive.

Kangas, S., Määttä, K. and Uusiautti, S. (2012) Alone and in a group: ethnographic research on autistic children's play. *International Journal of Play*, 1 (1): 37–50.

This study examines the play lives of children with Autistic Spectrum Disorder. Using ethnographic methods, the authors report that the children in their study expressed a variety of forms of lone play and group play, and show some progression in their play. On the basis of their findings, the authors argue for sensitive adult interventions to enhance the play of children with autism, using a range of pedagogical techniques. Contrast this study with Wood (2014) regarding the efficacy of free choice and free play.

Wood, E. (2014) Free choice and free play in early childhood education: troubling the discourse. *International Journal of Early Years Education*, 22 (1): 4–18.

Drawing on post-structural theories, Wood contests established assumptions about the efficacy of free choice and free play for young children. The research reveals how children's choices are situated within shifting power structures and relationships, involving conflict, negotiation, resistance and subversion. The conclusion problematizes the extent to which free choice and free play can be accommodated within the curriculum framework in England.

QUESTIONS FOR REFLECTION

1   Consider some of the definitions of play from your own reading and research. Why do you think that play is so difficult to define?
2   Think about your play life from childhood through to adulthood. Do you think that your definitions of play change according to different points in your play life?
3   Interpretive research is often criticized for its limitations: personal bias, subjectivity, reliability and generalizability. From your own reading and research, consider how these limitations are acknowledged and addressed in interpretivist research on play.
4   Consider some of the ethical concerns that have been identified in this chapter. How might you develop the ethical approaches identified by

Ebrahim (2010) with children who have disabilities and additional needs?
5   What are your own beliefs and values regarding play? How do you think these beliefs and values have influenced your interpretation and understanding of this chapter?

REFERENCES

Alcock, S. (2008) Young children being rhythmically playful: creating *musike* together. *Contemporary Issues in Early Childhood*, 9 (4): 328–337.

Alcock, S. (2010) Young children's playfully complex communication: distributed imagination. *European Early Childhood Education Research Journal*, 18 (2): 215–228.

Broadhead, P. (2004) *Early Years Play and Learning: Developing Social Skills and Co-operation*. London: RoutledgeFalmer.

Broadhead, P. (2006) Developing an understanding of young children's learning through play: the place of observation, interaction and reflection. *British Educational Research Journal*, 32 (2): 191–207.

Broadhead, P. and Burt, A. (2012) *Understanding Young Children's Learning through Play: Building Playful Pedagogies*. Abingdon: Routledge.

Brooker, L., Blaise, M. and Edwards, S. (eds) (2014) *The SAGE Handbook of Play and Learning in Early Childhood*. London: SAGE.

Chazan, S. E. (2012) The Children's Developmental Play Instrument (CDPI): a validity study. *International Journal of Play*, 1 (3): 297–310.

Davidson, C. (2010) Transcription matters: transcribing talk and interaction to facilitate conversation analysis of the taken-for-granted in young children's interactions. *Journal of Early Childhood Research*, 8 (2): 115–131.

Dell Clark, C. (2011) *In a Younger Voice: Doing Child-Centred Qualitative Research*. Oxford: Oxford University Press.

Ebrahim, H. B. (2010) Situated ethics: possibilities for young children as research participants in the South African context. *Early Child Development and Care*, 180 (3): 289–298.

Edmiston, B. (2008) *Forming Ethical Identities in Play*. Abingdon: Routledge.

Edmiston, B. (2010) Playing with children, answering with our lives: a Bakhtinian approach to coauthoring ethical identities in early childhood. *British Journal of Education Studies*, 58 (2): 197–211.

Edwards, S. (2013) Post-industrial play: understanding the relationship between traditional and converged forms of play in the early years. In J. Marsh and A. Burke (eds) *Children's Virtual Play Worlds: Culture, Learning, and Participation*, pp. 10–26. New York: Peter Lang.

Gallagher, M., Haywood, S., Jones, M. and Milne, S. (2010) Negotiating informed consent with children in school-based research: a critical review. *Children & Society*, 24: 471–482.

Grieshaber, S. and McArdle, F. (2010) *The Trouble with Play*. Maidenhead: Open University Press.

Hall, E. (2010) The communicative potential of young children's drawings. Unpublished PhD thesis, University of Exeter, UK.

Hill, M. (2014) Dead forever: young children building theories in a play-based classroom. Unpublished EdD thesis, University of Sheffield, UK.

Isaacs, S. (1933) *Social Development in Young Children*. London: Routledge & Kegan Paul.

Kangas, S., Määttä, K. and Uusiautti, S. (2012) Alone and in a group: ethnographic research on autistic children's play. *International Journal of Play*, 1 (1): 37–50.

Kelly-Byrne, D. (1989) *A Child's Play Life: An Ethnographic Study*. New York: Teachers College Press.

Levinson, M. P. (2005) The role of play in the formation and maintenance of cultural identity: Gypsy children in home and school contexts. *Journal of Contemporary Ethnography*, 34 (5): 499–532.

Levinson, M. P. (2008) Not just content but style: Gypsy children traversing boundaries. *Early Childhood Education and Care*, 3 (3): 235–249.

Lowenstein, A. E. (2011) Early care and education as educational panacea: what do we really know about its effectiveness? *Educational Policy*, 25: 92–114.

Marsh, J. (2010) Young children's play in online virtual worlds. *Journal of Early Childhood Research*, 8 (1): 23–39.

Marsh, J. and Burke, A. (eds) (2013) *Children's Virtual Play Worlds: Culture, Learning, and Participation*. New York: Peter Lang.

McPake, J., Plowman, L. and Stephen, C. (2012) Pre-school children creating and communicating with digital technologies in the home. *British Journal of Education Technology*, 44 (3): 421–431.

Moore, D. (2010) 'Only children can make secret places': children's secret business of place. Unpublished MEd thesis, Monash University, Victoria, Australia.

Papadopoulou, M. (2013) The ecology of role play: intentionality and cultural evolution. *British Educational Research Journal*, 38 (4): 575–592.

Pellegrini, A. D. (2009) *The Role of Play in Human Development*. Oxford: Oxford University Press.

Robson, S. (2010) Self-regulation and metacognition in young children's self-initiated play and Reflective Dialogue. *International Journal of Early Years Education*, 18 (3): 221–241.

Saracho, O. (2012) *An Integrated Play-based Curriculum for Young Children*. New York: Routledge.

Sellers, M. (2013) *Young Children Becoming Curriculum: Deleuze, Te Whāriki and Curricular Understandings*. Abingdon: Routledge.

Shin, M. (2010) Peeking at the relationship world of infant friends and caregivers. *Journal of Early Childhood Research*, 8 (3): 294–302.

Shonkoff, J. P. and Bales, S. N. (2011) Science does not speak for itself: translating child development research for the public and its policymakers. *Child Development*, 82: 17–32.

Sutton-Smith, B. (2001) *The Ambiguity of Play* (2nd edn). Cambridge, MA: Harvard University Press.

Swadener, B. B. and Mutua, K. (2007) Decolonizing research in cross-cultural contexts. In J. A. Hatch (ed.) *Early Childhood Qualitative Research*, pp. 185–205. New York: Routledge.

White, E. J. (2009) A Bakhtinian homecoming: operationalizing dialogism in the context of an early childhood education centre in Wellington, New Zealand. *Journal of Early Childhood Research*, 7 (3): 299–323.

Wohlwend, K. E. (2009) Mediated discourse analysis: researching young children's non-verbal interactions as social practice. *Journal of Early Childhood Research*, 7 (3): 228–243.

Wood, E. (2013a) *Play, Learning and the Early Childhood Curriculum* (3rd edn). London: SAGE.

Wood, E. (2013b) Contested concepts in educational play: a comparative analysis of early childhood policy frameworks in New Zealand and England. In J. Nuttall (ed.) *Weaving Te Whāriki: Aotearoa New Zealand's Early Childhood Curriculum Framework in Theory and Practice* (2nd edn). Wellington: NZCER Press.

Wood, E. (2014) Free choice and free play in early childhood education: troubling the discourse. *International Journal of Early Years Education*, 22 (1): 4–18.

Wood, E. and Hall, E. (2011) Drawings as spaces for intellectual play. *International Journal of Early Years Education*, 19 (3–4): 267–281.

19

Econometrics and the Study of Early Childhood: A Guide for Consumers

Gordon Cleveland

INTRODUCTION

In recent decades, econometrics has played a significant role in early childhood research and policy evaluation. 'Econometrics' refers to quantitative statistical analysis used by economists, although most of the statistical techniques used are not unique to economics or economists (see Cook and Campbell, 1979; Shadish et al., 2002). This chapter provides a guide for those who read, interpret and use statistical studies designed and/or conducted by economists in relation to early childhood.

Econometric research is not well known to early childhood researchers, many of whom have little acquaintance with economics. Economic models and econometric results are typically presented in mathematical form and statistical jargon that those in other disciplines may not find familiar. The purpose of this chapter is to provide a guide to some of the key approaches used in the econometric analysis of early childhood issues.

The chapter will emphasize the rationale for the statistical methods used, interpretation of results, and ways of judging the strengths and weaknesses of a particular study. To illustrate, the chapter will briefly discuss selected studies where these techniques have been used in early childhood research; in particular, research into the effects of child care and/or parental employment on children.

Measurement is predicated upon theory. Theory informs the processes, mechanisms and statistical techniques that are used to produce data. Economic theory on child development, with a particular focus on James Heckman and his co-authors, will be considered in the next section of the chapter.

If we are to draw conclusions about causal relationships between early childhood events and child outcomes, the central statistical problem we need to address is the issue of 'selection'. Most early childhood events or 'treatments' are not accidental; they are chosen (i.e., selected) by parents or children. If we are to estimate accurately the effect of parental employment on children's development, for example, we cannot ignore the fact that parental employment is chosen by parents, and that the characteristics of employed parents and their children are systematically different from those of parents who are not employed.

So too, if we are to accurately estimate the effects of early childhood care and education services on children's development, we cannot ignore the fact that the type, quality and amount of these services is chosen by parents and that the characteristics of parents and children using certain types, qualities and amounts of these services may be systematically different from those using different types, qualities and amounts. If we had data on all the systematic differences between those who select different alternatives, we could statistically control for these differences. However, it is unlikely that any data set will have information on all the important parent and child factors that affect a child's development – some of these factors will be observed (i.e., measured in our data set) and some will remain unobserved. Statistically, these unobserved systematic differences create the potential for biased estimates of any effects in which we are interested. The third section of this chapter describes what selection bias is and why dealing with potential selection bias is central to statistical studies of early childhood.

Using examples from reputable studies in early childhood, the fourth section of this chapter presents and discusses the key econometric research designs (see Angrist and Pischke, 2009; Blundell and Dias, 2009; Khandker et al., 2010; Dunning, 2012) that have been used to permit causal conclusions to be drawn from data about the correlates of children's development. These research designs include random assignment experiments, regressions using observational data but explicitly controlling for selection, propensity score matching methods, fixed-effects models, natural experiments with difference-in-differences analysis or regression discontinuity designs, use of instrumental variables

and use of quasi-structural models. In each case, the emphasis will not be on mathematics and statistical theory but on an assessment of the strengths of each technique, the kinds of data needed to use each technique, the appropriate interpretation of results from each technique and the weaknesses to look for in assessing the credibility of results coming from any particular study.

The final section of this chapter provides a brief summary of its main points, an assessment of the state of econometric research on early childhood and possible future directions.

ECONOMIC THEORIES OF CHILD DEVELOPMENT

Economic theories of child development are an extension of human capital theory, originally developed by Gary Becker (1964). According to human capital theory, every individual possesses a stock of knowledge, abilities and skills that permits that individual to be productive in the labor force, but also to interact socially, acquire new knowledge and skills through education and experience, and engage in activities that give direct satisfaction or utility. Individuals can increase or decrease their stocks of human capital over their lifetimes by investment in increasing their skills/abilities or by the depreciation of their skills/abilities. Human capital includes various cognitive and non-cognitive sets of skills as well as the individual's health characteristics.

Economic theory, in words and in mathematical form, seeks to explain how decisions are made (about having children, about investing in children, about entering the labor force, about getting married, etc.) by family members who seek to make themselves better off by using their existing resources to pursue goals that will give them satisfaction. Parents are seen to derive joy from consuming goods and services, from leisure time and from the rounded development of their children.

In general, parental time is the resource that parents have available to achieve the multiplicity of things that will give them satisfaction, including the development and happiness of their children. Given their tastes and abilities and the technology of child development, parents will seek to allocate their time to market work, child care and household time, and leisure time to maximize their joy/satisfaction. The implication is that families make decisions that affect child development, but all of these decisions reflect tradeoffs that are affected by parental tastes, parent abilities, child abilities and the characteristics of the child-abilities production function (i.e., the technology of child development – see below for details). Predictions from economic models are tested against data, often data from large sample surveys, using a variety of econometric techniques.

Most economists rely on mathematics rather than visual diagrams to express theory, but there is one very early and prominent exception. In a special issue of the *Journal of Political Economy* devoted to the economics of the family, Arleen Leibowitz (1974) depicted (part of) the human-capital model of child cognitive development.

According to Leibowitz's diagram, children have genetically-inherited abilities at birth (at this time, genetic and environmental factors were viewed as entirely separate). These abilities interact with parental investments of time and goods (and both the quantity and quality of these inputs matter) to affect the ultimate achievement level of children, measured by final schooling level. School achievement directly influences the ability to earn income. Since income is easy to measure and reflects a mix of social, emotional and cognitive skills, it has often been used by economists as a measure of the long-term effects of investment in child development.

Leibowitz's model is really only a part of human capital theory. It depicts what has been called the child-abilities production function (since she focuses on cognitive skills, we might refer to the cognitive-skills production function). In production theory, a production function is a technological relationship between inputs and outputs; it tells us what the output in a production process will be when we combine together inputs in different possible proportions. Learning is a less deterministic process than industrial production, of course, but economists find it useful to model child development as a relationship between inputs (e.g., different parental investments, initial child abilities) and outputs (some measure of child development).

A contemporary consensus version of the child-abilities production function (Todd and Wolpin, 2003; Bernal, 2008) would include four main groups of variables:

- parental time: investments of parental time that affect child development, including measures of both the quantity and quality of parental time. If we are considering the abilities of a child at age X, then we would be interested in the entire history of parental time investment from birth (or before birth) up to age X
- ECEC services: the quantity and quality of time spent in early childhood education and care services (i.e., non-parental time); again, we would be interested in the entire history of time spent in these services from birth
- goods and services: purchased goods and service inputs to child development. These inputs would include: the quantity and quality of housing purchased by the family, the characteristics of the neighbourhood, books and other learning materials, materials for play, computers and computer software, family vacations, ballet and sports lessons, etc. Again, the history of these inputs back to the child's birth might matter
- original child abilities: the inherent abilities (and disabilities) of the child. In other words, the stock of cognitive, non-cognitive and health characteristics of the child before experiences and investments begin to change the stocks of these abilities.

Any child outcome at a point in time is viewed as being systematically related to these four sets of variables. For example, child cognitive development is considered to be a knowledge acquisition process in which current and past inputs are combined with an individual's genetic endowment of ability-to-learn to produce a current cognitive outcome.

James Heckman and a host of co-authors (Heckman, 2007; Cunha et al., 2010; Heckman and Mosso, 2014) have pursued a somewhat distinct child development research agenda, with important amendments to this production-function framework. Adapting many insights from other disciplines, Heckman describes a revised technology of skill formation (his name for the child-abilities production function).

Within this paradigm, children have a set of capabilities at any age including pure cognitive abilities, non-cognitive abilities (including patience, self-control, temperament, etc.) and health. All of these capabilities are produced by a combination of investment, environment and genes. These capabilities will be used in different combinations in different tasks in school, in the labor market and in social life. The capability formation process proceeds in stages – each stage corresponds to a period in the life cycle of a child. Investments and inputs at each stage produce outputs (i.e., changes in capability) at the next stage.

The technology of development (i.e., the relation between inputs and the resulting outputs) is different at each stage. Some stages may be more productive in producing certain capabilities than other stages. If so, these stages are known as 'sensitive periods' for the development of those particular capabilities. If a capability can only be produced or affected in one particular stage, that stage is known as a 'critical period' for that capability. Capabilities at earlier stages affect capabilities at later stages; in other words, capabilities are self-productive, and the effects of early investment will persist (capabilities beget capabilities). Capabilities at one stage raise the productivity of investment at later stages; this is known as dynamic complementarity.

Heckman's technology of skill formation is distinct from a garden-variety child-abilities production function in that it emphasizes that it is not always possible to change the path of child development with later investments. Early experiences and early investments are especially important in a child's life both because some of these early stages are sensitive or critical for the development of capabilities, and also because the early development of capabilities makes it possible to grow these capabilities later, and makes later investments more productive for those children who have already accumulated sufficient skills, but less productive for those who have not. Many of Heckman's findings (Cunha et al., 2010) emphasize the importance of non-cognitive skills (i.e., personality, social and emotional traits) in supporting cognitive skill development.

SELECTION EFFECTS

The key statistical issue to address, in almost every study of early childhood, is 'selection'. The treatment that an individual receives (e.g., being employed, using child care) is not randomly assigned to the person; instead, it is selected by this individual and not selected by others. This problem comes under many guises and is described using different terms. Sometimes, there appears to be a multitude of problems, but all terms refer essentially to the same phenomenon. The problem can be referred to as the problem of endogeneity, the problem of selection effects, the problem of unobserved heterogeneity, the problem of identification, the assignment problem, non-ignorable treatment assignment or omitted variable bias. But these are the same problem in different guises.

We will use the language of clinical trials and refer to treatments and controls. A treatment is any potential input to child development outcomes in which we are interested. The group that receives this treatment will be described as the treatment group. The effect of the treatment will be determined by comparing, using some statistical method, the outcomes for the treatment group to those for a comparison group, generally known as the control group.

A useful way of thinking about the problem of making statistical inferences is to think about potential outcomes (Neyman, [1923] 1990; Rubin, 1974, 1978, 1990). To be concrete, imagine that we are concerned about the short-term effects on vocabulary for a group of 4-year-old children who may receive a year of high-quality preschool or may instead be cared for entirely by parents for that year. Each child has two potential outcomes: the effect of receiving the treatment (high-quality preschool) and the effect of receiving the control (exclusively parental care). Our statistical objective is to compare the average score of these children on some test of vocabulary when they receive the treatment to the score achieved by *the same children* when they receive the control. The average difference between these two potential outcomes will be interpreted as the short-term effect on vocabulary of this treatment.

However, it is not possible to collect data on both these potential outcomes for each child; each child receives either the treatment or control, not both. In order to make a statistical inference about the causal effects, we have to find a substitute for the missing information (known as the counterfactual). In particular, we need to find a valid comparison group for the group of children receiving the treatment. The ideal group will be one that is essentially identical to the treated group – identical in the factors that are likely to affect child development, both observed and unobserved. From the comparison group, the counterfactual can be statistically constructed; this counterfactual will stand in for the missing information on potential outcomes. This gives us a credible way of estimating the average potential outcome that would have happened in the absence of treatment.

However, we are rarely presented with this ideal comparison group. Instead, we have data on a group of children whose parents have chosen a certain treatment, and data on another group of children whose parents chose to do something else. The self-selected treatment group is, in general, systematically different from the comparison group in ways that will affect child outcomes. In other words, because of self-selection, the comparison group is not actually a good counterfactual for the treatment group. Simple analysis of the differences between treatment and comparison groups will give biased estimates of the effect of treatment.

Sometimes, the systematic differences between treatment and comparison groups are readily observable (mother's education level, her ability to earn a high wage, number of children in the family, ages of the children, presence of relatives available to provide childcare, mother's chronic health issues, single parent status, etc.). In this case, it may be possible to collect data on all of these factors responsible for the selection of, for example, employment or child care, and control explicitly, in a regression framework, for these factors.

On the other hand, perhaps the selection of, for example, employment status and type of child care are due to factors that are normally unobservable. In this context, 'unobservable' means unobservable to the researcher doing the study and implies that this is a factor that is either difficult or impossible to measure and collect data about. Unobservable factors that affect a mother's employment decision would include details about personal beliefs, temperament, health conditions, abilities or habits that might affect employability or the desire to be employed. These factors would also include unobservable characteristics of her children to which the mother might react in deciding whether to seek employment or use child care (e.g., problems of attachment or temperament, children's health problems, special abilities or disabilities that are known by the mother but unknown to the researcher).

If there are unobservable factors that are important in selection decisions (i.e., the decision to select or not select a certain treatment), then the treated group and the comparison group will be systematically different but in ways the researcher is unable to statistically control for. These unobserved differences may be correlated with different patterns or amounts of child development. A simple analysis that controls only for observable variables no longer measures a causal treatment effect. Any differences in child outcomes could be due to the treatment, but they could alternatively (or also) be due to the different unobserved family environments in which the two groups of children live.

Statistically speaking, the problem is one of bias. When receipt of the treatment is correlated with a set of unobserved factors that might themselves affect child outcomes, then a statistical estimation procedure that ignores this problem will produce biased estimates of the effect of the treatment. In other words, the estimates will not be valid causal estimates of the effect of the treatment.

A couple of possible scenarios can make the problem more concrete. Imagine that the true effect of high quality child care on children's cognitive and social development is positive, but small. Since the supply of high quality care is limited, parents who are highly child-focused may be especially likely to get their children into high quality centers. Those parents may also be the ones who make sure that the quality and quantity of parental time investments in children's development is particularly high. Most data sets do not have good detail on the quality and quantity of parental time investments in children. Since these unobserved parental investments may have strong positive effects on children, a simple regression of child outcomes on the quality of child care used will find very large positive effects. However, this would be an upward-biased estimate due to the positive correlation between center quality and unobserved (and very productive) parental investments.

Again, imagine that the true effect of high quality child care on children's cognitive and social development is positive, but small. Imagine also that a substantial number of children exhibit negative externalizing behaviors due to a combination of (unobserved) experiences very early in life and genetic disposition. These behaviors may be associated with slower cognitive and social development. Parents with these children may work very hard to make sure that they get access to the best quality child care available. When we do a simple regression of child outcomes on child care quality, we are likely to find that high quality in child care centers has little effect or even a negative effect on children's development. This would be a downward-biased estimate due to the correlation between high quality care and negative externalizing behaviors that slow children's development.

ECONOMETRIC APPROACHES TO THE STUDY OF EARLY CHILDHOOD

The best-known research design that deals with the potential bias of selection is the random assignment experiment.

Random Assignment Experiments

Random assignment experiments occur when individuals in a sample group are randomly assigned by the researcher to either receive the treatment (e.g., free preschool three days a week, smaller class size from kindergarten through Grade 3) or to be in the control group (i.e., no subsidization of preschool three days per week, larger class size in the early years of school). Random assignment experiments solve the central statistical problem we have been discussing because the assignment to treatment is uncorrelated with any of the family or school inputs (the unobserved characteristics of families and schools) that are in the residual term and cause estimates of the effects of the treatment to be biased. If random assignment is successful, the only systematic difference, either observed or unobserved, between the treatment group and the control group is that one receives the treatment and one does not. Therefore, the average difference in outcomes will provide a causal measure of treatment effects.

Project STAR was a social experiment carried out in 79 schools in Tennessee in the mid-1980s. Over 11,000 children, 60% white and 40% African-American, starting kindergarten in the 1985–86 school year were randomly assigned to either a small class (13 to 17 children) or a regular-sized class (22 to 25 children). Teachers were also randomly assigned to the teaching of either the small or the regular-sized class. The children were followed in the experiment from kindergarten through Grade 3, with children being kept in either the small or regular classes to which they had been assigned. This original experiment found that class size matters for child outcomes at Grade 3 completion (Krueger, 1999).

Dynarski, Hyman and Schanzenbach (2013) followed up on the Project STAR children about 25 years later to determine the long-term effects of being randomly assigned to a small class. Assignment to a small class in kindergarten and primary school is found to increase the probability of attending college by 2.7 percentage points and the likelihood of earning a college degree by 1.6 percentage points with substantially larger effects amongst black students.

In this case, random assignment allows for identification of a long-term effect that would otherwise be very difficult to distinguish from all the background factors affecting a multitude of inputs.

Random assignment experiments do not solve all statistical and inferential problems. First, it may be the case that individuals who are assigned to treatment or to control refuse to comply with this assignment. Those assigned to receive free preschool may decide to keep their child at home, for instance. Another issue is that, especially if the randomized sample is small, the sample may not be representative of the larger population for which the researcher is seeking to make statistical inferences (this is the issue of external validity). For instance, Janet Currie has argued that the findings of fadeout of positive effects amongst Head Start children were true in small randomized samples of low-income African-American children,

but not amongst children from other backgrounds in larger samples (see Currie and Thomas, 1995; Garces et al., 2002).

Random assignment experiments are inappropriate if the control group will be affected in any way by the treatment. For instance, someone assigned to the control group may experience regret at not receiving the treatment and change their behavior as a result (e.g., change the planned care arrangements for their child). Situations in which there are spillover effects from the treatment, or substitution as described above, or equilibrium effects will give biased estimates in a random assignment experiment.

Internal validity warrants that a study has sufficiently minimized the possibility of systematic bias in its estimates. External validity refers to the ability of researchers to generalize the results of a study to situations and people other than those in the study sample. Even if there are no issues of internal or external validity,[1] Todd and Wolpin (2003) remind us that random assignment experiments do not measure precisely the same effect (the same parameter) as a regression analysis does. Regression analysis, under perfect conditions, measures the effect of receiving the treatment with all other factors held constant. However, a random assignment experiment does not hold constant the reaction of parents, for instance, to the assignment to preschool or the assignment to a smaller class size. Parents might reduce their input to children's development, assuming that the enhanced preschool or school inputs make extra parental input unnecessary. The measured treatment effect in the random assignment experiment will combine both the effects of preschool and the effects of the parental reaction to it, or the effects of smaller class size and the change in parental input in reaction to it.

Including a Comprehensive Set of Regressors

At the opposite end of the spectrum from random assignment experiments in which control for selection is achieved by the pre-treatment design of the experiment, is regression analysis, where the control for selection is achieved by statistical manipulation after the treatment has occurred. One regression-based approach is to include a very wide range of variables in a regression to explain some child outcome. For instance, Blau (1999) uses this technique to look at the effects of inputs to child care quality (mainly group size, child–staff ratio and the training of caregivers) on measures of child behavioral problems, and early indicators of reading, math and vocabulary skills. Blau, using data from the National Longitudinal Study of Youth (NLSY), includes about 50 mother, family and child variables. The idea is to statistically control for (i.e., hold constant) any possible systematic differences between those receiving the treatment (higher child care quality) and those receiving lower child care quality. He concludes that child care inputs have little systematic effect on child outcomes.

Using a similar technique, NICHD-ECCRN and Duncan (2003) conclude that the effects of quality in child care centers are small (0.04 to 0.08 of a standard deviation on cognitive outcomes for children), but that, in addition, use of center-based care in the third and fourth years of a child's life has an independent effect of about 0.25 of a standard deviation on cognitive and academic achievement outcomes.

Magnuson, Ruhm and Waldfogel (2007) use data from the ECLS-K (Early Childhood Longitudinal Study-Kindergarten Cohort) to examine the effects of attending prekindergarten in the USA. Their regression estimates include an exceptionally detailed set of controls for child, family, background, school and neighborhood characteristics, including parenting practices, parental expectations for their children, parental depression, warmth and affection of the parent–child relationship, parental involvement in schooling, and other measures of home environment. They found improved reading and math skills at kindergarten for children attending

prekindergarten. However, attendance at pre-kindergarten was also predictive of higher levels of externalizing behaviors and lower levels of self-control. By first grade, the reading and math advantage was very substantially reduced, but behavior problems persisted. Negative behavioral effects were not significant for children who attended both prekindergarten and kindergarten in the same public school. The authors hypothesize that the higher quality of public school pre-kindergarten is responsible for the absence of negative behavioral effects.

The problem with this 'comprehensive set of regressors' technique is that there is no way of knowing whether the introduced variables have successfully controlled for the unobserved differences in parental inputs or initial child abilities that are correlated with the selection of treatment and may therefore produce bias. In fact, this technique relies on the assumption that the addition of sufficient variables can make these differences 'observed' (and therefore statistically controllable) rather than 'unobserved'. Researchers who adopt this technique for minimizing selection bias will often use other techniques as well, and argue that similar results across several techniques should increase our confidence that selection issues have been successfully addressed (Blau, 1999; NICHD-ECCRN and Duncan, 2003; Magnuson et al., 2007).

Propensity Score Matching

Propensity score matching is another research design that relies on the assumption that differences between treatment and control groups are observable, rather than unobservable. Propensity score matching improves on simple regression techniques in one important way, however. It makes its judgments about treatment effects only in groups that are, in observable ways, very similar to each other. In other words, matching estimators reweight the observations in a comparison group to create a counterfactual that is similar to the treated group.

One of the statistical problems that occurs when individuals or families choose their own treatments is that the treatment and the comparison groups may look very dissimilar. If the treatment is the use of private school (with an objective of determining the effect of attendance at private school on childhood relationships with peers), it may be true that most of those who use private schools will be systematically different on many observable dimensions from most of those who do not. A comparison between children who attend private schools and those who do not may seem like a comparison of apples and oranges. However, there are likely to be some children attending private schools who are quite similar to some children not attending private schools. A comparison of the peer relationships of these two sub-groups may be considered more reasonable.

A propensity score analysis compares the effects of private school on the dependent variable using groups that are similar on the relevant observable dimensions. This is achieved by calculating a propensity score – in our case, the propensity to use private school – using a regression of private school attendance on the observed variables that are presumed to affect the probability of attending private school. This regression generates the propensity score. Propensity scores are used to reweight the observations in the comparison group, so that it forms a reasonable counterfactual to the treated group for drawing causal conclusions. However, matching techniques such as propensity score matching assume that unobservable factors correlated with peer relationships are nonexistent or of minor importance. This assumption may or may not be a reasonable one (although the degree of reasonableness is testable – see Kottelenberg and Lehrer, 2013a).

Although a good propensity score analysis will discuss and justify the use of variables in calculating the propensity score, it is a matter of judgment whether the appropriate matching variables have been chosen (see Campolieti et al., 2014 for a good example, and discussion of alternative weighting estimators).

If not, the counterfactual may not be correctly measured. Several studies of the effects of early childhood education and care on children have used propensity score matching techniques (Hill et al., 2002; Warren and Haisken-DeNew, 2014). Kottelenberg and Lehrer (2013a) use inverse probability weighting (i.e., inverse propensity score weighting) methods that reweight both the treatment and comparison observations.

Fixed-Effects Models

If we can make accurate assumptions about the source of the selection bias, it may be possible to use a fixed-effects model to eliminate the potential bias. For example, imagine that the source of the bias is the correlation between treatment and unobservable parental time inputs; in general, parents whose children receive the treatment also spend more time reading to their children. However, if we are willing to assume that, within a family, parents will spend similar amounts and quality of time with each of their children, we can estimate a family fixed-effects model. This statistical model looks only at families in which at least one child receives the treatment and one does not. The average difference between the effect of the treatment on one child in each of these families in comparison to the absence of treatment on the other child in each family can be taken as an estimate of the effect of the treatment with parental inputs held constant. Other fixed-effect research designs compare the same child at two different points in time; in this case, the assumption that motivates and justifies a fixed-effects model is that selection bias does not vary over time.

Currie and Thomas (1995) used a family fixed-effects model (they call it a sibling fixed-effects model) to look at the long-term effects of Head Start programs in the USA on child outcomes. They compare outcomes of two siblings in the same family in which one sibling attended Head Start and the other did not. This controls for unmeasured family characteristics that might affect both Head Start enrolment and child outcomes. Currie and Thomas (1995) documented long-term (i.e., into the early school years) positive effects on school achievement for white Head Start attendees, but not for African American children. In a second paper using a similar technique, Currie and Thomas (1999) reported long-term positive effects on school achievement for Hispanics. In a follow-up study of effects at age 21 using a similar statistical technique, Garces, Currie and Thomas (2002) found that white children who attended Head Start were more likely to complete high school and to attend college, and to earn more than other white children who did not attend Head Start. African American children did not have the same school achievement gains, but were significantly less likely to be arrested for criminal activity than similar children in the same family who did not attend Head Start.

Fixed-effects models can produce strong results, but the results are no better than the assumptions on which they are based. The studies mentioned above rely on the assumption that unobserved parental investments are the same for both siblings. In other words, the model assumes that parental investments do not respond to previous differences between the children and do not vary even though the siblings are receiving different treatments (e.g., Head Start vs. any other care arrangements). If unobserved parental investments within a family vary systematically across siblings in a way that is correlated with the treatment, the fixed-effects model will also produce biased estimates. There is no way to test the basic assumption on which such fixed-effects models are based.

Dissatisfaction with the credibility of the assumptions upon which studies like these are based has led a number of economists to seek natural experiments that might shed unbiased light on the effects of early childhood events.

Natural Experiments – Difference-in-Differences

Human capital theory tells us that the skills and abilities of any child at any point in time are the product of a very large number of time and goods inputs and initial abilities throughout the lifetime of the child. Most of these inputs will be correlated with each other positively or negatively, and many of these inputs are unobserved by the researcher. Along with selection differences, this implies that it is quite difficult to avoid biased estimates using conventional forms of statistical manipulation. In reaction to these problems, there has been a major evolution in econometrics in the last couple of decades towards relying on natural experiments to make causal statistical inferences.

Natural experiments occur when some policy change or naturally-occurring event assigns a treatment to one group of people and not to another. Ideally, this assignment will be essentially random (i.e., as-if-random). If a natural experiment assigns treatment in a random way, then the observed *and* unobserved characteristics of the treated group and of the comparison group will be similar. And these characteristics will not be correlated with treatment, because treatment was assigned by some policy rule or uncontrollable event. Some researchers reserve the term 'natural experiment' for situations in which the assignment of subjects to treatment or control groups is demonstrably random, although this randomization is not done by the researcher. They then use the term quasi-experiment for assignment that is as-if-random. We use the term 'natural experiment' for both.

A useful way of thinking about natural experiments is that they provide a credible selection of a 'counterfactual' for the group that has received treatment. A natural experiment, then, can be thought of as an event (a naturally-occurring event – outside of the researcher's control) that simultaneously assigns a treatment to some individuals and creates a credible counterfactual group which is like the group receiving treatment, and would arguably have behaved similarly to the treatment group had treatment not been received. This counterfactual group becomes the comparison group for the analysis.

The concern with widespread selection effects biasing research results based on multiple regression analysis of observational data has led economists researching early childhood issues to turn towards natural experiments for more credible measures of the effects of different programs, policies and family choices. There are a number of research designs that depend on or attempt to mimic a natural experiment.

The most prominent of these is difference-in-differences analysis. A difference-in-differences analysis compares the change in a dependent variable for a group receiving a particular treatment to the change in that same dependent variable for a plausibly similar counterfactual group who did not receive the treatment.

Difference-in-differences analysis generally requires longitudinal data or repeated cross-sections of data so that pre vs. post can be compared between treated and not treated. Of course, if group A chooses the treatment and group B chooses not to receive the treatment, selection issues will be paramount. However, if the treatment is an unexpected and unchosen treatment given to some and not given to others in a plausibly random fashion, this natural experiment allows us to interpret the difference-in-differences results as causal estimates of the policy decision to make a certain group of people eligible for the treatment.

Difference-in-difference analysis is not a panacea, of course; analyses can be done well or poorly. The first issue is whether the policy change or naturally-occurring event distinguishes clearly between those who receive the treatment and those who do not. This requires that the event (e.g., rollout of a new child care program to some families but not to others, a flu epidemic affecting in-utero health for children in this flu season but not the previous one) does not have spillover effects or substitution effects that change the experience of control group members. The second issue is whether as-if-random assignment-to-treatment is successful, or only partially so. In other words, for example, given a particular policy change making a large number of families eligible for full-day kindergarten instead of part-day, do all or nearly all of those now eligible actually accept the treatment? If so, selection effects have been avoided and the results of the natural experiment can be interpreted as the causal effect of receiving the treatment. If many parents who are newly eligible for full-day kindergarten decide, nonetheless, to stick with part-day services, the average effect of the natural experiment must be interpreted as intention-to-treat effects, rather than treatment effects. Further statistical procedures may, under certain assumptions, be able to recover the treatment effects from this experiment.

Further, there are a couple of key assumptions that must be accepted as valid for a difference-in-differences analysis to produce casual estimates. One is that the treatment group and the control group were very similar before the treatment. This can be checked. A second is the common trends assumption. The natural experiment has produced a group that has been as-if-randomly assigned to treatment. The researcher has selected a comparison group that appears to be very similar in many ways to the treatment group except they did not receive the treatment. We are going to look at the change (before and after difference) in outcomes for the treated group in comparison to the change (before and after difference) in outcomes for the comparison group. The average difference between these differences will be our estimate of the effect of the treatment. However, the comparison group is only a valid counterfactual if, in the absence of treatment, the evolution of outcomes in response to various events for the treatment group and the comparison group would have been very similar. Usually, researchers look at the trends in outcomes for the treatment group and the comparison group before any treatment occurred to try to determine whether the assumption of common trends appears reasonable.

We can illustrate a couple of these issues by looking at the study by Baker, Gruber and Milligan (2008) on the effects of dramatic expansion of the availability of low-cost regulated child care in the province of Quebec, in Canada, in the late 1990s. They use data from the National Longitudinal Study of Children and Youth that collects information on a large sample of children and families across Canada every two years. Most of the measures are based on parental responses about socio-emotional and health outcomes of children and issues of maternal depression, family functioning, etc. These authors choose children in the rest of Canada, who did not benefit from the policy change in Quebec, as the primary control group (some analyses are also done using older children in Quebec for comparison).

The program led to large increases in maternal employment and in the use of non-parental child care. Using a difference-in-differences strategy, changes in outcomes are compared between children in Quebec (the treatment group) and the rest of Canada (the controls). The authors find significant negative effects of the program on a variety of socio-emotional and health outcomes of children under the age of 5 and on parents.

There are reasons for caution in accepting and interpreting these results. First, since the NLSCY only started collecting data in 1994–95, and because there is no history of similar studies in an earlier period in Canada, the authors only have two data points, 1994–95 and 1996–97, to establish that there would normally be common trends in outcomes and common response to shocks, in Quebec and in the rest of Canada. This is too little information to provide convincing evidence, so the assumption of common trends is left as an unsupported assumption. This issue is even more important because randomization is cluster randomization, and the two clusters (one receiving treatment and one acting

as the counterfactual) live in quite different cultural, linguistic and policy environments.

Second, in this case and somewhat frequently with natural policy experiments, the treatment is a complex one, so it becomes difficult or impossible to disentangle which specific factors are the cause of any effects. Baker, Gruber and Milligan (2008) suggest that the negative effects are the result of 'universal' child care. However, the treatment that these authors studied actually consisted of reducing the parent price to $5 per day for the existing group of regulated child care spaces (about 75,000 spaces) and expanding the supply of these regulated spaces by about 115,000 over a period of 8 years. Of this expansion about 67,000 were in family day care spots, 12,000 were in for-profit child care centers at poorer ratios and with worse training than the not-for-profit CPEs (*Centres de Petite Enfance* – Early Childhood Centres) and only 36,000 (or 31% of the increase in spaces) were in the not-for-profit CPEs (with better ratios and better-trained staff) that were intended to be the heart of the program. Further, the distribution of spaces was not even across income groups. And the expansion in child care spots was combined with a dramatic increase in maternal employment, particularly amongst mothers with relatively low levels of education. It is not clear what aspect of the reforms may have led to the observed negative effects.

The final point to note is that Baker, Gruber and Milligan's estimates are not estimates of treatment effects but of the intention-to-treat (i.e., of becoming eligible for access to a $5 per day child care space). Actual treatment (i.e., care in a $5 per day child care space) is only experienced by some children, so selection effects may influence the probability of being treated.

It is possible to move beyond 'intention-to-treat' analyses provided by a difference-in-differences technique (see below under 'Instrumental variables'). Kottelenberg and Lehrer (2013a, 2013b, 2013c) revisit Baker, Gruber and Milligan's (2008) findings about the natural experiment of the introduction of major child care and family policy reforms in Quebec (Canada). They confirm the negative intent-to-treat effects on child and family outcomes using additional cycles of data from the NLSCY. What is surprising, however, is the heterogeneity of effects they find when they examine the treatment effects of actually attending child care services.

In one paper (2013a), they find that even though the effects on families who are new to non-parental child care are strongly negative (a local average treatment effect analyzed using instrumental variables), the average treatment effects of attending child care (assessed with a propensity score technique) are strongly positive for MSD scores (a measure of motor, social and cognitive development of children 0–3) and there are significant positive effects in reducing maternal depression. None of the measures of child behavioral or cognitive development are negatively affected by child care in this latter analysis.

Kottelenberg and Lehrer's other papers (2013b, 2013c) find that the effects of child care vary substantially by age and by gender, with younger children and boys having a strong propensity to negative effects. Further, they conclude that the negative effects of Quebec's reforms are driven by dramatic declines in parental investments in their children's development by some Quebec parents as their children's use of child care increases.

Difference-in-differences analysis of natural experiments has been used to study the effects of maternal employment on children as well. For instance, Liu and Skans (2010) study the effects of a three-month increase (from 12 to 15 months) in partially-paid parental leave in Sweden in 1989. Mothers with children born in 1988 were given differential additional amounts of leave according to the month in which their children were born. Liu and Skans use this as an identification strategy for a difference-in-differences analysis of the effect on children of additional amounts of maternal time. The data is population-based, so the sample is sufficiently large to find effects. The outcome measures

are long-term – scholastic performance at age 16 – measured by test scores from national tests administered during the final compulsory school year in mathematics, Swedish and English. School grades in this same year are examined as well.

This is an interesting study because the alternative to maternal care for most families is high-quality Swedish child care, widely available for children of this age at subsidized prices. Liu and Skans (2010) find no effect of this expansion of maternity leave (relative to subsidized child care) on children's scholastic performance on average, but find positive effects for the children of well-educated mothers (the one-quarter of mothers with a tertiary education). This is a robust finding. No other heterogeneity in results is found, nor are there effects on other intermediate family outcomes. The authors conclude that longer parental leave reinforces the interaction between mother education and school outcomes.

Natural Experiments – Discontinuity Design

A second type of statistical analysis that relies on a natural experiment is known as discontinuity design, or sometimes regression discontinuity design. Discontinuity designs exploit natural discontinuities in the rules that assign some individuals to receive a certain treatment (e.g., to be eligible for a particular program) and other individuals to be just ineligible for the treatment. For example, the probability of being enrolled in a program may change discontinuously with respect to some continuous variable that determines eligibility (e.g., age, income, score on a test). Let us take the simple case where eligibility is very strictly enforced so that the age, or income, or test score rule for eligibility fully determines whether the treatment is received. In this case, the treated group is on one side of a line and the control group on another. However, arguably those who just qualified for the treatment are very similar/nearly identical to those who just failed to qualify. In many cases, those who just failed to qualify can serve as a plausible counterfactual group to determine the effects of the treatment on those who just succeeded in qualifying. This counterfactual strategy will be more convincing the narrower is the range considered on either side of the eligibility cut-off.

Gormley, Gayer, Phillips and Dawson (2005) used a regression discontinuity design to control for selection bias by comparing children using universal 4-year-old prekindergarten in Tulsa, Oklahoma, to those children just excluded from prekindergarten because of their age. The effects they find are very strong and not affected by narrowing the age bands considered until the treatment and control groups are of virtually identical ages. Using nationally-normed test instruments (Woodcock-Johnson subtests for letter-identification [pre-reading], spelling [pre-writing] and applied problems [pre-math]), the authors reported effect sizes from one year of attending a very good quality prekindergarten program of 0.79 of a standard deviation for pre-reading, 0.64 of a standard deviation for pre-writing and 0.38 of a standard deviation for pre-math.

The Oklahoma results were likely affected by the very high quality of the prekindergarten services provided in the schools by teachers who had both a teaching certificate and a certificate in early childhood education, and who were paid at public school rates. Classroom sizes were capped at 20 children, and, with one lesser-trained assistant, this meant that staff–child ratios were 1:10.

Statistical results from regression discontinuity design are not based on the entire population of those affected by a policy. Instead, the results are based on comparing the effects on those who are just eligible for the policy (e.g., just meet an age cut-off) to the effects on those who just fail to be eligible (narrowly miss an age cut-off). The effect uncovered with regression discontinuity design is called the Local Average Treatment Effect (the LATE) to reflect this restricted interpretation.

Instrumental Variables

The selection problem arises because the variable of interest (the treatment variable) is correlated with some other (usually unobserved) factor that also affects child outcomes. Instrumental variable techniques address this problem directly, generally by replacing the treatment variable with another variable that is reasonably well correlated with the treatment variable, but is not otherwise related to child outcomes or other variables that affect child outcomes.

A classic example is tobacco smoking across the 50 states in the USA. Clearly, tobacco-smoking is chosen by individuals, and this decision will be correlated with many other observable characteristics of individuals such as income, education, occupation and age, but also will be correlated with unobserved characteristics that might include degree of willingness to engage in risky behaviors. Variation in cancer rates across the states might be due to variations in smoking rates, but it might be due to the unobserved variations in the degree of willingness to engage in other risky behaviors (that also affect cancer rates). However, there is a part of the smoking rates that is independent of the willingness to engage in other risky behaviors. Instead, this part is due to the differences in the rates of taxation on tobacco across the states. We may, therefore, be able to use these rates of taxation as an instrument – in other words, take only the part of the variation in smoking rates that is correlated with taxation and use this to replace smoking rates in a regression looking at the impact of smoking on cancer. In effect, we are using the random nature of the variations in tobacco taxes as a natural experiment to purge the smoking variable of the part of it infected by selectivity.

As an example, Bernal and Keane (2010) use variations in state welfare rules in the USA as instruments for employment and child care decisions of sole parents in an analysis of the effects of these employment and child care decisions on children's cognitive development. The authors find that there are significant negative effects of full-time employment for sole mothers on the cognitive development of their children. However, the authors find evidence that negative effects are driven by the use of informal care; high quality center care does not have adverse effects.

In the context of a natural experiment, instrumental variable (IV) techniques may also be used to deepen the insights given by difference-in-differences analysis or regression discontinuity design. The problem this is designed to address emerges because treatment assignment is often not perfect. In other words, some individuals assigned to participate in a particular program will decide not to participate. Or, some individuals who are not given eligibility for a program or policy will nonetheless find a way of gaining access. One way of dealing with this problem is to ignore it. In that case, the difference-in-differences analysis or discontinuity design analysis becomes an analysis of the effects of the 'intention to treat' (often known as ITT) rather than the effects of treatment.

To push the analysis of this natural experiment further, instrumental variable analysis can be used to get at the effects of treatment. Under certain assumptions, the assignment to treatment can be used as an instrument for treatment itself (in effect, taking only the part of treatment influenced exclusively by assignment to treatment – or only those who were, on the margin, affected by treatment assignment [the 'compliers']) and an IV regression can be interpreted as causal for this group. Because these estimates only directly apply to a subset of the group being studied (the compliers), the results are known as the local average treatment effect (the LATE).

Instrumental variable estimates frequently encounter two problems. First, the assumption that the instrument has no independent effect on the outcome of interest may not hold. Second, the effects of the instruments may be limited to a relatively small subset of the group in which we are interested and the impact of the policy on these subgroups may

differ from those for the entire population of interest.

CONCLUSION

Economists have adopted a number of different statistical methods for addressing selection effects in studies of early childhood. Selection effects are the central impediment to drawing causal inferences from data about factors that affect children's early development. There is no perfect research design for eliminating selection effects to uncover true treatment effects; each method has strengths and weaknesses, is based on certain assumptions about the data and requires careful interpretation.

This chapter has provided a guide to the use of some econometric methods for researchers in the early childhood field who may be unfamiliar with the economists' approach. Random assignment experiments eliminate selection effects because the treatment is assigned rather than selected by parents. However, selection issues can re-emerge if some individuals do not accept the status to which they have been assigned. In that case, the researcher can examine the intention-to-treat instead, or can use treatment assignment as an instrument in an instrumental variable analysis.

Interest in natural experiments (sometimes known as quasi-experiments) has exploded in economics, because natural experiments may assign individuals as-if-randomly to receive a treatment or not. Natural experiments may arise when a policy change or a random health, weather or similar event assigns some individuals or groups to receive a treatment while similar individuals or groups do not. When data are available from before and after such an event, researchers can do a difference-in-differences analysis comparing the average change in the treatment group to the average change in the control group (often this is the difference in the conditional means, when other factors are held constant). Most of the potential concerns with difference-in-differences analysis relate to whether the control group chosen is a reasonable counterfactual for the natural experimentally treated group.

Some natural experiments lend themselves to regression-discontinuity-design analysis. This will occur when a particular value (or range of values) of a continuous variable is responsible for assigning some individuals to treatment while denying it to others. The individuals who by a narrow margin are just eligible will form the treatment group while those who just missed eligibility will form the counterfactual group.

Instrumental variable analysis can occur when the treatment variable of interest happens to be strongly correlated with another variable (i.e., the instrument), but the instrument is not correlated with selection (i.e., is exogenous). In effect, an instrumental variable analysis replaces the treatment variable with (a function of) its instrument. This purges the analysis of selection effects and allows for an unbiased estimate of the treatment effect. However, it is difficult to find instruments that are strongly correlated with the variable of interest and not themselves causally related to child development. Instrumental variable techniques will often be used within the context of a natural experiment to move from an intent-to-treat analysis towards an estimate of the average treatment effect.

Other econometric research designs may deal with selection effects, but only if certain assumptions about the nature and origins of the selection effects are true. So, for instance, a fixed-effects model may estimate a true treatment effect if the systematic differences in some unobservable variables that affect child development are normally correlated with treatment, but are not correlated with treatment within some institution (e.g., a family).

Using propensity score matching requires an assumption that factors affecting selection are exclusively, or very largely, observed within the data set being analyzed. A similar assumption is necessary if ordinary regression analysis is used with an extensive set of covariates.

The analysis by economists of the effects of mothers' employment and early childhood education and care on children's development has used all of these research designs to control for selection. In particular, natural experiments have become increasingly prominent.

Recent empirical estimates are, as a result, much more plausibly causal than those a couple of decades ago addressing similar questions. One fruit of the success in addressing selection effects is that researchers are realizing that treatment effects are much more heterogeneous – dependent on the details of the treatment, the family situation and the characteristics of the child – than was previously appreciated. Perhaps, as researchers, we have been looking for simple answers; increasingly the evidence suggests that simple answers are too simple. Reality – the reality of the effects of mothers' employment and early learning and care experiences on children – is complex.

The effects of maternal employment appear to be strongly dependent on the degree to which this employment affects the quality and quantity of parental time investments, on the quality of the care that the child receives as an alternative to maternal care, on the impacts of additional income on children's development and on the characteristics of the child herself.

Similarly, there is marked heterogeneity in the findings for the effects of early childhood education and care on children's development. The age of children seems to matter as well as the type and quality of ECEC service. Boys and girls may be differently affected. Children from different ethnic or racial backgrounds may be differently affected. Immigrant children may be affected differently from non-immigrant children. Children from disadvantaged backgrounds (however measured) may be affected differently than children from advantaged backgrounds. Some of this is due to the different types of alternative care these children would receive if they did not receive the 'treatment' type and quality of care.

On top of this, any particular early childhood education and care experience may affect different child (or family) outcomes differently. There are cognitive and non-cognitive outcomes, and quite diverse outcomes within each of these categories. There are short-term effects (before school age), medium-term effects (at entry to school or in school) and long-term effects (secondary or post-secondary achievement, labor market and social outcomes after school).

Future and current developments in the application of econometrics to early childhood emphasize the analysis of variations in outcomes. Research is examining the child, family, service and social characteristics that moderate effects of different treatments on children. Research is also looking beyond the conditional mean of the effects of a certain treatment, to see and characterize the entire distribution of treatment outcomes in early childhood.

FURTHER READING

Dunning, T. (2012) *Natural Experiments in the Social Sciences: A Design-Based Approach*. Cambridge: Cambridge University Press.

Kottelenberg, M. and Lehrer, S. (2013) The Gender Effect of Universal Child Care in Canada: Much Ado about Boys? Mimeo. Queen's University.

Manski, C.F. (2013) *Public Policy in an Uncertain World: Analysis and Decisions*. Cambridge, MA: Harvard University Press.

QUESTIONS FOR REFLECTION

1   If the statistical methods used in many disciplines are now much more likely to uncover causal relationships than they were before, why are empirical results on key questions not quickly converging? Is there much more heterogeneity in effects (e.g., on boys vs. girls, on low

income vs. higher income, on jurisdictions with different policy histories) than we previously imagined?

2   In assessing empirical work, always ask yourself: What is the comparison group (the counterfactual) to which the group receiving the treatment is being compared? Is the comparison group self-selected in some way? Is it reasonable to believe that this group represents what would have happened to the treatment group if it had not received the treatment?

3   The results of every statistical technique are only accurate if our assumptions about the ways in which the real world generates the data we analyze are correct. Always ask yourself: What is being assumed and do I think those assumptions are reasonable?

ACKNOWLEDGEMENTS

I am grateful to Michele Campolieti of the University of Toronto and Daniel Cloney of the University of Melbourne for detailed comments on earlier drafts. Neither one is responsible for my failure to incorporate completely their wise advice.

NOTE

1   When an eligibility rule is not sharp, so that individuals on either side of the cut-off have different probabilities of participation (but not 0/1 probabilities), the natural experiment is known as a fuzzy discontinuity design.

REFERENCES

Angrist, J. and Pischke, J.-S. (2009) *Mostly Harmless Econometrics: An Empiricist's Companion*. Princeton, NJ: Princeton University Press.

Baker, M., Gruber, J. and Milligan, K. (2008) Universal Childcare, Maternal Labor Supply and Family Well-being. *Journal of Political Economy*, 79, 709–45.

Becker, G. (1964) *Human Capital: A Theoretical and Empirical Analysis, with Special Reference to Education*. New York: National Bureau of Economic Research.

Bernal, R. (2008) The Effect of Maternal Employment and Childcare on Children's Cognitive Development. *International Economic Review* 49(4): 1173–1209.

Bernal, R., and Keane, M. (2010) Quasi-structural Estimation of a Model of Childcare Choices and Child Cognitive Ability Production. *Journal of Econometrics* 156: 164–89.

Blau, D. (1999) The Effect of Child Care Characteristics on Child Development. *Journal of Human Resources* 34(4): 786–822.

Blundell, R. and Dias, M. (2009) Alternative Approaches to Evaluation in Empirical Microeconomics. *Journal of Human Resources* 44(3): 565–640.

Campolieti, M., Gunderson, M. and Smith, J. (2014) The Effect of Vocational Rehabilitation on the Employment Outcomes of Disability Insurance Beneficiaries: New Evidence from Canada. *IZA Journal of Labor Policy* 3(10): 1–29.

Cook, T. and Campbell, D. (1979) *Quasi-Experimentation: Design and Analysis Issues for Field Settings*. Boston, MA: Houghton Mifflin.

Cunha, F., Heckman, J. and Schennach, S. (2010) Estimating the Technology of Cognitive and Noncognitive Skill Formation. *National Bureau of Economic Research Working Papers* No. 15664.

Currie, J. and Thomas, D. (1995) Does Head Start Make a Difference? *American Economic Review* 85: 341–64.

Currie, J. and Thomas, D. (1999) Does Head Start Help Hispanic Children? *Journal of Public Economics* 74(2): 235–62.

Dunning, T. (2012) *Natural Experiments in the Social Sciences: A Design-Based Approach*. Cambridge: Cambridge University Press.

Dynarski, S., Hyman, J. and Schanzenbach, D.W. (2013) Experimental Evidence on the Effects of Childhood Investments on Post-Secondary Attainment and Degree Completion. *Journal of Policy Analysis and Management* 32(4): 692–717.

Garces, E., Thomas, D. and Currie, J. (2002) Longer Term Effects of Head Start. *American Economic Review* 92: 999–1012.

Gormley, W.T. Jr., Gayer, T., Phillips, D. and Dawson, B. (2005) The Effects of Universal Pre-K on Cognitive Development. *Developmental Psychology* 41: 872–84.

Heckman, J. (2007) The Economics, Technology and Neuroscience of Human Capability Formation. *National Bureau of Economic Research Working Papers* No. 13195.

Heckman, J. and Mosso, S. (2014) The Economics of Human Development and Social Mobility. Working Paper No. 19925. New York: National Bureau of Economic Research.

Hill, J., Waldfogel, J. and Brooks-Gunn, J. (2002) Differential Effects of High-Quality Child Care. *Journal of Policy Analysis and Management* 21(4): 601–27.

Khandker, S., Koolwal, G. and Samad, H. (2010) *Handbook on Impact Evaluation: Quantitative Methods and Practices*. Washington, DC: The World Bank.

Kottelenberg, M. and Lehrer, S. (2013a) New Evidence on the Impacts of Access to and Attending Universal Child-Care in Canada. *Canadian Public Policy* 39(2): 263–85.

Kottelenberg, M. and Lehrer, S. (2013b) Do the Perils of Universal Child Care Depend on the Child's Age? Working Paper No. 132. Canadian Labour Market and Skills Researcher Network.

Kottelenberg, M. and Lehrer, S. (2013c) The Gender Effects of Universal Child Care in Canada: Much Ado about Boys? Mimeo. Queen's University.

Krueger, A. B. (1999) Experimental estimates of education production functions. *Quarterly Journal of Economics* 114: 497–532.

Leibowitz, A. (1974) Home Investments in Children, Part 2: Marriage, Family, Human Capital and Fertility. *Journal of Political Economy* 82(2): S111–S131.

Liu, Q. and Skans, O. (2010) The Duration of Paid Parental Leave and Children's Scholastic Performance. *B. E. Journal of Economic Analysis and Policy* 10(1): 1–33.

Magnuson, K.A., Ruhm, C. and Waldfogel, J. (2007) Does Pre-kindergarten Improve School Preparation and Performance? *Economics of Education Review* 26: 33–51.

Neyman, J., with Dabrowska, D. and Speed, T. ([1923] 1990) On the Application of Probability Theory to Agricultural Experiments: Essay on Principles. *Statistical*

Science 5(4): 465–72. [Originally published by Neyman in Polish in the *Annals of Agricultural Sciences*.]

NICHD-ECCRN and Duncan, G. (2003) Modeling the Impacts of Child care Quality on Children's Preschool Cognitive Development. *Child Development* 74: 1454–75.

Rubin, D. (1974) Estimating Causal Effects of Treatments in Randomized and Nonrandomized Studies. *Journal of Educational Psychology* 66: 688–701.

Rubin, D. (1978) Bayesian Inference for Causal Effects: The Role of Randomization. *Annals of Statistics* 6: 34–58.

Rubin, D. (1990) Comment: Neyman [1923] and Causal Inference in Experiments and Observational Studies. *Statistical Science* 5(4): 472–80.

Shadish, W., Cook, T. and Campbell, D. (2002) *Experimental and Quasi-Experimental Designs for Generalized Causal Inference*. Belmont, CA: Wadsworth Cengage Learning.

Todd, P. and Wolpin, K. (2003) On the Specification and Estimation of the Production Function for Cognitive Achievement. *The Economic Journal* 113: F3–F33.

Warren, D. and Haisken-DeNew, J. (2014) Early Bird Catches the Worm: The Causal Impact of Pre-school Participation and Teacher Qualifications on Year 3 National NAPLAN Cognitive Tests. Working Paper, Melbourne Institute, University of Melbourne.

PART IV

Applying Early Childhood Research

20

Contexts of Risk and Exploitation

Sibnath Deb and Anjali Gireesan

INTRODUCTION

Childhood has been considered to be a distinct developmental period from ancient times, regardless of empirical knowledge of children and their development across different regions. Childhood in itself has been divided into different stages. Across different theories, the term 'Early Childhood' refers to the period that may span birth to 8 years (OECD, 2006). There are geographical and regional variations in the definition of Early Childhood Development (ECD). In India, it is taken to be from birth to 6 years but for this chapter, birth to 8 years has been considered as the early childhood period. This is an important and distinct stage in childhood development. Early childhood development is influenced by an intricate web of factors and all these need to work in equilibrium to optimize an individual's development. As they are interconnected, a ripple in one of the domains affects the others. The complex and dynamic nature of early experience has attracted considerable theoretical and empirical attention.

While theories may provide conceptual understandings of early experience, research provides empirical evidence of the factors and mediators that influence experience and how these can be attenuated with children's changing environments, in order to ensure an optimal development. To take an example, a majority of theories such as Erikson's psychosocial stages of development (Erikson & Erikson, 1998), Vygotsky's socio-cultural theory (1978) and Bowlby's attachment theory (1958) emphasize the importance of early parental care-giving and responsiveness. Research has demonstrated that young children living in poor socio-economic conditions are predisposed towards risk factors such as abuse and neglect, harsh parenting, family and community violence, as well as physical hazards such as unhygienic and substandard housing (Lieberman et al., 2009) which has implications for the physical as well as mental health of an individual. This, again, is due to multiple effects, such as poverty, increasing psychological distress in parents which, in turn, might curb their provision of proper care; thus, predisposing them to other risk factors (McLoyd, 1990). Thus, we see how poverty, by influencing care-giving, may affect the development of the child. In a similar way, a combination of knowledge from both theory and research may help us in delineating the past, present and future of the development process and to intervene at appropriate points.

From the current theory as well as the research framework, early childhood development (ECD) has emerged as a critical age which has significant implications for all the other developmental stages. The risk and exploitation research alone gives us a view into this unfortunate reality that is not being given its due significance in practice. The problems faced by a child of this age can easily be hidden as they are unable to voice it in a manner that adults are able to comprehend. The identification process is the very basis of effective ECD. If it fails, it may be too late to prevent the harm from affecting the child and may result in irreversible damage. What needs to be understood are the different layers of protection and vulnerabilities that surround a child and then doing the needful to safeguard them to the extent possible. While the vast corpus of literature provides insight into the problem, what seems to be lacking is an adequate and effective system of awareness, resources and diffusion of responsibilities. The chapter now moves to enumerate key risk factors and to highlight the significance of ECD and its associated measures in addressing risk and exploitation in the Indian context.

MODELS OF CHILD MALTREATMENT

This section discusses key theoretical considerations relevant to the field of child maltreatment research. It begins with a consideration of the risk factors for exploitation and child maltreatment by drawing on various schools of thought from within the discipline of psychology, noting that the models that relate to these schools of thought have been reviewed systematically (see Table 20.1).

Child Sexual Abuse (CSA) may be considered as the most traumatic of all the forms of child maltreatment. The theories explaining its causation have most importantly concentrated upon the different characteristics of sexual offenders and how the offence is committed. Finkelhor's (1984) precondition theory states that for an offence to occur there is a set of four preconditions that need to be fulfilled in sequence: motivation to sexually abuse a child, overcoming internal inhibitions, overcoming external inhibitions and overcoming resistance to the abuse. These preconditions may further have an individual or a sociological basis. Individual factors might include alcohol consumption and societal factors might include child pornography. It is this interaction that might play a role in fulfilling the preconditions (Araji & Finkelhor, 1986; Hartman & Burgess, 1989). Ward and Siegert (2002) provide us with the Pathways model of child sexual abuse. Accordingly, there are four pathways: Intimacy Deficits, Deviant Sex Scripts, Emotional Dysregulation and Cognitive Distortion, all of which have their own unique group of primary causes that further interact to cause a sexual offence. For example, a person seen to have intimacy deficits may have an inappropriate choice of sexual partner. Within this approach, the causal factor resides with the type of attachment style that the individual has experienced in the past.

Child physical abuse is another form of maltreatment. A widely used model referred to in this context is the social information processing model of child physical abuse by Milner (2000). The theory states that abusive and non-abusive parents have a different pattern of cognition; and that abusive, compared to non-abusive, parents have more inaccurate and biased cognitive schemata which limit them in forming appropriate perceptions about their children. Their expectations of the child do not necessarily align with the child's developmental age. Also, there may be a pre-existing schema which validates their belief of physical punishment in the scenario of the

Table 20.1 Schools of thought on child maltreatment

Theory	Myth	Practice
Psychoanalytic: Child abuse is a product of parental psychopathology.	Parents who abuse children are 'ill' and require professional intervention for prevention and cure.	Psychotherapy and/or counseling.
Learning: Child abuse is a behavior learned from the experience of having been abused as a child. Parents model abusive parenting for their children.	Children who are abused grow up to abuse their own.	Parent education and re-education to learn non-abusing techniques
Attachment: Child abuse is a consequence of early separations between mother and child that interfere with the process of forming a protective bond of closeness and love.	Parents who abuse their children are not 'attached' to or do not love their children. There is a critical period during which attachment must occur.	Preventive attention to the provision of contact between mother and newborn, i.e. encouraging rooming in and handling.
Stress: Child abuse is a product of poverty and other factors that stress families, including sexual and economic inequality.	Short of a social revolution, preventing child abuse is impossible.	Advocacy to reduce or eliminate sources of stress in individual families. Political action directed toward social change. Community services to support persons in times of stress.
Labelling: A child abuser is a person to whom that label has been successfully applied. By labelling some (usually socially marginal) parents as deviant (i.e. abusive), others do not have to acknowledge their own abusiveness toward children, and their own personal and professional interests are served (e.g. it creates a need for the 'helping' professions).	Short of a social revolution, preventing child abuse is impossible.	Social action directed toward a change in values about violence and inequality in our society.

Source: Newberger & Newberger (1982)

child not performing to their expectations. The four stages within the model are:

- **Stage 1: Perception** – abusive parents are less attentive to and not very aware about their children
- **Stage 2: Interpretation and evaluation** – abusive parents are likely to interpret their child's behavior as wrong and more serious than non-abusive parents; they generally do not take environmental factors into consideration when a situation happens
- **Stage 3: Information integration and response evaluation** – even if information is perceived and interpreted properly, abusive parents may fail to integrate the information properly; they take the information that is consistent with their beliefs and cognitive disposition
- **Stage 4: Response implementation and monitoring** – physically abusive parents are not able to implement parenting skills according to the needs of the child.

Belsky (1993) gave us a developmental-ecological model which assumes that risk factors for physical abuse are encompassed within three domains. These are:

- **Developmental-psychological**: family characteristics (parental stress, history of abuse, etc.) as well as the child's characteristics (disruptive behavior, emotional problems)
- **Immediate**: the nature of the interaction between the child and the family
- **Broad**: the nature of the neighborhood and the community that the family and child live in.

Cicchetti and Lynch (1993) devised an organization-transaction model to explain the multiple causes of child maltreatment, regardless of any specific type of abuse. They emphasized the role of multiple risks that increase the vulnerability of the child and hence jeopardize their development. The above-mentioned models indicate the following:

- Different forms of child maltreatment have a set of similar as well as different factors.
- Both individual and environmental factors play a role in the manifestation of exploitation.
- The presence of multiple factors increases the chance of exploitation of children.

RISK FACTORS DURING EARLY CHILDHOOD

Biological and Physical Factors

There are certain biological factors that put early childhood development at considerable risk. If not taken seriously, they hinder the natural process of development in a myriad of ways.

Maternal Nutrition
A child's health in the early years is intricately linked to his/her mother's health. Animal studies show that both maternal under-nutrition and over-nutrition reduce placental-fetal blood flows and stunt fetal growth (Wu et al., 2004). Lack of proper maternal nutrition may lead to lower problem solving ability, diminished responsiveness and hindered motor development in the child.

Infectious Diseases
The occurrence of infectious disease also affects the process of development in children. Diarrhoeal disease forms one of the two major killer diseases in children under 5 years of age in the developing world (Ahmed et al., 2008). In 2002, in the developing countries, an estimated 1.6 million children died as a consequence of diarrhoeal disease. Diarrhoea increases a vulnerability to stunting and may have a negative impact on semantic fluency and verbal learning.

Malaria is a serious disease of childhood. There were an estimated 660,000 malaria deaths around the world in 2010, approximately 86% of which were in children under 5 years of age (WHO, 2013a). HIV, another grave infection in children, leads to cognitive impairments and lower mental as well as motor development. Malaria during pregnancy causes severe maternal illness and anaemia, and is also associated with low birth weight among newborn infants, a leading risk factor for infant mortality (UNICEF, 2000).

Every year, Acute Respiratory Infections (ARIs) in young children is responsible for an estimated 4.1 million deaths worldwide. In India, ARI constitutes a major public health problem and is the most important contributor to mortality and morbidity in children under 5 years, accounting for 15–34% of all childhood deaths (according to the WHO Bulletin, Health Situation in South East Asia Region 1994–1997, Regional office for SEAR, New Delhi, 1999). India accounted for 28% of the mortality and 30% of Disability Adjusted Life Years (DALYs) lost due to ARIs as stated in the WHO world health report, Bridging the Gaps (1995).

Environmental Toxins
These are also known as teratogens when one refers to them in the context of ECD. These toxins may enter an individual's body either during fetal development or during early childhood (Curl et al., 2003; Lanphear et al., 2002). Although environmental toxins are harmful for all, the way adults and children react to these toxins is different. A child is surrounded by three environments – the physical, biological and social, which together interact and influence them in all their developmental processes (Bearer, 1995).

Psycho-Social Factors

Poverty
Socio-economic status (SES) is as much of a developmental issue as it is a welfare and societal issue. Differences in the level of SES that children experience have direct as well as indirect implications for their development. The children of lower SES are observed

to suffer from nutritional deficiency (Miller & Korenman, 1994) which impairs the normal developmental process. Other domains that have been negatively influenced by low socio-economic status include cognitive and language development as well as social and motor development (Magill-Evans & Harrison, 2001; Petterson & Albers, 2001). Such children have problems in the acquisition of reading ability when compared to children from middle-class families and the effects crop up quite early on in childhood (Dickinson & Snow, 1987). The indirect implications can be viewed in the context of how SES affects parenting behavior and care-giving (Bradley & Corwyn, 2002).

The risk for maternal death (during pregnancy or childbirth) in Sub-Saharan Africa is 175 times higher than in developed countries. Neonatal deaths in developing countries account for 98% of worldwide yearly neonatal deaths (Filippi et al., 2006). That being said, poverty is detrimental to the health of both mother and child.

Parent–Child Interactions

A parent is the first social agent and primary caregiver in a child's life. This caregiver is instrumental in providing a secure base for the development of the child. Parent–child interactions form an important part of this relationship. The nature and frequency of these interactions have been empirically shown to impact on the social, cognitive and language development of the child (NICHD, Early Child Care Research Network, 1999). Maternal responsivity and parental sensitivity, in turn, can impact on such interactions; and have been studied extensively as influencing the language and cognitive development of the child (Barnard, 1997). Cleaver, Unell and Aldgate (2011) described the possible health, education and developmental impacts of parent behavior on child abuse and neglect; with children, unmet developmental needs in health and family relationships are exacerbated when parents engage in substance abuse or domestic violence (Cleaver et al., 2007).

Maternal Depression and Mental Health Problems

Maternal depression is a term used to describe a collection of depressive conditions experienced by mothers and mothers-to-be up to 12 months post-partum. The types of maternal depression include: prenatal depression; Baby blues; postpartum depression and postpartum psychosis (NIHCM Foundation, 2010). Maternal depression and mental health problems have been found to have adverse outcomes for early childhood development. Depressed mothers generally experience problems in exhibiting regular and 'normal' maternal behavior such as attending to the needs of the infant (Murray, 1992; Murray & Cooper, 1997). Long-term maternal depression, in turn, has been shown to have serious repercussions for cognitive and motor development for children between the ages of 28 and 50 months (Petterson & Albers, 2001).

Neglect, Discrimination and Abuse

Neglect

Malnutrition As per the United Nations Convention on the Rights of the Child, every infant and child has the right to good nutrition. Under-nutrition is associated with 45% of child deaths worldwide (WHO, 2013b). Globally, in 2012, 162 million children under 5 years were estimated to be stunted and almost 100 million had low weight-for-height, mostly as a consequence of poor feeding and repeated infections, while 44 million were overweight or obese. Only about 38% of infants at 0 to 6 months old are exclusively breastfed. The lives of about 220,000 children could be saved every year with the promotion of optimal breastfeeding and appropriate complementary feeding, and the provision of supplements in food-insecure populations (WHO, 2013b). It is relevant to note here that under-nutrition is associated with more than one-third of the global disease burden for children under 5 years (WHO, 2013b).

The majority of children in India have underprivileged childhoods, from birth. The infant mortality rate of Indian children is 44 and the under-5 mortality rate is 93, and 25% of newborn Indian children are underweight among other nutritional, immunization and educational deficiencies. Figures for India are substantially worse than the *developing country average* (UNICEF, 2001).

Given such a daunting challenge, the 'Integrated Child Development Services' (ICDS) scheme was first launched in 1975 by the Ministry of Women & Child Development, Government of India (2011), in accordance with the National Policy for Children in India (Kapil, 2002). Over the years, it has grown into one of the largest integrated family and community welfare schemes in the world (UNICEF, 2001). Given its effectiveness over the last few decades, the Government of India has committed to ensuring universal availability of the program.

Not Providing Colostrums and Inappropriate Breastfeeding The mortality rate of infants and children in India is 10–15 times higher than that of the developed world and this has been attributed to poor care and malnutrition (Shetty & Shetty, 2013). While colostrums have been attested as providing complete nutrition, protection from significant infections and reducing exposure to pathogens and even mortality, large numbers of mothers, especially those from rural areas with low educational backgrounds, do not provide colostrums to their newborn babies owing to a number of misconceptions. The most common misconception is that first breast milk is dirty and it might affect the stomach of the child (Deb, 2006), despite the evidence, from developing and industrialized countries, that early and continuous breastfeeding in the first six months protects children against gastrointestinal infections.

Not Given Immunization Due to Misplaced Beliefs Immunization is not given to small children because of lack of awareness, lack of accessibility to health centers and/ or false beliefs about immunization. About 2.5 million deaths a year continue to be caused by vaccine-preventable diseases, mainly in Africa and Asia, including India, among children less than 5 years old (WHO & UNICEF, 2005).

Discrimination

Female Feticide/Gender Preference In India, a most brutal form of female murder takes place, even before they have the opportunity to be born. In Indian society, women are pressured to have male children, as having a female child is considered to be a burden for the family (Ahmad, 2010). Females not only face inequality in this culture, they are even denied the right to be born. Aborting a female fetus is both practical and socially acceptable in India. Female feticide is driven by many factors, primarily by the perceived economic burden of the dowry. Sons are perceived to provide support for the family, to contribute income and to perform the relevant cultural rituals for parents after death. While abortion is legal in India, it is a crime to abort a pregnancy solely because the fetus is female. Strict laws and penalties are in place for violators. The decline in child-gender ratio in India is evident by comparing the census figures which point out the prevalence of both gender-selective abortion and female infanticide in India. In some areas, the gender ratio of males to females has dropped to less than 8000:1000 (Gupta, 2007).

Gender Discrimination in Terms of Nutrition and Education There is a strong preference for male children in countries such as India, Bangladesh and Pakistan, particularly in rural people; with educated people in some communities having a special preference for a male child with associated privileges in nutrition and education (NFHS III, 2005–2006). If a woman delivers a female child, she may experience mental torture at the hands of her in-laws and in some cases physical violence.

Abuse

Corporal Punishment Corporal punishment is a global problem, especially for children from developing countries such as India, Bangladesh and China. In developing countries, parents believe that punishing children is the best way to have control over them and/or to modify their behavior. A number of studies report a high incidence of corporal punishment in the family and in educational institutions in India (Deb & Modak, 2010; Deb & Walsh, 2011; Ministry of Women and Child Development, 2011; Raj, 2011). Studies have also found that children concede that parents and teachers have the right to punish them (Deb et al., 2012; Kumar et al., 2013).

Exposure to Violence Children experience violence in many forms. Their minds are still developing and cannot comprehend such actions and their associated consequences. But these situations leave a lasting impression on these children which affects their different domains of development, whether physical, psychological or moral (Garbarino et al., 1991; Ney et al., 1992). It has short-term as well as long-term effects. The manifestation of witnessing or experiencing violence may result in symptoms such as bedwetting or separation anxiety (Osofsky, 1995), which may hinder the child's socialization skills. It has also been linked to slower cognitive development and poor cognitive functioning.

Intimate Partner Violence (IPV) is defined as physical, sexual or psychological harm by a current or former intimate partner or spouse (Family Violence Prevention Fund, 2008). Children are generally silent observers of this type of violence but it creates an unforgettable and traumatic image in their minds. Children under the age of 6 are at a higher risk of witnessing IPV and domestic violence (Gjelsvik et al., 2003). Violence between caregivers affects the sense of security and

well-being of these children, which consequently influences the different stages of their developmental process (Carpenter & Stacks, 2009; Pepler et al., 2000).

Community violence refers to violence perpetuated outside the family by acquaintances or strangers. It involves acts such as robbery, homicide, rape and other associated and similar events. Exposure to community violence increases the risk of depressive symptoms and anxiety (Kliewer et al., 1998; Lynch & Cicchetti, 1998). These symptoms are observed to be more persisting when violence is perpetuated by acquaintances rather than strangers (Martinez & Richters, 1993); it also plays a role in the creation of a negative self-image which subsequently gives rise to internalizing problems (Fitzpatrick, 1993). It has further been found to have a negative influence on children's relationship formation (Osofsky, 1995).

Crimes Against Children A large number of children across the world experience various forms of criminal offences which include murder, rape, trafficking, kidnapping, sexual exploitation and feticide. In the case of India, there is no separate classification for offences against children. Generally, offences committed against children or crimes in which children are the victims are considered Crimes against Children. Indian penal code (IPC) and the various protective and preventive 'Special and Local Laws' (SLL) specifically mention those offences in which children are victims. The age of a 'child' varies as per the definition in the Acts and Sections but 'age of a child' has been defined to be below 18 years as per the Juvenile Justice Act 2000.

Crimes against children, whether it be murder, kidnapping or exploitation of any other kind, have increased substantially over the years, as indicated by secondary data. For example, a total of 26,694 cases of crimes against children were reported in the country during 2010 as compared to 24,201 cases during 2009, suggesting an increase of 10.3%. Among IPC crimes, the number of cases under Procuration of Minor Girls increased from 237 in 2009 to 679 in 2010, registering an increase of 186.5% over 2009. The crime rate has marginally increased from 2.1 in 2009 to 2.3 in 2010 in India. A total of 1,508 cases of murder of children (including infanticides) were reported in India, against 1,551 cases in 2009, resulting in a decrease of 2.8% in 2010 over 2009. A total of 100 infanticide cases were reported during 2010. Incidents increased in the year 2010 (100 cases) from 63 in the year 2009. A total of 5,484 cases of child rape were reported in the country during 2010, compared to 5,368 in 2009, accounting for an increase of 2.2% during the year, while a total of 10,670 cases of kidnapping and abduction of children were reported during the year, compared to 8,945 cases in the previous year, accounting for a significant increase of 19.3% (National Crime Records Bureau, 2010).

If we describe the disposal of crimes by police and courts, the picture is that the average rate of charge sheet for all the crimes against children (IPC and SLL) was 83.9% in 2010, the same as 2009. The highest charge-sheeting rate was observed in cases under 'Buying of Girls for Prostitution' (97.9%), followed by 'Rape' (97.5%), in comparison with the national-level charge-sheeting rate of 79.1% for IPC crimes and 94.7% for SLL crimes (National Crime Records Bureau, 2010).

Sacrificing Children for the Wellbeing of the Rest of the Family and/or Economic Prosperity of the Family Sacrificing children for religious reasons is still practiced in the 21st century by some communities in India. Sacrifice is the act of offering to a god, especially for the purpose of propitiation or homage: sacrifices were invaluable features of early religions. By this method, relationships with the gods were renewed and strengthened. Studies revealed the following as the causes of child sacrifice: economic factors, cultural beliefs, psychic factors and government negligence, ignorance, illiteracy and moral degeneration (Charles, 2011). In India, many cases of child sacrifice have been reported by the press and other forms of media. It is reported that the practice continues to exist due to blind superstition and widespread illiteracy among many rural Indian villages such as Khurja, UP (Charles, 2011). Today, society looks at human/child sacrifice as murder.

Vulnerable Children

Children who have been orphaned, children living outside of parental care or children in poor families are vulnerable to numerous risks and face social discrimination. Child sexual abuse and maltreatment and violence are predominant in Indian society and increase the vulnerability of children to being affected by HIV and AIDS. Children are especially vulnerable to exposure to HIV if they are involved in drugs and sexual abuse (Alliance & Save the Children, 2012).

Childhood obesity has become a global problem, 'one of the most serious public health challenges of the 21st century' (WHO, 2012). Obesity can harm a child's heart and lungs, muscles and bones, kidneys and digestive tract, as well as the hormones that control blood sugar and puberty, and can also take a heavy social and emotional toll (Ebbeling et al., 2002).

Globally, an estimated 43 million preschool children (under age 5) were overweight or obese in 2010, a 60% increase since 1990 (de Onis et al., 2010). The problem affects both developed and developing countries. Of the world's 43 million overweight and obese preschoolers, 35 million live in developing countries. By 2020, if the current epidemic continues unabated, 9% of all preschoolers will be overweight or obese – nearly 60 million children (de Onis et al., 2010). Although children in Asian countries are more vulnerable to anemia, older children are more prone to obesity (de Onis et al., 2010).

Children and HIV/AIDS

Incidence of HIV among mothers varies around the world, ranging from 1% to 40%, with African and Asian countries having the highest rates (McIntyre, 2005). HIV/AIDS can be transmitted to offspring during the prenatal period, childbirth or breastfeeding. If a mother is infected with the HIV/AIDS virus, there is a 25% chance that she will pass on the virus to her offspring, if she does not receive proper treatment during pregnancy; on the other hand, if a mother is treated during her pregnancy, there is a 98% chance that her baby will not become infected (NACO, 2006).

According to UNICEF, the last decade has seen a large increase in death among young children due to HIV/AIDS contracted from their parents (UNICEF, 2013), especially in countries where poverty is high and education levels are low (Toure et al., 2012).

HIV/AIDS infect and affect children both physically and mentally. Children with HIV/AIDS are vulnerable and are exploited and abused.

India has a low HIV prevalence of 0.34%. Yet in terms of individuals infected, India is home to the third largest number of people living with HIV in the world (NACO, 2006). Nearly 5% of infections are attributable to parent-to-child transmissions. Studies from India have documented mother-to-infant HIV transmission at rates between 36 and 48% (Dongaonkar et al., 2001).

Cultural Practices Concerning Children with Physical and Mental Disability

Children with disabilities are also at risk of victimization, especially in developing countries such as India. Stigmatizing practices may be based on the notion that disability is due to possession by spirits or one's own mistakes in the last life, or to attributed religious causes such as lack of faith in God or mistakes made by the parents (Berry & Dalai, 1994). The literature reveals that families with disabled children express fatalistic attitudes and external dependence, that is, they expect external agencies to cater to their rehabilitation needs (Dalal & Pande, 1999). For centuries, these beliefs have been embedded in folklore, religion and culture, resulting in patterns of thoughts, communications, actions, customs, beliefs and values that are related in society (Smith, 2002). In addition, family members blame the mother for the birth of a child with a disability (Edwardraj et al., 2010). Even today, disabled children are not accepted by society and schools refuse to admit these children.

Often, when it comes to delineating the risk factors that pose a threat to the development of children, there is a tendency to ignore the problems of vulnerable children as they remain macroscopically hidden. Neither their occurrence nor their effects are directly observable, unless they initiate a state of non-equilibrium epidemically. For example, in India, obese children are frequently termed as 'healthy'. Thus, obesity is not perceived to be a problem. Children with disability and HIV/AIDS tend to be hidden because of the fear of society and hence their problems cannot be suitably appraised. The greatest threat that these children face is lack of recognition of their problems that need to be addressed.

Cumulative Risk

A child has to develop in different domains to realize her/his maximum potential. According to the Every Child Matters agenda (DfES, 2006), there are five domains important for children:

- being healthy
- safety and security
- enjoying and achieving
- social and civic participation
- economic well-being.

Thus, a single risk factor is seen to be insufficient to influence or predict developmental outcomes. Cumulative disadvantage, together with compounding risk, is more likely to impact on child development than any one risk in isolation (Schoon, 2006). Cumulative risk, experienced from birth to early childhood, plays a major role and thus influences the entire development process of an individual (Osborne, 2008). It affects behavioral adjustment during childhood and psychosocial functioning and occupational efficacy during adulthood when the number of risks is greater in early childhood (Bynner et al., 2000; Schoon, 2006; Schoon et al., 2003). Single risk factor may not result in major developmental hazard but an accumulation of risk factors and a prevalence of multiple disadvantages have been observed to cause negative outcomes (Fergusson & Horwood, 2003; Gutman et al., 2002). These multiple factors generally include social and economic elements such as impaired parenting, neglectful and abusive home environments, marital conflict, family instability, family violence and high exposure to adverse family life events (Fergusson et al., 1994; Shaw et al., 1994). In general, the higher the number of risk factors, the more subsequent problems are observed (Masten & Sesma, 1999). In their work, Sabates and Dex (2012) observed that children living in low-income households and those living in families with multiple risks fared worse across all developmental outcomes than children living in families with no risk.

One of the major applications of cumulative risk research is seen in the field of child maltreatment, where multiple risk factors are seen to be better predictors of outcomes. It can be seen in various forms whether it be prevalence, etiology, consequences or outcomes. In essence, cumulative risk research accounts for the ambiguity of this phenomenon and sheds light on its emergence as well as its course (Masten & Wright, 1998).

POLICY AND PRACTICE WITH RESPECT TO EARLY CHILDHOOD DEVELOPMENT

Early childhood is embedded in a paradoxical context. It is the age at which the most

critical and rapid development takes place but it is an age that has been grossly neglected in terms of policy framework and subsequent service delivery. There are many policies that have been formulated in order to nurture and protect early childhood development, but what they lack is the essential foundation on which these policies need to be built and the important targets and goals that need to be focused on. Some of the lacunae are as follows:

- gaps in understanding the needs of early childhood
- lack of a proper approach towards early childhood development
- lack of emphasis on family and community.

POLICIES FOR PROTECTION OF CHILDREN IN INDIA

India is the second most populous country in the world where 13.12% of her population lies in the tender age bracket of 0–6 years, as per provisional 2011 Census figures. The decline in total child population since the Census of 2001 stands at 5,030,327, where the decline in rural child population is 8,885, in contrast to the increase in urban child population reported as 3,855 (Census of India, 2011).

A number of social measures have been adopted by the Government of India for ensuring proper growth and development of young children.

Integrated Child Development Scheme (ICDS)

This scheme was introduced in 1972 with the aim of improving mother and child health so that both achieve optimal functioning. Here, benefits and facilities provided for children include supplementary nutrition, immunization, basic health care, referral services to hospitals and health centers and non-formal pre-school education, whereas for mothers, tetanus immunization and for expectant mothers, supplementary nutrition and health education are provided (Muralialharari & Kaul, 1993). The ICDS program has been implemented and functioning for more than three decades now but it has not achieved its objectives to a satisfactory and trend-altering extent (Awofeso & Rammohan, 2011).

National Food Security Bill, 2013

Malnutrition is more prevalent in India than in Sub-Saharan Africa. In such a scenario, it was thought that a scheme to ensure food security for these children was essential. The National Food Security Bill, 2013 of the Government of India ensures an age-appropriate meal available free of charge to children in the age group of 6 months to 6 years.

Rajiv Gandhi Crèche Scheme

Today, work culture is prevalent among Indian women, but their responsibility towards their children and family remains a priority. In such a scenario, it was considered that a scheme that will help women realize these two different roles would be immensely beneficial. The Rajiv Gandhi crèche scheme has provisions for the development of effective day-care facilities that may share the burden of working mothers as well as help poor mothers who find it difficult to cope with all their difficulties beyond taking care of their children (Ministry of Human Resource Development, 2006). It includes supplementary nutrition, health care inputs such as immunization and polio drops, basic health monitoring and recreation. It is also a protection measure in addressing issues such as child labor, school drop-out, child prostitution, female illiteracy, and creating medical and health programs.

Indira Gandhi Matritva Sahyog Yojna (IGMSY)

Under-nutrition continues to adversely affect the majority of women in India. In India, every third woman is undernourished and every second woman is anemic (NFHS III, 2005–2006). An undernourished mother almost inevitably gives birth to a low-birthweight baby. The scheme is an initiative to promote safe and appropriate practices during and post pregnancy, including utilization of services available, promoting infant and young child feeding practices, as well as provision of cash incentives for accessing better health and nutrition facilities (Ministry of Women and Child Development, 2011). A similar scheme is Janani Suraksha Yojna, which provides protection to mothers under the National Rural Health Mission. IGMSY is a more comprehensive and encompassing scheme under the Ministry of Women and Child Development.

Integrated Child Protection Scheme

The Integrated Child Protection Scheme (ICPS) is a recent initiative by the Ministry of Women and Child Development, Government of India. It is an endeavor to bridge all the gaps that existed in all previous protection schemes by trying to ensure a substantial increase in the fund allocated towards this goal, as well as convergence of various services for children through an interconnected network between different bodies of state as well as central government.

The activities and programs of the ICPS are shown in Figure 20.1. These activities show that this policy is one of the most comprehensive schemes for the protection of children. One of the focal points is the care, support and rehabilitation services that seem to form the backbone of this program. These services, if carried out, may in essence perform a key role in safeguarding children in India.

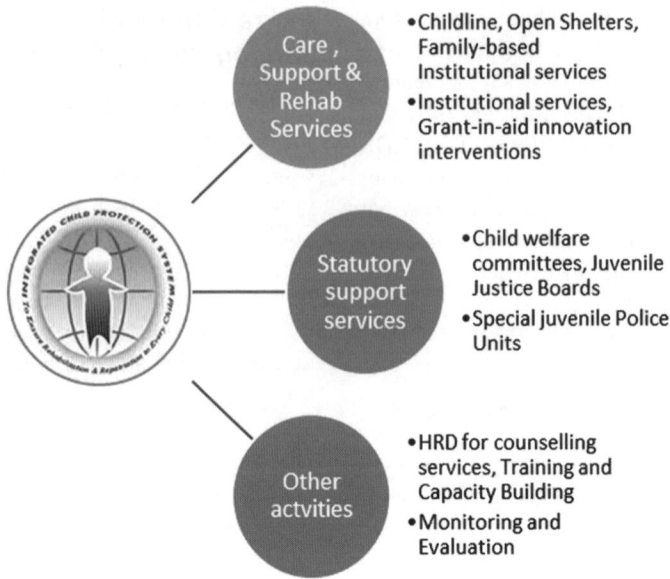

Figure 20.1 Programs and activities under ICPS

THRUST AREAS FOR PREVENTIVE INITIATIVE PROGRAMS OF THE GOVERNMENT OF INDIA

Convergence Structures and Monitoring Mechanisms

Indian legislation is one of the most comprehensive frameworks for the welfare and development of its children. The need of the hour is its effective implementation directed towards the right goal. This requires work from all levels of government as well as the community. To ensure a maximum outreach to beneficiaries, there should be monitoring at each level – national, state, district and village – through an integrated system of networks between all partners so that problems or loopholes at each stage can be identified and hence rectified. Thus, there needs to be multi-sectorial programming so that responsibilities and duties are properly distributed and authority is not exploited.

Knowledge and Awareness

Service delivery is successful when it is not only provided but also when beneficiaries and consumers of the service are aware that there are provisions to help them in the best possible manner. Different sources such as regular print and visual media, brochures, leaflets and awareness campaigns at each level should be organized so that people are aware of the legislation and various schemes.

Financial Investment in ECD

Early Childhood Development is an essential foundation on which our society is built. Investing in ECD has many advantages. It reduces child mortality, decreases gender-related inequalities, builds social capital and promotes the economic growth of society. Hence, there is an urgent requirement for intelligent financial investment in ECD which promotes all domains such as nutrition, health, education, safety and security, as well as care-giving.

Strengthening National Resource Capability and Institutions of Service Delivery

The tenets of service delivery are accessibility and outreach. Services can be delivered through home visits, various formal and informal learning centers, as well as any other centers or institutions constructed and initiated for this purpose (UNICEF, 2001). Services should be provided to the needy and not only to those people who come looking for services. Hence, vulnerable groups need to be identified and given necessary aid.

Programming Focus

Early childhood development programs cannot be thought about in isolation. The focus should not only be the child but other partners as well, such as families and home caregivers, community organizations, service delivery and a conducive environment. There needs to be parallel improvement in all these sectors in order to ensure an effective and successful ECD program that caters to the needs of all children.

CONCLUSION

A review of the evidence clearly indicates that, globally, a large number of young children experience various forms of risk, including malnutrition, obesity, HIV/AIDS, sexual exploitation, lack of immunization, female feticide, gender discrimination, corporal punishment, health problems such as diarrhea, malaria and acute respiratory infections, exposure to violence, disabilities, crimes such as rape, infanticide, murder, child trafficking and neglect (i.e., deprivation of care and basic support facilities, and so on). In other words, their rights are grossly violated. Young children in developing countries are more vulnerable to these risks compared to the young children of developed nations. Causal factors behind early childhood risk include maternal health, denial of colostrums, faulty breastfeeding practices, addiction among parents, mental health problems of immediate caregivers and interpersonal violence. Contributory factors include rising prices, cultural beliefs and practices with respect to child-rearing practices, migration, breakdown of family support, and social and political conflicts in many sectors of society.

Global experience demonstrates that ECD programs yield immediate results in addition to the expected long-term outcomes for children and communities. The Integrated Child Development Scheme (ICDS) of the Government of India and other social measures have helped thousands of mothers and children to improve their nutritional status and with other health-related issues. However, there is scope for further development of the situation, especially for small children in marginalized sectors of society, with parents working in the agricultural field, in brick and construction industries, for whom there is hardly any social support.

There is an urgent need to ensure the protection of young children through a participatory approach, organizing training of pre-school teachers and sensitization of parents and potential parents to the appropriate quality of child-rearing practices, and in this regard the media should take an active role in educating parents. In order to ensure child protection, it is very important to relook at some core issues, such as over-population, poverty, illiteracy, unemployment and cultural beliefs relating to child-rearing practices. At the same time, health workers and Anganwadi workers are to be empowered with knowledge and skills in order to educate parents. Health workers and Anganwadi workers can play a significant role since they have direct contact with community members. There is an urgent need for periodic monitoring of the performance and activities of ICDS workers at various levels.

Mapping of the research field of risk and exploitation gives rise to key recommendations designed to change the current child protection scenario in India and other Asian developing countries:

- Bringing the 'child protection issue' onto the national priority agenda.

- Ensuring implementation of policies and programs in the truest sense with more allocation of funds and infrastructure development across the country.
- Sensitization of policy makers to the necessity of child protection at all levels, and other stakeholders such as teachers, NGO personnel, the judiciary, doctors, parents, and so on.
- Pre-primary education strengthened across the country, making it mandatory for children aged 3–6 years, and brought under the Right to Education Act 2009. In the same law, education for children aged 6–14 is free and compulsory. This approach will facilitate the socialization process as well as early intervention for vulnerable and socio-economically disadvantaged children. Those working in pre-primary schools should be given due recognition for their services, and their remuneration and status should be commensurate with their skills and responsibilities.
- Establishment of child development resource centers at national and regional levels for training, research and documentation related to childhood. More funds should be allocated for research.
- Use of television channels for creating awareness about myths and misconceptions regarding child-rearing practices through culturally sensitive programs.
- Finally, there is an urgent need to adopt a comprehensive approach towards ensuring a sound foundation for survival, growth, protection, development and early learning for young children up to 6 years of age, particularly for marginalized children in developing countries. In addition, there should be conscious attempts to develop the understanding that Early Childhood Care and Education (ECCE) policy is the responsibility of both parents (not solely of the mother) and the community as a whole.

FURTHER READING

Edwards, S. (2009). *Early childhood education and care*. Pademelon Press.

Gillen, J., & Cameron, C. A. (2010). *International perspectives on early childhood research: A day in the life*. London: Palgrave Macmillan.

Greenspan, S. I., & Wieder, S. (2006). *Infant and early childhood mental health: A comprehensive developmental approach to assessment and intervention*. Washington DC: American Psychiatric Publishing Inc.

Mac Naughton, G., & Hughes, P. (2009). *Doing action research in early childhood studies: A*

step-by-step guide, England: McGraw-Hill Education.

Melhuish, E., & Petrogiannis, K. (eds.). (2006). *Early childhood care & education: International perspectives*. London: Routledge.

Messer, D. J. (2003). *Mastery motivation in early childhood: Development, measurement, and social processes*. London & New York: Routledge.

Plomin, Robert, John C. DeFries, & David W. Fulker (2006). *Nature and nurture during infancy and early childhood*. New York: Cambridge University Press.

QUESTIONS FOR REFLECTION

1 How can the knowledge of risk factors for neglect, abuse and exploitation during early childhood be instrumental in devising preventive measures for the same?
2 Are theoretical models of child maltreatment comprehensive and how can their implementation being improved?
3 Do the programs taken up by the Government of India for child protection address the need of the hour and is their periodic evaluation appropriate?
4 How can the cultural malpractices against children be reduced?
5 How can we ensure that significance of safety and proper care for all children during early childhood is realized on a global level?

REFERENCES

Ahmad, N. (2010). Female feticide in India. *Issues Law Med.* Summer, 26(1), 13–29.

Ahmed, S. F., Farheen, M. A., & Mattoo, G. M. (2008). Prevalence of diarrhoeal disease, its seasonal and age variations in under five in Kashmiar, India. *Int J Health Sci (Qassim)*, 2(2), 126–133.

Alliance & Save the Children (2012). Good practice HIV programming standards: Family-centred HIV programming for children. International HIV/AIDS Alliance, UK.

Araji, S., & Finkelhor, D. (1986). Abusers: A review of the research. In D. Finkelhor (ed.), *A sourcebook on child sexual abuse* (pp. 89–118). Beverly Hills, CA: SAGE.

Awofeso, N., & Rammohan, A. (2011). Three decades of the integrated child development services program in India: Progress and problems. In K. Smigorski (ed.), *Health management: Different approaches and solutions* (pp. 243–259). Rijeka: InTech.

Barnard, K. E. (1997). Influencing parent–child interactions for children at risk. In: M. Guralnick (ed.), *The Effectiveness of Early Intervention* (pp. 249–268). Baltimore, MD: Brookes.

Berry, J. W., & Dalai, A. (1994). Comparative studies of disability attitudes, beliefs and behaviors. In: *International Conference of International Association for Cross-Cultural Psychology*, Pamplona, July.

Bearer, C. F. (1995). Environmental health hazards: How children are different from adults. *The Future of Children*, 5(2), 11–26.

Belsky, J. (1993). Etiology of child maltreatment: A developmental and ecological analysis. *Psychological Bulletin*, 114(3), 413–434.

Bowlby, J. (1958). The nature of the child's tie to his mother. *International Journal of Psycho-Analysis*, 39, 350–373.

Bradley, R. H., & Corwyn, R. F. (2002). Socioeconomic status and child development. *Annual Review of Psychology*, 53(1), 371–399.

Bynner, J., Joshi, H., & Tsatsas, M. (2000). *Obstacles and opportunities on the route to adulthood*. London: Smith Institute.

Carpenter, G. L., & Stacks, A. M. (2009). Developmental effects of exposure to intimate partner violence in early childhood: A review of the literature. *Children and Youth Services Review*, 31(8), 831–839.

Census of India (2011). Office of the Registrar General, India, Ministry of Home Affairs, Government of India, New Delhi.

Charles, K. (2011). *Conflicts arising from child sacrifice in Mukono District*, A Master Dissertation submitted to the Department of Religion and Peace Studies, College of Humanities and Liberal Arts, Makerere University.

Cicchetti, D., & Lynch, M. (1993). Toward an ecological/transactional model of community violence and child maltreatment: Consequences for children's development. *Psychiatry-Washington-William Alanson White Psychiatric Foundation Then Washington School of Psychiatry*, 56, 96.

Cleaver, H., Nicholson, D., Tarr, S., & Cleaver, D. (2007). *Child protection, domestic violence and parental substance misuse: Family experiences and effective practice*. London: Jessica Kingsley.

Cleaver, H., Unell, I., & Aldgate, J. (2011) *Children's needs: Parenting capacity*, 2nd edition. London: TSO.

Curl, C. L., Fenske, R. A., & Elgethun, K. (2003). Organophosphorus pesticide exposure of urban and suburban preschool children with organic and conventional diets. *Environment Health Perspective*, 111, 377–382.

Dalal, A. K., & Pande, N. (1999). Cultural beliefs and family care of children with disability. *Psychology and Developing Societies*, 11(1), 55–75.

de Onis, M., Blossner, M., & Borghi, E. (2010). Global prevalence and trends of overweight and obesity among preschool children. *Am J Clin Nutr.*, 92, 1257–1264.

Deb, S. (2006). *Contemporary social problems in India*. New Delhi: Anmol.

Deb, S., & Modak, S. (2010). Prevalence of violence against children in families in tripura and its relationship with socio-economic, cultural and other factors. *Journal of Injury and Violence Research*, 2(1), 5–18.

Deb, S., & Walsh, K. (2011). Impact of physical, psychological, and sexual violence on social adjustment of school children in India. *School Psychology International*, 33(4), 391–415.

Deb, S., Kumar, A., Bhattacharyya, B., & Jiandong, S. (2012). Parents' perception about children's academic stress and child care related issues. *Indian Journal of Health and Wellbeing*, 3(3), 608–612.

Department for Education and Skills (DfES) (2006). *Every Child Matters: Integrated working to improve outcomes for children and young people*. London: DfES.

Dickinson, D. K., & Snow, C. E. (1987). Interrelationships among prereading and oral language skills in kindergartners from two social classes. *Early Childhood Research Quarterly*, 1, 1–25.

Dongaonkar, D., Jaykar, A. V., Angadi, S. A., Fernandes, C. S., & Subhash, K. (2001). Perinatal transmission of HIV infection in Mumbai, India. *J Obstet Gynaecol India*, 51, 56–60.

Ebbeling, C. B., Pawlak, D. B., & Ludwig, D. S. (2002). Childhood obesity: Public-health crisis, common sense cure. *Lancet*, 360, 473–482.

Edwardraj, S., Mumtaj, K., Prasad, J. H., Kuruvilla, A., & Jacob, K. S. (2010). Perceptions about intellectual disability: A qualitative study from Vellore, South India. *Journal of Intellectual Disability Research*, 54, 736–748.

Erikson, E. H., & Erikson, J. M. (1998). *The life cycle completed* (extended version). New York: W.W. Norton & Co.

Family Violence Prevention Fund (2008) Get the Facts: Domestic Violence is a Serious Widespread Social Problem in America. Retrieved from www.endabuse.org/userfiles/files/children_and_families/domestic violence.pdf

Fergusson, D. M., & Horwood, L. J. (2003) Resilience to childhood adversity: Results of a 21-year study. In: Lunthar, S. S. (ed.), *Resilience and vulnerability: Adaptation in the context of childhood adversities* (pp. 130–155). Cambridge: Cambridge University Press.

Fergusson, D. M., Horwood, L. J., & Lynskey, M. T. (1994). The childhoods of multiple problem adolescents: A 15-year longitudinal study. *Journal of Child Psychology and Psychiatry and Allied Disciplines*, 35, 1123–1140.

Filippi, V., Ronsmans, C., Campbell, O. M., Graham, W. J., Mills, A., Borghi, J., et al. (2006). Maternal health in poor countries: The broader context and a call for action. *The Lancet*, 368(9546), 1535–1541.

Finkelhor, D. (1984). *Child sexual abuse: New theory and research*. New York: Free Press.

Fitzpatrick, K. M. (1993). Exposure to violence and presence of depression among low-income, African-American youth. *Journal of Consulting and Clinical Psychology*, 61(3), 528–531.

Garbarino, J., Kostelny, K., & Dubrow, N. (1991). *No place to be a child: Growing up in a war zone*. Lexington, MA: Lexington Books.

Gjelsvik, A., Verhoek-Oftendahl, W., & Pearlman, D. N. (2003). Domestic violence with children witnesses: Findings from Rhode Island surveillance data. *Women's Health Issues*, 13, 68–72.

Gupta, A. (2007). Female foeticide in India. UNICEF press release. Retrieved from http://unicef.in/PressReleases/227/Female-foeticide-in-India

Gutman, L., Sameroff, A., & Eccles, J. (2002). The academic achievement of African-American students during early adolescence: An examination of multiple risk, promotive, and protective factors. *American Journal of Community Psychology*, 30, 367–399.

Hartman, C. R., & Burgess, A. W. (1989). Sexual abuse of children: Causes and consequences. In: D. Cicchetti and V. Carlson (eds), *Child maltreatment: Theory and research on the causes and consequences of child abuse and neglect* (pp. 95–128). New York: Cambridge University Press.

Kapil, U. (2002). Integrated Child Development Services (ICDS) scheme: A program for holistic development of children in India. *Indian Journal of Pediatrics*, 69(7), 597–601.

Kliewer, W., Lepore, S. J., Oskin, D., & Johnson, P. D. (1998). The role of social and cognitive processes in children's adjustment to community violence. *Journal of Consulting and Clinical Psychology*, 66(1), 199–209.

Kumar, A., Gireesan, A., & Deb, S. (2013). Students' perception of abuse and neglect. *Indian Journal of Positive Psychology*, 4(3), 1360–1365.

Lanphear, B. P., Hornung, R., Ho, M., Howard, C. R., Eberly, S., & Knauf, K. (2002). Environmental lead exposure during early childhood. *Journal of Pediatrics*, 140(1), 40–47.

Lieberman, A. F., & Osofsky, J. D. (2009). Poverty, trauma, and infant mental health. *Zero to Three*, 30(2), 54–58.

Lynch, M., & Cicchetti, D. (1998). An ecological-transactional analysis of children and contexts: The longitudinal interplay among child maltreatment, community violence, and children's symptomatology. *Development and Psychopathology*, 10(2), 235–257.

Martinez, P., & Richters, J. E. (1993). The NIMH community violence project, II: Children's distress symptoms associated with violence exposure. *Psychiatry-Washington-William Alanson White Psychiatric Foundation Then Washington School of Psychiatry*, 56, 22.

Magill-Evans, J., & Harrison, M. J. (2001). Parent–child interactions, parenting stress, and developmental outcomes at 4 years. *Children's Health Care*, 30(2), 135–150.

Masten, A. S., & Wright, M. O. D. (1998). Cumulative risk and protection models of child maltreatment. *Journal of Aggression, Maltreatment & Trauma*, 2(1), 7–30.

Masten, A. S., & Sesma, A. (1999). Risk and resilience among children homeless in Minneapolis. *CURA Reporter*, 29(1), 1–6.

McIntyre, J. (2005). Maternal health and HIV. *Reproductive Health Matters*, 13(25): 129–135.

McLoyd, V. C. (1990). The impact of economic hardship on black families and children: Psychological distress, parenting, and socioemotional development. *Child Development*, 61(2), 311–346.

Miller, J. E., & Korenman, S. (1994). Poverty and children's nutritional status in the United States. *American Journal of Epidemiology*, 140(3), 233–243.

Milner, J. S. (2000). Social information processing and child physical abuse: Theory and research. In: D. J. Hansen (ed.), *46th Annual Nebraska Symposium on Motivation: Motivation and child maltreatment* (pp. 39–84). Lincoln, NE: University of Nebraska Press.

Ministry of Human Resource Development (2006). Report of Working Group on Elementary Education and Literacy – For the 11th Five Year Plan, Government of India.

Ministry of Women and Child Development (2011). Indira Gandhi Matritva Sahyog Yojna, Government of India. Retrieved from http://wcd.nic.in/Schemelgmsy/IGMSYImpGuidelinesApr11.pdf

Muralialharari, R., & Kaul, V. (1993). Responding to children's needs: Integrated child development services in India. In: Elderling, L. and Leseman, P. (eds), *Early intervention and culture: Preparation for literacy – the interface between theory and practice*. Paris: UNESCO.

Murray, L. (1992). The impact of postnatal depression on infant development. *Journal of Child Psychology and Psychiatry*, 33(3), 543–561.

Murray, L., & Cooper, P. J. (1997). Effects of postnatal depression on infant development. *Archives of Disease in Childhood*, 77(2), 99–101.

NFHS III (2005–2006). *National Family Health Survey*. Mumbai: International Institute for Population Sciences and Macro International.

National Crime Records Bureau (2010). Crime in India, Ministry of Home Affairs, Government of India (ncrb.gov.in).

National AIDS Control Organisation (NACO) (2006). Strategy and Implementation Plan: National AIDS Control Programme Phase III [2007–2012]. New Delhi: NACO.

National Institute for Health Care Management (NIHCM) (2010). Identifying and treating maternal depression: Strategies and considerations for health plans, NIHCM Foundations, Washington DC.

Newberger, C. M., & Newberger, E. H. (1982). Prevention of child abuse: Theory, myth, practice. *Journal of Preventative Psychiatry*, 1, 443–451.

Ney, P., Fung, T., & Wickett, A. (1992). Causes of child abuse and neglect. *Canadian Journal of Psychiatry*, 37, 401–405.

NICHD Early Child Care Research Network (1999). Child outcomes when child care center classes meet recommended standards for quality. *American Journal of Public Health*, 89(7), 1072–1077.

OECD (2006). Starting strong II: Early childhood education and care, OECD, Paris.

Osborne, C. (2008). Changing Families, Changing Risks? Cumulative Risk Factors and Family Instability Among Urban Children. For consideration to present at the Annual Meeting of the Population Association of America, Population Research Center, University of Texas at Austin, September. Retrieved from http://paa2009.princeton.edu/papers/90525

Osofsky, J. D. (1995). The effect of exposure to violence on young children. *American Psychologist*, 50(9), 782–788.

Pepler, D. J., Catallo, R., & Moore, T. E. (2000). Consider the children: Research informing interventions for children exposed to domestic violence. *Journal of Aggression, Maltreatment & Trauma*, 3(1), 37–57.

Petterson, S. M., & Albers, A. B. (2001). Effects of poverty and maternal depression on early child development. *Child Development*, 72(6), 1794–1813.

Raj, L. (2011). Understanding corporate punishment in India. *Career Educator: An Interdisciplinary Education Journal*, 1, 3–18.

Sabates, R., & Dex, S. (2012). *Multiple risk factors in young children's development*. London: Centre for Longitudinal Studies, Institute of Education.

Schoon, I. (2006). *Risk and resilience: Adaptations to changing times*. Cambridge: Cambridge University Press.

Schoon, I., Sacker, A., & Bartley M. (2003). Socio-economic adversity and psychosocial adjustment: A developmental-contextual perspective. *Social Science and Medicine*, 57(6), 1001–1015.

Shaw, D. S., Vondra, J. I., Hommerding, K. D., Keenan, K., & Dunn, M. (1994). Chronic family adversity and early child behaviour problems: A longitudinal study of low income families. *Journal of Child Psychology and Psychiatry*, 35, 1109–1122.

Shetty, S. B., & Shetty, S.K. (2013). KAP study of factors promoting breastfeeding in nursing mothers and pregnant women. *Nitte University Journal of Health Science*, 3(3), 34–37.

Smith, J. D. (2002). The myth of mental retardation: Paradigm shifts, disaggregation, and developmental disabilities. *Mental Retardation*, 40, 62–4.

Toure, K., Sankore, R., Kuruvilla, S., Scolaro, E., Bustreo, F., & Osotimehin, B. (2012). Positioning women's and children's health in African union policy-making: A policy analysis. *Globalization and Health*, 8(3) [online].

UNICEF (2000). The Prescriber, UNICEF's Programme Division in cooperation with the World Health Organization, January, No. 8.

UNICEF (2001). The State of the World's Children: Panel 7 – Respecting the rights of the Indian child. Retrieved from www.unicef.org/sowc01/panels/panel7.htm

UNICEF (2013). *The state of the world's children 2013*. Geneva: UNICEF.

Vygotsky, L. S. (1978). *Mind in Society,* Harvard University Press, Cambridge, MA.

Ward, T., & Siegert, R. J. (2002). Toward a comprehensive theory of child sexual abuse: A theory knitting perspective. *Psychology, Crime and Law*, 8(4), 319–351.

WHO (1995). The world health report 1995: Bridging the gaps. Retrieved from www.who.int/whr/1995/en/

WHO (2012). Global strategy on diet, physical activity, and health: childhood overweight and obesity. Retrieved from www.who.int/dietphysicalactivity/childhood/en/

WHO (2013a). Malaria in children under 5. Retrieved from www.who.int/malaria/areas/high_risk_groups/children/en/index.htm

WHO (2013b). Infant and young child feeding, Fact Sheet No. 342, September.

WHO and UNICEF (2005). GIVS. *Global Immunization Vision and Strategy 2006-2015*. Geneva: UNICEF.

Wu, G., Bazer, F. W., Cudd, T. A., Meininger, C. J., & Spencer, T. E. (2004). Maternal nutrition and fetal development. *The Journal of Nutrition*, 134(9), 2169–2172.

21

Children in Conflict Situations: Applying Childhood Research with a Focus on the Early Years

Claire O'Kane

INTRODUCTION

This chapter focuses on applied childhood research concerning the early years in situations of armed conflict, post conflict and peace building. It critically reflects on theoretical and methodological approaches underpinning such efforts, as well as the ways in which applied research has informed policy and practice developments.

In addition, it draws upon other related applied research concerning the early years in disasters. Globally, just over 1 billion children under the age of 18 live in countries or territories affected by armed conflict – almost one sixth of the total world population (Office of the Special Representative of the Secretary-General for Children and Armed Conflict (SGCAC) in collaboration with UNICEF, 2009). Of these, approximately 300 million are under the age of 5 years (SGCAC and UNICEF, 2009). Armed conflict and its aftermath pose enormous challenges to the well-being of young children and their caregivers

(Wessells and Monteiro, 2008; SGCAC and UNICEF, 2009; the Consultative Group on Early Childhood Care and Development (CGECCD) and Inter-Agency Network for Education in Emergencies (INEE), 2009; Plan International, 2013). Despite increased efforts by governments, United Nations (UN) agencies, civil society organizations and academics to monitor, report, prevent and respond to grave violations affecting children in situations of armed conflict, research and programming relating to the early years has been under-resourced and under-developed (Bernard van Leer Foundation, 2005; Hart et al., 2007; Wessells and Monteiro, 2008; CGECCD and INEE, 2009; Lloyd and Penn, 2010; Akesson, 2012; Plan International, 2013; International Network on Peace Building with Young Children, 2010).

The research that is reviewed within this chapter has primarily been undertaken by international child rights organizations and broader coalitions, often in collaboration with academics to inform the development of Early Childhood Care and Development (ECCD) programming in conflict situations and to promote child rights and peace building. The research undertaken by child rights organizations is influenced by rights-based perspectives and ecological approaches recognizing the child in context, the agency of the child and the diversity of childhood experiences (James and Prout, 1990; Feinstein and O'Kane, 2008; Wessells and Monteiro, 2008; CGECCD and INEE, 2009; International Network on Peace Building with Young Children, 2010; Plan International, 2013). While the UN Convention on the Rights of the Child and theories concerning the diversity of childhood experiences emphasize the importance of listening to girls' and boys' perspectives, methodological and ethical approaches to research with children in situations of armed conflict are rarely sufficiently tailored to seek and respond adequately to the views of younger children. Reasons for such limitations are briefly explored in this chapter, including adult beliefs and perceptions, ethical concerns and methodological deliberations regarding appropriate methods to use in research with younger children. Moreover, lessons emerging from existing efforts to develop and apply methodological and ethical approaches to participatory and applied research with children in the early years are discussed, especially efforts to engage with younger children in situations of conflict and post-conflict (de Berry et al., 2003; Feinstein and O'Kane, 2008; Kostelny and Wessells, 2008). Emerging findings from a growing body of research in neuroscience are also briefly presented, as such research is propelling advocacy efforts to prevent and address direct and structural violence and conflict that adversely affect children and their well-being, particularly in early childhood (Yale University and ACEV Partnership, 2012; Early Childhood Peace Consortium (ECPC), 2013).

The latter part of the chapter outlines emerging themes from applied research concerning the early years in situations of conflict. The chapter explores ways in which these findings are reflected in current programming and policy developments by agencies and coalitions promoting ECCD in emergencies (INEE, 2010; International Network on Peace Building with Young Children, 2010; ECPC, 2013; Plan International, 2013). Moreover, various 'calls to action' are outlined which recognize and respond to gaps in research, practice and policy developments in ECCD in emergencies.

INCREASING FOCUS ON THE IMPACT OF ARMED CONFLICT ON CHILDREN, BUT LIMITED FOCUS ON THE EARLY YEARS

In 1996 the Graca Machel study on the impact of armed conflict was presented to the UN General Assembly. The report and its recommendations led to an increased focus on children (under 18 years), as a group requiring special attention. It was also instrumental in informing the establishment of a UN Security Council mechanism to monitor and report on six grave violations against children in situations of armed conflict, namely: killing or maiming; recruitment or use of children by armed forces and armed groups; attacks against schools or hospitals; rape and other forms of sexual violence; abduction; and denial of humanitarian access. While few of the recommendations from the Machel study were specifically focused on children in the early years, the study advocated for a multi-sector approach to address the health and nutrition of young children in emergencies (UN, 1996).

A decade later, a Strategic Review of the Machel Study (SGCAC and UNICEF, 2009) was undertaken to determine progress and ongoing challenges facing children affected by armed conflict. Armed conflict continues to result in direct violations of children's rights including: death, loss of parents/caregivers, displacement, loss of access to basic services (health, education, water and sanitation, protection), increased protection risks and emotional distress. The Review highlighted how the interruption and disintegration of basic services and sources of social protection during and after armed conflict lead to further violations of child rights – with repercussions that could last a lifetime. This was illustrated by data concerning the Millennium Development Goals (MDGs), which indicated that conflict-affected countries and territories have shown less progress towards the MDGs than many of their more fortunate counterparts (SGCAC and UNICEF, 2009). For example, analysis of data concerning the indicator of underweight prevalence, for children under 5, found that there are 98.5 million undernourished children below the age of 5 living in conflict-affected countries. This is more than two-thirds of the 143 million children under 5 globally who suffer from under-nutrition (SGCAC and UNICEF, 2009). The impact of exposure to prolonged stress, violence and conflict is especially salient in early childhood, where many effects are linked with the chronic activation of the body's stress response system. Recent research indicates that the most profound outcome is alteration to the trajectory of brain functioning, which can manifest later in childhood and throughout life as deficiencies and challenges to physical health, social-emotional well-being, memory and learning (CGECCD and INEE, 2009; Yale University and ACEV Partnership, 2012; ECPC, 2013).

The Machel review included a box to highlight the importance of 'giving children the right start in life, even in the midst of war' (SGCAC and UNICEF, 2009: 106). The boxed example drew upon research in neuroscience, outlining how brain development is influenced by a child's nutritional and health status, exposure to stimulation and interactions with people and objects. It describes how field experience and research conducted during the past few decades indicate that interventions to promote physical, intellectual and emotional development in early childhood, particularly in times of stress, make a difference for young children and their caregivers, both immediately and

in the long term. The Machel review emphasized the importance of understanding local cultural constructs of childhood, and using a variety of community-based approaches with children and their caregivers to ensure good care of children in the early years including: parenting classes, community-based centres, preschool programmes, psychosocial support and early stimulation and play activities (SGCAC and UNICEF, 2009). The chapter on 'children as peacemakers' in the Machel review also identified the need to address diversity and disparities in participation, recognizing factors such as age, gender, class, sibling order, etc. However, despite these inclusions, the Machel review has limited focus on the early years. While children and young people's views were sought as part of the strategic review process, few children under the age of 10 years were involved. Moreover, the lack of research concerning the impact of armed conflict on children in the early years and the need for increased human and financial investments in early childhood development programming is not adequately reflected in the Machel study review findings or recommendations.

Although there is a growing evidence base showing the importance of Early Childhood Care and Development (ECCD) in general, there is limited research, data and evaluations concerning ECCD in humanitarian situations (CGECCD and INEE, 2009; Lloyd and Penn, 2010; Plan International, 2013). For example, there have been no longitudinal or cost-benefit analyses for ECCD in emergencies (Plan International, 2013) and there is a dearth of evidence concerning the effectiveness of psychosocial interventions with younger children and their caregivers in contexts affected by armed conflict (Lloyd and Penn, 2010). An annotated bibliography concerning childhood care and development in emergencies (Hayden et al., 2010) reveals that there are fewer studies concerning the early years in situations affected by armed conflict, as compared to the early years and disaster situations. Moreover, many of the identified studies were focused on post-traumatic stress syndrome, a concept which has been critiqued for its western biases (Boyden and Mann, 2005; Lloyd and Penn, 2010).

CORE PERSPECTIVES SHAPING EARLY CHILDHOOD RESEARCH, POLICY AND PRACTICE

Woodhead (2007) identified four core perspectives that have been influential in shaping early childhood policies and practices:

1 *A developmental perspective* that emphasizes regularities in young children's physical and psychosocial growth during early childhood, as well as their vulnerabilities (and resilience) in this formative stage, which is reinforced by growing knowledge in neuroscience
2 *A political and economic perspective* which is informed by developmental principles, translated into social and educational interventions, and underpinned by economic models of human capital
3 *A social and cultural perspective* that draws attention to the way in which early childhood is a constructed status and to the diversities of ways it is understood and practised for, with and by young children, with implications for how goals, models and standards are defined, and by whom
4 *A human rights perspective* that reframes conventional approaches to theory, research policy and practice in ways that fully respect young children's dignity and their entitlements.

Donors supporting early childhood policy and programming developments, including the World Bank, the European Union and the Asian Development Bank tend to favour economic perspectives reflecting the human capital theory (Penn, 2011), as well as developmental perspectives. The World Bank places most emphasis on economic perspectives which primarily have been informed by research in the USA in the 1960s, 1970s and 1980s (Penn, 2011). The relevance and efficacy of applying such theories to diverse contexts in the global South has been questioned (see Penn, 2011; and Pence and Ashton, 2014).

In terms of applied research in conflict settings, although elements of each of these core perspectives (developmental, political and economic, social and cultural, and human rights) are evident, the most prominent framework used by child-focused agencies undertaking applied research is the human rights perspective. Rights-based agencies including Plan International, Save the Children and UNICEF apply the UN Convention on the Rights of the Child (UNCRC, 1989) as a tool, using the four general principles of child rights (survival and development, non-discrimination, participation and best interests) to inform programming and advocacy work. Due to the near universal ratification of the UNCRC,[1] it is an effective tool for awareness raising and advocacy work (Smith, 2007; Woodhead, 2007). Although the UNCRC has been criticized for its western bias (ethnocentric, imposition of individual autonomous rights versus collective, societal responsibilities), it remains a useful tool in working with childhood diversity if the general principles are taken seriously (O'Kane, 2003). Setting out from a starting point that every child is entitled to development without discrimination, we can gain an understanding of the complexities of local contexts by listening to the views and experiences of children and their caregivers, taking into consideration children's evolving capacities and local understandings of their best interests. A child rights-based approach recognizes children's agency and the social construction of childhoods, and approaches children in their wider socio-cultural, political and economic contexts (Smith, 2007; Woodhead, 2007; ARC, 2009). Thus, the rights-based perspective also embraces other core perspectives outlined by Woodhead (2007).

The UN Committee on the Rights of the Child (CRC) adopted General Comment No.7 on *Implementing Child Rights in Early Childhood* in September 2005. The General Comment aimed to strengthen understanding of the human rights of all young children and to draw governments' attention to their obligations towards young children. The Committee noted the growing body of theory and research that confirms that young children are best understood as social actors whose survival, well-being and development are dependent on and built around close relationships. The importance of prevention and intervention strategies during early childhood to address adversity, in order to impact positively on young children's current well-being and future prospects, was also highlighted. The Committee emphasized young children's vulnerability to risks when they are surrounded by conflict and violence or displaced from their homes as refugees. They also noted that 'Young children are especially at risk where parents or other caregivers are unable to offer adequate protection, whether due to illness, or death, or due to disruption to families or communities' (2005: 16). Recognizing the significance of young children's relationships and attachments with their parents or other primary caregivers, it is crucial to ensure that mothers, fathers and other caregivers receive necessary health, psychosocial and other necessary support during emergencies, in order that they may remain healthy and able to create a safe and supportive environment for their young children in the midst of crisis. When caregivers are secure and engaged, they are more likely to form the attachments and supportive relationships children need to overcome risk (Landers, 1998). Thus, increased attention to early childhood interventions including support to caregivers in conflict situations and other emergencies is needed (CGECCD and INEE, 2009).

LIMITED APPLIED RESEARCH INVOLVING YOUNG CHILDREN

Applied research involving young children in situations of armed conflict and post-conflict is limited. While there is increasing participatory research involving children and young people often undertaken from a rights-based perspective in diverse contexts around the world, much of this research has involved children older than 8 years (see MacNaughton

et al., 2007; Akesson, 2011; Johnson et al., 2014). Factors contributing to the exclusion of younger children include: adult beliefs and perceptions concerning younger children's lack of competency to engage meaningfully in research; difficulties in accessing and engaging with younger children without interference from their parents or caregivers; ethical concerns regarding informed consent and asking sensitive questions; and methodological concerns regarding appropriate and relevant methods to use with younger children (MacNaughton et al., 2007; Akesson, 2011; Johnson et al., 2014).

In recent years, there has however been a growing push for and experimentation in innovative participatory research involving younger children (see Save the Children, 2001; Clark and Moss, 2005; Lansdown, 2005; MacNaughton et al., 2007; Akesson, 2011; Harcourt and Einarsdottir, 2011; Johnson et al., 2014). Lansdown's (2005) work on children's evolving capacities has emphasized the importance of recognizing children as active agents in their own lives who are entitled to be listened to, respected and granted increasing autonomy in the exercise of rights, while also being entitled to protection in accordance with their relative immaturity and youth. The 'Mosaic approach' developed by Clark and Moss (2005) has been influential in encouraging other researchers and practitioners to engage with younger children with a focus on their abilities and competencies to engage in and influence research processes and outcomes. MacNaughton and colleagues (2007) describe recent developments in diverse disciplines, including sociology, developmental psychology and anthropology and from the consumer movement – in recognition of children as young citizens and social actors. They present a model of the young child that embodies and expresses three research-based ideas: young children can make valid meanings about the world and their place in it; children's knowledge of the world is different (not inferior) to adults' knowledge; and children's insights and perspectives on the world can improve adults' understandings of children's experiences (MacNaughton et al., 2007).

Undertaking applied research in contexts where children are affected by adversity, Boyden and Mann make the case for 'a dynamic, contextualized view of misfortune and suggests that children's experiences of adversity are mediated by a host of internal and external factors that are inseparable from the social, political, and economic contexts in which children live' (2005: 4). They call for greater attention to children's own understandings of their experience, and assert the need for research, policy and programmatic interventions to consider carefully the reality of children's lives in order to improve the effectiveness of interventions designed to assist them.

In undertaking research with children in situations affected by armed conflict, Hart and Tyrer also encourage researchers to 'avoid the view of children as inherently vulnerable' (2006: 10). They encourage a more nuanced approach recognizing how 'age, gender, class, education, language, particular setting, all position children differently with respect to the risks (and opportunities) created by conflict' (2006: 10).

While gender analysis has been relatively strong in applied research concerning children affected by armed conflict, analysis relating to age and in particular the experiences of younger children has been lacking. In research, policy and practice developments, there has been significant thematic focus and research on children associated with armed groups and gender-based violence, including sexual violence, which has been more associated with girls and boys above the age of 10 years – despite reports of rape of children under 6 years (Kostelny and Wessells, 2008).

In contexts affected by armed conflict, pragmatic, methodological and ethical considerations have further contributed to limited research with younger children. Hart and Tyrer have noted how the 'environment of armed conflict poses particular challenges for

safe, ethically responsible research involving children' (2006: 18). For example, participatory research approaches are generally group-focused, yet simply bringing children together may entail risk in a violent or unstable setting. Furthermore, encouraging open discussion might lead to the revelation of information that can put individual children, their families or the entire community at risk. Hart and Tyrer emphasize the need for good preparation, risk assessment and risk mitigation strategies but do not provide any specific guidance for involving younger children. One of the challenges they identify in undertaking research in environments of armed conflict is that parents, out of fear for their children's well-being, may severely limit children's engagement with society beyond the home. Thus, research undertaken with young children may require increased efforts to gain permission to meet with young children within their homes. However, Hart and Tyrer also note that children may not necessarily feel safe within their home, particularly if alcohol abuse has increased by caregivers as a result of the despair of living through conflict and upheaval, thus increasing risks of domestic abuse and violence against and neglect of children. Therefore, sensitive approaches to research with young children and caregivers are required, identifying and minimizing risks, and ensuring that researchers have established systems for support and back-up from appropriate trained local practitioners for situations where significant child abuse concerns are identified (see Hart and Tyrer, 2006).

LEARNING FROM APPLIED RESEARCH CONCERNING YOUNGER CHILDREN IN CONFLICT SITUATIONS

It is important to identify and build upon lessons learned from existing applied research and evaluation processes and findings concerning the early years in conflict situations. Applied research involving younger children aged 6 to 8 years, as well as older children, that are reviewed in this chapter include:

1 *The Children of Kabul* participatory research undertaken with girls and boys aged 6 to 18 years in Afghanistan by Save the Children US in 2002
2 Participatory research and evaluation on children's participation in armed conflict, post-conflict and peace building undertaken by Save the Children Norway in Bosnia-Herzegovina, Guatemala, Nepal and Uganda from 2006 to 2007
3 Outcome research on Child-Centered Spaces supported by Christian Children's Fund in Northern Uganda in 2007 which gathered evidence based on caregivers' views
4 A thesis by Ruskin (2009) examining the effectiveness of child-friendly spaces for 3–6- year-olds in fragile situations.

A brief overview of research findings from neuroscience and their relevance for peace building are also touched upon. Furthermore, in the latter part of the chapter, emerging themes from the applied research and some of their links to practice and policy developments concerning ECCD in emergencies are identified.

The Children of Kabul research was undertaken by Save the Children, with support from UNICEF, to listen to children's views and to hear about children's experiences of their daily lives in Kabul, in order to develop relevant programmes for war-affected children in Afghanistan (de Berry et al., 2003). The research was informed by a 'child rights-based perspective', recognizing children as right holders and social actors, and a 'psychosocial approach' that approached children in the context of their families, communities and cultural context to better understand their well-being, their experiences and their priorities in war-affected communities. The research sought to understand and build upon children's and adults' existing resources and positive coping strategies. In the latter stage of the research, children were supported to develop community-based action initiatives to address some of their priority concerns. For example, the children in one area prioritized awareness and action efforts to ensure that 'open wells' were closed; in another area, children prioritized traffic accidents and planned and implemented initiatives

to increase road safety in cooperation with community leaders and the traffic police.

The research used qualitative research methods including focus group discussions and child-friendly participatory tools involving over 600 people including girls and boys aged 6–12 years, adolescents aged 13–18 years, mothers, fathers, grandmothers and grandfathers. Forty-three groups of children were involved in the research, with each group participating in six two-hour research sessions. Each group had 10 to 15 children aged 6–13 years. The six sessions used *participatory activities* to explore the following topics:

1 Introduction to the project and children's involvement and ownership
2 Children's ideas about families and relationships – *drawing*
3 Children's ideas about risks and dangers – risk mapping to identify the risks and dangers in their homes and communities
4 Children's ideas about good and bad events and situations – *drawing happy or sad days*
5 Children's ideas about their bodies and feelings – *body mapping of likes and dislikes*
6 Children's ideas about their work and activities; feedback and close of the group.

While the research was initially designed for children aged 7 years and older, some 6-year-old girls and boys also participated in the research. Girls and boys aged 6–8 years were able to express themselves through drawings, mapping and orally as part of the focus group discussion. Participatory activities have been identified as effective tools to involve children more meaningfully in research in a range of studies, as they assist in transforming the power relations between adults and children, and are often found to be fun and interesting to use (see Boyden and Ennew, 1997; Hart and Tyrer, 2006; Tisdall et al., 2006; O'Kane, 2008; Johnson et al., 2014). In this study, use of participatory tools was identified as appropriate to ensure more sensitive, ethical research. Children found it easier to talk about their experiences, feelings and ideas when they were taking part in relevant activities such as drawing, mapping or story telling (de Berry et al., 2003). Furthermore, the children found the activities enjoyable and were thus willing and interested to participate in the research process that took place over a number of months. A commitment to a participatory research process and good facilitation skills are essential to the successful use of participatory research tools (O'Kane, 2008; Johnson et al., 2014). The researchers involved in the Kabul study highlighted: the significance of the friendliness, facilitation and listening skills of the researchers; the importance of starting with activities and easy questions which help younger children relax, before moving on to more personal or sensitive questions; and the importance of creating an environment where all children's ideas were respected, so that children did not feel any pressure to give a 'correct' or 'specific' answer (de Berry et al., 2003).

Key findings from the Children of Kabul research include:

- the importance of understanding cultural concepts concerning children's behaviour and well-being, which emphasize children's emotional and social development as well as their good health and physical survival
- the importance of positive and supportive relationships – especially with mothers, fathers, grandparents, brothers and sisters
- children's understanding of threats affecting their daily lives including: war, displacement, poverty, family loss and separation, harmful or exploitative work, violence, and dangers from the physical environment. For example, an 8-year-old boy drew a picture and described a sad day when he went to fly a kite, instead of going to weave carpets, and as a result was beaten by the carpet weaver instructor. A 7-year-old girl drew a picture of herself, explaining that 'the days when my mother and father don't fight, I am happy' (de Berry et al., 2003: 37)
- children's personal attitudes and social relations affect their ability to cope with adversity. Children were encouraged to express thankfulness, to be honest, to show faith and courage in time of adversity. In contrast, not telling the truth and adults' use of physical punishment and violence were identified as negative coping strategies
- children desired peace and security in their own homes. Children focused on their daily concerns and their immediate physical environment, including

the dangers of open wells and bad traffic, which caused worries, accidents, injuries and death.

Participatory research and evaluation on children's participation in armed conflict, post-conflict and peace building supported by Save the Children Norway was undertaken in Bosnia-Herzegovina, Guatemala, Nepal and Uganda from 2006 to 2007 (Feinstein and O'Kane, 2008). This research was also influenced by a human rights-based approach, including children's right to participate in decisions affecting them. Children and young people were actively involved as researchers, advisers and respondents to research, document and analyse projects and strategies supporting children's participation in peace building in countries affected by armed conflict and post-conflict. In Nepal and Uganda, the research primarily involved children aged 8 years and older, with insufficient attention given to the design or methods to involve younger children. However, the research in Bosnia-Herzegovina and Guatemala made more efforts to involve younger children aged 6–8 years, as well as older children aged 9–18 years. Ethical guidelines to ensure informed consent were applied and parents and caregivers' permission was sought to ensure support for children's participation. Furthermore, research activities were organized with and by children at times that they were more available, such as at weekends or during holidays. Children were actively involved as peer researchers and with child-friendly research tools including: body mapping on how the conflict affects children, risk and resource mapping, drawing, sharing stories of the most significant change, and human sculptures (of peace) were effectively used with younger children aged 6–8 years, especially when they were preceded by games to create a child-friendly environment.

In Bosnia-Herzegovina, the research team reported that younger children are able to play an important role in building peace by: socializing, communicating and playing with others in gentle, respectful and non-discriminatory ways; by influencing their family members and peers to be honest and forgiving; and by using non-violent communication methods to solve disputes or conflict in their daily lives. Inclusion of children with disabilities, and opportunities for children from different ethnic, religious and economic backgrounds to interact and be together in schools, communities, clubs and society, and efforts to address discrimination, were also identified by children as important to peace building. As part of the research in Guatemala, the team also reported on a peace campaign that was organized by children in Alta Verapaz to promote use of non-violent toys among children. The campaign provided an opportunity for children to exchange violent toys (such as toy guns, knives) for non-violent toys. Over 100 toy guns were collected and exchanged.

Across the four countries, a key research finding was the importance of ensuring increased adult support to value and support children's expression and participation. Parents and other adults tended to under-estimate children's abilities, particularly those of younger children, and thus did not take children's views and ideas seriously. Children of different ages, including younger children, emphasized the importance of peace in their families, schools and communities. Children would like their parents and other adults to be better role models, ensuring prevention of violence and conflict and using non-violent communication methods to resolve conflicts and to discipline children. A sense of love, care, safety, security and non-violence in the family is especially important to children who face insecurity and conflict in their wider environment.

Outcome research on Child-Centered Spaces in Northern Uganda was undertaken by the Christian Children's Fund[2] to determine the extent to which they contributed to the protection and psychosocial well-being of young children in settings affected by armed conflict and poverty (Kostelny and Wessells, 2008). Child-Centred Spaces (CCSs)[3] are a widely used intervention in emergency responses to address children's education, protection and psychosocial needs. Kostelny and Wessells (2008) describe how CCSs are often established during the acute phase of emergencies in open areas,

under trees or in already existing structures. Through community mobilization around children's needs, CCSs provide regular, structured activities for children, adolescents and parents of young children under the supervision of caring individuals from the community. Typically, they are organized and run by local people selected by the community as those who are trustworthy and motivated to support children.

In an effort to strengthen community systems of protection for children in Uganda, CCF established three CCSs in April 2006 in the Unyama Internally Displaced Persons (IDP) camp, in response to ongoing issues of protection for children living in the camp. The CCSs provided a safe, adult-supervised place for young children aged 3–6 years. While primary schools were available for children aged 7 years and older, supportive, developmentally appropriate activities were lacking for children under 7 years of age. The CCSs conducted activities for children from 7.30 a.m. to 1.00 p.m., Monday through Friday. Activities at the CCS included singing, counting, reciting the alphabet, listening to stories, organized games, learning hygiene skills, free play and helping pick up litter.

In 2007 outcome research was undertaken to compare the psychosocial well-being and protection benefits of 3–6-year-old children who either did or did not participate in CCSs. In terms of Woodhead's four perspectives (2007), this research was influenced by two perspectives: by a *developmental perspective* emphasizing regularities in young children's physical and psychosocial growth during early childhood, as well as their vulnerabilities and resilience; and by the *social and cultural perspective*, ensuring a better understanding of local understandings of childhood and better ways to support local people and communities to care for and protect children in situations of adversity. The study used a quasi-experimental design in order to separate intervention outcomes from those attributable to other variables, comparing the effects of the CCS intervention in the IDP camp where the CCSs were running with a comparison group in a nearby IDP camp where there were no organized activities for children. The emphasis was on caretakers' perceptions of children's well-being and safety, which reflected the extensive knowledge that caretakers have of their children. The researchers made the decision not to elicit children's responses, as children in the control group had no access to follow-up support and they wanted to avoid harm (Kostelny and Wessells, 2008). However, to demonstrate value for children's perspectives as rights holders and social actors, and to increase the validity of the findings, it would have been useful to elicit the views of young children in communities where the CCSs were organized to at least analyse the extent to which children's perspectives matched or differed from their caregivers' perspectives.

The qualitative data consisted of narratives from eight focus group discussions. The focus group discussions were conducted with separate groups of elderly caregivers, single mothers and widows, and camp leaders in both groups, with eight to ten participants in each group. In the CCS group, focus group discussions were also conducted with a group of child activity leaders and a group of Child Well-Being Committee members. The focus group discussions incorporated open-ended questions about risks and dangers to young children's well-being at the present time, risks and dangers that were present a year ago, and reasons why changes had occurred.

In the CCS group, 176 households from the three CCS centers were randomly selected from the CCS register. In the comparison group, 118 households with children aged 3–6 years of age were randomly selected from the ten zones in the comparison camp. A questionnaire was undertaken with these households gathering basic demographic information and information on locally generated questions concerning children's well-being (which were identified through analysis of the focus group discussions). These questions included information on: a child's play; a child's appetite; communication needs; how a child shares with or helps others; the extent to which a child is obedient and good mannered; whether a child knows how to use a latrine correctly; and whether the child washes

his or her hands after latrine use. In addition, two items relating to protection were identified by the senior child protection team: my child is safe at home; and my child is safe in the camp. All of these items were rated using a three-point Likert scale: 'Never', 'Some of the Time' and 'Most of the Time'.

Results from this mixture of qualitative and quantitative locally derived measures of child well-being showed that children who participated in CCSs were reported to be safer in their homes and camp, had more positive social interactions with peers and adults, and learnt more life skills than children from the comparison group (Kostelny and Wessells, 2008). One of the main reasons for children's increased safety and protection was that younger children were supervised at the CCS instead of being left alone at home, where they faced increased risks of accidents, injury and neglect, including risks of sexual abuse. Children attending CCSs had learned more about how to use a latrine and personal hygiene, which contributed to preventing ill-health and disease.

The process of developing locally relevant criteria of child well-being and the robustness of the research design in this study are useful to apply in other evaluation studies concerning early years programming. However, increased efforts are required to find appropriate and ethical ways to seek young children's perspectives.

A master's thesis by Ruskin (2009) further explored the 'Effectiveness of child friendly spaces in providing early childhood interventions for 3–6-year-olds in fragile situations'. Ruskin analysed existing research, field notes and agency guidelines relating to the effective provision of interventions targeted at 3–6-year-old children in 'child-friendly spaces' (CFS) in fragile situations concomitant with armed conflict and natural disasters. The recurring themes arising from the analysis were that, while CFS provide important physical space for play and other activities, the early years expertise of agency staff is often lacking. Ruskin recommended the recruitment of early years professionals and a clearer direction for advocacy. The study also highlighted the need to investigate the tensions that can arise between communities and agencies in relation to community ownership, cultural appropriateness and the new concepts that these early childhood interventions may introduce.

Together, these studies demonstrate the salience of attending to young children's views and experiences, as well as caregivers' perspectives, in situations of armed conflict and post-conflict. The studies show the potential to undertake relatively large-scale studies, using both qualitative and quantitative methods, with considerable attention to ethical issues in diverse socio-cultural contexts. Methodologies and methods, including the extent to which younger children are engaged as actors in research and evaluation processes, are influenced by the core perspectives described by Woodhead (2007). As illustrated in the first two studies by Save the Children (2001, 2008), when applying a human rights-based approach more efforts are made to develop and apply research processes, methods and ethical guidelines which support girls' and boys' active role in the research, as well as children's role in follow-up action or advocacy initiatives. In the CCF outcome study, which drew more on developmental and social/cultural perspectives, more emphasis was placed on listening to the views of caregivers, and children's views were not sought. Although the lack of children's engagement was justified on the basis of ethical reasons that the agency would be unable to follow up concerns raised by children in non-project site areas, the ethical and methodological concerns of not listening to children's views in project areas should also have been considered.

RESEARCH CONCERNING NEUROSCIENCE, WELL-BEING AND PEACE PROMOTION

Research informed by the *developmental perspective*, particularly by emerging evidence from development neurobiology, is propelling advocacy efforts to prevent and address violence and conflict that adversely affect children and their well-being, particularly in early childhood (ECPC, 2013). A growing body of knowledge on neuroscience is demonstrating how influential the early years are in terms of health, life skills and competences, which can have positive trans-generational effects in promoting development and peace (ECPC, 2013). However, there are also many scholars, including some eminent neuroscientists and philosophers, who have queried assumptions about the reach of neuroscience, particularly due to difficulties in the tracking and measurement of cellular activities (Bruer, 2011; Tallis, 2012).

Research in neurobiology provides evidence that key brain connections are made during the early years, which provide the foundations for a child's well-being, learning and development (Fox et al., 2010). Research has also shown that under-nutrition, stressful conditions and poor stimulation during these years can affect brain structure and function, with lasting cognitive and emotional effects (Grantham-McGregor et al., 2007).

Recent neuroscience research indicates how early life experiences, especially the initial bonds formed between infants and their caregivers, influence future interactions. Increased research is required concerning the physiology involved in early life bonding and the neuropeptide oxytocin (OT). The OT system is not only involved in the process of bonding, but also interacts with multiple neurophysiological systems in the brain and body. Recent discoveries in OT research point to OT system involvement in behaviours, including trust (Van Ijzendoorn and Bakermans-Kranenberg, 2012) and cooperation (de Dreu et al., 2011), that pertain to peace. Drawing upon such research, an Ecology of Peace conceptual framework has been developed, bringing together bio-behavioural and socio-ecological models of development, and a set of hypotheses are being explored to identify the viability of promoting peace through early childhood (Yale University and ACEV Partnership, 2012; ECPC, 2013). The set of hypotheses that are being piloted are rooted in neurobiology, affiliative bonding, parent education, early learning and grassroots movements. Robust research will be required to test these hypotheses, particularly in terms of overcoming challenges concerning the reach of neuroscience. Furthermore, the lack of attention to younger children's voices in such research needs to be addressed more systematically.

KEY FINDINGS FROM APPLIED RESEARCH AND THEIR LINKS TO PRACTICE AND POLICY RECOMMENDATIONS

Key findings from applied research involving younger children reveal the importance of a number of themes. As illustrated in Table 21.1, these themes are very much reflected in recent agency and coalition programming and policy initiatives to strengthen early childhood programming in countries affected by armed conflict or disasters. These themes are also reflected in the development and application of principles for ECCD programming in diverse settings (CGECCD and INEE, 2009), which emphasize the importance of: fostering the participation of individuals, families and communities; building upon the inherent strengths of local child-rearing practices; embracing diversity; seeking programme

Table 21.1   How emerging themes from research are being applied in programming and policy interventions?

Emerging themes from applied research concerning younger children in situations of armed conflict (de Berry et al., 2003; Feinstein and O'Kane, 2008; Kostelny and Wessells, 2008):	Common programming and policy interventions by agencies, coalitions and networks to increase early childhood programming in emergencies (CGECCD and INEE 2009; the International Network on Peace Building with Young Children, 2010; the Early Childhood Peace Consortium, 2013; Plan International, 2013):
The importance of: • increasing local understandings of childhood and building on the strengths of local child rearing practices; • encouraging active participation of younger children, youth, parents, caregivers, families and communities; and • providing psychosocial support to children's caregivers and to children.	• *Strengthening children's protective environment through parents and other caregivers* including: education sessions for mothers, fathers, grandparents, elder siblings and other caregivers on child development, breastfeeding and preventable diseases, nutrition, early stimulation and learning, and non-violent communication. • *Fostering children, caregiver and community participation in ECCD programming.* • *Decreasing stress and improving psychosocial wellbeing* of children and caregivers through developmentally and culturally appropriate activities to promote psychosocial wellbeing. The establishment of child development centres, child friendly/child centered spaces to organize regular games and activities with young children and their caregivers are encouraged.
The need to recognise children's holistic needs and to ensure integrated approaches to maternal and child health, nutrition, water and sanitation, education, protection and family livelihoods.	• *Supporting integrated early childhood care and development initiatives.* Community-based, non-formal child development centres to provide preschool learning activities through play that are integrated with health care, nutritious meals, clean water, latrines, and child safety initiatives. For example, practical guidance to integrate ECCD interventions into other humanitarian sector responses (e.g. water sanitation and hygiene, health, nutrition, education, protection) as part of the humanitarian response are outlined in the CGECCD and INEE (2009) publication *The Path of Most Resilience.*
The need to address immediate protection risks and threats facing girls and boys in their local environments.	• *Strengthening resilience and reducing vulnerability* by integrating disaster risk reduction and crisis-sensitive planning into all phases of programming. For example, through play based activities children as young as three years old can be involved in risk reduction initiatives in their homes, pre-schools and communities and can be better prepared for emergencies.
The importance of • preventing family violence and use of corporal punishment; and violence; • addressing discrimination; and • ensuring children's needs and rights are prioritized in reconstruction, peace and good governance processes.	• *Addressing discrimination due to gender, disability, HIV and other factors* to reduce vulnerability and to increase access of all children to basic services. • *Increasing peace building initiatives* with a focus on early childhood development, promoting effective non-violent communication in families, pre-schools, schools and communities and increasing human and financial investments in peace building initiatives at different levels (national, sub-national, local).

integration; and building child-focused partnerships.

Moreover, there is increased recognition that research, programming and policy developments concerning younger children and ECCD in emergencies are under-developed, thus contributing to a number of 'calls to action' for increased investments in this area.

'CALLS TO ACTION' TO MOVE THE AGENDA FORWARD

The lack of sufficient research and weak evidence base for ECCD in emergencies, as well as the failure of donors, governments and the humanitarian community to prioritize ECCD in emergencies, have been identified by the CGECCD and INEE (2009) and Plan International (2013) as two key interrelated obstacles, contributing to a lack of implementation of large-scale high quality ECCD programming in emergencies. Various 'calls to action' are being advocated for by different child rights agencies and coalitions (CGECCD and INEE, 2009; International Network on Peace Building with Young Children, 2010; ECPC, 2013; Plan International, 2013) to increase the scale and quality of interventions for young children affected by conflict and other emergencies.

Concerted advocacy and engagement with government stakeholders are called for, as governments are the primary duty bearers with responsibilities to develop and implement early childhood policies and programmes. It is recognized that advocacy started during an emergency response can prompt dialogue with government, which can eventually lead to increased commitment and longer-term investments in ECCD services and policies.

An overview of coalition and agency global initiatives on early childhood and emergencies

In 2009 the Consultative Group on Early Childhood Care and Development and the Inter-Agency Network for Education in Emergencies jointly published *The Path of Most Resilience: Early childhood care and development in emergencies – Principles and practice.* This Working Paper serves as a starting point, an opportunity to outline foundational principles of the field of early childhood care and development (ECCD) in emergencies. *Four Cornerstones to Secure a Strong Foundation for Young Children*, previously developed by the CGECCD, are interpreted and adapted for use in crisis situations. Furthermore, the principles and findings are being used to update a Good Practice Guide for ECCD in emergencies.

Plan International's (2013) *Investing in the Youngest: Early childhood care and development in emergencies* report promotes increased provision of immediate, life-saving, multi-sectoral support for young children from conception to 8 years, outlining eight key intervention areas. Plan advocates that ECCD in emergencies should last for more than a year, addressing children's multiple needs and strengthening their protective environment.

An Early Childhood Peace Consortium was launched in New York on 20 September 2013. The consortium currently brings together partners seeking to reduce violence and to promote and sustain peace in homes, schools, neighbourhoods and countries. It primarily draws upon emerging evidence from neurobiology indicating how our early life bonds (e.g., parents and children) can have an impact on our physiology in ways that influence peace building. The Early Childhood Peace Consortium seeks to partner with and complement the goals of other networks and organizations working to advance proven and sustainable early childhood interventions and peace building.

The International Network on Peace Building with Young Children was formed in November 2004 as a partnership between the World Forum Foundation and Early Years – the Organisation for Young Children. It consists of early childhood specialists, teachers, practitioners, academics and representatives from civil society organizations from the majority and minority world representing such conflict-affected regions. The Network has supported the development of programmatic and advocacy tools supporting innovation in the field of peace building in early childhood care and education (see International Network of Peace Building with Young Children, 2010) and has piloted a master's programme in Early Years and Conflict that encourages a rights-based approach and provides practitioners with a more focused knowledge of how to work with young children in conflict.

Common advocacy and policy recommendations urge donor agencies, governments and the humanitarian community to:

- increase financial and human resource investment in ECCD in emergencies
- increase research on early childhood in conflict, disaster and peace building settings, especially through coordinated initiatives involving academia, government and non-government agencies and donors. Greater efforts are needed to involve younger children and caregivers in research, and to undertake more research and evaluations, including longitudinal research to assess the impact of ECCD programmes on conflict, disaster and peace-building settings
- raise awareness around the importance of including ECCD programming in emergency situations to meet young children's diverse needs in each emergency phase, from emergency preparedness and planning to an actual emergency, transition, recovery, reconstruction and peace building
- establish global minimum standards and frameworks for ECCD in emergencies
- support coordination and inter-sector collaboration among the main actors in emergencies to ensure the holistic needs of young children are taken into account; and to integrate ECCD into national policies and plans across sectors.

CONCLUSION

There is growing recognition that there is insufficient research, programming and policy guidance to address the needs and rights of children in the early years in communities affected by armed conflict, insecurity and other emergencies (Bernard van Leer Foundation, 2005; Wessells and Monteiro, 2008; CGECCD and INEE, 2009; Akesson, 2012; Plan International, 2013). The first eight years of a child's life are the most critical in terms of cognitive, physical, social and emotional development (Grantham-McGregor et al., 2007; Fox et al., 2010). Armed conflict and insecurity, as well as conflict and violence in families, create stressful and detrimental conditions that adversely affect young children's development, well-being and

protection. Thus, it is critical that increased investments are made in research, practice and policy developments to increase the protection and fulfilment of children's rights in the early years in conflict, post-conflict and peace building.

All children have the right to access basic services, including in contexts affected by armed conflict, insecurity and/or disaster. Furthermore, it is recognized that emergencies provide a 'window of opportunity' to introduce or to strengthen ECCD provision and that minimum standards on early ECCD in emergencies are needed. As articulated by the CGECCD and INEE:

> Policy makers must rethink the way the emergency response is carried out so that the rights and needs of young children and their families are fully recognized and centred in humanitarian relief. Continued coordinated efforts must be made to make interventions effective and accountable, strengthen collective advocacy, and develop concrete policy and programmatic frameworks to prioritise ECCD as a core intervention in crisis settings. (2009: 4)

Participatory research and evaluations involving young girls and boys and their caregivers in conflict-affected communities can provide crucial insights and lessons learned to inform the development of minimum standards, as well as practice and policy guidance for early childhood initiatives in emergencies. Participatory research involving younger children and their caregivers can also inform the development of culturally appropriate indicators for ECCD services, ensuring disaggregated data concerning gender, ethnicity, religion, disability and other factors.

Ongoing efforts to apply a child rights and ecological framework which approaches young children in the context of their families, communities and wider socio-political, cultural and economic context are required to ensure systematic approaches to programming and advocacy which better support early childhood development in conflict-affected settings. Moreover, greater efforts are needed to develop and apply ethical and methodological approaches that support younger children's meaningful participation in applied research so that the lived experiences and perspectives of girls and boys in diverse contexts affected by insecurity and conflict can be better understood and responded to. The recent guidance developed by Johnson et al. (2014) provides a wealth of practical advice and innovative methods that can be applied to support such efforts. In recognizing the roles of older children in caring for younger siblings in many parts of the world, increased efforts should also be made to pilot child-to-child research methodologies, enabling slightly older children (for example, aged 9–17 years) to research and document the lives of younger children (aged 2–8 years) in their communities.

A number of agencies are mobilized to take forward their 'calls to action' for increased investment in ECCD in emergencies. Increased collaboration among these coalitions and networks, and stronger partnerships with academic institutions within each country and continent, will support innovation and scale-up in applied research, engaging younger children to better understand and respond to diverse childhood experiences in conflict settings.

FURTHER READING

Consultative Group on Early Childhood Care and Development (CGECCD) and the Inter-agency Network for Education in Emergencies (INEE) (2009) The Path of Most Resistance: Early Childhood Care and Development in Emergencies: Principles and Practice (www.ineesite.org/uploads/files/resources/ECCD_in_Emergencies_Principles_and_Practice_DRAFT_2503.pdf).

Johnson, V., Hart, R. and Colwell, J. (2014) *Steps to Engaging Young Children in Research. Volume I: The guide*. Brighton: University of Brighton, Education Research Centre and the Bernard van Leer Foundation (www.bernard-vanleer.org/files/Steps-to-Engaging-Young-Children-in-Research-vol-1.pdf).

Yale University and ACEV Partnership (2012) *The Ecology of Peace: Formative childhoods and peacebuilding*. A brief note, November.

New Haven, CT and Istanbul, Turkey: Yale-ACEV Partnership (www.acev.org/docs/ingilizce-kaynaklar/peacebuilding_ecd_briefnote.pdf?sfvrsn=2).

QUESTIONS FOR REFLECTION

1   How can donors and governments be encouraged to increase investments in applied research concerning the early years, conflict, post-conflict and peace building?
2   How can academia work in partnership with child-focused agencies and governments to increase ethical applied research with children in the early years in situations affected by conflict in diverse locations?
3   How can participatory research with children in settings affected by conflict be used to influence the development of culturally appropriate indicators for evaluating the effectiveness of ECCD services?
4   How can child-to-child research be better supported? For example, how can children and young people older than 8 years support the meaningful participation and engagement of younger children under 8 in participatory research processes?
5   What early experiences in the family act as resilience factors in the development of neuropeptide oxytocin (OT) functioning? How can findings from such applied research inform positive parenting and peace-building efforts?

NOTES

1   All governments have ratified the CRC except for the USA.
2   The organization is now known as Child Fund International.
3   Sometimes known as 'Child Friendly Spaces'.

REFERENCES

Action for the Rights of Children (ARC) (2009) ARC Resource Pack: A capacity building tool for child protection in and after emergencies (www.arc-online.org).

Akesson, B. (2011) *Research with Young Children affected by Family Violence:*

Proposing a robust research agenda. The Hague: Bernard van Leer Foundation.

Akesson, B. (2012) 'The concept and meaning of place for young children affected by political violence in the Occupied Palestine Territories: Spaces and flows', *An International Journal of Urban and Extra Urban Studies*, (2) 2: 245–56.

Bernard van Leer Foundation (2005) *Early Childhood Matters: Responses to young children in post-emergency situations*. The Hague: Bernard van Leer Foundation.

Boyden, J. and Ennew, J. (eds) (1997) *Children in Focus: A manual for experiential learning in participatory research with children*. Stockholm: Radda Barnen.

Boyden, J. and Mann, G. (2005) 'Children's risk, resilience, and coping in extreme situations', in M. Ungar (ed.), *Handbook for Working with Children and Youth: Pathways to resilience across cultures and contexts*. Thousand Oaks, CA: SAGE, pp. 3–25.

Bruer, J. (2011) *Revisiting the Myth of the First Three Years*. Paper presented at the University of Kent Parenting Conference, May (http://blogs.kent.ac.uk/parentingculturestudies/files/2011/09/Special-briefing-on-The-Myth.pdf).

Clark, A. and Moss, P. (2005) *Spaces to Play: More listening to young children using the Mosaic approach*. London: National Children's Bureau.

Consultative Group on Early Childhood Care and Development (CGECCD) and the Inter-Agency Network for Education in Emergencies (INEE) (2009) The Path of Most Resistance: Early Childhood Care and Development in Emergencies: Principles and Practice.

De Berry, J., Fazil, A., Farhad, S., Nasiry, F., Hashemi, S. and Hakimi, M. (2003) *The Children of Kabul: Discussions with Afghan families*. Kabul: Save the Children and UNICEF.

De Dreu, C.K., Greer, L.L., Van Kleef, G.A., Shalvi, S. and Handgraaf, M.J. (2011) 'Oxytocin promotes human ethnocentrism', *Proceedings of the National Academy of Sciences USA*, 108 (4): 1262–66.

Early Childhood Peace Consortium (ECPC) (2013) Concept Note, September.

Feinstein, C. and O'Kane, C. (2008) Global Report: Adults' War and Young Generations' Peace: Children's Participation in Armed Conflict, Post Conflict and Peace Building. Oslo: Save the Children Norway (http://resourcecentre.savethechildren.se/library/global-report-adults-war-and-young-generations-peace-childrens-participation-armed-conflict).

Fox, S., Levitt, P. and Nelson, C. (2010) 'How the timing and quality of early experiences influences the development of brain architecture', *Child Development*, 81 (1): 28–40.

Grantham-McGregor, S., Cheung, Y.B., Cueto, S., Glewwe, P., Richter, L. and Strupp, B. (2007) 'Developmental potential in the first five years for children in developing countries', *Lancet*, 369: 66–70.

Harcourt, D. and Einarsdottir, J. (2011) 'Introducing children's perspectives and participation into research', *European Early Childhood Education Research Journal*, 19 (3): 301–7.

Hart, J. and Tyrer, B. (2006) *Research with Children Living in Situations of Armed Conflict: Concepts, ethics and methods*. Oxford: Refugee Studies Centre, Working Paper No. 30.

Hart, J., Galappatti, A., Boyden, J. and Armstrong, M. (2007) 'Participatory tools for evaluating psychosocial work with children in areas of armed conflict: A pilot in eastern Sri Lanka', *Intervention*, 5 (1): 41–60.

Hayden, J., Dunn, R. and Cologen, K. (2010) 'Early Childhood Care and Development in Emergency Situations: Annotated Bibliography', prepared for the Inter-Agency Network on Education in Emergencies, the Early Childhood on Emergencies Working Group and the Consultative Group on Early Childhood Care and Development.

Inter-Agency Network on Education in Emergencies (INEE) (2010) INEE Minimum Standards for Education: Preparedness, Response and Recovery (www.ineesite.org/eietrainingmodule/cases/learningistheirfuture/pdf/Minimum_Standards_English_2010.pdf).

International Network on Peace Building with Young Children (2010) Paper One: Protecting and Providing for Young Children in Regions Affected by Conflict – A Framework for Practice, June (www.early-years.org/international/docs/protecting-and-providing-regions.pdf).

James, A. and Prout, A. (eds) (1990) *Constructing and Reconstructing Childhood*. London: Falmer Press.

Johnson, V., Hart, R. and Colwell, J. (2014) *Steps to Engaging Young Children in Research*. Brighton: University of Brighton,

Education Research Centre and the Bernard van Leer Foundation.

Kostelny, K. and Wessells, M. (2008) 'The protection and psychosocial well-being of young children following armed conflict: Outcome research on child-centered spaces in Northern Uganda', *Journal of Developmental Processes*, 3(2): 13–25.

Landers, C. (1998) *Listen to Me: Protecting the development of young children in armed conflict*. New York: UNICEF (Office of Emergency Programs Working Paper Series).

Lansdown, G. (2005) *The Evolving Capacities of the Child*. Innocenti Insight. Florence: UNICEF Innocenti Research Centre.

Lloyd, E. and Penn, H. (2010) 'Working with young children who are victims of armed conflict', *Contemporary Issues in Early Childhood*, 2 (3): 278–87.

MacNaughton, G., Hughes, P. and Smith, K. (2007) 'Young children's rights and public policy: Practices and possibilities for citizenship in the early years', *Children and Society*, 21: 458–69.

Office of the Special Representative of the Secretary-General for Children and Armed Conflict in collaboration with UNICEF (2009) Machel Study 10-Year Strategic Review: Children and Conflict in a Changing World (www.unicef.org/publications/index_49985. html).

O'Kane, C. (2003) 'Street and working children's participation in programming for their rights: Conflicts arising from diverse perspectives and directions for convergence', *Children, Youth and Environments*, 13(1), Spring.

O'Kane, C. (2008) 'The development of participatory techniques: Facilitating children's views about decisions which affect them', in P. Christensen and A. James (eds), *Research with Children: Perspectives and practice*, 2nd edn. London and New York: Routledge.

Pence, A. and Ashton, E. (2014) *The Whole of Humanity: Hearing Africa*.

Penn, H. (2011) 'Travelling policies and global buzzwords: How international non-governmental organisations and charities spread the word about early childhood in the global South', *Childhood*, 18 (1): 94–113.

Plan International (2013) *Investing in the Youngest: Early childhood care and development in emergencies*. Woking: Plan International.

Ruskin, L. A. (2009) 'Exploring the effectiveness of Child Friendly Spaces in providing Early Childhood Interventions for 3-6 year olds in fragile situations'. MA Education and International Development: 85, London: Institute of Education. *Unpublished*. Available at http://www.ineesite.org/uploads/files/resources/Ruskin_Dissertation_Exploring_the_effectiveness_of_Child_Friendly_Spaces_2009.pdf

Save the Children (2001) *Conversations with Families: To prepare for early childhood programming*. Participatory research handbook. Kathmandu: Save the Children.

Save the Children (2008) *Last in line, last in school: How donors can support education for children affected by conflict and emergencies*. London: Save the Children.

Smith, A. (2007) 'Children's rights and early childhood education links to theory and advocacy', *Australian Journal of Early Childhood*, 32 (3): 1–8.

Tallis, R. (2012) *Aping Mankind: Neuromania, Darwinitis, and the misrepresentation of humanity*. Bristol: Acumen.

Tisdall, K., Davis, J.M., Hill, M. and Prout, A. (eds) (2006) *Participation for What: Children, young people and social inclusion*. Bristol: Policy Press.

United Nations (UN) (1989) *UN Convention on the Rights of the Child*. Geneva: UNCRC.

United Nations (UN) (1996) Impact of Armed Conflict on Children: Report of the Expert of the Secretary-General, Ms Graça Machel, submitted pursuant to General Assembly Resolution 48/157, UN document A/51/306, New York, 26 August.

United Nations (UN) (2005) *Implementing Child Rights in Early Childhood, General Comment No. 7*. Geneva: UNCRC (www2.ohchr.org/english/bodies/crc/docs/AdvanceVersions/GeneralComment7Rev1.pdf).

Van Ijzendoorn, M.H. and Bakermans-Kranenberg, M.J. (2012) 'A sniff of trust: Meta-analysis of the effects of intranasal oxytocin administration on face recognition, trust to in-group, and trust to out-group', *Psychoneuroendrocrinology*, 37 (3): 438–43.

Wessells, M. and Monteiro, C. (2008) 'Supporting young children in conflict and post conflict situations: Child protection and psychosocial well-being in Angola', in M. Garcia, A. Pence and J.L. Evans (eds),

Africa's Future, Africa's Challenge: Early Childhood Care and Development in Sub-Saharan Africa. Washington, DC: The World Bank.

Woodhead, M. (2007) 'Changing perspectives on early childhood: Theory, research and policy', paper commissioned for the Education for All Global Monitoring Report 2007, Strong Foundations: Early childhood care and education.

Yale University and ACEV Partnership (2012) *The Ecology of Peace: Formative childhoods and peacebuilding*. A brief note. New Haven, CT and Istanbul, Turkey: Yale–ACEV Partnership.

22

Dual Language Learners

Eugene E. Garcia

INTRODUCTION

Millions of children around the globe are acquiring more than one language in the home and in early childhood education and care (ECEC) settings (McCabe et al., 2013). The growing body of evidence indicates that young children around the world can attain proficiency in more than one language at an early age (Baker, 2000; Barac and Bialystok, 2012; Genesee, 2010) and that instructional arrangements targeting these children specifically can produce positive developmental and learning outcomes (Calderón, 2010; California Department of Education, 2010; Castro et al., 2011; Chan, 2004; David and Wei, 2008; Fairbairn and Jones-Vo, 2010; Guofang et al., 2010; Oller and Eilers, 2002; Wright, 2010). Yet, the processes by which development and learning occur for young children acquiring two or more languages are quite complex.

Unfortunately, the mounting evidence indicates that dual language learners[1] (DLLs) – young children, birth to age 5, who are learning a majority language as a second language, while acquiring a minority language as their first, growing up between two cultures and languages – have the potential for low performance on developmental outcome assessments and later school failure (García and García, 2012). National statistics and evaluation studies in the USA indicate that DLLs of immigrants and indigenous families have lower school achievement than students who speak the dominant language as their only language. At the beginning and throughout their K-12 schooling, DLLs lag behind their monolingual, same age and grade peers at all proficiency levels of reading and mathematics, by at least a half of a standard deviation (García and Miller, 2008).

Although some of the differences are accounted for by socioeconomic variances between groups (on average, DLLs have lower socio-economic status (SES) and lower indicators of median family income and educational level of adult family members than monolingual whites and Asian-Americans), much of it is not (Reardon and Galindo, 2006). As early as 2001, the Early Childhood Longitudinal Study (NCES, 2001) reported that DLLs scored .3 to .5 of a standard deviation lower in mathematics and reading than their monolingual peers within all five SES quintiles (SES in ECLS-K is a composite of household income and parents' level of education and occupation). A separate analysis of ECLS-K data noted that these achievement differences by SES and race/ethnicity from kindergarten through first grade were attributable to processes within, between and out of school (Reardon, 2003). That is, practices in the home and school, including the use of a language other than English, bear meaningful influences on racial/ethnic and SES achievement gaps in early education.

Similar analysis of achievement gaps are not readily available in other countries, however significant research related to the linguistic, cognitive and socio-emotional development of DLLs has provided a more extensive view of bilingual development and is addressed in this review (Campbell and Sais, 1995; Carlson and Meltzoff, 2008; De Houwer, 1995; Döpke, 1998; Junker and Stockman, 2002; Kim, 2009). What is evident, internationally, is a deep concern for the absence of educational opportunities for the world's youngest children. UNESCO's report, *Education for All* (2001), indicated that over 100 million primary school age children are denied the chance to go to school, and by not attending to early schooling endeavors a significant human resource to our global wellbeing is placed at risk. At the same time, Malone (2001) reminds us that over 6000 languages are spoken worldwide, with an estimated 1 billion people who are speakers of lesser known languages, many of these unwritten. Despite the language and literacy educational agenda for our youngest children, language concerns, worldwide, are normally not at the forefront of planning and implementation of educational agendas (Cazden et al., 1990). UNICEF has addressed this issue in *The State of the World's Children* (1999) by pointing out that if the language of

formal instruction is not the language of the family, learning difficulties can accumulate over the child's educational experience. This UNICEF report also suggested that children who are provided with instruction in their 'mother' tongue are more likely to be successful in acquiring academic skill in a second language. This review will delve deeper into the circumstances initially addressed in this international report on linguistic diversity among our youngest children and their early educational experiences and outcomes.

In sum, with the growing numbers of DLLs in the USA and globally, the impact of dual language exposure on developmental and learning attributes and circumstances of this population is important for ECEC settings. Therefore, in this chapter an overview is provided of what is known about DLLs in ECEC settings. A historical overview of early learning circumstances in the USA sets the context for the discussion, highlighting programs and policies that have been influential in recent years, particularly those where attention to this population has grown significantly because of the large number of DLLs – some 25% of the overall 0–5 age range (García and García, 2012). The chapter then addresses what is currently known about DLLs in early education, specifically the research in the USA, as well as other countries, related to (1) program models in ECEC settings, (2) curricular and instructional best practices in ECEC, (3) early language and literacy development, and (4) the benefits of bilingualism. The chapter closes with a discussion of future directions necessary for improving not only ECEC circumstances of DLLs, but also for expanding what we know about and how we understand bilingual development and learning in early childhood.

HISTORICAL OVERVIEW: DLLs AND EARLY EDUCATION CIRCUMSTANCES IN THE USA

The common phrase, 'demography is destiny', is applicable to present educational circumstances. Currently, at least one in five children aged 5–17 in the USA has a foreign-born parent (Capps et al., 2005) and many of these children learn English as their additional language. The overall child population speaking a language other than English in the USA rose from 6% in 1979 to 14% in 2010 (García and Náñez, 2011). DLLs have been the fastest growing segment of the US population over the past few decades, due primarily to increased rates in (legal and illegal) immigration, as well as to high birth rates among immigrant families (Hernández et al., 2008). The representation of children who are developing English as an additional language in US schools has its highest concentration in early education (preschool and kindergarten). While the majority come from Spanish-speaking immigrant families, DLLs represent many national origins and more than 350 languages.

HEAD START: THE FEDERAL EFFORT IN THE USA AND DLLs

Historically in the USA, DLLs have been underrepresented in all forms of early learning provided in the private sector or in the public sector (state and locally funded efforts) including Head Start (García and García, 2012). However, their participation rates are steadily increasing. The percentage of Latino children in Head Start has grown steadily since 1992 when only about 19% of Latino children were served in the program, to 32% in 2007. Notwithstanding this steady progress, participation in Head Start remains a challenge for DLLs, particularly those who reside in states where immigrants have not traditionally targeted residence. In addition, a lack of resources to expand the Migrant and Seasonal Head Start and Early Head Start programs thwarts the participation of hundreds of thousands of DLLs eligible for these programs.

On 12 December 2007, President Bush signed into law the Improving Head Start for School Readiness Act of 2007 (P.L. 110–134). This was the first reauthorization of Head Start in nearly ten years. Various provisions were included in the new law, which helped to ensure that DLLs – the vast majority of whom are Latino – fully benefit from Head Start's services.

The Improving Head Start for School Readiness Act 2007 provides a framework for expanding Head Start in two important ways. First, it creates a mechanism for accurately determining the percentage of eligible children compared to the number of children served on a consistent basis. Second, the legislation requires that the US Health and Human Services Secretary ensures a plan be developed to identify and alleviate enrollment barriers to programs. The reauthorization and more recent investments in Head Start have improved the funding structure for all programs. This expansion and stability in Head Start has offered more opportunities related to early learning, specifically for the growing population of DLLs.

Accompanying these opportunity enhancements are adopted principles by Head Start with regard to DLLs. In the revised Multicultural Principles for Head Start Programs, several principles are outlined (García and Frede, 2010):

- Every individual is rooted in their culture and language.
- Every individual has the right to maintain his or her own identity while acquiring the skills required to function in a diverse society.
- Effective programs for children who speak languages other than English require development of the first language while the acquisition of English is facilitated.

Unfortunately, beyond Head Start, these principles are not adopted in many early learning venues serving DLLs in the USA (Espinosa, 2010a). However, emerging research has begun to shed light on the circumstances and effectiveness of early childhood education for DLLs.

CURRENT STATE OF KNOWLEDGE: DLLs IN ECEC SETTINGS – EARLY EDUCATION PROGRAM MODELS FOR DLLs

While there are many possible program options for bilingual students and children learning English as a second language in K–12 educational settings (García and García, 2012), the variation in program options for DLLs in ECEC settings is not as great. Typical programs include English Immersion, Transitional Bilingual Education and Dual Language Bilingual Education (DLBE). Each of these programs differs in the way in which it uses the language other than English and English during instruction and within the learning environment (Ovando et al., 2006). Each also differs in theoretical rationale, language goals, cultural goals, academic goals, student characteristics and instructional materials.

At one end of this continuum of programs are those characterized by minimal use of the students' home language (English immersion). At the other end of this continuum are programs that have as their goal bilingual proficiency DLBE. For all the programs, irrespective of their position on the continuum, optimizing individual achievement and literacy development is a critical feature. In the early years, a holistic approach is especially important. Variations across programs can be described by the ways in which programs support the development of the whole child and how language exposure and use (in one or more languages) sustain the cognitive, social, emotional and psychological development of DLLs. The extent to which a program is successful depends on local conditions, choices and innovations. Because communities differ (e.g., by socio-demographic conditions) and local and state policies demand assorted objectives from early learning environments, no single program works best in every situation.

Evidence in various US sites is beginning to emerge, indicating that DLBE can be an excellent model for academic achievement for both bilingual and monolingual children.

At the early education level, an experimental study compared the effects of a DLBE and a monolingual English immersion (EI) preschool program on children's learning (Barnett et al., 2007). Children in the study ($N = 150$) were from both English and Spanish home language backgrounds; 85 were randomly assigned to the DLBE program and 65 to the EI program in the same school district. The two programs were compared on measures of children's growth in language, emergent literacy and mathematics. Compared to those in the EI group, children in the DLBE program produced large and significant gains in Spanish vocabulary. In addition, all children (including native Spanish and native English speakers) in the DLBE program made greater phonological awareness gains in English, yet no group differences were found on measures of English language and literacy development. This study, therefore, suggests that early DLBE programs can provide support for home language development without sacrificing gains in English language development. Moreover, English monolingual children also made gains in Spanish language and literacy without hindering their English language development.

THE INTERNATIONAL EFFORTS OF MOTHER TONGUE INSTRUCTION

Outside of the USA, DLBE programs for young learners are often identified as mother tongue (MT) programs of instruction. Like DLBE programs in the USA, these ECEC efforts recognize that early instruction endeavors with children and families that speak a language that is not the predominant language of the schooling environment should receive instruction in one form or another in the home language (López, 2000). Reports from Northern Europe, which has seen migration of Turkish and Arabic speakers to that region, indicate that MT programs have been implemented with positive results for newly arrived immigrant populations

(Komarek, 1996; Verhoeven and Aarts, 2005). On the African continent where there is an abundance of linguistic and cultural diversity, and where more than one language is recognized as an 'official' national language, MT programs are aligned with the teacher preparation program to ensure implementation of the model (Wagner, 2005). Even in very diverse linguistic communities like those in Papua New Guinea, incorporation of various home languages into early instruction has proved to be beneficial (Klaus, 2001).

EFFECTIVE PRACTICES FOR DLLs IN EARLY EDUCATION

Features of high-quality early learning programs serving monolingual English speakers have been studied for some time (Barnett et al., 2007; Camilli et al., 2010; Dickinson, 2011; Dickinson and Neuman, 2006; Espinosa, 2003). There is an overlap between effective practices for DLLs and effective practices for all students (Espinosa, 2010b). However, the emerging research suggests that in order to create optimal development and learning environments, general best practices for ECEC must be enhanced for young students developing two languages simultaneously. These include bilingual exposure and use in early learning programs, bilingual instruction and assessment practices, and appropriate teacher training/development.

Language Exposure and Use

While the debate on bilingual education in the USA and other countries is often politically charged and often associated with debates about immigration and the status of immigrants in destination countries (Gándara and Hopkins, 2010; Skutnabb-Kangas, 1994) with varying profiles internationally (Genesee, 2010; Oller and Eilers, 2002), there is a general consensus across educators, researchers and policy makers that in order to

be successful in formal schooling, all students need to develop proficiency in the language[s] of the school. The debate focuses on how to best support young language learners' acquisition of schooling language; on whether academic proficiency in schooling must come at the cost of the loss of a student's home language or whether a student's home language can play a role in language and academic development in the formal education setting.

Specific to language use and exposure in ECEC settings in the USA, research indicates that supporting DLLs' home languages while adding English promotes higher levels of achievement in English (Barnett et al., 2007; Bernhard et al., 2006; Durán et al., 2010; Farver et al., 2009; Winsler et al., 1999). These studies reflect themes from separate meta-analysis on the effectiveness of bilingual instruction: at best, ECEC instruction that systematically includes a DLL's home language contributes to growth in both English and the home language; at worst, there is no difference in English achievement, but an advantage in home language development (Greene, 1998; Rolstad et al., 2005; Slavin and Cheung, 2005). On a more international scale, research evidence suggests highly positive benefits in areas of language and cognitive sensitivities and executive function for dual language instruction in ECEC settings (Yow and Markman, 2011; Zelazo et al., 2003).

Curriculum, Instruction and Assessment

Effective ECEC instructional practices in the USA appear to be beneficial for both English-only speaking students and DLLs (Farver et al., 2009; Jackson et al., 2006). Similar evidence is reported for this benefit in other countries (Luk and Bialystok, 2008; Romaine, 2004). However, some elements of effective teaching in ECEC settings prove to be especially necessary for DLLs. These include strategies to support comprehension, vocabulary development and literacy.

Effective strategies for developing comprehension for DLLs include supporting students' oral language skills. Shared reading and activities that promote listening compression have proven effective in this area (University of Chicago, 2010). Context-embedded learning also supports comprehension (Lindholm-Leary and Genesee, 2010; Mathematica Policy Research, 2010; Rasmussen et al., 2006). DLLs benefit from the use of visuals, songs, chants, rhymes, physical gestures and concrete objects. Strategies for developing comprehension, even through listening activities, will have lasting effects on students' reading comprehension abilities as they progress into elementary school. Another area linked to later reading success is vocabulary development. Strategies proven effective for DLLs include taking the time to explain new words encountered during reading, and helping students learn how words are used in different contexts (Collins, 2010; Kim, 2009; Paik and Mix, 2003).

Along with comprehension and vocabulary, there are strategies related to literacy development that are effective for DLLs. First, incorporating the home language and culture into learning engagements, such as read-alouds or curriculum themes, helps DLLs stay engaged and interested in learning (August and Shanahan, 2006; González et al., 2005). Teachers can use select words from a child's home language to activate prior knowledge and connect new learning to what a child already knows (Bransford et al., 2000; Gillanders and Castro, 2011).

Parallel to effective curriculum and instructional approaches, assessment practices must also be specific to DLLs. Unfortunately, assessments are not always available in languages other than English and/or have been normed to monolingual development (Espinosa and López, 2007). Without appropriate assessment measures, ECEC teachers and program developers cannot accurately assess DLLs' development and learning; ineffective assessments affect practice, as teachers may adjust instruction and curriculum based on incorrect assessment data.

While more appropriate measures are being developed, ECEC teachers must understand the ways in which assessments accurately and inaccurately portray bilingual development and learning. Once teachers have analyzed assessments for their appropriateness, they then need to assess and monitor bilingual and biliteracy development. Classroom assessments are necessary for adjustments to curriculum and for the identification of students who may need extra support (Lesaux and Siegel, 2003). In order for teachers to understand and use the effective practices discussed above, teacher preparation and teacher development programs must promote the qualities, knowledge and skills specific to working with young bilingual learners.

LANGUAGE AND LITERACY DEVELOPMENT

Research on the language and literacy development of DLLs is relatively new in comparison to the research that exists on the language and literacy development of monolingual language users. However, based on two recent, comprehensive reviews of the literature, there are some things we know about their language and literacy development. Hammer and colleagues (2014) note four key findings from their review of 139 peer-reviewed articles. First, through studies investigating phonology, grammar, vocabulary and pragmatics, strong evidence indicates that young bilingual learners know how to differentiate between the two languages from very early in life; that the two languages influence each other; and that they are not negatively affected by exposure to, and use of, two languages during the early developmental years. Second, development of abilities in the two languages varies depending on when students were exposed to each language and on the available opportunities to use both languages. Third, when compared to monolinguals, bilingual and biliteracy development differs in some important ways. With regard to phonological abilities, as infants, DLLs are behind monolinguals, but then catch up during the preschool years. Also, while their vocabulary in their individual languages is smaller than that of monolinguals, when both languages are combined, their vocabulary is equal to that of monolinguals. Finally, in relation to overall literacy development, there is evidence to suggest that often DLLs enter preschool with literacy skills in English that are lower than those of monolinguals. Hammer and colleagues end their review by noting that there is still much to learn about the language and literacy development of DLLs and that more research is needed (Hammer et al., 2014).

The second review, by Dixon and colleagues (2012), focused on literature about second language acquisition. Their review synthesized information from 71 empirical studies across four bodies of work: foreign language education, child language research, socio-cultural studies and psycholinguistics, to highlight an integrated understanding across typically isolated perspectives on the optimal conditions for second language acquisition. While this review focused on second language acquisition more broadly (studies included participants of all ages, infants to adults), there are implications from the review that can inform our understanding of the language and literacy development of DLLs. First, findings from the review suggest that strong home literacy practices in a learner's first language (L1) and strong L1 skills are characteristics of a successful second language (L2) acquisition experience. This is consistent with one of the key findings stated above, that the development of two languages does not hinder bilingual development, but, rather, strengthens language development in a second language. Dixon and colleagues also report that effective teachers of language learners are proficient in their students' first language. Effective teachers and caregivers know and use the languages of their young learners. Lastly, the review found that younger learners typically take longer to become proficient in a second language. This finding is pertinent to ECEC contexts (and correlates with the review by Hammer and colleagues) as it shows that while DLLs are developing two languages from birth to age 5, they may need additional time to reach proficiency in their two languages. Even though at the start of kindergarten, DLLs may appear behind their monolingual English-speaking peers, with time and opportunities for exposure and use of both languages, not only will they acquire proficiency in multiple languages but also catch up to their monolingual peers in regard to English language and literacy achievement. Problems with their bilingual development arise when support for their bilingualism is taken away. When classrooms place emphasis solely on English development as early as kindergarten, DLLs' development in their first language is stunted and their abilities in English continue to fall behind those of their English-speaking grade-level peers. Unfortunately, the disconnect between ECEC policies and practices and those typically used in K–12 classrooms means that once they enter kindergarten, DLLs are not provided with the time and support they need to reach their optimal development in either language. This means that they cannot reap the cognitive benefits that research on bilingualism has identified (see Bialystok et al., 2005; Kormi-Nouri, et al., 2008).

COGNITION

Given the specific issues related to bilingual development, attention to the cognitive intersections of bilingualism and instruction becomes a critical component. Reviewed more extensively elsewhere (Barac and Bialystok, 2012; García and Náñez, 2011), and summarized here, young bilinguals are more able to control their attention while engaged in nonverbal and linguistics tasks, such as mathematical problem solving and use of vocabulary with multiple meanings.

In doing so, they are more capable of attending to or controlling their attention to selective aspects of their environment (to focus on important and critical aspects of their surroundings that assist in making meaning), an inherent task in using two languages to communicate effectively. In addition, access to working memory seems to be enhanced for bilinguals. The ability to inhibit one language while using the other increases the efficiency of working memory. For example, bilingual children, in their communication activity, must determine what language and code within a language is needed to achieve a particular communication result. In some cases, they may even switch between their two languages within any one utterance to achieve more meaningful communication outcomes, identified as 'code-switching'.

Bilinguals also show advanced abilities to problem solve. This is particularly the case in executive control functions like planning, rule acquisition, abstract thinking and cognitive flexibility. Since bilinguals must choose between two languages and all the complexities related to the use of those languages, these executive functions are enhanced. Similarly, bilinguals have been identified with advantageous learning characteristics related to creative and divergent thinking and symbolic reasoning. Communicating in two languages often requires switching within those languages and the cognitive structures that underlie those languages. This may be related to the symbolic reasoning advantages for bilinguals.

Finally, there is the cognitive 'meta' – knowing about – advantages of bilingualism. The most common 'meta' attribute is related to awareness of cognitive operations – the awareness of one's own learning strategies, particularly related to self-regulation of the learning process. Processing of learning vocabulary, syntax, phonology and morphology in more than one language seems to provide bilinguals with a particularly enhanced set of insights into learning strategies that they are using. Instructionally, bilinguals may benefit more from strategies that examine the processing of learning, utilizing

reflections, examination and articulation of learning processes that the student may be engaged in at all levels of the curriculum. And of course, the 'meta' specific to linguistic repertoires can draw on the realization that words are arbitrary, that languages are rule governed (although the rules may be different) and that languages can be related in rule-governed ways to one another – for example, adding an 'o' to some English words makes them Spanish words. The clearest example of using metalingusitic awareness in instruction with bilinguals is exemplified in the instructional acknowledgement related to cognates in some languages. 'Science' in English has the same Latin roots and becomes 'sciencias' in Spanish. Cognates in Spanish and English are prolific in math, science, music and the arts.

FUTURE DIRECTIONS

The majority of current research compares the development and learning outcomes of young bilingual learners to that of monolingual, majority language speaking students (Hammer et al., 2014). In this vein, research aims to explain the low performance of DLLs, when compared to monolingual majority language populations, by focusing on what these children and their families are lacking. However, relying solely on a comparison methodology can lead to misinterpretations and biased conclusions about DLLs; understanding their development and learning must focus on the factors and experiences specific to young learners developing two or more languages simultaneously in ECEC settings.

A New Conceptual Model for Understanding the Development of Dual Language Learners

Along with considering the features specific to ECEC environments, in order to better understand and ultimately better support young DLLs, researchers and practitioners must consider the constellation of interrelated features that influence children's development and learning (McCabe et al., 2013). Recently, Castro and colleagues (Castro, Garcia, Espinosa, Gillanders, Hammer, LaForett, Peisner-Feinberg, and Tabors, 2015, in press) designed a conceptual framework for understanding the development of children growing up as DLLs. The framework is founded on socio-cultural and historical perspectives. As such, it emphasizes that an individual's development cannot be understood in isolation from the social, cultural and historical contexts in which it occurs (Vygotsky, 1978), and that children approach developmental tasks in particular situations based on the cultural practices in which they have previously participated (Rogoff, 2003). This perspective is particularly relevant for understanding the development of DLLs because these children's experiences differ in many ways from those of monolinguals.

We present their conceptual model as an archetype for future research, believing it is helpful for determining factors that need to be taken into consideration when designing, conducting and interpreting findings from new studies on early bilingual development. It moves research away from assumptions and expectations about developmental competencies rooted in monolingual perspectives and mainstream cultural practices. The model includes a constellation of interrelated features that may facilitate or impede DLLs' optimal development across society, community and family contexts; individual child characteristics; and early care contexts. The model created by Castro and colleagues broadens the view of development beyond the ECEC classroom.

With regard to features of development included in the society context, Castro and colleagues note that understanding the development of DLLs must include attention to social and educational policies and the immigration and integration history of their family. They advise that researchers critically examine educational policies, even those that promote high-quality early care and education,

noting that many times such initiatives do not include explicit provision to address the cultural, linguistic and educational needs of DLLs. Also, whether the DLL is the child of an immigrant or native-born parent, and the extent to which the DLL's family has integrated into mainstream society, are both associated with their development and learning (Castro et al., 2015, in press).

Features included in the community context are more immediate to DLLs' daily experience. For example, one feature highlighted in the conceptual model in the community context is the presence and value of different languages in a community as observed in spaces where the people who live in that community come together and interact. It is within these spaces that DLLs and their families have more or fewer opportunities to hear different languages, to interact with speakers of different languages and to observe everyday and academic uses of language and literacy. Opportunities for diverse and frequent linguistic interactions increase the likelihood that they will become bilingual. Along with language use, values related to bilingualism and multiculturalism and feelings of acceptance are features of development included in the community context.

The family context is also important in the development of young bilingual learners. Castro and colleagues emphasize that over-reliance on demographic characteristics may be insufficient for describing how family features influence development (Chang and Sandhofer, 2009). One example they give is how DLLs are more likely to live in homes with grandparents, other relatives or non-relatives, than their monolingual English-speaking peers. While such living environments may initially be viewed as overcrowded (and a detriment to development), upon further investigation, having more people living in the home may provide enriched language and other cultural experiences (Castro et al., 2015, in press). Beyond family demographics, other features in the family context include culture-specific parenting practices, beliefs and goals, as well as the language and literacy practices promoted in the home in both the home language and English.

The conceptual model (Castro et al., 2015, in press) encourages researchers in particular to consider a complexity of features, both within and outside of early education settings, to fully understand the development and learning of DLLs. In concert with the evidence that educational achievement patterns of virtually all racial/ethnic groups are established during the early years of school (and change little thereafter) and the significant population growth of DLLs, it is critical to understand the complexities surrounding their development and learning in ECEC settings, including the features that influence development in the society, community and family contexts. Without attention to these interrelated features, achievement gaps between DLLs and English-only students will continue to grow (Comeau and Genesee, 2001).

Along with changes to how researchers and practitioners approach the understanding of early bilingual development and learning, there is a critical need for education policies in early education to directly address language development issues and appropriate curricular and instructional approaches. While available evidence on schooling, language development and related policy remain limited – particularly in the development and testing of classroom strategies for diverse segments of the DLL population – current evidence suggests that rich language environments, DLBE programs, universal prekindergarten programs and high-quality teachers can improve learning opportunities and outcomes for these children (National Task Force on Early Childhood Education for Hispanics, 2007). In light of this, below we touch on recommendations for each area of government.

As the USA and other countries with large numbers of DLLs advance educational policy for students in an ever-diversified population, Wiley, Lee and Rumberger (2009) remind us that many nation-states deal with issues of children entering early care and education settings, as well as public schools, not speaking the language of the school. The United Nations has spoken directly to the right of a minority group to its language by explicitly indicating that utilization of an individual's heritage language is a basic human right.

Prohibiting the use of the language of a group in daily discourse or in schools or the printing and circulation of publications in the language of the group falls within agreed upon constraints regarding linguistic genocide (United Nations, 1948). In 1994, the UN Human Rights Committee spoke again to this international issue (United Nations, 1994). It is the most far-reaching human rights articulation of an international body addressing linguistic rights: 'In those states in which ethnic, religious or linguistic minorities exist, persons belonging to such minorities shall not be denied the right, in community with other members of their group, to enjoy their own culture, to profess and practice their own religion, or to use their own language' (United Nations, 1994, p. 794).

Skutnabb-Kangas (2000) has summarized this UN position as: (1) protecting all individuals on the State's territory or under its jurisdiction such as immigrants and refugees irrespective of their legal status, (2) recognizing the existence of a linguistic right, and (3) imposing positive obligations on the State to protect that right. Under this interpretation, the USA and many other countries might very well be in violation of the UN position.

Here I offer four related recommendations. First, I recommend that federal/national governments underwrite tests of programs designed to produce large increases in the number of culturally knowledgeable, bilingual preschool and early elementary teachers. The most fundamental element to the provision of rich language environments and high-quality programs for DLLs across the early care through 3rd grade spectrum (0–8 years old) is high-quality caregivers/teachers who are bilingual and knowledgeable regarding the cultural and linguistic circumstances of bilingual families and children. Indeed, research strongly suggests that the transfer of academic skills between languages is heightened and early achievement outcomes increased for young bilingual and emergent bilingual students when teachers use the child's native language in ECEC settings. The most successful caregivers and teachers are fluent in both languages, understand learning patterns associated with bilingual/second language acquisition, have a mastery of appropriate instructional strategies (i.e., cooperative learning, sheltered instruction, differentiated instruction and strategic teaching) and have strong organizational and communication skills.

Second, I recommend that the federal/national government fund and experiment with teacher preparation programs to recruit more early childhood bilingual teachers who are trained in bilingual acquisition to work as language specialists. The responsibility of 'language specialists' is to help classroom teachers in preschools with substantial numbers of DLLs to be responsive to students' linguistic and academic needs. Language specialists serve as consultants to teachers and aides in the classroom to help DLLs learn and achieve, recognizing and leveraging existent strengths. Having a language specialist in school can also help monolingual teachers make essential links with parents and families. Ongoing relationships with parents are an invaluable resource to connect educational practices between the home and school and thereby increase student engagement and learning.

Third, I recommend that the US federal government (through Head Start, Early Head Start and other grant programs) and similar national efforts in countries worldwide continue to explore and expand dual language and mother tongue programs. Young DLLs should have access to high-quality bilingual programs that teach home language skills through content. Integrating speakers of various languages in the same classroom with attention to the linguistic and cultural resources they bring to that classroom fosters linguistic and ethnic equity among children.

In most cases, the sort of work needed from state or regional governmental agencies necessitates meaningful collaborations with school-level efforts and other community-based organizations. First, these governments should collaborate with local communities to offer high-quality educational experiences with a variety of schedule options. DLLs aged 3 and 4 years should be given access to free, state-funded preschool. Evidence suggests that high-quality prekindergarten programs improve school readiness for DLL children and decrease achievement differences between racial/ethnic groups at kindergarten entry. As mentioned, these programs should have high-quality bilingual and culturally competent teachers and staff to effectively engage students and to develop sustainable relationships with family members. Governmental agencies should work alongside immigrant integration organizations and other community institutions to provide information to parents on these programs and encourage meaningful collaborations between home and school.

Second, state and regional governments should provide pay and benefits to qualified preschool teachers that are equal to those of elementary and secondary school teachers. This would provide the economic incentive to recruit and maintain a well-educated, reasonably stable group of preschool professionals.

Local governments should serve as a liaison between families and national, state and regional agencies. To this end, local governments can collaborate with national, state and regional agencies to provide information to parents. In the USA, this would include Pre-Kindergarten, Head Start and Early Head Start programs focusing on increasing the enrollment of DLLs. In other countries, universal and targeted early childhood and family interventions may be available (García and García, 2012). Continuing to increase early childhood enrollment remains important, considering the available evidence demonstrating improvements in school readiness for DLLs and decreases in achievement differences at school entry.

But the improvement of education for DLLs cannot occur without the involvement of non-governmental actors. The role of private foundations, community-based organizations and education researchers is highlighted in the next section.

Private foundations fund long-term efforts to design, test and evaluate language and academic development strategies for DLLs in early learning settings from all SES groups (particularly across levels of parent education and immigrant status). These include systematic, value-added studies to explore, develop and determine the efficacy and scalability of instructional and curricular approaches. In order to maximize the chances of determining if the strategies are able to contribute to improvements in school readiness at scale, funding for ten or more years of support for promising approaches should be made available. Additionally, private foundations should seriously consider creating two or three new foundations specialized in funding these areas, thereby ensuring that sustained investments in strategy development are made in the long term.

I am most familiar with the US context in which children of Mexican origin represent the largest group of DLLs nationwide. An approach to develop improved educational practices and student-learning opportunities during the early years of schooling (and across the early care-12 spectrum) is through bi-national collaborations between researchers, practitioners and policy makers in the USA and Mexico (Jensen, 2008). To date, the Foreign Affairs Office of the Mexican government has launched a number of programs (including teacher exchange, online courses, community plazas, the 'transfer document', among others) to enhance educational opportunities for Mexicans living in the USA (Gándara and Rumberger, 2009). A preliminary study of these programs found that they have a great deal of potential to serve Mexican American children and their families (not to mention the expansion of bi-national cooperation in education), but are constrained by low visibility, inadequate funding, poor integration with US institutions (particularly schools) and limited research and evaluation (Gándara and Rumberger, 2009). Ongoing study of programs like these is an example of the sort of innovation needed to enhance early educational opportunities for young bilingual children throughout the world.

CONCLUSION

With the increasing number of DLLs in ECEC settings, it is essential that researchers, practitioners and policy makers continue to expand on knowledge about early bilingual development and learning. From a developmental perspective, research, policy and practice have not conformed neatly to a cohesive framework that can be of benefit for better understanding and promotion of bilingual development and learning in early childhood.

This chapter has been about broadening the view of competencies to include aspects that are of particular interest in the study of young bilingual learners. To that end, the chapter has identified 'what we know about' and 'what we should do' through an expanded discussion of the key components of an emerging conceptual framework that identifies and takes into consideration key elements/contexts of the DLL experience: societal, community and family contexts; early childhood education and care contexts; child characteristics; and developmental competencies. This emerging conceptual framework is intended to help us better understand the integrated development and early learning knowledge base, identify gaps in knowledge and determine factors that need to be taken into account when designing, conducting and interpreting findings that could address issues of equity in the early care and education of DLLs.

To support the growing DLL population, ECEC teachers must be prepared with the additional qualities, knowledge and skills specific to young learners developing in two languages simultaneously. The curriculum, instruction and assessment practices used in ECEC settings should be those that have proven essential for the success of bilingual learners. Finally, researchers must promote new research that moves away from comparison models and towards efforts that aim to understand the specific complexities and uniqueness of the experience of young bilingual learners.

FURTHER READING

Bialystok, E., and Feng, X. (2011). Language proficiency and its implications for monolingual and bilingual children. In A. Y. Durgunoğlu and C. Goldenberg (eds), *Language and literacy development in bilingual settings* (pp. 121–138). New York: Guildford Press.

Genesee, F. (2010). Dual language development in preschool children. In E. García and E. Frede (eds), *Developing the research agenda for young English language learners*. New York: Teachers College Press.

McCabe, A., Tamis-Lemonde, C. S., Bornstein, M. H., Brockmeyer Cates, C., Golinkoff, R., Wishard Guerra, A., et al. (2013). Multilingual children: Beyond myths and toward best practices. *Social Policy Report*, 27(4), 1–29.

Rogoff, B., Moore, L., Najafi, B., Dexter, A., Correa-Chávez, M., and Solís, J. (2007). Children's development of cultural repertoires through participation in everyday routines and practices. In J. E. Grusec and P. D. Hastings (eds), *Handbook of socialization* (pp. 490–515). New York: Guilford Press.

NOTE

1 In this chapter, I purposely use the term dual language learners (DLLs) and not 'young bilingual learners' for a few reasons. First, not all DLLs are bilingual but all are growing up and developing in contexts where they are exposed to two languages. Second, using the term DLL is a way to distinguish research and literature about young children (ages birth to 5) from the research and literature on school-age (kindergarten through 12th grade) language learners, students typically referred to as bilingual or English-as-a-second-language learners. Finally, we use DLL because this is the term currently used by researchers and practitioners in the USA (Castro et al., 2011).

QUESTIONS FOR REFLECTION

1 Why is there a need for a new conceptual framework with regard to research with DLLs?
2 What linguistic, cognitive and social benefits can be linked to learning two languages in the early years?
3 What programs of instruction are promising with regard to the success of DLLs in early childhood education settings?

REFERENCES

August, D., and Shanahan, T. (eds) (2006). *Developing literacy in second language learners: Report of the National Literacy Panel on language-minority children and youth*. Mahwah, NJ: Lawrence Erlbaum.

Baker, C. (2000). *The care and education of young bilinguals: An introduction for professionals*. Clevedon: Multilingual Matters.

Barac, R., and Bialystok, E. (2012). Bilingual effects on cognitive and linguistic development: Role of language, cultural background, and education. *Child Development*, 83(2), 413–422.

Barac, R., Bailystok, E., Castro, D. C., and Sanchez, M. (2014). The cognitive development of young dual language learners: A critical review. *Early Childhood Research Quarterly*, 29, 699–714.

Barnett, W. S., Yarosz, D. J., Thomas, J., Jung, K., and Blanco, D. (2007). Two-way and monolingual English immersion in preschool education: An experimental comparison. *Early Childhood Research Quarterly*, 22, 277–293.

Bernhard, J. K., Cummins, J., Campoy, F. I., Ada, A. F., Winsler, A., and Bleiker, C. (2006). Identity texts and literacy development among preschool English language learners: Enhancing learning opportunities for children at risk for learning disabilities. *Teachers College Record*, 108(11), 2380–2405.

Bialystok, E., Craik, F. I. M., Grady, C., Chau, W., Ishii, R., Gunji, A., and Pantev, C. (2005). Effect of bilingualism on cognitive control in the Simon task: Evidence from MEG. *NeuroImage*, 24, 40–49.

Bransford, J. D., Brown, A. L., and Cocking, R. R. (eds) (2000). *How people learn: Brain, mind, experience, and school*. Expanded edition. Washington, DC: National Academy of Sciences.

Calderón, M. E. (2010). *Teaching reading and comprehension to English learners: K–5*. Bloomington, IN: Solution Tree.

California Department of Education (2010). *Improving education for English learners:*

Research-based approaches. Sacramento, CA: California Department of Education.

Camilli, G., Vargas, S., Ryan, S., and Barnett, W. S. (2010). Meta-analysis of the effects of early education interventions on cognitive and social development. *Teachers College Record*, 112(3), 579–620.

Campbell, R., and Sais, E. (1995). Accelerated metalinguistic (phonological) awareness in bilingual children. *British Journal of Developmental Psychology*, 13, 61–68.

Capps, R., Fix, M. E., Murray, J., Ost, J., Passel, J. S., and Hernández, S. H. (2005). *The new demography of America's schools: Immigration and the No Child Left Behind Act*. Urban Institute. Available at: www.urban.org/url.cfm?ID=311230

Carlson, S. M., and Meltzoff, A. N. (2008). Bilingual experience and executive functioning in young children. *Developmental Science*, 11, 282–298.

Castro, D. C., Páez, M., Dickinson, D., and Frede, E. (2011). Promoting language and literacy in dual language learners: Research, practice and policy. *Child Development Perspectives*, 5, 15–21.

Castro, D. C., Garcia, E. E., Espinosa, L. M., Genesee, F., Gillanders, C., Hammer, C. S., LaForett, D. R., Peisner-Feinberg, E., and Tabors, P. (2015) 'Conceptual Framework for the Study of Dual Language Learner Development' (in press, *Child Development*, 2015).

Cazden, C., Snow, C. E., and Heise-Baigorria, C. (1990). *Language planning in preschool education with annotated bibliography*. (Report prepared for the Consultative Group on Early Childhood Care and Development). New York: UNICEF.

Chan, A. (2004). Syntactic transfer: Evidence from the interlanguage of Hong Kong Chinese ESL learners. *The Modern Language Journal*, 88, 56–74.

Chang, A. and Sandhofer, C. (2009). Language differences in bilingual parent number speech to preschool-aged children. In N. A. Taatgen and H. van Rijn (eds), *Proceedings of the Thirty-first Annual Conference of the Cognitive Science Society* (pp. 887–892).

Collins, M. (2010). ELL preschoolers' English vocabulary acquisition from storybook reading. *Early Childhood Research Quarterly*, 25(1), 84–97.

Comeau, L., and Genesee, F. (2001). Bilingual children's repair strategies during dyadic communication. In J. Cenoz and F. Genesee (eds), *Trends in bilingual acquisition* (pp. 231–256). Amsterdam: John Benjamins.

David, A., and Wei, L. (2008). Individual differences in the lexical development of French-English bilingual children. *International Journal of Bilingual Education and Bilingualism*, 11(5), 598–618.

De Houwer, A. (1995). Bilingual language acquisition. In P. Fletcher and B. MacWhinney (eds), *The handbook of child language* (pp. 219–250). Oxford: Blackwell.

Dickinson, D. K. (2011). Teachers' language practices and academic outcomes of preschool children. *Science*, 333, 964–967.

Dickinson, D., and Neuman, S. B. (2006). *Handbook of early literacy research: Volume II*. New York: Guilford Press.

Dixon, L. Q., Zhao, J., Shin, Y., Wu, S., Su, J., Burgess-Brigham, R., et al. (2012). What we know about second language acquisition: A synthesis from four perspectives. *Review of Education Research*, 82(1), 5–60.

Döpke, S. (1998). Competing language structures: The acquisition of verb placement by bilingual German-English children. *Journal of Child Language*, 25, 555–584.

Durán, L., Roseth, C., and Hoffman, P. (2010). An experimental study comparing English-only and transitional bilingual education on Spanish-speaking preschoolers' early literacy development. *Early Childhood Research Quarterly*, 25(2), 207–217.

Espinosa, L. (2003). Preschool program quality: What it is and why it matters. *National Institute of Early Education Research Policy Brief*, 1(1), 1–12.

Espinosa, L. (2010a). *Getting it RIGHT for children from diverse backgrounds: Applying research to improve practice*. Upper Saddle River, NJ: Pearson.

Espinosa, L. (2010b). Assessment of young English-language learners. In García, E. E. and Frede, E. (eds), *Young English-language learners: Current research and emerging directions for practice and policy*. New York: Teachers College Press.

Espinosa, L. M., and López, M. (2007). *Assessment considerations for young English language learners across different levels of accountability*. Philadelphia: National Early Childhood Accountability Task Force.

Fairbairn, S., and Jones-Vo, S. (2010). *Differentiating instruction and assessment for English language learners: A guide for K–12 teachers*. Philadelphia: Caslon.

Farver, J. M., Lonigan, C. J., and Eppe, S. (2009). Effective early literacy skill development for young Spanish-speaking English language learners: An experimental study of two methods. *Child Development*, 80, 703–719.

Gándara, P., and Hopkins, M. (eds) (2010). *Forbidden languages: English learners and restrictive language policies*. New York: Teachers College Press.

Gándara, P., and Rumberger, R. (2009). Immigration, language, and education: How does language policy structure opportunity? In J. Holdaway and R. Alba (eds), *Education and immigrant youth: The role of institutions and agency*. New York: Social Science Research Council.

García E. E., and Frede E. C. (eds) (2010). *Young English language learners: Current research and emerging directions for practice and policy*. New York: Teachers College.

García, E. E., and García, E. (2012). *Understanding the language development and early education of Hispanic children*. New York: Teachers College Press.

García, E. E., and Miller, L. S. (2008). Findings and recommendations of the National Task Force on Early Childhood Education for Hispanics. *Child Development Perspectives*, 2(2), 53–58.

García, E. E., and Náñez, J. (2011). *Bilingualism and cognition: Joining cognitive psychology and education to enhance bilingual research, pedagogy and policy*. Washington, DC: American Psychological Association.

Genesee, F. (2010). Dual language development in preschool children. In E. E. García and E. C. Frede (eds), *Young English language learners* (pp. 59–79). New York: Teachers College Press.

Gillanders, C., and Castro, D. (2011). Storybook reading for young dual language learners. *Young Children*, 66(1), 91–95.

González, N., Moll, L., and Amanti, C. (2005). *Funds of knowledge: Theorizing practices, households, communities, and classrooms*. Mahwah, NJ: Lawrence Erlbaum Associates.

Greene, J. P. (1998). *A meta-analysis of the effectiveness of bilingual education*.

Claremont, CA: Thomas Rivera Policy Institute.

Guofang, L., Edwards, P. A., and Gunderson, L. (2010). *Best practices in ELL instruction*. New York: Guilford Press.

Hammer, C. S., Hoff, E., Uchikoshi, Y., Gillanders, C., Castro, D. C., and Sandilos, L. E. (2014). The language and literacy development of young dual language learners: A critical review. *Early Childhood Research Quarterly*, 29, 715–733.

Hernández, D. J., Denton, N. A., and Macartney, S. E. (2008). Children in immigrant families: Looking to America's future. *Social Policy Report*, 22(3), 1–24.

Jackson, B., Larzelere, R., St. Clair, L., Corr, M., Fichter, C., and Egertson, H. (2006). The impact of HeadsUp! reading on early childhood educators' literacy practices and preschool children's literacy skills. *Early Childhood Research Quarterly*, 21, 213–226.

Jensen, B. (2008). Immigration and language policy. In J. M. Gonzalez (ed.), *Encyclopedia of bilingual education*. London: SAGE.

Junker, D. A., and Stockman, I. J. (2002). Expressive vocabulary of German-English bilingual toddlers. *American Journal of Speech-Language Pathology*, 11(4), 381–394.

Kim, Y. (2009). Crosslinguistic influence on phonological awareness for Korean-English bilingual children. *Reading and Writing: An Interdisciplinary Journal*, 22(7), 843–861.

Klaus, D. (2001). The use of indigenous languages in early basic education in Papua New Guinea. Paper presented at the annual meeting of the Comparative and International Education Society, Washington, DC.

Komarek, K. (1996). *Mother-tongue education in sub-Saharan countries: Conceptual and strategic situations for promotion of mother-tongue education in Africa*. Eschborn, Germany: German Technical Cooperation Agency.

Kormi-Nouri, R., Shojaei, R. S., Moniri, S., Gholami, A. R., Moradi A. R., Akbari-Zardkhaneh, S., and Nilsson, L. G. (2008). The effect of childhood bilingualism on episodic and semantic memory tasks. *Scandinavian Journal of Psychology*, 49, 93–109.

Lesaux, N. K., and Siegel, L. S. (2003). The development of reading in children who speak English as a second language (ESL). *Developmental Psychology*, 39(6), 1005–1019.

Lindholm-Leary, K., and Genesee, F. (2010). Alternative educational programs for English language learners. In California Department of Education (ed.), *Improving education for English learners: Research-based approaches*. Sacramento: CDE Press.

López, L. E. (2000). Pedagogical issues in mother tongue and bilingual education. In *Language of instruction in basic education: Materials for distance learning course*. Washington, DC: World Bank Institute.

Luk, G., and Bialystok, E. (2008). Common and distinct cognitive bases for reading in English-Cantonese bilinguals. *Applied Psycholinguistics*, 29, 269–289.

Malone, S. E. (2001). When 'education for all' includes everyone: Providing relevant education for minority language communities. Paper presented at the World Bank Seminar on Language of Instruction, Washington, DC.

Mathematica Policy Research (2010). *Identifying enhanced instructional practices that support English language learners: Background literature review*. Washington, DC: Mathematica Policy Research.

McCabe, A., Tamis-Lemonde, C. S., Bornstein, M. H., Brockmeyer Cates, C., Golinkoff, R., Wishard Guerra, A., et al. (2013). Multilingual children: Beyond myths and toward best practices. *Social Policy Report*, 27(4), 1–29.

National Center for Education Statistics (NCES) (2001). The Condition of Education 2001. Washington, DC: National Center of Education Statistics, U.S. Department of Education. Available at: http://nces.ed.gov/programs/coe/2001/essay/index.asp

National Task Force on Early Childhood Education for Hispanics (2007). *Para nustros niños: Report of expanding and improving early education for Hispanics – Main report*. Tempe, AZ: National Task Force on Early Childhood Education for Hispanics. Available at: www.ecehispanic.org/work/expand_MainReport.pdf

Oller, D. K., and Eilers, R. E. (eds) (2002). *Language and literacy in bilingual children*. Clevedon: Multilingual Matters.

Ovando, C., Collier, V., and Combs, V. (2006). *Bilingual and ESL classrooms: Teaching in multicultural contexts*, 4th edn. New York: McGraw-Hill.

Paik, J. H., and Mix, K. S. (2003). US and Korean children's comprehension of fraction names: A re-examination of cross-national differences. *Child Development*, 74, 144–154.

Rasmussen, C., Ho, E., Nicoladis, E., Leung, J., and Bisanz, J. (2006) Is the Chinese number-naming system transparent? Evidence from Chinese-English bilingual children. *Canadian Journal of Experimental Psychology*, 60, 60–67.

Reardon, S. (2003). *Sources of educational inequality: The growth of racial/ethnic and socioeconomic test score gaps in kindergarten and first grade*. University Park, PA: Population Research Institute, Pennsylvania State University.

Reardon, S. F., and Galindo, C. (2006). *Patterns of Hispanic students' math and English literacy test scores*. Report to the National Task Force on Early Childhood Education for Hispanics. Tempe, AZ: Arizona State University.

Rogoff, B. (2003). *The cultural nature of human development*. Oxford: Oxford University Press.

Rolstad, K., Mahoney, K., and Glass, G. V. (2005). The big picture: A meta-analysis of program effectiveness research on English language learners. *Educational Policy*, 19(4), 572–594.

Romaine, S. (2004). The bilingual and multilingual community. In T. K. Bhatia and W. C. Ritchie (eds), *The handbook of bilingualism* (pp. 385–405). Oxford: Blackwell.

Skutnabb-Kangas, T. (1994). Mother tongue maintenance: The debate, linguistic human rights and minority education. *TESOL Quarterly*, 28(3), 624–628.

Skutnabb-Kangas, T. (2000). *Linguistic genocide in education – or worldwide diversity and human rights?* Mahwah, NJ: Lawrence Erlbaum Associates.

Slavin, R. E., and Cheung, A. (2005). A synthesis of research on language of reading instruction for English language learners. *Review of Education Research*, 75(2), 247–284.

UNESCO (2001). *Education for all: First anniversary of the World Education Forum*. April, no. 2001–65. Paris: UNESCO. Available at: www.unesco.org/opi/eng/unescopress/2001/01-65e.shtml

UNICEF (1999). *The state of the world's children*. New York: UNICEF.

United Nations. (1948). *The convention of the prevention and punishment of the crime of genocide*. New York: Author.

United Nations. (1994). *Convention on the prevention and punishment of the crime of genocide*. New York: Author.

University of Chicago (2010). *Getting on track early for school success: An assessment system to support effective instruction*. Technical report. Chicago, IL: University of Chicago.

Verhoeven, L., and Aarts, R. (2005). Attaining functional literacy in the Netherlands. In A. Y. Durgunoglu and L. Verhoeven (eds), *Literacy development in multilingual contexts: Cross-cultural perspectives* (pp. 111–134). Mahwah, NJ: Lawrence Erlbaum Associates.

Wagner, D. A. (2005). Putting second language first: Language and literacy learning in Morocco. In A. Y. Durgunoglu and L. Verhoeven (eds), *Literacy development in multilingual contexts: Cross-cultural perspectives* (pp. 169–183). Mahwah, NJ: Lawrence Erlbaum Associates.

Vygotsky, L. S. (1978). *Mind in society: The development of higher psychological processes*. Cambridge, MA: Harvard University Press.

Wiley, T. G., Lee, J. S., and Rumberger, R. W. (2009). *The education of language minority immigrants in the United States*. Buffalo, NY: Multilingual Matters.

Winsler, A., Diaz, R. M., Espinosa, L., and Rodriguez, J. (1999). When learning a second language does not mean losing the first: Bilingual language development in low-income, Spanish-speaking children attending bilingual preschool. *Child Development*, 70(2), 349–362.

Wright, W. E. (2010). *Foundations for teaching English language learners: Research, theory, policy and practice*. Philadelphia, PA: Caslon.

Yow, W. Q., and Markman, E. M. (2011) Young bilingual children's heightened sensitivity to referential cues. *Journal of Cognition and Development*, 12, 12–31.

Zelazo, P. D., Muller, U., Frye, D., and Marcovitch, S. (2003). The development of executive function in early childhood. *Monographs of the Society for Research in Child Development, Serial No. 274*. Boston, MA: Blackwell.

23

Early Childhood Research in Africa: The Need for a Chorus of Voices

Alan Pence and Emily Ashton

INTRODUCTION

Early childhood is a key focus of international research and international development. Such has not always been the case, as can be attested by those whose work predates approval of the Convention on the Rights of the Child (CRC) (United Nations, 1990) and the Education for All (EFA) initiative, which included the key words 'learning begins at birth' (UNESCO, 1990). At that point, the literature regarding early childhood education, care and development (ECD)[1] and international development was scarce – for some parts of the world that remains the case.

In this chapter, the authors argue 'that research on the whole of humanity is necessary for creating a science that truly represents the whole of humanity' (Arnett, 2008: 602). The majority of early childhood research has focused 'on a small corner of the human population – mainly, persons living in the United States', which represents only '5% of the world's total population' (2008: 602). Sub-Saharan Africa (SSA) is a key part of the

neglected 95% that Jeffrey Arnett argues warrants increased attention. Despite the fact that approximately 15% of humanity's children live in SSA, only a negligible percentage of the internationally accessible, published ECD literature focuses on the region. A point all the more critical, given the great diversity of cultures, traditions and languages found throughout Sub-Saharan Africa.

This chapter is integral to work that was initiated two decades ago with a focus on promoting capacity for local and country-led ECD initiatives in SSA, from policies to programs and, more recently, to research (Pence, 1999; Pence and Benner, 2015). From the beginning of that work, it has been clear that references and resource materials focusing on ECD in SSA, particularly materials with African lead authors, were very rare. And without such materials, Africa's ability to define its own way forward was restricted – a situation familiar in other parts of the Global South as well.

The invitation to submit a chapter to this volume occurred at the point when the authors, with funding as part of a collaborative project with the Aga Khan University Institute for Educational Development in Tanzania, had compiled an annotated list of more than 800 SSA-focused, ECD-relevant publications.[2] Such a trove of data is new and unique. This chapter establishes historical and conceptual foundations for further analyses of Africa's evolving ECD literature going forward.

The chapter begins with an historical analysis of ECD in SSA before the watershed period of 1990 referred to above. Earlier child studies research, in fields such as anthropology, cross-cultural psychology and culture and personality studies, produced a body of work which reveals much about African children, families, communities and culture before, during and after independence. The processes undertaken by those studies also speak to efforts to promote African-led scholarly capacity, a key theme throughout this review.

The chapter goes on to note that, for the most part, ECD in SSA had almost no global visibility until the early 1990s. At that point, several ECD-focused handbooks were published, each including one or more African countries with African lead authors. It was during that same period that one key African author initiated what would become, over time, an important 'stream' (or theme) of scholarly work; it is a stream that calls for an Africentric focus in the literature (Nsamenang, 1992). While A. Bame Nsamenang has continued to be active through to the present day, his critically focused 'Africentric stream' was not joined by a substantive collection of other African-led, Africa-focused research until the mid-2000s.

In the 2000s, a stream of SSA African-led research which focused on country-level issues of policy development was followed by publications attentive to the gap between policy and implementation. These policy-level analyses were accompanied by a wider range of ECD education, training, programming and curriculum-related publications. Most recently, critical reflections regarding SSA's approach to ECD have increased,

contributing substantially to the earlier call for an Africentric approach, and recalling an earlier emphasis on context, community and culture integral to key historical works described in the following section.

AFRICAN-BASED CHILD, FAMILY AND COMMUNITY RESEARCH

While a primary intent of this chapter is to provide a foundation for ECD research going forward in SSA, it is important to first explore the earlier history of child- and family-focused studies and scholarly writing. Such work brings one into contact with, among others, anthropologists and psychologists, extending a view of African-based child and family studies back in time several decades. Our starting point is the culture and personality movement made famous by the investigations of Margaret Mead and Ruth Benedict in the 1930s, but represented and reconceptualized in Africa most productively by John and Beatrice Whiting and their graduate student and research associate successors.[3] What the Whitings' decades-long commitment to comparative studies of children, families and communities around the world demonstrated is that researchers must take account of local contexts and ecological conditions on their own terms.

The Whitings led Harvard University's Laboratory of Human Development, which stood as 'the premier training base in comparative child development from 1950 through the 1980s, and then beyond under the leadership of Robert LeVine, one of their former students' (Edwards and Bloch, 2010: 485). Under the Whitings' direction, three important international, longitudinal projects were undertaken: (1) the Six Culture Study in which research teams compiled data of childrearing practices and children's socialization behavior from six countries; (2) the Child Development Research Unit (CDRU) at the University of Nairobi where local communities and local research assistants played key roles; and (3) the Harvard Comparative

Adolescence Project (Weisner, 2010; Weisner and Edwards, 2002). The first two projects are particularly relevant for our analysis.

The Six Culture Study of Socialization (SCS) was launched in 1954. The project involved collecting rich ethnographic studies from different parts of the world that would provide comparable data and suggest novel insights about childhood in a social and cultural context. The intensive multi-site fieldwork conducted from 1954 to 1957 included, for example, descriptions of child behaviors, caretaking practices, and cultural beliefs and ceremonies (Whiting, 1963; Whiting and Whiting, 1975). In 1955 Robert LeVine received a two-year grant to replicate the ongoing SCS ethnographic work in East Africa (LeVine and LeVine, 1966). His team spent 20 months generating data with the Gusii people of southwestern Kenya, and, on returning to Harvard, the Whitings decided to include the data in the larger study (LeVine, 2010). Ten years later, the Whiting and LeVine presence would again be felt in Kenya through the Child Development Research Unit (CDRU). Funded initially by the Carnegie Corporation, the CDRU was established as an international partnership and institutional capacity-building collaboration between Harvard University, the University of Nairobi and, subsequently, Kenyatta University.

Thomas Weisner (2010) described the research environment of the CDRU as exemplifying many of the Whitings' mentorship qualities. An explicit goal of the CDRU was to support, teach and collaborate with Kenyan university students 'so that they could become the next generation of social science researchers' (2010: 502). While such capacity-promoting work is laudable and was a key objective of the CDRU, the outcome based on published African-led studies alone was very limited. However, Caroline Pope Edwards and Beatrice Whiting (2004) clarify, noting the accomplishments of Kenyan women researchers affiliated with their CDRU work: 'All now have professional careers. They are successful lawyers, university professors, or

professionals in government. Some are senior executives at international organizations. One served as a high commissioner from Kenya to another African nation' (2004: 8).

Other key texts from this larger body of work include Robert LeVine and colleagues' *Child Care and Culture: Lessons from Africa* (1994) which bridges work undertaken for the SCS and the CDRU. The edited collection challenged the concept of a universal best child care, and further demonstrated how cultural priorities and social conditions complexly affect childrearing practices and priorities. The work of Charles Super and Sara Harkness, also working in SSA, provided researchers worldwide with the influential concept of 'developmental niche' (1986). Also important from this broader body of work were Weisner's studies of sibling caregiving as a widespread and valued practice. Although often dismissed in the Global North as too dangerous or as a form of child labor, Weisner and Ronald Gallimore (1977) importantly wrote 'My brother's keeper' to review the evidence, to situate care practices in context and to describe the advantages that this form of care can provide for both young children and their older sibling caretakers.

The impact of the Whitings' and their colleagues' work has touched many fields, including cross-cultural psychology, developmental psychology, anthropology, human and child development, comparative education and ECD (Edwards and Bloch, 2010). Over their long careers, the Whitings' persistent attention to cultural diversity and contextual variability marked a necessary challenge to the accelerating child development field that 'tended to regress to [a] monocultural perspective … [that] naively saw American children as representatives of a universal humanity and took no account of the rest of the world' (LeVine, 2010: 519). And while not all of their conceptual theorizations may have stood the test of time (Edwards and Bloch, 2010), their methodological experimentation and ethical practice remain relevant today.

Coterminous with the SCS and CDRU projects were several other longitudinal, multidisciplinary projects in other parts of Africa (Super et al., 2011). These include: the Piagetian-centered French-Swiss collaboration in the Ivory Coast (Dasen et al., 1978); observations of Ngecha infants in Kenya (Leiderman et al., 1973); the Kalahari studies directed by Irven DeVore and others (Konner, 1976); the caregiving practices of Efe peoples in the Ituri Forest project (Tronick et al., 1987); and the cultural-cognitive development of the Kpelle of Liberia (Cole et al., 1971). Another noteworthy contributor to pioneering cultural development research in SSA is the work of Robert Serpell in Zambia (1976, 1993).

TRANSITION FROM AFRICAN-BASED TO AFRICAN-LED RESEARCH

For the purposes of this chapter, it is important to note not only the relative invisibility of the studies noted above in contemporary, global discussions of ECD, but also the limitations of the projects to establish a globally recognized base of researchers from Sub-Saharan countries. Interestingly, through a very different set of circumstances an African-led scholarly stream of work does appear in the early 1990s; that particular stream, plus others, will be discussed in some detail later. But before that, and to shift water metaphors, a new wave appeared in the late 1980s – one that included African lead authors and which explicitly focused on ECD: international handbooks.

Early Childhood Handbooks

Over a period of five years (1989–93), four international handbooks on ECD were published. At the time, these collections represented the largest number of widely accessible African-authored contributions to the international literature.[4] The volumes by Patricia Olmsted and David Weikart (1989) and Michael Lamb, Kathleen Sternberg, Carl-Philip Hwang and Anders Broberg (1992)

were part of larger international projects. The volumes edited by Gary Woodill, Judith Bernhard and Larry Prochner (1992) and Moncrieff Cochran (1993) were intended primarily as student and library reference works.

Olmsted and Weikart's (1989) edited collection provided baseline profiles for an international pre-primary study by separately outlining 14 countries' care and education services, and situating pre-primary education within each country's larger historical context. Chapters authored by Olayemi M. Onibokun (Nigeria) and Pauline Riak, Ruth Rono, Florence Kragu and M. Nyukuri (Kenya) were the two African contributions to the volume. The handbook edited by Lamb, Sternberg, Hwang and Broberg (1992) was unique in that it did not focus primarily on country reports, but was instead organized by geographic region. Nsamenang, the sole African contributor, described the early years of Cameroonian childhoods. His chapter is followed by a larger-scale exposition of shared and sibling child care in East African countries by Harkness and Super, and a summative commentary by Serpell.

Woodill, Bernhard and Prochner's (1992) compilation includes the largest number of African contributors, but also the shortest submissions for each country, given that it includes the largest number of countries overall (45 in total). In the course of writing, all contributing authors were professors at African universities, and the countries included: Botswana (Ruth Monau), Kenya (George Godia), Liberia (J. Nyanquoi Gormuyor), Nigeria (Joseph Aghenta and J. Nesin Omatseye), Sudan (Gasim Badri) and Swaziland (Marissa Rollnick). The handbook edited by Cochran (1993) contains two chapters by African writers: Zimbabwe, Rosley Chada, and Kenya, Lea Kipkorir. Unlike the other handbooks, the Cochran volume included a workshop where the chapter authors met, shared draft copies, considered cross-country features and planned certain aspects of the final volume.

First and foremost, the importance of the handbooks stems from the fact that they collectively represent the first focused inclusion of African voices in ECD that were widely available to an international audience. Together, they provide a sound introduction to 10 Sub-Saharan countries' history of education, political structures and organization, policy frameworks, indigenous childrearing traditions, societal and familial change over time, ECD curricula and teacher education, and post-independence challenges. They remain an important reference with which to gauge the progress and challenges of ECD in the region.

SSA's Broader Watershed Period

During the same period that the ECD handbooks were being developed, other key international events were contributing to the rising prominence of early childhood on the international development stage. Two of those events were briefly alluded to in the introduction: the CRC and EFA. A third notable event was more specific to ECD and international development – the 1992 publication of *The Twelve Who Survive: Strengthening Programmes of Early Childhood Development in the Third World* (Myers, 1992).

Much has been written about the CRC and EFA in regards to their myriad impacts on childhoods internationally; as such, this chapter will only note that the worlds of ECD pre- and post-CRC and EFA are profoundly different. The before and after of Robert Myers' (1992) volume are more nuanced. *The Twelve Who Survive* makes the case for moving beyond improving child survival rates, to enhancing child well-being for the 12 out of 13 children who were surviving by 1991. The international ECD programs it highlights as exemplars present a more multifaceted understanding of ECD than the more singularly economic arguments often put forward later in the decade which, with the addition of a key, re-energized element of brain development, continues to form the dominant international discourse today.

This difference hinges on an acronym that could be called 'the 3Cs' of culture, context and community. The programs highlighted in *The Twelve Who Survive* are sensitive to these 3Cs, and in doing so they are reflective of what had come before in the child studies work discussed earlier. Additionally, evidenced by their long history of funding and publication support, the Bernard van Leer Foundation (BvLF) has been a forerunner at promoting a 3C- and African-led approach to work in the region. Any chronology of ECD in Africa would be remiss in not highlighting the work of this Foundation.

In 1971 the BvLF funded its first project in SSA, the Kenyan Pre-school Education Project, which aimed to transfer the post-independence spirit of Harambee (i.e., community self-help or 'all pull together') to ECD initiatives. Other BvLF contributions to ECD in SSA include support for Educare programs in apartheid South Africa, El-barta and Madrassa preschools in Kenya and community development programs for the San peoples of the Kalahari (Lanyasunya et al., 2001; Mwaura, 2003; LeRoux, 2002). In its key publication, *Building on People's Strengths: Early Childhood in Africa* (BvLF, 1994), the BvLF makes it clear that the 3Cs matter. The key message is that while there are many approaches to improving the status of young children in SSA, 'the basis must be building on what exists rather than imposing alien solutions' (1994: 1). BvLF does not advocate the rejection of all ECD models derived in the Global North, but clearly conveys the idea that local wisdom and traditional socialization practices must drive efforts to move forward. The report's introduction concludes with a prescient comment: 'Perhaps the continent's greatest weakness is that it does not recognize the much strength to be found with its own societies' (1994: 5). It is to the strengths of situated knowledge that this chapter now turns.

Emerging African Voices in the 1990s

As the reader will have noted, this chapter pays particular attention to the presence and absence of indigenous African voices in

SSA's ECD story. An important element of the broader watershed period was the emergence of a strong African voice in child development. A. Bame Nsamenang's first book appeared in 1992 and, with it, a challenge and a mission:

> The lopsidedness of developmental knowledge in favor of the West clearly provides the primary rationale for the focus of this book on the Third World Ecology. The exclusion of Third World ecologies from the bio-behavioral science certainly limits the evolution of a truly international psychology. (1992: 3)

A key concern of this chapter is not only that African perspectives were, and continue to be, largely absent in the internationally accessible literature, but that local researchers, those who understand local development as insiders, are a small minority of that small compendium. Nsamenang's voice is an important voice, not only for its rarity, but for its persistent critique of an unacceptable condition, and for its expanding range over time from child development to ECD and on to education more broadly.

Nsamenang's earliest work focused on the Nso peoples of Cameroon, in addition to other West African cultural groups. Much of his early writing highlighted the important caregiving function that older siblings fulfil in traditional caretaking practices (Nsamenang, 1992, 2005, 2006; Nsamenang and Dasen, 1993). His more recent ECD work argued for research and programmatic practices that recognize and celebrate children's agency (2008a), build on indigenous ways of living and learning (2008b), respect culture as a necessary correlate to quality ECD programming (2009) and recognize the complexity of Africa's triple heritage – Western, traditional African and Islamic educational traditions – in any and all efforts to create and implement ECD policy (Nsamenang, 2005, 2010; Pence and Nsamenang, 2008). Throughout his career, Nsamenang has been consistent in his critique of the imposition of Western theories, discourses and so-called best-practice models. Thus, he forcefully advocates for an African-led research agenda, generative of Africentric knowledge.[5]

The 1990s produced few other African single lead voices in ECD; however, a growing number of African co-author partnerships developed. Margaret Kabiru and Anne Njenga are two Kenyan authors with a substantial number of publications in the 'grey literature' extending back to the 1970s, and with an increasing number of internationally accessible publications from the 1990s forward (e.g., 2007 [1994]).[6] In particular, their partnership with American Beth Blue Swadener has proven fruitful. For instance, their book, *Does the Village Still Raise the Child? A Collaborative Study of Changing Child-Rearing and Early Education in Kenya* (Swadener et al., 2000), emerged from a 'year-long collaborative study of the impacts of rapid social and economic change on child-rearing, early education and community mobilization in Kenya' (Swadener et al., 1997: 285). The study reflected a conception of ECD that extended from center-based institutional settings to include traditional family and non-parental care practices, in addition to a demonstrated respect for the holistic and multifaceted development of children.

Kabiru was also a key contributor to the Early Childhood Development Network for Africa (ECDNA), whose establishment was in large part the result of Mauritian Cyril Dalais' ECD advocacy work at UNICEF's education cluster in the early 1990s. Dalais was joined by individuals such as Barnabas Otaala and Kabiru in advancing a series of activities that included the 'ECD: More and Better' initiative co-sponsored by BvLF and led by Kate Torkington, and co-sponsorship of a series of UNICEF-supported ECD capacity-promoting workshops led by Alan Pence (Victoria, Canada: 1995; Windhoek, Namibia: 1997; Banjul, The Gambia, 1998). In the late 1990s, the Association for the Development of Education in Africa (ADEA), along with the Dutch government, came forward to assume responsibility for ECDNA-type activities under a new name, the Working Group on ECD (WGECD). The WGECD, under

ADEA and with support from UNESCO-BREDA in Dakar, continued in that form until February 2015, when it became the Inter-Country Quality Node on Early Childhood Development, based in Mauritius.

Swadener's collaborative work increased throughout the 2000s, often co-authoring with doctoral students from SSA. She and her co-authors have addressed the effects of neoliberal discursive policies in Kenyan ECD (Swadener and Wachira, 2003; Swadener et al., 2008); community-derived initiatives, young mothers and the Mwana Mwende organization (Kabiru et al., 2003); critical, participative, decolonizing research methodologies for work in SSA and other majority (developing) world contexts (Mutua and Swadener, 2004); and critical disability studies, postcolonial legacies and inclusive education in Kenya (Mutua and Swadener, 2011).

Canadian academics Larry Prochner and Ailie Cleghorn have a history of collaboration with African colleagues that goes back to the handbook discussed earlier (see Woodill et al., 1992), but also includes Cleghorn's work on ECD teacher education and educational reform in Zimbabwe in 1992–97. Since that time they have co-authored with each other and with some other African colleagues (Cleghorn and Prochner, 1997, 2003; Cleghorn and Weber, 1995; Mtetwa and Cleghorn, 2004; Prochner and Kabiru, 2008). In working with African teachers, researchers and children, Cleghorn and Prochner advocate for the incorporation of traditional 'ways of knowing, doing, and believing' in African ECD (2003: 144).

In 1999 the World Bank received a proposal to develop an Early Childhood Development Virtual University (ECDVU) (Pence, 1999). Based on a series of SSA ECD seminars supported by UNICEF in the mid-1990s, and on the earlier development of a 'generative curriculum' approach with First Nations communities in Canada (Ball and Pence, 2006; Pence and McCallum, 1994), the ECDVU included ECD literature from the Global North but encouraged participants to consider that work in their own contexts and to generate approaches to ECD that reflected local understandings, traditions and values as well. The ECDVU created a space on its website for locally produced major papers (see www.ecdvu.org) and also included SSA students' work in a volume edited by Pence and Kofi Marfo (2004).

Mentorship was also taking place within certain SSA institutions of higher learning, but only two universities had graduate-level programs in ECD in the 1990s. One of those, Kenyatta University, created at a later point a compendium of the grey literature for the period 1990–2006 under the leadership of Barbara Koech (2008). Similar to another literature search project (King et al., 2009), most of Koech's findings focus on child health, survival and protection factors, largely falling outside the narrower focus for ECD provided here.

A challenge for research leaders and mentors, even those with strong ties to places in Africa, has been to ensure the audibility and sustainability of indigenous African voices in the published, international literature. The issue of how to effectively promote and expand African contributions to the internationally visible literature remains a key concern today, not only for academics, but also for international organizations. A number of those most closely associated with ECD will be examined in the next section.

International Organizations

The BvLF has already been noted as an important international presence in SSA in the pre-watershed years, supporting not only programs but also locally produced publications. A second noteworthy organization is the Aga Khan Development Network (AKDN), particularly in its development of Madrassa Resource Centres for ECD commencing in 1986 in Mombasa, Kenya.[7] And while international charities like Save the Children, PLAN International, Christian Children's Fund, World Vision and others have played important roles in a wide range of SSA countries in the twenty-first century, most had a limited presence in ECD before 2000.

To a certain degree, the same could be said of UNICEF and UNESCO, as both had broad engagements with children, addressing key issues of child survival, health and development before 2000, but with a restricted focus on ECD specifically. There were, however, exceptions, such as the East and Southern Africa Regional Office (ESARO) of UNICEF providing materials for ECD training as part of the 1979 'International Year of the Child' and a great deal of behind-the-scenes work between the leadership of UNICEF and the Consultative Group on Early Childhood Care and Development leading up to the CRC, EFA and the publication of *The Twelve Who Survive* (Dalais, personal communication, 21 November 2013).

In a number of respects, however, the greatest impact on ECD in SSA in the pre-2000 period came from a less likely, but very large player: the World Bank. Signaling the growing interest in ECD was a slim volume from the World Bank headquarters: *Early Childhood Development: Investing in the Future* (Young, 1996), and two Africa-focused reports (Colletta et al., 1996; Colletta and Reinhold, 1997). These publications aimed to provide up-to-date information on the condition of young children in SSA and review the ECD policies and programs currently in place. The release of the two reports concurred with the World Bank's emergence as a major funder/lender for ECD on a scale previously unimaginable. World Bank ECD funding projects in the 1990s included: the Kenyan Early Child Development Project (1997–2002) at US$35.1 million; the Ugandan Nutrition and Early Childhood Development Project (1998–2001) at US$40 million; and the partially ECD-related Nigerian Development Communication Pilot Project (1993–97) at US$10.2 million (World Bank, 2003).

As the World Bank became increasingly active in ECD during the mid- to late 1990s, the dominant discourse of ECD internationally and in SSA began to shift from the 3Cs narrative of culture, context and community to a more technically focused, neoliberal and socioeconomic set of arguments based in large part on a few cost-benefit analyses undertaken in the USA. Indeed, by the turn of the millennium it was doubtful that any Ministry of Education or Finance in SSA had not heard the ECD refrain 'for every X dollar spent, Y dollars will be saved'. While various authors have pointed out a disconnect between findings from American-based studies and the realities of Africa, the arguments continue to appear regularly in both international and SSA publications, though not without a growing number of critics. Helen Penn, herself a frequent contributor to the ECD in SSA literature, is one of the strongest of those critics (2002, 2011, 2012).

By 2000, the dynamics surrounding the early years and ECD in Africa bore little resemblance to those from just over a decade earlier. With various ECD initiatives underway in SSA in the late 1990s, including the large-scale World Bank loan agreements, it became clear that building capacity for ECD planning and implementation was a key issue in efforts to move forward. One such initiative was the World Bank's decision to sponsor the first African International ECD Conference to be held in Kampala, Uganda in 1999. By 2000, not only were numerous international agreements in place, but Africa had responded with its own documents: *African Charter on the Rights and Welfare of the Child* (African Union, 1990) and *Education for All: A Framework for Action in Sub-Saharan Africa – Education for African Renaissance in the Twenty-first Century* (Johannesburg, 1999).

AFRICAN-LED ECD LITERATURE IN THE TWENTY-FIRST CENTURY

The millennium dawned hopefully for ECD in SSA. As noted earlier in this chapter, actors and activities unknown barely a decade before had transformed possibilities. The ECD in SSA story becomes much more complex with considerable strength appearing in certain parts of the literature from approximately 2006 to the present, but with capacity differentials sharpening across countries and language groups. On the upside: by 2008, 19 countries had tabled ECD policies (up from just a few at the end of the 1990s), with another 20 countries engaged in preparations (UNESCO BREDA, 2012); the International ECD Conference series launched in 1999 continued with three more through 2009; and the ECD in SSA literature continued to grow. On the downside, the gap between policy and provision of services was apparent in many countries; the overall fabric of ECD in SSA, measured, for example, by the oscillating strength of the WGECD, remained uncertain; and the number of internationally published studies led by Africans remained dramatically low compared to Africa's percentage of the world's child population. In regards to the published literature: certain partnerships continued to be productive; some new ones were formed; key volumes were published; and identifiable streams of African-led literature appeared and grew, with one stream in particular opening up new possibilities, not only for Africa but for the international literature more broadly.

Reference was made earlier to the ECDNA, which was transformed in the late 1990s and renamed the Working Group on ECD (WGECD). With funding support provided by the Dutch government and the Association for the Development of Education in Africa (ADEA), the WGECD took on two key initiatives. The first was a major policy development project under the direction of Torkington (2001), with teams in Ghana, Mauritius and Namibia. Second, a follow-up project was implemented in three countries – Mauritania, Senegal and Burkina Faso – which resulted in the publication of *Planning Policies for Early Childhood Development: Guidelines for Action* (Vargas-Baron, 2005). Additionally, Karin Hyde (Hyde, 2008; Hyde and Kabiru, 2003) undertook multiple studies for the ADEA-WGECD which examined the early learning possibilities of increased national investment in ECD programs.

ADEA-WGECD also played a key role in providing support to the International ECD

Conference series, typically with strong on-the-ground support by ECDVU participants and their local colleagues. The first of the ADEA-supported conferences was the Eritrean government's hosting of the Second African International ECD Conference in 2002 in Asmara. Under the theme 'Health, Nutrition, ECD, and Children in Need of Special Protection', the Eritrean government was successful not only in hosting the conference, but in developing a *Declaration for ECD: Framework for Action*. The third conference in the series, 'Moving ECD Forward in Africa', was held in Accra, Ghana in 2005 and experienced a dramatic increase in the attendance of senior officials from SSA governments (from three in Kampala to over 30 in Accra). The fourth conference was held in Dakar, Senegal in 2009, with over 600 participants from 42 SSA countries. That conference also had a strong political and policy agenda, resulting in the development of a *Call to Action Communique* that was subsequently presented by the President of Senegal to the Africa Union.

A key output from the Accra 2005 conference, ready in time for the Dakar 2009 Conference, was a broadly inclusive edited volume, *Africa's Future, Africa's Challenge: Early Childhood Care and Development in Sub-Saharan Africa* (Garcia et al., 2008). The volume incorporates not only diversity in the geographic and disciplinary backgrounds of its authors, but also diversity in development philosophies and in topics that range from policies to programs and economic analyses to educational initiatives across SSA.

Policy development – as can be seen in the WGECD-supported projects, the frequency of sessions devoted to policy-related topics at the International ECD Conferences and the number of chapters in the *Africa's Future* volume – was a priority for work in SSA in the late 1990s into the 2000s. It is therefore not surprising that the first substantial wave of African-led and Africa-focused scholarly work appears soon after these seeding processes and focuses on policy-related issues. Further, given the ongoing challenges of building in-country capacity, it is also not surprising that a key theme that emerges early on is the gap between policy development and implementation. While such themes are presented as concerns, from the perspective of this chapter these publications are also grounds for celebration as, for the first time, there was a dramatic increase in the overall number of African authors and the number of SSA countries appearing in the internationally accessible ECD literature.

Policy-Related Literature

The majority of articles identified as this new stream of African-led scholarly work take the form of country-specific historical reviews of ECD with a focus on contemporary policy frameworks. The countries include: Ghana (Agbenyega, 2008), Nigeria (Akindele, 2012; Amali et al., 2012; Ejieh, 2006; Ifakachukwu, 2011; Nakpodia, 2011; Nakpodia and Achugbe, 2012; Oduolowu, 2009), Botswana (Bose, 2008), Ethiopia (Tigistu, 2013), Kenya (Nganga, 2009), Malawi (Kholowa and Maluwa-Bandam, 2008; Kholowa and Rose, 2007), Tanzania (Mtahabwa, 2009, 2010) and Zimbabwe (Moyo et al., 2012). While this listing is not exhaustive, it conveys the popularity of the topic. The focus of these articles is captured by Obielumani Ifakachukwu as a 'yawning gap between policy formulation and implementation' (2011: 30). What becomes clear is that despite the growing presence of progressive early years policies, ECD sectors in most SSA countries remain largely underdeveloped. Through multiple methodological strategies of surveys and questionnaires, focus group interviews and documentary reviews, two themes consistently appear in the articles: challenges and recommendations. A brief review of each follows.

The noted challenges to successful policy implementation include: a lack of governmental coordination, including policy monitoring; financial management and general political will; a lack of infrastructure, such as adequate facilities and expansion planning;

a lack of pedagogical supports, e.g., learning materials, small class sizes; and access to educational programs for children with special needs (Agbenyega, 2008; Akindele, 2012; Amali et al., 2012; Ifakachukwu, 2011; Nakpodia, 2011; Nganga, 2009; Moyo et al., 2012). Other challenges include: differences between rural and urban provision of services (Mtahabwa, 2010); the legacy of colonial influence (Nganga, 2009); and high educator shortage and turnover due to infrequent and/or low salaries (Nakpodia and Achugbe, 2012). While differences between and within the countries themselves should not be glossed over, when considered thematically these problematic conditions cross national boundaries. Furthermore, while the recommendations arise in response to the collective challenges, the proposed solutions are diverse.

When proposing solutions, many authors shift attention from issues of state and bureaucratic oversight to a focus on potential programming and training advancements. These proposed changes include: standardizing the curriculum to guide educator training (Bose, 2008); defining the roles and responsibilities of private ECD operators (Ejieh, 2006; Ifakachukwu, 2011; Tigistu, 2013); focusing resources on the most disadvantaged children and communities (Agbenyega, 2008); increasing enrolment on ECD post-secondary programs to address rural teacher shortages (Akindele, 2012); initiating public media campaigns to impart the importance of ECD (Akindele, 2012); implementing flexible training models that value the experience of educators currently in the field (Tigistu, 2013); and offering fair wages for ECD educators (Moyo et al., 2012).

Another set of recommendations begin to touch on issues that have been a long-standing subtext within SSA child-related literature: the importance of families, communities and culture (akin to the 3Cs discussed earlier). Examples from these publications include: greater consultation of families and communities in policy development and implementation activities (Agbenyega, 2008; Mtahabwa, 2009); state promotion and/or enforcement of the mother tongue as the medium of instruction policy (Ifakachukwu, 2011; Nakpodia, 2011); empowering of indigenous childrearing and educational practices (Tigistu, 2013); closer cooperation between ECD staff and families (Nakpodia and Achugbe, 2012); parental contributions in the form of locally sourced learning materials (Nakpodia and Achugbe, 2012); and the inclusion of parental desires and understandings of local realities in program development (Kholowa and Rose, 2007; Matafwali, 2011).

SSA is at a point where considerable value can be added to ECD research through the development of networks both within and across SSA countries. In 2013, scholars from 18 SSA countries met first online and then face to face for three days to share and discuss key ECD research issues in their countries and how a community of scholars could provide mutual support. The 18-country meeting was followed by a smaller meeting of seven countries from southern Africa focused on developing a multi-country, multi-institutional, multi-disciplinary regional proposal that could then be taken to international donor organizations. Work to build a supportive community of SSA-focused donors to support both regional and SSA-wide work is currently underway.

Another multi-country, combination online/face-to-face ECD initiative is the *Indigenous Early Childhood Care and Education (IECCE) Curriculum for Africa: A Focus on Context and Contents.* An initiative of UNESCO's International Institute for Capacity Building in Africa (IICBA) based in Addis Ababa, the curriculum has brought together approximately a dozen early childhood educational leaders from 11 SSA countries to plan and draft a training curriculum that is based on African understandings of care and development (UNESCO, 2013). The IECCE curriculum framework is designed to take account of the cultural context of the African child. As such, its seven modules are conceived as 'living documents' with a goal to capacitate parents, siblings, relatives, elders, community members, various stakeholders and ECD professionals to engage

with children's learning (2013: 3). The program is designed for 'home based, community based or institutional based' settings (2013: 4). Importantly, the child's mother tongue will be used in instruction, and pedagogical materials will be locally, and creatively, resourced.

The IICBA project reinforces a key stream within the ECD literature of Africa – a stream that began with Nsamenang's work in the 1990s. Nsamenang's strong, critical positioning, vis-à-vis the eclipse of African perspectives and understandings through the force (intended or otherwise) of the Global North, continues to resonate across the continent. Indeed, that critical positioning frames what, at present, could be considered SSA's most unique and powerful contribution to the international early childhood literature. The influence of diverse critical perspectives is apparent in the work of two very prolific African ECD scholars: Godfrey Ejuu of Uganda and Hasina Ebrahim of South Africa. With no direct connections between them, their different locations and influences suggest a broadly based interest in critical perspectives.

A New Generation of Critical Scholars

Godfrey Ejuu's work largely centers on ECD curricular-related activities, including the design of instructional materials, early learning and development standards (ELDS), teacher training and ECD program support. A thread weaving throughout Ejuu's publications is a critique of the silencing of indigenous care and learning practices in the adoption of best-practice models from the Global North. Ejuu, like Nsamenang, situates ECD interventions in SSA within 'broader historic geo-political activities that have contributed to the impoverishment of the continent' (2013: 7). To explore the postcolonial condition of ECD in Uganda, Ejuu employs multiple methodologies: statistical analyses (2011), qualitative interviews (2012a, 2012c), philosophical reflection (2013) and policy analysis (2012b). His findings reveal a devaluing of indigenous knowledge that has had detrimental effects for center-based programs (2012b), parental care practices (2012a), teacher education programs (2012c) and national policy frameworks (2102b).

With impressive volume and breadth in publication, Hasina Ebrahim had approximately 15 publications in the 2010–2013 period. Her recent work includes topics such as agentic children as research collaborators (2011a, 2011c), center-based programming and teacher practices (2010, 2011b), national policy and curricular frameworks (2012a, 2012b), philosophical, postcolonial, reconceptualist and critical insights (2012c, 2012d, 2013a, 2013b), and these are just her solo authored contributions. While much of her work is specific to the South African context, Ebrahim also contributes to the worldwide discussion on the politics of the globalization of childhood. She names the concept of global childhood as 'an essentialist, homogenizing and standardized view of childhood which privileges western ideals' (2012d: 80). That said, Ebrahim recognizes that research undertaken in the Global North may contain productive lessons for ECD in SSA so long as it is open to contestation and a 'critical exchange of ideas, reflection and debate by practitioners, academics and students in the field' (2012d: 81). It is in this call for an exchange, a fair and balanced interaction amongst diverse perspectives, that it is believed much can be achieved for the future of ECD and ECD research – not only in Africa, but globally.

CONCLUSION

While the text above ends on a hopeful note – the development of a critical, Africentric stream that represents not only a vibrant promise for the future of ECD scholarly work in SSA, but for international ECD as well – that optimism is not without very substantial challenges. One such challenge facing ECD research development in SSA is the paucity of funding support for African-led, African-identified and African-conceptualized research. The bulk of

African-based research continues to be identified and led externally, typically addressing an agenda conceptualized in the Global North. If Africans are involved, their role is too often primarily as data gatherers – a role whose relationship to colonial activities is clear – a condition that extends to many other parts of the Global South as well. Voices are lost where a diversity of voices is needed.

As long as ECD research is led by the 5% (Arnett, 2008), and with African capacity concerns addressed through a combination of knowledge transfer approaches and the removal of some of Africa's most capable researchers to institutions outside its borders, African ECD will remain in the image of the Global North. Such restrictions serve neither Africa nor the rest of the world well. Sub-Saharan Africa is a place of tremendous diversity in history, language and culture, with traditions that have served Africa in the past and could do so again. It is through promoting multiple ways of understanding and researching ECD, and ensuring that respectful spaces are created for knowledge exchange and generation, that innovative and productive ways to better address both the needs of and the possibilities for Africa's children will emerge. These spaces so envisioned are filled not with an echo of one voice, but a chorus of voices.

FURTHER READING

Okwany, A., Ngutuku, E. and Muhangi, A. (2011) *The Role of Local Knowledge and Culture in Child Care in Africa: A Sociological Study of Several Ethnic Groups in Kenya and Uganda*. Lewiston, NY: Edwin Mellen Press.

Pence, A. and Hix-Small, H. (2009) 'Global children in the shadow of the global child', *International Critical Childhood Policy Studies*, 2(1): 75–91.

Serpell, R. and Nasamenang, A. B. (2014) 'Locally relevant and quality ECCE programmes: Implications of research in indigenous African child development and socialization', *Early Childhood Care and Education Working Paper Series*. Paris: UNESCO.

QUESTIONS FOR REFLECTION

1 How can we insist on research that is based in lived realities and that recognizes, respects and honors indigenous African knowledges?

2 What counts as research in international settings? What knowledge is available in unpublished research reports, student dissertations and conference proceedings that we might not find in published journals and books? What efforts can be made to better include this grey literature going forward?

3 What are the priority research areas? Who decides? How might networks of African scholars be created, supported and sustained in the future?

NOTES

1 Early Childhood Education, Care and Development (ECD) is known by many names, including 'early childhood care and education', 'early childhood development', 'early childhood education', 'early learning and child care' and 'early childhood care and development'. What these terms share is concern for the care, education and development of young children. In this chapter, we use ECD to convey an inclusive concept that takes into account the connections between caretaking, learning, health, nutrition and community practices in relation to a child's overall well-being. It is also the acronym in common use in Sub-Saharan Africa.

2 The compendium referred to is an ongoing collection of journal articles, books, chapters, papers, conference proceedings and reports, accessible in a searchable database at ecdafricaresources.org. The collection focuses on ECD in SSA where the guiding conception of ECD is one that emphasizes the educational and care components of childhoods prior to school age. As such, areas such as child rights or health and nutrition are not the current focus. A limitation of this chapter's review of the SSA literature is the absence of historical studies from South Africa. As South Africa has a rich, published history of ECD in its own right, a separate review is necessary. With the exception of Hasina Ebrahim's work, this review does not reference ECD work undertaken in South Africa.

3 Graduate students of the Whitings who have made substantial contributions to interdisciplinary areas of child, family, community and culture studies include Robert LeVine, Thomas Weisner, Carolyn Pope Edwards, Sarah LeVine and Mimi Bloch, to name but a few.

4 For full references of individually authored chapters, please refer to the general citation for the edited volume.

5 According to Nsamenang and the HDRC, 'Africentric scholarship is borne out of a legitimate desire to document hitherto disregarded African visions and experiences; it is neither a rejection of nor a revolt against inescapable western knowledges and technologies. To be authentic Africans must transcend colonial knowledge systems and legacies deposited on the continent as natural and unquestionable ... African scholarship should not be undertaken in isolation, however. Our Africentric products make sense only within the exchange frameworks of trends in global knowledge waves and state-of-the-science scholarship and are designed to contribute to the corpus of universal human knowledge, where Africa deserves its own knowledge-niche' (HDRC, 'Vision', 2010).

6 Grey literature includes 'unpublished theses (master's and doctoral), working papers, technical research reports, conference proceedings, as well as scholarship appearing in periodicals/monographs with limited circulation beyond the issuing institution' (Marfo et al., 2011: 102). Most of the research, conducted by African scholars on ECD in SSA, is to be found here and as such should be a focus of future research.

7 The first Madrassa School, Khairat Nursery School, opened in Mombasa, Kenya in 1986 (Mwaura, 2003). The school was a community-based response to concerns of poverty, school readiness and the perceived loss of traditional cultural and religious teachings. The pre-school curriculum combines traditional stories and songs, Koranic teachings and values, and literary and numeracy activities. To date, there are over 200 pre-schools, educating nearly 50,000 children in Kenya, Uganda and Tanzania (Aga Khan, 'Education', 2007).

REFERENCES

African Union [Organization of African Unity] (1990) *African Charter on the Rights and Welfare of the Child*. Addis Ababa: Organization of African Unity.

Agbenyega, J. (2008) 'Development of early years policy and practice in Ghana: Can outcomes be improved for marginalized children?', *Contemporary Issues in Early Childhood*, 9(4): 400–5.

Akindele, I. (2012) 'Poverty in early childhood care, development, and education: The Nigeria case', *International Journal of Early Childhood Education Research*, 1(3): 20–36.

Amali, I., Muhinat, B. and Okafor, I. P. (2012) 'An assessment of pre-primary school programme activities in Kwara State, Nigeria', *European Scientific Journal*, 8(8): 73–82.

Arnett, J. (2008) 'The neglected 95%: Why American psychology needs to become less American', *The American Psychologist*, 63(7): 602–14.

Ball, J. and Pence, A. (2006) *Supporting Indigenous Children's Development*. Vancouver, BC: UBC Press.

Bernard van Leer Foundation (BvLF) (1994) *Building on People's Strengths: Early Childhood in Africa*. The Hague: BvLF.

Bose, K. (2008) 'Gaps and remedies of early childhood care and education (ECCE) programs of Botswana', *Educational Research and Reviews*, 3(3): 77–82.

Cleghorn, A. and Prochner, L. (1997) 'Early childhood education in Zimbabwe: Recent trends and prospects', *Early Education and Development*, 8(3): 337–50.

Cleghorn, A. and Prochner, L. (2003) 'Contrasting visions of childhood: Examples from early childhood settings in Zimbabwe and India', *Journal of Early Childhood Research*, 1(2): 131–53.

Cleghorn, A. and Weber, S. (1995) 'Early childhood teacher education in Zimbabwe: From grass roots to university-based training', *Canadian Journal of Research in Early Childhood Education*, 4(2): 56–60.

Cochran, M. (ed.) (1993) *International Handbook of Child Care Policies and Programs*. Westport, CT: Greenwood Press.

Cole, M., Gay, J., Glick, J. S. and Sharp, D. W. (1971) *The Cultural Context of Learning and Thinking*. New York: Basic Books.

Colletta, N. and Reinhold, A. (1997) 'Review of early childhood development policy and programs in Sub-Saharan Africa', *Working Paper Series*. Washington, DC: World Bank.

Colletta, N., Balachander, J. and Liang, X. (1996) 'The condition of young children in Sub-Saharan Africa: The convergence of health, nutrition, and early education', *Working Paper Series*. Washington, DC: World Bank.

Dasen, P., Inhelder, B., Lavallée, M. and Retschitzki, J. (1978) *Naissance de l'intelligence chez l'enfant baoulé de Côte d'Ivoire*. Berne: Hans Huber.

Ebrahim, H. (2010) 'Conflicting discourses of private nursery entrepreneurs in KwaZulu-Natal, South Africa', *Contemporary Issues in Early Childhood*, 11(1): 39–48.

Ebrahim, H. (2011a) 'Children as agents in early childhood education', *Education as Change*, 15(1): 121–31.

Ebrahim, H. (2011b) 'Levels of well-being and involvement in centre-based provision for birth to four years in the Free State in South Africa', *South African Journal of Childhood Education*, 1(2): 1–15.

Ebrahim, H. (2011c) 'Situated ethics: Possibilities for young children as research participants in the South Africa context', *Early Child Development and Care*, 18(3): 289–98.

Ebrahim, H. (2012a) 'Emerging models for early childhood development from birth to four in South Africa', in T. Papatheodorou (ed.), *Debates on Early Childhood Policies and Practices: Global Snapshots of Pedagogical Thinking and Encounter*. London: Routledge. pp. 62–71.

Ebrahim, H. (2012b) 'Foregrounding silences in the birth to four curriculum', *European Early Childhood Education Research Journal* (http://dx.doi.org/10.1080/1350293X.2012.738869).

Ebrahim, H. (2012c) 'Interrogating the current imagination of early childhood teacher education through dialogical processes', *Communitas*, 17: 101–15.

Ebrahim, H. (2012d) 'Tensions in incorporating global childhood with early childhood programs: The case of South Africa', *Australasian Journal of Early Childhood*, 37(3): 80–6.

Ebrahim, H. (2013a) 'Editorial', *European Early Childhood Education Research Journal*, 21(4): 455–8.

Ebrahim, H. (2013b) 'The role of play in fostering a creative culture: A South African perspective', in D. Guantlett and B. St. Jerne (eds), *Cultures of Creativities*. The Lego Foundation. pp. 20–3 (www.legofoundation.com/en-us/research/research-articles/).

Edwards, C. P. and Bloch, M. (2010) 'The Whitings' concepts of culture and how they have fared in contemporary psychology and anthropology', *Journal of Cross-Cultural Psychology*, 41: 485–98.

Edwards, C. P. and Whiting, B. (eds) (2004) *Ngecha: A Kenyan Village in a Time of Rapid Social Change*. Lincoln, NE: University of Nebraska Press.

Ejieh, M. (2006) 'Pre-primary education in Nigeria: Policy implication and problems',

Iköğretim Online/Elementary Education Online, 5(1): 58–64.

Ejuu, G. (2011) 'Determinants of public investment in early childhood development at local and national levels in Uganda', *Social Science Research Network* (http://ssrn.com/abstract=1761977).

Ejuu, G. (2012a) 'Cultural and parental standards as the benchmark for early learning and development standards in Africa', *International Journal of Current Research*, 4(4): 282–8.

Ejuu, G. (2012b) 'Early childhood development policy advances in Uganda', *Contemporary Issues in Early Childhood*, 13(2): 248–55.

Ejuu, G. (2012c) 'Implementing the early childhood development teacher training framework in Uganda: Gains and challenges', *Journal of Early Childhood Research*, 10(3): 282–93.

Ejuu, G. (2013) 'Rethinking early learning and development standards in the Ugandan context', *Childhood Education*, 89(1): 3–8.

Garcia, M., Pence, A. and Evans, J. (eds) (2008) *Africa's Future, Africa's Challenge: Early Childhood Care and Development in Sub-Saharan Africa*. Washington, DC: World Bank.

Human Development Resource Centre (HDRC) (2010) 'Vision' (thehdrc.org/openaccess.html).

Hyde, K. (2008) *Investing in Early Childhood Development: Benefits, Savings, and Financing Options*. Dakar: WGECD.

Hyde, K. and Kabiru, M. (2003) *Early Childhood Development as an Important Strategy to Improve Learning Outcomes*. Dakar: WGECD.

Ifakachukwu, O. (2011) 'Early childhood education: An overview', *International NGO Journal*, 6(1): 30–4.

Johannesburg (1999) 'Education for All: A framework for action in Sub-Saharan Africa – Education for African renaissance in the twenty-first century', report on the *All Sub-Saharan Conference on Education for All*, 6–10 December, Johannesburg, ARTG and UNICEF.

Kabiru, M. and Njenga, A. (eds) (2007 [1994]) *How Children Grow and Develop*. Nairobi: Nairobi KLB.

Kabiru, M., Njenga, A. and Swadener, B. B. (2003) 'Early childhood development in Kenya: Empowering young mothers, mobilizing a community', *Childhood Education*, 79(6): 358–63.

Kholowa, F. and Maluwa-Bandam, D. (2008) 'Early childhood education and development in Malawi: Major challenges and prospects', *Zimbabwe Journal of Educational Research*, 20(1): 11–21.

Kholowa, F. and Rose, P. (2007) 'Parental or policy maker misunderstandings? Contextual dilemmas of pre-schooling for poverty reduction in Malawi', *International Journal of Educational Development*, 27(4): 458–72.

King, M., September, R., Okarche, F. and Cardoso, C. (eds) (2009) *Child Research in Africa*. Dakar: Council for the Development of Social Science Research in Africa (CODESRIA).

Koech, B. (2008) National Council for Children's Services: Research Abstracts for the Consultancy Services on Research and Studies in Children Matters. Nairobi, Kenya (http://ecdvu.org/Africa_Pubs.php).

Konner, M. (1976) 'Maternal care, infant behavior and development among the !Kung', in R. Lee and I. DeVore (eds), *Kalahari Hunter-Gatherers*. Cambridge, MA: Harvard University Press. pp. 218–45.

Lamb, M., Sternberg, K., Hwang, C. and Broberg, A. (1992) *Child Care in Context: Cross-cultural Perspectives*. Hillsdale, NJ: Lawrence Erlbaum.

Lanyasunya, A. R., Lesolayia, M. S., with Neeto, T., Kamau, P., Senbeyo, M. and Lucy, L. (2001) *El-Barta Child and Family Project: Early Childhood Development*. Working Papers in Early Childhood Development No. 28. The Hague: BvLF.

Leiderman, P., Babu, B., Kagia, J., Kraemer, H. and Leiderman, G. (1973) 'African infant precocity and some social influences during the first year', *Nature*, 242: 247–9.

LeRoux, W. (2002) *The Challenges of Change: A Tracer Study of San Preschool Children in Botswana*. The Hague: BvLF.

LeVine, R. (2010) 'The Six Cultures Study: Prologue to a history of a landmark project', *Journal of Cross-Cultural Psychology*, 41: 513–21.

LeVine, R. and LeVine (Lloyd), B. (1966) *Nyansongo: A Gusii Community in Kenya*. New York: Krieger.

LeVine, R., Dixon, S., LeVine, S., Richman, A., Leiderman, P. and Keefer, C. (1994) *Child Care and Culture: Lessons from Africa*. New York: Cambridge University Press.

Marfo, K., Pence, A., LeVine, R. and LeVine, S. (2011) 'Strengthening Africa's contributions to child development research: Overview and ways forward', *Child Development Perspectives*, 5(2): 104–11.

Matafwali, B. (2011) 'Programmes in Zambia: A case of four selected districts', *Journal of Early Childhood Development*, 5: 109–31.

Moyo, J., Wadesango, N. and Kurebwa, M. (2012) 'Factors that affect the implementation of early childhood development programmes in Zimbabwe', *Studies of Tribes and Tribals*, 10(2): 141–9.

Mtahabwa, L. (2009) 'Early childhood cultural development in Tanzania: Reflections from key government documents', *Journal of Humanities*, 1(1): 43–54.

Mtahabwa, L. (2010) 'Pre-primary educational policy and practice in Tanzania: Observations from urban and rural pre-primary schools', *International Journal of Educational Development*, 30(3): 227–35.

Mtetwa, D. K. and Cleghorn, A. (2004) 'Structural aspects of primary mathematics lessons in Zimbabwe: Prospects for change?', *Education as Change*, 8(2): 92–104.

Mutua, K. and Swadener, B. B. (2004) 'Physical disability and the cultural construction of manhood: Dialectics of capitalism and post-coloniality', *Linking Research and Education in Special Education: An International Perspective*, 1(1): 16–29.

Mutua, K. and Swadener, B. B. (2011) 'Challenges to inclusive education in Kenya: Postcolonial perspectives and family narratives', in A. Artiles, E. Kozleski and F. Waitoller (eds), *Inclusive Education: Examining Equity on Five Continents*. Cambridge, MA: Harvard Education Press. pp. 201–22.

Mwaura, P. (2003) *Creating an Effective Early Childhood Education Programme: A Case of the Madrasa Resource Centre Programme*. The Hague: Madrasa Regional Research Programme and BvLF.

Myers, R. (1992) *The Twelve Who Survive: Strengthening Programmes of Early Childhood Development in the Third World*. London: Routledge.

Nakpodia, E. (2011) 'Early childhood education: Its policy formulation and implementation in Nigerian educational system', *African Journal of Political Science and International Relations*, 5(3): 159–63.

Nakpodia, E. and Achugbe, M. (2012) 'Problems encountered in the management of nursery and primary schools in Delta State, Nigeria', *African Journal of Political Science and International Relations*, 4(6): 140–8.

Nganga, L. (2009) 'Early childhood education programs in Kenya: Challenges and solutions', *Early Years: An International Research Journal*, 29(3): 227–36.

Nsamenang, A. B. (1992) *Human Development in Cultural Context: A Third World Perspective*. Newbury Park, CA: SAGE.

Nsamenang, A. B. (2005) *Developmental Psychology: Search for a Diversity Paradigm*. Bamenda, Cameroon: HDRC.

Nsamenang, A. B. (2006) 'Human ontogenesis: An Indigenous African view on development and intelligence', *International Journal of Psychology*, 41(4): 293–7.

Nsamenang, A. B. (2008a) '(Mis)Understanding ECD in Africa: The force of local and imposed motives', in M. Garcia, A. Pence and J. Evans (eds), *Africa's Future, Africa's Challenge: Early Childhood Care and Development in Sub-Saharan Africa*. Washington, DC: World Bank. pp. 135–49.

Nsamenang, A. B. (2008b) 'Agency in early childhood learning and development in Cameroon', *Contemporary Issues in Early Childhood Development*, 9(3): 211–23.

Nsamenang, A. B. (2009) 'Cultures of early childhood care and education', in M. Fleer, M. Hedegaard and J. Tudge (eds), *World Yearbook of Education 2009: Childhood Studies and the Impact of Globalization – Policies and Practices at Global and Local Levels*. New York: Routledge. pp. 23–45.

Nsamenang, A. B. (2010) 'Childhood within Africa's triple heritage', in G. Cannella and L. Soto (eds), *Childhoods: A Handbook*. New York: Peter Lang. pp. 39–54.

Nsamenang, A. B. and Dasen, P. (1993) 'Child development and national development in Cameroon', *Journal of Psychology in Africa*, 1(5): i–xvii.

Olmsted, P. and Weikart, D. (eds) (1989) *How Nations Serve Young Children: Profiles of Child Care and Education in 14 Countries*. Ypsilanti, MI: High/Scope Press.

Oduolowu, E. (2009) 'Early childhood care and Education for All in 2015: Is this a mirage in Nigeria?', *Journal of Global Initiatives: Policy, Pedagogy, Perspective*, 4 (http://digitalcommons.kennesaw.edu/jgi/vol4/iss1/2).

Pence, A. (1999) 'Developing an ECD virtual university', a proposal submitted to the World Bank, Washington, DC.

Pence, A. and Benner, A. (2015) *Complexities, Capacities, Communities: Challenging and Changing Development Narratives*. Victoria BC: University of Victoria. Manuscript submitted for publication.

Pence, A. and Marfo, K. (eds) (2004) 'Capacity building for early childhood education in Africa', *International Journal of Educational Policy, Research, and Practice*, 5(3): 5–12.

Pence, A. and McCallum, M. (1994) 'Developing cross-cultural partnerships: Implications for child care quality research and practice', in P. Moss and A. Pence (eds), *Valuing Quality in Early Childhood Services: New Approaches to Defining Quality*. New York: Teachers College Press. pp. 108–22.

Pence, A. and Nsamenang, A. B. (2008) *A Case for Early Childhood Development in Sub-Saharan Africa*. The Hague: BvLF.

Penn, H. (2002) 'The World Bank's view of early childhood', *Childhood*, 9: 118–32.

Penn, H. (2011) 'Travelling policies and global buzzwords: How international non-governmental organizations and charities spread the word about early childhood in the global South', *Childhood*, 18(1): 94–113.

Penn, H. (2012) 'The rhetoric and realities of early childhood programmes promoted by the World Bank', in A. Twum-Danso and R. Ame (eds), *Childhoods at the Intersection of the Local and the Global*. Basingstoke: Palgrave Macmillan. pp. 42–59.

Prochner, L. and Kabiru, M. (2008) 'Early childhood development in Africa: A historical perspective', in M. Garcia, A. Pence and J. Evans (eds), *Africa's Future, Africa's Challenge: Early Childhood Care and Development in Sub-Saharan Africa*. Washington: World Bank. pp. 117–33.

Serpell, R. (1976) *Culture's Influence on Behaviour*. London: Methuen.

Serpell, R. (1993) *The Significance of Schooling: Life-Journeys in an African Society*. Cambridge: Cambridge University Press.

Super, C. and Harkness, S. (1986) 'The developmental niche: A conceptualization at the interface of child and culture', *International Journal of Behavioral Development*, 9: 545–69.

Super, C., Harkness, S., Barry, O. and Zeitlin, M. (2011) 'Think locally, act globally: Contributions of African research to child development', *Child Development Perspectives*, 5(2): 119–25.

Swadener, B. B. and Wachira, P. (2003) 'Governing children and families in Kenya: Losing ground in neoliberal times', in M. N. Bloch, K. Hulqvist and T. Popkewitz (eds), *Restructuring the Governing Patterns of the Child, Education and the Welfare State*. New York/London: Palgrave Macmillan. pp. 231–57.

Swadener, B. B., Kabiru, M. and Njenga, A. (1997) 'Does the village still raise the child? A collaborative study in changing child-rearing in Kenya', *Early Education and Development*, 8(3): 285–306.

Swadener, B. B., Kabiru, M. and Njenga, A. (2000) *Does the Village Still Raise the Child? A Collaborative Study of Changing Childrearing and Early Education in Kenya*. Albany, NY: State University of New York Press.

Swadener, B. B., Wachira, P., Kabiru, M. and Njenga, A. (2008) 'Linking policy discourse to everyday life in Kenya: Impacts of neoliberal policies on early education and childrearing', in M. Garcia, A. Pence and J. Evans (eds), *Africa's Future, Africa's Challenge: Early Childhood Care and Development in Sub-Saharan Africa*. Washington, DC: World Bank. pp. 407–26.

Tigistu, K. (2013) 'Professionalism in early childhood education and care in Ethiopia: What are we talking about?', *Childhood Education*, 89(3): 152–8.

Torkington, K. (2001) *Working Group on Early Childhood Development Policy Project: A Synthesis Report*. Dakar: ADEA-WGECD.

Tronick, E. Z., Morelli, G. and Winn, S. (1987) 'Multiple caretaking of Efe (Pygmy) infants', *American Anthropologist*, 89: 96–106.

United Nations (1990) *Convention on the Rights of the Child*. New York: United Nations.

UNESCO (1990) World Declaration on Education for All (www.unesco.org/education/wef/en-conf/Jomtien%20Declaration%20eng.shtm).

UNESCO (2013) 'Draft concept note: Indigenous early childhood care and education (IECCE) for Africa pilot workshop on the delivery modules', *UNESCO Big Push Initiative* (www.unesco.org/new/en/dakar/about-this-office/single-view/news/big_push_workshop_to_accelerate_early_childhood_care_and_education_in_africa/).

UNESCO BREDA (2012) *Early Childhood Care and Education Regional Report: Africa*. Dakar: UNESCO.

Vargas-Baron, E. (2005) *Planning Policies for Early Childhood Development: Guidelines for*

Action. Paris: ADEA-WGECD, UNICEF and UNESCO.

Weisner, T. (2010) 'John and Beatrice Whiting's contributions to the cross-cultural study of human development: Their values, goals, norms, and practices', *Journal of Cross-Cultural Psychology*, 41(4): 499–509.

Weisner, T. and Edwards, C. P. (2002) 'Beatrice Whiting: Introduction', *Ethos*, 29(3): 239–46.

Weisner, T. and Gallimore, R. (1977) 'My brother's keeper: Child and sibling caretaking', *Current Anthropology*, 18: 169–90.

Whiting, B. (ed.) (1963) *Six Cultures: Studies of Child Rearing*. New York: Wiley.

Whiting, B. and Whiting, J. (eds) (1975) *Children in Six Cultures: A Psycho-Cultural Analysis*. Cambridge, MA: Harvard University Press.

World Bank (2003) *Global Directory of Early Childhood Development Projects*. Washington, DC: World Bank.

Woodill, G., Bernhard, J. and Prochner, L. (eds) (1992) *International Handbook of Early Childhood Education*. New York: Garland.

Young, M. (1996) *Early Child Development: Investing in the Future*. Washington, DC: World Bank.

24

Early Learning and Healthy Development in a Digital Age

Jason C. Yip, Michael H. Levine,
Alexis R. Lauricella and Ellen Wartella

INTRODUCTION

Children, especially in early childhood, are rapidly developing and highly influenced by their context. The study of early childhood learning and healthy development cannot take place today without considering the influence of pervasive digital media and technologies. In comparison to older children and adults, people often perceive young children as the most vulnerable and susceptible to the power of digital technology (Lemish, 2014). Over the past 50 years, new and repeated concerns have been noted from parents, policy makers, educators and other stakeholders regarding the impact that digital media may have on children's learning and development (see Wartella and Robb, 2008). For instance, in 1961 Commissioner Newton Minow of the USA Federal Communications Commission referred to the vast wasteland of quality content (e.g., sexual content, violence and immoral characters) available on broadcast television (Minow, 1961). Yet there is also great potential with each new technology to help children learn and develop.

In the mid-1960s, Joan Ganz Cooney and her colleagues at the Children's Television Workshop focused on the potential of television as a tool to engage and educate preschool children (Cooney, 1966). Together, Cooney and her colleagues created *Sesame Street*, a unique television program designed to educate preschool children while encouraging family co-viewing. The *Sesame Street* approach catalyzed an entire industry of educational media production that has consistently demonstrated that modern media can positively shape learning and development for millions of children in multiple international contexts (Fisch and Truglio, 2001; Mares and Pan, 2013).

Today, television is ubiquitous in the majority of homes across most countries and access to new mobile technologies (e.g., tablets, smartphones) is rapidly growing for children internationally (Gigli, 2004; Rideout, 2013). Furthermore, digital media now includes a plethora of interactive apps and games created for very young children (Guernsey et al., 2012; Shuler, 2009a, 2009b, 2010; Shuler et al., 2012). Unlike traditional television programming which was one-directional, these new mobile and interactive technologies include content that can be created by anyone and can now be personalized to meet the needs of each particular user, creating a two-way interaction in which the child directly impacts the content and the experience.

Given the dramatic change in available media technologies and the fact that young children all around the world are now spending around 2 or more hours a day with digital media (Gigli, 2004), it is essential to examine the impact of these technologies on young children's healthy development. While there is a large body of literature regarding the impact of television on child viewers, this chapter will focus primarily on the newer digital and mobile technologies (e.g., smartphones, tablets) and the role they may play in young children's learning and development.

The first section of this chapter addresses three key questions that define the contemporary technology and early learning landscape. First, we ask which factors shape young children's use of digital media (especially computers, smartphones and tablet computers). Second, caregivers and early childhood educators may be skeptical of new technologies for children. As such, we examine the question of what we know about the negative influences of using digital media on young children's development. Third, to allay some of the concerns about digital media and early childhood, we investigate the question, what are the positive influences of young children's digital media use on healthy development and learning? The second section utilizes a digital adaptation to Bronfenbrenner's (1977, 1979) ecological development theory (Takeuchi and Levine, 2014) to draw implications from the research for the broader field of early childhood practice, program design and public policy.

REVIEW OF THE LITERATURE

Which Factors Shape Young Children's Media Usage?

Today's young children are born into a world very different from the one in which their parents grew up. For instance, nearly all homes in the USA with children age 8 and under have a TV set (96%), 76% have a laptop or desktop computer, 63% have a smartphone and 40% have a tablet device (Rideout, 2013). While mobile device ownership has increased for families at all SES levels worldwide (Pew Global, 2014), a gap still exists as a function of family income. In the USA, only 20% of lower-income children have a tablet at home, whereas 63% of higher-income children do (Rideout, 2013). Rates of smartphone ownership are closer across income groups with 51% of lower-income families owning a smartphone compared to 65% of higher-income families (Rideout, 2013). Mobile devices (i.e., smartphones, cellular phones, mobile Internet) are more dominant in lower-income families in Asia (Qiu, 2014), Latin America (World Bank, 2012), North America (Smith, 2010) and Africa (Tortora and Rheault, 2011). However, mobile devices are restricted in their functions (e.g., limited applications) and mobile data caps can prevent downloads of large amounts of information (e.g., high-definition video streaming). A digital divide in access to technology still persists in the developing world, such as the lack of strong broadband Internet access in homes and schools in rural China (e.g., Li and Ranieri, 2013; Yang et al., 2013), India (e.g., Ale and Chib, 2011), Latin America (e.g., Carrasco and Torrecilla, 2012) and South Asia (e.g., Zhou et al., 2011).

Evidence also indicates that preschool children in the USA (Rideout, 2013) and other wealthy countries in Europe (e.g., Holloway et al., 2013; Mascheroni and Ólafsson, 2014) and Asia (e.g., Hong Kong Department of Health, 2009; Jie, 2012) are avid media users, spending about 2 hours per day with screen media. The use of newer mobile technologies is accelerating: 72% of children age 8 and under in the USA had used a mobile device in 2013, compared to only 38% in 2011 (Rideout, 2013). In Europe, the average age of first Internet usage is 8 years (Mascheroni and Ólafsson, 2014), and in South Korea (the country with the most high-speed Internet users) 93% of children aged 3–9 go online for an average of 8 to 9 hours a week (Jie, 2012).

Research has explored which factors are predictive of young children's media use. Studies have determined that in the USA, demographic factors like child age (Rideout, 2011), race (Rideout et al., 2011) and socio-economic status (SES) or parent education (Bittman et al., 2011) are predictive of child screen time, particularly for television. Beyond demographics, a child's desires and family culture shape media use (Stephen et al., 2013). Further, external factors including family conflict and stressors (e.g., poverty, depression) are negatively related to educational media usage in the USA (Vandewater and Bickham, 2004).

Research in North America, Asia and Europe demonstrates that parents' own media habits likely influence those of their young children as children's behaviors are often influenced by the observation of adults (Bleakley et al., 2013; Plowman and McPake, 2013; Wu et al., 2014). Parent media use is actually the strongest predictor of a child's use of both traditional technology (television, computers) and newer mobile media (smartphones, tablets), even when parent attitudes toward media technology are included in the models (Lauricella et al., resubmitted). This is particularly evident when parents are themselves heavy media users (e.g., Jago et al., 2010; Wartella et al., 2013; Woodard and Gridina, 2000).

More specifically, in a recent survey of parents in the USA, Wartella and colleagues (2013) found that media-centric families are composed of parents who reported spending an average of 11:04 (hours:minutes) a day with screen media, while their children aged

0 to 8 spend 4:29 a day. These families enjoy using media together and often use media as a tool to keep children occupied while they get other things done around the house. In contrast, 'media light' parents who reported spending less than 2 hours a day with screen media (1:48) have children who also spend less time with screen media – about an hour and a half per day. Further, other research conducted in the USA suggests that parent television time has a stronger relationship to child television time (for all ages) than access to television in the home or in the child's bedroom and parental rules of viewing (Bleakley et al., 2013). Overall, the impact that digital media have on the child's development is not predicated on access and usage alone, but is influenced by both the setting and the content (which we discuss in the next section) that children are experiencing (Guernsey, 2007).

What Concerns are Present About Children's Well-Being and Media Usage?

Over the past decade, concerns about young children's use of digital media and the impact on children's health and well-being have surfaced. Here, we examine the impact of media use on cognitive development, childhood obesity, musculoskeletal development and sleep.

Cognitive Development

Debates persist about the exact role media exposure has in normal cognitive development in babies and infants, particularly when it comes to attention problems. In 1999, the American Academy of Pediatrics (AAP) recommended that parents avoid television viewing for children under the age of 2 and stated that there is concern that overstimulation from high levels of media use might lead to attention deficit disorder or hyperactivity (AAP, 1999). Today, the AAP has adapted its stance to recognize distinctions in types of media experiences, but still discourages screen media use before the age of 2 (AAP, 2013).

Despite this recommendation, there is no reliable empirical evidence to demonstrate that viewing video causes attention problems (Courage and Howe, 2010; Courage and Setliff, 2010; Schmidt et al., 2009). One earlier study by Christakis and colleagues (2004) found an association between early media exposure and attention measures in children. However, Foster and Watkins (2010) reanalyzed the same dataset and found that when other appropriate control variables were included, the findings by Christakis and colleagues (2004) were no longer significant. Dutch researchers Huizinga, Nikkelen and Valkenburg's (2014) review of the literature calls for more research on whether individual factors (e.g., age, gender) specifically enhance media effects on attention deficit disorder behaviors. Currently, without more convincing evidence, it is unclear if there is any relationship between attention problems and media use. Rather, it may be that children exhibiting hyperactivity and problematic attention tend to either gravitate towards digital media or, perhaps, some parents use digital media as a way to calm hyperactive children.

Obesity

A childhood obesity epidemic has been on the rise for the past 30 years in the USA (Ogden et al., 2014) and, more recently, in other industrialized nations (World Health Organization, 2014). Researchers suggest there is no one cause for childhood obesity. Intertwining factors, such as screen media and sedentary behaviors (e.g., Byun et al., 2011; Strasburger, 2011), exposure to food advertisements and poor diet (e.g., Institute of Medicine, 2006), changing school cultures (e.g., less recess time) (e.g., Fernandes and Sturm, 2010) and home cultures (e.g., industrialized jobs vs. agrarian work) (Phillips, 2006), and children's sleep patterns (e.g., Cappuccio et al., 2008) all play a role in this health epidemic.

Given that young children often use media in a sedentary manner, many studies have examined the relationship between sedentary behavior and obesity. There is an apparent relationship between high levels of media use and higher weight levels or obesity in children. In Qatar, 80% of overweight and 80% of obese children spend more than 3 hours on the Internet each day, compared to 72% of normal weight children (Bener et al., 2012). A study of elementary school students in Canada demonstrated that children who spend 2 or more hours per day using screen media were more likely to 'sometimes' eat meals in front of the TV and have parents who are more sedentary themselves (He et al., 2010).

In addition to the relationship between sedentary behavior and obesity, food marketing via television, websites and apps, has been implicated in the obesity crisis. The Institute of Medicine (2006) report on *Food Marketing and the Diets of Children and Youth* conducted a systematic review of 123 American research studies on the relationship between television advertising and children's eating behaviors. The report found strong evidence for the effects of food and beverage marketing on children's food and beverage preferences, purchase requests and short-term food and beverage consumption for children aged 2 to 11. Increasingly, web video, online games with food themes and viral social media food marketing encourage young children to pass information on to other children (e.g., Cheyne et al., 2013; Harris et al., 2012). In short, young children in the digital age now navigate through many digital domains that target them as prospective consumers of unhealthy foods.

Musculoskeletal Development

Based on the previous research on the long and extended number of hours young children are exposed to screen time, there is a growing concern from researchers in ergonomics about the development of musculoskeletal disorders, especially for young children who are in a vulnerable stage of growth. When children use technology with poor posture or in constraining positions, problems in normal musculoskeletal development may occur (Straker et al., 2009).

Young children's use of technology across the world is more mobile (Groupe Speciale

Mobile Association, 2013): instead of being confined to a desktop computer, children's technology use can occur on the living room sofa, during car rides and in other environments that influence their physical positions and musculoskeletal development. However, little research has examined newer mobile technologies (e.g., smartphones, tablets) with respect to younger children's (ages 3–8) musculoskeletal development. One recent study does highlight ergonomic issues related to children's use of physical digital games (e.g., exergames). Straker and colleagues (2014) conducted an international review of the literature on digital games and children's health. They concluded that new digital games with more innovative and mobile controllers that allow 3D real-life body motion (e.g., *Kinect*), physical gestures (e.g., *WiiMote* controller) and repetitive motions, may impact young children's musculoskeletal health by causing repetitive strain in hands, awkward and sustained postures that increase musculoskeletal injury and high acceleration movements that increase the risk of accidental injury.

Sleep

Research has shown associations between digital media use and disruption of childhood sleep in wealthier nations (e.g., Anderson and Evans, 2001; Garrison et al., 2011; Haines et al., 2013; Higuchi et al., 2005; Owens et al., 1999; Paavonen et al., 2006). In the USA, Garrison et al. (2011) conducted a randomized control trial of children aged 3 to 5 that showed the watching of violent media content and evening use of technology were associated with disrupted sleep patterns. In contrast, daytime non-violent media content did not have any negative effects on sleep. Garrison and Christakis (2012) also found that reducing violent content can support better sleeping habits. Similarly, a study of children in Finland demonstrated that sleep disturbances are associated with higher levels of TV viewing and are particularly problematic when children are exposed to adult-targeted television programs (Paavonen et al., 2006).

Other research has examined the relationship between children's use of computers and video games and sleep patterns. In the USA, increased time spent on electronic games is associated with younger children's decreased total sleep time on weekends (Adam et al., 2007). In Japan, elementary school children's use of video games and of the Internet before bedtime was associated with negative sleep patterns, such as later wake-up times and shorter sleep duration (Oka et al., 2008). A strong predictor of sleep disturbances is the presence of television and other media technology in children's bedrooms. In the USA, Vandewater et al. (2007) found that one-fifth of children aged 0–2 and more than one-third of 3- to 6-year-olds have a television in their bedroom. However, the parental decision to put a TV in a child's bedroom goes against evidence that bedroom television may increase problems with sleep in young children (Anderson and Evans, 2001; Owens et al., 1999). More specifically, a study of students from Belgium found that children who had a TV set in their bedroom went to bed significantly later on both weekend and week days and spent less time in bed on weekdays than children without a TV in their bedroom (Van den Bulck, 2004). Similarly, the presence of computers in bedrooms has also been linked to sleep disruption in young Chinese children (Li et al., 2007).

What Positive Effects of Media and Technology are Present in Children's Healthy Development and Learning?

While there is evidence of significant concerns related to children's media use, not all media exposure has a negative impact on children's health and well-being. The history of children's viewing of educational television shows and use of other educational technologies has demonstrated the positive role media can play in young children's development. In a selective review of research, Guernsey (2007) demonstrated that children can and do learn from well-crafted, developmentally appropriate media content. She concluded that children's development and learning are influenced by '3 Cs': the *content* of the media they are using, the *context* in which they are using the media and the characteristics of the *child* (Guernsey, 2007). Following this useful framework, we first discuss the positive effects of media use on children's healthy development and learning for different age groups of children (specifically preschool children compared to infants and toddlers) and then examine the ways in which the content and context influence development and learning.

Preschool Learning

As children reach preschool and early elementary age, they begin to develop more advanced skills and are better able to learn from exposure to digital media. Empirical evidence indicates that preschoolers actively watch television (Anderson and Lorch, 1983) and that well-crafted, educational, preschool television viewing can be positively associated with academic performance and skills (Fisch and Truglio, 2001). For instance, decades of research in the USA with preschool-aged children demonstrates that watching educational media at home is positively associated with preschoolers' development of literacy, mathematics, science and prosocial behavior (e.g., Comstock and Scharrer, 2010; Fisch, 2014; Friedrich and Stein, 1973; Kirkorian et al., 2008). Importantly, the positive effects associated with viewing educational preschool television seem to be even more powerful for at-risk children in the USA (Fetler, 1984; Fisch and Truglio, 2001), and viewing educational TV can have long-term positive effects on academic performance (Anderson et al., 2001). Preschool children who were moderately at risk demonstrated gains across all areas of emergent literacy that were featured in the literacy show, *Between the Lions* (Linebarger et al., 2004).

It was the early success of *Sesame Street* in the 1970s that demonstrated the power of well-crafted educational media for teaching literacy skills to preschool children (Bogatz and Ball, 1971). Sesame Workshop (2014) has been a leader in promoting early childhood development with the assistance of educational media programs in countries such as Bangladesh (Kibria and Jain, 2009), Colombia (Céspedes et al., 2013), Egypt (Rimal et al., 2013), Indonesia (Borzekowski and Henry, 2011), Israel, Palestine and the West Bank (Brenick et al., 2010; Cole et al., 2003, 2008), Kosovo (Cole et al., 2008), Ireland (Connolly et al., 2008) and Tanzania (Borzekowski and Macha, 2010). These initiatives focus on early childhood learning and development as well as key global issues ranging from HIV-AIDS prevention to girls' education and conflict resolution.

In a recent independent analysis of programming in international settings, Mares and Pan (2013) examined *Sesame Street*'s impact on millions of children globally, including in some of the world's poorest regions. The meta-analysis examines the effects of children's exposure to international co-productions of *Sesame Street*, synthesizing the results of 24 studies, conducted with over 10,000 children in 15 countries. The results indicated significant positive effects of exposure to the program, aggregated across learning outcomes and within each of three outcome categories: cognitive outcomes, including literacy and numeracy; learning about the world, including health and safety knowledge; social reasoning and attitudes toward out-groups. The effects were significant across different methods and they were observed in both low- and middle-income countries and also in high-income countries.

Evidence suggests that carefully designed media may also encourage the development of positive emotional and social skills such as kindness, sharing and tolerance (Calvert and Kotler, 2003; Cole et al., 2008; Friedrich and Stein, 1973). More specifically, kindergartners who watched prosocial episodes of the USA show, *Mr. Rogers' Neighborhood* were more likely to help peers who were struggling with an art project (Friedrich and

Stein, 1975) than those who watched programming without the prosocial messages. More recently, researchers found that Israeli children who watched their local *Sesame Street* program, designed to teach tolerance between Jewish and Arabic children, held less negative stereotypes about people from other cultures (Cole et al., 2008).

Most of the research on preschool children's learning from media has focused on television as there is currently a lack of research studying the effects of learning from newer interactive digital technologies. However, the existing research supports the premise that developmentally appropriate content on interactive media, primarily computers, can have positive impacts on children's early learning (Jackson et al., 2006).

Infant and Toddler Learning

The research on infant and toddler learning is based on the decades of research on preschoolers' learning from television and other media. There appear to be clear age differences in children's learning from screen media, in which younger children face more challenges than their older preschool counterparts. While historically there has been a focus on the difficulties that infants and toddlers face when trying to learn from screen media (see Wartella et al., 2010 for a review), more recent research has begun to document the ways in which young children may be able to learn from visual digital content. Research suggests that screen media effects on infant and toddler learning are largely dependent on content and context. For learning to occur, young children need content that resembles infants and toddlers' real-life experience, repeated exposure to the content and a competent adult co-viewer who supports conversation and language learning (Linebarger and Vaala, 2010). Given the different challenges that infants and toddlers face compared to those of preschoolers and older children, we discuss some of the obstacles that young children face when learning from digital media and how they may be overcome.

The Obstacles Early research on infant and toddler media exposure found that young children learn better from a real-world adult than they do from a video presentation, which Anderson and Pempek (2005) labeled as the 'video deficit effect'. Evidence in support of the video deficit effect has been demonstrated in a range of experimental studies of 2- and 3-year-olds (Barr and Wyss, 2008; Schmidt and Vandewater, 2008; Strouse and Troseth, 2008). Imitation studies conducted with toddlers aged 12–30 months have demonstrated that learning of an imitation task is significantly better when the infant views the demonstration performance live by an adult as compared to the exact same demonstration performed on a screen (e.g., Barr and Hayne, 1999). Similar evidence has been found using object-search tasks, demonstrating that toddlers are better able to find hidden objects when information about their hiding places is provided by a live adult as compared to when it is given on screen (e.g., Deocampo and Hudson, 2005; Schmidt et al., 2007; Schmitt and Anderson, 2002). Finally, evidence also demonstrates that infants and toddlers learn language skills better from a live experience than from a video or televised presentation (e.g., Kuhl et al., 2003; Richert et al., 2010).

Even when the content is created to be educational and specifically designed for a very young audience, there are mixed results about whether infants and toddlers are able to learn language skills specifically from a video presentation. One study demonstrated that infants who were exposed to the program *Baby Einstein* at age 1 showed greater learning of specific words from the DVD compared to children in the control group who did not view the video (Vandewater, 2011). In contrast, multiple studies examining infants' language learning from commercially created infant-directed videos have failed to find evidence of language learning (DeLoache et al., 2010; Krcmar et al., 2007; Kuhl et al., 2003; Richert et al., 2010).

Overcoming the Challenges In contrast, some of the more recent research demonstrates that the video deficit effect can be ameliorated and in certain circumstances infants and toddlers can learn from digital visual media. More specifically, in some instances infants may in fact be able to learn language from programs created for them. Some studies have demonstrated that 2-year-olds can learn from video presentations even when tested 24 hours after exposure, however specific conditions need to exist (Barr and Wyss, 2008; Strouse and Troseth, 2008). For toddlers to learn from media, the content and the way the content is presented are particularly important. For example, the toddlers in Barr and Wyss's (2008) study successfully imitated the behaviors demonstrated on video when the video contained a voiceover that provided verbal labels to the actions that occurred during the demonstration. Similarly, infants can learn a cognitively meaningful seriation task (ordering objects according to size) better from a video presentation when the character on the screen is familiar compared to when the character is unfamiliar (Lauricella et al., 2011).

Adult Scaffolding and Joint Media Engagement

While age and developmental appropriate *content* is important for learning in digital media, the *context* in which children use technology also plays an important role in their ability to learn from the experience. One such context for learning is the use of parental scaffolding in helping infants and toddlers learn from media. For instance, when parents asked on-topic questions or labeled content while co-viewing a video, infants were more likely to interact with the video (Barr et al., 2008). Similarly, word learning from a DVD was improved when parents directed the child's attention to the DVD and repeated the words from the video (Krcmar et al., 2007). Adult scaffolding can also occur outside of the co-viewing context, as when an adult voiceover directs the child's attention to a video presentation (Barr and Wyss, 2008).

Scaffolding children's media use may be split into three types: cognitive, affective and technical scaffolding (Yelland and Masters, 2007). Cognitive scaffolding refers to providing aid in conceptual and procedural understanding. This can involve parents asking questions or calling attention to specific key parts of the story. Affective scaffolding refers to the positive encouragement and feedback needed to assist the child to persist in their media use. Finally, technical scaffolding refers to the features of a device that children need to learn to use (e.g., specific features of an app, how to touch the screen). Historically, research has called attention to the cognitive features of scaffolding and especially how parents and adults influence children's learning from media content.

For instance, with the introduction of *Sesame Street* in Israel, Salomon (1977) demonstrated that mothers from low SES backgrounds could help to increase their children's learning by showing positive encouragement in watching the show. Other studies on co-viewing *Sesame Street* showed learning and development gains in preschoolers when adults and children watched together (e.g., Reiser et al., 1984, 1988). More recently, Christakis et al. (2013) determined that an intervention to promote co-viewing of curriculum-based children's educational television shows and DVDs could modify the viewing habits of preschool-aged children and enhance their pro-social competence. Importantly, low-income boys experienced the greatest benefits of co-viewing (Christakis et al., 2013). However, co-viewing without active engagement and scaffolding has been demonstrated not to be helpful for children's learning (Ostrov et al., 2013; Warren, 2003).

In recent research, the definition of co-viewing has been expanded to focus on *joint media engagement* (Stevens and Penuel, 2010) and on how multiple people including caregivers, family members, siblings and peers actively interact together with media. Here, the context of parents engaging together with preschoolers and older children can positively influence children's learning from screen media through joint media engagement. Newer forms of digital media such as apps created for smartphones or tablets and video games present novel opportunities for joint media engagement for parents, caregivers and children. For instance, story creation apps on tablets allow for combinations of embodied modes (e.g., gestures, movements, physical touch), while integrated media (e.g., pictures, audio recordings, text) can mediate and shape the interaction between young children and caregivers (Kucirkova et al., 2013). Digital games can now present new support for parent–child dialogue, interactions, social connections and learning (e.g., Levine and Vaala, 2013). Even siblings' engagement in joint video game use has been shown to improve young children's strategies for game playing (Go et al., 2012).

New research examining reading on tablets and ebooks suggests that both the media and manner in which reading together occurs influence the effects of use. Moody, Justice and Cabell (2010) examined the reading behaviors of 25 preschool-aged children in the USA in three storybook reading conditions: adult-led ebook, child-led ebook and adult-led traditional print storybook. Findings show that when comparing the type of media (ebook vs. print), the children displayed higher persistence in their participation during reading tasks (such as pointing at pictures and words, turning pages, answering questions and positively commenting on the book) with the adult-led ebook than with the adult-led traditional book. However, children produced more communication initiations in the traditional storybook condition than in both of the ebook conditions. These findings suggest that interactive media can influence children's literacy and oral language development, particularly when dialogic co-reading with adults occurs (Chiong et al., 2012). Although ebooks provide ease and access to many stories, parent–child dialogue focused on the stories is important to make sure children are not distracted by the device and interactive media (Krcmar and Cingel, 2014).

Summary
In the above section, we reviewed the research on digital media, early childhood development, and health and learning. We focused on the factors that shape young children's media use, the concerns that are noted in the literature and the positive influences that exist (particularly with an emphasis on learning). We have shown examples of international research that indicate children as young as infants are directly interacting with new digital technologies that are affecting their well-being. While there are many concerns regarding the impact of media use on child health, the evidence on each of these concerns is limited and mixed at best. In contrast, there is evidence that when technology is developed and used appropriately, there are positive learning opportunities, especially for the most at-risk children. To date, we still need more research on the various types of media technology and longitudinal studies before any final conclusions can be drawn regarding the overall effects of young children's media use. Drawing from the research reviewed, we discuss the implications for policy and program development among leaders in the international early childhood community.

IMPLICATIONS FOR PRACTICE AND POLICY

Our consideration of the increasingly profound impact of digital technologies and media on early childhood development draws from Urie Bronfenbrenner's 'ecology of human development' (Bronfenbrenner, 1977, 1979). According to Bronfenbrenner's theory, children develop and grow within an ecosystem of interconnected and nested environments. The microsystem is the immediate environment young children reside in (e.g., homes, nurseries) and those domains contain the technologies they directly interact with (e.g., tablets, smartphones). The mesosystem is one system that bridges home and community environments.

A neighborhood, for example, contains several interconnected settings that a child inhabits such as the school, home and library. The macrosystem describes the overarching culture, values and policies that influence the developing child and family.

Takeuchi and Levine (2014) provide adaptations to Bronfenbrenner's (1979) influential 'ecological systems theory' within a modern-day learning ecology. Takeuchi and Levine show how children and families' interactions with digital media both shape and are being shaped by interconnected factors in the micro-, meso- and macrosystems. Using this adaptive framework as a guide, we examine several key leverage points, suggested by this research review, in which a modernized ecological systems perspective may inform future research, media design, practice and policy.

Microsystem Factors: Parental Demand for Information and Support

As we have shown in this review, media consumption all over the world is occurring in high numbers with young children aged 0–8, and parental involvement can play a pivotal role in whether media use has a positive or negative effect on child health, development and learning. Some observers have characterized this new digital world as the 'digital Wild West'[1] for parents seeking quality content for their young children (Guernsey et al., 2012). However, professionals have begun to establish some guidelines for teachers and practitioners on what constitutes the most effective use of media for learning and healthy development (NAEYC/Fred Rogers Center, 2012). A recently edited volume from pioneers in the early childhood field (Donohue, 2014) makes a compelling case for the use of digital technologies to spur interactive learning. Still, there is still much disagreement about the best ways to guide parents towards wise monitoring and scaffolding of experiences. Without guidance, parental practices around media use are

varied and often inconsistent. For example, in a 2010 survey of American parents of 3- to 10-year-olds, nearly two-thirds said they limit their children's media use on a case-by-case basis, versus only about one in five who reported setting overarching strict rules (Takeuchi, 2011).

A challenge for researchers and practitioners is to clearly articulate a useful framework for parents and caregivers that is usable across different situations and child developmental periods. New 'rating systems' and curation tools, based on scientific research standards and tied to child developmental stages, are now emerging to help parents and caregivers select media content, such as those organized by Common Sense Media, the National Association for the Education of Young Children and the Fred Rogers Center in the USA. However, these guidelines need to spread more quickly and globally to inform parents and caregivers about best practices including tips for parent–child interaction, joint media use and mediation of media experiences at the micro-system level including the home and school environments.

Mesosystem Factors: Integration of Digital Media use into Community Supports and Professional Practice Reforms

Bronfenbrenner's (1979) mesosystem focuses on the interactions that take place in one setting, which ultimately shape the interactions in another. For instance, what happens at home does affect behaviors and interactions at school. Studies of parent involvement in early learning and its influence on school performance indicate that alignment between home and school experiences is critical to later success (Henderson and Mapp, 2002). However, in the domain of digital learning, formal learning environments have not yet adapted to the types of digital media innovation which research suggests are needed to support learning and healthy child development. As we have shown in this review, young children before preschool are exposed to digital media both early and frequently in their lives. Early childhood teachers must now transform their practices in order to support young children's digital literacy practices. A recent survey found that 76% of American K–12 teachers are using digital media in their classroom with 33% of pre-K teachers using digital media (PBS and Grunwald Associates, 2010). Unfortunately, little is known about the content, context and effectiveness of this use.

Administrators, policy makers and curriculum developers would be well advised to explore ways to support early childhood teachers and their digital practices. As more early childhood teachers begin to use digital media, new innovative curricula need to be developed to integrate better digital pedagogical practices. For example, Penuel et al. (2010) explored the impact of a US preschool curriculum with digital content from two public television shows on increasing low-income children's interest in science. The study found that a combination of professional development with teachers, hands-on tasks and active classroom discussion using a digital media-rich curriculum could support increased science interest through more conversations with parents at home. Penuel et al.'s work shows that there is a need to better develop and integrate teacher education with higher quality 21st-century approaches to the learning and healthy development of young children.

Based on these needs, the Joan Ganz Cooney Center and Stanford University convened a task force to review research and to study emerging best practices in the teaching of young children with digital technologies. This report recently concluded that the integration of ubiquitous digital media (e.g., streaming educational videos, mobile devices, digital games) into early childhood learning environments could contribute to children's well-being, experiences and learning (Barron et al., 2011), but more research is needed in this area. Notably, implementation challenges associated with enhanced media usage continue to exist in early childhood settings in preschool especially. Guernsey (2014) and Blackwell et al. (2013), for example, cite a lack of preparation and professional development around technology for teachers as a key problem for supporting children's learning in preschool and the primary grades. Perhaps an ecological approach to deploy and effectively implement technologies across different settings (e.g., homes, libraries) would help support children's school success (Barron et al., 2011).

Macrosystem Factors: The Need for Equity Investments

The macrosystem (Bronfenbrenner, 1977, 1979) can impact on digital media practices in the micro- and meso-system levels through surrounding professional expectations, values and policies. For instance, research from Neuman and Celano (2012) and from Rideout (2013) suggests that low-income children from the USA face critical 'participation gaps' in receiving appropriate guidance and support in using new technologies to maximum advantage and we know that at-risk children gain the most from exposure to educational television programming (Fisch and Truglio, 2001). With child poverty on the rise in developed countries like the USA, Japan, Spain, Greece, Canada, Italy and the UK (Gould and Wething, 2012) and achievement and income gaps widening (Guttenplan, 2013), some prominent researchers have asked if unequal access to new technologies will exacerbate educational divides (Neuman and Celano, 2012). The research also indicates a lack of support for basic infrastructure to ensure that disadvantaged children and their families have access to the Internet, quality apps, well-equipped schools and community institutions. Guernsey (2014) argues that early learning centers need to be modernized to include a focus on access and equity. Further, it is essential to determine how to get the much-needed educational media content and supports to those who are the most likely to face academic and health challenges.

Basic technological infrastructure is not the only macro-system factor that plays an influential role. Bronfenbrenner (1977, 1979) argued that government investment in children's programs that provide adequate opportunities for young children to bond with their caregivers and early learning programs that support young children's developmental trajectory were an essential pathway to a decent society. In today's macro-system landscape, many countries are investing in early childhood programs. More than 30 governments have national policies for early childhood, 35 poverty reduction strategy papers include early childhood programs as a key component and more than 70 countries have national committees for early childhood development (UNICEF, 2007). However, in nearly all of these new country-specific plans for young children, the role of media and technology use for children's learning and professional reform is ignored. Global leaders in early childhood development should take stock of current efforts to inform low-income families about wise deployment of digital technologies at home and in school.

Similarly, government investments and programs will need to address the issue of information access for caregivers. Survey data in the USA (EDC/SRI, 2012; Rideout, 2014; Wartella et al., 2013) show that even though parents have a positive perception about the role that digital media may play in helping children learn, institutional problems of equity and information access persist. Parents, especially from low-income families in the USA, often cannot find appropriate guidance for choosing games and apps, but are looking for support from experts (Rideout, 2014). As noted before, some organizations have provided ratings and guidelines for parents and teachers, but often these sites cater to caregivers with access to the Internet, high reading levels in English and significant information capital. Foundations and global intermediaries such as UNICEF and OECD need to support greater efforts in policy development and institutional leadership to help expand the flow of information and technology access to the world's low-income communities.

Recommendations: More Precise, Targeted and Usable Research and Development

The selected research reviewed in this chapter provides evidence of both significant risks and important opportunities to deploy new technologies and media to promote learning and healthy development among young children and their families. We have noted throughout that there are key gaps in the research, especially regarding the newer digital media technologies. We make the following three recommendations based on our review of research and policies.

First, a rigorous, large-scale multinational research program is worth undertaking. Government bodies paired with foundation leaders could perhaps fund fellowships and model training programs to promote a new generation of researchers who specialize in the impacts of media and technological change on childhood well-being. A National Science Foundation (2008) task force recently advised that in order to open up research innovation on new technologies, we must agree to co-fund the development of new long-term partnerships with the private sector.

Since much of the research scholarship has focused on the USA and other wealthy nations, priority should be afforded to a global meta-analysis of existing research on the negative and positive impacts of digital media on children's health, well-being and learning, leading to recommendations for further research. The research portfolio should include investigations on the potential of specific new technologies for learning, parenting supports, health promotion and prevention. Finally, a global research entity, with support from philanthropic and policy leaders, could establish a 'best practice' initiative to disseminate effective uses of media and interactive technologies to both parents and practitioners for application across the ecological layers.

Second, our review leads us to believe that a reconfiguration of public and philanthropic investment in untapped potential of digitally enhanced learning may be necessary. For instance, in 2013, the US government invested less than $30 million in public media funds for programming for young children within the rubric of a 'Ready to Learn' broadcasting fund (US Department of Education, 2011). This current investment in public media funds is a pittance in comparison to the costs of early education programs in the USA, which the National Institute for Early Education Research estimated at over $12 billion in state preschool and federal Head Start funding in the USA in 2013 (National Institute for Early Education, 2013). A review of other countries' publicly supported investments in digital learning finds that most Ministries of Education, with some notable exceptions like the UK, Australia, the Netherlands and Canada, have made only very modest investments in children's educational media, leaving content creation largely to the private sector.[2] The public funds earmarked for early childhood initiatives must begin to accommodate rigorous research with digital media for curriculum and professional development, family engagement and assessment purposes. Additionally, wealthy nations, which have invested significant funds in their own early learning-oriented television production for young children, should immediately adopt initiatives to support wider experimentation with newer digital media forms.

Our third recommendation is for the creation of a global 'Fund' for educational media program development. Bringing together global leaders in the USA, Asia, Sub-Saharan Africa and the Caribbean Basin, this Fund could be operated by a global non-profit leader with a proven record of developing effective public–private partnerships. The Fund would establish shared curriculum, health promotion and financial sustainability goals informed by potent lessons for research, design, production and distribution provided by international producers with proven track records. Much can be learned from previous efforts by institutions

such as the US Agency for International Development's efforts to pursue localized versions of educational media programs such as *Sesame Street*.

CONCLUSION

In the first section of this chapter, we presented a brief overview of existing research on the relationship between technology and digital media for children's healthy development. We demonstrated that the digital landscape is shifting from passive television watching to more complex, multifaceted interactions around ubiquitous mobile technologies. Like all complex issues, there is no simple answer to whether or not digital media overall is an asset or a detriment to normative, constructive early childhood learning and well-being. The body of research points to three important factors to consider as well as to a social theory and action framework.

First, in order to understand the impact of digital media technology, we must begin to consider the developing child. Second, the content (independent of technological platform) should be both developmentally appropriate and engaging enough to compel children's attention and comprehension. Third, the context in which children are engaging with media technologies is critical. A nurturing context is important for young children's learning: optimal habits for young children include adult co-viewing, guidance and close monitoring whenever possible.

Finally, we offer a social theory as a useful action framework to situate childhood experiences with media and technology. Our review establishes that positive technology and digital media use depends on many factors, both personal (e.g., demographics, parental media habits) and ecological (e.g., institutional supports). We posit a digital era re-conception (Takeuchi and Levine, 2014) of Bronfenbrenner's (1977, 1979) human development theories to show that media use and influence on early childhood also depend on various micro- (e.g., parent engagement), meso- (e.g., community support, professional reform) and macrosystem factors (e.g., policies). We suggest that healthy learning and development in the decade ahead will depend on building new infrastructure for a shared future, including an emphasis on global investment in research and development, such as large-scale multinational research programs. Global investments across nations and media organizations to support early childhood learning are now increasingly timely.

The advancement of digital media and technology is rapidly changing early childhood experiences. At the beginning of this decade, the interactive touch-screen and smart mobile devices were barely launched; today, in wealthy countries, most children are exposed to the latest technological marvels at increasingly younger ages. As knowledge of the critical importance of early learning grows, so too must our dexterity in harnessing digital media technologies to accelerate young children's pathways to a healthy and productive future.

FURTHER READING

Calvert, S. and Wilson, B. (2008) *The Handbook of Children, Media, and Development*. Malden, MA: Wiley-Blackwell.

Jordan, A. and Romer, D. (2014) *Media and the Well-being of Children and Adolescents*. Oxford: Oxford University Press.

Lemish, D. (2013) *The Routledge International Handbook of Children, Adolescents, and Media*. New York: Routledge.

QUESTIONS FOR REFLECTION

1   Parents of children, especially those with limited access to financial resources and 'leisure time', often lead stressful lives. How can we help support efficient, informative use of digital media and new technologies for low-income and time-deficient parents? More generally, have we opened up a Pandora's Box: is the pace of technology development so rapid that most parents, caregivers and institutions cannot keep up with knowledge on how to support young children's well-being? How can we prioritize supports for parents and teachers in a 'digital Wild West?'

2   What are the implications of existing research for media and technology designers? Are there more inventive uses that industry creators can marshal, at low costs, to promote early learning and healthy development across the globe?

3   How can research on educational media and technology's potential for learning and healthy development among young children be best positioned in professional reforms? Are there new systems of professional development and knowledge transfer via technology that can spark increased sharing of best practice across countries and regions?

4   In an increasingly global and digital world, which new skill sets will emerge as vital for children to learn and be able to do over the next decade? How can these skill sets be advanced by playful learning experiences that are developmentally appropriate, but also thoroughly modern?

5   In what ways do different ecological layers – personal and community relationships and networks, national policies, cultural diversity and geographic factors influence early childhood use of media and new technologies? Are there new program or policy interventions to be designed for a digital age?

NOTES

1   The Wild West refers to the USA during the period of its Western settlement and the lawlessness of that time.

2   For more information, please refer to the World Bank website: www.worldbank.org/en/topic/edutech/brief/international-surveys-of-ict-use-in-education

REFERENCES

Adam, E. K., Snell, E. K. and Pendry, P. (2007) 'Sleep timing and quantity in ecological and family context: A nationally representative time-diary study', *Journal of Family Psychology*, 21(1): 4–19.

Ale, K. and Chib, A. (2011) 'Community factors in technology adoption in primary education: Perspectives from rural India', *Information Technologies & International Development*, 7(4): 53–68.

American Academy of Pedriatrics (AAP) (1999) 'Media education', *Pediatrics*, 104(2): 341–343.

American Academy of Pedriatrics (AAP) (2013) 'Children, adolescents, and the media', *Pediatrics*, 132(5): 958–961.

Anderson, D. R. and Evans, M. K. (2001) 'Peril and potential of media for infants and toddlers', *Zero to Three*, 22(2): 10–16.

Anderson, D. R. and Lorch, E. P. (1983) 'Looking at television: Action or reaction', in J. Bryant and D. R. Anderson (Eds.), *Children's Understanding of Television: Research on Attention and Comprehension*. New York: Academic. pp. 1–33.

Anderson, D. R. and Pempek, T. A. (2005) 'Television and very young children', *American Behavioral Scientist*, 48(5): 505–522.

Anderson, D. R., Huston, A. C., Schmitt, K. L., Linebarger, D. L., Wright, J. C. and Larson, R. (2001) 'Early childhood television viewing and adolescent behavior: The recontact study', *Monographs of the Society for Research in Child Development*, 66(1): i–154.

Barr, R. and Hayne, H. (1999) 'Developmental changes in imitation from television during infancy', *Child Development*, 70(5): 1067–1081.

Barr, R. and Wyss, N. (2008) 'Reenactment of televised content by 2-year olds: Toddlers use language learned from television to solve a difficult imitation problem', *Infant Behavior and Development*, 31(4): 696–703.

Barr, R., Zack, E., Garcia, A. and Muentener, P. (2008) 'Infants' attention and responsiveness to television increases with prior exposure and parental interaction', *Infancy*, 13(1): 30–56.

Barron, B., Copple, C., Cayton-Hodges, G., Darling-Hammond, L., Bofferding, L. and Levine, M. H. (2011) *Take a Giant Step: A Blueprint for Teaching Young Children in a Digital Age*. New York: Joan Ganz Cooney Center at Sesame Workshop.

Bener, A., Al-Mahdi, H. S., Al-Nufal, M., Ali, A. I., Vachhani, P. J. and Tewfik, I. (2012) 'Association between childhood computer use and risk of obesity and low vision', *Public Health Frontier*, 66–72.

Bittman, M., Rutherford, L., Brown, J. and Unsworth, L. (2011) 'Digital natives? New and old media and children's outcomes', *Australian Journal of Education*, 55(2): 161–175.

Blackwell, C. K., Lauricella, A. R., Wartella, E., Robb, M. and Schomburg, R. (2013) 'Adoption and use of technology in early education: The interplay of extrinsic barriers and teacher attitudes', *Computers & Education*, 69: 310–319.

Bleakley, A., Jordan, A. B. and Hennessy, M. (2013) 'The relationship between parents' and children's television viewing', *Pediatrics*, 132(2): e364–e371.

Bogatz, G. A. and Ball, S. (1971) The second year of Sesame Street: A continuing evaluation (http://eric.ed.gov/?id=ED122800).

Borzekowski, D. L. G. and Henry, H. K. (2011) 'The impact of Jalan Sesama on the educational and healthy development of Indonesian preschool children: An experimental study', *International Journal of Behavioral Development*, 35(2): 169–179.

Borzekowski, D. L. and Macha, J. E. (2010) 'The role of Kilimani Sesame in the healthy development of Tanzanian preschool children', *Journal of Applied Developmental Psychology*, 31(4): 298–305.

Brenick, A., Killen, M., Lee-Kim, J., Fox, N., Leavitt, L., Raviv, A., et al. (2010) 'Social understanding in young Israeli-Jewish, Israeli-Palestinian, Palestinian, and Jordanian children: Moral judgments and stereotypes', *Early Education and Development*, 21(6): 886–911.

Bronfenbrenner, U. (1977) 'Toward an experimental ecology of human development', *American Psychologist*, 32(7): 513–531.

Bronfenbrenner, U. (1979) 'Contexts of child rearing: Problems and prospects', *American Psychologist*, 34(10): 844–850.

Byun, W., Dowda, M. and Pate, R. R. (2011) 'Correlates of objectively measured sedentary behavior in US preschool children', *Pediatrics*, 128(5): 937–945.

Calvert, S. L. and Kotler, J. A. (2003) 'Lessons from children's television: The impact of the Children's Television Act on children's learning', *Journal of Applied Developmental Psychology*, 24(3): 275–335.

Cappuccio, F. P., Taggart, F. M., Kandala, N.-B., Currie, A., Peile, E., Stranges, S. and Miller, M. (2008) 'Meta-analysis of short sleep duration and obesity in children and adults', *Sleep*, 31(5): 619–626.

Carrasco, M. R. and Torrecilla, F. J. M. (2012) 'Learning environments with technological resources: A look at their contribution to student performance in Latin American elementary schools', *Educational Technology Research and Development*, 60(6): 1107–1128.

Céspedes, J., Briceño, G., Farkouh, M. E., Vedanthan, R., Baxter, J., Leal, M., et al. (2013) 'Targeting preschool children to promote cardiovascular health: Cluster randomized trial', *The American Journal of Medicine*, 126(1): 27–35.

Cheyne, A. D., Dorfman, L., Bukofzer, E. and Harris, J. L. (2013) 'Marketing sugary cereals to children in the digital age: A content analysis of 17 child-targeted websites', *Journal of Health Communication*, 18(5): 563–582.

Chiong, C., Rhee, J., Takeuchi, L. and Erickson, I. (2012) *Print Books vs. eBooks*. New York: Joan Ganz Cooney Center at Sesame Workshop.

Christakis, D. A., Ebel, B. E., Rivara, F. P. and Zimmerman, F. J. (2004) 'Television, video, and computer game usage in children under 11 years of age', *The Journal of Pediatrics*, 145(5): 652–656.

Christakis, D. A., Garrison, M. M., Herrenkohl, T., Haggerty, K., Rivara, F. P., Zhou, C. and Liekweg, K. (2013) 'Modifying media content for preschool children: A randomized controlled trial', *Pediatrics*, 131(3): 431–438.

Cole, C., Arafat, C., Tidhar, C., Tafesh, W. Z., Fox, N., Killen, M., et al. (2003) 'The educational impact of Rechov Sumsum/Shara'a Simsim: A Sesame Street television series to promote respect and understanding among children living in Israel, the West Bank, and Gaza', *International Journal of Behavioral Development*, 27(5): 409–422.

Cole, C. F., Labin, D. B. and Galarza, M. del R. (2008) 'Begin with the children: What research on Sesame Street's international coproductions reveals about using media to promote a new more peaceful world', *International Journal of Behavioral Development*, 32(4): 359–365.

Comstock, G. and Scharrer, E. (2010) *Media and the American Child*. New York: Academic Press.

Connolly, P., Kehoe, S., Larkin, E. and Galanouli, D. (2008) *A cluster randomised controlled trial evaluation of the effects of watching Sesame Tree on young children's attitudes and awareness (report 1)*. Belfast, Ireland: Centre for Effective Education, Queen's University Belfast.

Cooney, J. G. (1966) *The Potential Uses of Television in Preschool Education*. New York: Carnegie Corporation (http://eric.ed.gov/?id=ED122803).

Courage, M. L. and Howe, M. L. (2010) 'To watch or not to watch: Infants and toddlers in a brave new electronic world', *Developmental Review*, 30(2): 101–115.

Courage, M. L. and Setliff, A. E. (2010) 'When babies watch television: Attention-getting, attention-holding, and the implications for learning from video material', *Developmental Review*, 30(2): 220–238.

DeLoache, J. S., Chiong, C., Sherman, K., Islam, N., Vanderborght, M., Troseth, G. L., et al. (2010) 'Do babies learn from baby media?', *Psychological Science*, 21(11): 1570–1574.

Deocampo, J. A. and Hudson, J. A. (2005) 'When seeing is not believing: Two-year-olds' use of video representations to find a hidden toy', *Journal of Cognition and Development*, 6(2): 229–258.

Donohue, C. (Ed.) (2014) *Technology and Digital Media in the Early Years: Tools for Teaching and Learning*. New York: Routledge.

EDC/SRI (2012) *EDC/SRI Year 2 Ready to Learn Research and Evaluation Summary Report*. Education Development Center and SRI International (www-tc.pbskids.org/lab/media/pdfs/research/Y2-EDC-SRI-Year_2_Summary_Report.pdf).

Fernandes, M. and Sturm, R. (2010) 'Facility provision in elementary schools: Correlates with physical education, recess, and obesity', *Preventive Medicine*, 50: S30–S35.

Fetler, M. (1984) 'Television viewing and school achievement', *Journal of Communication*, 34(2): 104–118.

Fisch, S. M. (2014) *Children's Learning from Educational Television: Sesame Street and Beyond*. New York: Routledge.

Fisch, S. M. and Truglio, R. T. (2001) 'Why children learn from Sesame Street', in S. M. Fisch and R. T. Truglio (Eds.), *G is for Growing: Thirty Years of Research on Children and Sesame Street*. Mahwah, NJ: Lawrence Erlbaum Associates. pp. 233–244.

Foster, E. M. and Watkins, S. (2010) 'The value of reanalysis: TV viewing and attention problems', *Child Development*, 81(1): 368–375.

Friedrich, L. K. and Stein, A. H. (1973) 'Aggressive and prosocial television programs and the natural behavior of preschool children',

Monographs of the Society for Research in Child Development, 1–64.

Friedrich, L. K. and Stein, A. H. (1975) 'Prosocial television and young children: The effects of verbal labeling and role playing on learning and behavior', *Child Development*, 27–38.

Garrison, M. M. and Christakis, D. A. (2012) 'The impact of a healthy media use intervention on sleep in preschool children', *Pediatrics*, 130(3): 492–499.

Garrison, M. M., Liekweg, K. and Christakis, D. A. (2011) 'Media use and child sleep: The impact of content, timing, and environment', *Pediatrics*, 128(1): 29–35.

Gigli, S. (2004) *Children, Youth, and Media around the World: An Overview of Trends and Issues*. New York: UNICEF.

Go, J., Ballagas, R. and Spasojevic, M. (2012) 'Brothers and sisters at play: Exploring game play with siblings', in *Proceedings of the ACM 2012 Conference on Computer Supported Cooperative Work*. pp. 739–748.

Gould, E. and Wething, H. (2012) 'US poverty rates higher, safety net weaker than in peer countries', Economic Policy Institute (www. Epi.org/publication/ib339-Us-Poverty-Higher-Safety-Net-Weaker).

Groupe Speciale Mobile Association (GSMA) (2013) *Children's Use of Mobile Phones: An International Comparison 2012*. GSMA (www.gsma.com/latinamerica/childrens-use-mobile-phones-international-comparison-2012).

Guernsey, L. (2007) *Into the Minds of Babes: How Screen Time Affects Children from Birth to Age Five*. New York: Basic Books.

Guernsey, L. (2014) *Envisioning a Digital Age Architecture for Early Education*. Washington, DC: New America Foundation (www. newamerica.net/sites/newamerica.net/files/policydocs/DigitalArchitecture-20140326.pdf).

Guernsey, L., Levine, M., Chiong, C. and Severns, M. (2012) *Pioneering Literacy in the Digital Wild West: Empowering Parents and Educators*. New York: Joan Ganz Cooney Center at Sesame Workshop.

Guttenplan, D. D. (2013) 'OECD warns West on education gaps', *The New York Times*, 8 December (www.nytimes.com/2013/12/09/world/asia/oecd-warns-west-on-education-gaps.html).

Haines, J., McDonald, J., O'Brien A., Sherry, B. Bottino, C.J., Schmidt, M.E. and Taveras, E.M. (2013) 'Healthy habits, happy homes: Randomized trial to improve household routines for obesity prevention among preschool-aged children', *JAMA Pediatrics*, 167(11):1072–1079.

Harris, J. L., Speers, S. E., Schwartz, M. B. and Brownell, K. D. (2012) 'US food company branded advergames on the Internet: Children's exposure and effects on snack consumption', *Journal of Children and Media*, 6(1): 51–68.

He, M., Piché, L., Beynon, C. and Harris, S. (2010) 'Screen-related sedentary behaviors: Children's and parents' attitudes, motivations, and practices', *Journal of Nutrition Education and Behavior*, 42(1): 17–25.

Henderson, A. T. and Mapp, K. L. (2002) *A New Wave of Evidence: The Impact of School, Family, and Community Connections on Student Achievement*. Austin, TX: National Center for Family and Community Connections with Schools (www.sedl.org/connections/resources/introduction.pdf).

Higuchi, S., Motohashi, Y., Liu, Y. L. and Maeda, A. (2005) 'Effects of playing a computer game using a bright display on presleep physiological variables, sleep latency, slow wave sleep and REM sleep', *Journal of Sleep Research*, 14(3): 267–273.

Holloway, D., Green, L. and Livingstone, S. (2013) *Zero to Eight: Young Children and their Internet Use*. LSE, London: EU Kids Online (www.cci.edu.au/reports/ZerotoEight.pdf).

Hong Kong Department of Health (2009) *Child Health Survey 2005–2006*. Hong Kong: Surveillance and Epidemiology Branch Centre for Health Protection, Department of Health.

Huizinga, M., Nikkelen, S. W. C. and Valkenburg, P. M. (2014) 'Children's media use and its relation to attention, hyperactivity, and impulsivity', in D. Lemish (Ed.), *The Routledge International Handbook of Children, Adolescents, and Media*. London: Routledge. pp. 179–185.

Institute of Medicine (2006) *Food Marketing to Children and Youth: Threat or Opportunity?* Washington, DC: National Academies Press.

Jackson, L. A., von Eye, A., Biocca, F. A., Barbatsis, G., Zhao, Y. and Fitzgerald, H. E. (2006) 'Does home internet use influence the academic performance of low-income children?', *Developmental Psychology*, 42(3): 429–435.

Jago, R., Fox, K. R., Page, A. S., Brockman, R. and Thompson, J. L. (2010) 'Parent and child physical activity and sedentary time: Do active parents foster active children?', *BMC Public Health*, 10(1): 194.

Jie, S. H. (2012) ICT Use Statistics of Households and Individuals in Korea. Presented at the 10th World Telecommunication/ICT Indicators Meeting (WTIM-12), Bangkok, Thailand (www.itu.int/ITU-D/ict/wtim12/documents/cont/029_E_doc.pdf).

Kibria, N. and Jain, S. (2009) 'Cultural impacts of Sisimpur, Sesame Street, in Bangladesh: Views of caregivers of children in rural Bangladesh', *Journal of Comparative Family Studies*, 40: 57–75.

Kirkorian, H. L., Wartella, E. A. and Anderson, D. R. (2008) 'Media and young children's learning', *The Future of Children*, 18(1): 39–61.

Krcmar, M. and Cingel, D. P. (2014) 'Parent–child joint reading in traditional and electronic formats', *Media Psychology*, 17(3), 262–281.

Krcmar, M., Grela, B. and Lin, K. (2007) 'Can toddlers learn vocabulary from television? An experimental approach', *Media Psychology*, 10(1), 41–63.

Kucirkova, N., Messer, D., Sheehy, K. and Flewitt, R. (2013) 'Sharing personalised stories on iPads: A close look at one parent–child interaction', *Literacy*, 47(3): 115–122.

Kuhl, P. K., Tsao, F.-M. and Liu, H.-M. (2003) 'Foreign-language experience in infancy: Effects of short-term exposure and social interaction on phonetic learning', *Proceedings of the National Academy of Sciences*, 100(15): 9096–9101.

Lauricella, A. R., Gola, A. A. H. and Calvert, S. L. (2011) 'Toddlers' learning from socially meaningful video characters', *Media Psychology*, 14(2): 216–232.

Lauricella, A., Wartella, E., and Rideout, V. (resubmitted) 'Children's screen time: The role of parent media use', *Journal of Applied Developmental Psychology*.

Lemish, D. (Ed.) (2014) *The Routledge International Handbook of Children, Adolescents and Media*. New York: Routledge.

Levine, M. H. and Vaala, S. E. (2013) 'Games for learning: Vast wasteland or a digital promise?', *New Directions for Child and Adolescent Development*, 71–82.

Linebarger, D. L. and Vaala, S. E. (2010) 'Screen media and language development in infants and toddlers: An ecological perspective', *Developmental Review*, 30(2): 176–202.

Linebarger, D. L., Kosanic, A. Z., Greenwood, C. R. and Doku, N. S. (2004) 'Effects of viewing the television program Between the Lions on the emergent literacy skills of young children', *Journal of Educational Psychology*, 96(2): 297–308.

Li, S., Jin, X., Wu, S., Jiang, F., Yan, C. and Shen, X. (2007) 'The impact of media use on sleep patterns and sleep disorders among school-aged children in China', *Sleep*, 30(3): 361–367.

Li, Y. and Ranieri, M. (2013) 'Educational and social correlates of the digital divide for rural and urban children: A study on primary school students in a provincial city of China', *Computers & Education*, 60(1): 197–209.

Mares, M.-L. and Pan, Z. (2013) 'Effects of Sesame Street: A meta-analysis of children's learning in 15 countries', *Journal of Applied Developmental Psychology*, 34(3): 140–151.

Mascheroni, G. and Ólafsson, K. (2014) *Net Children Go Mobile: Risks and Opportunities* (2nd edition). Milano: Educatt.

Minow, N. N. (1961) 'Television and the public interest', speech presented at the National Association of Broadcasters, Washington, DC.

Moody, A. K., Justice, L. M. and Cabell, S. Q. (2010) 'Electronic versus traditional storybooks: Relative influence on preschool children's engagement and communication', *Journal of Early Childhood Literacy*, 10(3): 294–313.

NAEYC/Fred Rogers Center (2012) Key Messages of the NAEYC/Fred Rogers Center Position Statement on Technology and Interactive Media in Early Childhood Programs (www.naeyc.org/files/naeyc/file/positions/KeyMessages_Technology.pdf).

National Institute for Early Education (2013) The State of Preschool 2013 (http://nieer.org/publications/state-preschool-2013).

National Science Foundation (2008) *Fostering Learning in the Networked World: The Cyberlearning Opportunity and Challenge*. Arlington, VA: National Science Foundation.

Neuman, S. B. and Celano, D. (2012) *Giving Our Children a Fighting Chance: Poverty, Literacy, and the Development of Information Capital*. New York: Teachers College Press.

Ogden C.L., Carroll, M. D., Kit, B. K. and Flegal, K. M. (2014) 'Prevalence of childhood and adult obesity in the United States, 2011–2012', *JAMA*, 311(8): 806–814.

Oka, Y., Suzuki, S. and Inoue, Y. (2008) 'Bedtime activities, sleep environment, and sleep/wake patterns of Japanese elementary school children', *Behavioral Sleep Medicine*, 6(4): 220–233.

Ostrov, J. M., Gentile, D. A. and Mullins, A. D. (2013) 'Evaluating the effect of educational media exposure on aggression in early childhood', *Journal of Applied Developmental Psychology*, 34(1): 38–44.

Owens, J., Maxim, R., McGuinn, M., Nobile, C., Msall, M. and Alario, A. (1999) 'Television-viewing habits and sleep disturbance in school children', *Pediatrics*, 104(3): e27.

Paavonen, E. J., Pennonen, M., Roine, M., Valkonen, S. and Lahikainen, A. R. (2006) 'TV exposure associated with sleep disturbances in 5- to 6-year-old children', *Journal of Sleep Research*, 15(2): 154–161.

PBS and Grunwald Associates (2010) *Deepening Connections: Teachers Increasingly Rely on Media and Technology*, Washington, DC: PBS.

Penuel, W. R., Bates, L., Pasnik, S., Townsend, E., Gallagher, L. P., Llorente, C. and Hupert, N. (2010) 'The impact of a media-rich science curriculum on low-income preschoolers' science talk at home', in *Proceedings of the 9th International Conference of the Learning Sciences: Volume 1*, International Society of the Learning Sciences. pp. 238–245.

Pew Global (2014) *Emerging Nations Embrace Internet, Mobile Technology: Cell Phones Nearly Ubiquitous in Many Countries* (www.pewglobal.org/2014/02/13/emerging-nations-embrace-internet-mobile-technology/).

Phillips, L. (2006) 'Food and globalization', *Annu. Rev. Anthropol.*, 35: 37–57.

Plowman, L. and McPake, J. (2013) 'Seven myths about young children and technology', *Childhood Education*, 89(1): 27–33.

Qiu, J. L. (2014) '"Power to the people!": Mobiles, migrants, and social movements in Asia', *International Journal of Communication*, 8: 376–391.

Reiser, R. A., Tessmer, M. A. and Phelps, P. C. (1984) 'Adult–child interaction in children's learning from "Sesame Street"', *Education Technology Research & Development*, 32(4): 217–223.

Reiser, R. A., Williamson, N. and Suzuki, K. (1988) 'Using "Sesame Street" to facilitate children's recognition of letters and numbers', *ECTJ*, 36(1): 15–21.

Richert, R. A., Robb, M. B., Fender, J. G. and Wartella, E. (2010) 'Word learning from baby videos', *Archives of Pediatrics & Adolescent Medicine*, 164(5): 432–437.

Rideout, V. J. (2011) *Zero to Eight: Children's Media Use in America 2011*. San Francisco, CA: Common Sense Media.

Rideout, V. J. (2013) *Zero to Eight: Children's Media Use in America 2013*. San Francisco, CA: Common Sense Media (www.commonsensemedia.org/about-us/news/press-releases/new-research-from-common-sense-media-reveals-mobile-media-use-among-you).

Rideout, V. J. (2014) *Learning at Home: Families' Educational Media Use in America*. New York: Joan Ganz Cooney Center at Sesame Workshop.

Rideout, V., Lauricella, A. and Wartella, E. (2011) *Children, Media, and Race: Media Use Among White, Black, Hispanic, and Asian American Children*. Evanston, IL: Northwestern University.

Rimal, R. N., Figueroa, M. E. and Storey, J. D. (2013) 'Character recognition as an alternate measure of television exposure among children: Findings from the Alam Simsim program in Egypt', *Journal of Health Communication*, 18(5): 594–609.

Salomon, G. (1977) 'Effects of encouraging Israeli mothers to co-observe "Sesame Street" with their five-year-olds', *Child Development*, 1146–1151.

Schmidt, M. E. and Vandewater, E. A. (2008) 'Media and attention, cognition, and school achievement', *The Future of Children*, 18(1): 63–85.

Schmidt, M. E., Crawley-Davis, A. M. and Anderson, D. R. (2007) 'Two-year-olds' object retrieval based on television: Testing a perceptual account', *Media Psychology*, 9(2): 389–409.

Schmidt, M. E., Rich, M., Rifas-Shiman, S. L., Oken, E. and Taveras, E. M. (2009) 'Television viewing in infancy and child cognition at 3 years of age in a US cohort', *Pediatrics*, 123(3): e370–e375.

Schmitt, K. L. and Anderson, D. R. (2002) 'Television and reality: Toddlers' use of visual information from video to guide behavior', *Media Psychology*, 4(1): 51–76.

Sesame Workshop (2014) Our Results: Sesame Workshop (www.sesameworkshop.org/what-we-do/our-results/).

Shuler, C. (2009a) *D is For Digital*. New York: Joan Ganz Cooney Center at Sesame Workshop.

Shuler, C. (2009b) *iLearn: A Content Analysis of the iTunes App Store's Education Section*. New York: Joan Ganz Cooney Center at Sesame Workshop.

Shuler, C. (2010) *Pockets for Potential*. New York: Joan Ganz Cooney Center at Sesame Workshop.

Shuler, C., Levine, Z. and Ree, J. (2012) *iLearn II: An Analysis of the Education Category of Apple's App Store*. New York: Joan Ganz Cooney Center at Sesame Workshop.

Smith, A. (2010) *Mobile Access 2010*. Pew Internet & American Life Project (www.pewinternet.org/2010/07/07/mobile-access-2010/).

Stephen, C., Stevenson, O. and Adey, C. (2013) 'Young children engaging with technologies at home: The influence of family context', *Journal of Early Childhood Research*, 11(2): 149–164.

Stevens, R. and Penuel, W. R. (2010) 'Studying and fostering learning through joint media engagement', in *Principal Investigators Meeting of the National Science Foundation's Science of Learning Centers*, Arlington, VA.

Straker, L., Abbott, R., Collins, R. and Campbell, A. (2014) 'Evidence-based guidelines for wise use of electronic games by children', *Ergonomics*, 57(4): 471–489.

Straker, L., Pollock, C. and Maslen, B. (2009) 'Principles for the wise use of computers by children', *Ergonomics*, 52(11): 1386–1401.

Strasburger, V. C. (2011) 'Children, adolescents, obesity, and the media', *Pediatrics*, 128(1): 201–208.

Strouse, G. A. and Troseth, G. L. (2008) '"Don't try this at home": Toddlers' imitation of new skills from people on video', *Journal of Experimental Child Psychology*, 101(4): 262–280.

Takeuchi, L. (2011) *Families Matter: Designing Media for a Digital Age*. New York: Joan Ganz Cooney Center at Sesame Workshop.

Takeuchi, L. and Levine, M. (2014) 'Learning in a digital age', in A. B. Jordan and D. R. Romer (Eds.), *Media and the Well-being of Children and Adolescents*. Oxford: Oxford University Press.

Tortora, B. and Rheault, M. (2011) *Mobile Phone Access Varies Widely in Sub-Saharan Africa*. Gallup World (www.gallup.com/poll/149519/mobile-phone-access-varies-widely-sub-saharan-africa.aspx).

UNICEF (2007) Early Childhood Policies for Early Childhood Development (www.unicef.org/earlychildhood/index_40752.html).

US Department of Education (2011) Funding Status: Ready to Learn television, 15 June (www2.ed.gov/programs/rtltv/funding.html).

Van den Bulck, J. (2004) 'Television viewing, computer game playing, and Internet use and self-reported time to bed and time out of bed in secondary-school children', *Sleep*, 27(1): 101–104.

Vandewater, E. A. (2011) 'Infant word learning from commercially available video in the US', *Journal of Children and Media*, 5(3): 248–266.

Vandewater, E. A. and Bickham, D. S. (2004) 'The impact of educational television on young children's reading in the context of family stress', *Journal of Applied Developmental Psychology*, 25(6): 717–728.

Vandewater, E. A., Rideout, V. J., Wartella, E. A., Huang, X., Lee, J. H. and Shim, M. (2007) 'Digital childhood: Electronic media and technology use among infants, toddlers, and preschoolers', *Pediatrics*, 119(5): e1006–e1015.

Warren, R. (2003) 'Parental mediation of preschool children's television viewing', *Journal of Broadcasting & Electronic Media*, 47(3): 394–417.

Wartella, E. and Robb, M. (2008) 'Historical and recurring concerns about children's use of the mass media', in S. L. Calvert and B. J. Wilson (eds.), *The Handbook of Children, Media, and Development*. Chichester: Wiley. pp. 7–26.

Wartella, E., Richert, R. A., and Robb, M. B. (2010). 'Babies, television and videos: How did we get here?', *Developmental Review*, 30:116–127.

Wartella, E., Rideout, V., Lauricella, A. and Connell, S. (2013) *Parenting in the Age of Digital Technology: A National Survey*. Evanston, IL: Center on Media and Human Development, Northwestern University.

Woodard, E. H. and Gridina, N. (2000) *Media in the Home 2000: The Fifth Annual Survey of Parents and Children*. Philadelphia, PA: Annenberg Public Policy Center of the University of Pennsylvania.

World Bank (2012) *Latin America Leads Global Mobile Growth* (www.worldbank.org/en/news/feature/2012/07/18/america-latina-telefonos-celulares).

World Health Organization (WHO) (2014) *World Health Statistics 2014*. Geneva, Switzerland: WHO.

Wu, C.S.T., Fowler, C., Lam, W.Y.Y., Wong, H.T., Wong, C.H.M. and Loke, A.Y. (2014) 'Parenting approaches and digital technology use of preschool age children in a Chinese community', *Italian Journal of Pediatrics*, 40(44): 1–8.

Yang, Y., Hu, X., Qu, Q., Lai, F., Shi, Y., Boswell, M. and Rozelle, S. (2013) 'Roots of tomorrow's digital divide: Documenting computer use and Internet access in China's elementary schools today', *China & World Economy*, 21(3): 61–79.

Yelland, N. and Masters, J. (2007) 'Rethinking scaffolding in the information age', *Computers & Education*, 48(3): 362–382.

Zhou, Y., Singh, N. and Kaushik, P. D. (2011) 'The digital divide in rural South Asia: Survey evidence from Bangladesh, Nepal and Sri Lanka', *IIMB Management Review*, 23(1): 15–29.

25

Using Early Childhood Research to Inform and Influence Public Policy: An Example from Brazil

Irene Rizzini and Malcolm Bush

INTRODUCTION

The large body of international research on what impacts on early childhood development has implications for children in all countries. However, the contexts in which children grow up vary quite significantly in different countries and, as a result, different aspects of that body of research are more important than others in different countries. The ways in which the research is used may also differ. This chapter will concentrate on the context of early childhood in Brazil as it affects the production and use of early childhood research. In particular, it will discuss the ways in which early childhood research can be used to inform and influence public policy.

This chapter's concentration on the use of research in one country, Brazil, reflects the authors' experience that contexts vary dramatically, even among southern-tier countries and that any attempt to summarize the Global South will obscure key details and

make for a misleadingly simplistic overview. The use of international research, therefore, requires, at the same time, an understanding of the particular conditions on the ground of an individual country and an assessment of how different country contexts may frame research conducted in other countries more or less pertinent in the home country. Any multiple country research aggregated to the level of a group of countries is likely to make the research less valuable as that level of aggregation obscures vital local conditions and between-country differences.

Early childhood research from around the world demonstrates the critical importance of the first few years of a child's life for later childhood development and adult outcomes. The following are a few of the most striking findings and serve as the research backdrop for the chapter:

1 Ability gaps between individuals and across socioeconomic groups open up at early ages, for both cognitive and non-cognitive skills, as do gaps in

health status, and these differences increase with age. (Heckman, 2007: 13250–13255)

2   A study from Chile measured psychomotor development at 18 months and following. It showed that: 40% of children from poor families were developmentally delayed by age 5; 50% were delayed in language development; 30% in visual and motor development; and 17% in gross motor development. (Sequel et al., 2002)

3   Children aged 5 years in the highest-income quintile had language performance between 0.5 and 1.5 standard deviations higher than those in the lowest-income quintile in Ethiopia, India, Peru and Vietnam. (Engle et al., 2011)

4   Young children exposed to societal violence show insecure attachments, increased risk of behavior problems, reduced levels of pro-social behavior and increased aggressive behavior. (Engle et al., 2011: 10)

5   There are large differences in the number of shocks and adverse events suffered by low-income families with young children in Ethiopia; for example, the number of shocks is much higher in rural than in urban communities. (Woodhead et al., 2013: 13)

6   Children who have stunted growth at age 1 but physically recover by age 5 have similar test results as children who were never stunted. (Woodhead et al., 2013: 30)

7   Center-based early learning programs usually improve children's cognitive functioning, readiness for school and school performance. These effects are larger for children from disadvantaged backgrounds and larger in higher quality programs, whether those programs are formal or informal. (Engle et al., 2011: 4)

This selection of findings is chosen from a wide range in order to emphasize the underlying importance of poverty, the importance of social contexts and, in the last two items, the promise of some programs to ameliorate the impact of harsh conditions.

Below, the chapter lays out the context of early childhood in Brazil, with statistical information about the challenges facing many children and their families and the rise of a rights-based discourse in children's policies and practices. With this background, the chapter goes on to address the role of research and researchers in influencing policy and practice. It considers the advantages

and challenges of active engagement with communities, civil society and policy makers, as well as dilemmas of methodologies and methods that are robust, participative and persuasive. The chapter ends by advocating the inclusion of children's research, with other discourses, within public policy.

THE CONTEXT OF EARLY CHILDHOOD IN BRAZIL

Brazil is a country of around 200 million people, and despite a high aggregate GDP, it has a low per capita GDP, ranking it at about 100 among countries on this measure (de Sainte Croix, 2012). Sixteen million Brazilians still live on less than US$1.30 a day. About 35% of Brazilian children aged 0–6 years live in households where the household income is below half the minimum wage, a wage which is currently about US$210 a month, (US$1 = RS$ 3.5) i.e., the minimum wage itself is about US$210. About 15% live in families where the household income is below a quarter of the minimum wage or US$52 a month (International Center for Research and Policy on Childhood (CIESPI) Social Indicators 2012). These are extreme rates of poverty that impact on many aspects of a child's life and development. The poverty is accompanied by other dangerous conditions. One such condition is basic domestic sanitation. Over 50% of children aged 0–3 in urban Brazil live in households with inadequate sanitation. Between 1999 and 2009, the percentage declined from 63% to 55% nationwide, although in more recent years the figure was 95% in rural Brazil (CIESPI Data Resource 2014). Even more recent apparent improvements in this statistic are due to a change in definition, where all three characteristics of poor sanitation have to be present rather just one to determine that a household has inadequate sanitation. The government has similarly disguised the real situation of poverty by substituting the measure of extreme poverty as the measure for general poverty.

While Brazil, in the last decade, has seen a decline in income inequality, income inequality is still high. In 2011, for example, on the major index of income inequality (the Gini Coefficient of Income Inequality) that ranges from 0 to 1 with 0 being no inequality and 1 complete inequality, Germany scored 0.27 and Brazil 0.50.[1] The decline in income inequality, which has been modest, has been due to a mixture of government income policy including income support in the shape of the *Bolsa Familia* or family stipend, consistent efforts to raise the minimum wage and an expanding economy.[2] The continuing barriers to wage inequality include the over 40% of the population who work in the informal economy and who, therefore, lack any work-related legal protection or insurance,[3] the gross inadequacy of the public education system (most Brazilian children in both the public and the private sector only attend school for half a day), the difficulty of escaping life in low-income communities to enter the mainstream economy and high barriers to entrepreneurship in the formal sector. The deficiencies of the public education system are illustrated by the fact that Brazil's burgeoning off-sea oil industry has to recruit oil-platform staff from around the world despite federal rules that require that 90% of such crews be Brazilian.

Another key characteristic of poverty in Brazil which impacts on young children is the high degree of urbanization and the high concentration of low-income populations in low-income communities. Sometimes popularly called *favelas*, urban low-income communities are characterized by: poor sanitation; a degree of overcrowding that blocks air circulation and the sun from many dwellings; high levels of domestic violence and violence from drug traffickers, informal militias and the police; poor access to public transportation, and many houses only accessible by alleys or steps; few safe places for children to play; high rates of infectious diseases; and low-quality public services.

Two caveats need to be made to this picture. The first is that low-income communities vary widely even in urban Brazil. In Rio de Janeiro, for example, low-income communities adjacent to middle-income areas have many small-scale businesses, opportunities for women to work as domestic help and men in low-skilled public employment, and some public transit access to middle-income neighborhoods. Some low-income communities on the periphery of the city have little economic life, tenuous connections to middle-income neighborhoods, high rates of extreme poverty and few role models for an alternative future.

The second caveat is that in some cities, and Rio is a prime example, there have been serious public sector efforts to improve life in low-income communities. These include what are known as 'urbanization' programs to improve infrastructure, and community policing programs which in Rio are called UPP or 'units of pacifying police'. This second program is the subject of much controversy. In the communities it has been implemented, many drug traffickers have been chased out and residents report enormous relief at their absence. Crime rates are reported to have dropped and economic conditions in surrounding communities have improved. Summarizing a number of resident surveys, a recent report shows in general that a large majority of residents are very grateful for the significant reduction in violent crime and flying bullets (Cano, 2012). High numbers report the disappearance of violent drug gangs. A series of quantitative analyses showed the number of violent deaths in the UPP communities was reduced by almost 75% with the number of violent deaths caused by the police reduced to almost zero. However, the disappearance of the drug gangs resulted in an increase in other crimes that the traffickers had kept in check through vigilante violence, and it is generally agreed that the community-building aspects of UPP disappeared very quickly and that there are still significant levels of police violence.

Residents of UPP communities have another concern. They fear that after the Rio Olympics in 2016, a number of crime-reduction programs will be abandoned, so too will UPP after which the drug traffickers will come back and severely punish those who cooperated with the police. The residents of other non-UPP low-income communities note a related increase in trafficker violence in their neighborhoods as the traffickers move out of UPP neighborhoods into their communities.

Areas where aspects of family life have improved greatly are demonstrated in such indicators as infant mortality, maternal morbidity and the numbers of young children attending preschool and first grade. The improvements in these measures in the last ten years are very large. In 2001, 11% of the population of children aged 0–3 years attended crèche compared to 21% in 2011. In the earlier year, 66% of 4–6-year-olds attended preschool or school, a figure that rose to 83% in 2011 (CIESPI Indicators, 2014). The number of young children in crèche and preschool is still, however, very much affected by family income, with lower-income children having much lower rates of attendance.

DISCOURSE OF IMPROVING THE LIVES OF CHILDREN IN BRAZIL

While research has its own well-developed discourse and practices, other discourses are important influences on the practice of research, on the way it is discussed and disseminated and on public policy. In Brazil, as part of the huge re-examination of many aspects of society during the comparatively recent return to democracy, the situation of children and children's policies and practices are debated and decided upon in the language of rights to a much greater degree than in other countries.[4] In the USA, for example, the language of rights is much more likely to be used for issues of 'negative liberty', i.e., freedom from unlawful restraints, than for issues of 'positive liberty', i.e., issues of enhancing well-being. Brazil is a country with exceptionally strong constitutional and legal protections for children and youth and

an increasing number of policies and programs to fulfill those rights in practice. In modern times, the critical event in the development of the contemporary rights language was the long struggle to overthrow the military dictatorship which seized power in 1964 and ended in 1985. The new guarantees are enshrined in the 1988 Constitution and the 1990 Statute of the Child and Adolescent which itself was inspired by the United Nations Convention on the Rights of the Child (UNCRC) (1989). The current Brazilian Constitution was adopted in 1988 and contains a sweeping clause about the rights of all children. Article 227 of the Constitution states:

> It is the duty of the family, society and the state to assure with absolute priority the rights of children and adolescents to life, health, food, education, leisure, occupational training, culture, dignity, respect, freedom, and family and community life, and in addition to protect them from all forms of negligence, discrimination, exploitation, violence, cruelty and oppression. (Federal Government of Brazil, Preamble to Article 227 of the Brazilian Constitution, 1988)

The 1990 Brazilian Statute of the Child and Adolescent marked a major step forward in the establishment of legal rights for children (Federal Government of Brazil, 1990). It was the result of years of mobilization on behalf of children. The critical change the Statute made was the provision that children and adolescents were, henceforth, to be 'the subject of rights' and citizens, albeit citizens with additional rights to protect their full development (Federal Government of Brazil, 1990: 30–32). The Statute made a clean break with the former legal status of children which, to the degree it was spelt out in law, was concerned with those children the state found a challenge under the 'Doctrine of [children in an] Irregular Situation', i.e., a situation that required judicial intervention. This former status labeled such children as sources of danger to the public order and not as persons with rights.

Just as the Constitution contained a sweeping statement about children's rights so did the Statute. Articles 3–4 of the Statute established the basic principles of the law:[5]

Art. 3. Without prejudice to the full protection covered in this Law, the child and adolescent shall enjoy all the fundamental rights inherent to the human person and, by law or other means, are ensured of all opportunities and facilities so as to entitle them to physical, mental, moral, spiritual and social development, in conditions of freedom and dignity.

Art. 4. It is the duty of the family, community, society in general and the public authority to ensure, with absolute priority, effective implementation of the rights to life, health, nutrition, education, sports, leisure, vocational training, culture, dignity, respect, freedom and family and community living.

This is powerful language, especially the notion of society's responsibility to ensure these rights as a matter of absolute priority. The notion of rights is the context in which Brazil thinks about, talks about and acts on social issues. The language of rights is, in short, the key discourse for setting out the need for social change. While there is a vast gap between the guarantee of rights and the reality of rights, particularly for low-income children, the language is ubiquitous and provides justification for all manner of attempts to improve the condition of children. Unfortunately, the broadness of the language and the failure to guarantee rights in practice also permit both defenders and opponents of the status quo to use the apparent impossibility of implementing them all to accept the status quo. Allied to this problem is the existence of national plans on various topics that affect children that contain a breathtaking number of recommendations, and the lack of experience in the nonprofit sector in developing disciplined shortlists of priorities that facilitate immediate action.

EARLY CHILDHOOD IN BRAZIL: A RECENT PRIORITY

Elevating early childhood up the political and policy agenda in Brazil is a recent

development. While an emphasis on the rights of children and youth in Brazil dates from the passage of the Statute of the Child and Adolescent in 1990, young children were not a priority in the realm of public policy until the first decade of the 21st century.

One important step towards prioritizing early childhood came in 2006 with educational reforms, which folded preschool education into the ambit of compulsory education and which included legal provision for the funding of preschool.[6] This action represented a promise by the federal government to include children aged 4 and 5 in the provision of publicly funded education and to extend the public reach to crèches.

In addition to this public action, different sectors of civil society geared up to meet the large demand for early childhood education. Various nonprofit organizations organized themselves into forums on early childhood education at municipal, state and national levels in order to participate in setting the public agenda, monitor the quality and adequacy of organizations that served young children and fight for improved education and better conditions for professionals in the field of early education. The law also mandated the inclusion of young children with special needs and, slowly, changes are being made to include these children in early childhood education opportunities.

These policy steps represent an important advance despite the continuing struggle to provide places for all 4–5-year-old children in early childhood education and to improve the quality of that education (Kramer et al., 2013). Data from the 2010 census indicate that 73% of the population of children aged 4–5 had some access to early childhood education though this percentage differs by income and region of the country (CIESPI Indicators, 3.5.1 to 3.5.2). On the other hand, the percentage of children aged 0–3 years attending crèche was much lower at 18% (IBGE, 2010). In a recent study coordinated by Kaya, Bennet and Moss involving Brazil and eight other countries, the authors concluded that the principal challenge in early childhood policy was working on all other aspects of a young child's life that affect development in the early years (Kaya et al., 2010).

Another important milestone in the increasing interest in early childhood education in Brazil was the launching of the National Plan for Early Childhood (PNPI) in 2010. This document was the result of the formation of the National Network on Early Childhood in 2006 which, in a very short space of time, became an important voice in national debates. At the present time, the network includes some 150 organizations from around the country and has an agenda concentrated on the well-being of children in the first six years of their lives. The National Plan is a political and technical document which aims to orient the actions of government and civil society towards the promotion and defense of the rights of the child up to 7 years of age. This plan 'draws up general rules, objectives and methods through which the country should fulfill each of the rights established by the Federal Constitution and by the Statute on the Rights of the Child' (Rede Nacional Primeira Infância, 2010: 12).

Building from the National Plan, representative government and non-government organizations began constructing plans for early childhood at the municipal level. The city of Rio de Janeiro was the first municipality to approve such a plan and this plan was approved by the public assembly of the Children's Rights Council on 11 November 2013 (Conselho Municipal dos Direitos da Criança e do Adolescente, 2013). The approval of the Rio Plan was an important step in prioritizing young children. A number of the priorities included in the Plan are rights provided in the federal Constitution and federal law, but still lacking implementation. The construction and approval of the Plan was also an important opportunity to link together diverse groups of people in the public and civil sectors in a discussion of early childhood issues and the development of priorities. It is worth noting that the process included listening to children's voices as children aged 3–9 from different parts of the city were consulted about what was important in their daily lives and what they thought was needed to improve the chances of small children growing up happy. Their participation enriched the final document and served as an example of how to include children's voices in the 6000 other municipalities in the country.

At national level, there have been other indications of this new focus on a political agenda for very young children. In 2010, the Parliamentary Front for Early Childhood was formed to coordinate the activities of various parliamentarians interested in defending the rights of young children. Among the results of this collaboration was an increase in investment in programs aimed at young children. One of these programs, *O Brasil Carinhoso* (Caring Brazil), launched by President Dilma Rouseff in 2012, spelt out three areas of activities – social development, health and education – with a special emphasis on children considered most vulnerable.

In general, the country has advanced significantly legally and conceptually to advance the well-being of young children. Today, there is a much greater awareness of the importance of the early years of life and the need to create conditions to promote full development. There are also concrete investments to protect children's development which did not exist a decade ago. However, in terms of concrete achievements, while there are major results in some areas, there is little sign of improvement in others. The big change in the reduction of infant and maternal mortality, for example, still leaves high rates of inadequate domestic sanitation and high levels of violence.

USING RESEARCH TO IMPACT ON POLICY

Brazilian university-based children's researchers have an advantage that does not exist in all countries. The very adverse situation of some children and the emphasis on civic action that followed the end of the dictatorship permit researchers who so wish to engage in actively injecting their research and policy work into the public debate and into those forums where policy and practice decisions are actually made. An important part of this advantage is the ability not just to communicate with public leaders and administrators in private, but also to engage the range of civic forums that debate policy issues. The authors' research institute, the International Center for Research and Policy on Childhood at the Pontifical Catholic University of Rio de Janeiro (CIESPI at PUC-Rio), has always taken advantage of this attitude toward engagement.[7]

Key vehicles for civil engagement in Brazil are the federally mandated rights councils which exist at the federal, state and municipal levels. Separate councils exist on different topics including children's rights. Many countries have commissions of various kinds that oversee aspects of public life but these commissions are usually appointed by the executive or legislative branches of government. The Brazilian Children's Rights Councils spring from a more general provision contained in the Brazilian Constitution known generically as Oversight Councils for Social Policy (Conselhos Gestores de Políticas Sociais). The civil society members (half of the membership, with public officials making up the rest) are elected by a very select electorate: that is, civil society organizations that are registered by the Councils as organizations that provide services to children and youth.

What is unusual about the Children's Rights Councils is that they are one of two types of Oversight Councils that have the power to formulate policy as well as consult on policy (Secretaria de Direitos Humanos, 2010). This power is spelt out in Article 88 of the Statute of the Child and Adolescent which states that Children's Rights Councils are decision-making and monitoring bodies (órgãos deliberativos e controladores) (Federal Government of Brazil, 1990). We should note that the Councils are but one part of a theoretically

comprehensive system in Brazil for implementing rights known as the System for the Guarantee of Rights (Sistema de Garantia de Direitos). This System encompasses all the public and nonprofit sector actors responsible for guaranteeing the rights of all citizens.[8] Two examples of CIESPI's work through the Council mechanism illustrate the possibilities of using them to inject research and policy knowledge into public decision making about children. The first is about a group of very vulnerable children and youth and the second about children aged 0–6. For many years, CIESPI has worked with the Rede Rio Criança (the Rio Children's Network), the major coalition of organizations in Rio on street children, and in 2007 started a new initiative with the coalition to press the municipal Children's Rights Council to develop an effective policy to improve the condition of Rio's street children. Such a policy was passed in 2009, representing the first time that any municipality in the country had passed such a policy through the Children's Rights Council process.[9] The Council set up an implementation committee on which CIESPI staff had a seat but little was done to press for the implementation of the policy. The election of a new Council brought new opportunities and, in consequence, in October 2013, CIESPI started a deliberate strategy of trying to extend the coalition by bringing in powerful new allies to assist in implementation. Since then, CIESPI has played a major role in bringing senior officials from the Health and Culture Secretariats into the discussion, both departments key to improving the condition of street children, and also the Defensoria Pública, or Public Defender's Office, a department with broad responsibilities for the guaranteeing of human rights. It has also encouraged the participation of the Federal Prosecutor's Office or Ministério Público.

The Center has played a similar role, both in using its database on indicators and research findings to inform the new policy and in developing a group of organizations who successfully pressed for the development and passage of a policy on early childhood.

In some ways, work on this policy initiative was easier than the policy initiative on street children. There was an obvious group of colleague organizations from the Rio members of the National Network on Early Childhood, and early childhood policy in Brazil does not attract the kind of law and order opposition groups that work on street children attracts. The key challenge was different – working with the group to narrow down the large number of possible initiatives so that the priority agenda was small enough to be actionable in a reasonable time frame. The work started appropriately enough for a research organization with a scan of the international research on early childhood development and then fashioning this into a summary that could be read and understood by a broad audience of interested parties. This summary became part of the CIESPI website section, the Context of Early Childhood (Ambiente da Primeira Infância, www.ciespi.org.br/primeira_infancia/).

At CIESPI-convened meetings, the group then fashioned a workable, short agenda for improving the lives of young children in the city, and suggested this as a basis for the Children's Rights Council to develop its own official policy. This group then divided responsibility among itself for building support among Children's Rights Council members to examine the possibility of adopting a policy on early childhood. Senior CIESPI staff attended the decision-making body of the Council, the Public Assembly, along with coalition members, to make the case for such a policy and the Council subsequently set up a working group to develop a policy with the explicit instruction of the Assembly to finish its work in a short period of time. The working group, of which coalition members and CIESPI staff were a part, did just that, and at another meeting of the Assembly, the proposed policy was adopted and an implementation group, again with coalition and CIESPI staff on it, was established to oversee implementation.

This degree of involvement with the dissemination of research and with facilitating organizations to develop and press for policies that reflect the broad research consensus on early childhood may seem unusual to some children's research centers. And this account is not intended to be in any degree prescriptive. But it should be understood in the context of a country: where many young children grow up in environments that put their development at risk; where civic engagement is, following the end of dictatorship, seen as an opportunity and a duty; and where the nonprofit sector is comparatively new following centuries of colonial, imperial, oligarchic and military rule. In countries with a richer nonprofit tradition, there exist organizations outside of universities with a mission to perform, summarize and disseminate children's research in pursuit of the improvement of children's policies and practices.[10]

We should, however, note that the decision to take dissemination so seriously has consequences for a research center. The process of building and maintaining networks to press for policy change, and the process of engaging public bodies and assemblies to make a reasoned case for change is enormously time-consuming and operates on a different timetable than research. Deliberative bodies have processes that are no respecter of academic and legislative timetables or priorities. Showing up at long meetings is a *sine qua non* for gaining respect and a voice, and coalition strategy discussions can and do take place at any time of day and night. Furthermore, research staff also have to have qualities that enable them to be effective in coalition and public discussions. But all these real costs have proven worthwhile in CIESPI's case, both because they have resulted in policies based on serious research and knowledge and because participants have often expressed their appreciation of having a safe, respectful and serious forum in a university setting for discussing the children's issues they face every day and for developing strategies for change.

RELATIONS WITH COMMUNITY RESIDENTS AND CHILDREN

Children's researchers face numerous questions about how to conduct their work. One of the more important is their relationship to the subjects of their work. This question can be approached in a number of ways including ethical, political, methodological and epistemological considerations. The CIESPI team has chosen to maintain close contact with representative actors in low-income communities including children and youth. CIESPI staff have, for example, over the years, helped with the development of play and learning centers for young children, created advisory groups of residents for different projects and maintained close links with one particular low-income community in Rio de Janeiro, Rocinha, one of the largest slums in South America.

CIESPI staff articulate several reasons for this practice. Our recent children's research in Rocinha has focused on how parents and youth perceive the challenges of growing up in a difficult environment.[11] This issue involves trying to understand how residents perceive their reality and the best, though not infallible, sources of that understanding are the residents themselves. As one philosopher has put it:

> There is a sense in which phenomenological facts are perfectly objective: one person can know or say of another what the quality of the other's experience is. They are subjective, however, in the sense that even this objective ascription of experience is possible only for someone sufficiently similar to the object of ascription to be able to adopt his point of view – to understand the ascription in the first person as well as in the third, so to speak. The more different from oneself the other experiencer is, the less success one can expect with this enterprise. (Nagel, 1974: 437)

A distinguished US sociologist, declining to answer the question of the research subject's view of his or her life on epistemological or moral grounds, instead argued the case for close involvement in subjects' lives on the grounds of the likelihood of finding out more about the subjects than by other techniques:

> In contrast [to the quantitative analysts] fieldworkers cannot insulate themselves from data. As long as they are 'in the field' they will see and hear things which ought to be entered into their field notes. If they are conscientious, or experienced enough to know that they had better put it all in, even what they think might be useless and keep on doing that until they know for sure that they will never use data on certain subjects. They thus allow themselves to become aware of things they had not anticipated which may have a bearing on their subject. They expect to continually add variables and ideas to their models. (Becker, 1996: n.p.)

He went on to argue that researchers ascribe meanings to the actions of their subjects, so it is better to start off with the meanings people ascribe to their own actions and beliefs.

In Brazil, the political/democratic reasons for involving the subjects of research are perhaps more salient than in other countries. One of the elements of creating a democracy after the military dictatorship was to establish strategies for civic involvement in public decision making. The Rights Councils described above are one outcome of these attempts. Brazil suffers not only from a large gap between the promise of rights and their implementation but also in trust between the government and the governed. This mistrust on the part of ordinary citizens easily transfers to a mistrust of researchers, so the creation of some sort of partnership between researchers and the subjects of their research is necessary to gain access to communities and the lives of their residents.

The long-term partnership between CIESPI and some key residents of Rocinha is a two-way street. The key residents provide access to residents in a variety of settings, and CIESPI assists the residents in a variety of ways including in the provision of organizational and technical assistance in several children and youth settings. But most important, the key residents are a constant source of day-to-day information about what is happening in the community, which is critical to understand how residents experience various effects of the UPP and massive public works targeted at the Mayor and the Governor's priorities, rather than the community's.[12]

For its research and policy development on early childhood, CIESPI, with the assistance of its community contacts, has been able to set up a series of interviews and focus groups with parents and youth (adolescents and young adults) about the challenges facing young children. The trust allows for a very frank dialogue and some very innovative ways of collecting information which can be fed back to the community. One of these was the writing, production and dissemination online of a sketch created by young people in the community about the enormous challenges of making it to adulthood through a host of difficulties and dangers.[13] The young actors portrayed the dangers of physical abuse, of adults screaming at them, of menial work, but also the power of friendship to help with hard situations. The sketch both allowed glimpses into the inner lives of young people in the community and is also a powerful drama that will speak to interested parties in Brazil. In the same way, the Rio Coalition on Early Childhood brought children to the Public Assembly of the Children's Rights Council to talk about their experiences of growing up in low-income communities.

Such contacts also permit access to very powerful stories that would not appear in quantitative data or even in simple surveys. Teachers told CIESPI staff about a 6-year-old who vomited out of fear on her way to school because of nearby gunfire and the presence of armed drug dealers. A school principal recounted how difficult it was to retain competent staff when such staff could easily find a job in the middle-class beach community of Copacabana and be on the beach within five minutes of the end of school. Parents complained that there was not a single outdoor space in the community that was safe for their young children to play in as they showed the researchers the few regular streets in the community which were packed with cars, buses and motorbikes, and the dark, steep dangerous alleyways that are the only means of access to the majority of houses. In another encounter, CIESPI staff celebrating the opening of a children's library watched as young, masked men armed with AK 47s walked outside the library door as a

reminder of the power of the drug traffickers. The on-the-ground presence not only elicits key facts and events that might otherwise go unnoticed but gives the researcher something of the emotional valence of those facts that parents and children would feel, a valence that maintains a sense of urgency and interest and helps sort out what is important and not so important in the lives of low-income families.

While using these varied methodologies, some of which involve close connection with the young people and communities in question, CIESPI remains aware that it is first and foremost a research center and is always responsible for the robustness of the data it presents and for the validity of the conclusions it reaches. Such an approach also requires that some staff have particular skills in working in the communities, providing technical assistance to various community endeavors, while others are more highly trained researchers. Some of the researchers need to be comfortable and skilled in collecting qualitative data from community settings and from those settings where public debate and decision making occur. This latter observation is not a comment on the comparative merits of qualitative and quantitative data. The Center holds that different data and information require different methodologies. We do note, however, that there is a too infrequent use of relevant change-in-time quantitative data in public debates and media reports on young children in Brazil. The same may also be said of other countries.

An important consequence of this approach is that the Center has to be a place where this kind of diversity is honored and where there is space for the different points of view arising from this diversity to be heard and discussed. The tolerance of such diversity is not achieved without a conscious effort and recognition that the diversity adds greatly to the richness of the Center's understandings and effectiveness. Debate among staff with different approaches and discourses can be contentious and difficult, but it can also be very rewarding.

As with participation in coalitions and other groups to disseminate research findings to decision-making bodies, this participation with and consultation of children, families and communities takes consistent time and energy and a staff with the qualities to build such relationships. Listening to the targets of policy changes, however, adds another element of realism to the research and policy development and that, in turn, should make the resulting policies more attuned to the realities of the target populations and, hence, more effective.

CONCLUSION

In the USA and elsewhere, researchers, particularly those engaged in quantitative children's research, use the terms data- or evidence-based practice. These terms show up regularly, for example, in schools of social work. The intent is laudable, that public policies and practices should be shaped by research on the nature of the problems to be addressed and the relationship between problems and proposed solutions. But as this chapter shows, the relationship between research knowledge and public policy is really more complicated. The slogans in themselves suggest that policy makers and practitioners should listen more to researchers than the reverse. The slogans also suggest that the discourse of children's research has insights that are superior to other discourses relevant to public policy as opposed to being contributory. What this chapter suggests is an ongoing interplay of ideas, values, priorities and knowledge among the subjects of research, the research findings, the political values of a nation, the particular situation the nation finds itself in as regards the conditions of young children, the particular political mechanisms that fashion policies and their implementation, and the epistemological and human values placed on the insights of 'subjects'. Research on the impacts of early life conditions on the present and future status of children is crucial to improving these conditions. The international research sets out starkly the consequences for their future development of children growing up in harsh conditions. But the ways in which the research gets used and its relevance to a particular situation will depend on other important factors.

Brazil faces large challenges in its now explicit attempts to improve the conditions of all its young children. International children's research points to the enormous harm of not making that attempt. But the success of the enterprise will depend on: Brazil's continuing legal and theoretical emphasis on human rights; the establishment of institutional and legal mechanisms to promote implementation; the monitoring of policies and programs; and the exploitation of a quite unusual commitment to participatory democracy exemplified quite recently by the massive demonstrations for human rights that began in June 2013 and which continue today. As this chapter shows, another critical element in Brazil is the research community's willingness to participate as one of a number of other legitimate players and, as individual members of that community, to choose to take on additional roles to make sure that research findings make it into decision-making forums.

FURTHER READING

The following titles are available in pdf form at www.ciespi.org.br under Publications:

Bush, M. and Rizzini, I. (2011) *Closing the Gap between Rights and Realities for Children and Youth in Urban Brazil: Reflections on a Brazilian project to improve policies for street children*. Rio de Janeiro: CIESPI-PUC-Rio.

Kaufman, N.H. and Rizzini, I. (eds) (2002) *Globalization and Children: Exploring potentials for enhancing opportunities in the lives of children and youth*. New York/London: Kluwer Academic/Plenum Publishers.

Kramer, S. (2014) 'Early Childhood Education: Difficulties creating and changing daily practice', *Creative Education*, 5: 386–395.

QUESTIONS FOR REFLECTION

1   What are the most urgent public policy issues affecting early childhood in your country and are the policy priorities in line with the research evidence on the greatest harms to young children?
2   Is there sufficient understanding in your country of the enormous negative influence on young children's development of growing up in contexts of violence, poverty and stress?
3   Does the university system in your country encourage or discourage researchers' active involvement in policy debates and decisions?
4   Do university researchers consider that they should only inform the research community about their research, that community and political and civil service leaders, or all the interested public including community groups and advocacy organizations?
5   Is there interest and are there sources of funding for research centers to engage in serious, as opposed to *pro forma*, dissemination and policy debate?

NOTES

1   There are a number of ways of measuring this coefficient and these figures are taken from a list of several ways of measuring it at http://en.wikipedia.org/wiki/List_of_countries_by_income_equality (accessed 30 June 2014).
2   The *Bolsa Família* has been consistently raised by the federal government of President Dilma Rousseff, and was last raised on 1 May 2014 by 10%, an increase which assisted the 36 million families that received the allowance (Dame, 2014: 3).
3   Statistics, 2012, accessed at http://laborsta.ilo.org/applv8/data/INFORMAL_ECONOMY/2012-06-Statistical%20update%20-%20v2.pdf0,5April2014. Note the difference between informal employment, the figure cited here, and employment in the informal sector, a much lower percentage.
4   A major example of the use of this language is to be found in the publication, *Direitos Humanos de Criancas e Adolescentes, 20 Anos do Estatuto* (The Human Rights of Children and Adolescents: Twenty Years of the Statute), Secretaria de Direitos Humanos, 2010. This publication is a review of improvements in the condition of children and youth since the passage of the Statute of the Child and Adolescent in 1990.
5   Taken from an English language version of the Statute at www.eca.org.br/ecai.htm (accessed 18 March 2011).
6   Early childhood education seen as the first stage of basic education is mentioned in the federal provisions, Rules for the Provision of Education (LDB 9.394/96). With the constitutional amendment No. 53 in 2006, early childhood education in creche and preschool is guaranteed up to the age of 5 (Leite Filho and Nunes, 2013: 71).
7   For more information about CIESPI at the Pontifical Catholic University of Rio de Janeiro/PUC-Rio, see www.ciespi.org.br. This site has both a Portuguese and English language account of the research and activities of the Center.
8   The System for the Guarantee of Rights is described in detail as it relates to children in a publication of the Brazilian Association of Magistrates, Prosecutors and Public Defenders of the Child and the Adolescent (Associação Brasileira de Magistrados, Promotores de Justiça e Defensores Públicos da Infância e da Juventude), 2008.
9   See Bush and Rizzini, 2011, which was published with the support of the Oak Foundation, Geneva, Switzerland.
10   See, e.g., in the USA, the Children's Defense Fund at national level and organizations such as Voices for Illinois Children at state level.
11   In this initiative, adolescents and young adults aged 17–22 were involved and some of these were parents of young children. CIESPI staff also interviewed other parents of young children.
12   The classic example of this mismatch is the public investment in a *teleférico* or cable car through the community, while residents insist that covering up and replacing open sewers, a major source of ill-health, is their priority. Residents point out that *teleférico* mechanisms are not suitable for access by people carrying e.g., shopping bags, are not accessible to the very young, the old or disabled, and are routed in such a way as to promote tourism, not to permit residents the inter- and intra-community transit they need.
13   The video sketch was named 'Na Corda Bamba' or The Tight Rope and can be downloaded at http://vimeo.com/81461735.

REFERENCES

Becker, H.S. (1996) The Epistemology of Qualitative Research (https://connect.ssri.duke.edu/sites/connect.ssri.duke.edu/files/upload/help-resource/Becker.Epistemology%20of%20Qualitative%20Research.pdf).

Brazilian Institute on Geography and Statistics (IBGE) (2010). *Censo*. Rio de Janeiro: IBGE.

Bush, M. and Rizzini, I. (2011). *Closing the Gap between Rights and Realities for Children and Youth in Urban Brazil: Reflections on a*

Brazilian project to improve policies for street children. Rio de Janeiro: CIESPI-PUC-Rio.

Cano, I. (2012). Os donos do morro: Uma avaliação exploratória do impacto das Unidades de Polícia Pacificadora (UPPs) no Rio de Janeiro (http://riorealblog.files.wordpress.com/2012/07/relatc3b3riofinalcaf13.pdf, accessed 5 February 2014).

Conselho Municipal dos Direitos da Criança e do Adolescente (2013). Deliberação N.° 1.042/2013 DS/CMDCA, Rio de Janeiro.

Dame, L. (2014). 'Dilma parte "pra cima"', *O Globo*, 1 May, p. 3.

de Sainte Croix, S. (2012). 'Brazil Strives for Economic Equality', *Rio Times Online*, 7 February (http://riotimesonline.com/brazil-news/rio-business/brazil-strives-for-economic-equality).

Engle, P., Fernald, L.C.H., Alderman, H., Behrman, J., O'Gara, C., Yousafzai, A., et al. (2011). 'The Global Child Development Steering Group: Strategies for reducing inequalities and improving developmental outcomes for young children in low-income and middle-income countries', *The Lancet*, 378(9799): 1339–1353.

Federal Government of Brazil (1988). Constituição da República Federativa do Brasil de 1988, Capítulo VII, Art. 227 (www.planalto.gov.br/ccivil_03/constituicao/constitui%C3%A7ao_compilado.htm).

Federal Government of Brazil (1990). Statute of the Child and Adolescent (www.planalto.gov.br/ccivil_03/Leis/L8069.htm).

Heckman, J.J. (2007). 'The Economics, Technology, and Neuroscience of Human Capability Formation', *Proceedings of the National Academy of Sciences of the United States*, 14 August, 104 (33): 13250–13255.

Kaya, Y., Bennet, J. and Moss, P. (2010). *Caring and Learning Together: A cross-national study on the integration of early childhood care and education within education*. Paris: UNESCO.

Kramer, S., Nunes, M.F. and Carvalho, M.C. (eds) (2013). *Educação infantil: formação e responsabilidade*. Campinas: Papirus.

Leite Filho, A. and Nunes, F. (2013). 'Rights of the Child and Early Education: Reflections on the history and the politics', in S. Kramer, M.F. Nunes and M.C. Carvalho (eds), *Educação infantil: formação e responsabilidade*. Campinas: Papirus.

Nagel, T. (1974). 'What is it Like to Be a Bat?', *Philosophical Review*, pp. 435–50.

Rede Nacional Primeira Infância (RNPI) (National Network on Early Childhood) (2010). *Plano Nacional pela Primeira Infância (PNPI) (National Plan for Early Childhood)*. Rio de Janeiro: RNPI.

Secretaria de Direitos Humanos (SDH) (2010). *20 Anos de Estatuto: Direitos humanos de crianças e Adolescentes*. Brasília: SDH.

Sequel, X.T., Izquierdo, T. and Edwards, M. (2002). Diagnostico Nacional y Elaboracion del Plan de Accion para el Decenio en el area del desarrollo infantil y familiar. Santiago, Chile: United Nations Children's Fund.

United Nations (1989). *Convention on the Rights of the Child*. New York: United Nations.

Woodhead, M., Dornan, P. and Murray, H. (2013). *What Inequality Means for Children: Evidence from the Young Lives Project*. Oxford: Oxford University Press.

26

Rethinking Epistemology and Methodology in Early Childhood Research in Africa

Auma Okwany and Hasina Ebrahim

INTRODUCTION

Africa has an extremely high and disproportionate representation of young children who bear the greatest risk of failure to achieve their developmental potential due to limitations in health, nutrition, education and care services. There has been increasing attention from international organizations, donor agencies and foundations on the development of policies and programs for young children in the last two decades. However, these programs and policies are based on the dominant narrative on early childhood development, which is the product of Euro-American culture and storyline, and which promotes a model of childhood from the Global North (Ebrahim, 2014; Nsamenang, 2005, 2009; Okwany et al., 2011; Pence, 2013; Penn, 2012; Twum Danso-Imoh and Ames, 2012).

Our starting point in this chapter is a concern with this disproportionate dominance and influence of Western scholarship on early childhood research, discourse and policy in Africa and the epistemic inequality in which the contribution of local scholars and activists is subordinated. As noted by Nsamenang (2009), these decontextualized 'best practices' condemn and exclude Africa's developmental theories and educational praxes rather than seeking to understand and improve them. While we confront the partiality of this dominant framing and critique how it is held up as the yardstick for all countries to emulate, our emphasis is on the need for countervailing efforts to go beyond advocacy for an Africentric narrative. Indeed, in maintaining the need to rethink epistemology and research methods in early education care and research in Africa, we argue for the imperative of decentering universals and the recognition of a multi-polar world and plurality of voice and space within both the Eurocentric and Africentric narratives.

Our main argument is that the dominant narrative in child development knowledge production and practice influences the way in which ECD is read, interpreted, practiced and researched. We aim to provide a perspective on how the dominant often marginalizes local narratives and how this not only constitutes epistemological injustice, but also has implications for context-specific approaches to early care education and research in Africa. We demonstrate how this not only constrains the space for knowledge production but also eschews a focus on the situated and contextual knowledge of marginalized scholars and communities with a specific focus on Africa.

In challenging dominant discourses, our aim is to make visible the role of power in the generation of ECD knowledge in diverse contexts. We posit that valuing particular ECD knowledge at the expense of the less dominant knowledge leads to constructions of truth and narratives (grand) which fail to consider diverse ethnicities, contexts (both material and other) and complexities of childhood. In so doing, we are writing ourselves as part of an emerging constituency of African scholars who seek a space for scholars from the Global South to be seen as *speaking subjects* in ECD knowledge production and who have argued for child development practice that is contextual and situated (Marfo et al., 2011; Nsamenang and Tchombe, 2011; Odora Hoppers, 2010; Shiva, 2000; Smith, 1999). We join these voices in an attempt to give 'voice to the 'voiceless', to 'secure representation' of alternative voices in ECD research and practice, and at the same time to reveal the stunting impacts of this received ECD knowledge (Nsamenang, 2008; Otterstad, 2005; Pence, 2013; Penn, 2012).

CROSS-CULTURAL UNIVERSALS: TRANSCENDING GLOBAL AND LOCAL DIVIDES

In arguing for the need to move beyond polarized grand narratives, we do not consider Africa as a monolithic entity and argue for a recognition that the continent works at multiple levels – global, regional, national and local. In this chapter, we recognize that knowledge in Africa is not homogenous and we posit that just as there are different cultures, communities and idiosyncrasies in Africa, there is also diversity within Africa with regard to ways of knowing. Indeed, viewing Africa as 'local' serves to confirm that only the Euro-American is 'global', which glosses over the fluid and dynamic interplay between local and global which are interrelated in an economy of time and space. We draw on the contention by Chakrabarty (2000) in his book, *Provincializing Europe*, in which he troubles conceptual Europe and the dominant Euro-American framing of history of progress, modernity and capital. He notes that this modern history is not universal, but is a provincial history particular to those specific regions, which subordinate 'minority histories' or 'histories from below' that are basic elements of 'liberal-democratic struggles for inclusion and representation' (2000: 97). Equally importantly, he points out that this dominant 'European thought is at once both indispensable and inadequate in helping us to think through the experiences of political modernity in non-Western nations, and provincializing Europe becomes the task of exploring how this thought … may be renewed from and for the margins' (2000: 16).

We view this distinction as useful for laying emphasis on the need to focus on in-between perspectives in the early childhood care and education spaces between the polarity of dominant and Africentric narratives. We argue that it is critical to pay attention to the people in these spaces, their practices, beliefs and interpretations as sites where global and local forces converge or diverge. This enables us to pluralize time and space (both global and local) and ground it in practice. We thus emphasize the imperative of engaging from a complementary rather than a duality perspective.

While providing a perspective on the tyranny of the dominant on Africa's way of knowing, we join with other scholars (Ngutuku, 2010; Nsamenang, 2006a; Pence and Nsamenang, 2008; Odora Hoppers, 2009; Okwany et al., 2011; Oudenhoven and Wazir, 2006) when we say that the dominant narrative, which is a product of Western forms of epistemology in ECD, is in itself not a problem, but rather its claims to universality should not be used to deprive other cultures of their heritage in childcare. We also argue that the global and the local are not dichotomous categories and that the West is not just a geographical category. Guided by the conceptualization of Hall, we view the West as a system that wields power over what is seen as valid knowledge when he states:

> The idea of 'the West,' once produced, became productive in its turn. It had real effects: it enabled people to know or speak of certain things in certain ways. It produced knowledge. It became both the organizing factor in a system of global power relations and the organizing concept or term in a whole way of thinking and speaking. (1992: 187)

The West/Western is therefore not just geographical but is an idea or a concept and a language for imagining complex stories, ideas, historical events and social relationships. In Africa, the history and legacy of colonialism have interacted with the dominant narrative to inform the child development landscape, leading to a kind of 'cultural incapacity' that negatively impacts on child welfare and development. We contend that the West, which produces the dominant narrative, is itself not homogenous, but has internal heterogeneity and significant populations of minority groups who are 'othered' and whose ways of knowing have also been devalued and marginalized. Child welfare reformers have noted the danger of cultural incapacity among these groups with similarly devastating effects (Dahlberg et al., 2007; Dennis and Lourie, 2006; Denzin et al., 2007). In her comparison of children's lives in Howa, Sudan and Harlem in New York City, Katz (2004) highlights the nuanced ways in which the effects of global capitalism and neo-liberalism have impacted on children's wellbeing in both settings. Her rich analysis succeeds in not only moving beyond

polarizing North/South divides, but also elucidates the convergences and divergences in both settings, illuminating the voicelessness of children and caregivers in both African and North American settings.

The need for a contextual and situated ECD is thus not quintessentially an African clamour. Care, stimulation and learning are essentially cultural concepts. A substantial body of anthropological and psychological evidence (DeLoache and Gottlieb, 2000; Gottlieb, 2004; LeVine, 2004) suggests that patterns of care, stimulation and learning are intrinsically contextual. This being the case, we follow the thinking of critical and postcolonial theorists (Appiah, 1997; Fanon, 1963; Mbembe, 2001; Nyamjoh, 2012; Odora Hoppers, 2010; Said, 2003; Spivak, 1999; Viruru, 2001; wa Thiong'o, 1986, 2012) who have called for the need to challenge universal representations. Chakrabarty notes the importance of context in the writings of such postcolonial theorists who 'refer us to the plurality that inheres in the "now", the lack of totality, the constant fragmentariness that constitutes one's present' (2000: 243). We are also influenced by reconceptualist authors such as Lubeck (2000), Penn (2005, 2012), Swadener and Kessler (1991) and Swadener and Mutua (2008) who challenge conventional methods and knowledge in ECD including Developmentally Appropriate Practice, arguing that it was ethnocentric and ignored the situated experiences of children from different backgrounds. In calling for Afrocentric ECD practice and research, the argument is not for 'an additive epistemology' but for a dialogue between the dominant and marginalized knowledge in ECD practice and research and an epistemological shift in representations.

The development niche, a framework expounded by Harkness and Super (1992, 1996; Harkness et al., 2009), is illustrative in showing the diversity of ways in which children are nurtured in specific cultural spheres. The development niche consists of three subsystems: the physical and social settings of daily life; the customs and practices of care; and parental ethnotheories (cultural beliefs) which operate in harmony with but are also influenced by the larger culture and economy. They are replete with modes of knowledge that are articulated in a multiplicity of ways and include an array of indigenous resources. The framework is useful for a cross-cultural examination of care, policy and practice, which are cultural products in all contexts, and is thus helpful for moving us beyond artificial global–local divides.

We support our arguments by drawing examples from our research on the situated experiences of young children, households and communities in East and South Africa, as well as from diverse empirical research in Africa that foreground the voices and experiences of marginalized communities including young children. In articulation with debates around early childhood epistemology and research methods, we challenge the pervasive influence of the dominant ways of knowing on early education and care practices and research. We provide counter-narratives to highlight the importance of promoting research that is embedded in caregivers' and young children's contextual realities and local ways of knowing. In this way, the analysis contributes to a more nuanced and situated conceptualization of early education and care, epistemology and methodology.

PERSPECTIVE ON THE UNIVERSAL AS THE NORM IN THE METANARRATIVE OF ECD

Metanarratives or grand narratives function to universalize some truth held by dominant groups over other truths. A master narrative is a script that specifies and controls how social processes are carried out (Stanely, 2007). We argue in this chapter that the grand/dominant narrative operating in ECD often defines and limits what is valued as knowledge and practice and who is entitled to create that knowledge. Indeed, according

to Oudenhoven and Wazir (2006), the field of childhood studies is dominated by scholars who trace the intellectual roots of their arguments to Western discourses on childhood. These scholars generate knowledge that is deemed valid in early care and education and we argue that there is an exclusion of the voices, perspectives and input of African scholars in the shaping of this master narrative.

The standards and measurements developed from the West are used as a yardstick and the norm in ECD in Africa. The development of the early learning standards in the Global South is a case-in-point. Ebrahim (2012) notes how initial processes to establish early learning standards in six countries in the Global South, including South Africa, led to child development knowledge transfer, which required adaptations to national priorities rather than fundamental generative engagements in what children should know and be able to do in contexts that shape early care and education.

This illustrates how the dominant narrative is not cognizant of a multicultural universe and the diversity of local narratives, including local competing discourses and notions of childhood and childcare, with dire consequences for contextually appropriate policy/practice. This is consistent with the critique by Nsamenang (2006b: 296) that 'Whenever Euro-American ECD programs are applied as the gold standards by which to measure forms of Africa's ECD, they forcibly deny equity to and recognition of Africa's ways of provisioning for its young, thereby depriving the continent a niche in global ECD knowledge'. We concur with him and join scholars who argue that there is a need for 'emancipation from hearing only the voices of Western Europe/North America, emancipation from generations of silence, and emancipation from seeing the world in one color' (Guba and Lincoln, 2005: 212). Similarly, Pence (2013) argues for the imperative of listening to unheard voices when he underscores the importance of critical and indigenous perspectives.

WHOSE ECD? WHOSE GOOD START?

According to Okwany et al. (2011: 128), the dominant narrative in ECD revolves around giving children a 'good start'. However, the pervasiveness of the dominant narrative means that most projects have tended to discursively construct the needs of children and communities, often portraying them as passive recipients of aid or assistance. This good start is thus often out of touch with local realities because it has been constructed from the outside (based on Eurocentric models) and implemented from the top, often based on assumed and not articulated needs. In an EFA assessment at the turn of the century, Myers (2000: 25) noted the contextual differences in knowledge and values informing programmes for early care and development:

> Frameworks and knowledge – the basis for lobbying and constructing ECCD programmes – continue to originate, the most part, in the Minority World. Accordingly, a tension often arises between 'received truth' linked to the Minority World knowledge base and values guiding an agency, and local knowledge linked to another set of values rooted in some part of the Majority World. These may overlap but they are different.

Thus, a critical question that remains unanswered is: whose ECD and whose good start? Indeed for too long, the story of children in Africa has been told by those in positions of power, and in this naming, African ways of rearing their children have been abstracted and some of them seen as gothic and deficient when measured against the dominant norms (Okwany et al., 2011: 131). We trouble the pathologizing of African childhoods and childcare and contend that within the dominant narrative of ECD and childhood in general, African children have been (mis) represented as victims of retrogressive cultures, in deficient communities. They are thus seen as mere voiceless objects (of the Victorian-appropriated view to be seen and not heard) in need of salvation through various ECD interventions. Even as we confront this (mis) representation of African childhoods and

critique these problematic 'salvation interventions', we draw from Woodhead (2006) who cautions that we should be cognizant of the serious economic inequalities and social exclusion challenges that remain entrenched for many young children in the Global South and of the need for interventions to combat their negative impacts.

Our critique is consistent with the reminder by Pence (2013) and Penn (2012) that the science of child development has its roots in a Western 'civilizing' imperative based on an image of deficiency. Indeed, we argue that the fervor with which African children and childhoods have been (mis)represented is akin to the representation of pre-colonial societies by some missionaries, whereby the worse the rendering of indigenous people, the greater the urgency to save them. Differences stemming from local ideas and practices embedded in local ways of knowing and doing are seen as fault lines and deficiencies that need to be corrected. According to Harkness et al. (2013) and Nsamenang (2008), though culture determines the nature of many dimensions of children's development niches, the gap between African children's conditions and the theories applied to them persist because universalized responses are applied to problems that have local characteristics, ignoring the diverse, embedded contextual realities of childhood and the range of ECD experiences therein.

(RE)FRAMING KNOWLEDGE PRODUCTION

Our contention in this chapter is that the pervasiveness of dominant ways of knowing are infused in the knowledge production process and, therefore, require ideological shifts in research through critical reflexivity to trouble hidden assumptions. We note that the dominant narrative affects research questions, the choice of analytical categories and theories, and ultimately underpins the knowledge and power relations that are (re)produced.

Investigative methods in ECD also fail to nuance childcare contexts and we concur with Odora Hoppers (2010) who questions the power embedded in investigative methods of research, and we highlight several reasons for the prevalence of universal norms in ECD research.

One of the main reasons is that research regarding the impacts of a broad set of interventions and programs is commissioned and funded by the international donor community (Ebrahim and Penn, 2011; Pence and Nsamenang, 2008). Ebrahim and Penn (2011) reflect on evaluation research commissioned by UNICEF on ECD among poor and vulnerable children in South Africa, which is illustrative of the effects of the pervasiveness of donor influence on research. The study, Ebrahim notes, was aimed at providing contextual accounts of ECD and thus utilized a qualitative approach and was sensitive to translation, language and ethical issues. All this was useful in unearthing contextual factors. However, despite government attention and support, financial constrains meant that programming was dependent on donor funding. Penn asserts that this external aid comes with imported ideologies on ECD based on scientific approaches from Euro-American perspectives, which framed how the research was carried out. In her critical reflection, Penn provides an outsiders' perspective, arguing that the methodological approach did not critically problematize the existing dominant assumptions within ECD that are promoted by INGOs like UNICEF, hence the research produced grey literature. Additionally, by adhering to a dominant framing of researching ECD, the study fails to challenge the assumptions on community involvement and identification of ECD gatekeepers who frame young children as 'becomings' and hence without much agency. As such, the approach further reinforced a compensatory approach to ECD as opposed to a complementary one.

According to Marfo et al. (2011), a lack of sufficient local expertise capable of conducting conceptually and methodologically sound research means that there are constrained opportunities for African and other majority world researchers to contribute to a truly global ECD discussion. It also means that inquiry needed to generate a locally relevant knowledge base to guide policies and interventions cannot be sustained. Pence (2013) powerfully illustrates this epistemic inequality when he notes that despite the demographic dominance of children in Africa, none of the numerous studies included in the prominent medical journal the *Lancet* series, which summarize substantial quantitative evidence of the developmental risks faced by children in the majority world, was led by an African scholar. This epistemic injustice is problematic and we assert that there is a need to challenge the power dynamics of who produces what knowledge about whom and to expand the space for alternatives not only to expose but also to influence ECD policy and practice.

Ebrahim and Penn (2011) note that conducting research in the Global South and in poor communities may have its own sensibilities, which, in turn, may contradict dominant framing, and a key consideration should be structured by local contexts and ways of knowing. Neuroscientific research emphasizes that stimulation of the brain in very early childhood through appropriate caregiving will stimulate brain development. However, an over-reliance on these findings of early intervention and brain research is problematic for several reasons: first, the research has been largely carried out in the USA, thus it ignores the fact that 'the scientific basis' of such research is transposed from one context to another without taking into consideration contextual factors (2011: 195); second, Penn (2012) notes that even some of the key proponents of brain research (Shonkoff and Phillips, 2000) have not only stated that brain research is in its early stages, but they are clear that harmful environments have detrimental effects on very young children. Indeed, Shonkoff (2010: 363) notes that there is still no research on the effects of childrearing beliefs and practices on brain development.

Penn (2012) provides a strong critique of the World Bank's uncritical promotion of early intervention and brain research and troubles the emphasis on mothers/caregivers' action in care and stimulation as central to early childhood development, while ignoring extreme poverty as a structural issue within the care context. This is consistent with the critique by George (2010: 15) of analyses of poverty, including those in the *Lancet* series, in which the locus of poverty is on poor children, their caregivers and their low-income 'unstimulating' homes, while ignoring the deficits in global and national structures that generate poverty, exclusion and inequality.

Nsamenang (2009) argues that the reliance on the universal may be occasioned by the fact that African 'differentness' breeds ambiguity due to the plural realities, which are often difficult to tolerate or to put in simple measurement criteria. Bar-On's (2004) examination of early care and education in Botswana deepens the point in relation to early socialization. He contends that in Western societies there is an individualist response to the meaning and direction of life. This stems from both the Judeo-Christian ethos and capitalist assumptions. These assumptions make salient the fact that each person is an independent moral entity who is unique and that history, relationships and contexts do not matter. Each person is entitled to choose how they live their lives and the preparation for adulthood is directed toward building independence and autonomy. It is not surprising then that pedagogical activities in early childhood centers place a great deal of emphasis on curiosity and exploration. In Sub-Saharan Africa, Bar-On (2004) contends that social networks, especially kinship, are of utmost importance. These networks are overburdened in the contemporary context, but nonetheless kinship networks provide a different reading of how children are readied for society. Thus, it is not so much about children discovering their talents but rather about them internalizing the expected norms and values of their society (Doob, 1985). Socialization in this context is associated with discipline and control, and children are expected to be obedient and responsible in the eyes of those preparing them for adulthood.

This difficulty in handling contradictions often leads to a tendency to homogenize into a single Euro-American referential frame. A prototype emerges and becomes a site for manipulation for intervention in early care and education. Relying on 'expertise' from the West also buttresses the reliance on the dominant framing of ECD, and, as Nsamenang (2009) argues, the failure or inability to translate foreign ECD ideas into the local language leads to a hiring of foreign consultants who may not be sensitive to local realities. Additionally, this prototypical practice within the donor community hampers the need to develop local research capacity and local researchers are used mostly as data gatherers. This minimalist role discounts the need to develop research where full capacity building of local researchers is part of the outcomes. In the sections that follow, we provide evidence of how African researchers are providing counter-narratives in ECD epistemology, and how these narratives allow them to argue within and against the dominant narrative.

CAREGIVERS AS SPEAKING SUBJECTS

In this section, we counter the dominance of normative framing in the ECD research process by presenting examples of ECD research that incorporate participatory research methodology with caregivers. Smith (1999), talking about research among the Maoris, argues that research is the dirtiest vocabulary that Indigenous people have ever heard and that master narratives about them have been derived from Eurocentric accounts, while Maori accounts have remained as oral stories.

In her research conducted in the urban poor locales of Nairobi, Kenya, Munene (2013) troubles the dominance of Western-adapted ideologies in child healthcare policy (for children aged 0–3 years) that is promoted by international donor organizations and not adequately contextualized by state child health policy makers. These policies are selective and pay minimal attention to the structural and institutional constraints (formal and informal rules) which caregivers in these locales face, thereby silencing their voices in policy and practice. Yet these informal efforts make a critical contribution to child health and wellbeing in these local contexts in which state provisioning of social development is minimal. As such, the indirect or direct silencing of caregivers enhances exclusionary mechanisms that inhibit the responsiveness of the existing care systems and networks, thereby denying children holistic health and development. By critically analyzing the intra-household, inter-household and state healthcare providers' interactions using in-depth interviews, participant observation and focused groups, she is able to bring out the muted/unheard voices of caregivers. These speaking subjects include men, women, private unregistered and registered health practitioners, and indigenous health practitioners and community health workers. The experiences of these caregivers as they interact with each other's diverse epistemologies of caregiving reveal points of tension, of convergence and divergence in these care spaces. These experiences further reveal not only the material deficiencies in these locales and how they shape caregiving, but also the diverse wealth of care practices and sense of communal participatory care that caregivers provide in these locales on a daily basis. The findings reveal that through meaningful participatory research and engagement, these speaking subjects can enrich child healthcare policy and practice in Kenya and make them more responsive and transformative.

Caregivers are thus speaking subjects who have important information to share about their children, family and community life. Another illustrative research project is a large qualitative study on mapping barriers to education in the context of HIV/AIDs, supported by the National Research Foundation in South Africa, which also involved investigating early education (Muthukrishna and Ebrahim, 2006). The research was designed by a small team of university staff who worked closely with the socio-economically deprived Richmond community in KwaZulu-Natal. The team attempted to partly address the cultural impositions in community development and research. In early education, it was important to listen to the voices of caregivers. Participatory techniques provided opportunities for caregivers' words, ideas and understandings to come to the fore. Through a transect walk and social mapping exercise, caregivers were able to discuss information about the community, identify resources and explain the effects on children and family life. They also completed a vulnerability matrix in which they identified barriers to the care and development of children in the community. Through ranking exercises, caregivers were able to rank the sources of support and focus group discussions in local languages which helped the caregivers to support each other and to share their ways of knowing and doing. Listening to the voices of caregivers assisted in the development of an intervention plan, which was proposed for the next phase of the study.

Similarly, in a year-long study which examined the role of local ways of knowing in early childhood education and care among several communities in Kenya and Uganda, Okwany et al. (2011) used a generative participatory research approach, which went beyond data mining or collection to data production. They present a proverb from one of the study communities in Kenya, the Bukusu, which avers: 'Every mother dances her baby.' The literal meaning of this proverb is that the size of the baby does not hinder the parent/caregiver from nurturing it. The underlying meaning of the proverb is that all communities, families and households have distinct and valued ways of early childhood education and care, which have been passed down from one generation to another. The authors note that this singularity speaks to the socially constructed nature of childhood, which varies between societies, social groups, by gender, cross-culturally and over time. Similarly, the system of care also varies over time and space, implying both a distinctiveness and diversity of socio-cultural contexts and circumstances (2011: 2).

Our emphasis in this chapter is thus that the dominant narrative of childhood obscures and even erodes this diversity and distinctiveness of childhoods and childcare contexts. This calls for generative methodologies that are qualitative and participatory. Okwany et al. (2011) present data on how communities in Kenya and Uganda draw upon their valued ways of knowing and doing and employ a range of indigenous and local resources in the care and socialization of their children. These diverse ways of 'dancing' children comprise childrearing practices, socialization strategies and diverse methods of scaffolding children including proverbs, songs and games. They also include culturally responsive conceptions of child rights and child protection, as well as a resilient social protection system rooted in reciprocity, mutuality and social justice. This bolsters the assertion by Nsamenang (2008) that African approaches to ECD are withering, but nowhere have they entirely disappeared; rather, they have shown unusual resilience in the face of extraordinary measures to suppress them into extinction.

This externally funded research involved a careful maneuvering of donor processes that initially expected the study to be finalized in four months. The methodology employed for the year-long research was based on strengthening what was there, and through this appreciative, intergenerational inquiry the researchers present the continuities and discontinuities of local ways of care and education of young children across three generations of caregivers, thereby affirming caregivers as epistemic subjects in ECD research. The empowering nature of the research methods and continuous interaction with caregivers during the process of research through progressive verification enabled the study participants to recognize the *tyranny* of dominant discourses in policy and programming, which had denied parents and caregivers a role in knowledge production. Smith (1999, cited in Odora Hoppers, 2010: 80–81) notes that: 'it galls non-Western societies that Western researchers, intellectuals and scientists trained in that tradition, can claim to know all that there is to know about other societies, on the basis of brief and superficial encounters with those societies'. The research, therefore, gave the caregivers an opportunity not only to challenge the dominant received ECD knowledge, but also to 'talk back to its power' and to 'look it in the eye' (hooks, 1989).

By taking into account caregivers' ethnotheories within their settings and listening to their valued ways of caregiving, the research validated them as 'speaking subjects'. This challenges the regimes of truth within which ECD programmes are embedded, which exclude caregivers as foundational teachers (Nsamenang, 2008). It also demonstrates that research in ECD should be participatory and that researchers do not have a prerogative right to oversee, name and claim (Smith, 1999). To the communities that participated in this research, research was not the 'dirtiest' word in their vocabulary (1999: 1) but something that was experienced as liberating. It was a case of listening to the voices of caregivers 'without imperialism'.

By involving the participants in the entire process of setting the research questions, improving on data collection methods and validating findings, the research methodology heeded to the call of Wilson (2008) that research (in Africans' way of rearing their children) should be a ceremony, and that researchers should maintain accountability to the communities who should be involved in generating research questions. By using different contextually sensitive methods of data collection, such as storytelling, community dialogue, conversation, music and proverbs, the research also responds to the assertion by Tchombe (2008) that African philosophies need to be incorporated into data collection methods.

CHILDREN AS SPEAKING SUBJECTS

Most ECD studies have failed to incorporate children as subjects in the research; neither have they been attentive to children's subjective views including their voice and action. Drawing on her research with very young children, Ebrahim (2007, 2011) provides a theoretical and methodological illustration of how to challenge the dominant narrative. Her ethnographic research approach shows that when the researcher's gaze shifts from children as adults-in-the-making to experts in childhood, young children under 5 years are not passive targets but become agents actively engaged in constructing their own childhoods against the structure laid out within early childhood centers. She notes that the methods used to invite young children's participation should not only take into account their ways of knowing and sharing but also the cultural views that frame the early socialization of children (see Ebrahim, 2011).

In a contextual analysis of how poverty and AIDs challenge childhood in South Africa, Swift and Maher (2008) argue that the lack of focus on participation of very young children could be attributed to the need for adults to exert authority over child submissiveness in the context of violence against women and children. Their interview of Tebello Masita from an early childhood non-governmental organization presents another dimension that is critical in ECD intervention programs:

> You can't say children's participation happens in some cultures but not in African culture. We had children's participation but it had a different form. It was participation in the sense of taking part in what was going on – it was not about what came out of the child's mouth but about what the child would do. If you want to bring in children's participation in the children's rights sense, you have to respect the context in which this intervention has to be made. You have to say, these are people and they have been living like this and then ask yourself, how do we begin to support them? (2008: 165)

The role of older children in the distributed caregiving network that characterizes many African contexts, as well as the supervisory role of parents in these arrangements, has been understated in the dominant narrative. We point to the need for sensitivity on how socio-economic and cultural contexts support the place, action and voice of older children within the caregiving system in early childhood care and education. Nsamenang (2008) draws attention to the critical role of older siblings in the care of young children in contexts where caregiving and tasks are distributed across the social network. Indeed, in child-to-child participation, older children assist in developing the values and skills of younger children. In a study of a child-to-child program run by a local non-governmental organization in rural KwaZulu-Natal, James and Ebrahim (2012) used a qualitative approach including semi-structured interviews and observation of older children to highlight the role they played in care and early stimulation in a poor and vulnerable community where access to early childhood centers was problematic. Within these fluid learning environments, older children created learning opportunities for early literacy, numeracy and creative arts. The fun-filled environments encouraged generational participation and the spirit of *ubuntu* – living in interconnected ways. The implicit support within the communal system was critical for child-to-child caregiving, highlighting it as an important component of early childhood care, education and social cohesion.

In systematic comparisons of early childhood experiences across the North and South, LeVine et al. (1994) show how a focus on individual children and enabling them to express their sense of self through sharing their opinions and preferences is a particularly Euro-American concept. They note how children's participation in activities in and around the household offers emotional security without verbal expressiveness by the mother and other caregivers. This raises questions of the moral complexities that confront early childhood researchers when children are positioned as speaking subjects. It also draws attention to the fact that there is no single morality that researchers can use to capture the diversity of the lives of children. Drawing on post-foundational theories, Ebrahim (2010) shows the salience of situated ethics and critical reflexivity when young children are positioned as subjects in early childhood research. Sensitivities to the lived realities of childhood require a negotiated ethical framework that is flexible and responsive.

We, thus, underscore the importance of research that takes into account the narratives of caregivers and children in early education and care as a starting point, including their perceptions and experiences of poverty and the intersection between external and local agendas. The Young Lives project, a 15-year longitudinal study on childhood poverty research in four countries, is illustrative. The project heeds calls in the child poverty indicator's movement for a shift in poverty measures beyond material to non-material measures. These include holistic explorations of wellbeing and diverse methodological techniques, to capture children's subjective views as well as their lived experiences and voice.

SPEAKING BACK TO DOMINANT EVIDENCE: AFRICAN-LED CHILD-RELATED MEASUREMENT AND TESTING

As noted by Pence and Nsamenang (2008), ECD in Africa has been based on extrapolated evidence. We assert that, more often than not, this evidence is out of touch with local realities in Africa and is removed from their context. Over-reliance on external evidence as the yardstick is akin to the advice to anthropologists by Tylor (1881, cited in Śarana, 1977: 276) 'to avoid that error which the proverb calls measuring other people's corn by one's own bushel.' We highlight the need to reclaim and reposition the representation of indigenous ways of knowing and doing that have been pushed to the margins

and excluded. We however do not reclaim a romanticized representation that is stuck in the past, but rather argue for a culturally competent discourse and local ways of knowing and doing that have evolved over time and have been regenerated, appropriated and incorporated into hybrid coping strategies and social support networks (Okwany et al., 2011). Nsamenang and Lo-oh (2009) note that African knowledge and social thought are embedded in such non-Western sources of knowledge as folklore, idioms, spatial use of cues, touch, garden metaphors and participatory processes that most current psychological instruments and techniques do not aptly measure.

In their impact assessment research of the Madrasa Resource Centres in East Africa, Mwaura and Marfo (2011) draw attention to the problems related to measurement tools. They note that selection of the instruments for impact assessment was not based on their contextual appropriateness but on availability in the absence of locally validated tools. Local relevance of research is thus impeded by dependence on imported instruments that are not adequately adapted to the local context. Additionally, there is a lack of collaborative research partnerships to design contextually relevant instruments that can measure a broad range of developmental and learning outcomes. The latter is needed for expansion of the scope of outcome assessments beyond the cognitive and academic domains.

This is consistent with the argument by Fenald et al. (2009) about the need for adaptation of tools used to measure children's development in low-income countries. The authors outline several steps in the adaptation process and advise the following: accurate interpretation of the test and underlying construct(s), sensitivity to the local context, adaptation of procedures to the local context, conducting of pilots and testing of the assessment. This process is lengthy and expensive. It is also problematic in the sense that it makes assumptions about children and childhood, about how different stakeholders conceptualize them and how they are reared in cultural contexts in specific historical times. Nonetheless, it is a better option than the uncritical borrowing of decontextualized measurement tools.

The Birth to Ten longitudinal studies of children growing up in post-apartheid South Africa show the researchers' attempts to develop more locally validated tools (Barbarin and Richter, 2001). The researchers engaged with the limitations of concepts derived from Western frameworks to measure specific aspects of child development and argued that the unique cultural and social conditions in Africa contribute to alternative conceptualizations of people, their abilities and competences. These notions are not only different in themselves from Western views but also in relation to the aspects under investigation. In order to test whether African cultural perspectives of childhood lead parents to hold distinctive views of what constitutes disordered behavioral and emotional processes in children, they constructed prototypes of childhood dysregulation using parental descriptions of problem children. For an insider perspective on dysregulation, they asked parents to describe specific children they assumed to have problems that might impact on their development over time. This information was collected through focus group discussions with study participants from diverse ethnic groups, including the Zulu, Tswana, Xhosa and Colored. The researchers found that whilst the answers were consistent with Western views of self-regulation, local nuances came to the fore. For example, emotional and behavioral functioning was less distinct in parental conceptions of child adjustment than in Western formulations.

Similarly, normative measures of intelligence and achievement are restrictive and ill-suited for many African contexts because they are based on a deficit model of difference. According to Berry (1974) and Sterberg (1984, cited in Kathuria and Serpell, 1998: 228), the very concept of intelligence is so deeply embedded in complex networks of interactions among the values, practices and technology of Western culture that it may be counterproductive to seek a culture-free definition of what it means and there is no one-on-one correspondence in different cultures. In responding to this cultural bias in assessment of intelligence, longitudinal studies (1971–2008) carried out in Zambia (Serpell, 2011) and rooted in local knowledge have generated African contributions to developmental science, including contextually sensitive testing for intelligence among children in rural, often marginalized areas. The findings reveal the inadequacies of conventional assessment tools of intelligence, which narrowly measure cognitive skills and knowledge acquisition. In sharp contrast, the longitudinal studies reveal that intelligence in the local community or *nzelu* is a blend of cognitive alacrity and social responsibility and forms a central part of socialization, which prompted Serpell to note the credibility gap for public education with respect to the values and aspirations of parents and local communities (2011: 128). We draw on these findings to contend that when the constructs are changed, the strengths of children come to the fore, showing that assets exist if the tools are responsive to the socio-cultural context.

Adala and Okwany (2009: 111), argue that the search for long-lasting solutions and sustainable development in Africa must include a widening of the learning base and a drawing from structures that extend to the rediscovery of suppressed local ways of knowing and doing to confront the myriad challenges that impede learning systems in Africa. This is consistent with the assertion by Nsamenang and Tchombe that 'no people entirely dislodged from their ancestral roots have ever made collective progress with development' (2011: xxvii). In responding to this challenge, their edited handbook, *African Educational Theory and Practices*, aims to fill the gap with an Africentric approach in both educational research and practice in the region. The nine sections of the handbook provide curricular suggestions based on grounded research by a range of scholars and educators in specific cultural contexts in Africa. This approach is consistent with the generative curriculum model of the Early Childhood Development Virtual University (ECDVU) which offers a pathway to integrating indigenous knowledge in early childhood development and making policy, programming and research responsive to and inclusive of local input.

CONCLUSION

We concur with Marfo and Pence (2009) that there is no single narrative on early childhood education and care and that the normative childhood model should supplement and not supplant local narratives. In being attentive to contextual differences and African ways of knowing, a critical question is what knowledge we should seek in ECD so that research can be attentive to contextual differences and complexities, as well as represent local voices including positioning both caregivers and children as speaking subjects. To this end, our argument is consistent with Marfo et al. (2011: 108) who propose multiple methods to highlight the importance of a diversity of epistemological and theoretical perspectives and we emphasize the rationale of methodologies of participation such as ethnography (Ebrahim, 2012: 85).

Clearly, there is a need to challenge power dynamics in relation to who produces what knowledge about whom. The challenge is also to expand the space for alternatives that we have exposed here, to influence ECD policy and practice. In this epistemological shift, we agree with the reasoning of Spivak (1999: 60), who argues that 'the question is not so much who should speak but more of who is listening'. We contend that scholars in the Global South need to be listened to seriously but not with 'benevolent imperialism' (Smith, 1999: 15). Equally importantly, children, caregivers and communities should not be seen as objects in the epistemological domains of

ECD. To counter what Choi (2006) calls the 'schoolification' of early learning that is so pervasive in Africa, we propose the harnessing of responsive socialization strategies including participatory pedagogical tools such as proverbs, songs, riddles and games, and the critical need to strengthen the role of parents and caregivers as foundational teachers. There is also a need for the contextualization of theory and, more importantly, for the 'culturalization' of methods and assessment techniques. We are also calling for research to address the assumptions of dominant discourses and to foreground contextually relevant insights and counter-narratives to open up new perspectives.

The Global North should help the Global South in its quest for child wellbeing by supporting Africa's efforts to hear its own voices and seek its own way forward. In the words of Lyotard (cited in Odora Hoppers, 2010: 81), grand narratives should give way to '*petits récits*', or more modest and 'localised' narratives. We are calling for a relinquishing of this monopoly on ECD and for the importance of listening to the discordant voices of the 'other' in Africa. We cite Odora Hoppers in her quest for cognitive justice as she notes:

> An experiment in cognitive justice can turn this hierarchy into a circle. The search becomes not just one for equality, but for a method of dialogue. Only with a method for exploring difference and providing for reciprocity and empathy is fraternity at the cognitive level born. It is not just respect for the knowledge system. It is understanding of the life forms, a livelihood and a way of life … It is here that cognitive justice i.e., the right of different forms of knowledge to survive – and survive creatively and sustainably – emerge as the most important criteria of fraternity of knowledge. (2010: 87, 90)

Caregivers and communities as 'epistemic subjects' should be given an opportunity to have a say in whether they should be written about, what should be written about them and how it should be written and disseminated. They should also have the option of being trained to conduct research and to be co-creators of knowledge on ECD. We propose embracing a socially constructivist approach which shows that the reality of childhood is dependent on the context within which it is experienced.

In this chapter, we set out to argue for the need to rethink epistemology and research methods in early childhood development in Africa. We confronted the dominant Euro-American narrative of childhood, which has been exported and internationalized and is now held up as the standard for policy, practice and research. We have confronted the partiality of this grand narrative and argued for the need to avoid a reactive Africentrism, but rather pushed for a more textured in-between framing that is respectful of the diversity of narratives and voices in ECD research. We contend that it is this multivocality in the research space that is imperative for dealing with the complexities that characterize the lives of young children in Africa. Many questions still remain, including the ones we raise here.

FURTHER READING

Garcia, M., Pence, A. and Evans, J. (eds) (2009) *Africa's Future, Africa's Challenge*. Washington: The World Bank.

Mutua, K. and Swadener, B. (2004) *Decolonizing Research in Cross-Cultural Contexts: Critical Personal Narratives*. New York: SUNY Press.

Okwany, A. Ngutuku, E. and Muhangi, A. (2011) *The Role of Local Knowledge and Culture in Child Care in Africa: A Sociological Study of Several Ethnic groups in Kenya and Uganda*. Lewiston, NY: Edwin Mellen Press.

QUESTIONS FOR REFLECTION

1 What are the intended and unintended forces emanating from the West that eclipse African perspectives and understandings in early childhood care, education and research? What are the effects of the power relations? How do we address the issue of knowledge transfer from the North to the South for a respectful knowledge exchange?

2 How do we problematize 'knowing' itself as a purpose of research to address the silences in the dominant framing of '*what we know* about early childhood care, education and research'?

3 What are the naturalized ways of doing research with young children and their caregivers? How do we (re)produce forms of exclusion through our research activities with them? What epistemological and methodological insights does the local cultural context offer to address these forms of exclusion?

4 In what ways can African research institutions offering multi-disciplinary early childhood care mobilize to promote African conceptualized research led by African researchers and scholars? What needs to be done to make this agenda attractive to funding support?

REFERENCES

Adala, A. and Okwany, A. (2009) 'From Schooling for Some to Lifelong Learning for All: A Paradigm Shift for Education and Development in Africa', in M. Amutabi and M. Okech (eds) *Studies in Lifelong Learning in Africa: From Ethnic Traditions to Technological Innovations*. Lewiston, NY: Edwin Mellen Press.

Appiah, A.K. (1997) 'Europe upside down: Fallacies of the new Afrocentrism', in R.R. Grinker and C.B. Steiner (eds) *Perspectives on Africa* (pp. 728–731). London: Blackwell.

Barbarin, O.A. and Richter, L. (2001) *Mandela's Children: Growing Up in Post-Apartheid South Africa*. New York and London: Routledge.

Bar-On, A. (2004) 'Early childhood care and education in Africa: The case of Botswana', *Journal of Early Childhood Research*, 2 (1): 67–84.

Chakrabarty, D. (2000) *Provincializing Europe: Postcolonial Thought and Historical Difference*. Princeton, NJ: Princeton University Press.

Choi, S. (2006) 'Bite off only as much as you can chew: Gambia's policy of early childhood development', UNESCO policy brief on Early Childhood Development No. 34. Paris: UNESCO.

Dahlberg, G., Moss, P. and Pence, A. (2007) *Beyond Quality in Early Childhood Education and Care: Languages of Evaluation* (2nd edn). London: Falmer Press.

DeLoache, J. and Gottlieb, A. (eds) (2000) *A World of Babies: Imagined Childcare Guides for Seven Societies*. Cambridge: Cambridge University Press.

Dennis, W. and Lourie, S. (2006) *Everything is Normal until Proven Otherwise: A Book about Wraparound Services*. Washington, DC: CWLA Press.

Denzin, N.K., Lincoln, Y.S. and Smith, L.T. (2007) *Handbook of Critical and Indigenous Methodologies*. Thousand Oaks, CA: SAGE.

Doob, L.W. (1985) 'Psychology', in R.A. Lystad (ed.) *The African World: A Survey of Social Research*. New York: Praeger.

Ebrahim, H. (2007) Constructions of childhood for and by children in two early childhood centers in the province of KwaZulu-Natal, South Africa: An ethnographic study. Unpublished thesis, University of KwaZulu-Natal.

Ebrahim, H. (2010) 'Situated ethics: Possibilities for young children as research participants in the South African context', *Early Child Development and Care*, 180(3): 289–298.

Ebrahim, H. (2011) 'Children as agents in early childhood education', *Education as Change*, 15(1): 121–131.

Ebrahim, H. (2012) 'Tensions in incorporating global childhood into early childhood programmes: The case of South Africa', *Australasian Journal of Early Childhood*, 37(3): 80–86.

Ebrahim, H. (2014) 'Foregrounding silences in the South African National Early Learning Standards for birth to four years', *European Early Childhood Education Research Journal*, 22(1): 67–76.

Ebrahim, H. and Penn, H. (2011) 'Research on early childhood in KwaZulu-Natal, South Africa', in A. Halai and D. Williams (eds) *Researching Methodologies in the South*. Pakistan: Oxford University Press.

Fanon, F. (1963) *The Wretched of the Earth*. New York: Grove Press.

Fenald, L.C.H., Kariger, P., Engle, P. and Raikes, A. (2009) *Examining Early Childhood Development in Low-income Countries: A Toolkit for the Assessment of Children in the First Five Years of Life*. Washington, DC: The International Bank for Reconstruction and Development/The World Bank.

George, S. (2010) Wasted Childhoods? Beyond the Pathologization of Poor Children and their Families. Paper presented at 'The Doors of Perception: Viewing Anthropology through the Eyes of Children' conference, Vrije Universiteit, Amsterdam, 30 September/1 October.

Gottlieb, A. (2004) *The After-life is Where we Come from: The Culture of Infancy in West Africa*. Chicago: University of Chicago Press.

Guba, E. and Lincoln, Yvonna S. (2005) 'Paradigmatic Controversies, and Emerging Confluences', in N.K. Denzin and Y.S. Lincoln (eds), *Handbook of Qualitative Research,* 3rd Edition (pp. 191–216). Thousand Oaks, CA: Sage.

Hall, S. (1992) 'The West and the rest: Discourse and power', in S. Hall and B. Gieben (eds) *Formations of Modernity*. Cambridge: Polity Press.

Harkness, S. and Super, C.M. (1992) 'The developmental niche: A theoretical framework for analyzing the household production of health', *Social Science and Medicine*, 38(2): 217–226.

Harkness, S. and Super, C.M. (eds) (1996) *Parents' Cultural Belief Systems: Their Origins, Expressions, and Consequences*. New York: Guilford.

Harkness, S., Super, C.M., Barry, O. and Zeitlin, M. and Long J. (2009) 'Assessing the environment of children's learning: The developmental niche in Africa', in E. Grigorenko (ed.) *Multicultural Psychoeducational Assessment* (pp. 133–155). New York: Springer.

Harkness, S., Super, C.M., Mavridis, J.C., Barry, O. and Zetlin, M. (2013) 'Culture and Early Childhood Education Programs: Implications for Policy and Programs', in P. Rebello Britto, P. Engle and C. Harkness (eds) *Handbook of Early Childhood Development Research and its Impact on Global Policy*. Oxford: Oxford University Press.

hooks, b. (1989) *Talking Back: Thinking Feminist, Thinking Black*. New York: South End Press.

James, M. and Ebrahim, H. (2012) 'Pedagogic activities for early education in a child to child programme in South Africa', in T. Papatheodorou and J. Moyles (eds) *Cross-cultural Perspectives on Early Childhood*. London: Routledge.

Katz, C. (2004) *Growing up Global: Economic Restructuring and Children's Everyday Lives*. Minneapolis, MN: University of Minnesota Press.

Kathuria, R. and Serpell, R. (1998) 'Standardization of the Panga Munthu test: A nonverbal cognitive test developed in Zambia', *Journal of Negro Education*, 67(3): 228–241.

LeVine, R., Dixon, S., LeVine, S., Richman, A., Leiderman, P., Keefer, C. and Brazleton, T. (1994) *Childcare and Culture: Lessons from Africa*. Cambridge: Cambridge University Press.

LeVine, R. A. (2004). 'Challenging Expert Knowledge: Findings from an African Study of Infant Care and Development', in U.P. Gielen and J. Roopnarine (eds) *Childhood and Adolescence: Cross-Cultural Perspectives and Applications* (pp. 149–65). Westport, CT: Praeger.

Lubeck, S. (2000) 'On reassessing the relevance of the child development knowledge base to education: A response – Invited commentary', *Human Development*, 43(4–5): 273–278.

Marfo, K. and Pence, A. (2009) Strengthening Africa's Contributions to Child Development Research. A small-group invitational conference project sponsored by the Society for Research in Child Development (SRCD), final project, June.

Marfo, K., Pence, A., LeVine, R. and LeVine S. (2011) 'Strengthening Africa's contributions to child development research: Overview and ways forward', *Child Development Perspectives*, 5(2): 104–111.

Mbembe, A. (2001) *On the Post Colony*. Berkeley, CA: University of California Press.

Mwaura, P.A.M. and Marfo, K. (2011) 'Bridging culture, research and practice in early childhood development: The Madrasa Resource Centers in East Africa', *Child Development Perspectives*, 2: 134–139.

Munene, A. (2013) A Troubling Start: Exposing processes of exclusion for children aged 0–3 years in urban poor locales in Kenya. Unpublished master's thesis. The Hague: International Institute of Social Studies/ Rotterdam: Erasmus University.

Muthukrishna, N. and Ebrahim, H. (2006) 'Experiencing education in school and community in the early years', in N. Muthukrisha (ed.) *Mapping Barriers to Basic Education in the Context of HIV and AIDS*. Pietermaritzburg: University of KwaZulu-Natal.

Myers, R. (2000) *Thematic Studies: Early Childhood Care and Development*. Paris: UNESCO.

Ngutuku, E. (2010) 'Re-imagining development: Working within and against the Metanarrative', Nascent RDO (http://nascent-rdo.org/article.html).

Nsamenang, A.B. (2005) 'Education in African family traditions', in C. Fisher and R. Lerner (eds) *Encyclopedia of Applied Developmental Science* (pp. 61–62). Thousand Oaks, CA: SAGE.

Nsamenang, B. (2006a) *Meaning and Role of Measurement in ECD: Problematizing an Africentric Glimpse*. Quebec: Centre for Excellence on Early Childhood Development.

Nsamenang, B. (2006b) 'Human ontogenesis: An indigenous African view on development and intelligence', *International Journal of Psychology*, 41: 293–297.

Nsamenang, B. (2008) '(Mis)Understanding ECD in Africa: The force of local and global motives', in M. Garcia, A. Pence and J. Evans (eds) *Africa's Future, Africa's Challenge*. Washington, DC: The World Bank.

Nsamenang, B. (2009) 'A critical peek at early childhood care and education in Africa', *Child Health and Education*, 1(1): 44–55.

Nsamenang, B. and Lo-oh, J. (2009) 'Afrique Noire', in M. Borstein (ed.) *Handbook of Cross-cultural Development* (pp. 383–407). London: Taylor Francis.

Nsamenang, B. and Tchombe, S. (2011) *Handbook of African Educational Theories and Practices: A Generative Teacher Education Curriculum*. Yaoundé, Cameroon: Presses Universitaires d'Afrique.

Nyamjoh, F. (2012) 'Potted plants in greenhouses: A critical reflection on the resilience of colonial education in Africa', *Journal of Asian and African Studies*, 47(2): 129–154.

Odora Hoppers, C. (2009) Development Education and Transition from Triage Society to a Moral and Cognitive Reconstruction of Citizenship: Keynote Address at The International Conference on Critical Thinking and Development Education: Moving From Evaluation to Research. 3rd–4th October. University of South Africa.

Odora Hoppers, C. (2010) 'Renegotiating agency in knowledge production, innovation and Africa's development in the context of the triage society', *Critical Literacy: Theories and Practices*, 4(1): 78–94.

Okwany, A. Ngutuku, E. and Muhangi, A. (2011) *The Role of Local Knowledge and Culture in Child Care in Africa: A Sociological Study of Several Ethnic Groups in Kenya and Uganda*. Lewiston, NY: Edwin Mellen Press.

Otterstad, M. (2005) 'Different "reading" of the multicultural within early childhood (con) texts', *Barn* nr. 3: 27–50. Norsk Senter for Barneforskning.

Oudenhoven, N.J.A. and Wazir, R. (2006) *Newly Emerging Needs of Children: An Exploration*. Antwerp: Garant.

Pence, A. (2013) 'Voices less heard: The importance of critical and "indigenous" perspectives', in P. Rebello Britto, P. Engle and C. Harkness (eds) *Handbook of Early Childhood Development Research and its Impact on Global Policy*. Oxford: Oxford University Press.

Pence, A. and Nsamenang, B. (2008) *A Case of Early Childhood Development in Sub-Saharan Africa*. The Hague: Bernard van Leer Foundation.

Penn, H. (2005) *Unequal Childhoods: Young Children's Lives in Poor Countries*. London and New York: Routledge.

Penn, H. (2012) 'The rhetoric and realities of early childhood programmes promoted by the World Bank', in A. Twum Danso-Imoh and R. Ames (eds) *Childhood at the Intersection of the Local and Global*. Basingstoke: Palgrave MacMillan.

Said, E.W. (2003) *Orientalism*. Penguin Classics. London: Penguin.

Śarana, G. (1977) Do Anthropologists Explain? in Bernardo Bernardi (ed.) *The Concept and Dynamics of Culture* (pp. 263–282). The Hague: Mouton Publishers.

Serpell, R. (2011) 'Social responsibility as a dimension of intelligence and an educational goal: Insights from programmatic research in African society', *Child Development Perspectives*, 5(2): 126–133.

Shiva, V. (2000) 'Foreword', in G.J. Sefa Dei, B. Hall and D.G. Rosenberg (eds) *Indigenous Knowledges in Global Contexts*. Toronto, ON: University of Toronto Press.

Shonkoff, P. (2010) 'Building a new bio-developmental framework to guide the future of early childhood policy', *Child Development*, 81(1): 357–367.

Shonkoff, P. and Phillips, A. (eds) (2000) *From Neurons to Neighborhoods: The Science of Early Child Development*. Washington, DC: National Academy Press (www.nap.edu/).

Smith, T.L. (1999) *Decolonizing Methodologies: Research and Indigenous Peoples*. London: Zed Books.

Spivak, C. (1999) *A Critique of Postcolonial Reason: Towards a History of the Vanishing Present*. Cambridge, MA: Harvard University Press.

Stanely, C. (2007) 'When counter narratives meet master narratives in the journal editorial-review process', *Educational Researcher*, 36(1): 14–24.

Swadener, B. and Kessler, S. (eds) (1991) 'Reconceptualizing early childhood education' [Special Issue]. *Early Education and Development*, 2(2).

Swadener, B. and Mutua, K. (2008) 'Decolonizing performances: Deconstructing the global postcolonial', in N.K. Denzin, Y.S. Lincoln and L.T. Smith (eds) *Handbook of Critical and Indigenous Methodologies* (pp. 31–43). Thousand Oaks, CA: SAGE.

Swift, A. and Maher, S. (2008) *Growing Pains: How Poverty and AIDS are Challenging Childhood*. London: Panos.

Tchombe, T.M.S. (2008) Education Research in West Africa: The Role of Wera in Fostering Research. http://citeseerx.ist.psu.edu/viewdoc/download?doi=10.1.1.503.2590&rep=rep1&type=pdf

Twum Danso-Imoh, A. and Ames, R. (2012) *Childhood at the Intersection of the Local and Global*. Basingstoke: Palgrave MacMillan.

Viruru, R. (2001) *Early Childhood Education: Postcolonial Perspectives from India*. London: SAGE.

wa Thiong'o, N. (1986) *Decolonizing the Mind: The Politics of Language in African Literature*. New York: Heinemann.

wa Thiong'o, N. (2012) *Globalectics: Theory and the Politics of Knowing*. New York: Columbia University Press.

Wilson, S. (2008). *Research is Ceremony: Indigenous Research Methods*. Halifax, Canada: Fernwood Publishing.

Woodhead, M. (2006) 'Changing Perspectives on Early Childhood: Theory, Research and Policy', *International Journal of Equity and Innovation in Early Childhood,* 4(2): 1–43.

27

Cognitive Research in Developing Countries

Nirmala Rao, Jin Sun and Ying Wang

INTRODUCTION

'Cognitive development' refers to the improvement in perception, memory, reasoning, problem-solving, language, and self-regulatory skills with increasing age (Gupta and Richardson, 1995). It is particularly important that children make the expected levels of progress in language, thinking, and understanding during the preschool period, as age-appropriate development of cognitive skills is critical for school readiness and, in turn, for school success. Early cognitive development predicts school progress, and if a child fails to reach his/her developmental potential, this may lead to a vicious cycle of low educational attainment and the intergenerational transmission of poverty (Grantham-McGregor et al., 2007).

Contemporary basic research on cognitive development has focused on the following questions: (1) Do all cognitive competencies develop at the same rate or do certain ones develop particularly rapidly at certain periods of development? (2) How do genetic and environmental factors influence patterns of change in cognitive development? (3) How effective are interventions designed to enhance cognitive development? This chapter focuses on research that has evaluated the effectiveness of early childhood interventions on the cognitive development of children from disadvantaged families in developing countries.

Socio-economic gradients in early development and learning exist within all countries, and priority has been accorded to dealing with the challenges associated with these gradients in both developed and developing countries. However, children from economically disadvantaged families in developing countries typically experience even less stimulating environments than those in developed countries, resulting in sub-optimal early-development and learning outcomes for economically disadvantaged children in developing countries (i.e., Alderman, 2011; Baker-Henningham and Boo, 2010; Walker et al., 2007). Indeed, more than

200 million children in developing countries do not achieve the expected levels of cognitive development due to poverty, stunted growth, and the associated lack of early learning opportunities (Grantham-McGregor et al., 2007). The discrepancies in cognitive development and school achievement between children in developed and developing countries are of considerable global concern, and efforts have been made to provide interventions to mitigate these disparities.

Against this backdrop, researchers have placed considerable emphasis on understanding which types of programs are effective in promoting cognitive development in developing countries. In this chapter, we draw upon a rigorous review of the literature on early childhood interventions and cognitive development in developing countries conducted for the Department for International Development (DFID) in the UK (Rao et al., 2014b). Before presenting the findings of the review, we consider the indicators of cognitive development and the processes through which early interventions are assumed to impact on cognitive development.

INDICATORS OF COGNITIVE DEVELOPMENT

IQ and/or achievement test scores are often used as indicators of children's cognitive development. Compared to IQ tests, which assess skills learned incidentally and are likely to be affected by children's neurological maturation, achievement tests assess skills taught intentionally and are more sensitive to the effects of learning experiences in both home and school contexts (Fernald et al., 2009a). IQ tests typically assess the following competencies: verbal comprehension, working memory, problem-solving, non-verbal reasoning, spatial skills, cognitive control, and acquired knowledge. Some cognitive development tests focus on only one cognitive competency, such as non-verbal reasoning ability, and some tests tap a combination

of such competencies. Achievement tests may also be used in the assessment of cognitive development. Such tests may focus on one domain, such as mathematics, or a combination of developmental domains, such as literacy, mathematics, and school readiness. Although the type of information derived from IQ tests is assumed to be less affected by family, educational, and community environments than the results of achievement tests, the effects of environmental deprivation cannot be underestimated.

Clearly, indicators of cognitive development change as children mature. For example, given the limited verbal capabilities of infants and toddlers, their cognitive development is assessed by evaluating their ability to solve problems with objects. For infants/toddlers (birth to 36 months), a comprehensive assessment of development (including motor, language, cognition, socio-emotional development and problem-solving skills) is desirable. Children over 3 years of age are expected to be capable of solving simple puzzles, identifying letters or words, matching colors or shapes, problem-solving, and reasoning, or a combination of these (Fernald et al., 2009b). Tests from developed countries may be inappropriate indicators of the cognitive development of children from developing countries, as children from developing countries may not have received either training in basic concept knowledge or exposure to print, as their parents often have lower levels of education than their counterparts in developed countries. Furthermore, as expectations of typical development are derived from studies conducted in developed countries, they are often inappropriate for children from socially disadvantaged families in developing countries because of cultural and contextual variations. For example, parents may not be able to teach reading and writing to facilitate children's language and cognitive development in developing countries, as parents in developed countries often do (Guldan et al., 1993; UNICEF, 2001). Thus, indicators of cognitive development in developing countries need to be contextually appropriate.

Information on children's cognitive development has also been garnered from parent and teacher reports and direct observation of individual children. For example, the Early Development Instrument (EDI) (Janus and Offord, 2007) relies on teachers' reports to assess various dimensions of children's school readiness, and has been implemented in many countries. In contrast, assessments based on the framework of the Early Learning and Development Standards (Kagan and Britto, 2005), which have been developed in over 40 developing countries, operationalize culturally appropriate expectations and involve direct assessment of children's cognitive and other competencies. The East Asia Pacific Early Child Development Scales, which have been recently validated, are one example of such an effort (Rao et al., 2014a).

HOW DO EARLY CHILDHOOD INTERVENTIONS INFLUENCE COGNITIVE DEVELOPMENT?

We draw upon Gottlieb's experiential canalization model (1991, 1997), Blair and Raver's analysis (2012), and the work of Walker et al. (2011) to describe the processes through which early childhood interventions are assumed to affect cognitive development. In Gottlieb's experiential canalization model (1991, 1997), biology and experience mutually influence each other during the developmental process. Adversity releases stress hormones that influence neural systems, which, in turn, affect cognitive and socioemotional development (Blair and Raver, 2012). Walker et al. (2011) identify several developmental-risk and protective factors that affect the brain at different developmentally sensitive periods. Early-intervention programs promote cognitive development by mitigating the risk factors associated with poor cognitive outcomes or by enhancing the protective factors that promote cognitive development. While large-scale studies conducted in developed countries have provided evidence of the effectiveness of preschool participation in improving cognitive development and academic achievement (e.g., Loeb et al., 2004, 2007; NICHD ECCRN, 2005; Sylva et al., 2011), there is a dearth of similar large-scale studies in developing countries. However, researchers have identified some key risk factors which prevent children from low-income families in developing countries from attaining their developmental potential, resulting in disparities between children from low-income families in developed and developing countries in early learning and development, including cognitive development. These risk factors include stunting, inadequate cognitive stimulation, iodine deficiency, and iron-deficiency anemia, some micronutrients, malaria, HIV infection, exposure to violence, and maternal depression (Walker et al., 2007, 2011). Poor children are particularly challenged because risks tend to occur together, and these risks have a cumulative effect.

Children from economically disadvantaged families usually experience less cognitively stimulating environments than their more advantaged peers. They are likely to have fewer age-appropriate toys, to experience less responsive parenting, and are less likely to attend high-quality early learning programs than other children. Further, their families may experience poverty-related chronic stress (Evans and Kim, 2013). All these factors adversely affect children's cognitive development. Indeed, children from disadvantaged families have lower levels of speech and language processing skills than their peers from advantaged backgrounds in the same country, reflecting the possible influence of environmental stimulation (Roy and Chiat, 2013). Children's behaviors and characteristics also influence the amount of stimulation they receive. For example, a child whose parents talk to her frequently is likely to be more verbal and to elicit even more stimulation from her parents. On the other hand, a child whose parents do not talk to her frequently has less opportunity to develop speech and communicative competencies as she experiences less stimulation in the environment (Demir and Küntay, 2014).

Interventions that aim to reduce children's exposure to risk factors, increase the influence of protective factors, and promote cognitive development in developing countries, are urgently needed, and there is accumulated evidence of their effectiveness. For example, cortisol levels affect children's behaviors and emotional regulation, while community-level support for children living in poverty is associated with lower average cortisol levels (Fernald and Gunnar, 2009). In addition, preschool attendance has been shown to facilitate cognitive development including literacy, vocabulary, mathematics, and the quantitative reasoning of children from disadvantaged families in both developed and developing countries (see, for example, Rao et al., 2012b; Sammons et al., 2007). Although examining the effectiveness of interventions designed to promote early development and learning has been one of the key imperatives of contemporary research on cognitive development in developing countries, no study has provided a systematic narrative synthesis of the existing research. We attempt to do so in this chapter.

EARLY CHILDHOOD INTERVENTIONS AND COGNITIVE DEVELOPMENT IN DEVELOPING COUNTRIES

This chapter considers studies that have evaluated the effect of early childhood interventions (parent-focused interventions, child-focused educational interventions, nutrition and health interventions, income-supplementation programs, and comprehensive programs) on cognitive outcomes in developing countries. We conducted a meta-analysis of the evidence and prepared narrative summaries of high-quality interventions carried out in developing countries in various regions of the world. We report on the latter and describe the range of methodologies used in these studies and identify the factors associated with program effectiveness.

Method

We searched (i) nine electronic databases (Academic Search Elite/EBSCOhost, the Cochrane Reviews, Google Scholar, JSTOR, ProQuest, PubMed, Web of Science, PsycINFO, and The University of Hong Kong Libraries Catalogue); (ii) reference lists of journals; and (iii) specialist websites (UNICEF Evaluation Database, UNESCO, the World Bank, the Brookings Institute, Save the Children, Bernard van Leer, the National Institute of Early Education Research, The Consultative Group on Early Childhood Care and Development, Young Lives, Pratham, 3ie International Initiative for Impact Evaluation, the Open Society Institute, and Plan International) to include studies which evaluated the impact of early childhood interventions on the cognitive development and learning achievement of young children conducted in either developed or developing countries. The key variables of interest were *Early Childhood Development* and *Cognitive Development*. Search terms for the former included the following phrases: early childhood program, preschool experience, early intervention, early childhood education, early learning, early cognitive stimulation, nutritional supplementation, early childhood health intervention, home-visiting program, parental support and education, early reading program, breakfast program, lunch program, income supplement, and cash transfer. Search terms used for the variable, *Cognitive Development*, included: school readiness, cognitive development, academic achievement, learning outcomes, child development, intelligence, language development, literacy, mathematics achievement, problem solving skills, attention and executive functions, basic concepts, IQ, DQ, thinking, communication skills, vocabulary, brain development, and neural development.

A total of 3431 articles were initially identified, but after title and abstract screening, 3289 studies were excluded for not meeting the required selection criteria. The full text of 142 publications was screened and assessed to determine whether or not the study should be included for quality assessment, systematic review, and meta-analysis, respectively. A total of 111 studies, published between 1992 and 2013 and conducted in 40 developing countries, were selected for inclusion in the rigorous literature review. Most (*n* = 82) of these studies were peer-reviewed journal articles. The rest were program evaluation reports (*n* = 19), working or discussion papers (*n* = 8), a conference paper (*n* = 1), and a policy brief (*n* = 1). These 111 studies were coded to specify their quality including their rigor and soundness (level of reliability and validity). Five major types of early childhood interventions were identified and examined in terms of their effects on children's cognitive outcomes: parent-focused interventions, child-focused educational interventions, nutrition and health interventions, income-supplementation programs, and comprehensive programs (see Table 27.1). All of these studies had a comparison group.

We coded the following aspects of each study: the intervention design (case study, single group before and after comparison, prospective quasi-experimental design, quasi-experimental design, or randomized controlled trial); fidelity of implementation (monitoring of the extent to which intervention offered to recipients complied with requirements in delivering the intervention); location (where the intervention was conducted); dosage and intensity of the intervention (hours per week and length of the intervention); qualification(s) of the change agent, i.e., the person who instructs recipients about the intervention; age and gender of the target children; and effectiveness of the intervention (negative, potentially negative, no discernible, mixed, potentially positive, or positive effects). Since there was often more than one reported intervention in each study, we further used the specific intervention, rather than the study per se, as the unit of analysis. For example, a study could have a control group and two intervention groups. In such a situation, the study was considered to have two interventions. Coding

was undertaken by six raters, and all coders underwent training given by one member of the team who was considered the gold standard. Over half of the coding was randomly selected and checked by the gold standard to ensure consistency and accuracy in coding. A high level (over 95%) of inter-rater agreement was achieved for the quality of the studies and for at least one major take-home message derived from the reported interventions.

Results

Table 27.1 presents the broad characteristics of the five types of interventions based on the coding scheme described above. Parent-focused interventions were represented in 25 studies; 32 documented child-focused educational interventions; 32 reported on nutrition and health interventions; 11 described income-supplementation interventions; and 11 documented comprehensive interventions. In the following section, we consider each of the five types of interventions. The meta-analysis of the studies presented in this review found that effect sizes for comprehensive programs were the highest, followed by child-focused educational interventions, parent-focused interventions, income-supplementation programs, and nutrition and health interventions, respectively (Rao et al., 2014b).

PARENT-FOCUSED INTERVENTIONS

The mere provision of information about how to enhance child development (nutrition, childcare and management of common illness) and about services and opportunities available (health services, education and employment prospects) to parents of young children is one of the most common forms of early childhood intervention in developing countries (Evans and Stansbery, 1998). This is because there are a large number of poor and illiterate parents who are often unaware of the need to provide stimulating experiences for young children or

Table 27.1   Number and types of early childhood interventions reviewed

Type of intervention	Number of studies	Country distribution	Study design	Fidelity of implementation	Effects of intervention
Parent-focused	25	Bangladesh, China, Chile, Ethiopia, India, Brazil, Jamaica, Saint Lucia, Turkey, Vietnam, Honduras	RCT: 64% QED: 5% PQED: 26% RD: 5%	High: 77% Low: 5% NI: 18%	PE: 72% PPE: 15%; ME: 3% NDE: 10%
Child-focused educational	32	Cambodia, China, Chile, Costa Rica, India, Bangladesh, the Democratic Republic of the Congo, Tajikistan and Yemen, Kenya, Uganda and Tanzania/ Zanzibar, Cape Verde and Guinea, Mozambique, Botswana, Ethiopia, Uruguay, Nepal, Myanmar, Zambia, Mexico, Turkey, Indonesia	RCT: 27% QED: 5% PQED: 35% RD: 29% SG pre- and post-tests: 4%	High: 46% NI: 54%	PE: 60% PPE: 23% ME: 5% NDE: 11% PNE: 2%
Nutrition and health	32	Guatemala, Colombia, Peru, Brazil, Chile, Kenya, Gambia, Tanzania/Zanzibar, Nepal, Thailand, China, Vietnam, Indonesia, India, Bangladesh	RCT: 93% QED: 2% PQED: 4% RD: 3%	High: 72% NI: 28%	PE: 7% PPE: 24% ME: 7% NDE: 57% PNE: 4%
Income- supplementation	11	Ecuador, Nicaragua, Mexico, Bolivia	RCT: 55% QED: 18% PQED: 9% RD: 18%	High: 54% Low: 18% NI: 27%	PE: 36% PPE: 46% NDE: 18%
Comprehensive	11	Albania, Colombia, Peru, Philippines, Paraguay, India	RCT: 9% QED: 27% RD: 64%	High: 50% NI: 50%	PE: 75% PPE: 13% ME: 12%

Notes: NI = Not indicated; RCT = randomized controlled trial; QED = quasi-experimental design; PQED = prospective quasi-experimental design; RD = retrospective design; SG pre- and post-tests = single-group pre- and post-tests; PE = positive effects; PPE = potentially positive effects; ME = mixed effects; NDE = no discernible effects; PNE = potentially negative effects

are uninformed about methods of providing such stimulation (Guldan et al., 1993; UNICEF, 2001). Most parent-focused interventions included in our study were designed to promote parent–child interaction through psychosocial stimulation to improve children's cognitive and language abilities, but other topics, such as hygiene, feeding, positive discipline, and/or gender equality were also covered in intervention sessions.

As noted earlier, there was often more than one reported intervention in each study and we further used the specific intervention rather than the study as the unit of analysis. A total of 38 parent-focused interventions were reported from 25 studies, with 10 to 184 parent participants in intervention groups. Among the 25 studies, change agents worked with either parents or caregivers only

in five while they worked with both parents/ caregivers and children together in 20 of them. Among these 20 studies, six included a comparison group of children who received nutritional supplements in addition to the parent–child intervention.

The interventions were typically implemented at home by the parents (usually mothers) of the children. The parents of the target children varied greatly in their educational backgrounds. Support for the parents was usually provided through home visits, group sessions, and a combination of home visits, group sessions, community activities, and primary healthcare and nutritional services. These programs typically engaged parents or caregivers and children at the same time, and were most commonly used with parents of children under 3 years.

These interventions targeted children in deprived environments and attempted to mitigate the negative effects associated with risk factors such as poverty, low birth-weight (Gardner et al., 2003; Walker et al., 2004, 2010), iron deficiency (Lozoff et al., 2010), undernutrition (Gardner et al., 2005; Nahar et al., 2008), and growth retardation (Grantham-McGregor et al., 1997; Walker et al., 2000, 2005).

As many of these interventions were designed taking into account existing health service systems, professional or parapro-fessional community health workers were employed as instructors. Other interventions typically relied on trained village women (peer educators), who either received a small honorarium or worked on a voluntary basis. The training provided for parents took many forms and varied considerably in duration; some training schemes began only a few days before the interventions, while some involved continuous training and supervision by pro-gram leaders for up to two years. Most of the interventions were found to have positive effects on children's cognitive development (see Table 27.1). Almost all of the parenting interventions focused on teaching parents to stimulate children through play, often utiliz-ing homemade toys or other readily available household items. All interventions had key messages and/or defined curricula.

Most of the studies were not representative of the population of the countries, did not use random assignment to groups and only demonstrated short-term effects on young children's cognitive development. However, three interventions showed significant and positive long-term effects. Two longitudinal intervention trials were conducted in Jamaica to combat the cognitive deficits of low birth-weight (Gardner et al., 2003; Walker et al., 2004, 2010) and stunted infants/toddlers (Grantham-McGregor et al., 1997; Walker et al., 2000, 2005), respectively. Both interven-tions comprised weekly home visits for two years by community health workers, who demonstrated play techniques to the mother and taught concepts of color, shape, size, and

position. Significant main effects on cogni-tion (including attention, memory, vocabu-lary, reading skills and problem solving) were found in both low-birthweight and stunted children in the intervention groups four years after the intervention ended. Stunted children whose parents received such intervention in early childhood showed sustained cognitive and educational benefits even at age 17–18.

Significant long-term positive effects were also found in another two-year intervention for mothers of children aged 3–5 years. The Turkish Early Enrichment Project (TEEP) was designed to help mothers deal appro-priately with the needs of their children (Kagitcibasi et al., 2001, 2009). Mothers participated weekly and training occurred at home one week and in a group setting the following week. Depending on their educa-tional levels, local women were trained either as 'mother's aides' who visited the mothers at home, or as coordinators who conducted group meetings and supervised the mother aides. The cognitive skills, social relations, and school adjustment of children whose mothers were involved in TEEP were sig-nificantly higher than those of their peers in a control group, even seven years after the end of intervention. They were also more likely to attend college and have jobs of significantly higher status 19 years after the end of TEEP than children in the control group.

The positive effects of some parent-focused interventions led to improvements in parent–child relationships and the home envi-ronment. These changes were noted through observations of the home environment and in responses to questions during parent inter-views. These positive changes appeared to be sustained beyond the intervention period.

In general, parent-focused interventions had positive effects on young children's cog-nitive development in developing country contexts, and were especially effective in compensating for delays in cognitive devel-opment in malnourished children. Short-term interventions were effective for children under 18 months, but interventions that lasted at least two years were shown to have sustainable positive effects on older children. The most effective programs were those with culturally appropriate materials, opportunities for sharing, discussion, and guided parental practice with children. Therefore, parent-focused interventions present a cost-effective option in promoting cognitive development in developing country contexts.

CHILD-FOCUSED EDUCATIONAL INTERVENTIONS

Child-focused educational interventions target infants (under 1 year), toddlers (between 1 and 3 years), and preschoolers (3 years or older). They include formal (e.g., preschools) and informal early learning programs (e.g., home-based learning programs) and target children's cognitive, socio-emotional, or schooling outcomes. We included 32 studies which reported on the effectiveness of child-focused educational interventions in our review. Most of these interventions were conducted in Asia and Africa (see Table 27.1).

The scale of the interventions varied greatly, ranging from those with fewer than 20 child participants (e.g., Piramal and Law, 2010) to one intervention that involved more than 10,000 child participants (e.g., Behrman et al., 2004). The majority of child-focused educational interventions that included children under 3 were center-based (Berument et al., 2012; Leroy et al., 2012; Taneja et al., 2002, 2005), often targeting children in orphanages (Berument et al., 2012; Taneja et al., 2002, 2005) as parents were not available to offer early stimulation at home, and the majority of interventions for children over 3 years were provided almost exclusively in preschools (e.g., Aboud, 2006; Aboud and Hossain, 2011; Aboud et al., 2008; American Institutes for Research, 2012; Berlinski et al., 2008; Education Development Center, 2009; He et al., 2009; Malmberg et al., 2011; Martinez et al., 2012; Moore et al., 2008; Mwaura et al., 2008; Nonoyama-Tarumi and Bredenberg, 2009; Opel et al., 2009; Piramal

and Law, 2010; Rao et al., 2012 a, b; Rolla et al., 2006; Save the Children, 2003, 2004; Woldehanna, 2011) or in day-care centres (e.g., Education Development Center, 2009; Jaramillo and Tietjen, 2001; Taiwo and Tyolo, 2002; Zuilkowski et al., 2012). Only one of these interventions was implemented in the home setting and it involved watching a television program to enhance cognitive and socio-emotional skills (Baydar et al., 2008). The other interventions were implemented in a center or preschool. The length of the intervention varied from one hour per week to 30 hours per week, but most of the studies did not provide information about the number of hours per week that children attended, which is actually an important variable in relation to program efficacy. The duration of the intervention also varied considerably from one month in Bangladesh (Opel et al., 2009) to three academic years in Uruguay (Berlinski et al., 2008), Ethiopia (Woldehanna, 2011), Kenya, Tanzania/Zanzibar, and Uganda (Malmberg et al., 2011).

The persons responsible for the child-focused interventions (change agents) tended to be early childhood educators/teachers. Most had received at least secondary-school education, and many received ongoing training even after they started teaching. The majority of child-focused interventions were found to have positive effects on cognitive development (see Table 27.1). It is important to note that program effectiveness, which was evaluated by comparing children's performance before and after intervention programs, was affected by the quality of the preschool programs, which was associated with the qualifications and training of the change agents, the program structure, and the extent to which the curricula and instruction were child appropriate. For example, the findings of studies from Bangladesh (Aboud and Hossain, 2011), China (Rao et al., 2012b), and Costa Rica (Rolla et al., 2006) all showed that children demonstrated larger cognitive benefits when they were enrolled in programs that provided higher-quality stimulation, including more responsive teacher–child interactions, more structured learning activities, more age-appropriate learning materials, and more qualified early childhood educators than in other programs. Program effectiveness was limited if the interventions did not emphasize stimulation quality but merely encouraged children's participation.

There is limited research that systematically examines the relationships among the dosage of early childhood intervention, the nature of preschool experiences in different forms of preschool programs, and children's cognitive development in developing countries. A caveat is that quality matters and that structured programs with well-qualified change agents are associated with better outcomes. This is not to state that informal programs should not be scaled up – indeed, there were no significant differences in school readiness between children who attended home-based programs and those who attended center-based community programs in Cambodia (Rao et al., 2012a), but this may be because sufficient support was provided to the change agents in home-based programs. However, the qualifications of change agents are significantly associated with quality and child outcomes, and formal programs typically have better qualified educators.

NUTRITION AND HEALTH INTERVENTIONS

Nutrition and health interventions have long-term effects on health, learning, and behavior (e.g., Barker, 1995, 1999; Barker et al., 1990; Eriksson et al., 2010), and nutrition inputs such as iron, zinc, and folic acid are critical to child development. In nutrition and health interventions, children (or pregnant women) were most often given the supplements at home by parents/caregivers and/or other persons such as community health workers and midwives. Ten of the 32 studies of nutrition and health interventions reported positive effects on children's cognitive development, including language and numeracy skills, intellectual functioning,

and school achievement. Moreover, interventions that commenced during pregnancy showed that some interventions could protect children from the detrimental effects of maternal under-nutrition.

The delivery of the nutrition and health interventions was straightforward. Children (or pregnant women) were usually given the supplements at home by parents/caregivers or other change agents such as community health workers and midwives. Supplements, breakfasts, and lunches were also distributed in preschools or day-care centers by teachers or other people. In addition, the interventions were delivered at the community level by field workers.

The outcomes of interventions that commenced during pregnancy showed that some nutrients may be more effective than others in protecting children from the detrimental effects of maternal under-nutrition on children's motor and cognitive development. In Bangladesh (Tofail et al., 2008) and China (Li et al., 2009), prenatal multi-micronutrient (MM) supplementation (versus iron or folic supplementation) which was provided during pregnancy was found to have minor benefits for infants. The effects of iron and zinc supplementations were most commonly studied in the intervention trials directly supplementing young children since infancy (≤ 2 years) in developing countries. However, the results of the five studies included suggested that the supplements were only beneficial in terms of growth, not cognitive development. The few trials that targeted older children aged 6–8 years had somewhat more positive outcomes. For example, MM-fortified biscuits were found to be associated with potentially positive effects on the school performance of 6- to 8-year-olds (Nga et al., 2011). Other interventions, such as an iron supplementation and a deworming-drug program for 2- to 6-year-olds in India (Bobonis et al., 2006) and subsidized school meals in Kenya (Vermeersch and Kremer, 2004), did not enhance cognitive performance but led to substantial gains in child weight and preschool participation. Extant evidence precludes conclusions about the optimal timing of nutritional supplementation to promote cognitive development.

It should be noted that the effectiveness of nutrition and health interventions was also often dependent on the capacity to plan, manage, deliver, and monitor these services. Furthermore, the positive effects of nutritional interventions on cognitive development may only be apparent in long-term studies, not short-term ones. For example, in one study a number of six-month-olds were given micronutrient-fortified food until they were 2 years old. Results indicated that these children showed significantly higher cognitive development at 4 and 6 years compared to children who did not receive the intervention (Chen et al., 2010).

Although different types of supplementation were used in the interventions, and the effects of nutrition and health interventions on children's cognitive development are inconsistent, it is important to be cognizant of several issues when considering the effectiveness of these types of interventions. The findings in our review showed that the positive effects of nutrition and health interventions depended not only on the type of supplementation provided, but also on whether the children benefited from a supportive learning environment (Mitter et al., 2012; Pollitt et al., 1993; Stein et al., 2008). This is because the 'particular socio-environmental factors which led to the development of early clinical malnutrition in some children and not in others in the same family or in the same community may also have contributed directly to the reduced intellectual performance observed' (Ricciuti, 1981). In addition, the studies reviewed tended to focus on a single input intervention and a single outcome (cognitive development) and they did not consider the interactive influences of different facets of early experience (nutrition, poverty, exposure to toxins and child–adult interaction) on brain development. Therefore, not only is better understanding needed of the combined or interactive effects of different nutrients and of the most effective timing for nutritional supplementation of cognitive

development, but further information is also required on the interactive effects of nutrition and other early experiences on the cognitive development of young children.

INCOME-SUPPLEMENTATION PROGRAMS

Income-supplementation programs, particularly Conditional Cash Transfer (CCT) programs, have been widely used in Latin America as a poverty-alleviation strategy. The beneficiaries of traditional (unconditional) cash transfer programs receive monies solely to supplement their low-income level. In contrast, conditional cash transfer programs require families to comply with certain requirements to qualify for benefits. For instance, parents are commonly required to take their children for health checks, send their children to school, or attend parenting programs. Cash transfer programs differ from supply-side interventions such as the provision of preschool education or food supplementation in that they allow parents to choose the investments they make in their children. Young children's cognitive development may be directly facilitated because parents choose to purchase more nutritious food, improve the quality of the home environment, or send their children to early childhood programs. Moreover, cognitive development may be indirectly facilitated by enhancing the psychological and physical well-being of mothers, decreasing financial strain, and improving maternal nutrition. Whilst the positive impact of CCTs on children's health and nutrition has been documented in earlier work, the influence of CCTs on children's early cognitive development has only recently been evaluated (i.e., Behrman et al., 2004; Fernald and Hidrobo, 2011; Paxson and Schady, 2010).

Eleven studies were included in the review. Each had an income-supplementation component and the effect of this component on children's cognitive development was investigated. All studies were large-scale interventions, and the number of children sampled in the intervention groups ranged from 797 (Fernald and Hidrobo, 2011) to 65,259 (Behrman et al., 2004). Six studies reported positive effects of the income-supplementation intervention on children's cognitive development or learning achievement (see Table 27.1). Among these, four showed small[1] effects (Fernald et al., 2009a; Fernald and Hidrobo, 2011; Gertler and Fernald, 2004; Paxson and Schady, 2010) and two showed medium and positive effects (Behrman et al., 2004; Fernald et al., 2008). The variations might be because of the location and evaluation of the intervention programs, and programs also differ in terms of how much, when and how the beneficiaries are given the cash.

The best-known income-supplementation intervention is Mexico's *Oportunidades* program, one of the first CCT programs to be implemented in a developing country context. Evaluations indicate that the program enhanced the cognitive development of children whose mothers had received no formal education (Fernald et al., 2009a; Leroy et al., 2012). The cash component of the program was associated with improved outcomes in child height, cognition, and language development in preschool-aged children who had been enrolled since birth (Fernald et al., 2008). Previous studies had also shown that cumulative cash transfers had significant and positive effects on cognitive development (Behrman et al., 2004; Fernald et al., 2008, 2009a). Variations in the effectiveness of cash transfer programs are assumed to be a function of the age of the child when the program starts and household demographic characteristics.

It is difficult to isolate the effect of cash transfers on cognitive development for several reasons. First, parents may engage in one or more behaviors, each of which could independently enhance children's cognitive development. For example, parents may purchase more nutritious food for their children, improve the quality of their home environment, or enroll their children in early childhood programs. Second, cash transfers may improve mothers' psychological and physical well-being by decreasing financial strain and improving maternal health. These changes in maternal well-being may indirectly facilitate children's cognitive development. Furthermore, cash incentives are usually conditional on medical checks, parental counseling, or program attendance, and these requirements are themselves interventions. Therefore, it is difficult to pinpoint the precise mechanism by which CCT programs produce effects.

COMPREHENSIVE PROGRAMS

Comprehensive programs usually take an integrated approach to intervention and combine several components: a safe environment for all participating children, early childhood learning (including motor, cognitive, affective, and social domains), nutrition, health, and parental support. The activities and learning materials associated with such programs are appropriate for children of different ages and incorporate local customs and traditions. Comprehensive programs adopt a variety of approaches to delivering services and include center-based (e.g., day-care centers, pre-schools, health stations), home-based (e.g., family day-care programs where a childminder takes care of a group of children from the community at his/her home), and community-based interventions (Armecin et al., 2006; Cueto et al., 2009). Most of these programs are 'Head Start'-type programs.[2] A few comprehensive early intervention programs have been evaluated in some developing countries. Despite the small number of programs evaluated, the results strongly support the claim that children benefit from comprehensive intervention programs that support child development in developing countries. These programs had important positive impacts on children's cognitive, motor, language and social development, and nutritional status, with some suggestion that the duration of exposure increases the program impacts (Armecin et al., 2006; Gultiano and King, 2006; Peairson et al., 2008). Research on the effectiveness of these programs also showed that positive program effects vary depending on the child's age. Children under 4 years exhibit faster rates of change in psycho-social development than do children over 4 years, and thus may be more receptive to interventions that aim to improve developmental outcomes (Armecin et al., 2006).

However, these findings are largely based on an analysis of secondary data with constructed comparison groups. Such designs are less rigorous than those used to evaluate other interventions (see Table 27.1). It should also be noted that all of the comprehensive programs reviewed were large-scale projects, which are typically government-funded. In addition, these comprehensive intervention programs have been faulted for a variety of reasons, including operating as feeding centers, neglecting preschool education, some failing to reach the most disadvantaged sections of society (Hazarika and Viren, 2010; Rao, 2010), and providing early childhood educators with insufficient training.

LIMITATIONS AND IMPLICATIONS

While research on cognitive development and its facilitation has received increased attention in developing country contexts, there are research gaps. First, there are large variations in the rigor of program evaluations. Second, few studies focus on the long-term effects of early childhood interventions. Third, studies do not reflect the population distributions of children in developing countries. For example, most of the studies included in this review were conducted in Latin America and the Caribbean (38%) and South Asia (28%), while studies conducted in Africa, East Asia and the Pacific, Central and Eastern Europe, and the Commonwealth of Independent States only accounted for 34% of the total number of studies. Fourth,

further work is needed to develop contextually appropriate interventions to promote cognitive development and to develop culturally appropriate tools to assess the effects of these interventions on cognitive development and school readiness. Last but not least, to increase the number and quality of evaluation studies, researchers in developing countries should also be empowered and funded to conduct systematic, rigorous research to develop and evaluate programs in order to make evidence-based decisions about promoting early development and learning.

CONCLUSION

Cognitive development involves gains in language, thinking and understanding. Contemporary research on cognitive development in developing countries has focused on the assessment of interventions that promote early cognitive development and learning.

In this chapter, we have drawn upon a rigorous review of the literature on early childhood intervention and cognitive development in developing countries. Results indicate that early childhood development interventions in developing countries have generally had positive effects on cognitive development.

We presented highlights from narrative summaries of high-quality studies of the five major types of early childhood interventions (parent-focused, child-focused educational, nutrition and health, income-supplementation, and comprehensive programs) and their effects on cognitive outcomes in developing countries.

FURTHER READING

The two series on Child Development in Developing Countries published in *The Lancet* are highly recommended:

Series 1

Engle, P. L., Black, M. M., Behrman, J. R., Cabral de Mello, M., Gertler, P. J., Kapiriri, L., et al. (2007). Strategies to avoid the loss of developmental potential in more than 200 million children in the developing world. *The Lancet*, 369, 229–42.

Grantham-McGregor, S., Cheung, Y. B., Cueto, S., Glewwe, P., Richter, L. and Strupp, B. (2007). Developmental potential in the first 5 years for children in developing countries. *The Lancet*, 369, 60–70.

Walker, S. P., Wachs, T. D., Gardner, J. M., Lozoff, B., Wasserman, G. A., Pollitt, E., et al. (2007). Child development: Risk factors for adverse outcomes in developing countries. *The Lancet*, 369, 145–57.

Series 2

Engle, P., Fernald, L. C. H., Alderman, H., Behrman, J. R., O'Gara, C., Yousafzai, A., et al. (2011). Strategies for reducing inequalities and improving developmental outcomes for young children in low-income and middle-income countries. *The Lancet*, 378, 1339–53.

Walker, S. P., Wachs, T. D., Grantham-McGregor, S., Black, M. M., Nelson, C. A., Huffman, S. L., et al. (2011). Inequality in early childhood: Risk and protective factors for early child development. *The Lancet*, 378, 1325–38.

QUESTIONS FOR REFLECTION

1   Produce a list of factors that facilitate/hinder cognitive development in developing country contexts. Explain the process by which each factor affects cognitive development (for example, nutrition intervention → more energy and increased responsiveness to stimulation → better learning outcomes).

2   Which factors need to be considered when developing tools to evaluate cognitive development in developing country contexts?

3   What types of research designs have been used to evaluate the effects of early childhood interventions on cognitive development? What problems may be associated with implementing rigorous experimental designs in developing countries?

4   How does participation in early-intervention programs help to protect and realize children's rights as specified by the UN Convention on the Rights of the Child (United Nations, 1989)?

NOTES

1   The interpretation of the unbiased effect size of each intervention was based on Cohen's (1988) benchmark: .20 was small, .50 was medium and .80 was large.

2   Head Start, a US federal program that provides a variety of services (e.g., preschool education and childcare, healthcare, nutrition, and parent education and involvement) to low-income families with children, is one of the best-known early-years interventions in the world.

ACKNOWLEDGMENT

This chapter is based on the following report, and some sections of the chapter are taken directly from the report: Rao, N., Sun, J., Wong, J. M. S., Weekes, B., Ip, P., Shaeffer, S., et al. (2014). *Early childhood development and cognitive development in developing countries: A rigorous literature review*. London: Department for International Development (http://eppi.ioe.ac.uk/cms/Default.aspx?tabid=3465).

REFERENCES

Aboud, F. E. (2006). Evaluation of an early childhood preschool program in rural Bangladesh. *Early Childhood Research Quarterly*, 21(1), 46–60.

Aboud, F. E. and Hossain, K. (2011). The impact of preprimary school on primary school achievement in Bangladesh. *Early Childhood Research Quarterly*, 26(2), 237–46.

Aboud, F. E., Hossain, K. and O'Gara, C. (2008). The Succeed Project: Challenging early school failure in Bangladesh. *Research in Comparative and International Education*, 3(3), 295–307.

Alderman, H. (ed.) (2011). *No small matter: The impact of poverty, shock, and human capital investments in early childhood development*. Washington, DC: The World Bank.

American Institutes for Research (2012). *Getting ready for school: A child-to-child approach, program evaluation for year one grade one outcomes*. New York: UNICEF.

Armecin, G., Behrman, J. R., Duazo, P., Ghuman, S., Gultiano, S., King, E. M. and Lee, N. (2006). *Early childhood development through an integrated program: Evidence from the Philippines* (Policy Research Working Paper 3922). Washington, DC: The World Bank.

Baker-Henningham, H. and Boo, F. L. (2010). *Early childhood stimulation interventions in developing countries: A comprehensive literature review*. Bonn, Germany: Inter-American Development Bank. Retrieved from http://idbdocs.iadb.org/wsdocs/getdocument.aspx?docnum=35349131

Barker, D. J. P. (1995). Fetal origins of coronary heart disease. *British Medical Journal*, 311, 171–4.

Barker, D. J. P. (1999). Early growth and cardiovascular disease. *Archives of Disease in Childhood*, 80, 305–7.

Barker, D. J. P., Bull, A. R., Osmond, C. and Simmonds, S. J. (1990). Fetal and placental size and risk of hypertension in adult life. *British Medical Journal*, 301, 259–62.

Baydar, N., Kağitçibaşi, Ç., Küntay, A. C. and Gökşen, F. (2008). Effects of an educational television program on preschoolers: Variability in benefits. *Journal of Applied Developmental Psychology*, 29(5), 349–60.

Behrman, J. R., Cheng, Y. and Todd, P. E. (2004). Evaluating preschool programs when length of exposure to the program varies: A nonparametric approach. *Review of Economics and Statistics*, 86(1), 108–32.

Berlinski, S., Galiani, S. and Manacorda, M. (2008). Giving children a better start: Preschool attendance and school-age profiles. *Journal of Public Economics*, 92(5), 1416–40.

Berument, S. K., Sönmez, D. and Eyüpoğlu, H. (2012). Supporting language and cognitive development of infants and young children living in children's homes in Turkey. *Child: Care, Health and Development*, 38(5), 743–52.

Blair, C. and Raver, C. C. (2012). Child development in the context of adversity: Experiential canalization of brain and behaviour. *American Psychologist*, 67, 309–318.

Bobonis, G. J., Miguel, E. and Puri-Sharma, C. (2006). Anemia and school participation. *Journal of Human Resources*, XLI(4), 692–721.

Chen, C. M., Wang, Y. Y. and Chang, S. Y. (2010). Effect of in-home fortification of complementary feeding on intellectual development of Chinese children. *Biomedical and Environmental Sciences*, 23(2), 83–91.

Cohen, J. (1988). *Statistical power analysis for the behavioral sciences* (2nd edition). Hillsdale, NJ: Lawrence Erlbaum.

Cueto, S., Guerrero, G., Leon, J., Zevallos, A. and Sugimaru, C. (2009). *Promoting early childhood development through a public program: Wawa Wasi in Peru* (Working Paper No. 51). Oxford: Young Lives.

Demir, Ö. E. and Küntay, A. C. (2014). Cognitive and neural mechanisms underlying socioeconomic gradients in language development: New answers to old questions. *Child Development Perspectives*, 8(2), 113–18.

Education Development Center (EDC) (2009). *Radio instruction to strengthen education (RISE) in Zanzibar*. Boston: EDC.

Eriksson, J. G., Kajantie, E., Osmond, C., Thornburg, K. and Barker, D. J. P. (2010). Boys live dangerously in the womb. *American Journal of Human Biology*, 22(3), 330–5.

Evans, G. W. and Kim, P. (2013). Childhood poverty, chronic stress, self-regulation, and coping. *Child Development Perspectives*, 7(1), 43–8.

Evans, J. L. and Stansbery, P. S. (1998). *Parenting in the early years: A review of programs for parents of children from birth to three years of age*. Washington, DC: The World Bank.

Fernald, L.C.H and Gunnar, M. R. (2009). Poverty-alleviation program participation and salivary cortisol in very low-income children. *Social Science and Medicine*, 68(2), 180–2, 189.

Fernald, L. C. H. and Hidrobo, M. (2011). Effect of Ecuador's cash transfer program (Bono de Desarrollo Humano) on child development in infants and toddlers: A randomized effectiveness trial. *Social Science and Medicine*, 72(9), 1437–46.

Fernald, L. C., Gertler, P. J. and Neufeld, L. M. (2008). Role of cash in conditional cash transfer programmes for child health, growth, and development: An analysis of Mexico's Oportunidades. *The Lancet*, 371(9615), 828–37.

Fernald, L. C., Gertler, P. J. and Neufeld, L. M. (2009a). 10-year effect of Oportunidades, Mexico's conditional cash transfer programme, on child growth, cognition, language, and behaviour: A longitudinal follow-up study. *The Lancet*, 374(9706), 1997–2005.

Fernald, L. C. H., Kariger, P., Engle, P. and Raikes, A. (2009b). *Examining early child development in low-income countries: A toolkit for the assessment of children in the first five years of life.* Washington, DC: The World Bank.

Gardner, J. M. M., Powell, C. A., Baker-Henningham, H., Walker, S. P., Cole, T. J. and Grantham-McGregor, S. M. (2005). Zinc supplementation and psychosocial stimulation: Effects on the development of undernourished Jamaican children. *American Journal of Clinical Nutrition*, 82(2), 399–405.

Gardner, J. M., Walker, S. P., Powell, C. A. and Grantham-McGregor, S. (2003). A randomized controlled trial of a home-visiting intervention on cognition and behavior in term low birth weight infants. *Journal of Pediatrics*, 143(5), 634–9.

Gertler, P. J. and Fernald, L. C. (2004). *The medium term impact of Oportunidades on child development in rural areas.* Unpublished manuscript, University of California, Berkeley.

Gottlieb, G. (1991). Experiential canalization of behavioral development: Theory. *Developmental Psychology*, 27, 4–13. doi:10.1037/0012-1649.27.1.4

Gottlieb, G. (1997). *Synthesizing nature–nurture: Prenatal roots of instinctive behavior.* Mahwah, NJ: Erlbaum.

Grantham-McGregor, S., Cheung, Y. B., Cueto, S., Glewwe, P., Richter, L. and Strupp, B. (2007). Developmental potential in the first 5 years for children in developing countries. *The Lancet*, 369, 60–70.

Grantham-McGregor, S. M., Walker, S. P., Chang, S. M. and Powell, C. A. (1997). Effects of early childhood supplementation with and without stimulation on later development in stunted Jamaican children. *American Journal of Clinical Nutrition*, 66(2), 247–53.

Guldan, G. S., Zeitlin, M. F., Beiser, A. S., Super, C. M., Gershoff, S. N. and Datta, S. (1993). Maternal education and child feeding practices in rural Bangladesh. *Social Science and Medicine*, 36, 925–35.

Gultiano, S. A. and King, E. M. (2006). A better start in life: Evaluation results from an early childhood development program. *Philippine Journal of Development*, 33(1–2), 101–28.

Gupta, P. D. and Richardson, K. (1995). Theories of cognitive development. In V. Lee and P. D. Gupta (eds) *Children's cognitive and language development.* Milton Keynes: Open University Educational Enterprises Ltd.

Hazarika, G. and Viren, V. (2010). *The effect of early childhood developmental program attendance on future school enrollment and grade progression in rural north India.* Bonn: IZA.

He, F., Linden, L. L. and MacLeod, M. (2009). *A better way to teach children to read? Evidence from a randomized controlled trial.* Cambridge, MA: Abdul Latif Jameel Poverty Action Lab (JPAL).

Janus, M. and Offord, D. R. (2007). Development and psychometric properties of the early development instrument (EDI): A measure of children's school readiness. *Canadian Journal of Behavioural Science*, 39, 1–22.

Jaramillo, A. and Tietjen, K. (2001). *Early childhood development in Africa: Can we do more for less? A look at the impact and implications of preschools in Cape Verde and Guinea.* Washington, DC: The World Bank, Africa Region.

Kagan, S. L. and Britto, P. R. (2005). *Going global with early learning and development standards: Final report to UNICEF.* New York: The National Center for Children and Families, Teachers College, Columbia University.

Kagitcibasi, C., Sunar, D. and Bekman, S. (2001). Long-term effects of early intervention: Turkish low-income mothers and children. *Journal of Applied Developmental Psychology*, 22(4), 333–61.

Kagitcibasi, C., Sunar, D., Bekman, S., Baydar, N. and Cemalcilar, Z. (2009). Continuing effects of early enrichment in adult life: The Turkish Early Enrichment Project 22 years later. *Journal of Applied Developmental Psychology*, 30(6), 764–79.

Leroy, J. L., Gertler, P. and Martinez, S. (2012). *The impact of day care on maternal labor supply and child development in Mexico: Final data analysis report.* Mexico: Instituto Nacional de Salud Pública.

Li, Q., Yan, H., Zeng, L., Cheng, Y., Liang, W., Dang, S., et al. (2009). Effects of maternal multimicronutrient supplementation on the mental development of infants in rural Western China: Follow-up evaluation of a double-blind, randomized, controlled trial. *Pediatrics*, 123, 685–92.

Loeb, S., Bridges, M., Bassok, D., Fulle, B. and Rumberger, R. W. (2007). How much is too much? The influence of preschool centers on children's social and cognitive development. *Economics of Education Review*, 26(1), 52–66.

Loeb, S., Fuller, B., Kagan, S. L. and Carrol, B. (2004). Child care in poor communities: Early learning effects of type, quality, and stability. *Child Development*, 75, 47–65.

Lozoff, B., Smith, J. B., Clark, K. M., Perales, C. G., Rivera, F., and Castillo, M. (2010). Home intervention improves cognitive and social-emotional scores in iron-deficient anemic infants. *Pediatrics*, 126(4), e884–e894.

Malmberg, L.-E., Mwaura, P. and Sylva, K. (2011). Effects of a preschool intervention on cognitive development among East-African preschool children: A flexibly time-coded growth model. *Early Childhood Research Quarterly*, 26(1), 124–33.

Martinez, S., Naudeau, S. and Pereira, V. (2012). *The promise of preschool in Africa: A randomized impact evaluation of ECD in rural Mozambique*. New Delhi, India: International Initiative for Impact Evaluation (3ie).

Mitter, S. S., Oriá, R. B., Kvalsund, M. P., Pamplona, P., Joventino, E. S., Mota, R., ... and Lima, A. A. (2012). Apolipoprotein E4 influences growth and cognitive responses to micronutrient supplementation in shanty-town children from northeast Brazil. *Clinics*, 67(1), 11–18.

Moore, A. C., Akhter, S. and Aboud, F. E. (2008). Evaluating an improved quality preschool program in rural Bangladesh. *International Journal of Educational Development*, 28(2), 118–31.

Mwaura, P. A., Sylva, K. and Malmberg, L. E. (2008). Evaluating the Madrasa preschool programme in East Africa: A quasi-experimental study. *International Journal of Early Years Education*, 16(3), 237–55.

Nahar, B., Hamadani, J. D., Ahmed, T., Tofail, F., Rahman, A., Huda, S. N. and Grantham-McGregor, S. M. (2008). Effects of psychosocial stimulation on growth and development of severely malnourished children in a nutrition unit in Bangladesh. *European Journal of Clinical Nutrition*, 63(6), 725–31.

Nga, T. T., Winichagoon, P., Dijkhuizen, M. A., Khan, N. C., Wasantwisut, E. and Wieringa, F. T. (2011). Decreased parasite load and improved cognitive outcomes caused by deworming and consumption of multi-micronutrient fortified biscuits in rural Vietnamese school children. *American Journal of Tropical Medicine and Hygiene*, 85(2), 333–40.

NICHD Early Child Care Research Network (ECCRN) (2005). *Child care and child development: Results from the NICHD study of early child care and youth development*. New York: Guildford.

Nonoyama-Tarumi, Y. and Bredenberg, K. (2009). Impact of school readiness program interventions on children's learning in Cambodia. *International Journal of Educational Development*, 29(1), 39–45.

Opel, A., Ameer, S. S. and Aboud, F. E. (2009). The effect of preschool dialogic reading on vocabulary among rural Bangladeshi children. *International Journal of Educational Research*, 48(1), 12–20.

Paxson, C. and Schady, N. (2010). Does money matter? The effects of cash transfers on child development in rural Ecuador. *Economic Development and Cultural Change*, 59(1), 187–229.

Peairson, S., Austin, A. M. B., de Aquino, C. N. and de Burró, E. U. (2008). Cognitive development and home environment of rural Paraguayan infants and toddlers participating in Pastoral del Niño, an early child development program. *Journal of Research in Childhood Education*, 22(4), 343–62.

Piramal, R. and Law, J. (2010). Evaluating a programme to enhance vocabulary development in pre-schoolers. *International Journal of Language and Communication Disorders*, 36(s1), 222–7.

Pollitt, E., Gorman, K. S., Engle, P. L., Martorell, R. and Rivera, J. (1993). Early supplementary feeding and cognition: Effects over two decades. *Monographs of the Society for Research in Child Development* Serial No. 235: 58(7).

Rao, N. (2010). Preschool quality and the development of children from economically disadvantaged families in India. *Early Education and Development*, 21(2), 167–85.

Rao, N., Sun, J., Pearson, V., Pearson, E., Liu, H., Constas, M. A. and Engle, P. L. (2012a). Is something better than nothing? An evaluation of early childhood programs in Cambodia. *Child Development*, 83(3), 864–76.

Rao, N., Sun, J., Zhou, J. and Zhang, Li. (2012b). Early achievement in rural China:

The role of preschool experience. *Early Childhood Research Quarterly*, 27, 66–76.

Rao, N., Sun, J., Ng, M., Becher, Y., Lee, D., Ip, P. and Bacon-Shone, J. (2014a). *Validation, finalization and adoption of the East Asia-Pacific early child development scales (EAP-ECDS)*. New York: UNICEF.

Rao, N., Sun, J., Wong, J. M. S., Weekes, B., Ip, P., Shaeffer, S., et al. (2014b). *Early childhood development and cognitive development in developing countries: A rigorous literature review*. London: Department for International Development (http://eppi.ioe.ac.uk/cms/Default.aspx?tabid=3465).

Ricciuti, H. N. (1981). Adverse environmental and nutritional influences on mental development: A perspective. *Journal of the American Dietetic Association*, 79(2), 115–20.

Rolla, A., Arias, M., Villers, R. and Snow, C. (2006). Evaluating the impact of different early literacy interventions on low-income Costa Rican kindergarteners. *International Journal of Educational Research*, 45(3), 188–201.

Roy, P. and Chiat, S. (2013). Teasing apart disadvantage from disorder: The case of poor language. In C. Marshall (ed.) *Current issues in developmental disorders*. London: Psychology Press.

Sammons, P., Sylva, K., Melhuish, E., Siraj-Blatchford, I., Taggart, B., Grabbe, Y., and Barreau, S. (2007). The Effective Pre-school and Primary Education 3–11 Project (EPPE 3–11): Influences on children's attainment and progress in Key Stage 2: Cognitive outcomes in Year 5. London: DfES / Institute of Education, University of London.

Save the Children (2003). *What's the difference? The impact of early childhood development programs. A study from Nepal of the effects for children, their families and communities*. Kathmandu, Nepal: Save the Children.

Save the Children (2004). *Early childhood care and development: A positive impact, Myanmar. A study from Myanmar of the effects for children, their families and communities*. Myanmar: Save the Children.

Stein, A. D., Wang, M., DiGirolamo, A., Grajeda, R., Ramakrishnan, U., Ramirez-Zea, M. … and Martorell, R. (2008). Nutritional supplementation in early childhood, schooling, and intellectual functioning in adulthood: a prospective study in Guatemala. *Archives of Pediatrics & Adolescent Medicine*, 162(7), 612–18.

Sylva, K., Melhuish, E., Sammons, P., Siraj-Blatchford, I. and Taggart, B. (2011). Preschool quality and educational outcomes at age 11: Low quality has little benefit. *Journal of Early Childhood Research*, 9, 109–24.

Taiwo, A. A. and Tyolo, J. B. (2002). The effect of pre-school education on academic performance in primary school: A case study of grade one pupils in Botswana. *International Journal of Educational Development*, 22(2), 169–80.

Taneja, V., Aggarwal, R., Beri, R. S. and Puliyel, J. M. (2005). Not by bread alone project: A 2-year follow-up report. *Child: Care, Health and Development*, 31(6), 703–6.

Taneja, V., Sriram, S., Beri, R. S., Sreenivas, V., Aggarwal, R. and Kaur, R. (2002). 'Not by bread alone': Impact of a structured 90-minute play session on development of children in an orphanage. *Child: Care, Health and Development*, 28(1), 95–100.

Tofail, F., Persson, L. A., El Arifeen, S., Hamadani, J. D., Mehrin, F., Rideout, D., et al. (2008). Effects of prenatal food and micronutrient supplementation on infant development: A randomized trial from the Maternal and Infant Nutrition Interventions, Matlab (MINIMat) study. *American Journal of Clinical Nutrition*, 87(3), 704–11.

UNICEF (2001). *Baseline survey of caregivers' KAP on early childhood development in Bangladesh*. Dhaka, Bangladesh: UNICEF.

Vermeersch, C. and Kremer, M. (2004). School meals, educational achievement and school competition: Evidence from a randomized evaluation. Unpublished manuscript.

Walker, S. P., Chang, S. M., Powell, C. A. and Grantham-McGregor, S. M. (2004). Psychosocial intervention improves the development of term low-birth-weight infants. *Journal of Nutrition*, 134(6), 1417–23.

Walker, S. P., Chang, S. M., Powell, C. A. and Grantham-McGregor, S. M. (2005). Effects of early childhood psychosocial stimulation and nutritional supplementation on cognition and education in growth-retarded Jamaican children: Prospective cohort study. *The Lancet*, 1–8.

Walker, S. P., Chang, S. M., Younger, N. and Grantham-McGregor, S. M. (2010). The effect of psychosocial stimulation on cognition and behaviour at 6 years in a cohort of term, low-birth weight Jamaican children. *Developmental Medicine and Child Neurology*, 52(7), e148–e154.

Walker, S. P., Grantham-McGregor, S. M., Powell, C. A. and Chang, S. M. (2000). Effects of growth restriction in early childhood on growth, IQ, and cognition at age 11 to 12 years and the benefits of nutritional supplementation and psychosocial stimulation. *Journal of Pediatrics*, 137 (1), 36–41.

Walker, S. P., Wachs, T. D., Gardner, J. M., Lozoff, B., Wasserman, G. A., Pollitt, E., et al. (2007). Child development: Risk factors for adverse outcomes in developing countries. *The Lancet*, 369, 145–57.

Walker, S. P., Wachs, T. D., Grantham-McGregor, S., Black, M. M., Nelson, C. A., Huffman, S. L., et al. (2011). Inequality in early childhood: Risk and protective factors for early child development. *The Lancet*, 378, 1325–38.

Woldehanna, T. (2011). The effects of early childhood education attendance on cognitive development: Evidence from urban Ethiopia. Paper presented at the CSAE Conference on Economic Development in Africa, St Catherine's College, Oxford, 20–22 March.

Zuilkowski, S. S., Fink, G., Moucheraud, C. and Matafwali, B. (2012). Early childhood education, child development and school readiness: Evidence from Zambia. *South African Journal of Childhood Education*, 2(2), 117.

PART V

Considering the Future of Early Childhood Research

28

Social and Political Landscapes of Childhood

Helen Penn

INTRODUCTION

This chapter offers an overview of the research on early childhood in low- and middle-income countries. It locates the discussion about early childhood in the wider context of development aid, and reflects on some of the highly problematic and contentious general debates about how rich nations might best offer support to poor nations and, thus, seek to redress inequality. One of the arguments advanced in this chapter is that the early childhood research community is by and large unaware of this wider debate, and, as a result, although well-meaning and with humanitarian intentions, it tends to frame questions, use research methodologies, make predictions and advance solutions which may be too narrow or too naïve, thereby precluding other interpretations. It over-relies on research paradigms which may be appropriate to high-income countries, with high levels of resources, but may even be harmful in very different circumstances. Paradoxically,

the early childhood research community ignores much of the research that is generated in such high-income countries. It raises questions about whether there is a hierarchy of research models and whether research needs to be led from high-income countries, as charitable funders and bilateral funders, as well as research departments based in prestigious universities, readily assume (Hulme and Edwards, 1997; Pogge, 2009).

CONTEMPORARY RESEARCH IN EARLY CHILDHOOD IN LOW- AND MIDDLE-INCOME COUNTRIES

The most recent research compendium at the time of writing is that by Rebello Britto et al. (2013a), the rather grandly titled *Handbook of Early Childhood Development Research and its Impact on Global Policy*. The contributions are by scholars (mainly from the USA) and cover a variety of fields, theoretical as well as programmatic. The book explores broad research avenues and research findings mainly within the framework of internationally agreed policies such as the Millennium Development Goals and the UN Convention on the Rights of the Child. The handbook refers to 'Early Child Development (ECD)', the preferred title used by most international agencies because of its paediatric overlap. The emphasis on early child *development* is a specific reference to the importance of health and healthy development as an aspect of child well-being. Agencies such as UNICEF, the World Bank and the World Health Organization (WHO) use the acronym ECD. However, UNESCO, because its primary reference point is education, categorizes the field as 'Early Childhood Care and Education'.

There is a significant series of papers in *The Lancet* on child survival and healthy development (Chan, 2013; Engle et al., 2007, 2011; Grantham-McGregor et al., 2007) and, in particular, on the growth of very young children and the training of mothers in providing adequate care and nutrition. The *Lancet* papers were, in turn, the focus of an international conference, Promises for Preschoolers (IFS/3ie/UCL, 2012), in June 2012, organized jointly by the Institute of Fiscal Studies, the Department of Development Economics at UCL and 3ie, an American Institute committed to systematic review and evidence-based policy. The original *Lancet* papers were primarily concerned with nutritional interventions and drew heavily on medical evidence, and in particular rely on randomized controlled trials (RCTs). The subsequent papers reviewed at the conference focused mainly on the economic costs and consequences of particular kinds of early childhood development interventions, which went beyond paediatric interventions.

Slightly earlier, there was a book edited for the World Bank by Marito Garcia, a leading development economist, entitled *Africa's Future, Africa's Challenge* (Garcia et al., 2008), another work which sought to summarize the economic arguments for intervention.

The chapters in this book hypothesized about the causal links between interventions and subsequent outcomes.

The Organisation for Economic Co-operation and Development (OECD), as a voice for high-income countries, by contrast, refers to early childhood education and childcare (ECEC) as a single issue (OECD, 2013, 2014). The European Union (EU) similarly refers to ECEC and is currently funding a comprehensive series of data collection and research programmes on governance, training, access and other aspects of ECEC (European Commission, 2014; European Commission et al., 2014). Both the OECD and the EU maintain comprehensive databases on ECEC which are readily accessible and provide very useful comparative material (Penn, 2014). The research cited above discusses 'the global reach' of international development policy on early childhood, but none of it refers to either the OECD or the EU, although some middle-income countries are members of the OECD and some Eastern European countries in the EU are also middle income.

The major difference between the 'global reach' of the ECD literature discussed above and the focus of the EU and the OECD on early childhood, is in their approach to gender issues. For instance, a paper for UNICEF-IRC by Rebello Britto et al. (2013b) claims to map early childhood services in low-income countries, but singularly omits *any* consideration of childcare. Yet the evidence about working women in low- and middle-income countries points to the 'feminization of poverty' and the way in which global economic changes have led to significant pressures on women to work to support their young children and the burdens of childcare that arise (Heymann, 2003, 2006; Razavi, 2011a, 2011b).

Mahon (2011) suggests that the 'Washington consensus', the group of international agencies working closely with and taking their lead from the World Bank, which includes UNICEF and other major donors, reflects the USA's priorities and programming in early childhood. The USA, more than most other high-income countries, lacks coherent government-led early education and childcare policies (Zigler et al., 2009). Historians and social scientists investigating mothering in the USA have argued that the strength of maternalistic viewpoints – a woman's place in the home – has mitigated against the development of childcare services. It is an entrenched position that women carry the main responsibility for childrearing (or paying for help with childrearing) and that such a responsibility should not be shouldered by the state except in extreme circumstances (Kamerman and Gatenio-Gabel, 2007; Michel, 1999; Michel and Mahon, 2002). This position in the USA is implicitly taken as the norm, rather than as the exception, by many development agencies, and any kind of government-led, universalistic approach is seen as an unacceptable burden on tax payers and as simply impractical in low-income countries. It is left up to philanthropic organizations and private companies to fill any perceived gaps in provision. Mostly these gaps are assumed to be about improving mothering, rather than relieving the burdens of mothering. Most of the research findings on ECD, for instance the *Lancet* series, concern interventions to help poor women become better mothers; it discounts their voices and does not recognize their needs or circumstances other than their attitudes towards and their care of their children.

As argued below, the latest version of this long-running negative conception of state intervention in early childhood is the way in which economic and neuroscientific arguments have been fused to justify targeted spending on particular kinds of interventions in early childhood.

RESEARCH METHODS, ETHICS AND FUNDING

There is now a wide range of methodological experimentation and evaluative techniques on which researchers and aid agencies can draw. They are potentially complementary rather than in opposition (Boyden and Bourdillon, 2012). Although there is considerable research sophistication, I argue here that this research palette is often narrowly used, because of the dogmas governing ECD research in low- and middle-income countries. An extremely brief introduction to research approaches, ethics and funding is offered here.

Demographic Data

There is an increased emphasis on sophisticated household survey data which can be used as a benchmark for measuring the impact of government policies on households and for disaggregating the position of women or children within households (Atkinson and Marlier, 2012; Milanovic, 2011; Stiglitz et al., 2009). Household surveys, although they may be done at long intervals in low- and middle-income countries, or else have to be specially set up, may provide essential core data. For example, a recent survey of child disability in Iraq (Alborz et al., 2011), the Department for International Development (DFID) Young Lives project (Jones and Sumner, 2011) and recent work in South Africa (Dawes et al., 2007) have all used household surveys and other demographic data as a means of establishing benchmarks for their projects. Maggi et al. (2005), in their report for WHO, argue that sophisticated demographic data is needed to identify and target the most vulnerable communities, and they outline methodologies for doing so. UNICEF commissions specific household survey data on children in order to compile its country indicators – for instance, the Multiple Indicator Cluster Survey (MICS) data for the CEE/CIS region which has enabled UNICEF to track what has been happening to children and their access to relevant services in the period since the fall of communism (their position became much worse but is now improving again, though slowly). Demographic data are essential to contextualizing any evaluation, and, over time, can offer a standardized measure of change across recognized indicators of well-being and development.

Randomized Controlled Trials and Systematic Reviews

The most rigorous methodology is generally regarded as the randomized controlled trial (RCT), where there are two randomly selected groups, and one receives the intervention and the other does not. The results between the two groups are then compared, and if the group that received the intervention does better, the intervention is seen to have an effect. The randomized controlled trial is regarded as a gold standard for investigation in medicine, but its efficacy as a method in the social sciences also depends on context – on the scope of what is being investigated and the range of methods used within the trial (White, 2013).

A cousin of RCTs is the systematic review; that, is a review of evidence on a particular topic, according to agreed protocols. The evidence reviewed is usually from randomized controlled trials but could include other sources if the protocols are carefully constructed. These reviews are now regarded as essential in the field of medicine for assessing interventions. The reviews are extremely thorough in the way in which they compare the range of methods used, the nature of the intervention and the outcomes. An overall body, the Campbell collaboration, acts as a conduit and an additional scrutiny for published reviews (Gough et al., 2012). The use of RCTs and systematic reviews is often referred to as 'evidence-based policy'.

Randomized controlled trials and systematic reviews weight the evidence, but do not necessarily exclude qualitative evidence (White, 2013). The organization 3ie has made a particular point of carrying out systematic reviews in the field of early childhood interventions in developing countries, but points out, in a recent systematic review, that often

randomized controlled trials do not compare like with like. Leroy et al. (2011) compared day-care interventions in low-income countries and concluded that the interventions were of differing kinds and targeted at different groups, so much so that it was impossible to draw concrete conclusions. I return to this point below in discussing the interventions drawn on by Heckman as a basis for economic arguments for early childhood.

Participatory Methods

Asking the recipients of an intervention what they think the problems are, and how they might be solved, is now an accepted procedure in development interventions. Pioneered in the field of agriculture by Chambers (1997, 2012), participatory methods attempt to provide alternative situational analysis to those of experts and consultants, who Chambers provocatively describes as 'developmental tourists'. These methods are now widely used, for example in the second volume of the World Bank Study of Poverty, *Voices of the Poor* (Narayan and Chambers, 2000). They have been extensively used in the DfID Young Lives project, a longitudinal study of 12,000 children in four countries – Vietnam, Peru, Ethiopia and the Andhra Pradesh region of India.

It is only relatively recently that such methods have been incorporated alongside demographic information and RCTs, and the emphasis on research on development interventions has become one of methodological heterogeneity. As discussed below, participatory methods have been remarkably absent from much of the literature cited as evidence for early childhood interventions.

Theory of Change and Other Evaluations

Typically, evaluations of early childhood interventions by aid agencies, especially smaller agencies, have been post hoc. A consultant (often already known to the agency) is hired to review the project and give an opinion of its efficacy. This has advantages in terms of local connections and local knowledge, but is highly problematic (Ebrahim and Penn, 2012). More recently, it has been accepted that evaluation needs to be planned from the beginning as part of an intervention, and information needs to be systematically collected as the project proceeds. One current approach, adopted, for example, by UNICEF, is known as the *Theory of Change*. This sets out the objectives of the intervention, attempts to define the processes which are taking place to reach the objectives and identifies the ways in which outcomes can be measured. A recent review of the *Theory of Change* commissioned by DfID (Vogel, 2012) suggests that it is a somewhat open-ended approach and has been used as a 'catch-all' for a variety of methods. However, its main virtue is in accepting a planned and more rigorous approach to the evaluation of aid interventions.

Anthropology

Anthropology is the antithesis of RCTs. It is about near total immersion in a local context for a substantial period of time in order to try to understand and record that context. In the phrase of the famous anthropologist Clifford Geertz, it is about 'thick description' (1973). Critics, some from within the discipline (such as Clifford and Marcus, 1986), argue that it is impossible to supress one's own feelings and culture in order to observe that of others, and in any case the traffic is usually one way, with those who are educated in rich nations speculating about the poor of other countries, rather than vice versa. But anthropology is still regarded as an important means of understanding situations and ways of thinking that are very unfamiliar. There are some important studies of children carried out within this situation, for example the work of LeVine (2003; LeVine and New, 2008), who worked in East Africa, Gottlieb (2004) in West Africa, and Punch (2007) in

South America. In these studies, the relationships of children and adults in family and village contexts illustrate, by contrast, the idiosyncratic and particular expectations of Euro-American culture, as much as the culture of those being investigated (Hobart, 1993).

Ethics

This variety of methodologies, and the particular tensions of researchers working among poor households in low-income countries, give rise to a range of ethical issues, not least that of reciprocity – what participants might expect from taking part. These have been discussed at some length by Morrow (2013). Medical research protocols emphasize informed consent, confidentiality and avoidance of harm, but in local contexts there may be unforeseen or changing circumstances not covered by the original ethical agreement. Allowing for local context and changing circumstances in this way is sometimes called *situated ethics*, which is a view of ethics as an ongoing practice. Working with young children and their parents raises many questions about consent, about how understandings are shared and translated, about how feedback is given and about who is responsible for the child and how much their views may differ from those of the child. Morrow suggests that the over-riding principles should be justice, respect and avoidance of harm, but the details of these need to be worked out at a local level, and the many conflictual situations that are likely to arise should be carefully considered and recorded within the project.

Research Funding

Research is governed by the available funding, and research projects which span several countries are usually expensive. Most large research grants from bilateral and other international agencies are awarded by tender, on the model of business contracts. The EU, for example, solicits tenders for all its research projects, in Europe as well as in low- and middle-income countries. The Department for International Development in the UK (DfID) similarly solicits competitive tenders, as do UNICEF and many other agencies. It is a rigid process; the contractual requirements are very precisely set out and must be followed to the letter, and a breach of a small unnoticed clause may cause the project to be rejected, however good it is in principle or however much the situation in the field changes. There are always strict confidentiality clauses, to protect competitors, and the process can never be scrutinized by outsiders. Tendering has led to a preponderance of bids from commercial companies and consultancy firms, who have specialized in bidding for large grants and whose familiarity with the process gives them an advantage. As someone who has acted both as a contract researcher under such conditions and as an assessor for international education bids, I have found the tendering process most problematic.

An additional complication is the status of in-country researchers. Competitive tenders are usually costed on the basis of international rates for senior researchers, but local country rates for basic researchers may be very meagre in countries where the research is being carried out. Moreover, the research project is invariably devised, submitted and controlled from rich countries, with very little contribution from those on the ground, who may be offered token 'training' as compensation. There is an in-built colonial approach to the question of knowledge gathering and knowledge transfer (Silova and Steiner-Khamsi, 2008), which mirrors the wider development aid field, discussed below.

PROBLEMS OF DEVELOPMENT AID

There has been a longstanding and often extremely critical commentary on the role of rich (high-income) countries in relation to poor (low-income) countries. It is a critique of the process of 'development' itself. Its most severe critics suggest that development aid is now little more than a new form of colonialism, continuing to excuse and underwrite the worst kinds of extractive capitalism. The eminent Harvard political scientist and agrarian specialist, James C. Scott (2013) has argued, for example, that the history of 'development' can be compressed into a history of violence, conflict and resistance in response to 'the appetite of states for trade goods, slaves and precious ores' and to 'the appetite of capitalism'. These wide-ranging critiques, based on serious and original scholarship, point to the: crippling legacy of colonialism; exploitation and theft of mineral resources; appropriation of land; imposition of alien and inappropriate structures of government based on promotion of complaisant male elites; indentured labour and slavery (Chambers, 1997, 2012; Chang, 2008; George, 1990; Gibson et al., 2005; Mamdani, 1996, 2012; Pogge, 2009; Rahnema, 1997; Rist, 1997; Rodney, 1972; Sachs, 1992; Sklair, 1994; Wolf, 1997). These historical critiques, of which only a tiny selection is given here, demonstrate how the past has emphatically shaped the present, and raise questions of justice and restitution as part of any attempt to address present inequalities.

Other scholars, whose work overlaps with this historical critique, have commented on the belittling of non-European cultures in the social and scientific literature. They argue that the languages and cultural innovation of non-European cultures have been systematically devalued, ignored or obliterated and the process of development has been one of increasing homogeneity towards the adoption of Euro-American norms (Achebe, 2011; Connell, 2007; Hobart, 1993; Nederveen Pieterse and Parekh, 1995; Quarles van Ufford and Giri, 2003; Said, 2003; Sen, 2005; Taussig, 2003). This failure to understand the extent and porousness of cultural diversity has also been discussed in regard to early childhood (Penn, 2012).

At its most radical and profound, the critique of development is devastating and requires the world to change. But even if it were possible to disregard this depth of criticism, there is still a very substantial case made by highly respected economists – some of them Nobel prize winners and/or ex-World Bank economists – for challenging the current economic status quo. The economic debate centres on inequality and the huge disparities in wealth both between low-income and high-income countries, and between rich and poor households within countries. It is in part a debate about the relentlessness of capitalist consumption of global resources and the state's role in guaranteeing such consumption, made manifest in issues such as environmental pollution – the degradation of extractive industries, such as oil, diamonds and precious metals, or in the monoculture of large-scale agriculture. The resulting degree of inequality embitters and distorts relationships and ultimately rebounds on the rich – in terms of unrest, poor health, corruption, crime and warfare (Collier, 2007, 2011; Kumar, 2003; Milanovic, 2010; Reinert, 2008; Sen, 2010; Stiglitz, 2012; Stiglitz and Kaldor, 2013). Small-scale aid efforts – like early childhood interventions – can do very little to influence wider political and economic realities, but at least in being aware of them, they will not make disproportionate claims for intervention, and interventions as a result may be more effective (Edwards, 2011; Jones et al., 2013).

AMBITIONS FOR EARLY CHILDHOOD DEVELOPMENT

Much of the debate about early childhood intervention implicitly or explicitly centres on views about the nature of the young child and the mother's role in relation to her children. The rationales for studying – and intervening – in early childhood have shifted considerably over time. In the aftermath of two world wars, for instance, a key focus of much research was aggression and the conditions under which it was produced in young children. Piaget's work was an explicit attempt to investigate the growth of rationality and logic in young children, to counteract the irrational aggressiveness of wartime (Piaget, 1934). Subsequently, much of the research focus shifted to attachment theory and the consequences of women leaving their children in day care in order to work (Penn, 2009).

The current trope for investigating early childhood development is productivity, a direct reflection of the concerns of a neo-liberal economy that individuals should stand on their own feet and not be dependent on the state, since vulnerability costs taxpayers money. Making sure children, especially poor children, adopt positive habits when they are little, will save on paying out money later for correction, on dealing with school failure, criminality and a general lack of success. Much recent research, in high-income countries, but especially in low-income countries, has been economic research focused on testing the idea that early childhood holds the key to productivity (and curing poverty) in later life. Those children, especially poor children, who have received some kind of external intervention in their early life, will achieve more – and be more productive and less problematic adults than they would have been without the intervention.

To paraphrase the leading theorist in the field, James Heckman, a Nobel prize-winning economist and his colleagues, education perseverance and motivation are major factors determining productivity both in the workforce and beyond it. Heckman's analysis is located within a neo-liberal and maternalistic framework, in which successful competition in the labour market is a key issue. By this reckoning, the poor are principally responsible for their own shortcomings and can be taught to perform better. The family is the major producer of these skills which are indispensable for students and workers. Unfortunately, many families have failed to perform this task well in recent years. This retards the growth of the quality of the workforce. Dysfunctional families are also a major determinant of child participation in crime and other costly pathological behaviour. On productivity grounds alone, it appears to make sound sense to invest in young children from disadvantaged environments. An accumulating body of evidence suggests that early childhood interventions are more effective than remedies that attempt to compensate for early neglect later in life (Heckman and Masterov, 2005).

It has become a commonplace in the early childhood literature that early childhood interventions are cost-effective. The figure frequently cited is $7 spent for every $1 saved. Heckman, in his original formulations about cost-effectiveness, relied mainly on three studies which have measured cost benefits over a period of longer than 10 years: the Perry High Scope, which was begun in the 1960s; the Abecedarian which was begun in the 1970s; and the Chicago Child–Parent Centres, begun in the 1980s. They all show some long-term benefits for children, but they are different programmes run for different age groups, for different amounts of time, and have different outcomes. They were all intensive and expensive programmes (Baker, 2011). The studies were carried out with African American and Hispanic children at a time when and in places where racism was pervasive, yet there is little or no acknowledgement that racism might have shaped both the research questions and the results.

The figure quoted on the basis of these *three* studies is that investing $1 in early childhood brings a return of $7 when the children grow up, *mainly* because they are less likely to commit crimes or other misdemeanours. However, crime rates among the African American population in the USA, and levels of victim compensation, are far higher than anywhere else in the developed world, and these savings on crime account for 40–60 per cent of the $7 saved. This figure varies between the three studies, but in any case it is a ball-park figure which does not represent the range of variation within and between the three studies or the *highly specific* circumstances in which the studies were carried out.

There is no explanation of causality, and the voices of the poor themselves are nowhere to be heard. The High Scope subjects, for example, have purportedly been followed up for 40 years, but there is not one study where their comments on participation (or on non-participation for group members who did not receive the intervention) have been explored (Penn et al., 2006).

As Baker (2011) has commented, it is extremely difficult to extrapolate from these studies any clear idea of what programmes work best, or what should be replicated, or how programmes might be 'scaled up' given the original costs of the interventions. Yet the original proposition that savings in national budgets could be made by investing in targeted programmes for disadvantaged children in very poor districts of the USA has been taken to hold good for any country, in any circumstances and with whatever programme has been introduced.

These economic arguments, allied with the neuroscientific arguments discussed below, have been taken as irrefutable evidence for the advantages of investing in early childhood. But at best they are very general arguments for targeting poor and disadvantaged children and their families. The argument put forward here is that this research is located within a long tradition of animosity towards welfare support for poor and disadvantaged children and their families, especially towards those who are not white, and in the resistance towards any kind of equality agenda (Penn and Lloyd, 2007; Penn et al., 2006). These economic arguments for investing in young children are unfortunately not arguments for social inclusion, for redressing inequality, for addressing gender disparities or for understanding cultural diversity.

EARLY CHILDHOOD INTERVENTIONS AND RESEARCH IN LOW- AND MIDDLE-INCOME COUNTRIES

This rationale of economic productivity for early childhood intervention now dominates discussions about early childhood education and care interventions in poor countries. Investment in the early years brings a good rate of return; it will improve the life chances of very poor children and save governments money in the long term. The mechanisms by which this transformation happens – from poor and problematic child to relatively successful adult – are unclear but the argument relies heavily on the analogy of nutrition. Children's physical growth and development depend on nutritious intake; malnourished children tend to be badly stunted and underweight. By analogy, if children's brains are stimulated through early childhood programmes, their neuronal development will lead to and enhance subsequent learning; but without this stimulation their neural circuits will fail to develop, or in extreme cases atrophy (Allen, 2011).

Heckman's arguments, then, have been given extra substance and extra reach in poor and low-income countries, by extrapolating from the neurosciences. It is frequently posited that 'science has proved' that neuronal growth is greatest in the first few years of life and that this growth is greatly enhanced by good nutrition and adult stimulation of young infants. Therefore, any early childhood intervention programme which offers nutritional supplements and teaches mothers or caregivers to stimulate their infants is likely to be successful in terms of later development (Engle et al., 2011; Grantham-McGregor et al., 2007; Shonkoff and Richter, 2013; Young and Mustard, 2008). This argument assumes that the scientific case for stimulation which can enhance neural growth patterns is proven beyond all doubt. This statement, in a World Bank publication, suggests how breath-taking – and ahistorical – the claim is: 'For especially poor countries, investing in ECD can overcome the major deficits caused by poverty, disease and social disruption' (Young and Mustard, 2008: 88).

Other commentators are more cautious. Although not challenging the basic hypothesis that young children's brains are changed by early childhood interventions, and that

they will become more productive citizens as a result, a recent review, published in the Rebello Britto volume, says: 'Some systematic evidence suggests that ECD programmes in developing countries may have substantial positive effects in some contexts … but we are struck by how much we do not know as compared with what we do know' (Behrman and Urzia, 2013: 135).

The basis of the argument, that neuroscience is the missing link and can explain why investment in the early years is apparently so important, is not necessarily held within the field of neuroscience itself. There are many scholars, including some eminent neuroscientists and philosophers, who have queried these assumptions about the reach of neuroscience (Bennett and Hacker, 2003; Karmiloff and Karmiloff-Smith, 2001; Rose, 2005; Tallis, 2014). Tallis points to the very great difficulties of tracking and measuring cellular activities, and observes that neuronal studies have low levels of statistical certainty. Bruer (1999), in his book *The Myth of the First Three Years*, explores the limitations of the neuroscientific evidence. The evidence relies on three main assumptions:

- brain connectivity – the development of synaptic connections – equals greater learning
- there are critical periods, after which it becomes harder to establish such synaptic connections
- an enriched environment can promote faster and denser neural connections.

Bruer systematically explored the evidence underlying these assumptions and concluded that the existing neuroscientific evidence was too general, too unspecific and too weak to substantiate such assumptions (1999, 2011). He tracked and analysed commentaries in the national press and in professional journals and concluded that the claims of neuroscience were blown out of all proportion by advocates keen to argue for better early childhood provision in the USA, where welfare support for early education and childcare has generally been regarded as a low – or worse, unacceptable – priority. Other eminent developmental psychologists, such as Kagan (1998) and Zigler et al. (2009), have made similar comments.

Despite the cautions and sceptical views of many neuroscientists themselves about the limitations of what they know, despite the near impossibility of providing an explanatory framework which relates the incredibly complex physiological and chemical processes of the brain to behaviour and consciousness, and despite the well-documented difficulties in accurately measuring neuronal activity, the early years community has latched on to 'brain research'. Such research seems to prove that early childhood is a valuable time and this adds weight to the argument that investment in early childhood is a social, economic and even moral necessity. There is virtually no direct evidence about the relationship between behaviour and brain development. The highly specific and limited work which does exist has not been carried out in low-income countries.

Yet these arguments, first developed in the USA in relation to poor black and Hispanic children, have now been extrapolated from their original context and are taken to apply generally to children growing up in poor nations as well as to children growing up in poor neighbourhoods in the USA or the UK. Despite its current popularity and contemporary findings, the view that poor children's brains are atrophying from a lack of stimulation has a long history, rooted in racial stereotyping, which predates neuroscientific research:

> The Black child has no toys. He does not find around him any occasion to rouse his intellect ... the early childhood of the Black always take place in an environment intellectually *inferior* to *any imaginable in Europe* ... The Black child remains inactive for long hours. He thus undergoes a terrifying head shrinking from which it is virtually impossible to recover. The neural centres of his cortex which should normally be used for exercise, do not receive the necessary stimuli for their development. (Maistriaux, 1955, cited in Erny, 1981: 88)

Much of the discussion about 'scientific understandings' of early childhood is simplistic and is itself framed within other, unacknowledged assumptions and histories.

WHAT KIND OF ECD INTERVENTION?

The arguments for ECD interventions in poor and low-income countries are based on the assumption that all interventions make a difference, and the younger the child, the better. One implication of the 'scientific' understanding of childhood which informs interventions is that there is also a 'scientific' repertoire of activities which constitute a remedy. In the studies on which Heckman's analysis principally relies, the Perry High Scope, the Abecedarian and the Chicago, the interventions have in common that they are very expensive, but they differ in all other respects – in the age groups of those who received the intervention, the duration of the intervention, the type of intervention and the outcomes measured (Penn et al., 2006). Most of the recent interventions carried out in low- and middle-income countries target children much younger than those in the studies considered by Heckman, and are very much cheaper to implement, yet identical claims are made for their economic efficacy.

Most studies carried out in high-income countries suggest that 'quality' matters (MacCartney, 2004). Quality is usually described in terms of structural and process variables. These include good child–staff ratios, well-trained staff, age-appropriate curricula and warm interactions. The precise nature of the variables, especially the notion of 'age-related curricula', is also open to discussion (Nsamenang, 2008). But these kinds of 'high quality' interventions rarely exist in low-income countries, especially since, by default, most provision is in the for-profit sector (Woodhead and Streuli, 2013). Anglo-European standards may be found in high-end, expensive centre-based care in urban settings in most low-income countries, for the elite and expatriates who can afford the fees, but access to quality childcare is contingent on the ability to pay and for the poor such provision is rarely available (Penn, 2011; Penn and Maynard, 2010; Woodhead and Streuli, 2013). Rao (2010) has explored whether quality provision can be provided in resource-poor settings.

Early childhood interventions for young children, especially for those under 3, tend to be very cheap, in many cases relying entirely on voluntary contributions of time from women who apparently have no other occupation. Much of the work described in the Rebello Britto handbook (2013a), and in the *Lancet* series, describes nutritional interventions targeted at the very poor, with additional home-visiting programmes, staffed by volunteers, to teach mothers how better to feed their children and 'stimulate' their cognition.

As well as the instrumental view of children being acted upon in order to manipulate their development, a striking aspect of this research is the absolute lack of voice of those mothers/families who are being targeted. It is possible to argue that such studies are discriminatory against women, in that these economist approaches do not acknowledge the contribution of women to the economy through unpaid caring work, or indeed the burdens poor women face (Bakker and Silvey, 2008; Razavi, 2011a, 2011b).

This ignorance, in relation to women's caring responsibilities and how they impact on their lives and those of their children, affects poor women more than it does wealthier professional women. Women with reasonable incomes can rely on servants and other forms of domestic help. Women domestics, by contrast, often tend to be internal or external migrants – who may even find themselves neglecting or abandoning their own children in order to earn a living by looking after other women's children (Heymann, 2003, 2006; Hochschild and Ehrenreich, 2003; Razavi, 2011a, 2011b).

To summarize, the main rationale given for interventions in the field of early childhood development is that the long-term productivity of the children on whom the intervention is focused will be transformed. At its most crude, the explanation for this supposed transformation is that very young children's brains will be altered by the intervention. But the interventions themselves are not coherent or consistent; they are almost always cheap or 'cost-effective' and they rely heavily on volunteers to change mothers' behaviour. They do not match the notions of 'high quality' that are the cornerstone of research formulations in rich countries. The research methods used to monitor the interventions, often randomized controlled trials led by economists, are frequently contextless and narrow and produced with little or no reference to the wider political, economic, historical and anthropological contexts of the countries and communities for whom they are prescribed (Burman, 2008; Hulme, 2010; Jones and Vilar, 2008; LeVine, 2003; Minjuin and Nandy, 2012; O'Riordan et al., 2013; Penn, 2005, 2011; Twum Danso-Imoh and Ames, 2012).

CONCLUSION

Detailed studies of inequality within countries, and of chronic childhood poverty in low- and middle-income countries, suggest that understanding, charting and ameliorating childhood poverty and improving childhood well-being is a highly complex process. The history of development aid also serves as a warning about highly problematic, post-colonial relationships. A sole focus on early childhood, and extravagant claims for the efficacy of interventions, serve to distract from these complexities.

Research also suggests that the poor, those who are the subjects of interventions, have useful comments to make about the processes in which they are involved. Scott (1985, 2012) goes further and argues that understanding the strategies and subterfuges that very poor people use to resist the demands that are made upon them, by those who are wealthier or more powerful, is essential to any attempt at bringing about change. This is particularly important because so much of the research on ECD makes assumptions about mothers' availability and their circumstances, their willingness to take part in projects and their understanding of what might be involved, even though mothers are perceived to be the main agents for bringing about change.

Recent work on methodology and ethics – the randomized controlled trials and systematic reviews which are the backbone of evidence-based policy – has led to a more rigorous approach to evaluation. The post-hoc in-house evaluations by consultants, which were a main source of information about the efficacy of aid projects, are gradually being replaced by more robust approaches. But RCTs and systematic reviews are as good as the questions they set out to investigate, and if the research questions are themselves narrowly framed, the evidence produced, however robust, will be similarly narrow.

It is possible as well as productive to combine methodologies and incorporate a variety of approaches within an evidence-based framework. The DfID Young Lives project, which followed up 12,000 children in four countries over 15 years, from the age of 5 into adulthood, using household data, personal accounts from children and their parents, and longitudinal mapping, is an exemplar in this respect. It has produced very rich data across a plethora of circumstances, but on a scale which makes extrapolation of data robust beyond casual generalization.

This chapter then suggests that much of the recent work on early childhood interventions in low- and middle-income countries is based on premises which, although popular and widely held, tend to be North American in orientation and relatively limited in reach. Alternative approaches do not easily gain traction. Contextual understanding which takes into account political, historical, economic and cultural circumstances; a greater and more careful focus on the household data; a fuller understanding of the status, values, opinions and needs of mothers whose children are subject to interventions – all of these

are part of the process. The 'global reach' of early child development research is unfortunately, as yet, far from being truly global.

FURTHER READING

Department for International Development (DfID) (2001–) Young Lives: An International Study of Childhood Poverty – various papers (http://www.younglives.org.uk/publications).

Razavi, S. (2014) Making Unpaid Care Work Count in the Post-2015 Framework. Video of presentation given at Rutgers University, 12 March (www.youtube.com/watch?v=niLU3e_-TvA).

Rebello Britto, P., Engle, P. and Harkness, C. (eds) (2013) Handbook of Early Childhood Development Research and its Impact on Global Policy. Oxford: Oxford University Press.

QUESTIONS FOR REFLECTION

1 How pervasive is inequality?
2 What kind of role do wealthy philanthropic organizations such as the Bill and Melissa Gates Foundation or international non-governmental organizations like UNICEF or UNESCO or financial institutions like the World Bank, have in developing and sustaining early childhood interventions?
3 Is there a role for the market in developing early childhood services?

REFERENCES

Achebe, C. (2011) The Education of a British Protected Child. London: Penguin.

Alborz, A., Al-Hashemy, J., Al-Obaidi, K., Brooker, E., Miles, S., Penn, H., and Slee, R. (2011) A Study of Mainstream Education Opportunities for Disabled Children and Youth and Early Childhood Development in Iraq. Final report, 31 March. London: CARA.

Allen, G. (2011) Early Intervention: The Next Steps. London: The Cabinet Office.

Atkinson, A. and Marlier, E. (eds) (2012) *Income and Living Conditions in Europe*. Brussels: Eurostat/EU Commission.

Baker, M. (2011) 'Universal early childhood interventions: what is the evidence base?', *Canadian Journal of Economics*, 44(4): 1069–1105.

Bakker, I. and Silvey, R. (2008) *Beyond States and Markets: The Challenges of Social Reproduction*. London: Routledge.

Behrman, J. and Urzia, S. (2013) 'Economic perspectives on some important dimensions of early childhood development in developing countries', in P. Rebello Britto, P. Engle and C. Harkness (eds) *Handbook of Early Childhood Development Research and its Impact on Global Policy*. Oxford: Oxford University Press. pp. 123–141.

Bennett, M. and Hacker, P. (2003) *The Philosophical Foundations of Neuroscience*. Oxford: Blackwell.

Boyden, J. and Bourdillon, M. (eds) (2012) *Childhood Poverty: Multidisciplinary Approaches*. London: Palgrave Macmillan.

Bruer, J. (1999) *The Myth of the First Three Years*. New York: The Free Press.

Bruer, J. (2011) Revisiting the Myth of the First Three Years. Paper given at the University of Kent parenting conference, May (http://blogs.kent.ac.uk/parentingculturestudies/files/2011/09/Special-briefing-on-The-Myth.pdf).

Burman, E. (2008) *Developments: Child, Image, Nation*. London: Routledge.

Chambers, R. (1997) *Whose Reality Counts? Putting the First Last*. Rugby: Intermediate Technology Publications.

Chambers, R. (2012) *Provocations for Development*. Rugby: Practical Action Publishing.

Chan, M. (2013) 'Linking child survival and child development for health', *The Lancet*, 381(9877): 1514–1515.

Chang, H.-J. (2008) *Bad Samaritans: Guilty Secrets of Rich Nations and the Threat to Global Prosperity*. London: Random House.

Clifford, J. and Marcus, G. (1986) *Writing Culture: The Poetics and Politics of Ethnography*. Berkeley, CA: University of California Press.

Collier, P. (2007) *The Bottom Billion*. London: Oxford University Press.

Collier, P. (2011) *The Plundered Planet: How to Reconcile Prosperity with Nature*. London: Penguin.

Connell, R. (2007) *Southern Theory*. Cambridge: Polity Press.

Dawes, A., Bray, R. and van der Merwe, A. (eds) (2007) *Monitoring Child Well-being: A South African Rights Based Approach*. Cape Town: HSRC/SCF Sweden.

Ebrahim, H. and Penn, H. (2012) 'Undertaking research on early childhood in KwaZulu-Natal in South Africa', in A. Halai and D. Williams (eds) *Research Methodologies in the South*. Pakistan: Oxford University Press.

Edwards, M. (2011) 'Thick problems and thin solutions: how NGOs can bridge the gap', Future Calling – Think Piece, Hivos (www.hivos.net/Hivos-Knowledge-Programme/Themes/Future-Calling/Short-Reflections/Thick-Problems-and-Thin-Solutions).

Engle, P.L., Black, M.M., Behrman, J.R., Cabral de Mello, M., Gertler, P.J., Kapiriri, L., et al. (2007) 'Child development in developing countries 3: Strategies to avoid the loss of development potential in more than 200 million children in the developing world', *The Lancet*, 369: 229–242.

Engle, P.L., Fernald, L.C.H., Alderman, H., Behrman, J., O'Gara, C., Yousafzai, A., et al. (2011) 'Strategies for reducing inequalities and improving development outcomes for young children in low-income and middle-income countries', *The Lancet*, 378: 1339–1353.

Erny, P. (1981) *The Child and his Environment in Black Africa*. Translated and abridged by G.J. Wanjoh. Nairobi: Oxford University Press.

European Commission (2014) *Towards a European Quality Framework in Early Childhood Education and Care*. Director General Education and Culture, ECEC/ESL stakeholder meeting, 31 March.

European Commission/EACEA/Eurydice/Eurostat (2014) *Key Data on Early Childhood Education and Care in Europe*. Eurydice and Eurostat report. Luxembourg: Publications Office of the European Union (http://eacea.ec.europa.eu/education/eurydice/documents/key_data_series/166EN.pdf).

Garcia, M., Pence, A. and Evans, J. (2008) *Africa's Future, Africa's Challenge*. Washington, DC: The World Bank.

Geertz, C. (1973) *The Interpretation of Cultures*. London: Fontana.

George, S. (1990) *Ill Fares the Land*. London: Penguin.

Gibson, C., Andersson, K., Ostrom, E. and Shivakumar, S. (2005) *The Samaritans Dilemma: The Political Economy of Development Aid.* Oxford: Oxford University Press.

Gottlieb, A. (2004) *The Afterlife is Where We Come From: The Culture of Infancy in West Africa.* Chicago: University of Chicago Press.

Gough, D., Oliver, S. and Thomas, J. (2012) *An Introduction to Systematic Reviews.* London: SAGE.

Grantham-McGregor, S., Cheung, Y.B., Cuerto, S., Glewwe, P., Richter, L., Strupp, B. and the International Child Development Steering Group (2007) 'Child development in developing countries 1: Development potential in the first five years for children in developing countries', *The Lancet*, 369: 60–70.

Heckman, J.J. and Masterov, D.V. (2005) *The Productivity Argument for Investing in Young Children.* Available at: http://jenni.uchicago.edu/human-inequality/papers/Heckman_final_all_wp_2007-03-22c_jsb.pdf

Heymann, J. (2003) *The Role of ECCE in Ensuring Equal Opportunity.* Policy brief no. 18. Paris: UNESCO.

Heymann, J. (2006) *Forgotten Families: Ending the Growing Crisis Confronting Children and Working Parents in the Global Economy.* Oxford: Oxford University Press.

Hobart, M. (ed.) (1993) *An Anthropological Critique of Development: The Growth of Ignorance.* London: Routledge.

Hochschild, A. and Ehrenreich, B. (eds) (2003) *Global Woman: Nannies, Maids and Sex Workers in the New Economy.* New York: Metropolitan Books.

Hulme, D. (2010) *Global Poverty.* London and New York: Routledge.

Hulme, D. and Edwards, M. (eds) (1997) *NGOs, States and Donors: Too Close for Comfort?* Basingstoke: MacMillan Press/SCF.

IFS/3ie/UCL (2012) Promises for Preschoolers: Early Childhood Development and Human Capital Accumulation Conference, UCL, 25–26 June (www.ucl.ac.uk/economics/ecd).

Jones, N. and Sumner, A. (2011) *Child Poverty, Evidence and Policy.* Cambridge: Polity Press.

Jones, N. and Vilar, E. (2008) 'Situating children in international development policy: challenges involved in successful evidence-informed policy making', *Evidence and Policy*, 4(1): 31–51.

Jones, H., Jones, N., Shaxson, L. and Walker, D. (2013) *Knowledge, Policy and Power in International Development: A Practical Guide.* Bristol: Policy Press.

Kagan, J. (1998) *Three Seductive Ideas.* Cambridge, MA: Harvard University Press.

Kamerman, S.B. and Gatenio-Gabel, S. (2007) 'Early childhood education and care in the United States: an overview of the current policy picture', *International Journal of Child Care and Education Policy*, VI(1): 23–34.

Karmiloff, K. and Karmiloff-Smith, A. (2001) *Pathways to Language: From Fetus to Adolescent.* Cambridge, MA: Harvard University Press.

Kumar, A. (2003) *World Bank Literature.* Minneapolis, MN: University of Minnesota.

Leroy, J., Gadsden, P. and Guijarro, M. (2011) *The Impact of Daycare Programmes on Child Health, Nutrition and Development in Developing Countries: A Systematic Review.* London: International Initiative for Impact Evaluation (3ie).

LeVine, R. (2003) *Chidhood Socialization: Comparative Studies of Parenting, Learning and Educational Change.* Hong Kong: Comparative Education Research Centre.

LeVine, R. and New, R. (eds) (2008) *Anthropology of Child Development: A Cross Cultural Reader.* London: Blackwell.

MacCartney, K. (2004) 'Current research on childcare effects', in R.E. Tremblay, R.G. Barr and R. DeV Peters (eds) Encyclopedia on Early Child Development. Montreal: Centre of Excellence for Early Child Development.

Maggi, S., Irwin, L., Siddiqui A., Poureslami, I., Herzman E. and Herzman, C. (2005) International Perspectives on Early Child Development: Analytic and Strategic Review Paper. Geneva: WHO.

Mahon, R. (2011) 'After neo-liberalism? The OECD, the World Bank and the child', *Global Social Policy*, pp. 172–192.

Mamdani, M. (1996) *Citizen and Subject: Contemporary Africa and the Legacy of Late Colonialism.* Princeton, NJ: Princeton University Press.

Mamdani, M. (2012) *Define and Rule.* Cambridge, MA: Harvard University Press.

Michel, S. (1999) *Children's Interests/Mothers' Rights: The Shaping of America's Child Care Policy.* New Haven, CT: Yale University Press.

Michel, S. and Mahon, R. (eds) (2002) *Child Care Policy at the Crossroads: Gender and*

Welfare State Restructuring. New York: Routledge.

Milanovic, B. (2010) *The Haves and the Have Nots*. New York: Basic Books.

Milanovic, B. (2011) *Worlds Apart: Measuring International and Global Inequality*. Princeton, NJ: Princeton University Press.

Minjuin, A. and Nandy, S. (eds) (2012) *Global Child Poverty and Well-Being: Measurement, Concepts and Action*. Bristol: Policy Press.

Morrow, V. (2013) 'Practical ethics in social research with children and families in young lives: a longitudinal study of childhood poverty in Ethiopia, Andhra Pradesh (India), Peru and Vietnam', *Methodological Innovations Online*, 8(2): 21–35.

Narayan, D. and Chambers, R. (eds) (2000) *Voices of the Poor, Vol. 2: Crying Out for Change*. Oxford: Oxford University Press.

Nederveen Pieterse, J. and Parekh, B. (eds) (1995) *The Decolonization of Imagination: Culture, Knowledge and Power*. London: Zed Books.

Nsamenang, A. (2008) '(Mis)Understanding ECD in Africa: the force of local and global motives', in M. Garcia, A. Pence and J. Evans (eds) *Africa's Future, Africa's Challenge*. Washington, DC: The World Bank.

O'Riordan, J., Hogan, D. and Martin, S. (eds) (2013) *Early Childhoods in the Global South: Local and International Contexts*. Oxford: Peter Lang.

OECD (2013) *Education Indicators in Focus: How do early childhood education and care (ECEC) policies, systems and quality vary across OECD countries?* Paris: OECD (www.oecd.org/education/skills-beyond-school/EDIF11.pdf).

OECD (2014) *Family Database*. Paris: OECD, Social Policy Division, Directorate of Employment, Labour and Social Affairs (www.oecd.org/els/social/family/database).

Penn, H. (2005) *Unequal Childhoods: Young Children's Lives in Poor Countries*. London: Routledge/Falmer.

Penn, H. (2009) 'Public and private: the history of early education and care institutions in the UK', in K. Schweie and H. Willekens (eds) *Childcare and Pre-school Development in Europe*. Basingstoke: Palgrave Macmillan. pp. 105–125.

Penn, H. (2011) 'Travelling policies and global buzzwords: how international non-governmental organizations and charities spread the word about early childhood in the Global South', *Childhood*, 18(1): 94–113.

Penn, H. (2012) 'The rhetoric and realities of early childhood programmes promoted by the World Bank in Mali', in R. Ames and A. Twum Danso-Imoh (eds) *Childhoods at the Intersection of the Local and the Global*. Basingstoke: Palgrave MacMillan. pp. 75–93.

Penn, H. (2014) 'International indicators as a measure of national policies', *International Journal of Early Childhood*, 46(1): 33–46.

Penn, H. and Lloyd, E. (2007) 'Richness or rigour? A discussion of systematic reviews and evidence based policy in early childhood', *Contemporary Issues in Early Childhood*, 8(1): 3–18.

Penn, H. and Maynard, T. (2010) *Siyabonana: Building Better Childhoods in South Africa*. Edinburgh: Children in Scotland.

Penn, H., Burton, V., Lloyd, E., Mugford, M., Potter, S. and Sayeed, Z. (2006) *A Systematic Review of the Economic Impact of Long-term Centre-based Early Childhood Interventions*. Research Evidence in Education Library. London: Social Science Research Unit, Institute of Education (www.eppi.ioe.ac.uk).

Piaget, J. (1934) *Rapport du directeur: cinquieme reunion du Conseil*. Geneva: Bureau international d'education.

Pogge, T. (2009) *Politics as Usual: What Lies Behind the Pro-Poor Rhetoric?* Cambridge: Polity Press.

Punch, S. (2007) 'Generational power relations in rural Bolivia', in R. Panelli, S. Punch, E. Robson (eds) *Global Perspectives on Rural Childhood and Youth: Young Rural Lives*. Abingdon, Oxon: Taylor & Francis. pp. 151–164.

Quarles van Ufford, P. and Giri, A.K. (2003) *A Moral Critique of Development: In Search of Global Responsibilities*. London: Routledge.

Rahnema, M. (ed.) (1997) *The Post Development Reader*. London: Zed Books.

Rao, N. (2010) Quality Matters: Observations from Early Childhood Programs in Low Resource Environments in Asia. Key speech at the World Conference on Early Childhood Care and Education: Building the Wealth of Nations, Moscow, Russian Federation, 27–29 September.

Razavi, S. (2011a) 'Rethinking care in a development context', *Development and Change*, 42(4): 873–904.

Razavi, S. (2011b) *World Development Report 2012: Gender Equality and Development – An Opportunity Both Welcome and Missed*. 7 October, Geneva: UNRISD (www.unrisd.org).

Rebello Britto, P. Engle, P. and Harkness, C. (2013a) *Handbook of Early Childhood Development Research and its Impact on Global Policy*. Oxford: Oxford University Press.

Rebello Britto, P., Yoshikawa, H., Van Ravens, J., Ponguta, L.A., Soojin, S. Oh, R.D. and Seder, R.C. (2013b) *Understanding Governance of ECD and Education Systems and Services in Low Income Countries*. Innocenti Working Paper No. WP-213-07, June. Florence: UNICEF Office of Research.

Reinert, E. (2008) *How Rich Countries Got Rich and Why Poor Countries Stay Poor*. London: Constable.

Rist, G. (1997) *The History of Development: From Western Origins to Global Faith*. London: Zed Books.

Rodney, W. (1972) *How Europe Under Developed Africa*. London: Bogle L'Ouverture Publications.

Rose, S. (2005) *The 21st Century Brain: Explaining, Mending and Manipulating the Mind*. London: Jonathan Cape.

Sachs, W. (1992) *Planet Dialectic: Exploration in Environment and Development*. London: Zed Books.

Said, E. (2003) *Orientalism*. London: Penguin.

Scott, J.C. (1985) *Weapons of the Weak: Everyday Forms of Peasant Resistance*. New Haven, CT: Yale University Press.

Scott, J.C. (2012) *Decoding Subaltern Politics: Ideology, Disguise, and Resistance in Agrarian Politics*. London: Routledge.

Scott, J.C. (2013) 'Crops, towns, government', *London Review of Books*, 35(22): 13–15.

Sen, A. (2005) *The Argumentative Indian*. London: Allen Lane.

Sen, A. (2010) *The Idea of Justice*. London: Penguin.

Shonkoff, J. and Richter, L. (2013) 'The powerful reach of early child development: a science-based foundation for sound investment', in P. Rebello Britto, P. Engle and C. Harkness (eds) (2013) *Handbook of Early Childhood Development Research and its Impact on Global Policy*. Oxford: Oxford University Press. pp. 24–34.

Silova, I. and Steiner-Khamsi, G. (eds) (2008) *How NGOs React: Globalization and Education Reform in the Caucasus, Central Asia and Mongolia*. Bloomfield, CT: Kumarian Press.

Sklair, L. (ed.) (1994) *Capitalism and Development*. London: Routledge.

Stiglitz, J. (2012) *The Price of Inequality*. London: Penguin.

Stiglitz, J. and Kaldor, M. (eds) (2013) *The Quest for Security: Protection without Protectionism and the Challenge of Global Governance*. New York: Columbia University Press.

Stiglitz, J., Sen, A. and Fitoussi, J. (2009) *Report of the Commission on the Measurement of Economic Performance and Social Progress*. Paris (www.stiglitz-sen-fitoussi.fr).

Tallis, R. (2014) *Aping Mankind: Neuromania, Darwinitis and the Misrepresentation of Humanity*. Bristol: Acumen.

Taussig, M. (2003) *Law in a Lawless Land*. Chicago: University of Chicago Press.

Twum Danso-Imoh, A. and Ames, R. (2012) *Childhood at the Intersection of the Local and Global*. Basingstoke: Palgrave Macmillan. pp. 121–142.

Vogel, I. (2012) *Review of the Use of 'Theory of Change' in International Development*. Glasgow: Department of International Development (http://r4d.dfid.gov.uk/pdf/outputs/mis_spc/DFID_ToC_Review_VogelV7.pdf).

White, H. (2013) 'An introduction to the use of randomized controlled trials to evaluate development interventions', *Journal of Development Effectiveness*, 5(1): 30–49.

Wolf, E. (1997) *Europe and the People without History*. Berkeley, CA: University of California Press.

Woodhead, M. and Streuli, N. (2013) 'Early education for all: is there a role for the private sector?', in P. Rebello Britto, P. Engle and C. Harkness (eds) *Handbook of Early Childhood Development Research and its Impact on Global Policy*. Oxford: Oxford University Press.

Young, M.E. and Mustard, F. (2008) 'Brain development and ECD: a case for investment', in M. Garcia, A. Pence and J. Evans (eds) *Africa's Future, Africa's Challenge*. Washington, DC: The World Bank. pp. 71–92.

Zigler, E., Marsland, K.W. and Lord, H. (2009) *The Tragedy of Child Care in America*. New Haven, CT: Yale University Press.

29

Researching Technologies in Children's Worlds and Futures

Jackie Marsh

INTRODUCTION

Research on young children's engagement with digital technologies has been a growing area of study over the past decade, as researchers and early childhood educators have become increasingly aware of the significance of changing technologies for children's lives and learning. This chapter reflects on the theoretical and methodological approaches utilized across a range of studies and draws out some of the key findings from this research. It takes an international perspective, recognizing the complexities inherent in the interplay between the Global North and the Global South. The chapter acknowledges the interdisciplinary nature of studies in this field and considers theoretical frameworks emerging from psychology, sociology, linguistics and cultural studies, amongst other disciplines. It is important to note that this is not a comprehensive review of the research undertaken in this area. There is no intention to provide a complete record of relevant studies; rather, the aim is to draw out some of the key findings identified to date and to indicate the direction of travel for research in this area in order to signal the research questions that will require focusing upon in the years ahead if we are to gain a fuller understanding of the implications of technological changes in children's lives.

In the first section of the chapter, research that has examined children's use of technologies in homes and community spaces is reviewed. This research has explored access and use, and has also examined parental involvement in children's use of technologies. It is argued that this research has offered a significant contribution to the development of an understanding of the ubiquitous nature of technology in contemporary children's lives. The challenge for future work in this area, it is proposed, lies in broadening the methodologies and methods utilized to understand in greater depth children's motivations for the use of particular technologies and in tracing the changes in children's use of technologies over time and space.

The chapter moves on to consider research that has focused on the use of technologies in early childhood settings. The concepts of *assimilation* and *accommodation* in the use of technologies in classrooms are examined (Reinking et al., 2000) and studies that have offered insights into how technologies can be used in a transformational manner in early childhood classrooms, in order that children can become early apprentices in the 'participatory culture' (Jenkins et al., 2006) of the new media age, are considered in some detail.

The final section of the chapter reflects on recent technological developments that may well prove to have a significant impact on the worlds of young children across the globe in the decades ahead. It is argued that early childhood researchers will need to develop an understanding of the nature of these changes and their implications for the lives of children and their families in a global context and that urgent attention should be paid to the way in which more equitable practice can be developed. To begin with, however, a review of research on children's engagement with technologies in homes and community settings is undertaken.

RESEARCHING TECHNOLOGIES IN CHILDREN'S HOMES AND COMMUNITIES

There have been a large number of studies in this area that have provided evidence of the way in which technologies are embedded in the everyday lives of young children. These studies can be grouped into two distinct categories. First, there is a body of work that has utilized quantitative methodologies to provide large-scale data on children's access to and use of technologies; some of these have included a mixed-method approach in order to pursue particular aspects of technological use in greater depth. Second, a number of studies have consisted of case studies of specific families and/or children, in which qualitative methods have informed understanding

of the use of technologies in everyday lives. The majority of studies across both categories have been undertaken in the Global North and the review therefore focuses on this geographical region, whilst recognizing that there is an urgent need to undertake further research in this area in the Global South.

Large-scale studies in the field have identified that children are engaged in the use of a wide range of technologies from birth. The first large-scale studies of this age group emerged in the first years of the twenty-first century. Rideout, Vandewater and Wartella (2003) detailed the findings from a telephone survey of 1,065 families in the USA and England. Marsh et al. (2005) analyzed the responses of 1,852 parents who reported on their 0–6-year-olds' media use. These studies identified that young children were engaged in the use of a range of technologies including TV, computers and laptops, electronic toys, radios and music players, console games and mobile telephones, and developed a range of skills and knowledge in this use. Usage differed in relation to social class, age and gender across different forms of media. Between then and 2012, large-scale surveys of the use of technologies of children under 8 years were rarely undertaken outside of the USA, but over the past two years, that situation has changed, perhaps due to an increasing recognition of the extent to which technology is now permeating daily life.

Recent quantitative studies continue to demonstrate the way in which children have access to and use the technologies identified above, in addition to more recently developed technological artefacts, such as tablets and smartphones. In relation to tablets, Ofcom's (2014) survey of children and parents' use of media in the UK found that 62% of 5–15-year-olds use a tablet computer in the home, whilst 38% of 3- and 4-year-olds use one. In addition, many parents report that they feel tablets are beneficial for their children to use. Neumann (2014) surveyed 109 parents of children aged 3–5 years in Australia in order to determine how touch-screen technology impacted upon emergent literacy. She found that there was a positive relationship between access to tablets and higher letter sound and name writing skills, although this may be related to associated economic status. Neumann found that 69% of parents stated that the tablets were easy for young children to operate and 70% felt that they were beneficial for young children's literacy learning. There are concerns, however, about unequal access to such technologies. Rideout (2013), in a report for Common Sense Media on a national study of 0–8-year-olds' media use in the USA, points to the 'app gap' that may lead to inequity in access to tablets. It was found that whilst only 20% of children living in lower-income families have access to a tablet device at home, 63% of higher-income children have.

Tablet and smartphone use is growing rapidly among this age group. The Common Sense Media survey found a five-fold increase in ownership of tablet devices such as iPads in families with children under 8 from 2011 to 2013, whilst ownership of 'smart' mobile devices, which includes mobile phones, jumped from 52% of families in 2011 to 75% of families in 2013 (Rideout, 2013). Similarly, Ofcom (2014) reported that tablet use amongst 5–15-year-olds in the UK had increased by an additional 20% from 2013 to 2014, having tripled in use between 2012 to 2013. This points to the relative ease with which children can use tablets, and there is a growing market for apps for the under-8s. This widespread adoption of tablets is likely to continue to increase, with implications for future research required in this area, given the paucity of current studies that examine children's use of tablets in the home.

A similar trajectory can be seen in the numbers of children under 8 who now have access to the Internet. In the UK, 29% of 3- and 4-year-olds and 62% of 5–7s use the Internet at home. In Europe, Holloway, Green and Livingstone (2013) report that in Germany, 21% of 6–7-year-olds are online, in comparison to 64% of Finnish 7-year-olds;

and 70% of pre-schoolers in Belgium and Sweden and 78% of children of this age group in the Netherlands use the Internet (Holloway et al., 2013), whilst in the USA, 69% of parents of under-8s report having Internet access (Rideout, 2013). In Australia, 86% of 5–8-year-olds have access to the Internet at home and 22% of that access is via a mobile phone (Australian Bureau of Statistics, 2012). Figures for this age group's Internet access in many countries outside of Australia, Europe and the USA are difficult to locate, although Jie (2012) reports that 66% of 3–5-year-olds in Korea had Internet access in 2011. UNESCO (2012: 20) states that data for children under 5 is difficult to locate outside of Korea and the USA, and its study of child Internet safety more generally confirms that children and young people's access to the Internet in the Global South is more limited than in the Global North.

These quantitative studies have primarily relied on parental reporting of children's use of technologies. This is, obviously, necessary, given the age of the children involved and the focus of the surveys on use and access, but these studies need to be considered alongside more detailed qualitative studies of children's engagement with technologies in the home. A few studies have employed mixed methods, including Marsh et al. (2005) and Plowman, McPake and Stephen (2008), but the majority of studies of this age group have focused on qualitative case studies. This has enabled a rich picture to be developed of the way in which children engage in the use of digital technologies in home and community contexts. A range of theoretical frameworks, which are reviewed below, has informed the studies of this use.

The theoretical frameworks that have underpinned the study of young children's engagement with technologies draw primarily from the disciplines of psychology, linguistics, sociology and cultural studies. In terms of theoretical frameworks emerging from the discipline of psychology, the work of Bronfenbenner has been significant. For example, Marsh (2013a) reports on children's digital practices by drawing on Bronfenbrenner's (1979) concepts of the nested structures of the microsystem (the child's immediate surroundings), the mesosystem (which links two different microsystems together), the exosystem (contexts external to the child but which impact on her/his life) and the macrosystem (the social and cultural context). Ecological theories relating to engagement with technology indicate that attention needs to be paid to the interrelation of a range of factors shaping individuals' engagement with technology. Nardi and O'Day (1999: 49), for example, suggest that an ecology is 'a system of people, practices, values, and technologies in a particular local environment'. Interaction with technology is never context-free and the relationships between social agents, tools, technological practices and local contexts are complex. Table 29.1 provides an example of how children's uses of technology might be mapped across Bronfenbrenner's systems.

Wong (2013) conducted an ecological inquiry that was informed by complexity theory. Complexity theory informs the study of complex adaptive systems and attempts to explain how order emerges from apparently chaotic systems such as ecologies and markets. Drawing on participant observation of children's use of media and technologies in the home in Canada, Wong suggested that children can be competent users of a range of technologies, including iPads and laptops, and that they are able to develop a range of operational skills whilst using these objects, findings that correlate with data from the large-scale studies identified previously. Similarly, Plowman and colleagues (2011) used an ecocultural approach (Tudge, 2008) to examine children's home use of technology in 54 families in Scotland. Researchers on the project participated in tours of homes conducted by children and other methods used included mobile phone diaries, videos recorded by families and interviews, which were all used to develop an ecological picture of children in naturalistic settings in their homes. Plowman et al. (2011) suggest that this approach enabled them to document how children's uses of technology are regulated by parents in terms of the time children are allowed to engage with it (e.g., watch television or use a computer), the spaces parents make available for this use and the resources they provide for their children.

This ecological model emphasizes the way in which children are embedded in digital literacy practices across a range of domains from their first entry into the world. Just as

Table 29.1   Bronfenbrenner's ecological framework as a tool for the analysis of children's use of technologies

Microsystem	Mesosystem	Exosystem	Macrosystem
Children's use of technologies in the home, e.g. • Televisions/ DVDs • Computers/ laptops • Tablets • Smartphones • Handheld computers • Console games • Musical hardware, e.g. CD players/ radios/karaoke machines • Electronic games • Domestic electronic devices, e.g. microwave, washing machine	Community spaces that parents visit with the child, in which children may engage in the use of technologies, such as parent/toddler groups, community 'self-help' groups or social action groups	Parents' employment outside of the home, which may impact upon parental confidence with technologies and thus shape parent/child interactions	Societal attitudes to technology, which may impact upon parental understandings, e.g. 'moral panics' which appear in the media with regard to young children and technology

the literature on *emergent literacy* in the mid-1980s demonstrated that young children are introduced to literacy in naturalistic ways in everyday family life, through activities such as writing shopping lists or sending postcards to family members (Teale and Sulzby, 1986), so recent ecological studies point to the way in which children now engage in what might be characterized as *emergent digital literacy* practices (Marsh et al., 2015), as they observe family members shopping on eBay or writing text messages to others.

It is worth noting that the use of an ecological framework for the analysis of children and young people's engagement with technologies has been subject to critique in recent years. Carrington (2013) argues that an ecological framework suggests balance and coherence, whereas use of technology is much more eclectic, fast-moving and multi-layered. She proposes, drawing on Deleuze and Guattari (1987: 4), the use of the term 'assemblages' to account for the poly-centricity and multi-layeredness of media supersystems:

> While an ecological framing looks to find a contributory role for all components, an assemblage has room for tension, mismatch and ongoing reconfiguration. There is not a sense of creating and then maintaining a balanced symbiosis of parts. As a result of this heterogeneity and independence, assemblages dismantle and reassemble in different combinations as context and requirements shift. (Carrington, 2013: 209)

Other psychology-based theoretical tools that are drawn upon in an analysis of children's use of technology in the home include those that are located within sociocultural perspectives. For example, Edwards (2011) draws on Vygotsky's (1978) theories of play as a leading activity in cognitive and imaginative development and argues that contemporary digital cultures provide rich opportunities for the promotion of play that is rooted in children's everyday experiences. This is not, she suggests, an inferior form of play; rather, it sits alongside more traditional play activities and is important for creative development. This is an argument developed in her later

work. In a study of children's technology use in ten families in Australia, Edwards (2013) contends that there is a need to reconsider the relationship between traditional play (e.g., construction play, pretend play) and 'converged play' in post-industrial times. By converged play, she refers to play that is related to children's popular cultural artefacts and texts, including digital media. Rather than viewing the two types of players as oppositional, Edwards argues that they are interrelated and that it is no longer appropriate to view traditional play as the highest quality form, given that converged play leads to imaginative play.

Similarly, Teichert and Anderson (2014) suggest that technology and play are not oppositional. They report on an in-depth case study of a 5-year-old girl in Canada in which they traced the role of digital media in her everyday life. Drawing on a sociocultural lens, they demonstrate how the child's interactions with technology were embedded in her everyday life, and whilst technology was important, including the use of an iPad for drawing, the child had numerous other interests and was not solely focused on technology. This is a consistent theme in research in this area. Contrary to concerns that children may be 'addicted' to technologies (Palmer, 2006), numerous studies indicate that children move across digital and non-digital artefacts, such as dolls and cars, construction toys, drawing materials, dressing-up clothes and so on, and that media is not over-dominant in the majority of children's lives (Chaudron et al., 2015; Marsh et al., 2005; Stephen et al., 2013).

Other studies drawing from sociocultural theories have examined children's use of technologies in relation to other members of the family and have analyzed the attitudes of parents to this use. Numerous studies have found that many parents have a balanced attitude towards young children's use of new technologies and feel that they can be advantageous to children's development (e.g., Marsh et al., 2005; Palaiologou, 2014). Verenikina and Kervin (2011) interviewed parents in three families in which children aged 3 and 4 used iPads to play a range of games. Parents noted that the children enjoyed playing a range of games and that these promoted imaginative and physical play. The parents also emphasized the need for children to use apps that were educational in nature, rather than simply playing with digital technologies.

Other studies have also identified a parental emphasis on the educational value of technology, although projects have found differences across families in terms of their attitudes and experiences. Stephen, Stevenson and Adey (2013) report on research with four children and their families who were involved in a larger study of children's learning with toys and technology in Scotland. They found that parents differed in their perspectives on the value of play with technological toys, in their understandings about how learning should be supported and in their ways of interacting with their children and managing family life (p. 157). These differences shaped the individual differences between children's technological play. A further aspect impacting on the distinctions between children's use of technologies was the children's individual interests and temperaments.

Studies drawing from a sociocultural framework frequently emphasize the way in which children's use of technology becomes integrated into their everyday family relationships. For example, Kelly (2013) outlines a case study of one family's use of technology in which the use of Skype enabled intersubjectivity to be developed between grandparents and a 4-year-old girl who lived in a different part of the world from them. During Skype sessions using a laptop, the English grandparents played hide and seek with their Australian grandchild as she hid in various parts of the room and her mother pointed the laptop camera to areas where she was not hiding, eventually allowing the child to be 'spotted'. The game was then reversed and the mother hid the laptop, as the child left the room, returning soon afterwards to find grandma and granddad's faces appearing on the laptop screen, hidden behind a curtain or under the bed. These games were initiated

by the child and this vignette offers a rich example of the way in which technology is becoming deeply embedded in the lifeworlds of young children, such that its use for this kind of play becomes unremarkable to the families involved.

Theoretical frameworks that draw on the field of linguistics and applied linguistics have offered valuable insights into young children's competence in managing technology from a very young age. Danby et al. (2013), Davidson (2009, 2011, 2012), and Spink and colleagues (2010) have conducted studies in which they have used interactional analysis theories to interrogate children's interactional competence as they interact with parents in the use of technology in the home. This work demonstrates that young children are skilled in drawing on a range of interactional resources as they use computers, seeking help when they need to and using talk and non-verbal actions to collaborate with others.

Related to the field of linguistics, but extending analysis to children's communication using a range of modes, a social semiotic theory of multimodality (Kress, 2010) has informed a number of studies of children's home use of technologies. A multimodal approach enables an examination of children's meaning making that moves beyond language to include images, sound, gesture and so on. An example of this approach is a study that examined 3- and 4- year-olds' engagement with multimodal texts at home and in an early childhood setting (Flewitt, 2011; Wolfe and Flewitt, 2010). The study found that children's 'reading' of multimodal texts was supported by parents, who used gestures and a range of non-verbal cues to facilitate children's engagement in multimodal, multimedia texts. The range of multimedia texts children used was broad, as was found in a case study undertaken in Canada of one 7-year-old, Tara, whose reading at home included informational texts on websites, written and visual instructions for game playing on the computer and manipulating virtual objects as she played the computer game 'Sims' (McTavish, 2014). Further, studies using a social semiotic theory of multimodality have extended the focus beyond the home and into the community. Yamada-Rice (2013) examined how seven children aged between 3 and 6 years living in Japan interacted with and comprehended the visual mode in the community environment. She found that these young children were sophisticated meaning-makers who were able to make sense of a range of multimodal texts and signs. Yamada-Rice argues that early childhood scholars need to move away from an over-emphasis on environmental print, which privileges the written word, to a recognition of the importance of children's interactions with a range of modes in homes and community spaces.

Moving on, sociological analyses have focused on examining the way in which young children's digital use is shaped by sociocultural factors that emanate from societal structures. For example, Marsh (2011) has drawn upon Bourdieu's (1986) work on forms of capital to examine the relationship between children's offline and online activities in virtual worlds. Economic, cultural and social capital shape the way in which ecological systems, outlined in Table 29.1, work together (or not, as the case may be) to determine children's technological experiences. Each child's engagement with technology is unique to her/his context and the economic, social and cultural capital of family and this will inform how children's engagement with technology is shaped. This is an approach also taken by Savage (2012) in a study of young multilingual children's digital literacy practices in homes in Qatar.

Finally, theories from cultural studies have informed an understanding of how young children's use of technologies is deeply embedded in their everyday worlds. In a longitudinal ethnographic study of children playing in school playgrounds, Willett and colleagues (2013) draw on Du Gay et al.'s (1997) notion of the 'circuit of culture' model, which was developed to examine the social and cultural practices embedded in the use of the Sony Walkman. The circuit consists of key elements that circulate in

media production and consumption, which are: representation, identity, production, consumption and regulation. This model makes it clear that in any cultural event, complex factors intersect. Whilst not located in the home, the Willet et al. (2013) study was informative in relation to how children's out-of-school media and technological practices inform their play in school playgrounds. Children's folkloric culture, as evidenced in the playground, is produced through the dynamic that occurs in the interaction of the elements of the circuit of culture; children's *productions* are related to *consumption* of a range of media, and, through the *representations* offered and contested in that media, their *identities* are forged. *Regulation* impacts on children's cultural production in numerous ways and obviously, in the playground, the regulation of play and bodies can be observed. The study found that there was a rich and complex relationship between children's playground games and rhymes and their home use of digital media, and children drew extensively from their experiences with the latter in their play. Cultural study theories have also informed studies of young children's home use of technologies that are rooted in everyday popular culture (Marsh, 2014, 2015).

This theoretical overview of studies of young children's use of technologies in homes and communities is not exhaustive, but it outlines how diverse the theoretical frameworks are that inform this field and the extent to which there is now a rich and extensive body of work that informs an understanding of the topic. It should also be made clear that many scholars draw on multiple frameworks in their analysis of data, so, for, example, McTavish's (2013) study of Tara used both sociocultural theory and a social semiotic theory of multimodality. Indeed, it is important that this theoretical bricolage takes place, as it enables data sets to be viewed from a range of angles and issues of relationships, power, identity and communicative practices to be considered simultaneously.

In terms of the methodologies employed in research studies on young children's use of technologies in the home, again there is a diversity of approaches that have been utilized such as ethnography, surveys and case studies. Methods used include observation, sometimes videoed, diaries, interviews and analysis of the artefacts and texts children produce. Some of the studies have involved parents and children as active researchers in the process. For example, Marsh et al. (2015) involved parents in a study in which they filmed and kept diaries of their own children's digital literacy practices. Plowman et al. (2011) engaged both children and parents in their project through the use of techno-tours led by children and mobile phone diaries kept by parents of children's media use. Willet et al. (2013) involved children in filming their own playground activities and in the Sheffield school participating in that study, children kept ethnographic notes of their observations in the playground (Marsh, 2013b). However, there is further scope in the future for engaging children as co-researchers in projects that are focused on their use of technologies in the home, given the now extensive knowledge base regarding how this might be undertaken (see Tisdall, et al., 2009).

From this overview of the theoretical and methodological approaches used in studies of children's use of technologies in the home, a number of key findings can be summarized thus, at least in relation to the Global North: (i) technologies are an embedded and ubiquitous element in children's everyday lifeworlds; (ii) children display competency in the use of technologies from a very young age; (iii) access to and use of technologies is shaped by factors such as socio-economic status, gender and age, but not exclusively so in that other factors are important, such as the values and confidence of parents and their previous use of technologies; (iv) the majority of children use technology as part of a well-balanced diet of leisure activities and do not focus on technology use to the exclusion of other pleasures; (v) parents and other family members support children's engagement and learning with technologies in a variety of ways.

This analysis has highlighted the need for further research in this field on the Global South, given that most of the studies conducted so far have been concentrated in Australia, Europe and the USA. In addition, few studies have considered children's use of media and technologies in the home over time and longitudinal studies that offer insights into changes and developments in this use would be valuable. Finally, studies which involve analysis of children's use of technologies across domains would be of value, as most consider their use in homes and early childhood settings separately, with a few exceptions (e.g., Levy, 2011; McTavish, 2013). In the following section, research that has focused upon institutional settings is considered.

RESEARCHING THE USE OF TECHNOLOGIES IN EARLY CHILDHOOD SETTINGS

Numerous systematic and narrative reviews of the use of technologies in early childhood settings have pointed to the limited number of studies compared to other age groups (Blackwell et al., 2013; Burnett, 2010; Burnett and Merchant, 2013; Levy and Marsh, 2011; Levy et al., 2012). Nevertheless, there has been some significant work undertaken in this field, which has tended to fall into two quite separate paradigms, outlined below.

Drawing on Piagetian (1936) concepts, Reinking, Labbo and McKenna (2000) point to two ways in which technology has normally been adopted in classrooms. The first mode can be characterized as 'assimiliation', that is when technology 'is implemented in ways that conform to existing curriculum, pedagogical goals, and instructional activities that are comfortable and familiar' (Reinking et al., 2000: 112). In this model, technology does not transform traditional practices, but rather is used in ways that conform to long-established pedagogies and/or used to support the acquisition of skills and knowledge that have been previously acquired through non-technological means. In contrast, 'Accommodation implies that new information and experiences lead to a fundamental restructuring of thinking and a re-orientation that allows for viewing the world in new terms' (Reinking et al., 2000: 114), and thus can be seen as more transformational in character.

There are a number of reviews of the use of technologies in early childhood that outline the assimilation model (e.g., Belo et al., 2013). The research that is identified in these studies frequently draws from a psychological theoretical framework in order to identify the way in which technology can enhance cognitive processes and learning (e.g., De Graaff et al., 2007; Macaruso and Rodman, 2011). Some of this work is informed by developmental theories (Korat and Blau, 2010) and thus is concerned to identify 'developmentally appropriate practice'. This refers to an emphasis on determining the developmental stage of the child and choosing technologies to employ that can be assessed as appropriate for this stage (see the NAEYC and Fred Rogers Center Joint Position Statement, 2012). Inevitably, this approach has been widely critiqued, given that children's development is a complex process (Burman, 2007; Cannella, 1997; O'Brien, 2000), and whilst a technology might appear at first assessment to be too challenging for a particular age group, indeed some children may be able to use the technology in ways that are appropriate to their needs (Yelland et al., 2008).

Recent studies on young children's engagement with technologies in early childhood settings that could be characterized as promoting an 'accommodation' model of technology adoption (Reinking et al., 2000) draw largely from sociocultural and social-constructionist theories to emphasize the way in which technologies can promote learning if used in ways that enhance creativity and social interaction. Given that a number of recent reviews of work in this field have

been undertaken (Bers and Kazakoff, 2013; Blanchard and Moore, 2010; Burnett and Merchant, 2013; Levy and Marsh, 2011; Levy et al., 2012), this section will only consider research published since 2012. This review thus focuses on recent work that demonstrates how learning in early childhood can be supported through innovative and creative use of technologies.

The use of social networking tools, such as blogs and Twitter, allows early childhood classrooms to link to the outside world and thus promotes intergenerational communication. Marsh and Yamada-Rice (2013) report on a study in which multilingual 3- and 4-year-olds in an early childhood sitting in the North of England used blogging software to share their iPad drawings, digital photographs and podcasts, all created when visiting a city farm. They suggest that through the publishing of the children's work on the blog, the early childhood teachers in this setting enabled the children to communicate directly with a 'real' audience external to the nursery, thus providing an authentic context for reading and writing.

There are studies, however, that suggest that not all early childhood educators feel confident to adopt these approaches and there is a need for professional development and support in this area (Arrow and Finch, 2013). Roberts-Holmes (2013) conducted a one-year qualitative study of a nursery that used ICT and the input of a digital media consultant to transform the early years curriculum. Activities included children making mini movies and avatars, which were uploaded onto the nursery website. Roberts-Holmes found that these activities promoted sustained shared thinking between teachers and children, and suggests that 'Genuine learning and co-construction of knowledge occurred between children and teachers as they played and experimented with making mini-movies together' (Roberts-Holmes, 2013: 13). The presence of a digital media consultant was central to the development of teachers' confident practice.

In the years ahead, one of the foci for studies of innovative use of technologies in early childhood classrooms will be the deployment of tablet technologies, given the affordances of touch-screen for young children. Studies of the use of iPads in the early classroom are emerging. In Canada, Reid, Reid and Ostashewski (2013) found that iPads could be used successfully to support digital storytelling in an early learning environment through the use of an animation app. Whilst children enjoy the use of tablets and find them motivating (Verenikina and Kervin, 2011), in one American study Shifflet et al. (2012) observed that children moved easily from the use of iPads to other areas of the pre-school classroom, such as the construction area, which again appears to debunk myths regarding children's obsession with this technology (Palmer, 2006).

Lynch and Redpath (2014) conducted a year-long ethnographic study of one early childhood setting's use of iPads over a 16-month period. The authors examined apps in terms of their 'openness' or 'closedness'. Apps that were more open were found to be ones with more opportunities for user-driven creativity, whereas closed apps give the user few freedoms in use. They argue that the use of open apps may mirror some of the children's out-of-school digital practices and that innovative use of tablets could link home and school domains:

> Within early years literacy, the authors believe that 'smart' touch-screen devices, such as the iPad, can be used to begin to bridge the gap between emerging home literacies and the techno-literacy practices of the early years classroom, and through this to support new forms of cultural participation and learner identity. (Lynch and Redpath, 2014: 170)

Additional studies that draw on a sociocultural and/or social-constructionist model of learning likewise emphasize the potential value that tablets have for children's engagement and social interaction in the classroom, and stress that appropriate adult scaffolding in their use is required (Dezuanni et al., 2015; Flewitt et al., 2014b). Tablets also appear to have valuable affordances when used with young children with special educational needs (Flewitt et al., 2014a).

Other theoretical models used in the 'accommodation-ist' paradigm of young children's engagement in technologies in early childhood classrooms include a social semiotic theory of multimodality, nexus theory and spatial theories. These have been drawn upon to explore the complexities of children's navigation of a range of modes across space and time as children use technology to go online in classrooms and early childhood settings. Nexus theory focuses on an analysis of the practices that are used to produce cultural meanings in a given instance (Scollon and Scollon, 2004) and it enables an analysis of the power relationships embedded in those practices. The value of a multimodal approach combined with nexus theory is that it enables an understanding of how children navigate social interaction in virtual spaces. The use of spatiality theory (Leander and Sheehy, 2004) can also inform an understanding of how children's social interaction and learning operate across online and offline spaces. Drawing on Jones (2009), Wohlwend and Kargin (2013) point out that analyses of space in online environments should connect five different spaces:

1 Physical/body space (interactional between social actors, actors on computers)
2 Discursive space (an ideological space that justifies valued practices and available modes)
3 Virtual space (computer interface with network of other computers)
4 Screen space (user–computer interface, audible, visible locus of communication)
5 Relational space (interactional, between participants on screen)

Wohlwend and Kargin use nexus theory, in combination with multimodal analysis (the analysis of multiple modes such as word, image, sound and movement), to report on the study of an after-school club for 5–8-year-olds in the USA. They examine children's interactions on screen when using the virtual world 'Club Penguin', addressing all five spaces outlined above. Using these theoretical and analytical tools, they note that the children's interactions spread well beyond the virtual world itself:

> Club Penguin peer cultures are created and maintained in and around the commercial infrastructure of the game, but they also extend beyond the reach of the networked servers and associated official websites into fan sites where events are resemiotized and nexus are extended though 'unauthorized' activities such as flash mobs at particular in-world locations. Through these official and unofficial global networks, affinity groups make particular actions and artifacts more valued than others, creating potential cultural capital with potential for positioning peers. (Wohlwend and Kargin, 2013)

Wohlwend and Kargin (2013) argue that issues of digital equity are significant when children do not have opportunities to engage in play in such digital spaces at home and suggest that early childhood settings provide valuable opportunities for children to engage in these practices.

In terms of methodological approaches used across these studies, it is worth noting that the vast majority of studies emerging from the 'accommodation-ist' model have utilized qualitative methods, such as observations, interviews and micro-analyses of young children's digital projects and products. Studies that use experimental quasi-experimental designs to examine the efficacy of the use of technologies in early childhood classrooms have largely been located within an assimilationist framework (e.g., Penuel et al., 2012; Savage et al., 2009). It is arguably the case that policy makers are more influenced by these kinds of studies and there is, therefore, a question about whether or not early childhood researchers who work from an 'accommodation-ist' model should adopt these approaches if governments are to embrace the innovative and transformative use of digital technologies in early childhood settings more readily than is currently the case.

Recent studies in children's use of technologies in early childhood settings and classrooms have, as can be seen, identified a range of ways in which innovative and creative uses of a variety of tools including computers, laptops and mobile technologies, such as phones, tablets and digital cameras, can promote the development of a range of skills and knowledge and engage children in meaningful interactions in which their agency is paramount. In the following section, the chapter moves on to consider potential future developments in research on young children's engagement in technologies across domains and reflects on the theoretical and methodological challenges these bring.

THE FUTURE OF RESEARCH ON TECHNOLOGIES IN CHILDREN'S WORLDS AND FUTURES

It is clear from this review of recent research on young children's engagement with technologies in homes, communities and early years settings that there is a growing understanding of significance of this area of children's lives. In the years ahead, there will be a need to undertake research in order to understand a number of emerging areas of interest. First, it is clear that tablets are becoming increasingly prevalent in the homes of families with young children, as identified previously in the chapter. There is a need for studies of very young children's (aged 0–3) use of tablets, in addition to more detailed studies of 4–8-year-old children's interactions with a variety of apps. There is, as yet, little understanding of how access to apps on tablets impacts on children's use of other media and technologies, and this will need to be a focus of study. For example, does children's use of apps related to their favorite television programs impact on their engagement with those programs in any way? Do apps that link to children's virtual worlds provide children with the same pleasures as participating in the virtual worlds? How do children move across platforms? There are also numerous questions related to the educational use of tablets and apps in early childhood settings that will become significant in the future. First, further understanding is needed of the types of apps that are most productive for particular types of learning in early childhood. There needs to be additional knowledge developed with regard to the affordances of apps for promoting an enjoyment of reading. There are numerous e-books appearing as apps (Yokota and Teale, 2014) and yet there is little research on how children respond to these (for a review of research to date, see Miller and Warschauer, 2014). It would also be useful to develop research that can inform an understanding of how tablets can be used to provide greater integration between home and school learning for children, given their mobility. There are, inevitably, so many other questions that need to be asked, but these are the areas in which there is, at present, limited understanding.

As identified in recent research, the boundaries between young children's online and offline spaces are becoming more diffuse over time (Burke and Marsh, 2013) and this will continue to be an area in which we see rapid developments. There will be interesting changes in this area as augmented-reality apps on tablets become more sophisticated and enable children to engage with a range of texts in different ways. This will be of interest in relation to storybooks, of course, as children become able to link an app to a book and bring the characters to life. There are already a few examples of this technology in existence, but it is fledgling days in this regard and the kinds of interaction possible between physical texts and artefacts and virtual characters and settings are limited. As technological capacity grows, research will be needed to identify how augmented-reality apps enable children to engage in play and literacy practices in which the virtual and physical can interact in interesting ways.

I have discussed elsewhere other developments in the years ahead which may impact on young children's engagement with technologies, such as the use of wearable technologies, widening access to 3D printers as they become more affordable and the increasing sophistication of robots, which will be able to interact with children in a range of ways (see Marsh, 2014). Early childhood researchers interested in the way in which technology is changing the social and cultural landscape of children's lives should be alert to these developments and focus attention on how such technology shapes children's play and learning.

CONCLUSION

In this chapter, research that has examined the extent, role and nature of technologies in children's worlds has been explored. Whilst research in some areas is still limited, there is a strong body of evidence, from the Global North, that use of technologies is well-embedded into many children's daily lives, but that there is also somewhat of a disconnect between how technologies are used in homes and community settings and the extent to which early childhood educators draw on the affordances of various technologies in order to offer creative, participatory and innovative learning experiences. There are obvious implications for policy makers in that there is a need to develop approaches that foster the *accommodation* of technologies into the curriculum rather than their *assimilation* (Reinking et al., 2000).

There are also important implications of this analysis for global initiatives. Whilst some technologies are in widespread use across the Global North and South, such as the use of mobile phones, there is a great disparity between countries in terms of access and use (UNESCO, 2012). This situation will only exacerbate global inequities in relation to economic wealth, given that skills and knowledge in the use of technologies lead to a creative economy and sociological developments. Initiatives such as the 'One laptop per child'[1] scheme are commendable, but there is also an urgent need to ensure that early childhood educators' initial training programs across the world provide sufficient information and opportunities to enable any technologies that can be accessed to be used effectively. Given developments in open learning, such as massive open online courses (MOOCs), there are now many more opportunities than ever before to share knowledge and expertise across countries.[2] In the increasingly networked age in the decades ahead, there should be no excuse for the persistent disparities in access to knowledge and understanding with regard to research on the use and impact of technologies in young children's lifeworlds.

FURTHER READING

Burke, A. and Marsh, J. (eds) (2013) *Children's Virtual Play Worlds: Culture, Learning and Participation*. New York: Peter Lang.

Plowman, L., Stephen, C. and McPake, J. (2010) *Growing Up With Technology: Young Children Learning in a Digital World*. London: Routledge.

Yelland, N., Lee, L., O'Rourke, M. and Harrison, C. (2008) *Rethinking Learning in Early Childhood Education*. Maidstone: Open University Press.

QUESTIONS FOR REFLECTION

1   What approaches to teacher education need to be taken in order to ensure that all early childhood educators feel able to use technologies appropriately in teaching and learning? Can, for example, collaborative research projects with parents and children inform understanding?

2   What kinds of ethical issues arise in research on young children's engagement with technologies and how might these be addressed?

3   What theoretical frameworks can be drawn upon to inform an understanding of developments in children's use of emerging technologies, such as augmented reality apps, wearable technologies and robots?

4   How can research on young children's engagement with technologies inform parents' and families' interactions with children?

5   What strategies can be used to extend knowledge and understanding in this area and promote greater exchange in research and practice communities across the Global North and Global South?

NOTES

1   See http://one.laptop.org
2   See 'Digital Futures in Teacher Education' for an example of this kind of initiative: www.digital futures.org

REFERENCES

Arrow, A.W. and Finch, B.T. (2013) Multimedia literacy practices in beginning classrooms and at home: The differences in practices and beliefs. *Literacy*, 27(3): 131–141.

Australian Bureau of Statistics (2012) Children's participation in cultural and leisure activities. Accessed at: www.abs.gov.au/AUSSTATS/abs@.nsf/DetailsPage/4901.0Apr%202012?OpenDocument

Belo, N.A.H., McKenney, S.E. and Voogt, J.M. (2013) Towards a knowledge base for using ICT to foster early literacy development: A review study. Paper presented at the EARLI conference, 27–31 August, Munich.

Bers, M.U. and Kazakoff, E.R. (2013) Techno-tykes: Digital technologies in early childhood. *Handbook of Research on the Education of Young Children* (pp. 197–205). London/New York: Routledge.

Blackwell, C.K., Lauricella, A.R., Wartella, E., Robb, M. and Schomburg, R. (2013) Adoption and use of technology in early education: The interplay of extrinsic barriers and teacher attitudes. *Computers and Education,* 69(1): 310–319.

Blanchard, J. and Moore, T. (2010) *The Digital World of Young Children: Impact on Emergent Literacy.* Pearson Foundation White Paper. Accessed at: www.pearsonfoundation.org/PDF/EmergentLiteracy-WhitePaper.pdf

Bourdieu, P. (1986) The forms of capital. In J. Richardson, Ed. *Handbook of Theory and Research for the Sociology of Education* (pp. 241–258). New York: Greenwood Press.

Bronfenbrenner, U. (1979) *The Ecology of Human Development: Experiments by Nature and Design*. Cambridge, MA: Harvard University Press.

Burke, A. and Marsh, J. (eds) (2013) *Children's Virtual Play Worlds: Culture, Learning and Participation*. New York: Peter Lang.

Burman, E. (2007) *Deconstructing Developmental Psychology*, 2nd edn. London: Routledge.

Burnett, C. (2010) Technology and literacy in early childhood educational settings: A review of research. *Journal of Early Childhood Literacy*, 10(3): 247–270.

Burnett, C. and Merchant, G. (2013) Learning, literacies and new technologies: The current context and future possibilities. In J. Larson and J. Marsh (eds) *Handbook of Early Childhood Literacy*, 2nd edn (pp. 575 – 586). London, New Dehli, Thousand Oaks, CA: SAGE.

Cannella, G.S. (1997) *Deconstructing Early Childhood Education: Social Justice and Revolution*. New York: Peter Lang.

Carrington, V. (2013) An argument for assemblage theory: Integrated spaces, mobility and polycentricity. In A. Burke and J. Marsh (eds) *Children's Virtual Play Worlds: Culture, Learning and Participation*. (pp 200–216). New York: Peter Lang.

Chaudron, S. et al. (2015). Young Children (0–8) and Digital Technology: A qualitative exploratory study across seven countries. European Union Joint Research Centre, Science and Policy Reports. Luxembourg: Publications Office of the European Union. http://publications.jrc.ec.europa.eu/repository/handle/JRC93239 doi:10.2788/00749

Danby, S., Davidson, C., Theobald, M., Scriven, B., Cobb-Moore, C., Houen, S., et al. (2013) Talk in activity during young children's use of digital technologies at home. *Australian Journal of Communication*, 40(2). Available at: http://austjourcomm.org/index.php/ajc/article/view/4/122

Davidson, C. (2009) Young children's engagement with digital texts and literacies in the home: Pressing matters for the teaching of English in the early years of schooling. *English Teaching: Practice and Critique*, 8(3): 36–54.

Davidson, C. (2011) Seeking the green basilisk lizard: Acquiring digital literacy practices in the home. *Journal of Early Childhood Literacy*, 12(1): 24–45.

Davidson, C. (2012) The social organisation of help during young children's use of the computer. *Contemporary Issues in Early Childhood*, 13(3): 187–199.

De Graaff, S., Verhoeven, L., Bosman, A.M.T. and Hasselman, F. (2007) Integrated pictorial mnemonics and stimulus fading: Teaching kindergartners letter sounds. *British Journal of Educational Psychology*, 77(3): 519–539.

Deleuze, G. and Guattari, F. (1987) *A Thousand Plateaus: Capitalism and Schizophrenia*. London: Continuum.

Dezuanni, M., Dooley, K., Gattenhof, S. and Knight, L. (eds) (2015) *iPads in the Early Years: Developing Literacy and Creativity*. United Kingdom: Routledge.

Du Gay, P., Hall, S., Janes, L., Mackay, H. and Negus, K. (1997) *Doing Cultural Studies: The Story of the Sony Walkman*. London: SAGE/Open University.

Edwards, S. (2011) Lessons from 'a really useful engine'™: Using Thomas the Tank Engine™ to examine the relationship between play as a leading activity, imagination and reality in children's contemporary play worlds. *Cambridge Journal of Education*, 41(2): 195–219.

Edwards, S. (2013) Post-industrial play: Understanding the relationship between traditional and converged forms of play in the early years. In A. Burke and J. Marsh (eds) *Children's Virtual Play Worlds: Culture, Learning and Participation*. New York: Peter Lang.

Flewitt, R.S. (2011) Bringing ethnography to a multimodal investigation of early literacy in a digital age. *Qualitative Research Special Issue – Multimodality and Ethnography: Working at the Intersection*, 3: 293–310.

Flewitt, R.S., Kucirkova, N. and Messer, D. (2014a) Touching the virtual, touching the real: iPads and enabling literacy for students with learning disabilities. *Australian Journal of Language and Literacy*, Special Issue, 37: 107–116.

Flewitt, R.S., Messer, D. and Kucirkova, N. (2014b) New directions for early literacy in a digital age: the iPad. *Journal of Early Childhood Literacy*.

Holloway, D., Green, L. and Livingstone, S. (2013) *Zero to Eight: Young Children and their Internet Use*. London: LSE/EU Kids Online (http://eprints.lse.ac.uk/52630/).

Jenkins, H., Clinton, K., Purushotma, R., Robison, A. and Weigel, M. (2006) *Confronting the Challenges of Participatory Culture: Media Education for the 21st Century*. An Occasional

Paper on Digital Media and Learning. The John D. and Catherine T. MacArthur Foundation. Available at: http://digitallearning. macfound.org/site/c.enJLKQNlFiG/ b.2108773/apps/nl/content2.asp?content_ id={CD911571-0240-4714-A93B-1D0C07C7B6C1}andnotoc=1

Jie, S.H. (2012) ICT Use Statistics of Households and Individuals in Korea. 10th World Telecommunication/ICT Indicators Meeting (WTIM-12) Bangkok, Thailand, 25–27 September. Accessed at: www.itu.int/ITU-D/ ict/wtim12/documents/cont/029_E_doc.pdf

Jones, R. (2009) Cyberspace and physical space: Attention structures in computer-mediated communication. In A. Jaworski and C. Thurlow (eds) *Semiotic Landscapes: Language, Image, Space* (pp. 151–167). London: Curriculum.

Kelly, C. (2013) 'Let's do some jumping together': Intergenerational participation in the use of remote technology to co-construct social relations over distance. *Journal of Early Childhood Research*, pp. 1–18.

Kress, G.R. (2010) *Multimodality: A Social Semiotic Approach to Contemporary Communication*. London: Routledge.

Korat, O. and Blau, H. (2010) Repeated reading of CD ROM storybook as a support for emergent literacy: A developmental perspective in two SES groups. *Journal of Educational Computing Research*, 43(4): 445–466.

Leander, K.M. and Sheehy, M. (eds) (2004) *Spatializing Literacy Research and Practice*. New York: Peter Lang.

Levy, R. (2011) *Young Children Reading at Home and at School*. London: SAGE.

Levy, R. and Marsh, J. (2011) Literacy and ICT in the early years. In D. Lapp and D. Fisher (eds) *Handbook of Research on Teaching the English Language Arts* (pp. 168–174). New York: Routledge.

Levy, R., Yamada-Rice, D. and Marsh, J. (2012) Digital literacy in primary classrooms. In B. Comber, T. Cremin, K. Hall and L. Moll (eds) *International Handbook of Research on Children's Literacy, Learning, and Culture*. London: SAGE.

Lynch, J. and Redpath, T. (2014) 'Smart' technologies in early years literacy education: A meta-narrative of paradigmatic tensions in iPad use in an Australian preparatory classroom. *Journal of Early Childhood Literacy*, 14(2): 147–174.

Macaruso, P. and Rodman, A. (2011) Efficacy of computer-assisted instruction for the development of early literacy skills in young children. *Reading Psychology*, 32(2): 172–196.

Marsh, J. (2011) Young children's literacy practices in a virtual world: Establishing an online interaction order. *Reading Research Quarterly*, 46(2): 101–118.

Marsh, J. (2013a) Childhood in the digital age. In T. Maynard and N. Thomas (eds) *An Introduction to Early Childhood Studies*, 3rd edn. London: SAGE.

Marsh, J. (2013b) Children as knowledge brokers. *Childhood*, 19(4): 508–522.

Marsh, J. (2014) Media, childhood and play. In L. Brooker, S. Edwards and M. Blaise (eds) *Handbook of Play and Learning in Early Childhood* (pp. 403–414). London: SAGE.

Marsh, J. (2015). 'Unboxing' Videos: Co-construction of the child as cyberflâneur. *Discourse: Studies in the Cultural Politics of Education.* Published online ahead of print, 25 June 2015. DOI:10.1080/01596306. 2015.1041457

Marsh, J., Brooks, G., Hughes, J., Ritchie, L. and Roberts, S. (2005) *Digital Beginnings: Young Children's Use of Popular Culture, Media and New Technologies*. Sheffield: University of Sheffield. Accessed at: www.digitalbeginnings.shef.ac.uk/DigitalBeginningsReport.pdf

Marsh, J., Hannon, P., Lewis, M. and Ritchie, L. (2015) Young children's initiation into family literacy practices in the digital age. *Journal of Early Childhood Research*. First published online 18 June 2015. DOI: 10.1177/ 1476718X15582095

Marsh, J. and Yamada-Rice, D. (2013) Early literacy development in the digital age. In D.M. Barone and M.H. Mallette (eds) *Best Practices in Early Literacy Instruction* (pp. 79–95). New York: Guilford Press.

McTavish, M. (2014) 'I'll do it my own way!': A young child's appropriation and recontextualization of school literacy practices in out-of-school spaces. *Journal of Early Childhood Literacy,* 14(3): 319–344.

Miller, E. and Warschauer, M. (2014) Young children and e-reading: Research to date and questions for the future. *Learning, Media and Technology,* 39(3): 383–305.

Nardi, B.A. and O'Day, V. (1999) *Information Ecologies: Using Technology with Heart*. Cambridge, MA: MIT Press.

National Association for the Education of Young Children (NAEYC) and the Fred Rogers Center for Early Learning and Children's Media at Saint Vincent College (2012) Technology and interactive media as tools in early childhood programs serving children from birth through age 8. Joint Position Statement, January. Accessed at: www.naeyc.org/files/naeyc/file/positions/PS_technology_WEB2.pdf

Neumann, M.M. (2014) An examination of touch screen tablets and emergent literacy in Australian pre-school children. Australian Journal of Education, 58(2): 108–122.

O'Brien, L.M. (2000) Engaged pedagogy: One alternative to 'indoctrination' into DAP. Childhood Education, 76(5): 283–288.

Ofcom (2014) Children and Parents: Media Use and Attitudes Report. Available at: http://stakeholders.ofcom.org.uk/binaries/research/media-literacy/media-use-attitudes-14/Childrens_2014_Report.pdf

Palaiologou, I. (2014) Children under five and digital technologies: Implications for early years pedagogy. European Early Childhood Education Research Journal. Published online before print, 24 June 2014. DOI:10.1080/1350293X.2014.929876

Palmer, S. (2006) Toxic Childhood. London: Orion Press.

Penuel, W.R., Bates, L., Gallagher, L.P., Pasnik, S., Llorente, C., Townsend, E., et al. (2012) Supplementing literacy instruction with a media-rich intervention: Results of a randomized controlled trial. Early Childhood Research Quarterly, 27(1): 115–127.

Piaget, J. (1936) Origins of Intelligence in the Child. London: Routledge & Kegan Paul.

Plowman, L., McPake, J. and Stephen, C. (2008) Just picking it up? Young children learning with technology at home. Cambridge Journal of Education, 38(3): 303–319.

Plowman, L., Stevenson, O., McPake, J., Stephen, C. and Adey, C. (2011) Parents, pre-schoolers and learning with technology at home: Some implications for policy. Journal of Computer Assisted Learning, 27(4): 361–371.

Reid, D., Reid, E. and Ostashewski, N. (2013) Combining iPads and slowmation: Developing in an early learning environment. In J. Herrington et al. (eds) Proceedings of World Conference on Educational Multimedia, Hypermedia and Telecommunications

(pp. 1539–1543). Chesapeake, VA: AACE. Accessed at: www.editlib.org/p/112164

Reinking, D., Labbo, L.D. and McKenna, M.C. (2000) From assimilation to accommodation: A developmental framework for integrating digital technologies into literacy research and instruction. Journal of Research in Reading, 23(2): 110–122.

Rideout, V.J. (2013) Zero to Eight: Children's Media Use in America. San Francisco, CA: Common Sense Media.

Rideout, V.J., Vandewater, E.A. and Wartella, E.A. (2003) Zero to Six: Electronic Media in the Lives of Infants, Toddlers and Preschoolers. Washington, DC: Kaiser Foundation.

Roberts-Holmes, G. (2013) Playful and creative ICT pedagogical framing: A nursery school case study. Early Child Development and Care, 184(1): 1–14.

Savage, M. (2012) Home literacy and agency: An ethnographic approach to studying the home literacy practices of six multiliterate children in Qatar. Unpublished EdD thesis, University of Sheffield.

Savage, R.S., Abrami, P., Hipps, G. and Deault, L. (2009) A randomized controlled trial study of the ABRACADABRA reading intervention program in Grade 1. Journal of Educational Psychology, 101(3): 590–604.

Scollon, R. and Scollon, S.W. (2004) Nexus Analysis: Discourse and the Emerging Internet. New York: Routledge.

Shifflet, R., Toledo, C. and Mattoon, C. (2012) Touch tablet surprises: A preschool teacher's story. Young Children, 67(3): 36–41.

Spink, A., Danby, S., Mallan, K. and Butler, C. (2010) Exploring young children's web searching and technoliteracy. Journal of Documentation, 66(2): 91–206.

Stephen, C., Stevenson, O. and Adey, C. (2013) Young children engaging with technologies at home: The influence of family context. Journal of Early Childhood Research, 11(2): 149–164.

Teale, W. and Sulzby, E. (1986) Emergent Literacy: Writing and Reading. Norwood, NJ: Ablex Publishing Corporation.

Teichert, L. and Anderson, A. (2014) 'I don't even know what blogging is': The role of digital media in a five-year-old girl's life. Early Child Development and Care, 184(11): 1677–1691.

Tisdall, K., Davis, J. and Gallagher M. (eds) (2009) Researching with Children and Young

People: Research Design, Methods and Analysis (pp. 154–167). London: SAGE.

Tudge, J. (2008) *The Everyday Lives of Young Children*. Cambridge: Cambridge University Press.

UNESCO (2012) Child Safety Online: Global Challenges and Strategies. Technical report, UNICEF. Accessed at: www.unicef-irc.org/publications/pdf/ict_techreport3_eng.pdf

Verenikina, I. and Kervin, L. (2011) iPads, digital play and preschoolers. *He Kupu*, 2(5): 4–19.

Vygotsky, L. (1978) *Mind in Society* (trans. M. Cole). Cambridge, MA: Harvard University Press.

Willett, R., Richards, C., Marsh. J., Burn, A. and Bishop, J. (2013) *Children, Media and Playground Cultures: Ethnographic Studies of School Playtimes*. Basingstoke: Palgrave Macmillan.

Wohlwend, K.E. and Kargin, T. (2013) 'Cause I know how to get friends – plus they like my dancing': (L)Earning the nexus of practice in Club Penguin. In A. Burke and J. Marsh (eds) *Children's Virtual Play Worlds: Culture,*
Learning and Participation (pp. 79–98). New York: Peter Lang.

Wolfe, S. and Flewitt, R.S. (2010) New technologies, new multimodal literacy practices and young children's metacognitive development. *Cambridge Journal of Education*, 40: 387–399.

Wong, S.S. (2013) Hop on Pop, Click on Poptropica: Preschoolers' multiliteracy practices at home. *Early Childhood Education*, 41(1): 25–29.

Yamada-Rice, D. (2013) The semiotic landscape and three-year-olds' emerging understanding of multimodal communication practices. *Journal of Early Childhood Research,* 12(2): 154–184.

Yelland, N., Lee, L., O'Rourke, M. and Harrison, C. (2008) *Rethinking Learning in Early Childhood Education*. Maidstone: Open University Press.

Yokota, J. and Teale, W.H. (2014) Picture books and the digital world: Educators making informed choices. *The Reading Teacher*, 67(8): 577–585.

30

What is the Future of Sustainability in Early Childhood?

Ingrid Pramling Samuelsson

INTRODUCTION

We live in a world that is economically, socially and environmentally unsustainable, a world that severely compromises the next generation's chances of living a healthy, safe and enjoyable life. Such a scenario was articulated, more than 40 years ago, by the Brundtland Commission in the 1970s, in the report *Our Common Future* (1978). Since then, a number of international agreements have committed to a more sustainable and democratic world, yet without appreciable impact. In most of these agreements, for example *Education for All* (EFA), *The Millennium Development Goals* (MDG), the *Literacy DECADE* (UN), and the *DECADE for Education for Sustainable Development* (ESD), children below the age of primary school have been largely overlooked. It took until 2008 before the first UNESCO report in the area of sustainability was published with a focus on the youngest age group, with the

title *The Role of Early Childhood Education for a Sustainable Society* (Pramling Samuelsson and Kaga, 2008). It is peculiar that it has taken so long, given the plethora of research studies from medicine and from the social and behavioral sciences that attest to the benefit of early learning around sustainability (Britto and Ulkuer, 2012; Pramling Samuelsson and Wagner, 2012). So too, the field of economics shows that a society benefits more from investment in the youngest children compared to later education levels (Chua and Heckman, 2007), and continues to provide a set of arguments to which governments tend to listen and respond. There is, therefore, compelling evidence that experiences before school are critical for laying the foundation for a sustainable future. Despite these arguments, the latest UNESCO survey on change in ESD during the decade shows that ECEC has the lowest rate of investment compared to other levels of education (UNESCO, 2014).

In light of this context, this chapter will examine sustainability in early years education from two perspectives: (1) through policy – by optimal enrolments of children in an Early Childhood Education and Care[1] program which recognizes them as holistic persons in their own right. In turn, it implies that ECEC should be related to health, nutrition, parent education, care, play and education. In contemporary societies, ECEC plays an important role for the whole family system as a sustainability factor, particularly so in developing countries. Contemporary families in Western industrialized societies need such support, which in extended families would likely have come from elder family members; (2) ECEC can ensure that the program addresses sustainability through content and through everyday practices in settings, where education takes on a transformative approach (Wals, 2006). Families can be guided towards sustainability, while ECEC can adhere to mandatory frameworks for sustainability, as a requirement akin to teaching literacy in primary school.

THE SITUATION FOR THE WORLD'S CHILDREN

Today children live in the most unsustainable world in history. They will reap the consequences of the problems the current generation has created. It is timely, therefore, to look closely at reports such as *The Future We Want* (United Nations, 2012) and to begin to work towards whatever is possible in our generation, economically, socially and environmentally. A priority is to educate children to meet their future, since no advances in sustainable development will occur in the coming decades without multiple generations contributing to societal improvement. Moreover, beyond sheer survival, children have a right to thrive, to develop their full potential and to live in a sustainable world. Children's health, learning and behavior during the early years are the foundation for later school success and completion, close nurturing relationships with peers and adults, and the capacity to participate in their community, the workplace and society (SDSN, 2013).

In a recent survey conducted for the UN Decade of Education for Sustainable Development, the Ministries of Education, Environment and Sustainable Development in 97 UN Member States identified *poverty* as the highest priority area to be addressed in achieving Sustainable Development. Poverty was rated above Climate Change and Agricultural and Food Security as a priority. This leads us to focus on those children in the world living in poverty – 6.6 million children die every year before the age of 5 years, that is, around 18,000 die every day (http://unicef.se/fakta/barns-ovrlevnad). One of the goals of the MDG was to reduce early deaths by half. While the goal was achieved, the question of survival requires there being a world worth surviving and allowing the child to develop his/her full potential (UNICEF, 2012). The most important international agreements, *Human Rights* (UN, 1948) and *Convention on the Rights of the Child* (UN, 1989), articulate this right.

Inequity is a key factor, both between countries and within countries. Wilkinson and Pickett (2010) compared the richest 20% in countries with the poorest 20% and examined the gap between the two groups. They found that the larger the gap was between rich and poor, the more problems there were among the population related to: level of trust, mental illness (including drug and alcohol addiction), life expectancy and infant mortality, obesity, children's educational performance, teenage births, homicide, imprisonment rates, and lack of social mobility.

If we now focus on education for children below primary school age, we see differences between various regions in the world, particularly with respect to what is included in pre-primary education. In some countries, it means a year of pre-primary school. In others, for example the Nordic countries, it means a place for all children in

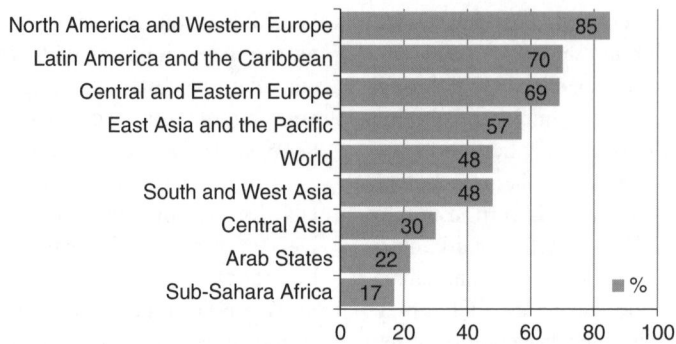

Figure 30.1   Pre-primary gross enrollment ratio (GER)

Source: UNESCO, 2012: 193/209

early childhood education from 1 year of age (Swedish National Agency for Education, 2011). Figure 30.1 shows the inequality between countries, where about half of the world's children have some kind of access to ECEC.

Inequity is not only between countries, it is also within. Statistics from 28 of the world's developing countries show that children from the richest families in these countries are 10 times more likely to get a chance to participate in an early childhood education program than are the poorest children. The richest families are also much more likely to have someone taking care of their youngest children, while the poorest are left alone or with siblings when parents work (UNICEF, 2012). It may also mean that girls do not get a proper education, since they take care of their siblings, becoming a double inequality (for families and for girls).

The next generation of the United Nations' development goals, 15 years ahead, are: an integrative approach to health and learning; support of parenting and early childhood education; social protection, workforce development and non-formal education; social inclusion for the most vulnerable; and measurement of early childhood development to track progress on sustainability. When components targeting cognitive stimulation and responsiveness during feeding are added to nutritional supplementation interventions,

positive effects on parents and on child health and cognitive outcomes are seen to be strong (SDSN, 2013). One such intervention in Jamaica had remarkable effects 20 years on – as participants reached young adulthood, their anxiety, depression and violent behavior were reduced, and their educational attainment increased, as well as earnings and IQ (Grantham-McGregor et al., 2007). Similar results were found in the earlier Perry High/ Scope study in the USA (Weikart, 1989).

Health and education are closely linked for young children. System and infrastructural improvements contribute not only to sustainability but also to child survival. WASH (water, sanitation and hygiene) interventions are found to be effective in reducing risks for diarrhea and attendant morbidity and mortality. Hygiene interventions, providing education and encouraging hand washing, and the provision of sanitation facilities have positive effects on diarrheal as well as asthma and other respiratory diseases. OMEP (Organisation Mondiale pour l'Éducation Prescolare) has initiatives for early years to be included in the extended UNICEF project WASH in schools (UNICEF, 2014), with the introduction of hand-washing days/weeks in ECEC in many countries. OMEP's interest in the project came from a preschool teacher in Kenya, who worked with her village children on sustainability through the purification of water (Siraj-Blatchford et al., 2010).

In developed countries such as Sweden, pre-school children's health improved dramatically by focusing on teaching children good manners about hand washing in preschool (Västra Götalands Regionen, 2014).

Learning in early childhood is a multi-generational enterprise. Learning is largely built through interactions with caring adults and peers, regardless of the setting or the child's home – a village communal space; a social network of parents; a media-based interactive environment; or an out-of-home care or pre-primary education setting. Learning and development in early childhood are supported by the sum of caring adult and peer interactions that a child encounters in the settings of daily home life, childcare and early childhood education. Only through attention to all the settings of early childhood can developmental potential, and subsequent sustainable development, be assured. Supporting a young child's development is thus a community responsibility that requires and benefits from opportunities to increase adult learning (SDSN, 2013; Sylva et al., 2010). Recent evidence suggests the benefits of encouraging caregiving roles and skills that are both culturally and developmentally specific. Although the developmental importance of responsive caregiving has been established across many cultures, there is variation in the forms that reciprocal, responsive interactions in caregiving can take, depending on the developmental stage of the child, the specific settings of family and community life, and values and beliefs of what constitutes successful development. For example, cultures vary in the extent to which interdependence versus autonomy are encouraged in children's relations with one another and with adults (Pramling Samuelsson and Siraj-Blatchford, 2014).

Successful programs balance these foci in ways sensitive to the ecological and cultural context. A parenting program in Turkey, for example, found-long term positive effects from a parenting approach focused on intentionally integrated interdependence and autonomy with sensitivity to the child (Kagitcibasi et al., 2001). The program operated in light of the particular sociocultural and historical context of the low-income families and communities it served. As children's behavior and cognitive capacities become more complex over the first five years of life, their integration into family and community life changes in nature. Successful programs are contextually sensitive to these changes. Programs to improve parents' or caregivers' interactions with preschool-aged children, for example, have emphasized to different degrees a reduction in acting-out or aggressive behaviors; the encouragement of autonomy and initiative; and the inclusion of those who are excluded from social interactions.

Approaches to training and professional development for those who provide caregiving and parenting support to family health educators, home visitors and community parents are showing evidence of success. For example, an intensive two-year professional development and education program for community mothers engaged in home-based care in Colombia produced increases in the observed quality of caregiving as well as in child health and behavior (Landaeta and Cardenas, 2013). In turn, a program in Pakistan tailored a Care for Child Development module to provide intensive professional development and supervision to community health workers, encouraging responsiveness and stimulation in mothers' interactions with their children, in health workers' interactions with the mothers, and in the interactions of the trainers with the health workers, many of whom had relatively low levels of education. In the Pakistan program, positive effects were observed in caregiving as well as in children's cognitive, language and motor skills at ages 12 and 24 months (Yousafzai et al., 2012).

In considering the major questions in the world for children, it is evident that the most fundamental, the provision of adequate support for ECEC itself, requires sustainable development (Pramling Samuelsson and Siraj-Blatchford, 2014). Whatever the form taken by programs to support families in support of children's learning, it needs to be viewed in a broad sense and be related to health and parents, caregivers and teachers' attitudes and skills. It is not a question of providing all children access to *any* early program, it is the quality that makes the difference in later success for children (Sylva et al., 2010). That said, one can claim that, for children in developing countries, an average quality program is better for children than not being taken care of or being cared for by siblings (UNICEF, 2012).

In summarizing, one can claim that there is enough research evidence and many international agreements for providing safe, secure and health-giving care and education for young children. There is also research evidence that ECEC can be a stepping stone for sustainability. There are, however, no clear roads or agreements on how an ECEC for sustainability should become a reality for all children.

SUSTAINABLE DEVELOPMENT RESTS UPON STRONG FOUNDATIONS, BEGINNING IN EARLY CHILDHOOD

The United Nations in New York (December 2013) hosted a seminar for a group of NGOs entitled *Post-2015 Global Policy Agenda: Early Childhood Development as a Foundation for Sustainable Development*. The message for politicians was clear and stated that hundreds of millions of children (aged 0–8) will not have the best start in life and develop to their potential because they grow up facing a broad range of risks, most notably poverty; poor health including HIV/AIDS and malnutrition; high levels of family and environmental stress; exposure to violence, abuse, neglect, exploitation; and inadequate levels of care and learning opportunities. This includes risks that result from emergencies related to conflict, climate change and global demographic shifts through migration and urbanization (Engle et al., 2007, 2011).

A compelling body of cross-disciplinary research and practice highlights the importance of investing in the early childhood

years, especially during critical and unique periods of brain development. Adverse risks and experiences can be mitigated by strengthening the environments in which young children grow through evidence-based strategies, i.e., parent support; early detection and intervention for developmental delays and disabilities; early childhood programs of care, support and learning; targeted health, nutrition, sanitation and social protection services; and good quality preschool and early primary-grade experiences.

Investment in development and learning during early childhood results in greater cost savings than investment later on in the life cycle (Heckman et al., 2012), with a return ranging from $8 to $18 for every dollar invested. Good quality early primary education (grades 1–3) combined with quality early childhood services, prior to children entering school, improves the efficiency of the schooling system and saves money by reducing repetition and drop-out and improving completion rates and achievement, especially for girls and other marginalized groups.

A measurable and actionable Early Childhood Development (ECD) goal – that all children get the best start in life and for learning in order to reach their development potential through ECD policies and programs – is part of a human development and rights-based framework that promotes equitable and sustainable development and that needs to be implemented in partnership with multiple sectors and partners. This kind of effort will help advance other important development goals – in particular, improving birth and achieving key health outcomes, improving access to quality basic education and learning outcomes, promoting social justice, advancing women's rights and gender equality, and ultimately reducing inequality and poverty. The conclusions of the workshop are:

- Early child development[2] should be included on the global development agenda.
- Given what we know in the area of brain science, we must start as young as possible to focus on

families, recognizing indigenous knowledge and practices, and go beyond education to address ECD across multiple sectors.

- There must be a focus on child development and on nurturing human capital along the life course through investment in ECD.
- The goal of reducing poverty and inequality must directly impact on children and strengthen families and social protection mechanisms.
- There must be integration of the most disadvantaged children in ECD.
- Pia Britto, Senior Advisor, Early Childhood Development Unit Programme Division at UN, mentioned the high correlation between the ECD Index and the Human Development Index – the more investment in ECD, the higher a country ranks on the HDI. She said: 'Young children are a living message for a world we may never see.' (Minutes from the meeting by Louise Zimanyl)

These conclusions can be seen as arguments for giving all children in the world a chance to participate in ECEC in order to achieve a more sustainable world. As UNICEF (2013) has stated: 'Sustainable Development starts and ends with safe, healthy and well-educated children.' Politicians have to look at what the barriers and challenges are for each country, as well as for the whole world, since we all are dependent on each other globally. With all the evidence around giving children a proper start in life, how can we afford not to spend money on the youngest age group?

In the next section of the chapter, we will discuss what can be done within ECEC for developing programs that intend to lead towards future sustainability.

PRACTICE IN EARLY CHILDHOOD EDUCATION AND CARE

If we managed to get all children into an ECEC setting,[3] how would this contribute to a sustainable world? What should be focused on and what possibilities and opportunities have to be included for education in the early years? There is evidence on the Internet for ECEC programs supporting sustainability work, and it is impressive how many good

examples there are from all over the world. One can also find organizations driving large projects in the area.

As we see it, sustainability questions in the early years need to be addressed in terms of content and learning objects, and in terms of pedagogy or, as we say in the Nordic countries, didactics (see Pramling and Pramling Samuelsson, 2011), which should be carried out in cooperation with young children. The word 'didactics' is used differently in the Nordic countries than in the English-speaking world (Pramling and Pramling Samuelsson, 2011), where it is related to instruction. When we in the Nordic countries talk about didactics we lean on the Greek origin, where it stands for 'pointing something out to someone' (Nordkvelle, 2003), and the whole *German bildung tradition* (Broström and Vejleskov, 2009), where care, play and learning are integrated in informal and non-formal ways. Although content and form are sometimes interrelated in early childhood, we will here separate them and discuss one at a time.

CONTENT OF SUSTAINABILITY IN THE EARLY YEARS

UNESCO's (2004–2014) dimensions of social/cultural factors, the environment and the economy have informed the visual representation of integrated sustainability in the early years (see Figure 30.2). There is, however, today sometimes a fourth dimension of children's rights

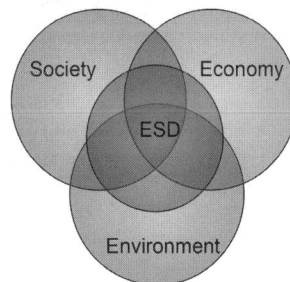

Figure 30.2 A simplified picture of ESD

Source: UNESCO, 2004–2014

and participation – that of course by necessity is in the core of sustainability.

First of all, the field of ECEC has a tradition of focusing on nature, typified as early as the 19th century in the work of Froebel (2004/1826). The move from a focus on nature to the environment was a small step, with environmental questions the most common aspect of the sustainability picture today. This is shown by the research of Davis (2009), with a focus on the environment and natural sciences, where she states that environmental questions have brought human, social aspects to the natural sciences.

Second, a focus on society and social-cultural approaches to ECEC must include a consideration of how to behave towards others, as well as matters of democracy and solidarity (Emilson and Johansson, in press). When parents are asked about their expectations of ECEC for their children, they most often put socialization at the top of their priority list (Ivarson-Jansson, 2001). Given that ECEC is a collective arena involving socializing with others beyond the family, it can be viewed as a micro society with its own norms, values and rules – which could be used in education as such.

Finally, the third dimension, the economy, has been largely overlooked in ECEC, yet is increasingly important. Case studies conducted in nine countries to test the OMEP Environmental Rating Scale for Sustainable Development in Early Childhood (ERS-SDEC), showed that teachers had their greatest problem with the notion of the economy (Siraj-Blatchford et al., in press). It may be that economics is seen as a family matter, much like religion, which is not easily discussed in ECEC, but on discussion preschool teachers could easily see how the economy could be brought up in everyday life with children in preschool (Kultti et al., in press). There are also excellent examples of OMEP world projects on 'equality for sustainability', where teachers work with inequality questions related to work, money and food from the starting point of a full and an empty fridge (Hammond et al., 2014).

In summary, sustainability questions in ECEC deal with all three aspects: society, the environment and the economy. Each can benefit from the others to form an integrated thematic approach. Working in preschool with themes or projects can integrate each of the ESD aspects. However, the learning object, that is, what we want to make visible to the child in creating a possibility for learning, can be narrow and focused on a specific meaning, at the same time as the child is viewed as a 'playing learning child' in a broader sense (Pramling Samuelsson and Asplund Carlsson, 2008).

Figure 30.3   OMEP logo for the first world project

OMEP[4] has had four world projects on ESD, where the overall aim has been to enhance the awareness of ESD with young children and their teachers in ECEC. The aim of ESD project Part 1, *Child interviews*, was to collect data on young children's thoughts, comments and understanding of the picture of the earth (see Figure 30.3): 9,142 children and 641 adults in 385 schools in 28 countries took part (Engdahl and Rabušicová, 2011). The aim of Part 2, *ESD in practice*, was to implement ESD together with children in early childhood education practices. But a further aim was to collect information for a greater understanding of young children's ideas and actions for ESD: 30,714 children and 12,075 adults in 29 countries participated in 396 projects. In Part 3, *Intergenerational dialogues for ESD*, the perspectives were broadened and extended beyond the pre-school/school. Children and teachers were asked to engage in intergenerational dialogues around three specific goals for a sustainable lifestyle. Such dialogues were found to bring mutual benefits for the young children and their teachers and caregivers, based on the local context and including indigenous and traditional knowledge. Intergenerational learning is a process through which people from all generations acquire skills and knowledge, and develop their attitudes and values. It takes place in everyday life and on all sorts of occasions. Intergenerational learning is not restricted to any specific age or to the view that you must learn specific things in specific ways. It recognizes and accepts learning as a relational process and that we all learn differently. Intergenerational dialogue as a method within the OMEP world project was introduced to clarify the links between ESD and lifelong learning. In total, 209 projects were conducted with 4475 children, 509 teachers, 2737 grandparents and 2389 parents involved (Engdahl and Rabušicová, 2013). Part 4, *Equality for sustainability*, involved 13 countries in 87 different projects, covering topics such as attitudes, the poor–rich and indigenous knowledge. This initiative was exemplified by the economy being placed on the agenda. The four world projects, involving children, teachers, childcare workers and parents, are making ECEC aware of sustainability questions and of the role of young children in sustainable futures (see www.worldomep.org, under Projects).

The ECEC sustainability agenda is also seen in the Early Childhood Australia Sustainability Interest Group (Young and Moore, 2010). The group's focus on biodiversity includes: (a) decay, scavenging, conservation, protection, hibernation, habitats; (b) making compost, worm farms and vegetable patches; (c) life and food cycles; (d) prey, predators and camouflage; (e) conducting biodiversity audits of the play space; (f) planting a diverse range of plants; (g) discussing plant and animal conservation; (h) sponsorship of an endangered or local species; (i) creation of frog bogs, bird baths and feeders; and (j) play space design discussions. These aspects are pertinent to ECEC practice.

In short, the content of ESD in ECEC covers relationships and values, including the relationship between human beings and nature, and the relationship between the economy and living conditions. It is also concerned with promoting children's awareness of inequality and unsustainability (Pramling Samuelsson, 2011). A topic that can be content related as well as pedagogical is the child's right to participate in decisions and in influencing their own learning, as well as in collective decisions and negotiations, not least for practicing and developing critical thinking.

WHAT IS A GOOD PEDAGOGY OR DIDACTICS FOR PROMOTING SUSTAINABILITY IN THE EARLY YEARS?

The Gothenburg Recommendations on Education for Sustainable Development (Ottosson and Samuelsson, 2008) identified six characteristics of ESD pedagogy in ECEC:

- building upon the everyday experiences of children
- curriculum integration and creativity

- intergenerational problem solving and solution seeking
- promotion of intercultural understanding and recognition of interdependency
- involvement of the wider community
- active citizenship in the early years.

Building upon everyday experiences of children is today a well-established approach in ECEC (Sommer et al., 2010). A child-centered pedagogy where the child is more important than the content taught has a long tradition within early childhood. To adapt to the child's world also means to allow for play and to recognize the individual child's experiences (Foss and Lillemyr, 2013). It is also a question of listening to the child to let the child's voice come through (Rinaldi, 2012; UNCRC, 1989).

Curriculum integration and creativity have a long tradition in ECEC. In the 19th century, this was sometimes called 'centres of interest' (Doverborg et al., 1987) – what today are labeled themes or projects (Katz and Chard, 1989). This means that there is an overriding topic that the work is united around, like the forest, the sea, communications, etc. within which all different learning objects could be focused (Pramling Samuelsson and Asplund Carlsson, 2008). Creative work is central in ECEC, not only in approaches like Reggio Emilia, but as far back as the most important issues arrived in early years, and as a source for creating meaning about the content worked on (Pramling and Pramling Samuelsson, 2011).

The Swedish-certified Green Flag preschools (Eco-preschools) constitute an example of a curriculum for ESD. In these preschools, priority is given to active environmental work in everyday life – towards ESD, democracy and participation. Children have to cover one of the following themes – the life cycle, water, energy, forests or lifestyle and health – for at least six months. An example of this is a preschool working through the following five topics over the course of a year: (1) sorting, (2) how a worm's compost functions, (3) the degradation process

in the forest, (4) from seed to seedling, and (5) environment-marked products.

Intergenerational problem solving and solution seeking is a main task in ESD, since sustainability is a complex question and it is why problem solving should be a topic as well as a method to focus on in the early years. By working on problems, children develop problem-solving strategies, which may not be those one needs for solving future problems, but being able to create solutions to solve problems is a key skill to develop early, and something which may be more important than knowing facts of various kinds. Problem solving is close to creativity, which may be what we need the most for taking action in response to various future problems (Robinson, 2000).

Promotion of intercultural understanding and recognition of interdependency. Many ECEC programs have children from diverse ethnic backgrounds. In such contexts, an everyday understanding of different cultures begins, by children seeing both the similarities between children and the differences in family experiences (Kultti, 2012). This aspect of interdependence can be highlighted in relations between human beings and nature, as an interrelationship, but also related to how people are dependent on each other in various ways (Hundeide, 2006).

Involvement of the wider community can be viewed as 'children as global citizens'. This means giving children support to recognize the need for sustainable development, for equality globally and locally. It also points to the values, responsibilities and rights of the child and of those around them. An important issue today is preparing children for all kinds of risks and disasters, without scaring them (Pramling Samuelsson and Siraj-Blatchford, 2014). Disaster risk reduction (DRR) aims at reducing risks and strengthening supports in order to mitigate the impact of these disasters. In the context of ECEC, this involves ensuring that the preschools, ECD centers, health services, orphanages and homes of young children are hazard resistant. Research in this area has shown that children also have a role as risk communicators, supporting the behavioral changes required of other people in their communities (Tanner, 2010).

Active citizenship in the early years sees children as competent persons who can influence their neighborhood and family (Kurt Lewin Foundation, 2012), but also ECEC as such. In a study in Sweden, children were involved in remodeling their own preschool yard. From interviews and observation of children's play outdoors, the dialogue between teachers and children framed an outdoor environment which was much more in accordance with what children really wanted than before the dialogue took place (Engdahl and Ärlemalm-Hagsér, 2010). In another study, together with their teachers, children in one preschool managed to change the routine in buying eggs of a better quality after a long project where children studied both eggs and the hens' living conditions (Pramling Samuelson and Kaga, 2010). Related to questions of sustainability, the idea of preschool children as agents for change has to be a strong element in pedagogy (Ärlemalm-Hagsér, 2013; Caiman and Lunnegård, 2013).

CONCLUSION

If we are to take children seriously, as claimed by the European Panel for Sustainable Development (EPSD, 2010: 7), we need 'to realize that the process towards sustainable development lies in the capabilities of our children, but also in that we as adults recognize them and take them seriously'. We do that by making it possible for an acceptable start in life where ECEC operates as one important and necessary contribution. Different actors need to be involved in young children's life around sustainability questions. An excellent example of this is the Leuchtpol (Lighthouse) project in Germany (Stoltenberg et al., 2013) where the University of Lüneburg, an environmental organization and the energy concern E.ON contributed to the project with the aim of implementing

sustainable development at the level of ECEC; 4000 preschool teachers and their children were involved in the project. The evaluation showed a deeper understanding among staff as well as children, but also changed behavior in families and in the preschool teachers' lives outside work. This unusual collaboration between different actors is what we need a lot more of in the future. Everyone must be involved in young children's life – it is everyone's business!

To develop ECEC with a sustainable perspective, we must both look at policy questions and ensure that every child has a good start in life and has access to ECEC. The ECEC setting, however labeled, needs to have intentions of both care and education, since education starts at birth in communication and interaction with caregivers. It is also a policy question of how curricula or frameworks for the youngest children are formulated, and where sustainability is introduced (Ärlemalm-Hagsér and Davis, 2014). ESD is argued here to be a worldwide priority, in all curricula. However slow a process, drawing on more examples of projects, teachers may be inclined to tackle questions of sustainability (Kultti et al., in press). It is, however, also important that everyday life in ECEC, led by staff, adapts into a sustainable mode by, for example, sorting and composting, and saving electricity, making these things habitual for children. All of this needs to be regulated by policy!

One problem for practice within ECEC in the developing world is that most staff working there have very little or no education of their own. Even in developed countries, this group of staff often has a lower educational background than have primary school teachers (Education International, 2010). This has nothing to do with facts, but with status! Whatever the educational level of teachers, there are a lot of content areas that could be covered, wherever the ECEC setting is located. With modern technology coming to most countries, it is easy to stay in contact with preschools in other parts of the world, which has been shown to inspire and challenge both children and teachers in their daily work (Siraj-Blatchford et al., 2010).

CRITICAL REFLECTIONS FOR FUTURE SUSTAINABILITY QUESTIONS IN ECEC

At the same time as we want a sustainable world, shown in many international policy agreements (Pramling Samuelsson, 2011), we also know that the notion of sustainability is not an easy one. It has been interpreted in many different ways (Knutsson, 2011). It is also a notion that is framed in policy and ideology, which has to be interpreted for each context or research project. The fact that policy, ideology and various national contexts vary makes it hard to point to the core of it all, which also has consequences for research in the area.

Large-scale reputable research studies are few. This might be related to the fact that ESD in itself is a multidisciplinary question, but also that it demands longitudinal studies that are extremely expensive and difficult to carry out with all the variables that are involved in ESD. Hence, although publications from UNESCO and others, as well as journal articles, are accumulating, they are still few and far between compared to those on many other issues relating to children. According to Hedefalk, Almqvist and Östman (2014), articles on ECEC and ESD either focus on the implementation of ESD in ECEC or on teacher competences or the lack of them.

While there is no universal agreement that ESD should begin in ECEC, many argue for it (Pramling Samuelsson, 2011). Arguments for not involving young children are that adults have caused the problems of unsustainability and should therefore have to solve them, or that children should live a happy life without needing to tackle such problems (Björneloo, 2006). The fact remains that children are already involved, in the course of their everyday lives. In the knowledge society of today, we need evidence, not only of what children

need to grow up and become able to use their full potential, but also of what the various experiences of the early years lead to in terms of attitudes and values, and not least of what contributes to supporting children as agents for change (Ärlemalm-Hagsér, 2013). Some teachers seem to think that children need facts, others that children have to be controlled in their behavior, as, for example, in making sure they pick up rubbish. Finally, some teachers claim that children have to be involved in negotiation to develop critical thinking (see Flogaitis and Agelidou, 2003; Sandberg and Ärlemalm-Hagsér, 2011). What the consequences are of these different strategies for children's learning in, about and for ESD have not yet been evaluated. The only thing we know is that we need children capable of confronting various problems in the future, since these problems are not going to be solved by the time they are grown up. What we also know is that there is no one single way to prepare children for this, but children are children today and not tomorrow, or, as one of our teachers said: 'Working with young children is like being in direct broadcasting all the time – and it cannot be changed by words.'

FURTHER READING

Davis, J. (eds.) (2014) *Young Children and the Environment: Early Education for Sustainable Development* (2nd edition). Cambridge: Cambridge University Press.

Pramling, N. and Pramling Samuelsson, I. (eds.) (2011) *Educational Encounters: Nordic Studies in Early Childhood Didactics*. Dordrecht: Springer.

Pramling Samuelsson, I. and Asplund Carlsson, M. (2008) 'The playing learning child: Towards a pedagogy of early childhood', *Scandinavian Journal of Educational Research*, 52(6), 623–641.

QUESTIONS FOR REFLECTION

1   How can we develop indicators for measuring the status of ESD in ECEC?

2　How can ECEC be a forerunner in ESD?
3　In what ways are ECEC and ESD dealt with in your country's curriculum for ESD?
4　What is the difference between a high quality program and an ESD-based program?
5　How can we make visible what it looks like to make young children agents for change?

NOTES

1　Definitions of early childhood education and care vary in different countries and regions, according to local traditions and the organization of primary school systems. It is also labelled differently. Here, however, we mean all kinds of setting before school-entry age, which varies in different countries.
2　The UN uses the term Early Child Development, where they include ECEC.
3　An ECEC setting can mean different things in different cultures, but it has to be a caring, nurturing, healthy and educative provision in the community context.
4　OMEP is an international, non-governmental and non-profit organisation (NGO) founded in 1948 with the objective to defend and promote the rights of the child from birth to 8 years to high quality education and care worldwide. OMEP is currently established in over 70 countries and holds a consultative status within UNESCO, UNICEF and the European Council.

REFERENCES

Ärlemalm-Hagsér, E. (2013) Engagerade i världens bästa? Lärande för hållbarhet i förskolan [An interest in the best for the world? Education for sustainability in the Swedish preschool] (Doctoral thesis, Gothenburg Studies in Educational Sciences 335). Gothenburg, Sweden: University of Gothenburg.

Ärlemalm-Hagsér, E. and Davis, J. (2014) 'Examining the rhetoric: A comparison of how sustainability and young children's participation and agency are framed in Australian and Swedish early childhood education curricula', *Contemporary Issues in Early Childhood*, 15(3), 231–244.

Björneloo, I. (2006) *Innebörder av hållbar utveckling: En studie om lärares utsagor om undervisning* [Meaning of sustainable development: A study of teachers' expressions]. Gothenburg, Sweden: University of Gothenburg.

Britto, P. and Ulkuer, N. (2012) 'Child development in developing countries: Child rights and policy implementations', *Child Development*, 83(1), 92–103.

Broström, S. and Vejleskov, H. (2009) *Didaktik i børnehaven: Planer, principper og praksis* [Didaktik in preschool: Plans, principles and practice]. Frederikshavn, Denmark: Dafolo.

Brundtland Commission (1978) *Report of the World Commission on Environment and Development: Our Common Future*. Oxford: Oxford University Press.

Caiman, C. and Lunnegård, L. (2013) 'Pre-school children's agency in learning for sustainable development', *Environmental Education Research*.

Chua, F. and Heckman, J. (2007) The technology of skill formation. Institute for the Study of Labor discussion papers (ftp://ftp.iza.org/SSRN/pdf/dp2550.pdf).

Davis, J. (2009) 'Revealing the research 'hole' of early childhood education for sustainability: A preliminary survey of the literature', *Environmental Education Research*, 15(2), 227–241.

Doverborg, E., Pramling, I. and Qvarsell, B. (1987) *Inlärning och utveckling: Barnet, förskolan och skolan* [Learning and development: The child, preschool and school]. Stockholm: Liber.

Education International (2010) Early childhood education: A global scenario. A study conducted by the Education International ECE Task Force, June (http://download.ei-ie.org/Docs/WebDepot/ECE_A_global_scenario_EN.PDF).

Emilson, A. and Johansson, E. (in press) 'Values in Nordic early childhood education: Democracy and the child's perspective', in M. Fleer and B. van Oers (eds.), *International Handbook on Early Childhood Education and Development*. Dordrecht: Springer.

Engdahl, I. and Rabušicová, M. (2011) 'Children's voices about the state of the earth', *International Journal of Early Childhood*, 43, 153–176.

Engdahl, I. and Rabušicová, M. (2013) *Report on the OMEP World Project on Education for Sustainable Development 2009–2013* (www.worldomep.org/en/education-for-sustainable-development/).

Engdahl, I. and Ärlemalm-Hagsér, E. (2010) *Barns delaktighet i det fysiska rummet: Svenska*

OMEP:s utvecklingsprojekt med stöd av Allmänna arvsfonden 2007–2010 [Child participation outdoors in the Swedish preschool: A development project from OMEP Sweden supported by The Swedish Inheritage Fund 2007–2009]. Stockholm: OMEP.

Engle, P., Black, M., Behrman, J., Cabral de Mello, M., Gertler, P., Kapiriri, L., et al. (2007) 'Strategies to avoid the loss of developmental potential in more than 200 million children in the developing world', *The Lancet*, 369, 229–242.

Engle, P., Fernald, L., Alderman, H., Behrman, J., O'Gara, C., Yousafza, A., et al. (2011) 'Strategies for reducing inequalities and improving developmental outcomes for young children in low-income and middle-income countries', *The Lancet*, 378, 1339–1353.

European Panel for Sustainable Development (EPSD) (2010) *Taking children seriously: How the EU can invest in early childhood education for a sustainable future.* Centre for Environment and Sustainability, Chalmers/University of Gothenburg (www.ufn.gu.se/digitalAssets/1324/1324488_epsd_report4.pdf).

Flogaitis, E. and Agelidou, E. (2003) 'Kindergarten teachers' conceptions about nature and the environment', *Environmental Education Research*, 9(4), 461–478.

Foss, E. and Lillemyr, O.F. (eds.) (2013) *Till barnas beste: Veier til omsorg og lek, laering og danning* [To the wellbeing of children: Ways to care and play, learning and development]. Oslo: Gyldendahl Akademisk.

Froebel, F. (2004/1826) *Människans utbildning* [On the Education of Man] (Die Menschenerziehung). Keilhau/Leipzig: Wienbrach.

Grantham-McGregor, S., Cheung, P.B., Cueto, S., Glewwe, P., Richter, L. and Strupp, B. (2007) 'Developmental potential in the first 5 years for children in developing countries', *The Lancet*, 369, 60–70.

Hammond, L.-L., Hesterman, S., Knaus, M. and Vajda, M. (2014) *Children's ideas about families' access to food from a perspective of wealth and poverty.* OMEP World Project: Equality for Sustainability, presented at the OMEP conference in Cork, 3 July.

Heckman, J.J., Pinto, R. and Savelyev, P. (2012) Understanding the Mechanisms through Which an Influential Early Childhood Program Boosted Adult Outcomes. NBER Working

Paper No. 18581, November (www.nber.org/papers/w18581).

Hedefalk, M., Almqvist, J. and Östman, L. (2014) Education for sustainable development in early childhood education: A review of the research literature. *Environmental Education Research*. Available at: http://www.tandfonline.com/doi/full/10.1080/13504622.2014.971716

Hundeide, K. (2006) *Sociokulturella ramar för barns utveckling: barns livsvärldar* [Sociocultural frames for children's development: Children's life worlds]. Lund, Sweden: Studentlitteratur.

Ivarson-Jansson, E. (2001) *Relationen hem–förskola* [The relationship of preschool–home]. Umeå: Pedagogiska Institutionen, Umeå Universitet.

Kagitcibasi, C., Unar, D. and Bekman, S. (2001) 'Long-term effects of early intervention: Turkish low income mothers and children', *Applied Developmental Psychology*, 22, 333–361.

Katz, L. and Chard, S. (1989) *Engaging Children's Minds: The Project Approach*. Norwood, NJ: Ablex.

Knutsson, B. (2011) *Curriculum in the Era of Global Development: Historical Legacies and Contemporary Approaches*. Gothenburg, Sweden: University of Gothenburg.

Kultti, A. (2012) *Flerskpråkiga barn i förskolan: Villkor för deltagande och lärande* [Multilingual children in preschool: Conditions for participation and learning]. Gothenburg, Sweden: University of Gothenburg.

Kultti, A., Ärlemalm-Hagsér, E., Larsson, J. and Pramling Samuelsson, I. (in press) 'Education for sustainability in Swedish early childhood education', in J. Siraj-Blatchford, E. Park and C. Mogrerraban (eds.) *Developing a Research Programme for Education for Sustainable Development in Early Childhood*. Dordrecht: Springer.

Kurt Lewin Foundation (2012) *Youth and active citizenship* (www.opensocietyfoundations.org/reports/youth-and-active-citizenship).

Landaeta, D. and Cardenas, A. (2013) Prevención de Enfermedades Infecciosas En La Población Infantil de Colombia, División de Salud Comunitaria.

Nordkvelle, Y.T. (2003) 'Didactics: From classical rhetoric to kitchen Latin', *Pedagogy, Culture & Society*, 11(3), 315–330.

Ottosson, P. and Samuelsson, B. (eds) (2008) *The Gothenburg Recommendations on Education for Sustainable Development*. Centre for Environment and Sustainability (GMV), Chalmers/University of Gothenburg, Sweden.

Pramling, N. and Pramling Samuelsson, I. (eds) (2011) *Educational Encounters: Nordic Studies in Early Childhood Didactics*. Dordrecht: Springer.

Pramling Samuelsson, I. (2011) 'Why we should begin early with ESD: The role of early childhood education', *International Journal of Early Childhood*, 43(2), 103–118.

Pramling Samuelsson, I. and Asplund Carlsson, M. (2008) 'The playing learning child: Towards a pedagogy of early childhood', *Scandinavian Journal of Educational Research*, 52(6), 623–641.

Pramling Samuelsson, I. and Kaga, Y. (eds) (2008) *The Contribution of Early Childhood Education to a Sustainable Society*. Paris: UNESCO (http://unesdoc.unesco.org/images/0015/001593/159355e.pdf).

Pramling Samuelsson, I. and Kaga, Y. (2010) 'Early childhood education to transform cultures for sustainability', in *State of the World 2010: Transforming Cultures – From Consumerism to Sustainability* (pp. 57–61). Worldwatch Institute (www.worldwatch.org).

Pramling Samuelsson, I. and Siraj-Blatchford, J. (2014) Education for Sustainable Development in Early Childhood Care and Education. A UNESCO Background Paper.

Pramling Samuelsson, I. and Wagner, J. (2012) 'Open appeal to local, national, regional and global leaders to secure the world's future', *International Journal of Early Childhood*, 44(3), 341–346.

Robinson, K. (2000) *Ken Robinson says schools kill creativity*. Accessed at: www.ted.com/talks/ken_robinson_says_schools_kill_creativity.html

Rinaldi, C. (2012) *In Dialogue with Reggio Emilia: Listening, Researching and Learning*. London: Routledge.

Sandberg, A. and Ärlemalm-Hagsér, E. (2011) 'The Swedish national curriculum: Play and learning with fundamental values in focus', *Australian Journal of Early Childhood*, 36(1), 44–50.

Sommer, D., Pramling Samuelsson, I. and Hundeide, K. (2010) *Child Perspectives and Children's Perspectives in Theory and Practice*. New York: Springer.

Siraj-Blachford, J., Park, E. and Mogrerraban, C. (eds) (in press) *Developing a Research Programme for Education for Sustainable Development in Early Childhood*. New York: Springer.

Siraj-Blatchford, J., Smith, K.C. and Pramling Samuelsson, I. (2010) *Education for Sustainable Development in the Early Years*. Göteborg, Sweden: Svenska OMEP.

Stoltenberg, U., Benoist, B. and Koster, T. (2013) *Modellprojekte verändern die Bildungdlandschaft: Am Beispiel des Projekys Leuchtpol*. Hamburg: VAS-Verlag für Akademische Schriften.

Sustainable Development Solutions Network (SDSN) (2013) *A Global Initiative for the United Nations: The Future of Our Children: Lifelong, Multi-Generational Learning for Sustainable Development*. Thematic group report (http://unsdsn.org/).

Swedish National Agency for Education (Skolverket) (2011) *The Curriculum for the Preschool*, Lpfö 98 (www.skolverket.se/om-skolverket/andra-sprak-och-lattlast/in-english/the-swedish-education-system/preschool).

Sylva, K., Melhuish, E., Simmons, P., Siraj-Blatchford, I. and Taggart, B. (2010) *Early Childhood Matters: Evidence from the Effective Pre-school and Primary Education Project*. London: Routledge.

Tanner, T. (2010) 'Shifting the narrative: Child-led responses to climate change and disasters in El Salvador and the Philippines', *Children & Society*, 24, 339–351.

UNESCO (2012) Opportunities lost: The impact of grade repetition and early school leaving (www.uis.unesco.org/Education/GED%20Documents%20C/GED-2012-Complete-Web3.pdf).

UNESCO (2014) Results from the ESD UNESCO Questionnaire 2: Input from online survey for Member States, Key Stakeholders and UN Agencies, January.

UNICEF (2012) *Inequities in Early Childhood Development: What the Data Say*. Evidence from the Multiple Indicator Cluster Surveys, February.

UNICEF (2013) Sustainable development starts and ends with safe, healthy and well-educated children: A post-2015 world fit for children, May (www.unicef.org/post2015/files/Sustainable_Development_post_2015.pdf).

UNICEF (2014) WASH in schools: About water, sanitation and hygiene (www.unicef.org/wash/schools/).

United Nations (UN) (1948) *The Universal Declaration of Human Rights* (www.un.org/en/documents/udhr/).

United Nations (UN) (1989) *UN Convention on the Rights of the Child (UNCRC)*. New York: United Nations.

United Nations (UN) (2012) *The Future We Want*. A/RES/66/288 (https://sustainabledevelopment.un.org/futurewewant.html).

Västra Götalands Regionen (2014) Tvätta, tvätta liten hand: Hygiensjuksköterska i förskolan [Wash, wash the little hand: Hygiene nurse in preschool]. www.vgregion.se/upload/Smittskyddsenheten/Projekt/

Wals, A. (2006) *The end of ESD… the beginning of transformative learning – emphasizing the E in ESD*. Paper presented at the Gothenburg Consultation on Sustainability in Higher Education.

Weikart, D. (1989) *Quality Pre-school Programs: A Long-term Social Investment*. Occasional Paper 5, Ford Foundation.

Wilkinson, R. and Pickett, K. (2010) *Why Equality is Better for Everyone*. London: Penguin.

Young, T. and Moore, D. (2010) Healthy biodiversity is no luxury: It's the foundation of all life on earth. Early Childhood Australia Sustainability Interest Group, accessed at: www.earlychildhoodaustralia.org.au/wp-content/uploads/2015/04/Biodiveristy_fact_sheet.pdf

Yousafzai, A.K., Rasheed, M.A. and Bhutta, Z.A. (2012) 'Annual research review: Improved nutrition – a pathway to resilience', *Journal of Child Psychology and Psychiatry*, 54, 367–377.

31

Future Directions in Early Childhood Research: Addressing Next-Step Imperatives

Sharon Lynn Kagan, E. Kay M. Tisdall and Ann Farrell

INTRODUCTION

To paraphrase Dickens, in many ways, this may be the best of times to produce a new volume on early childhood research, and, in some ways, it may be the worst. Early childhood research is at a critical juncture; it is a time laden with opportunities and challenges. With regard to opportunities, the research field is rapidly expanding, encouraged by political concerns about children as future citizens and by new and well-popularized concepts such as children's well-being, children's rights, and children as social actors. This era is also characterized by methodological innovations in both quantitative and qualitative research, which are joined by inventive approaches to conceptualizing and conducting research in diverse contexts. Drawing on new theories and disciplines, including neuroscience and economics that complement its more traditional research disciplines, notably education and developmental psychology, early childhood

education (ECE) research is expanding and gaining worldwide momentum. These broadened lines of inquiry inspire new thinking and perspectives along with some new opportunities for funding and influencing practice and policy.

But such expansion also breeds new challenges regarding what is researched, who are researchers, how research is conceptualized, how it is carried out, and how it is used. Contemporary ECE research also sits amidst increasingly complex social, political, and environmental contexts that contour the research enterprise and present formidable challenges. In concluding the volume, this chapter seeks to address both the opportunities and the challenges; more specifically, it aims to review succinctly the major opportunities facing those engaged in ECE research and the major challenges with which they will be forced to contend. Although not fully inclusive of all the issues addressed in this volume, this chapter highlights some of the major themes evoked by the volume's authors and discerned by its editors for early childhood research. This chapter, much like the volume itself, is predicated on the stance that research is not simply an element of ECE, but rather is a necessary elixir for its improvement.

THE CHANGING CONTEMPORARY CONTEXT FOR ECE RESEARCH INTERNATIONALLY

Increasingly complex, many themes characterize the contemporary context for ECE research, some with historic roots and others emanating from 21st-century phenomena. Four themes, especially pertinent to the contemporary context, will be discussed: (i) the rise in social commitments to young children, generally; (ii) the consequences of these ideological and socio-political changes; (iii) the changing nature of the social context; and (iv) the increasing demand for usable research on young children and their families.

The Rise in Social Commitments to Young Children Generally

Throughout most of the world, interest in the well-being, care, health, and/or education of young children (defined as birth to age 8) has escalated to the top of the political agenda. Certainly, not all countries share the same motivations for this interest, nor do they share the same programmatic or policy strategies to bolster that interest. They do, however, learn and policy borrow from each other (Steiner-Khamsi and Waldow, 2012), and so, although armed with different intents and approaches, countries around the world are vastly increasing their interest and investments in young children.

Be it in the Global South or the Global North, emerging or established economies, or conservative or liberal political regimes, new commitments to young children are prevalent.

Such commitments are in part due to the increased visibility, both conceptually and practically, and to the prevalence and popularization of research on young children. Such research includes findings from pedagogical and social science research that affirm the importance of quality education and care, and demonstrate its impact on child well-being. Emanating from diverse disciplines including economics, political science, developmental psychology, neurobiology, and pedagogical theory, a cascade of positive empirical findings, strengthened by the diversity of the disciplines, has verified the effect of quality ECE (Camilli et al., 2010; Karoly, 2006; King, 2006; Shonkoff and Phillips, 2000; Weiland and Yoshikawa, 2013). So strong and diverse are the data that it is impossible to responsibly refute the benefits and cost-effectiveness of high-quality ECE for the development of young children or the accrued benefits to their societies (Chetty et al., 2011; Heckman, 2006; Heckman et al., 2010).

This surging interest in young children and ECE research is also propelled by the changing social context. For families, mothers' increasing labor force participation, particularly in the Global North, extends the need for quality childcare and early education services and research attendant to them. From the perspective of increasing global competitiveness, amply bolstered by league tables including children's well-being report cards of the United Nations Children's Fund (UNICEF) and the Programme for International Student Assessment (PISA), there is evidence of both inequitable access to services and significant disparities in children's outcomes. Together, these drivers encourage more attention to ECE settings and more efforts to make them accessible to young children. As Qvortrup (1994) notes, while ideologically children may remain within the family, children are in practice being increasingly individualized and institutionalized in ECE settings. ECE service expansion, then, also propels the call for more ECE research.

Such interest in research, however, should not be confused with agreement regarding its content or methods. Indeed, much of the ECE research, replete with its nuanced findings, is somewhat inconclusive; indeed, controversy persists regarding every examined element that the research touches: the nature of quality, the requisite amount of investment necessary, the preferred pedagogical approaches, and the ideal timing and duration of precise early childhood interventions (Besharov and Ramey, 2008; Brooker and Woodhead, 2013; Dahlberg and Lenz-Taguchi, 1994; Fuller, 2007; Walker and Chang, 2013; Zaslow et al., 2010). Divergent results cannot mask, and may even fuel, escalating interest in services and supports for young children.

Empirical data do not stand alone. Buttressing it, documents from major international organizations including the United Nations and its allied agencies (UNESCO, 2010a, 2010b; UNICEF, 2014), the Organization for Economic Cooperation and Development (OECD, 2012), the European Union, philanthropic entities, and foundations have conspired to increase the prominence of early childhood education and young children in international circles (Naudeau et al., 2011). Seminal documents, including the United Nations Convention on the Rights of the Child, the Millennium Development Goals, Education for All, and A World Fit for Children, all speak to the importance of education and of health, beginning early in life. Adding weight and visibility to the attention being accorded ECE, the business community in the USA has weighed in on the importance of the early years (Committee for Economic Development, 2006). Accompanying these documents, many of their organizational sponsors have proffered implementation supports in the form of grants, awards, and fiscal incentives to boost further investments in young children.

Finally, with increased sophistication, social advocates have turned to the media to popularize these efforts, increasing further public/private interests and investments in young children. Although, historically, important developmental research has existed, its applicability to practice and policy has been somewhat limited because of its comparative inaccessibility, with major publication efforts typically taking the form of scholarly journal articles or academic presentations. Presently, with the advancement of technology and the commitment of scholars to having their research used to advance social well-being, a new era in scientific communication has emerged, with data on young children and their families being regularly popularized in popular magazines, television broadcasts, social media, and the blogosphere. Governments, too, have increased their use of the media, seeking to highlight the importance of early childhood and their efforts to advance child and family well-being. In many countries, ECE, once barely discussed, has become a mainstay of electoral campaigns.

The Consequences of Increased Social Commitments

Covering a broad swath of society, the above efforts have all been powerful elixirs in elevating young children to the social agenda, but with what consequences? Although such attention fosters growing awareness, it does not fall on a tabula rosa; individuals, countries, and governments have historic ideas about how they 'hold' children and childhood. Insight from childhood studies (e.g., James and Prout, 1990; Mayall, 2002; Wyness, 2015) suggests that how children and childhood are understood and socially constructed, in any particular context, have considerable implications for the policies, services, and practices that frame children's lives. For example, in the Global North, 'traditional' ideas about children, and particularly young children, characterized them as innocent, passive, and dependent on adults. As a result, it was believed that young children were to be protected and instructed, with pedagogical ideas of an 'empty vessel' where children were to be filled with information, skills, and social graces that would move them from the unruly years of childhood into the world of the fully socialized adult. Childhood studies, aligned with children's rights and other initiatives, have argued for alternative constructions of childhood and, particularly, for children to be seen as social actors, who are 'active in the construction of their own lives, the lives of those around them and of the societies in which they live' (James and Prout, 1990: 8).

Children are now seen as possessing capabilities, intentions, and desires; they are regarded as influencers of their relationships, as actors in their social dramas, and as sculptors of their lives and destinies. Children are increasingly seen as vital human capital with the potential to shape the destiny of a country. More than ever before, children are regarded as active participants in society, entitled to the rights and privileges thereof.

Given that young children are no longer metaphorically sequestered, but are racing to the fore of public discourse, societies are forced to reckon with them. New questions are being asked and new stances are being negotiated: what should a society do for its youngest citizens? What can it do, in light of other social demands and needs? Are young children a public responsibility or a private obligation of their families? If they are a matter of public concern and social destiny, what is the government's appropriate level of engagement, for whom and under what conditions, and how is it best to distribute these services among levels of government (local, regional, and national) and its diverse ministries? What is the role of the private sector and of civic society, and should and how should private sector and/or civic society involvement be incentivized? In short, the increased attention to young children as rights bearers has raised new and perhaps more challenging questions than it has answered. Such questions transcend conventional topics, including the pedagogy of the program, and cut to the core of fundamental challenges facing a new and expanded vision of children and childhood, with many of these issues challenging long-held cultural values, social norms, and conventional political commitments to children that differ

considerably within and across countries. As such, contemporary early childhood is raising both new and highly provocative questions, many of which beg for new and different conceptualizations of childhood as well as new and different forms of research (Kagan and Gomez, 2015).

Rethinking the Social Context from a Child-Rights Perspective

It is axiomatic, if not somewhat plebeian, to note that, like the conceptions of children and childhood, the social context has changed dramatically. Indeed, globalization has made the world smaller and flatter, and technological advances have whittled geographic distances and time differences down, if not away. Amidst the rhetorical call for ECE to become a right of all children (United Nations, 2014; Voipio, 2012; White, 2007), however, reality happens: wars persist, children continue to live lives compromised by exploitative adults, and natural disasters condemn millions of youngsters annually to compromised health, sanitation, and safety conditions. So pervasive that they are unable to be ignored, these contextual realities challenge conventional thinking, research, and policy paradigms. As such, they must be considered as ECE research matures.

Data play a critical role in fusing conventional and paradigmatic thinking. Increasing numbers of international data sets, many of them used in this volume, render researchers and policy makers far more aware of the life conditions of children globally. Data now routinely convey the status of young children, noting their neglect, malnourishment, and proneness to disease. Data also convey the widely disparate access to services and the highly varied quality of such services. The availability of such data, and the technology to manipulate them, reveals embarrassing international comparisons. This, coupled with the increased zest for definitive accountability reporting in many nations, suggests that country 'secrets' about children's status are being eradicated. Transparency is a new norm and, with such transparency, comes the sometimes shocking awareness that the conditions of children, much less their inherent rights, are compromised.

Concurrently, the prevalence of rich demographic data not only reveals important population shifts, but it also reveals a new understanding of children as a social imperative. In many European countries, for example, the population is aging, with declining overall populations notable. In these contexts, children are highly valued for the joys they evoke as children, but also as potential and precious transmitters of culture and tradition. In other countries, populations are diversifying, buoyed by influxes of immigrants, or by escalating birth rates among some segments of the population (McLanahan, 2004). Whether it be the 'graying' or the 'multicoloring' of societies, children are caught in the vortex. For countries with graying populations, pronatalist incentives are emerging, as well as incentives to support young families and their children. For countries with multicoloring and sometimes burgeoning populations of young children, efforts to create access to and manage equitable services and supports are not distributed evenly among the population (Chandy and Gertz, 2011; Lee and Burkam, 2002; Narayan, 2012). New understandings about emerging demographic changes position young children at the center of debate, policy, practice, and research in unprecedented ways. Although different approaches are taken to meet children's rights, the need to regard children with respect and as rights bearers is fueled by changing demographics.

Rethinking the Social Context from a Research Perspective

The combination of increased technological capacity and the need for prudent public and private investments has accelerated an international accountability movement that perpetually demands new data, new and sophisticated data systems, and increasingly usable research. Calls for 'research-based' investments and policy herald this movement and, along with them, the press for more usable research. No longer content to have research sit in scholarly journals, the current social context is holding data and research to a more practicable level of accountability. Governments and major funding entities are interested: in program evaluations; in ongoing longitudinal data on the performance of children, students, and their families; and in chronicles and costs associated with the services provided. The international accountability movement potentially provides a boost to research and researchers, while it also imposes new demands on children, practitioners, researchers, and policy makers.

Examples of the press for usable data and research, mentioned throughout this volume, are plentiful. Among them is the call for new approaches and techniques for conducting quantitative research. Indeed, this call has yielded many inventive statistical approaches that serve to both extend and complicate research realms and confidences. Simultaneously, a call for renewed focus on new and different forms of qualitative research is emerging, in part as an antidote to finely calibrated and increasingly sophisticated quantitative methodologies. As demonstrated in many chapters in this volume, qualitative research in particular, and quantitative research to some extent, has argued for research *with*, rather than *on*, children. This seeks to respect children's own meanings, views, and experiences, in contrast to extractive research that treats children as objects or only uses their parents' responses as proxies. Mixed-method studies are emerging in increasing numbers. Along with such methodological diversification, new ethical issues are being raised, as traditional ethical issues maintain their currency.

Researchers are also diversifying their units of analysis and expanding their domains of inquiry. For example, the conventional focus on individual children and programs is being augmented by new emphases on ECE systems and systemic infrastructure.

These emphases are enhancing the already diverse disciplines represented in ECE research. Logical in part because young children are not the purview of any single discipline, interest from the medical and health, education and pedagogical, psychological, social science and mental health communities is part of the richly diverse traditional research ethos. Less conventional, however, is the research focus of economists, political scientists, environmentalists, implementation and evaluation scientists, and the neuroscientific community. Through their diverse lens, each discipline sees a piece of the child, recalling the proverbial elephant who looks and feels different depending on whether his trunk, ear, or leg is touched. The challenge is seeing the 'elephant', or the child, as a whole and not privileging any single research tradition or discipline, no matter how highly esteemed. For research on young children, this is complex. Some research disciplines are traditionally more respected for the scientific nature of their inquiry and for the precise protocols associated with their research traditions. For example, economists' data carry a great deal of weight: they can boost or dismantle direct services to young children, based on economic rationalism and cost-effectiveness studies that may lead to reductions in services that are costly but otherwise effective. The challenge is compounded because new research disciplines are emerging and have not had the time to establish the status associated with more highly perfected, scientific methodologies and instruments associated with some disciplines. However welcome, the vast amounts of emerging research from diverse disciplines will need to be considered. Honoring the contributions of each, while entwining the work of all, remains a large challenge in early childhood research.

Rethinking the Social Context: A Summary

Increased attention to young children and early childhood is now pervasive in diverse countries throughout the world. Fueled by demographic changes, advancements in technology, and economic and social globalization, children, and research about them, have escalated in importance. Research has also expanded and diversified, creating new methodological and content challenges. In turn, this emerging zeitgeist has rendered this volume and the need to examine the challenges of producing and using research on young children from ethical, methodological, and diverse disciplinary perspectives an extremely salient and prescient issue. It is to those issues that this chapter now turns.

THE CHALLENGE OF *PRODUCING* RESEARCH FOR INTERNATIONAL ECE

For convenience, the challenges associated with producing research for young children and early childhood education research can be broken down into three distinct categories: (i) endemic challenges, (ii) methodological and funding challenges, and (iii) content challenges. The endemic challenges are related to the nature of children and childhood and the field, itself. The methodological challenges embrace issues associated with *how* research is carried out; more specifically, the nature of research traditions, tools, biases, and approaches. Finally, the content challenges address *what* is to be researched.

Endemic Challenges

Conducting research on young children and the environments in which they are served, by definition, is complicated and is sometimes more challenging than conducting research on populations of older children. Indeed, the very nature of young children's development and their life conditions complicates data collection for research purposes (Snow, 2011). Young children, for example, have very rapid rates of growth and development, rendering data collected at one point in time reflective of only that moment, and not of children's potential for development. Moreover, young children's learning is somewhat episodic, that is they often learn something, forget it, and then quite naturally re-learn it. This, too, makes capturing accurate data very difficult. Additionally, young children may be restless and anxious in new settings with unknown adults, making them poor test-takers, [...] age-appropriate [...] commodious c[...] Council, 2008). [...]

If research a[...] dren's full range [...] additional chal[...] grow physically [...] and cognitively [...] to chronicle all [...] above, various [...] on one of these dimensions, rendering [...]gs that are not representative of all domains of development. Research is then compromised because assumptions regarding overall development cannot be, but often are generalized from any single domain.

[handwritten note: these domains can dominate as "the" ways can are known d named]

ECE research is also challenging because the very meaning and intent of early childhood education differ dramatically within and among countries. In some nations, ECE is regarded as the period preceding entry into formal schooling, which itself may vary among countries, roughly including the years from birth to 5, 6, or 7 years. But in some cases, preschool is considered as only the year/s immediately preceding entry to school, and does not include infants and toddlers. In other countries, the early years embrace the first few years of primary schooling, roughly including the ages from birth to age 8, the frame we have used in this volume. Confusing matters, the nature of services associated with ECE may vary, embracing health, education, care, and protective services. ECE may include or exclude parenting education and family support; it may include or exclude services for children with disabilities or for those whose home language

is not the language of the dominant culture. It may include services for children in formal settings or services in both formal and informal settings. Defining the universe that is ECE embraces and is an endemic challenge, forcing each researcher or research team to consider which parameters it will set for its research (Goffin and Washington, 2007). This, of course, makes data generalization very difficult within and across countries. Beyond this, the names that are associated with the different ages and forms of care are highly inconsistent, varying from early childhood education to early childhood development, and early care and education, along with a multitude of other variants.

If such definitional ambiguities were not complex enough, there are large structural challenges emanating from different endemic understandings of ECE. The holistic orientation of young children's development means that services to support that development are spawned across diverse ministries, which may have their own cultures, missions, rules, regulations, budgets, and operational strategies. Often, these diverse ministries do not communicate effectively with one another, leaving ECE providers straddling two or three different sets of obligations that often have different ideologies about how best to serve young children and whether children or families are the primary service recipients. Moreover, ideas about research and about how to use research may differ. These differences exist despite prominent coordination efforts that now exist in the literature (Bergenholtz, 2011) and that are currently underway in the field to create coordinating bodies and structures (Neuman and Devercelli, 2013; Vargas-Barón, 2013).

Beyond the complications of dealing with diverse ministries, ECE is also handicapped because different ideologies co-exist regarding the appropriate role of the state in family affairs. Social democracies and some communist countries regard this as more inclusive, while many mercantile democracies favor a sharing of responsibility among families, communities, and the public sector (Kamerman and Kahn, 1978). These different perceptions of the state's role can complicate research design, access, and the utilization of data (Kagan and Gomez, 2015). As endemic features of children, of the field, and of governments, these elements are less porous and subject to change than the challenges discussed below.

Methodological and Funding Challenges

Framed by the above endemic challenges, the research enterprise has its own complications, some immediately and uniquely germane to ECE and others more general in nature. Looking first at the more general considerations, ECE research is faced with scientific traditions, with diverse standards of evidence, and with diverse research biases. More germane to ECE, the research community faces technical issues related to the paucity of tools, instruments, functional data systems, and limited funding commitments to ECE research.

Scientific traditions that transcend ECE also influence it. Debates about the value of qualitative as well as quantitative research continue, particularly for policy-oriented funding. In such circles, quantitative research has been considered the 'gold standard', with ECE increasingly being called upon to design studies with this tradition in mind. Having noted some of the challenges in dealing with young children, the quantitative gold standard is hard and expensive to achieve. Moreover, it does not always shed light on some of the influential nuances that can only be captured by qualitative research. Similarly, in much of social science research, discerning outcomes and effects is privileged over examining inputs and/or the processes that lead to the outcomes. Most fields dealing with human endeavors benefit from a blend of both quantitative and qualitative research, and ECE is not an exception. This volume demonstrates some of the rich traditions and emerging research areas using a range of qualitative methods, from ethnography to narrative inquiry. Like many fields, ECE must design a balanced repertoire of studies so that the benefits of both qualitative and quantitative research can be achieved.

Discerning appropriate standards of evidence is a methodological challenge that simultaneously plagues and defines research trajectories. In the field of comparative international research, this paradox persists. Internationalists examine how and to what degree cultural variation impacts evidence standards; they ask is there, and can there really be, one standard, given the diverse international contexts in which comparative research is conducted? This line of inquiry raises important issues regarding the viability of a single evidence standard and who gets to determine that standard. Moreover, it reprises the need for, and content of, an international 'gold' standard of research.

Closely related to standards of evidence issues are those that address research biases. Researchers, unwittingly or not, come to their work with biases, often influenced by culture, geographic locale, socio-political considerations, and disciplinary traditions. Such biases are hard to shake off, but acknowledgement of them, though often called for, is challenging to do. Often, the very populations studied, the research questions posed, and the choice of methods used are filtered through the lens of culture and experience, all of which can induce unintended bias. All research and all researchers deal with this as studies are designed and carried out, and as data are analyzed. In some research paradigms, the important challenge is recognizing the value-laden nature of research and working to control for bias. In other research paradigms, the 'reflexive' turn encourages recognizing such subjectivity, as a resource to aid in construction and reconstruction of research knowledge (e.g., see May and Perry, 2011).

For those interested in researching ECE, all these issues pertain, along with others. As a comparatively new field, ECE does not have a long history with tools, data systems, mixed-service delivery modes, and 'uncontaminated' or partially treated populations. More sophisticated than instruments to assess and measure socio-emotional development or approaches toward learning, ECE does have some solid tools to capture changes in children's language, physical, and cognitive development. Yet, because of their importance to overall development, the absence of tools that address socio-emotional development and approaches toward learning is a Herculean hole. Moreover, the lack of research tools that acknowledge the holistic nature of children's development and childhood makes the garnering of appropriate data on young children especially problematic. While challenging, efforts to assuage this paucity are taking hold.

The lack of effective ECE data systems is common and is improving, but at a snail's pace in comparison to the development of data systems in other areas of social endeavor. In part, the development of effective systems is complicated by the multidisciplinary, multi-ministry nature of ECE services. Establishing complex and comprehensive data systems that span ministries and that deal with the multiple challenges associated with data collection for young children already discussed, makes this challenging. Moreover, given that universal services for young children are rare, many countries favor investing in immediate and direct services to reach underserved populations of children over investments in data that sometimes appear to be of questionable utility.

Because ECE is emerging so rapidly and because it deals with emerging boundary-spanning issues, often the research needed is very cutting edge. This is to say that, sometimes, workable protocols have not been devised to address the most trenchant ECE challenges: systemic planning, multi-sectorial initiatives, cultural variation, and new methods of governance, finance, and professional certification and development. These lacks are not totally unique to ECE, but because of its embryonic and fast-emerging status, research on these issues is both essential and sorely lacking. Without such research, the field is 'building a plane, while flying it'.

Finally, ECE research is more precariously funded than other domains of inquiry, despite its increased prominence as a growth field. For example, in the USA, historically ECE research has been funded primarily by private-sector dollars. With the call for more gold standard research that has applicability across contexts and cultures, the costs are escalating, causing scholars to seek public support sometimes manifest in the form of public–private partnerships to carry out such research. In the USA, outlets for ECE research are less robust than for other fields, as are training and professional development funds for supporting young scholars in the field. Funding for research exchanges is limited for those who invest their lives in the scholarly pursuit of information regarding this age population. Other countries have their own funding variations and practical challenges, such as the risk that early years research funding is a current 'fad' due to policy interest but one which may fade over time. As discussed in this volume, researchers from parts of the Global South seek to establish their own research priorities and methodologies, but find it challenging to tap into the international development and research funding. In short, methodological and funding issues encase ECE research, but ECE research is not circumscribed by them. Rather, due to the embryonic and precarious nature of ECE research, ECE scholars face a myriad of additional challenges.

Content Challenges

Despite the proliferation of ECE research, some of it documented in this volume, three areas of significance need far greater attention: (i) responsiveness to cultural variation; (ii) systemic structures and elements, including governance, finance, professional development, accountability, and family engagement; and (iii) global comparisons. For each of these categories, far greater attention is needed to implementation sciences and to better understanding not only the outcomes associated with these variables, but also the processes and factors that facilitate or inhibit such outcomes.

With regard to cultural variation, more research is needed to learn about the cultural variants that influence children's learning and the evolution of systems. Special attention should be accorded to within-country cultural variation in addition to cross-country variation. Moreover, attention should be accorded to the parameters that comprise cultural variation, with specific attention to how they are expressed in standards, curriculum, and assessments. Calls in this volume come for culturally appropriate and relevant research agendas and methodologies, which are suitable for the particular context rather than imposed by external bodies – government, international agencies, and/or funders. These calls come particularly from parts of the Global South that have found conceptualizations of childhood, and subsequently ECE, imposed on them rather than starting from their own constructions and contexts.

With ECE investments evolving at unprecedented rates, much more research is needed on systems development and implementation, on the nature of how services are delivered, and on the degree to which governance and fiscal investments matter. More research is needed on boundary-spanning mechanisms and on inventive ways to govern and finance ECE, including efforts to blend public and private resources (Kagan and Cohen, 1996; Yoshikawa et al., 2014). Far more investigation must be expended on the equitable distribution of services, as well as on their sustainability and elements of systemic development. Of particular importance, additional research is needed on the qualities, competencies, and capacities of those who work with young children and on how best to prepare and induct them into the profession (Bernal, 2012; Kagan et al., 2008).

Finally, developing the capacity to collect global information on young children that can foster accurate comparisons of the status of children globally is essential. Diverse data sets, measurement criteria, and standards saturate the world with data, but, due to their lack of common definitions and common metrics, leave a befuddled legacy that, while data abundant, is information poor.

Rethinking The Production of Research: A Summary

To produce high-quality, usable ECE research, three areas need attention: endemic challenges, methodological challenges, and content challenges. None of these is impossible to overcome but, to gain strides, a serious commitment to enhancing the ECE research enterprise will be necessary. Endemic challenges may be the most difficult to overcome, but they should be addressed. Methodological challenges, some germane to educational/social science research in general, and some specific to ECE, warrant attention, with a particular focus on elevating the status of diverse research approaches, developing new research tools, and according vigorous attention to human capacity development in order to support the growth and quality of the ECE research enterprise. Once these are attended to, there will be a greater chance of addressing the critical, and sadly overlooked, research topics.

THE CHALLENGE OF *USING* RESEARCH FOR INTERNATIONAL ECE

If the challenges of *producing* quality research are legion, so too are the challenges associated with its effective *use*. Research can have different and overlapping functions: for example, it can seek to develop theory, methods, and methodology and/or to answer practical and policy questions. Research cultures vary considerably across disciplines, organizations, and countries, on the extent to which research impact is valued and part of research design. For example, some chapters in this volume arise from practitioners and activists in the field, who undertake research with policy and practice very much in mind. Their networks and settings ensure their research is current and has impact, but their research does not always permeate more academic research circles. Other chapters are written by academic researchers who seek to ensure that their research has practical impact, but such practical engagement may not be rewarded or even supported within their academic arenas. Such chapters contribute to the broader literature on 'knowledge exchange', which aims to move beyond the limited, one-way concept of dissemination. Instead, knowledge exchange values genuine collaboration and dialogue between researchers and private, public, and/or civil society sectors to make research more meaningful to policy and practice (e.g., Economic and Social Research Council, 2015).

Considering the chapters in this volume, at least three issues arise for ECE research seeking to realize productive knowledge exchange: (i) conceptualizing and framing of research questions so the results are optimally usable, (ii) communicating results in accessible formats and outlets, and (iii) applying the results over time and across populations.

Conceptualizing and Framing Research

To render research results optimally usable, the guiding conceptualization of the analysis, as well as the research questions that operationalize the study, must be framed by utility considerations. Traditionally, academic empirical studies were incepted with the interests or intentions of the researcher in mind, with far less attention accorded to the end users of the results. To combat this, as studies are developed, their application must be considered, as much as the needs of the end users of the information. Indeed, many scholars are not trained to adapt their theoretical orientations and their research paradigms to practice and/or policy. Clearly, not all research studies will be generated with the

improvement of practice in mind, but those that are must consider their audience and uses. This is easier said than done because many scholars have not been trained to begin their analytic work with such a practical orientation. This means that professional development efforts must prepare researchers with these ends in mind. To date, understanding the importance of empirical research to policy and practice, professional organizations are infusing their conferences, webinars, and other public communications with research findings to foster greater social use.

Communicating Results in Accessible Formats and Outlets

Generating usable research is not the only problem; communicating results effectively and in the proper outlets is also necessary. Academic incentivization schemes, including the pressure to publish articles in scholarly journals, sometimes impede the widespread dissemination of the results. Often written for technical audiences, the articles are suitable for consumption by other scholars, but not by those invested in improving practice and policy. Even if they have the requisite skills to understand complex research methodologies, practitioners are often more interested in the implications of the findings than in the methods used to evoke the results. They tend to want more direct, clear recommendations, rather than the nuanced 'on-the-one-hand; on-the-other-hand' analyses rendered by those whom policy makers often term 'two-handed-scholars'. Such communication is not remediated by adding a practice/policy coda to an otherwise practice/policy-irrelevant study. Efforts of this ilk can both water down the impact of the analysis and render irrelevant recommendations.

Beyond the way research is conceptualized and where it is presented, the way it is written matters. Because practitioners and policy makers do not tend to read scholarly journals, writing practice and policy briefs is important if scholars hope to reach this audience. But writing a policy brief demands different skills from those for which academics are conventionally trained; writing more succinctly, using less technical jargon, and taking very clear stances on next-step efforts are critical communication tools for this kind of writing. Such communication tools are being recognized now, with more scholars being trained to write and orally communicate more succinctly. Composing 'elevator' speeches, or those that can be communicated in 2 minutes or the time it takes to ride in an elevator, is becoming an essential skill for the effective communication of research. To this end, many professional organizations and training programs are stressing the importance of effective communication in practice-salient forms and outlets. Researchers and research are not only found in academia, but in a range of governmental and non-governmental settings. The skills developed in these non-academic settings can be usefully shared with those who have kept their careers in academia and may have less opportunity and inclination to write for policy consumers.

Applying the Results Over Time and Across Populations

Of particular relevance for ECE is the degree to which these skills and orientations have been mastered. Indeed, the reason so much attention has been accorded ECE has to do, in part, with effective communication. In tandem with using the media effectively is the need to use it responsibly. Yet, ECE is particularly vulnerable to over-generalization. Such over-generalization can take three forms. First, data can be over-generalized beyond the context for which it was generated. Indeed, the vast variations in ECE programs, contexts, and populations may not render all studies suitable for across-the-board generalization or wide-scale application. For example, research generated in health settings may not have applicability in childcare settings. Moreover, and particularly germane to this volume, research generated in one country or for one culture may not have cross-national or cross-cultural applicability. Clearly, with a field as vast and as somewhat ill-defined as ECE, consideration must be given to those contexts where results will have applicability.

Timing is a second generalizability issue. The scholarly and publication processes often deter information consumption by months and years beyond when the data were collected. Just as it is inappropriate to generalize from one context to another, it is unwise to generalize from one time period to another. This is true in fields where the pace of change is slow, but is particularly important to bear in mind in a field like ECE, one that is in flux and where change is the norm. Moreover, such temporal factors may inhibit when and how data are used. Data produced at one point in time may lose their relevance over time as situations, practices, or policies change.

Finally, a third challenge related to generalizability is one that is acute in ECE. While much of the data do indicate considerable advances for children and families, many of the generalizations emanating from the data fail to underscore the contribution of *high-quality* ECE to the outcomes being popularized. This leaves the false impression that ECE can produce results, even if the programs are not of quality, and can reduce attention to necessary and known quality production variables. Examples of over-stating the results, while understating their elixirs, commit twin faults: omission of critical information and tacitly conveying erroneous policy information. The overselling or over-generalization of the efficacy of ECE is of concern, particularly when quality elements are either avoided or given short shrift. Indeed, over-promising and under-funding ECE is a recipe for ECE failure over time.

Using Research: A Summary

Throughout this volume, contributors have raised challenges regarding the effective use

of data. Three of importance have been highlighted here, including: conceptualizing and framing research with an eye toward its application; communicating results in accessible formats and outlets; and applying the results appropriately. Although somewhat complex, the utilization of research for practice and policy is something to which ECE scholars and practitioners should attend. New approaches are being developed that warrant attention: including practitioners, parents, and/or children in conceptualizing new studies, collaborations of researchers within and outside academia, and training of junior academics to render their work and their publications suitable for popularization and application. Having noted these advancements, it is equally important to acknowledge that scholarship, as we know it, has a role in social advancement. It allows assumptions and programmatic efforts to be tested and reconsidered, it builds and affirms new knowledge and, with care, it can give voice to those whose culture and work have been underrepresented in the literature and in policy, historically. As such, research is a powerful accelerator of higher quality, and more equitably distributed and sustainable services for young children. The challenge, to which we now turn, is how to accomplish this.

LOOKING FORWARD: NEW POSSIBILITIES

Improving the quality of ECE research, as well as its usability, is not a simple task that can be accomplished overnight by any one field, organization, or association. Rather, it is a complex and durable task that has been addressed by the majority of authors in this volume. There is no one right strategy, but we offer a considered approach based on the diverse ideas represented in this volume. The contents of this volume suggest three main focal areas: (i) addressing under-considered areas; (ii) enhancing research methodologies, tools, and approaches; and (iii) applying

research results more systematically and judiciously.

Addressing Under-Considered Areas

In a field as fertile and as evolving as ECE, areas for new research abound. We have already suggested three areas that need attention: (i) responsiveness to cultural and ability variation; (ii) systemic structures and elements, including governance, finance, professional development, accountability, family engagement; and (iii) global comparisons and trends. While it is not our intent to reprise these areas, we do want to underscore that for each, there are multiple options for the expansion of the research agenda. In addition to these areas, we also want to suggest that greater research must be accorded the three trenchant themes associated with contemporary ECE, notably the quality of services, their equitable distribution, and their sustainability.

With regard to the quality of services, far more theoretical attention should be paid to improving pedagogical opportunities across age and context. Conventionally, quality has been conceptualized as a constant, meaning that what is quality in one context has applicability in all contexts. Some in ECE have boldly questioned this conceptualization, but more evidence is needed that speaks to how quality may vary, depending on the ages and capabilities of children (Odom et al., 2005) and on the diverse contexts in which they develop (Moss, 2014). That is to say, new and more nuanced ways of conceptualizing quality should be considered. For example, while much global attention has been focused on improving the quality of preschool settings, too little has been accorded to settings for infants and toddlers. Moreover, issues related to quality in diverse kinds of ECE services should be forefronted in future research; for example, building on work being undertaken, consideration should be given to the improvement of parenting education and to supporting child–parent centers (Temple and

Reynolds, 2007), to the inclusion of early stimulation efforts (Baker-Henningham and Lopez-Boo, 2010), and to the advancement of physical health and mental health services as a normative element of mainstream educational programming. Discerning how best to improve services within and across disciplines and institutions merits more work (McCabe and Sipple, 2011). Linkages across the age spectrum should be addressed more systematically, so that gains achieved for one age group will be sustained as children and their families move through the developmental continuum, from birth to age 8. Quality also needs to be examined from the perspective of those adults whose lives impact on children. More attention needs to be paid to teacher/practitioner preparation for different ages of children and for different populations of youngsters, most notably children at risk. Because ECE is so intimately linked with families and communities, far more work on the ways in which families and communities are mobilized and empowered should be considered within the ECE research agenda.

Throughout the world, with only a few exceptions, services for young children are not equitably distributed, with children from more affluent families and communities often having far better access to services than their less advantaged counterparts (UNICEF, 2012; Vegas and Santibanez, 2010). Reasons for this differ, but they do involve the ways in which services are funded and governed, and the ways in which countries hold young children. Examining service equity from a rights-driven perspective would be a fruitful line of inquiry, as would discerning economic models that could reliably estimate the costs of universal services often associated with a rights perspective. Having data that would quantify the expenditures and the savings from universality could be helpful in fostering a rights-driven ECE approach.

Further, greater attention needs to be accorded to the sustainability of ECE services (Vargas-Barón, 2007). Often conceptualized by one political regime and denigrated by the next, ECE is far too vulnerable to political ideology. Examining what it would take to position ECE more centrally as part of countries' normative agenda should be considered. Such positioning involves far more than publically sponsored service provision. There may be inventive models of service provision that are sustainable through public–private partnerships. Moreover, sustainability cannot be manufactured without rigorous attention to the infrastructure that supports comprehensive ECE. Less is known about systems theory and development and about policy transferability in this field than in others. In short, there are cascades of areas where new research content should and could be undertaken. In addition to attending to under-addressed areas, we suggest that focusing research on advancing the quality, equity, and sustainability of ECE might be a useful frame for considering future research topics.

Finally, it is important to underscore that research regarding young children needs to be conceptualized within, and constructed about, the context of their real-time, real-place experiences. The emergence of new, and now near-global, technology influences the content and process of children's communication. Similarly, capitalist markets and accompanying consumerism have widespread effects on young children, either directly in terms of consumption or more indirectly in terms of inequality or the political economies of ECE. Environmental realities – from housing to natural disasters, from wars to levels of pollution – affect young children, their families, and communities. Yet young children have not always been considered in research agendas on such issues, as documented in this volume. As such, future research must explore children with an understanding of and interest in their contemporary and broad contexts.

Enhancing Research Methodologies, Tools, and Approaches

Discussed above, there is clearly a need to make research more central to current debates

regarding the future of ECE. ECE research should be considered as important to the agenda as are quality teachers and quality facilities. To achieve this new level of appreciation, the entire ECE research enterprise must be 'opened up' and made more porous. New players should be induced into research efforts, including honoring children's, parents', and practitioners' views and engagement. New technologies should be used, so that research capitalizes on the ability to collect, chronicle, and analyze data with more speed and accuracy. Diverse methodologies need to be accorded greater respect and tolerated with more openness. This is not to suggest that methodological safeguards, including ethical regulation and peer reviews, should be limited; rather, it is to suggest that such safeguards be applied appropriately to a wider range of research protocols and strategies. According more weight to field-based and qualitative work in the construction of policy should be considered.

Indeed, now that ECE research has made its way onto the policy agenda, it is time to assess the current arguments and methodologies to see what new orientations and stances will best advance young children's lives. To do this, developing and sustaining data systems that are usable, inclusive, and aligned with ECE populations must be a focus of next-step research endeavors. Developing new approaches to understanding transferability, scalability, and sustainability are critical as well. Finally, those who fund research must be enlisted to provide more and diverse training and resources to junior-level researchers so that their work and careers are focused on the production of research that will be directed toward child and service enhancements.

Applying Research Results More Systematically and Judiciously

The social utility of research is not limited to the content it addresses or the methods it uses; rather, social utility is predicated on according weight and resources to thinking thoughtfully about audience and dissemination as integral elements of any research endeavor. This means that more examples of how research can and does shape a practice and policy agenda should be chronicled and made known. Supporting a call for data-driven decision making supports this stance, as does a focus on ensuring that the public is aware of the potency of high-quality research. Position statements of national and international organizations should be reviewed to discern their stance on the production, dissemination, and use of research, with the goal of having all organizations whose lives touch young children incorporate statements regarding the importance of research. Similarly, the position statements and long-range ECE plans of individual countries should incorporate a commitment to data, evaluation, and research. Such plans should be accompanied by a fiscal commitment to generating new research and a cadre of new scholars to conduct and apply research and data to ECE developments and enhancements. Similarly, philanthropic efforts to support the sharing of innovative research methodologies and results should be considered. Advancing the calls for, and support of, ECE research is essential to the improvement of children's lives, service practices, and countries' policies related to young children and their families.

Next Steps: A Summary

Implementing an ECE research agenda is not a short-term or piecemeal undertaking. To achieve the development and use of research, multiple strategies need to be undertaken. As a prelude to further advancing this goal, this volume has been undertaken with the intention of helping to broadly define ECE research and to present the work of some of its most noted scholars globally. We do not suggest that ECE research be delimited to the topics or the methods presented. Rather, we intend for this volume to spur on discourse regarding the merits of current research practices and to prelude discussions regarding how to more wisely and durably position the emerging field of international early childhood research. In editing this volume, we hope to have raised critical issues, provoked controversial thinking, and, above all, helped move ECE research to its rightful place amidst meaningful, sustainable, and effective policy and practice agendas.

REFERENCES

Baker-Henningham, H. and Lopez-Boo, F. (2010). *Early childhood stimulation interventions in developing countries: A comprehensive literature review.* IDB Working Paper Series, IDB-WP-213.

Bergenholtz, C. (2011). Knowledge brokering: Spanning technological and network boundaries. *European Journal of Innovation Management,* 14(1), 74–92. Retrieved from www.emeraldinsight.com/doi/abs/10.1108/14601061111104706

Bernal, R. (2012). The impact of a professional-technical training program for childcare providers on children's well-being. Retrieved from http://econweb.umd.edu/~urzua/Bernal.pdf

Besharov, D. and Ramey, C. (2008). Preschool puzzle. *Education Next,* 8(4), 61–69. Retrieved from http://educationnext.org/preschool-puzzle/

Brooker, L. and Woodhead, M. (2013). *The right to play. Early childhood in focus,* 9. Retrieved from www.bernardvanleer.org/English/Home/News/Home-News-2013/Early-Childhood-in-Focus-on-The-Right-to-Play.html

Camilli, G., Vargas, S., Ryan, S. and Barnett, W. S. (2010). Meta-analysis of the effects of early education interventions on cognitive and social development. *Teachers College Record,* 112(3), 579–620. Retrieved from http://rci.rutgers.edu/~camilli/Papers/38_15440.pdf

Chandy, L. and Gertz, G. (2011). Poverty in numbers: The changing state of global poverty. In I. Ortiz, L. Daniels and S. Enfilbertsdottir (Eds.), *Child poverty and inequity: New perspectives.* New York: UNICEF, Division of Policy and Practice.

Chetty, R., Friedman, J. N., Hilger, N., Saez, E., Whitmore Schanzenbach, D. and Yagan, D. (2011). How does your kindergarten classroom affect your earnings? Evidence from Project Star. *Quarterly Journal of Economics,* 126(4), 1593–1660. Retrieved from www.nber.org/papers/w16381

Committee for Economic Development. (2006). *The economic promise of investing in high-quality preschool: Using early education to improve economic growth and the fiscal sustainability of states and the nation.* Washington, DC: Author.

Dahlberg, G., and Lenz-Taguchi, H. (1994). *Förskola och skola: om två skilda traditioner och om visionen av en mötesplats.* (Preschool and school: Two different traditions and the vision of a meeting place). Stockholm: HLS Förlag.

Economic and Social Research Council (2015). The Benefits of Collaboration. Retrieved from www.esrc.ac.uk/collaboration/knowledge-exchange/

Fuller, B. (2007). *Standardized childhood: The political and cultural struggle over early education.* Stanford, CA: Stanford University Press.

Goffin, S. and Washington, V. (2007). *Ready or not: Leadership choices in early care and education.* New York: Teachers College Press.

Heckman, J. J. (2006). Skill formation and the economics of investing in disadvantaged children. *Science,* 312(5782), 1900–1902.

Heckman, J. J., Moon, S., Pinto, R., Savelyev, P. and Yavitz, A. (2010). The rate of return to the High Scope Perry Preschool Program. *Journal of Public Economics,* 94(1–2), 114–128.

James, A. and Prout, A. (1990). *Constructing and reconstructing childhood.* London: Falmer.

Kagan, S. L. and Cohen, N. (Eds.). (1996). *Reinventing early care and education: A vision for a quality system.* San Francisco, CA: Jossey-Bass.

Kagan, S. L. and Gomez, R. E. (Eds.). (2015). *Early childhood governance: Choices and consequences.* New York: Teachers College Press.

Kagan, S. L., Kauerz, K. and Tarrant, K. (2008). *The early care and education teaching workforce: An agenda for reform.* New York: Teachers College Press.

Kamerman, S. B. and Kahn, A. J. (1978). *Family policy: Government and families in fourteen countries.* New York: Columbia University Press.

Karoly, L. (2006). *Poverty alleviation through early childhood education*. Santa Monica, CA: Rand Corp.

King, J. (2006). *Closing the achievement gap through expanded access to quality early education in grades PK-3* (Issue Brief No. 3). Washington, DC: New American Foundation Early Education Initiative.

Lee, V. E. and Burkam, D. T. (2002). *Inequality at the starting gate: Social background differences in achievement as children begin school*. Washington, DC: Economic Policy.

McCabe, L. A. and Sipple, J. W. (2011). Colliding worlds: Practical and political tensions of pre-kindergarten implementation in public schools. *Educational Policy*, 25(1), e1–e26.

McLanahan, S. (2004). Diverging destinies: How children are faring under the second demographic transition. *Demography*, 41(4), 607–627.

May, T. and Perry, B. (2011). *Social research and reflexivity: Content, consequences and context*. London: SAGE.

Mayall, B. (2002). *Towards a sociology of childhood: Thinking from children's lives*. Buckingham: Open University Press.

Moss, P. (2014). *Transformative change in real utopias in early childhood education: A story of democracy, experimentation and potentiality*. London: Routledge.

Narayan, D. (2012). The dynamics of poverty. In I. Ortiz, L. Daniels and S. Enfilbertsdottir (Eds.), *Child poverty and inequity: New perspectives*. New York: UNICEF, Division of Policy and Practice.

National Research Council (2008). *Early childhood assessment: Why, what and how*. Committee on Developmental Outcomes and Assessments for Young Children, C. E. Snow and S. B. Van Hemel (Eds.), Board on Children, Youth, and Families, Board on Testing and Assessment, Divisions of Behavioral and Social Sciences and Education, Washington, DC: The National Academies Press.

Naudeau, S., Kataoka, N., Valerio, A., Neuman, M. and Elder, L. (2011). *Investing in young children: An early childhood development guide for policy dialogue and project preparation*. Washington, DC: The World Bank.

Neuman, M. and Devercelli, A. E. (2013). *What matters most for early childhood development: A framework paper* (Working Paper No. 5). Retrieved from http://wbgfiles.world-bank.org/documents/hdn/ed/saber/supporting_doc/Background/ECD/Framework_SABER-ECD.pdf

Odom, S. L., Brantlinger, E., Gersten, R., Horner, R. H., Thompson, B. and Harris, K. K. (2005). Research in special education: Scientific methods and evidence-based practices. *Exceptional Children*, 71(2), 137–148. Retrieved from www.cecdr.org/pdf/Research_in_Sped.pdf

Organization for Economic Cooperation and Development (OECD). (2012). Executive summary. *Starting strong III: A quality toolbox for early childhood education and care*. Paris: OECD.

Qvortrup, J. (1994). Childhood matters: An introduction. In J. Qvortrup, M. Bardy, G. Sgritta and H. Wintersberger (Eds.), *Childhood matters: Social theory, practice and politics* (pp. 1–24). European Centre, Vienna. Aldershot: Avebury.

Shonkoff, J. and Phillips, D. (Eds.). (2000). *From neurons to neighborhoods: The science of early childhood development*. Washington, DC: National Academy Press.

Snow, K. (2011). *Developing kindergarten readiness and other large-scale assessment systems: Necessary considerations for the assessment of young children*. Washington, DC: NAEYC.

Steiner-Khamsi, G. and Waldow, F. (Eds.). (2012). *Policy borrowing and lending: World yearbook of education 2012*. London: Routledge.

Temple, J. A. and Reynolds, A. J. (2007). Benefits and costs of investments in preschool education: Evidence from the Child-Parent Centers and related programs. *Economics of Education Review*, 26(1), 126–144.

United Nations (2014). The millennium development goals report 2014. Retrieved from www.un.org/millenniumgoals/2014%20MDG%20report/MDG%202014%20English%20web.pdf

United Nations Children's Fund (UNICEF) (2012). Inequities in early childhood development: What the data say. Evidence from the Multiple Indicator Cluster Surveys. New York: UNICEF. Retrieved from www.unicef.org/lac/Inequities_in_Early_Childhood_Development_LoRes_PDF_EN_02082012%281%29.pdf

United Nations Children's Fund (UNICEF) (2014). *The state of the world's children 2014 in numbers: Every child counts*. New York: UNICEF.

United Nations Educational, Scientific and Cultural Organization (UNESCO) (2010a). *Early childhood care and education regional report: Arab states*. Paris: UNESCO.

United Nations Educational, Scientific and Cultural Organization (UNESCO). (2010b). *Early childhood care and education regional report: Asia and the Pacific*. Paris: UNESCO.

Vargas-Barón, E. (2007). *Going to scale and achieving sustainability in selected early childhood programs of Latin America*. Washington, DC: The RISE Institute.

Vargas-Barón, E. (2013). Building and strengthening national systems for early childhood development. In P. Britto, P. Engle and C. M. Super (Eds.), *Handbook of early childhood development research and its impact on global policy* (pp. 443–466). New York: Oxford University Press.

Vegas, E. and Santibanez, L. (2010). *The promise of early childhood development in Latin America and the Caribbean*. Washington, DC: The World Bank.

Voipio, T. (2012). Social protection for all: An agenda for pro-child growth and child rights. In I. Ortiz, L. Daniels and S. Engilbertsdóttir (Eds.), *Child poverty and inequity: New perspectives* (pp. 118–124). New York: UNICEF, Division of Policy and Practice.

Walker, S. and Chang, S. (2013). Effectiveness of parent support programs in enhancing learning in the under-3 group. *Early Childhood Matters*, June. Retrieved from http://earlychildhoodmagazine.org/effectiveness-of-parent-support-programmes-in-enhancing-learning-in-the-under-3-age-group/

Weiland, C. and Yoshikawa, H. (2013). Impacts of a prekindergarten program on children's mathematics, language, literacy, executive function, and emotional skills. *Child Development*, 84(6), 2112–2130.

White, A. K. (2007). General comment 7: Implementing child rights in early childhood. *Coordinators Notebook*, 29, 35–37.

Wyness, M. (2015). *Childhood*. Bristol: Polity Press.

Yoshikawa, H., Ponguta, A., Nieto, A. M., van Ravens, J., Portilla, X., Rebello Britto, P. and Leyva, D. (2014). *Evaluación de los mecanismos de implementación, gobernanza, financiación y sostenibilidad de la Estrategia Integral de Desarrollo de la Primera Infancia en Colombia De Cero a Siempre*. (mimeo)

Zaslow, M., Anderson, R., Redd, Z., Wessel, J., Tarullo, L. and Burchinal, M. (2010). *Quality dosage, thresholds, and features in early childhood settings: A review of the literature*. OPRE 2011–5. Washington, DC: Office of Planning, Research and Evaluation, Administration for Children and Families, US Department of Health and Human Services.

Index

Page references to Figures or Tables will be in *italics*. ECE stands for early childhood education, ECD for early childhood development, ECEC for Early Childhood Education and Care (wherever they appear in the index). References to Notes will be followed by the letter 'n'.